Post-Conflict Rebuilding and International Law

The International Law of Peace and Security

Series Editor: Professor Nigel White

Post-Conflict Rebuilding and International Law

Edited by

Ray Murphy

National University of Ireland Galway, Ireland

ASHGATE

Wherever possible, these reprints are made from a copy of the original printing, but these can themselves be of very variable quality. Whilst the publisher has made every effort to ensure the quality of the reprint, some variability may inevitably remain.

Published by
Ashgate Publishing Limited
Wey Court East
Union Road
Farnham
Surrey GU9 7PT
England

Ashgate Publishing Company
Suite 420
101 Cherry Street
Burlington
VT 05401-4405
USA

www.ashgate.com

British Library Cataloguing in Publication Data
Post-conflict peacebuilding and international law. – (The
    international law of peace and security)
    1. Peace-building–Case studies. 2. Postwar
    reconstruction–Case studies. 3. Intervention
    (International law)
    I. Series II. Murphy, Ray, Dr.
    341.5'84–dc22

Library of Congress Control Number: 2011930086

ISBN 9780754629573

MIX
Paper from responsible sources
FSC
www.fsc.org   FSC® C013056

Printed and bound in Great Britain by
TJ International Ltd, Padstow, Cornwall.

Contents

Acknowledgements

The editor and publishers wish to thank the following for permission to use copyright material.

Cambridge University Press for the essays: Max Du Plessis and Jolyon Ford (2009), 'Transitional Justice: A Future Truth Commission for Zimbabwe?', *International and Comparative Law Quarterly*, **58**, pp. 73–117. Copyright © 2009 British Institute of International and Comparative Law; Amy Maguire (2009), '"Security Starts with the Law": The Role of International Law in the Protection of Women's Security Post-Conflict', in B. Bowden, H. Charlesworth and J. Farrell (eds), *The Role of Law in Rebuilding Societies after Conflict*, New York: Cambridge University Press, pp. 218–43. Copyright © 2009 Cambridge University Press.

Copyright Clearance Center for the essays: Jennifer Widner (2001), 'Courts and Democracy in Postconflict Transitions: A Social Scientist's Perspective on the African Case', *American Journal of International Law*, **95**, pp. 64–75. Copyright © 2001 American Society of International Law; Erika de Wet (2009), 'The Governance of Kosovo: Security Council Resolution 1244 and the Establishment and Functioning of EULEX', *American Journal of International Law*, **103**, pp. 83–96. Copyright © 2009 American Society of International Law; Gregory L. Naarden and Jeffrey B. Locke (2004), 'Peacekeeping and Prosecutorial Policy: Lessons from Kosovo', *American Journal of International Law*, **98**, pp. 727–43. Copyright © 2004 American Society of International Law; Hansjörg Strohmeyer (2001), 'Collapse and Reconstruction of a Judicial System: The United Nations Missions in Kosovo and East Timor', *American Journal of International Law*, **95**, pp. 46–63. Copyright © 2001 American Society of International Law; Christine Bell (2006), 'Peace Agreements: Their Nature and Legal Status', *American Journal of International Law*, **100**, pp. 373–412. Copyright © 2006 American Society of International Law; David Marshall and Shelley Inglis (2003), 'The Disempowerment of Human Rights-Based Justice in the United Nations Mission in Kosovo', *Harvard Human Rights Journal*, **16**, pp. 95–146. Copyright © 2003 Harvard University Law School; David Tolbert with Andrew Solomon (2006), 'United Nations Reform and Supporting the Rule of Law in Post-Conflict Societies', *Harvard Human Rights Journal*, **19**, pp. 29–62. Copyright © 2006 Harvard University Law School.

Journal of International Law and International Relations for the essay: Simon Chesterman (2005), 'From State Failure to State-Building: Problems and Prospects for a United Nations Peacebuilding Commission', *Journal of International Law and Relations*, **2**, pp. 155–75.

Oxford University Press for the essays: Richard Sannerholm (2007), 'Legal, Judicial and Administrative Reforms in Post-Conflict Societies: Beyond the Rule of Law Template', *Journal of Conflict and Security Law*, **12**, pp. 65–93. Copyright © 2007 Oxford University

Press; Carsten Stahn (2006), "'*Jus ad Bellum*", "*Jus in Bello*"…"*Jus post Bellum*"? Rethinking the Conception of the Law of Armed Force', *European Journal of International Law*, **17**, pp. 921–43. Copyright © 2007 Oxford University Press.

Taylor & Francis for the essays: Matteo Tondini (2008), 'From Neo-Colonialism to a "Light-Footprint Approach": Restoring Justice Systems', *International Peacekeeping*, **15**, pp. 237–51; Victoria K. Holt and Alix J. Boucher (2009), 'Framing the Issue: UN Responses to Corruption and Criminal Networks in Post-Conflict Settings', *International Peacekeeping*, **16**, pp. 20–32; Philippe Le Billon (2008), 'Corrupting Peace? Peacebuilding and Post-Conflict Corruption', *International Peacekeeping*, **15**, pp. 344–61; Robert Muggah and Keith Krause (2009), 'Closing the Gap between Peace Operations and Post-Conflict Insecurity: Towards a Violence Reduction Agenda', *International Peacekeeping*, **16**, pp. 136–50.

Every effort has been made to trace all the copyright holders, but if any have been inadvertently overlooked the publishers will be pleased to make the necessary arrangement at the first opportunity.

Series Preface

The essays collected in the four volumes of this reprint series, The International Law of Peace and Security, focus on a number of facets of international law concerned with peace and security. Clearly there are existing volumes in the Library of Essays on International Law (series editor Robert McCorquodale) that are essential reading for anyone interested in this area of international law, primarily *Collective Security Law*, edited by Nigel White, and *International Peacekeeping*, edited by Boris Kondoch. However, the aim of this series is not simply to develop and deepen the reader's understanding of international law in the area of peace and security, but to introduce new areas and concepts, namely the international laws that purport to govern and regulate arms control, counter-terrorism, the use of force, and peace-building. The focus will be on peace and security rather than on conflict, as the law of armed conflict has already been covered in the aforementioned series, in *Humanitarian Law* edited by Judith Gardam.

The international laws in the area of peace and security are essentially different from those that apply in conflicts – basically, the difference is between the law of peace and the law of war. Simply put, the law of war is concerned with regulating warfare – its means, methods, and issues of targeting and protecting persons – thereby upholding principles of humanity while recognizing the dictates of military necessity. The law of peace and security is about preventing conflicts and wars, and is increasingly concerned with rebuilding a situation of peace and security on the other side of the conflict following a ceasefire and peace agreement. Of course, it is not always possible to maintain a clear line between the *jus ad bellum*, *jus in bello* and *jus post bellum* – an issue raised by the controversial 'war on terror', but coming through more practically in specific instances such as the application of international humanitarian law to peacekeepers. In addition, the series only considers issues of international criminal justice when analysing the rebuilding of a post-conflict state or as an element of counter-terrorism, thus giving rise to little overlap with the collection in the aforementioned series, *The International Criminal Court* edited by Olympia Bekou and Robert Cryer.

The focus of these four volumes is essentially on the law of peace, more specifically those laws and legal regimes that underpin peace by means of controlling the spread of dangerous weapons and by limiting the occasions when states can use force on the international stage, or restoring it when that peace has been broken. In times of peace the main fear is of sudden attacks, possibly by the use of WMD or by terrorists, signifying that arms control law, the law regulating the use of force and anti-terrorist laws are all potentially applicable. In post-conflict situations, peace is being restored usually with the involvement of international actors, which raises a whole host of legal issues, including the applicability of human rights law within the unstable post-conflict state and the principles governing international intervention and involvement. The presence of the UN Security Council, as principal international guarantor and guardian of peace and security, in each of the four volumes is not only illustrative of the unifying theme of peace and security, but also raises concerns and issues about the central role of this most political of bodies in this area of law.

In considering the four volumes in this series individually, it can be seen that the volume edited by Dan Joyner – *Arms Control Law* – is a pretty unique collection of secondary sources collected from both legal and non-legal areas. The essays in this collection review and analyse the major arms control treaties and institutions including the Security Council. The contribution of arms control law to international peace and security is a key theme.

In *The Use of Force and International Law*, Tarcisio Gazzini and Nikolaos Tsagourias have carefully selected essays from a vast range of literature to reflect the debates and controversies of this most fundamental, but much contested, area. The rules on when states and organizations can use or authorize the use of force is not only confined to the primary international treaty governing peace and security – the UN Charter – but also includes different viewpoints on controversial (customary) exceptions such as humanitarian intervention, as well as the more recent debates on the responsibility to protect. All this again requires attention to be given to the Security Council.

In *Counter-Terrorism and International Law*, Katja Samuel and Nigel White consider the problem of international terrorism (embodied in the struggle to define it) and the range of responses crafted by states and international organizations in order to try to respond to it, ranging from declaring 'war' to consensual cooperative criminal justice-type measures. The role of the Security Council in developing the legal regimes here, by use for example of targeted sanctions, is considered against the backdrop of existing conventions and practices. The contribution of these measures to the goals of peace and security embodied in the UN Charter is central to this collection.

Finally, *Post-Conflict Rebuilding and International Law*, edited by Ray Murphy, comprises an interesting collection of essays illustrating the phenomenon of rebuilding peace within different regions, followed by a consideration of the general normative framework including the arguments for and against recognizing (the need for) a *jus post bellum*. The essays review and analyse various types, stages and institutions involved in post-conflict peace-building from an international law perspective. They include discussion of rebuilding and peace operations (a much wider concept than peacekeeping operations), electoral support, humanitarian assistance and rule-of-law capacity-building. Post-conflict accountability mechanisms (amnesties, truth commissions, criminal tribunals) and their contribution to peace-building, as well as the wider restoration of peace and security, are also covered. Because this area is new and still developing there will be a need to identify the applicable principles of international law (for example, human rights including economic, social and cultural rights and the right of self-determination, but also the right to security), and the possible development of a *jus post bellum*, but Ray Murphy identifies a number of other challenges to this most difficult of tasks – rebuilding peace.

Each volume of collected essays is of immense value in itself, but each is also supplemented by an introduction by the volume editors and a selected bibliography, both of which add considerably to the usefulness of the collections to the reader.

NIGEL D. WHITE
Series Editor
University of Nottingham

Introduction

Peace-building, like the concept of peace-keeping, is neither defined nor specifically provided for in the UN Charter (see United Nations, 1996, pp. 3–9; White, 1997, pp. 207–84; Azimi and Lin, 2000; Paris, 2007; Simma, 2007, pp. 648–700). While intrinsically linked, neither concept lends itself to precise definition and may include myriad tasks. Peace-building is not an entirely recent phenomenon. The UN played such a role in the Congo in the early 1960s, while the United States and its allies rebuilt Germany and Japan in the aftermath of World War II.

As the dynamic of conflict in the world changed, so too did the response of the UN, and other international organizations and states (International Commission on Intervention and State Sovereignty, 2001, pp. 8–9; Holzgrefe and Keohane, 2003; Johnstone, 2004, p. 823). Since 1985 there has been a significant increase in the number of peace-keeping missions established, with a corresponding increase in the complexity of the mandates. These are often referred to as 'second generation' peace-keeping operations (United Nations, 1996, p. 5). The traditionally passive role of peacekeepers has been replaced by a more active role involving, *inter alia*, national reconstruction, facilitating transition to democracy and providing humanitarian assistance (Roper *et al.*, 1993, p. 4).

The resolution of internal or domestic conflict has been a dominant feature of recent peace-keeping operations and has involved the establishment of 'democratic' governments culminating in the nation-building attempted in Somalia, Kosovo, Afghanistan and Iraq. International administration of this kind is not subject to a clear UN doctrine. Operations in Eastern Slavonia, Bosnia-Herzegovina, Kosovo and East Timor (Timor-Leste) have been characterized by the UN and other international organizations assuming responsibilities that evoke the historically sensitive concepts of trusteeship and protectorate (Berdal and Caplan, 2004).

Although the UN has little experience in the actual governance of territories, such activity is consistent with the objects and purpose of the Charter (see Matheson, 2001, p. 83). Making international administrations accountable and preventing them from adopting neo-colonial roles is imperative and a major challenge for contemporary peace-building operations (see Mégret and Hoffmann, 2003; Cerone, 2005, p. 42; Kondoch, 2005, p. 19; Verdirame, 2005, p. 81; Mansson, 2008; Murphy, 2008, p. 75; Devereux, 2009, p. 198). While the UN has little experience in the actual governance of territories, it has been an integral part of post-conflict peace-building efforts and the need for co-ordination of post-conflict strategies was evident for some time. Maintaining impartiality can present peacekeepers with a dilemma, especially when they confront situations in which civilians are victimized, or when UN forces are themselves the subject of attack (United Nations, 1996, p. 5). Similar challenges exist for peace-building operations where the question of the consent of the host state or parties to a conflict to a UN presence is particularly problematic.

The UN and Peace-Building

In June 1992, then UN Secretary-General Boutros Boutros-Ghali published *An Agenda for Peace*.[1] The report expressed the optimism and confidence of the time, but these were to be short lived. Subsequent events highlighted the deficiencies in the UN system, in particular the controversy over UN policy in Somalia and Rwanda, and the failure to secure peace and protect Bosnia in the former Yugoslavia. However, the report stimulated a major international debate about the role of the UN, and the international community, in securing and maintaining peace in the post-Cold War era. The Secretary-General recognized the need not only to end conflicts but also to rebuild communities and prevent the resurgence of violence. Henceforth post-conflict peace-building became part of the lexicon and *raison d'être* of UN peace-keeping. This marked a major development in UN policy and a similar shift in thinking which was reflected in the view of the Secretary-General emphasized in 1993: 'U.N. operations now may involve nothing less than the reconstruction of an entire society and state', for an extended period involving 'social, economic, political, and cultural aspects far beyond [the] traditional military dimension' (Boutros-Ghali, 2003, p. 115). In this way, the Security Council came to add the crucial task of post-conflict peace-building to its peace-keeping operations and this soon became a UN priority (see United Nations, 1992, paras 55–59, introducing post-conflict peace-building as a UN priority). Consequently, the mandate of peace-keeping evolved from comprising lightly armed interpositionary forces monitoring a truce, into a new spectrum of responsibilities, 'including supervising and running elections, upholding human rights, overseeing land reform, delivering humanitarian aid under fire, [and] rebuilding failed states' (Tharoor, 1995, p. 411; Wedgwood, 1995, p. 635). Today, peace-keeping includes a range of multidimensional tasks from building peace to establishing a system of international administration that entails all of the responsibilities of governance. Peace-building should be seen as complementary to peace-making (bringing an end to hostilities) and peace-keeping (maintaining peace through military force to separate conflicting parties). As such, peace-building aims to foster and create the means to sustain peace in a post-conflict environment without the need for a peace support operation.

The UN Secretary-General has described post-conflict peace-building in the following terms:

> By post-conflict peace-building, I mean actions undertaken at the end of a conflict to consolidate peace and prevent a recurrence of armed confrontation. Experience has shown ... that an integrated peace-building effort is needed to address the various factors that have caused or are threatening a conflict. Peace-building may involve the creation or strengthening of national institutions, monitoring elections, promoting human rights, providing for reintegration and rehabilitation programmes, and creating conditions for resumed development. Peace-building does not replace ongoing humanitarian and development activities in countries emerging from crisis. It aims rather to build on, add to, or reorient such activities in ways designed to reduce the risk of a resumption of

---

[1]   The report aimed to provide 'analysis and recommendations on ways of strengthening and making more efficient ... the capacity of the UN for preventive diplomacy, for peacemaking and for peacekeeping'.

conflict and contribute to creating the conditions most conducive to reconciliation, reconstruction and recovery. (United Nations, 1998, para. 63)

With regard to post-conflict peace-building, Franck (2002, p. 31; see also International Commission on Intervention and State Sovereignty, 2001, pp. 39–45) has referred to the need to support the emergence of a 'holistic approach to humanitarian rescue' which can act in the short-term to save lives, while supporting the longer-term restoration of political stability. The UN Secretary-General has outlined the following priorities for post-conflict peace-building:

> To avoid a return to conflict while laying a solid foundation for development, emphasis must be placed on critical priorities such as encouraging reconciliation and demonstrating respect for human rights; fostering political inclusiveness and promoting national unity; ensuring the safe, smooth and early repatriation and resettlement of refugees and displaced persons; reintegrating ex-combatants and others into productive society; curtailing the availability of small arms; and mobilizing the domestic and international resources for reconstruction and economic recovery. Every priority is linked to every other, and success will require a concerted and coordinated effort on all fronts. (United Nations, 1998, para. 66)

The end of the Cold War also heralded a significant increase in the UN's willingness to pursue its role in the maintenance of international peace and security by the adoption of military solutions. The UN and the international system seemed unprepared and ill-equipped for the potential consequences of the 'new world order'. Not surprisingly, the UN has come under considerable criticism. However, there is sometimes a failure to distinguish between the UN and its separate organs, especially the Security Council. In this context, there is merit in remembering that the institution is only as strong or effective as its member states will allow. Therefore, some of the blame for ineffectiveness can be laid at the feet of the member states that vote to take action, but then fail in subsequent resolutions to provide the means to support the very operations they had earlier deemed critical. The establishment of the Peace-building Commission was an attempt to plug one gap in the UN post-conflict reconstruction strategy.[2] Simon Chesterman, 'From State Failure to State-Building' (Chapter 14), considers state-building efforts and prospects for the Commission. He points out that generally it is not the state that 'fails' – it is the government or individual leaders. He concludes that the evolution of the Commission is a somewhat typical example of ideas being diluted as the negotiation process progressed through the labyrinth of policy and intergovernmental machinery (p. 360). Despite its broad mandate, early warning and formulating strategy were

---

[2]   In the enabling resolutions establishing the Peace-building Commission, resolution 60/180 and resolution 1645 (2005) of 20 December 2005, the United Nations General Assembly and the Security Council mandated it, *inter alia*, to bring together all relevant actors to marshal resources and to advise on the proposed integrated strategies for post-conflict peace-building and recovery; to help ensure predictable financing for early recovery activities and sustained financial investment over the medium to long-term; and to develop best practices on issues in collaboration with political, security, humanitarian and development actors. The resolutions also identify the need for the Commission to extend the period of international attention on post-conflict countries and where necessary, highlight any gaps which threaten to undermine peace-building.

initial casualties making it look more like a standing conference. In addition to clarity of purpose, success requires time and money. Lengthy engagement in the past did not ensure success, but premature departure guaranteed failure (p. 354). Yet the Commission remains a significant development for facilitating co-ordination and highlighting the need for a sustained post-conflict peace-building effort.

The adoption by the UN of resolutions under Chapter VII of the Charter involving enforcement measures has been one of its most controversial actions in recent years. The real problem is not the legality of such activity, but the question of which states decide when it is appropriate and the criteria used to form that decision.[3] This is so despite the fact that the practice of the Security Council authorization for states to use armed force does not correspond to the express text of Chapter VII of the Charter. The current practice allows the permanent members of the Council to determine the agenda, thus facilitating a very selective, secretive and undemocratic response to international crises. The situation is made worse by the ambiguity surrounding the extent to which peaceful settlement procedures, including diplomatic efforts must be exhausted before military sanctions are applied.[4] The problem has been compounded by the willingness of states to take action outside the framework of the UN such as occurred in Iraq (2003) and Kosovo (1999), and the role of a select industrialized group of nations, especially in relation to Kosovo, which has been to function as a kind of shadow Security Council, but with no real accountability. All of these factors impact on UN peace-building efforts. If military intervention is contemplated, then it must take account of post-intervention strategy (International Commission on Intervention and State Sovereignty, 2001, para. 5.3). The object being to ensure the reasons that necessitated the intervention do not arise again. In this way the responsibility to protect or react implies a similar responsibility to follow through and rebuild International Commission on Intervention and State Sovereignty, 2001, para. 5.1). Failed states are inevitably associated with internal and endogenous problems, though they may have cross frontier dimensions (Ramcharan, 1996, p. 143; Thurer, 1999, p. 731). The situation is one of implosion rather than explosion of the structures of power and authority. An initial priority must be the provision of security, including disarmament, demobilization and re-integration and rebuilding of national forces. This should be followed by a justice and reconciliation policy to include the right of returnees and refugees, and lastly a development policy aimed at improving the overall economic climate (see Tschirgi, 2003).

UN High-Level Panel on Threats, Challenges and Change

Post-conflict peace-building has been adopted to describe the assumption of governance functions by the UN that is, 'action to identify and support structures which will tend to strengthen and solidify peace in order to avoid a relapse into conflict' (Boutros-Ghali, 1992,

---

    [3]   This is so despite the fact that the practice of the Security Council authorization for states to use armed force does not correspond to the express text of Chapter VII of the Charter.

    [4]   This was a source of controversy and debate before the adoption of SC Resolution 678 (1991), which authorized collective measures against Iraq and led to Operation Desert Storm (see Green, 1991, p. 560; Schachter, 1991, p. 452).

para. 21).[5] The expansion of the Security Council's mandate has focused attention on whether the underlying legal authority for peace-keeping provides a legitimate foundation for these new missions (see for example, Ratner, 1995, pp. 58–60). As the mechanisms of Security Council action under Chapters VI and VII of the UN Charter were established with more traditional peace-keeping in mind rather than post-conflict peace-building, practitioners and commentators have considered an alternative framework for intervention. This would replace the current rather *ad hoc* system of Security Council action. Some commentators (Mohamed, 2005, p. 809; see also International Commission on Intervention and State Sovereignty, 2001, paras 5.22–5.24) have recommended transferring the administration and reconstruction of collapsed states to the now-dormant Trusteeship Council, the UN organ responsible for steering dependent territories to independence.[6]

In 2000, the UN Secretary-General convened an expert Panel on United Nations Peace Operations to make recommendations for reform of the peace-keeping system. The final report ('Brahimi Report') outlined a wide range of proposals for reform. It also contained blunt criticisms and warned that without significant institutional change, the UN would not be capable of executing the critical peace-keeping and peace-building tasks that the member states assign (United Nations, 2000, paras 1, 8; see also United Nations, 2001, para. 21).

The *High-Level Panel on Threats, Challenges and Change* (United Nations, 2004) evaluated UN policies with regard to collective security and provided recommendations for strengthening the organization taking into account twenty-first-century challenges to global security. It offered a blue print for reform, while acknowledging the strengths of the organization.

> The [UN's] role in this area arises from its international legitimacy; the impartiality of its personnel; its ability to draw on personnel with broad cultural understanding and experience of a wider range of administrative systems, including the developing world; and its recent experience in organizing transitional administration and transitional authority operation. (United Nations, 2004, para. 262)

The High-Level Panel recognized that peace-building is essential given contemporary challenges, but deplored that work and resources in this area remain too dispersed. It concluded that there was 'no place in the United Nations system explicitly designed to avoid state collapse ... or to assist countries in their transition from war to peace' (United Nations, 2004, para. 261). Amongst its proposals was the establishment of a Peace-Building Commission dedicated to supporting states in their reconstruction and development efforts. This was later endorsed by the Secretary-General and in a subsequent report entitled *In Larger*

---

5   See also United Nations (2004, para. 229): '[T]he core task of peacebuilding is to build effective public institutions that, through negotiations with civil society, can establish a consensual framework for governing within the rule of law.'

6   Personal interview, DPKO official, UN headquarters, New York, December 2009. The Trusteeship Council was responsible for colonies and territories that at the end of World War I were 'inhabited by peoples not yet able to stand by themselves under the strenuous conditions of the modern world' (see Sayre, 1948, pp. 263–68; Abbot and Snidal, 1998, p. 20). The panel convened by the Secretary-General, *Report of the High-Level Panel on Threats, Challenges and Change*, proposed abolishing the Trusteeship Council (United Nations, 2004, para. 299).

Freedom: Towards Development, Security and Human Rights for All, the Secretary-General recommended the establishment of a Rule of Law Assistance Unit within the Peace-Building Commission 'to assist national efforts to re-establish the rule of law in conflict and post-conflict societies' (United Nations, 2005a, p. 36).[7]

Rule of Law[8]

The establishment of the rule of law is vital for all those involved in post-conflict peace-building (see O'Connor, 2005; O'Connor and Rausch, 2007, p. 3). Prisons, police stations and court houses may be destroyed. Lawyers, judges and police may have fled leading to a situation where the criminal justice system is dysfunctional or has ceased to function completely. According to David Tolbert and Andrew Solomon, 'United Nations Reform and Supporting the Rule of Law in Post-Conflict Societies' (Chapter 9), the phrase 'rule of law' became part of the lexicon of post-conflict peace-building and is accepted by many commentators as central to the rebuilding process (p. 209). The current rule of law promotion field began in the mid-1980s in Latin America and has since expanded to include Eastern Europe, the former Soviet Union, Asia and sub-Saharan Africa (Thomas Carothers, 'Promoting the Rule of Law Abroad' (Chapter 7, p. 186)). However, there is still some confusion and scepticism about what rule of law means in practice and if the various programmes achieve anything.[9] Lord Ashdown (2002, p. A2), then High Representative for Bosnia-Herzegovina, is on record as saying:

> In hindsight, we should have put the establishment of the rule of law first, for everything else depends on it: a functioning economy, a free and fair political system, the development of civil society, public confidence in the police and courts.

Hansjörg Strohmeyer came to a similar conclusion based on his study, 'Collapse and Reconstruction of a Judicial System' (Chapter 8), when considering the UN missions in Kosovo and East Timor. The administration of justice must be a top priority from the outset and he proposes a number of practical recommendations to achieve this goal. This is no simple task when there is no system to be administered, no qualified personnel available and no physical structure left intact.

The UN Secretary-General has defined rule of law as follows:

---

[7]   See also the Secretary-General's Remarks on the Launch of the Peace-Building Fund, New York, 11 October 2006.

[8]   See Carlson (2006); Stomseth *et al.* (2006).

[9]   'When rule-of-law practitioners gather among themselves to reflect on their work, they often express contradictory thoughts. On the one hand they talk with enthusiasm and interest about what they do, believing that the field of rule-of-law assistance is extremely important. Many feel it is at the cutting edge of international efforts to promote both development and democracy abroad. On the other hand, when pressed, they admit that the base of knowledge from which they are operating is startlingly thin. As a colleague who has been closely involved in rule-of-law work in Latin America for many years said to me recently, "we know how to do a lot of things, but deep down we don't really know what we are doing"' (Carothers, Chapter 7, p. 180).

The rule of law is a concept at the very heart of the Organization's mission. It refers to a principle of governance in which all persons, institutions and entities, public and private, including the State itself, are accountable to laws that are publicly promulgated, equally enforced and independently adjudicated, and which are consistent with international human rights norms and standards. It requires, as well, measures to ensure adherence to the principles of law, equality before the law, accountability to the law, fairness in the application of the law, legal certainty, avoidance of arbitrariness and procedural and legal transparency. (UNSC, 2004, para. 5)

Although this may have been viewed as a somewhat narrow and legal perspective on the rule of law, by definition it must be embedded in legal principles. This begs the question, which legal principles? The rule of law is a key element in the UN's post-conflict agenda. The two central tenets espoused as part of this agenda are: the promotion of international norms and standards and facilitating the development of local ownership (Vig, 2009). However, this is likely to lead to situations where both components cannot be satisfied simultaneously.

Brahimi advocated, *inter alia*, a 'light footed' and bottom-up approach by the UN to post-conflict rebuilding based on his own experience in missions such as Afghanistan. This approach should minimize the UN and other international presence while facilitating local ownership (Schmemann, 2001, p. B4; Vig, 2009, p. 138). Avoidance of adopting a neo-colonial approach and ensuring the creation of a sustainable post-conflict society are paramount considerations. However, these must be reconciled with the imperative of creating a framework based on international norms and standards espoused in the 2004 report *The Rule of Law and Transitional Justice in Conflict and Post-Conflict Societies* (UNSC, 2004, p. 3; see generally Aersten *et al.*, 2008). This report constitutes the foundation of UN peace-building theory and represented a new approach to rule of law policy in post-conflict societies. An obvious problem with international norms is that they are easy to sign up to but much more difficult to live up to.

Finding means of engaging national stakeholders is crucial to the success of any strategy devised to promote legitimacy and sustainability. Such stakeholders include justice sector officials, civil society, professional associations, traditional leaders, women, minorities, displaced persons and refugees (UNSC, 2004, p. 6; see also Lopes and Theisohn, 2003, p. 29; Chesterman, 2007, pp. 1, 3, 8). These must be given a real say in driving the process of reform. Identifying national partners and recognizing their leadership role should be a priority task for those involved in peace operations (Brahimi, 2007, p. 3). This will require cultivation of support among all sectors, former combatants and social elites and those marginalized under previous regimes.

International missions in Somalia, Bosnia, East Timor and Kosovo have been characterized by international officials participating fully in policy-making and in the process acting as kinds of trustees. New laws and codes were introduced that were described by Matteo Tondini in 'From Neocolonialism to a "Light-Footed" Approach' (Chapter 10), as having 'the ring of authoritarianism and appear to be dropped in from on high' (p. 243, but see Strohmeyer, Chapter 8). The need for some form of intervention in failed states does not bestow authority or grant a licence on those intervening to do what they will. A central objection against UN action in post-conflict societies is that 'rich and powerful states perpetuate their domination, fulfill their own foreign policy objectives, and impose their own models of government and society under the veil of the UN' (Han, 1994, p. 888).

In Rwanda, the widespread engagement of international actors in justice system reform was said to have created a 'donor-driven justice' (Oomen, 2005, p. 894), completely separated from the country's legal tradition. In Afghanistan, on the other hand, the justice system has been shaped in a manner that paid due attention to the legal and judicial systems formerly in place (Tondini, p. 243; see also Schoiswohl, 2006). This placed primary responsibility for the restoration of the sector on the Afghan government (at least formally), with international actors performing a limited co-ordination role which the UN termed adopting the so called 'light-footprint approach' (United Nations, 2002, p. 16). This approach, despite criticisms, builds on the premise that the UN is a partner in the process, rather than sovereign administrator (Chesterman, Chapter 14, p. 349; see also Chesterman, 2005, p. 339; Chesterman, 2007, p. 9). Both Afghanistan and Iraq are examples of 'post-conquest peace-building' which raise legitimate fears of the peace-building project being overtaken by other agendas (see Tschirgi, 2004, p. 1). In theory, democratic institutions and structures put in place should continue after the departure of the UN. However, Afghanistan remains a test case and at the time of writing it is not clear if the peace-building mission there, which amounts to state-building and the promotion of good governance by means of democratic institutions, will succeed (see also Rand Corporation, 2005; Schoiswohl, 2006).

Carothers (Chapter 7) has drawn attention to the weakness of many rule of law programmes and the lack of knowledge at many levels of conception, operation and evaluation. Among the most common lessons learned, for example, are 'programs must be shaped to fit the local environment' and 'law reformers should not simply import laws from other countries' (p. 186). The fact that common sense lessons of this type are put forward by institutions as lessons learned is an unfortunate indicator of the weakness of many such efforts.

Jennifer Widner, 'Courts and Democracy in Postconflict Transitions' (Chapter 2), offers a social scientist's perspective of the role courts in achieving peace and building new democracies in Africa. She focuses on how law plays a central but delicate role in many peace settlements and democratic transitions on the African continent. She cautions against placing too much faith in courts as their relationship with post-conflict stabilization is not always straightforward. There are no 'quick fix' solutions. The attitude of other social actors, the efficacy of the courts in indicating their ambition for intervention, the character of the law itself and mobilization of resources all impact on the contribution the courts can make (p. 60).

Legal reforms and situations to date indicate that finding a formula that has universal application is not possible. However, achieving a stable political and security situation is imperative in any post-conflict reconstruction (CSIS and AUSA, 2003, p. 7). Efforts to identify the applicable law have often been haphazard and *ad hoc* in nature. This question has now been resolved with the publication of the Model Codes for Post-Conflict Criminal Justice. These sought to address one of the most daunting and fundamental challenges confronting and peace-building mission that is, identifying and applying a relevant and acceptable code of law. While establishing a legal framework is essential, Tolbert and Solomon (Chapter 9) point out that it is also necessary to ensure an independent and competent judiciary, legal profession and reputable schools for training lawyers (pp. 224–30). Closely linked to the Rule of Law is that of transitional justice. This can take many forms which combine 'prosecutorial styles of justice, local mechanisms for truth recovery and a progamme for criminal justice reforms' (McEvoy, 2007, p. 412). Issues of good governance are uppermost on the agenda of transitional administrations. Unfortunately, the mandates of those administrations are often ambiguous and broad. They are the result of political compromise. Nevertheless, this has been identified for some time as a weakness in peace-keeping missions. Security Council resolutions are too ambitious to provide secure guidance for post-conflict justice (Stahn, 2004–05, p. 320).

The expansion of the UN's role in peace operations was accompanied by a new emphasis on 'human rights' and the 'rule of law' (Correl, 2005, p. 31). Carsten Stahn, '"Jus ad Bellum", "Jus in Bello" … "Jus post Bellum"?' (Chapter 12), recommends that the existing international law framework needs to be extended beyond the boundaries of the dualist conception of *jus ad bello* and *jus in bellum* (pp. 298–99).[10] He suggests a new approach to determining the legal framework applicable to post-conflict situations and proposes the development of an *ius post bellum*, that is, a specific post-conflict regime with the potential to draw on both human rights and humanitarian law in peace-building. This argument certainly has appeal. The ultimate purpose of fair and just peace-making is to remove the causes of violence. This will mean more than a return to the *status quo ante* but the positive transformation of the domestic order of a society. Ideally this will endeavour to achieve a higher level of human rights protection, accountability and good governance than had existed before (p. 294). There is also a move from collective to individual responsibility (Orend, 2000, p. 232). Modern international practice, particularly in the area of peace-building, appears to focus on a model involving targeted accountability in peace processes. This involves amnesties for less serious crimes, and the establishment of truth and reconciliation commissions with a functioning criminal justice system (Stahn, Chapter 12, p. 299). Lastly, he also suggests that it include provision for 'people centred government': 'Peace-making, more than ever before, is tied to the ending of autocratic, undemocratic and oppressive regimes, and directed towards the ideal of "popular sovereignty" held by individuals instead of states or elites' (p. 299).

Lessons from UNMIK

David Marshall and Shelley Inglis's study of United Nations Interim Administration Mission in Kosovo (UNMIK), 'The Disempowerment of Human Rights-Based Justice in the United Nations Mission in Kosovo' (Chapter 6), found that establishing a *de facto* government incorporating a new justice system is a significant challenge in any situation, but especially when a society is nursing deep wounds from recent conflict (p. 174; see generally Murphy,

---

[10]   Stahn recommends the *ius post bellum* includes a move from collective to individual accountability and the harmonization of justice and reconciliation. He also suggests provision for 'people centred government' that would 'create, *inter alia*, a duty for domestic or international holders of public authority in situations of transition to institute political structures that embody mechanisms of accountability *vis-à-vis* the governed population and timelines to gradually transfer power from political elites to elected representatives' (p. 299; see also Roberts, 2006, p. 580, at pp. 595–90). Roberts is pessimistic about the possibilities of developing a more coherent *jus post bellum* regime either through *ad hoc* modification or formal revision of existing regimes.

2007). In spite of the achievement in Kosovo, UNMIK provides some sobering lessons in the area of criminal justice and human rights from which future post-conflict peace-building operations could learn. The mission failed to establish a framework based on international human rights standards within which UNMIK and Kosovo Force (KFOR) could determine the extent and quality of their actions (p. 126). Long-term strategic goals were unclear, especially in regard to the justice sector, and there was no consistent, transparent and inclusive process. UNMIK created a system of governance whereby it was effectively above the law and even the human rights components of the mission were marginalized in the legislative process (p. 128). This made reviewing proposals for human rights compliance almost non-existent.

Peace-building missions need to recognize that developing a justice system based on the rule of law and human rights is the cornerstone of a successful transition to democracy. International administration must be structured to limit the amount of power vested in the transitional administrator and ensure a system of checks and balances. A clear legal framework is needed, and an independent courts system must be an essential element in this (p. 174). It is inevitable that certain peace-building missions will require the vesting of supreme powers in an administrator. Where this occurs it is imperative that an effective system of checks and balances is put in place to ensure that fundamental principles of good governance are adhered to. A legal framework based on international standards can provide the benchmark by which to measure compliance by civilian and security components of peace-building missions. Such a framework must be supported by an effective court system incorporating an overarching constitutional or Supreme Court with appropriate jurisdiction (p. 174). The design of a constitution and the process leading to its adoption is identified by Kirsti Samuels, 'Post-Conflict Peace-Building and Constitution-Making' (Chapter 11), as an integral and difficult part of the peace-building process (p. 277). The adoption of institutional structures that promote moderate behaviour is a crucial aspect of the architecture of governance in post-conflict environments. This is especially so in relation to electoral and power-sharing models chosen. Unfortunately, short-term political goals may mitigate against long-term institution-building needs. Indentifying best practice is fraught with practical difficulties owing to the multiplicity of factors impacting on the outcome (Widner, 2007–08, p. 1537).

Gregory Naarden and Jeffrey Locke's study of the UNMIK experience, 'Peacekeeping and Prosecutorial Policy' (Chapter 5), demonstrates that it has been a test case for the viability of including a prosecutorial component in transitional criminal justice systems. Future missions must evaluate the criminal justice environment before international prosecutors are introduced. There must be an analysis of the nature of the crimes that affect the peace process and the ability of law enforcement agencies to deal with those crimes. The ability to prosecute dangerous crimes was fundamental to ensuring peace and security. This required a comprehensive framework and strategy to ensure UNMIK reforms became institutionalized. However, corruption hinders the development of effective, legitimate and transparent public institutions in Kosovo (p. 110). Success can be measured by the degree to which local prosecutors are willing to pursue prosecutions in the absence of international assistance.

Erika de Wet, 'The Governance of Kosovo' (Chapter 4), analyses the challenges to the governance of Kosovo arising from the establishment of the European Union Rule of Law Mission in Kosovo (EULEX). The deployment of EULEX raised a significant controversy in regard to its reconcilability with UN Security Council Resolution 1244. Russia persisted in questioning its legality, a position supported by the Serbian minority in Kosovo. The evolution of the mandate for civil administration in Kosovo demonstrates the difficulties that arise in the face of such an open-ended mandate under Chapter VII of the Charter. Changed circumstances require an amendment, but political realities and the risk of a reverse veto currently preclude exercising such an option. In order for EULEX to exercise its mandate in accordance with Resolution 1244, all stakeholders must be willing to compromise. De Wet also analyses the challenges of co-ordinating the international responsibility of UNMIK and EULEX and the implications of the *Behrami* decision of the European Court of Human Rights.[11] If EULEX and its member states try to shield themselves behind this decision, an accountability vacuum will result as no other entity is likely to take responsibility.

Threat from Corruption

Corruption is acknowledged to be a significant factor in determining the success or otherwise of peace-building missions (United Nations, 2005b; Le Billon, Chapter 17, p 407). In his essay, 'Corrupting Peace?' (Chapter 17), Le Billon presents some of the arguments linking liberal peace-building with higher levels of corruption (p. 413). Corruption and conflict are often perceived to be synonymous during the post-conflict reconstruction phase.[12] It weakens the legitimacy and effectiveness of the architecture of good governance, creates obstacles to economic recovery and international investment and facilitates a return to violence. This in turn marginalizes local populations leading to disempowerment and political unrest (Bolongaita, 2005; Le Billon, 2005a, 2005b; Boucher *et al.*, 2007; O'Donnell, 2008). According to the UN Secretary-General, 'corruption, illicit trade and money-laundering contribute to state weakness, impede economic growth and undermine democracy. These activities thus create a permissive environment for civil conflict' (United Nations, 2004, para. 23).

The pervasiveness of corruption in Bosnia and Herzegovina is often cited as a major factor in the country's political and economic setbacks since the 1995 Dayton Accord (General Accounting Office (GAO), 2000; International Crisis Group (ICG), 2002; Devine, 2005). The Brahimi Report on peace operations advocates 'support for the fight against corruption' and stressed that it is the first priority among the 'essential complements to effective peace-building' (United Nations, 2000, p. 24). Richard Sannerholm, 'Legal, Judicial and Administrative Reforms in Post-Conflict Societies' (Chapter 3), has criticized the rule of law template as not sufficiently broad to deal with post-conflict reconstruction (p. 88; see generally Clark, 2009). The emphasis has been on security and law and order, and the protection of civil and political rights, while deficient in relation to other sectors of the state. This has resulted in widespread corruption and embezzlement of state assets in war-torn societies. A new trend is, however, 'vaguely discernable' in the practice of international actors engaged in peace-building

---

[11] *Behrami & Behrami* v. *France*; *Saramati* v. *France*, Joint App. Nos. 71412/01 & 78166/01, Admissibility Decision (31 May 2007), at: http://echr.coe.int/echr/en/hudoc.

[12] See for example, opinion polls: 'South East Europe Public Agenda Survey' by the South East Europe Democracy Support, 2002; Nicaragua, 'National Integrity Survey', CIET International, 1998; 'Governance and Anti-Corruption Report for Sierra Leone', World Bank, 2003; 'Cambodia Governance and Corruption Diagnostic', World Bank, May 2000.

that gives priority to the rule of law in public sector reform, including governance and economic management issues (p. 81; see also Agbakwa, 2003).

Victoria Holt and Alix Boucher, 'Framing the Issue' (Chapter 16), argue that there is an implicit link between the objectives of UN peace operations and rule of law missions intended to combat transnational crime (p. 394).[13] The UN's definition of transnational crime is broad and based on the 2000 UN Convention on Transnational Crime.[14] This definition has led to scholars adopting phrases such as 'illicit networks', 'transnational crime', 'illicit enterprise and illegal economies' (see Standing, 2003), to describe modern global networks and how these affect global economies and societies, especially their ability to maintain and build peace (Cockayne, 2007).

Corruption, similarly, is seen as the abuse of entrusted office for illegitimate private gain, as well as both a cause of conflict and an impediment to peace-building (US Agency for International Development (USAID), 2005, pp. 5–8). Combined with involvement in illicit networks, it can lead to renewed grievances and conflict (Boucher *et al.*, 2007). Together, they undermine peace-building efforts and the rule of law.

The negative impact of continued criminal activity by rebel groups was evident in Liberia (International Crisis Group (ICG), 2005, p. 30; United Nations, 2003, para. 15; United Nations, 2006, paras 24–25, 102). Post-conflict structures can institutionalize corruption. Government and rebel forces can be involved in illegal trading of weapons and commodities such as diamonds, timber and gold. Unfortunately, UN forces and personnel can also be a source of instability and corruption.[15]

There are inconsistencies and contradictions in the role of UN peace operations and panels of experts in addressing corruption and transnational crime. Panels of experts are small fact-finding teams appointed by the Security Council to monitor and investigate how UN targeted sanctions such as embargoes on arms, diamonds and timber, asset freezes and travel bans, are violated.[16] Holt and Boucher (Chapter 16) have highlighted the work of such panels in tracking transnational criminal networks (p. 398). However, no single tool is

---

[13]   UN involvement in tackling transnational crime and corruption are centred on a range of offices outside headquarters from the UN Office on Drugs and Crime (UNODC) to the UN Development Programme (UNDP), with some liaison and co-ordination with Interpol and other international bodies, such as the Organization for Security and Co-operation in Europe (OSCE).

[14]   United Nations Convention Against Transnational Organized Crime (2000), articles 2–3. A crime is transnational when it is planned, committed and has effects in more than one state. It considers an organized criminal group as a 'structured group of three or more persons, existing for a period of time and acting in concert with the aim of committing one or more serious crimes or offenses established in accordance with this Convention'.

[15]   In November 2007, over 100 Sri Lankan peacekeepers were sent home from the UN mission in Haiti for suspected involvement in sexual exploitation of local women. Similarly, a Pakistani unit deployed with the UN mission in the Democratic Republic of the Congo (DRC) was investigated for trafficking gold and weapons with militia groups in that country (see Vandenberg, 2002; Mendelson, 2005; Plaut, 2007a, 2007b; UN, IRIN, 2007).

[16]   Panels of experts were initially created to monitor the arms embargo on Rwanda and then sanctions on Angola. Panels of experts have since looked into how sanctions are violated in Sierra Leone, Liberia, the DRC, Cote d'Ivoire, Sudan and Somalia, and by Al Qaida and the Taliban. The panels were among the first to link criminal networks to continuing conflict, detailing how spoilers

designed to address the variety of vexing problems associated with criminal networks and corruption. Nonetheless, co-operation between panels of experts and peace operations could be more extensive and arrangements more systematic. Their combined effort in the field, such as occurred in Liberia, has the potential to enhance successful outcomes (p. 401). Before this can happen, transnational crime must be identified as the threat it is to peace and stability, and institutional co-operation between the UN Peace-Building Commission and agencies like Interpol increased. Panels of experts are like all UN creations, they need resourcing, planning and support from the Security Council. Ultimately better tools and systems will produce improved results.

Gender and Peace-Building

Gender is a term often used in the context of peace-building, but not frequently explained. Gender analysis involves understanding the differences between men and women.[17] Ensuring women's voices are heard is crucial in war-torn societies. They have separate and distinct sets of roles and experiences in times of conflict and Amy Maguire, '"Security Starts with the Law"' (Chapter 15), inquires into the role of international law in the protection of women's security in post-conflict societies. Research was conducted in three societies at various stages of post-conflict transition: Northern Ireland; Lebanon; and South Africa. As Mazurana (2005) notes, irrespective of the positive impact women can have in times of conflict:

> post-conflict reconstruction processes and peacekeeping operations routinely fail to see the larger
> gendered political and economic structures supporting the armed conflict or the value of women's
> peacebuilding work at local and regional levels. Because for the most part the politics of gender are
> not recognised and gendered causes and consequences are overlooked, the few international and
> national policies and programs developed to empower women or promote them in peacebuilding
> too often remain superficial, because they do little to challenge and dismantle the structures that
> caused and fuelled the violent conflict. Rather the conditions for inequality and refuelling the
> violence remain in place. (p. 4)

Awareness that gender involves socially constructed roles of men and women is particularly important in this context. What men and women do in society, their position, roles and status, cannot be attributed in sole part to their inherent nature. It is also shaped by the norms and hierarchy of a predominantly masculine society (Puechguirbal, 2004). In the context of peace-building, gender should be seen as ensuring that projects and programmes are executed in an effective manner, without perpetuating existing discrimination, or inadvertently harming

secure arms and undermine peace, and in some cases how governments use these networks to continue war.

17   Pankhurst (2003, p. 166) defines gender in the following manner: 'Gender is a term used in contrast to sex, to draw attention to the social roles and interactions between women and men .... Gender relations are social relations, which include the ways in which the social categories of male and female interact in every sphere of social activity, such as those who determine access to resources, power, and participation in political, cultural and religious activities.'

men or women, and promoting equality, human rights and internationally mandated values (Anderlini, 2007). Unfortunately, in 1992 *An Agenda for Peace* (Boutros-Ghali, 1992) did not formulate peace-building though the lens of gender analysis (see generally Chinkin, 2004; Paris, 2004). Confirmation that this had occurred at an international level was with the landmark Security Council Resolution 1325 (2000), which called for a gender perspective to be incorporated into the policy and practice of reconstruction and peace-building.[18]

Case studies show that despite the political legitimacy conferred on women's activism by Resolution 1325, and efforts to integrate these into the political process at national level, old obstacles to participation remain (Puechguirbal, 2004). Some cross-cutting issues were noted from a case study of Burundi, the Democratic Republic of Congo, Liberia and Sierra Leone. Common to these post-conflict situations was that provisions in the peace agreements reached failed to make adequate reference to women's agency and capacity for instigating change. Women are still grouped in the vulnerable 'women-and-children' category. This constructs the woman in terms of her passivity and dependence on men, and relegates her out of the political sphere. Some of the main obstacles to involvement of women in peace processes noted in the context of the above countries were: lack of political literacy and strategy; lack of experience in formal political techniques; a lack of visibility of women's conflict-resolution activities; insufficient material and financial resources; and the utilization of inappropriate methods of expression for formal negotiations. As well as this the onus on women to return to more traditional roles after the peace process has ended makes it more difficult to re-engage when reconstruction begins (Puechguirbal, 2004, p. 59).

Zimbabwe

In this volume, Max Du Plessis and Jolyon Ford, 'Transitional Justice' (Chapter 1), consider the complex variety of challenges confronting Zimbabwe and the extent to which an international legal framework not only forms a backdrop to national choices on justice and reconciliation, but may shape and constrain the institutional and procedural options available. They reflect on a variety of transitional justice experiences and conclude that three main avenues are now used to formally address injustices relating to past violence: criminal trials (the majority of these operations have seen the use of 'mixed' internationally–nationally staffed tribunals); truth for amnesty commissions; and a hybrid strategy entailing both conditional amnesties and selective prosecutions. Despite the growth in 'best practices' and guidelines, transitional justice choices remain eclectic. They argue that peace-building institutions extend a margin of appreciation to transitional societies to find their own ways to reconcile with the past as part of building a sustainable future peace. As the normative framework is evolving, bona fide national measures must be respected. The real challenge is to adopt a strategy to address

---

[18]   UN Security Council Resolution 1325, 31 October 2000. For more background see the Inter-Agency Network on Women and Gender Equality (IANWGE), Taskforce on Women, Peace and Security, 'From the Charter to Security Council Resolution 1325' at: www.womenwatch.org/womenwatch/ ianwge/taskforces/wps/history.html. The Security Council has since adopted three more resolutions on women peace and security in order to expand and complement the content of Resolution 1325, namely Resolution 1820, 1888 and 1889.

a diverse range of past human rights tragedies from torture to land disputes and economic deprivation. The choice is not between peace or justice and there is a need to move on from the simplistic analysis that presents these as mutually inconsistent objectives in a post-conflict environment (see generally Williams and Scharf, 2002; Siels and Weirda, 2005; Grono and O'Brien, 2008).

Conclusion

The UN is often required to play multiple roles in post-conflict environments. These are not always consistent and on occasion can come into conflict. This was nowhere more evident than in Sudan where, among other things, the Security Council established a Chapter VII peace-keeping operation in conjunction with the African Union but on terms dictated by the Sudanese government, while at the same time it referred the situation in Darfur to the International Criminal Court.

The record of peace-building, like that of peace-keeping, is varied (Paris, 2007, p. 416). The UN can go from being a peace-keeper under Chapter VI to a peace-enforcer under Chapter VII, and back again. While enforcing the peace and rule of law in places like Kosovo, it can at the same time decline to arrest suspected war criminals (Lyck, 2007). This can give mixed messages to national and international stakeholders, in addition to being confusing for UN staff on the ground.

The UN is increasingly overstretched in terms of its current commitments, while in Timor-Leste and Bosnia-Herzegovina, it has learnt to its cost the importance of a long-term commitment. Sometimes it seems like the Security Council has lost touch with reality. Despite an inability to find enough troops and helicopters for the mission in Sudan, the Council continued to approve missions elsewhere (Center on International Cooperation, 2009, p. 2). Operations have increased in size and complexity, while UN personnel on the ground are required to face ever-increasing challenges from insecure environments to multi-dimensional mandates.

The mandates for current peace operations cover a wide spectrum from traditional peace-keeping and monitoring of ceasefire arrangements (United Nations Disengagement Observer Force (UNDOF) on the Golan Heights) to assisting with the organization of elections and the rebuilding of national institutions (as in the DRC), to administering territory such as Kosovo under complex legal and political arrangements. In addition to struggling to implement these broad mandates, the UN has to integrate a wide range of activities with other UN programmes and agencies, and international and local actors.

The UN itself is a large bureaucracy and post-conflict interventions can be challenging on every front. 'Integration' and 'coherence' have been identified as critical for peace-building as is the engagement of a broad range of actors, including national authorities and the local population.[19] In response, the UN has developed a series of 'integration reforms' aimed at enhancing its capacity to integrate post-conflict efforts into a single coherent strategy (Campbell, 2008). At the level of the UN Secretariat, reforms have led to the creation of

---

[19] UN Secretary-General, 'Note of Guidance on Integrated Missions', 17 January 2006, para. 2.

offices dedicated to strengthening the rule of law, and increasing the capacity of Department of Peace-Keeping Operations (DPKOs) to deal with contemporary issues.[20]

Peace-building, at least initially, will exist in the grey zone between war and peace where lines are blurred as to where one ends and the other begins (Plunkett, 1998, p. 63). While UN involvement remains central, the organization can be hindered by bureaucracy and inertia. It is difficult to mobilize its resources to best effect, while its management culture and internal accountability mechanisms can be deficient.[21] Its diversity too can be a weakness, with meritocracy being supplanted by patronage and political necessity.

Peace-building will always be linked to the peace process that preceded it and any agreement concluded. The terms used can evoke conflicting perceptions about the process undertaken. In this way, according to Christine Bell, 'Peace Agreements' (Chapter 13), a peace agreement may be perceived as a 'ceasefire agreement' by some and as 'surrender' by others (p. 303; see further Bell, 2000). Bell provides a comprehensive analysis of the nature and legal status of peace agreements. She argues that peace agreements have produced practices of legalization marked by some consistency across varying peace processes and that this constitutes an emerging 'law of peace makers (*pax pacificatoria*)'. The main factors affecting the likelihood of parties remaining committed to a peace agreement include the dynamics of third-party interventions; the structural characteristics of conflict processes; the changing regional/systemic power relationships and balances; and the range of issues covered by the agreement. Many variables can influence the outcome, including regime change, environmental changes and economic uncertainty. In places like Afghanistan, the regional context cannot be ignored and security issues in parts of Pakistan have a direct impact. The potential negative role of so-called 'spoilers', individuals or parties who work against a peace process, must also be taken into account (see Zartman, 1989; Brown, 1996; Stedman, 1997; Greenhill and Major, 2006).

Robert Muggah and Keith Krause, 'Closing the Gap between Peace Operations and Post-Conflict Insecurity' (Chapter 18), highlight how instruments for addressing the sources of armed conflict need to include the development of practical armed violence prevention and reduction programmes that draw upon scholarship and practice from criminal justice and health sectors. They point out the deficiencies of small arms control programmes and recommend ways to promote more comprehensive approaches to armed violence reduction in post-conflict or violent environments.

Tondini (Chapter 10) analyses peace-building theories and methods, as applied to justice system reform in post-conflict societies. The evidence available indicates the need for a change of strategy in the approach adopted to the reform of justice in war-torn societies, as interventions tend to be largely ineffective (p. 253). It is imperative that the UN deal with

---

[20]   The UN created an Office of Rule of Law and Security Institutions (OROLSI) in the DPKO (see 'UN Rule of Law, Security Officials Outline Key Priorities for 2008', *UN News Service*). Another initiative was the creation of a Rule of Law Co-ordination and Resource Group, which gathers the heads of eight UN departments, including DPKO, UNDP, UNODC, to discuss better integration of rule-of-law efforts (Migiro, 2008, 'Rule of Law Drives Work and Mission of UN', *UN News Service*).

[21]   Independent Inquiry Committee into the United Nations Oil-for-Food Programme (2005), esp. vol. 1, *Report on the Management of the United Nations Oil-for-Food Programme*, 7 September 2005, at: http://www.iic-offp.org/Mgmt_Report.htm.

the challenges presented by transnational crime and its impact on peace-building and the rule of law. The success rate of peace-building missions in the re-establishment of justice systems does not appear encouraging. The situation in Africa is especially critical (p. 252). The 'war on terror' has remedied the traditional neglect of the continent, but interventions have more to do with strategic priorities of powerful states rather than needs (Chesterman, 2007, p. 5). Likewise, there should be no dilution of criminal accountability for violations of international human rights or humanitarian law. Such short-term expediency can unravel the successes and achievements of post-conflict peace-building. This is why establishing an effective legal framework within which an independent judiciary and legal profession can function is essential.

The rule of law assistance programme may not be assumed to be a coherent field of international aid as it still lacks a well grounded rationale and proven analytic method (Carothers, Chapter 7, pp. 188–89). The notion that specific improvements in the rule of law will provide the necessary 'quick fix' to achieve democracy is dangerously simplistic, as in Western countries '[d]emocracy often, in fact usually, co-exists with substantial shortcomings in the rule of law' (p. 182). Rule of law is just one element in the peace building process. It cannot compensate for or resolve the political problems involved in peace-building and post-war reconstruction (Chandler, 2004, p. 314; Chandler, 2006, p. 483).

While a secure environment is essential for peace-building, state-centric security concerns have led some governments to compromise on commitments to human rights, good governance and the rule of law. A state of emergency precipitating an intervention cannot be allowed to justify the suspension of fundamental rights and guarantees, however challenging a task a peace-building mission may prove to be. Field missions must endeavour to have personnel with relevant expertise at both the legislative proposal and implementation stages. This requires judges, prosecutors and investigators of international standing from the earliest stage in the mission. National 'ownership' by key stakeholders is a critical component in ensuring the sustainability of initiatives aimed at developing a justice system. In Somalia, the re-establishment of the national police forces was prioritized over judicial systems (Kelly, 1999, p. 78). Shortage of resources often leads to such decisions, but a better strategy would be to view both as essential and in partnership.

UN mandates are often ambiguous and in practice this may mean that UN administrations grant themselves far-reaching legislative, executive and judicial powers as occurred in East Timor and Kosovo. Although some may question if the UN should be so deeply involved in transitional administration (United Nations, 2000, para. 78; Stahn, 2004–05, p. 326), there seems little alternative. The experience to date demonstrates that justice can be a malleable concept. Establishing basic judicial functions and safeguards remains a fundament priority. But it must take into account domestic particularities. International and national bodies must be accountable. International standards should be the benchmark to scrutinize actions, especially those outlining the minimum protections for human rights.

Peace-building has become a matter of state-building with the UN and similar international organizations promoting democratic institutions as a basis for good governance (Johnstone, 2004, p. 823; Schoiswohl, 2006, p. 821). It is ironic that what were deemed free and fair elections in Palestine in 2006 were rejected by the United States and Europe when they did not like the outcome. The 'war on terrorism' has meant that military responses dominated strategies in both Iraq and Afghanistan. The causes of terrorism are complex and multi-faceted, but contemporary peace-building seeks to address these while at the same time transforming environments that allow terrorism to grow.

The ideas of reconstruction, justice and reconciliation are often put forward as merits of sustainable peace-making, however, they are also a *post hoc* means of justifying liberal interventions (Stahn, 2004–05, p. 315). In some cases, public affirmations of the local ownership of state-building processes may be a mask behind which international actors protect themselves in case of failure. Moreover, '[w]hen delays, obstacles, and drawbacks cannot be ignored any longer; they are blamed on the local actors' (Belloni, 2007, p. 107). Mistakes are often repeated by the same or different entities; this need not be the case (UNSC, 2004, para. 14–3). The Peace-Building Commission, despite its broad but somewhat ill-defined mandate and some deserved criticism, remains a significant development for facilitating co-ordination and focusing on the need for a sustained post-conflict peace-building effort. While it should remedy the 'strategic deficit' highlighted in recent studies (Smith, 2004; Verstegen *et al.*, 2005), the Commission needs a charismatic leader, enhanced budget, role and revised terms of reference (Otobo, 2010; Salomons, 2010). International law can provide a framework for an enhanced role. It is not a solution in itself. This will only be found when peace-building incorporates social and economic reconstruction that takes account of the historical context, and the range of political, social, economic and environmental factors that contributed to this.

Bibliography

Abbot, K.W. and Snidal, D. (1998), 'Why States Act through Formal International Organizations', *Journal of Conflict Resolution*, **42**, pp. 3–32.

Aersten, I., Arsovska, J., Rohne, H.-C., Valinas, M. and Vanspauwen, K. (eds) (2008), *Restoring Justice after Large Scale Violent Conflicts: Kosovo, DR Congo and the Israeli-Palestinian Case*, Cullompton: Willian Publishing.

Agbakwa, S.C. (2003), 'A Path Least Taken: Economic and Social Rights and the Prospects of Conflict Prevention and Peacebuilding in Africa', *Journal of African Law*, **47**, pp. 38–64.

Anderlini, S. (2007), 'How the International System Lets Women Down', in *Women Building Peace: What They Do, Why It Matters*, Boulder, CO: Lynne Rienner, pp. 191–232.

Ashdown, P. (2002), 'What I Learned in Bosnia', *New York Times*, 28 October, p. A2.

Azimi, N. and Lin, C. (eds) (2000), *The Nexus between Peacekeeping and Peacebuilding: Debriefing and Lessons*, Hague: Kluwer.

Bell, C. (2000), *Peace Agreements and Human Rights*, New York: Oxford University Press.

Belloni, R. (2007), 'Rethinking "Nation-Building": The Contradictions of the Neo-Wilsonian Approach to Democracy Promotion', *Whitehead Journal of Diplomacy and International Relations*, **8**, pp. 97–109.

Berdal, M. and Caplan, R. (2004), 'The Politics of International Administration', *Global Governance*, **10**, pp. 1–5.

Bolongaita, E. (2005), *Controlling Corruption in Post-Conflict Countries*, Kroc Institute Occasional Paper No. 26.

Boucher, A., Durch, W.J., Midyette, M., Rose, S. and Terry, J. (2006), *Mapping and Fighting Corruption in War-Torn States*, Washington, DC: Henry L. Stimson Centre.

Boutros-Ghali, B. (1992), *An Agenda for Peace: Preventive Diplomacy, Peacemaking and Peace-Keeping*, Report of the Secretary-General, UN Doc. A/47/277–S/24111.

Boutros-Ghali, B. (2003), 'Beyond Peacekeeping', *New York University Journal of International Law and Politics*, **25**, p. 113–22.

Brahimi, L. (2007), 'State-Building in Crisis and Post-Conflict Countries', *7th Global Forum on Reinventing Government Building Trust in Government*, Austria: Vienna, 26–29 June.

Brown, M.E. (ed.) (1996), *The International Dimensions of Internal Conflict*, Cambridge, MA: MIT Press.

Campbell, C. (2000), 'Peace and the Laws of War: The Role of Humanitarian Law in Post-Conflict Environment', *International Review of the Red Cross*, **839**, pp. 527–51.

Campbell, S.P. (2008), '(Dis)integration, Incoherence and Complexity in UN Post-Conflict Interventions', *International Peacekeeping*, **14**, pp. 556–69.

Carlson, S.N. (2006), *Legal and Judicial Rule of Law Work in Multi-Dimensional Peacekeeping Operations: Lessons Learned Study*, New York: UN Peacekeeping Best Practices Unit.

Center for Strategic and International Studies (CSIS) and the Association of the US Army (AUSA) (2003), *Play to Win: Final Report of the Bi-Partisan Commission on Post-Conflict Reconstruction*, Arlington, VA: CSIS and Washington, DC: AUSA.

Center on International Cooperation (2009), *Annual Review of Global Peacekeeping 2009*, Boulder, CO: Lynne Rienner.

Cerone, J. (2005), 'Reasonable Measures in Unreasonable Circumstances: A Legal Responsibility Framework for Human Rights Violations in Post-Conflict Territories under UN Administration', in N.D. White and D. Klaasen (eds), *The UN, Human Rights and Post-Conflict Situations*, Manchester: Manchester University Press, pp. 42–80.

Chandler, D. (2004), 'Imposing the "Rule of Law": The Lessons of BiH for Peacebuilding in Iraq', *International Peacekeeping*, **11**, pp. 312–33.

Chandler, D. (2006), 'Back to the Future? The Limits of Neo-Wilsonian Ideals of Exporting Democracy', *Review of International Studies*, **32**, pp. 475–94.

Chesterman, S. (2005), 'Transitional Administration State Building and the U.N.', in S. Chesterman *et al.*, *Making States Work, State Failure and the Crisis of Governance*, New York: United Nations University Press, pp. 339–58.

Chesterman, S. (2007), 'Ownership in Theory and Practice: Transfer of Authority in UN Statebuilding Operations', *Journal of Intervention and Statebuilding*, **1**, pp. 3–26.

Chesterman, S., Ignatieff, M. and Thakur, R. (2005), *Making States Work, State Failure and the Crisis of Governance*, New York: United Nations University.

Chinkin, C. (2004), *International Legal Framework and Peacebuilding: Gender and Peacebuilding in Africa*, Working Paper for the Norwegian Institute of International Affairs (NUPI), Oslo.

Clark, J.N. (2009), 'The Limits of Retributive Justice: Findings of an Empirical Study in Bosnia and Hercegovina', *Journal of International Criminal Justice*, 7, pp. 463–87.

Cockayne, J. (2007), *Transnational Organized Crime: Multilateral Response to a Rising Threat*, New York: International Peace Academy.

Correl, H. (2005), 'Authorization for State-Building Missions: Legal Issues Related to Their Creation and Management', *American Society of International Law Proceedings*, **99**, pp. 31–35.

Devereux, A. (2009), 'Selective Universality? Human-Rights Accountability of the UN in Post-Conflict Operations', in B. Bowden, H. Charlesworth and J. Farrell (eds), *The Role of International Law in Rebuilding Societies after Conflict: Great Expectations*, New York: Cambridge University Press, pp. 198–217.

Devine, V. (2005), 'Corruption in Post-War Reconstruction: The Experience of Bosnia and Herzegovina', in D. Large (ed.), *Corruption in Post War Reconstruction: Confronting the Vicious Circle*, Beirut: Lebanese Transparency Association, TIRI and UNDP.

Thomas M. Franck (1998), 'A Holistic Approach to Building Peace', in O.A. Otunnu and M.W. Doyle (eds) *Peacemaking and Peacekeeping for the New Century*, Lanham, MD: Rowman and Littlefield, pp. 275–96.

General Accounting Office (GAO) (2000), *Bosnia Peace Operation: Crime and Corruption Threaten Successful Implementation of the Dayton Peace Agreement*, GAO/NSIAD-00-156, Washington, DC: GAO.

Green, L.C. (1991), 'Iraq, the U.N. and the Law', *Alberta Law Review*, **29**, pp. 560–83.

Greenhill, K.M. and Major, S. (2006), 'The Perils of Profiling: Civil War Spoilers and the Collapse of Intrastate Peace Accords', *International Security*, **31**, pp. 7–40.

Grono, N. and O'Brien, A. (2008), 'Justice in Conflict? The ICC and Peace Processes', in *Courting Conflict? Justice, Peace and the ICC in Africa*. London: Royal African Society, pp. 13–20.

Han, S.K. (1994), 'Building a Peace That Lasts: The United Nations and Post-Civil War Peace-Building', *New York University Journal of International Law and Politics*, **26**, pp. 837–92.

Holzgrefe, J.L. and Keohane, R.O. (eds) (2003), *Humanitarian Intervention*, Cambridge: Cambridge University Press.

Hurwitz, A. and Huang, R. (eds) (2008), *Civil War and the Rule of Law*, Boulder, CO: Lynne Rienner.

International Commission on Intervention and State Sovereignty (2001), *The Responsibility to Protect: Report of the International Commission on Intervention and State Sovereignty*, Ottawa, ON: International Development Research Centre.

International Crisis Group (ICG) (2002), *Courting Disaster: The Misrule of Law in Bosnia and Herzegovina, Balkans*, Report No. 127, Brussels: ICG.

International Crisis Group (ICG) (2005), *The Congo's Transition Is Failing: Crisis in the Kivus*, Africa Report, No. 91, Brussels: ICG.

Johnstone, I. (2004), 'US–UN Relations after Iraq: The End of the World (Order) as We Know It?', *European Journal of International Law*, **15**, pp. 813–38.

Kelly, M.J. (1999), *Restoring and Maintaining Order in Complex Peace Operations: The Search for a Legal Framework*, Hague, Kluwer.

Kondoch, B. (2005), 'Human Rights Law and UN Peace Operations in Post-Conflict Situations', in N.D. White and D. Klaasen (eds), *The UN, Human Rights and Post-conflict Situations*, Manchester: Manchester University Press, pp. 19–41.

Le Billon, P. (2005a), 'Corruption, Reconstruction and Oil Governance in Iraq', *Third World Quarterly*, **26**, pp. 679–98.

Le Billon, P. (2005b), 'Overcoming Corruption in the Wake of Conflict', in *Global Corruption Report*, Berlin: Transparency International, pp. 73–82.

Lopes, C. and Theisohn, T. (2003), *Ownership, Leadership and Transformation: Can We Do Better for Capacity Development?*, New York: Earthscan.

Lyck, M. (2007), 'International Peace Enforcers and Indicted War Criminals: The Case of Ramush Haradinaj', *International Peacekeeping*, **14**, pp. 418–32.

Mansson, K. (2008), 'Integration of Human Rights in Peace Operations', in R. Murphy and K. Mansson (eds), *Peace Operations and Human Rights*, New York: Routledge, pp. 91–107.

Matheson, M.J. (2001), 'United Nations Governance of Postconflict Societies', *American Journal of International Law*, **95**, pp. 76–85.

Mazurana, D. (2005), 'Introduction', in D. Mazurana, A. Raven-Roberts and J. Parpart (eds), *Gender Conflict and Peacekeeping*, Lanham, MD: Rowman and Littlefield, pp. 1–28.

Mazurana, D., Raven-Roberts, A. and Parpart, J. (eds) (2005), *Gender Conflict and Peacekeeping*, Lanham, MD: Rowman and Littlefield.

McEvoy, K. (2007), 'Beyond Legalism: Towards a Thicker Understanding of Transitional Justice', *Journal of Law and Society*, **34**, pp. 411–40.

Mégret, F. and Hoffmann, F. (2003), 'The UN as a Human Rights Violator? Some Reflections on the United Nations Changing Human Rights Responsibilities', *Human Rights Quarterly*, **25**, pp. 314–45.

Mendelson, S. (2005), *Barracks and Brothels: Peacekeepers and Human Trafficking in the Balkans*, Washington, DC: Center for Strategic and International Studies.

Mohamed, S. (2005), 'From Keeping Peace to Building Peace: A Proposal for a Revitalized United Nations Trusteeship Council', *Columbia Law Review*, **105**, pp. 809–40.

Murphy, R. (2007), *UN Peacekeeping in Lebanon, Somalia and Kosovo: Legal and Operational Issues in Context*, New York: Cambridge University Press.

Murphy, R. (2008), 'An Assessment of UN Efforts to address Sexual Misconduct by UN Personnel', in R. Murphy and K. Mansson (eds), *Peace Operations and Human Rights*, New York: Routledge, pp. 75–90.

O'Connor, V. (2005), 'Traversing the Rocky Road of Law Reform in Conflict and Post-Conflict States: Model Codes for Post-conflict Criminal Justice as a Tool of Assistance', *Criminal Law Forum*, **16**, pp. 231–55.

O'Connor, V. and Rausch, C. (eds) (2007), *Model Codes for Post-Conflict Criminal Justice* (Vol. 1), Washington, DC: United States Institute of Peace.

O'Donnell, M. (2008), 'Post-Conflict Corruption: A Rule of Law Agenda?', in A. Hurwitz and R. Huang (eds), *Civil War and the Rule of Law*, Boulder, CO: Lynne Rienner, pp. 225–67.

Oomen, B. (2005), 'Donor-Driven Justice and Its Discontents: The Case of Rwanda', *Development and Change*, **36**, pp. 887–910.

Orend, B. (2000), *War and International Justice: A Kantian Perspective*, Waterloo, ON: Wilfrid Laurier University Press.

Otobo, E.E. (2010), 'The New Peacebuilding Architecture: An Institutional Innovation of the United Nations', in P.G. Danchin and H. Fischer (eds), *United Nations Reform and Collective Security*, New York: Cambridge University Press, pp. 212–33.

Pankhurst, D. (2003), 'The "Sex" War and Other Wars: Towards a Feminist Approach to Peace Building', *Development in Practice*, **13**, pp. 154–77.

Paris, R. (2004), *At War's End: Building Peace after Civil Conflict*, Cambridge: Cambridge University Press.

Paris, R. (2007), 'Post-Conflict Peacebuilding', in T. Weiss and S. Daws (eds), *The Oxford Handbook on the United Nations*, New York: Oxford University Press, pp. 404–26.

Plaut, M. (2007a), 'Eastern DRC, UN Troops "Traded Gold for Guns"', 23 May, *BBC News*.

Plaut, M. (2007b), 'Trading Guns for Gold: Pakistani Peacekeepers in the Congo', *Review of African Political Economy*, **34**, pp. 580–88.

Plunkett, M. (1998), 'Reestablishing Law and Order in Peace-Maintenance', *Global Governance*, **4**, pp. 61–79.

Puechguirbal, N. (2004), *Involving Women in Peace Processes: Lessons from Four African Countries (Burundi, DRC, Liberia and Sierra Leone) in Gender and Peace-Building in Africa*, Working Paper for the Norwegian Institute of International Affairs (NUPI), Oslo.

Ramcharan, B. (1996), 'UN Policies and Strategies: Preventing State Failures and Rebuilding Societies', *Journal of International Law and International Relations*, **2**, pp. 141–54.

Rand Corporation (2005), *The UN's Role in Nation Building: From the Congo to Iraq*, Santa Monica, CA: Rand Corporation.

Ratner, S.R. (1995), *The New UN Peacekeeping: Building Peace in Lands of Conflict after the Cold War*, New York: St Martin's Press.

Roberts, A. (2006), 'Transformative Military Occupation: Applying the Law of War and Human Rights', *American Journal of International Law*, **100**, pp. 580–622.

Roper, J., Nishihara, M., Otunnu, O. and Schoettle, E. (1993), *Keeping the Peace in the Post-Cold War Era: Strengthening Multilateral Peacekeeping*, A Report of the Trilateral Commission, **43**, New York: Trilateral Commission.

Salomons, D. (2010), 'On the Far Side of Conflict: The UN Peacebuilding Commission as Optical Illusion', in P.G. Danchin and H. Fischer (eds), *United Nations Reform and Collective Security*, New York: Cambridge University Press, pp. 195–211.

Sayre, F.B. (1948), 'Legal Problems Arising from the United Nations Trusteeship System', *American Journal of International Law*, **42**, pp. 263–98.

Schachter, O. (1991), 'United Nations Law in the Gulf Conflict', *American Journal of International Law*, **85**, pp. 452–73.

Schmemann, S. (2001), 'U.N. Envoy Says All Options Are Open on a Post-Taliban Afghanistan', *New York Times*, 18 October, p. B4.

Schoiswohl, M. (2006), 'Linking the International Legal Framework to Building the Formal Foundations of a "State at Risk": Constitution Making and International Law in Post-Conflict Afghanistan', *Vanderbildt Journal of Transnational Law*, **39**, pp. 819–63.

Siels, P. and Weirda, M. (2005), *The International Criminal Court and Conflict Mediation*, New York: International Centre for Transitional Justice.

Simma, B. (ed.) (2007), *The Charter of the United Nations: A Commentary* (2nd edn), Oxford: Oxford University Press.

Smith, D. (2004), *Towards a Strategic Framework for Peacebuilding: Getting Their Act Together*, Overview Report of the Joint Ustein Study of Peacebuilding, Brattvaag, Norway: Royal Norwegian Ministry of Foreign Affairs.

Stahn, C. (2004–05), 'Justice under Transitional Administration: Contours and Critique of a Paradigm', *Houston Journal of International Law*, **27**, pp. 311–44.

Standing, A. (2003), *Rival Views of Organized Crime*, Monograph 77, Pretoria: Institute for Security Studies.

Stedman, S. (1997), 'Spoilers Problems in Peace Processes', *International Security*, **22**, pp. 5–53.

Stromseth, J., Wippman, D. and Brooks, R. (2006), *Can Might Make Rights? Building the Rule of Law after Military Intervention*, New York: Cambridge University Press.

Tharoor, S. (1995), 'The Changing Face of Peace-Keeping and Peace-Enforcement', *Fordham International Law Journal*, **19**, pp. 408–26.

Thurer, D. (1999), 'The "Failed State" and International Law', *International Review of the Red Cross*, **81**, pp. 731–61.

Tschirgi, N. (2003), *Peacebuilding as a Link between Security and Development: Is the Window of Opportunity Closing?*, New York: International Peace Academy.

Tschirgi, N. (2004), 'Post-Conflict Peacebuilding Revisited: Achievements, Limitations and Challenges', International Peace Academy, Prepared for the WSP International/IPA Peacebuilding Forum Conference, New York, 7 October.

United Nations (1992), *An Agenda for Peace*, A/47/277 – S/24111, New York: United Nations.

United Nations (1996), *The Blue Helmets: A Review of United Nations Peacekeeping* (3rd edn), New York: United Nations.

United Nations (1998), *The Causes of Conflict and the Promotion of Durable Peace and Sustainable Development in Africa*, Report of the Secretary-General on the Work of the Organization, UN Doc. A/52/871–S/1998/318, 13, New York: United Nations.

United Nations (2000), *Report of the Panel on UN Peacekeeping Operations* (Brahimi Report), UN Doc. A/55/305-S/2000/809, New York: United Nations.

United Nations (2001), *No Exit without Strategy: Security Council Decision-Making and the Closure or Transition of United Nations Peacekeeping Operations: Report of the Secretary-General*, UN Doc. S/2001/394, New York: United Nations.

United Nations (2002), *The Situation in Afghanistan and Its Implications for International Peace and Security*, Report of the Secretary-General, UN Doc. A/56/875–S/2002/278, New York: United Nations.

United Nations (2003), *Report of the Secretary-General to the Security Council on Liberia*, UN Doc. S/2003/875, New York: United Nations.

United Nations (2004), *A More Secure World: Our Shared Responsibility – Report of the High-Level Panel on Threats, Challenges and Change*, UN Doc. A/59/565, New York: United Nations.

United Nations (2004), *Report of the Secretary-General: The Rule of Law and Transitional Justice in Conflict and Post-Conflict Societies*, 23 August, UN Doc. S/2004/616.

United Nations (2005a), *In Larger Freedom: Towards Development, Security and Human Rights for All – Report of the Secretary-General*, UN Doc. A/59/2005, New York: United Nations.

United Nations (2005b), *Corruption: Threats and Trends in the Twenty-first Century*, UN Doc. A/CONF.203/6, New York: United Nations.

United Nations (2006), *Report of the Panel of Experts on Liberia*, UN Doc. S/2006/379, New York: United Nations.

United Nations, IRIN (2007), *DRC: Probe into MONUC Gold, Arms Trafficking Allegations "Well Advanced"*, 25 May, Kenya: Integrated Regional Information Networks (IRIN).

US Agency for International Development (USAID) (2005), *Anticorruption Strategy*, Washington, DC: USAID.

Vandenberg, M. (2002), *Testimony on Trafficking of Women and Girls to Bosnia and Herzegovina*, House Committee on International Relations Subcommittee on International Operations and Human Rights, at: http://hrw.org/backgrounder/wrd/ trafficking-testim-april.pdf.

Verdirame, G. (2005), 'UN Accountability for Human Rights Violations in Post-Conflict Situations', in N.D. White and D. Klaasen (eds), *The UN, Human Rights and Post-conflict Situations*, Manchester: Manchester University Press, pp. 81–97.

Verstegen, S., van de Goor, L. and de Zeeuw, J. (2005), *The Stability Assessment Framework: Designing Integrated Responses for Security, Governance and Development*, Prepared by the Clingendael Institute for the Netherlands Ministry of Foreign Affairs, January.

Vig, S. (2009), 'The Conflictual Promises of the United Nations' Rule of Law Agenda: Challenges for Post-Conflict Societies', *Journal of International Peacekeeping*, **13**, pp. 131–58.

Wedgwood, R. (1995), 'The Evolution of United Nations Peacekeeping', *Cornell International Law Journal*, **28**, pp. 631–43.

Weiss, T. and Daws, S. (eds) (2007), *The Oxford Handbook on the United Nations*, New York: Oxford University Press.

White, N.D. (1997), *Keeping the Peace* (2nd edn), Manchester: Manchester University Press.

White, N.D. and Klaasen, D. (eds) (2005), *The UN, Human Rights and Post-conflict Situations*, Manchester: Manchester University Press.

Widner, J. (2007–08), 'Constitution Writing in Post-Conflict Settings: An Overview', *William and Mary Law Review*, **49**, pp. 1513–41.

Williams, P. and Scharf, M. (2002), *Peace with Justice? War Crimes and Accountability in the Former Yugoslavia*, Lanham, MD: Rowman & Littlefield.

Zartman, I.W. (1989), *Ripe for Resolution: Conflict and Intervention in Africa*, New York: Oxford University Press.

Part I
Africa

[1]

TRANSITIONAL JUSTICE: A FUTURE TRUTH COMMISSION FOR ZIMBABWE?

MAX DU PLESSIS* AND JOLYON FORD**

Abstract An eventual sustained democratic transition process in Zimbabwe may include a 'truth and reconciliation' commission. The need for—and possible form of—any such institution is situated in a number of discussions: the balance of principle and pragmatism that peace deals sometimes require; comparative experiences in other societies and the promise and limits of institutional modelling; the dynamic between global expectations or pre-scriptions and ground-level exigencies; the interface of international criminal law and institutions with national-level justice processes; the content of the State's international legal duty to afford a remedy. In considering the extent of an international normative framework limiting the justice options of transitional States, a certain margin of appreciation may be appropriate or necessary to enable a society to reconcile with its violent past on its own terms.

I. INTRODUCTION

What lessons about formally accounting for past systematic and widespread human rights abuses can Zimbabweans learn from other societies that have undergone political transition? If there is a sociological and political case for a deliberative national process of remembering, dwelling, telling, uncovering, admitting, accusing, apologising, what international legal considerations attend these questions or affect the forms that such processes might conceivably take? In 2008, and expressly in an endeavour to avoid the internationalization of criminal justice issues in a future Zimbabwe, the main opposition party have said that their transitional justice policy, if in government, would meet 'international standards'.[1] As part of the September 2008 agreement intended to break the political deadlock that followed the March 2008 elections, the parties have agreed to 'give consideration to the setting up of a mechanism to properly advise on what measures might be necessary and practicable to achieve national healing, cohesion and unity in respect of victims of pre- and

---

* Max du Plessis is a Associate Professor at the Faculty of Law at the University of KwaZulu-Natal, Durban; Senior Research Associate, Institute for Security Studies, Pretoria; Advocate & Associate Member of the Durban Bar.
** Centre for International Governance & Justice, Australian National University.
[1] *MDC Policy 2008* (Movement for Democratic Change, Harare), discussed further at (n 18) below.

post independence political conflicts.'[2] While its subject-matter relates to an evolving political context, this article is an attempt to stand back and consider the extent and content of international legal standards against which to assess any future victim-related truth, peace or justice mechanism that may be created as part of Zimbabwe's ongoing political settlement process.

One purpose of this article is to consider the extent to which an international legal framework not only forms a backdrop to national choices on justice and reconciliation, but may shape and even constrain the institutional and procedural options available. In the context of decades of violence and impunity in Zimbabwe, and in anticipation of an eventual democratization of political life there, we reflect on a variety of comparative transitional justice experiences such as those of Argentina, Cambodia, Chile, El Salvador, Guatemala, South Africa, Sierra Leone and Timor-Leste. Three main avenues are now used to formally address injustices relating to past violence: criminal trials (sometimes wholly or partly internationalized), truth-for-amnesty commissions, and a hybrid strategy entailing both conditional amnesties and selective prosecutions. A survey of the variety of mandates and procedures adopted and practices followed in various States reveals that notwithstanding the growth of a body of 'best practices' and guidelines, transitional justice choices remain eclectic. Within certain limits mandated by respect for universal norms, we argue that this is not only inevitable but may (with some caution) be preferable. There are limits to the appropriateness of foreign institutional formulae for pursuing locally legitimate and relevant justice and reconciliation. Provided the State's duty to afford an effective remedy is fulfilled, international peacebuilding institutions (and international law itself) currently does—and ought to—extend a margin of appreciation to transitional societies, where appropriate, to find their own ways to reconcile with the past as part of building a sustainable future peace. Comparative experience is thus simultaneously of significance and of limited utility in the design and conduct of any future institution in Zimbabwe. International legal principles certainly inform issues and available choices, but aside from the issue of purported national amnesty for international crimes, provide less by way of mandatory parameters than might be expected in relation to the content of the state's duty to afford a remedy for human rights abuse.

In the first part of this article (sections II to IV below) we consider debates on the utility, rationale and justification of establishing 'truth and reconciliation' bodies. While certain precautions are noted, these generic considerations and the particular context of Zimbabwe suggest, in our view, that such a body may be one viable or commendable component of any transitional justice strategy in that country. The second part of the article (sections V

---

[2] 'Agreement between ZANU-PF and the Two MDC Formations on Resolving the Challenges Facing Zimbabwe' (Harare, 15 September 2008) available at www.allafrica.com/stories/200809151361.html.

to VIII below) considers the legal framework possibly affecting national transitional justice strategies. Consideration is given to comparative experiences in terms of the mandate and procedures of truth commissions, and in particular the options available in terms of amnesties from prosecution. What will become clear is that the complexity and idiosyncrasy of these issues and the range of legitimate (but often incompatible) considerations, described in the first part, is a primary explanation for the lack of evolution of a detailed, prescriptive normative framework at the international level. Those interested in promoting international transitional justice solutions are prone to asserting the existence and certainty of international standards on the forms of transitional justice despite the variety of practices followed around the world, and despite the risk that global expectations might distort local exigencies for peace and reconciliation.

Before proceeding it ought to be emphasised that a range of difficult questions will undoubtedly arise for Zimbabweans as they grapple with transition away from the crisis and the 2008 horse-trading towards a new future. These reveal that social discourse on 'justice' involves, but is not always reducible to, legal or doctrinal issues.[3] In any interim phase, how will negotiations on 'transitional justice' persuade the powerful and prosecutable that it is safe to cooperate? How do we balance the need for restorative justice with solemn principles pointing to criminal trials and retributive justice? To what extent should society be looking back rather than concentrating its energies on the future? How far back does 'the past' really go? What is the status in law of pardons and amnesties given in the past? What would be required for future national amnesties to have international legal validity and afford immunity from prosecution? What is the place of international criminal justice mechanisms where a national process is in place? What is the relevance, utility or propriety of calls for international prosecutions? How would such a process deal—if at all—with any process on land claims between communities, or with wrongs that have a predominantly economic dimension: at least in relation to remedial measures? Can many of the intra-communal acts of violence be separated from an enquiry into questions of landholding and title? If there is 'no peace without justice', who can or should decide on justice? Is there a role for outsiders and, if not, who in Zimbabwe would have the moral authority to guide any process? With an economy in freefall, what priority of resources and national attention should a backward-looking process have, and what room to manoeuvre does international law allow a State in such situations?

The list of questions alone indicates the complexity of the debate. We modestly engage with these and other questions, placing our discussion of

---

[3] On the limits of a legalistic approach to understanding or ensuring justice, see Kieran McEvoy's excellent 'Beyond Legalism: Towards a Thicker Understanding of Transitional Justice' (2007) 34(4) Journal of Law and Society 411.

what might be drawn from comparative experiences within a wider approach which privileges seeking to solve problems according to local needs rather than becoming wedded to particular forms of institution. We consider whether local solutions nevertheless take place within the context of some degree of emerging consensus discernible on international minimum standards on truth commissions, amnesties and concurrent criminal prosecutions. It is important to comment at this stage that we do not necessarily subscribe, in reviewing options for approaches to dealing with the past, to the view that there is a need to choose starkly between 'peace' and 'justice'.[4] While there are certainly tensions between the two concepts, and often the price of peace is to accept that justice might need to be stayed against important stakeholders in the peace,[5] there is a recognized need now to move beyond a simplistic dichotomy that presents these two ideals as mutually inconsistent objectives where there has been conflict. Some aggrieved parties will not be able to contemplate peace without justice being seen to be done. These deep and real feelings cannot be denied simply on the basis that academic scholarship has moved beyond any simple dichotomy. Nevertheless, it is often an abdication of the duty to seek imaginative, tailored solutions to simply assert that justice and peace are incompatible objectives in most transitional settings: 'to place prosecutorial justice and the attainment of peace into opposed, abstract categories comes at the expense of an informed analysis of where tensions do, and do not, exist on the ground.'[6]

II. THE CONTEXT: POLITICAL VIOLENCE AND HUMAN RIGHTS ABUSE IN ZIMBABWE

The suggestion that a truth commission may be an important instrument for Zimbabweans in their transition from autocracy proceeds from two premises: first, that the human rights abuses that have occurred in Zimbabwe's modern history have been widespread, persistent, serious, systemic and systematic, and attended by a pattern of amnesty and lack of remedial action; secondly,

---

[4] N Biggar 'Making Peace or Doing Justice: Must we Choose?' in Biggar (ed) *Making Peace and Doing Justice after Civil Conflict* (Georgetown University Press, Washington DC, 2001) 6–13. See too V Nesiah, 'Truth vs. Justice' in Helsing and Mertus (eds.) *Human Rights and Conflict* (United States Institute of Peace, Washington DC, 2005), and generally Roht-Arrazia and Mariezcurrena *Transitional Justice in the 21st Century: Beyond Truth versus Justice* (Cambridge University Press, 2006).

[5] For a recent thorough survey of the issues, see N Grono and A O'Brien 'Justice in Conflict? The ICC and Peace Processes' in *Courting Conflict? Justice, Peace and the ICC in Africa* (Royal African Society, London, 2008). As the authors maintain, difficult choices will arise however nuanced the approach is, since it will simply be impossible to simultaneously pursue peace and justice objectives in complex cases. See also P Siels and M Weirda, 'The International Criminal Court and Conflict Mediation' (International Centre for Transitional Justice, New York, 2005).

[6] Justice Albie Sachs (Constitutional Court of South Africa) in *Courting Conflict?* (n 5), 'Foreword'. Polarised debates about the supposed incompatibilities between 'peace' and 'justice' have obscured efforts to consider these issues in a more integrated way and to recognise the potential for these goals to be compatible and mutually reinforcing: G Simpson, 'One among Many: the ICC as a Tool of Justice during Transition' also in *Courting Conflict*, Chapter 9.

Transitional Justice 77

that a truth commission would be a valuable and acceptable ingredient in addressing the violations and injustice and permitting a sustainable national peace. The second premise is the topic of the next section.

In relation to the first premise, human rights abuses perpetrated, encouraged or tolerated in particular by the State and its agents since at least February 2000, and which continued to worsen through 2008, have constituted constitutional, criminal and civil wrongs in Zimbabwean law and have in any event created pain, loss, grief, distrust, uncertainty, suspicion, grievance, anger and dislocation. The period has been marked by the consistency and level of State intimidation and brutality, involving widespread victimization; the partly covert nature of direct State abuses and indirect action at State instigation; the large number of low-level perpetrators especially among the youth militias; secrecy and denial on the part of the regime; a culture of impunity reinforced by pardons and general amnesties over many years; and the lack of remedial options. These factors all suggest the need for a formal national justice mechanism accompanying (and partly enabling) any future political transition to legitimate government. These abusive practices have been fairly well chronicled (although part of the point is that much is, of course, not known or presently knowable) and are only summarized here in order to properly situate our discussion. While formal denials, secrecy and the difficulty of cataloguing cases prevents a full assessment, a number of credible sources have reported that Zimbabwe's Government has been directly or indirectly responsible for murder, disappearances, rape, torture, beatings and other humiliating inhumane or degrading treatment, arbitrary detentions, denial of due process rights, group punishment including use of food as a political weapon, selective non-distribution of famine relief, mass displacement and forced removal, and other human rights abuses falling within well recognized 'categories' in international law.[7]

---

[7] See for example 'Justice in Zimbabwe' (Legal Resources Foundation, Harare, 2002); *Playing with Fire* (Zimbabwe Institute, Harare, 2004); 'Resolution on the Situation of Human Rights in Zimbabwe' African Commission on Human and People's Rights, Banjul, 5 December 2005; monthly and annual reports of the Zimbabwe Human Rights NGO Forum www.hrforumzim.com; shadow reports and other reports of the Human Rights Trust of Southern Africa www.sahrit.org; 'Policing the State' (November 2006, with Solidarity Peace Trust) and the 'Zimbabwe Monitor' both of the Institute for Justice and Reconciliation (Cape Town) www.ijr.org.za/transitionaljustice/zimbabwe-monitor; Human Rights Watch world reports and occasional reports on Zimbabwe www.hrw.org/africa/zimbabwe.php, including the then influential June 2003 HRW Report 'Under the Shadow: civil and political rights in Zimbabwe' and more recent reports, most recently in June 2008 (www.hrw.org/reports/zimbabwe/0608/); annual and occasional country reports of Amnesty International www.amnesty.org/en/region/africa/southern-africa/zimbabwe; US State Department, Country Reports (Human Rights), 2000—present www.state.gov/g/drl/rls/hrrpt/; United Kingdom Government (Foreign & Commonwealth Office), Human Rights Report (2002–2007). See also the evidence brought before the US Federal District Court for the Southern District of New York in the case of *Tachiona v Mugabe* (2001) 169 F.Supp.2d 259. See too B Raftopoulos & T Savage (eds) *Zimbabwe: Injustice and Political Reconciliation* (Weaver Press, Harare; African Books Collective, Oxford; 2005). We note that the ZANU PF and the MDC parties have in respect of the post-March 2008 election period recorded

From the available reports it is possible to identify three groupings of widespread violations since 2000. First, beginning shortly before the parliamentary elections of June 2000, and in response to both the rising popularity of the opposition Movement for Democratic Change (MDC) and to the ZANU-PF Government's defeat in the February 2000 constitutional referendum, Zimbabweans have witnessed nearly a decade of direct abuses on the part of the security services, as well sometimes less subtle abuses by ZANU-PF supporters and youths, with State facilitation, encouragement or instigation. Impunity has marked both sources of violence and intimidation, which have peaked in and around elections including the most recent (March and June) 2008 elections. The State and the party have been indistinguishable in Zimbabwean political life. Secondly, spontaneous as well as State-sponsored invasions of mainly white-owned commercial farms began in 2000: the Government perpetrated or incited (or at least failed to prevent, condemn or act against) the accompanying violence, property offences, mass displacement and lawlessness, the primary victims of which were thousands of farm workers. Impunity for criminal acts since 2000 was first formalized by a presidential decree of October 2000 granting amnesty, and followed by subsequent clemency orders including a substantial one in 2002. In those rare cases where a criminal conviction has been obtained against State agents, presidential pardons have been given to many actors responsible for political violence. Thirdly, there have been systematic forced displacements of urban dwellers pursuant to a deliberate political strategy: one official operation in the winter of 2005, condemned around the world, led to the forcible displacement of as many as 700,000 people.[8]

State human rights abuses have occurred in earlier periods of Zimbabwe's history too, and the extent to which these periods are to be addressed presents a difficult issue in the design of any future truth commission. Any truth commission today might not seek to address alleged war crimes and serious human rights abuses committed on all sides during the Rhodesian civil war leading to Zimbabwe's 1980 independence, for various reasons given later in this article. Of a different order is the question of whether and how to formally deal with allegations of grave crimes and human rights abuses arising from the Zimbabwean army's *gukurahundi* campaign in Matabeleland in the south of

---

themselves as being '[g]ravely concerned by the displacement of scores of people after the election of March 29, 2008 as a result of politically motivated violence' (see Article 18.2 of the Agreement of 15 September 2008 (n 2). The agreement is a political settlement and carefully avoids laying responsibility for the violence at the door of any one party.

    [8] Launched in 2005, *Operation Murambatsvina* (this ChiShona language term has a 'clean up' connotation) involved razing of settlements in and around the capital, Harare, allegedly in an attempt to intimidate the urban civilian population and to force some to move to rural areas where a higher level of state control was thought possible; see *Order out of Chaos, or Chaos out of Order? A Preliminary Report on Operation Murambatsvina* (ZHR NGO Forum, June 2005); 'Report of the Fact-Finding Commission of the UN Special Envoy on Human Settlement Issues' (July 2005) www.un.org/News/dh/infocus/zimbabwe/zimbabwe_rpt.pdf.

the country in 1983–4.[9] The campaign coincided with a period in the new Zimbabwe during which the political and ethnic balance of power between the dominant ZANU-PF party and the ZAPU party was still crystallizing. The south of the country, ZAPU's support base, was subject to sporadic violent attacks by, amongst others, dissident ZAPU fighters. In response from January to April 1983 (and to a lesser extent throughout the rest of that year), the Matabeleland North area was subject to a state of emergency marked by waves of direct state violence against the civilian population: mass killings, disappearances, murder, group beatings, rape, destruction of property, intimidation, detentions, and torture. The overwhelming majority of abuses were committed by members of the uniformed services or the intelligence service. Between at least February and April 1984, the same units were deployed in Matabeleland South. It is thought that more than 10,000 people died as a direct result of the operations, while many more suffered serious human rights abuses.

There has been no official or formal communal action in relation to this period. Findings of an official January 1984 inquiry into Matabeleland (the Chihambakwe Commission) were never published.[10] Until the independent 1997 Catholic Commission for Justice and Peace report, *Breaking the Silence, Building True Peace*,[11] the story of the 1983–4 period remained almost entirely unspoken and unheard in Zimbabwe. The report was based on detailed survey work sampling a few affected communities in Matabeleland. In just the two formally sampled districts, the report recorded 2000 confirmed dead, 3–4000 'almost certain' dead, 10,000 arbitrarily detained, and 7,000 beaten or tortured. A copy of the report was sent to President Mugabe and to members of the Cabinet. No official comment was ever received. As part of the Unity Accord signed on 22 December 1987, a general amnesty under Zimbabwean law was granted to dissidents on Independence Day on 18 April 1988. This was extended in June 1988 to members of the security services in relation to the *gukurahundi* operational area.

---

[9] *Gukurahundi* is a ChiShona word for a seasonal phenomenon and is usually translated as 'the rain which washes away the chaff before the spring rains.' It was the name given, reportedly by President Mugabe himself, to the new Zimbabwe army's 5th Brigade which, alongside police, intelligence and other entities was primarily responsible for the violence against civilians in Matabeleland in 1983–4. The insinuation was that there needed to be a 'cleansing' of the community which the government held responsible for harbouring a small number of dissident militant elements from the minority Ndebele-speaking group.

[10] It was announced in November 1985 that the findings of the report would not be released; in 2004 the Supreme Court dismissed an application for the State to be compelled to release the report: *Zimbabwe Lawyers for Human Rights v President of Zimbabwe & Anor*, S-12-03; Civ. App. 311/99.

[11] Catholic Commission for Justice and Peace; Legal Resources Centre (Harare, 1997); see also 'Choosing the Path to Peace and Development: Coming to Terms with Human Rights Violations of the 1982–1987 Conflict in Matabeleland and Midlands Provinces' (Zimbabwe Human Rights Association, Harare, 1999).

The *Breaking the Silence* report suggests that there remain serious matters to be unearthed and resolved in Zimbabwe, including possible international crimes. Apart from the obvious serious physical and psychological harms, loss of family members (many of whom are missing or in mass graves), property destruction, and so on, there is a general lack of knowledge about 'what happened', accompanied by the fact that the violence and impunity marking the period has not been forgotten by its victim communities. There remain a number of practical and legal difficulties for families who were unable to obtain a death certificate for missing persons or persons buried in mass graves. There has been no formal apology or explanation and no redress or reparation for victims. No compensation scheme has ever been implemented despite a 1996 undertaking by the Government.[12]

In this context, there have been a number of calls for any 'transition' in Zimbabwe to be marked by a truth and reconciliation commission as one component of a comprehensive approach to justice and peace.[13] The debate has been largely confined to a small group of local civil society activists and lawyers.[14] Nevertheless, since at least August 2003, when over 70 civil society organizations met in Johannesburg for a 'Symposium on Civil Society and Justice in Zimbabwe', the general preference has been for what that symposium called a 'Truth, Justice and Reconciliation Commission' as the main mechanism for redress, while expressly not discounting the possibility of

[12] The *Breaking the Silence* report had recommended that if individual compensation was not possible (as indeed it suggested it was not), a form of communal reparation should be pursued (by targeted development or communal reparation), and proposed a Reconciliation ('Uxolelwano') Trust for this purpose. One recommendation was to extend the benefits of the existing *War Victims Compensation Act* (relating to the Rhodesia-era conflict) to *gukurahundi* victims. The Act had a number of difficulties, and its related fund has been subject to plunder and abuse by high-level officials. The commonly held view in Zimbabwe is that the Act and perhaps the idea of such a scheme now has no 'moral credibility': W Buford and H van der Merwe 'Reparations in Southern Africa' (2004) *Cahiers d'Etudes Africaines* 44(1–2).

[13] Some observers are of the view that Zimbabweans are 'cynical' about reconciliation and the concept has been 'widely devalued, perhaps irrevocably' and 'remains polluted as a result of its expedient political manipulation and its failure to deliver meaningful results': *Exploring Transitional Justice Options in Contemporary Zimbabwe* (Zimbabwe Human Rights NGO Forum, Harare, 2006) 7, 21; also 'Zimbabwe: Why Reconciliation Failed' in *Reconciliation After Conflict: A Handbook* (International Institute for Democracy and Electoral Assistance, Stockholm, 2003) 34–39. We are not sure that this precludes such an institution. It rather depends on the form and practice of the institution and the prevailing political situation at the time of its establishment. The IDEA Handbook opines that the preference in 1980 for a 'shallow, cheap form of reconciliation without historic, restorative or economic justice' has devalued the notion of reconciliation in Zimbabwe. Other agree that by choosing 'reconciliation' over true 'reparation' in 1980, a dangerous culture of apathy and impunity was created: see Buford and van der Merwe (n 12) at fn 151; see also the record of an interview of July 2003 with former Archbishop Ncube in A Iliff 'Arresting Impunity: Towards a Transitional Justice Paradigm for Zimbabwe' (Honours Thesis, Harvard University, March 2004; unpublished).

[14] The preference apparent in the Zimbabwe Human Rights NGO Forum's 2006 consultant's study (above) was, if anything, for prosecutions. While the report's cover quotes the Nuremberg Tribunal, it acknowledges that the scale of violations, while widespread and systematic has not, since 1983–4, been of the gravest extent of international crimes.

criminal prosecutions.[15] The draft alternative Zimbabwean constitution of the unofficial National Constitutional Assembly has since 2001 provided for a 'Truth, Justice, Reconciliation and Conflict Prevention Commission' in its Chapter 9.[16] The opposition MDC party has in the past received generic advice on transitional justice options. It has consistently followed a fairly conciliatory line on future justice issues, though not without some ambiguities. For example, in its major 2003 Congress the MDC mentioned the intention to establish mechanisms in future for 'truth, justice, reconciliation and restitution'. At that time, one ambiguous position adopted was that 'general provisions of amnesty for prisoners will continue' although the party would nevertheless 'ensure that due legal process is applied to all human rights abuses.'[17]

In its latest (2008) policy statement the MDC does not mention a legal or policy position on past amnesties at all, and mentions future amnesties only obliquely.[18] The MDC policy says it will 'make a clean break with that past and establish a strong human rights culture' but that it 'will be necessary to deal with all past abuses'. It proposes a 'Truth and Justice Commission' to hear, in public formal recorded sessions, 'the stories of the victims and to identify those responsible for human rights abuses and any associated criminal acts', as well as mechanisms to prevent future abuses and 're-orientation programmes for all those affected'. Based on the four 'rights' expressed to underlie it,[19] the policy purports to deal with all episodes of political violence in Zimbabwe since 1980. It states that the MDC is committed to 'dealing with the needs of the victims' of all post-1980 abuses 'in a holistic and comprehensive way' by giving 'those affected by the abuse of their rights the satisfaction of knowing that the truth about what happened has been revealed and

---

[15] The Symposium condemned the pattern of amnesties and culture of impunity in Zimbabwean and Rhodesian history, and expressed the view that gross violations should never be subject of an amnesty; it noted that victims of all past human rights abuses have a right to redress and to be consulted about the nature of mechanisms what will be established to address their needs.

[16] The proposed institution would sit for five years, with options to renew it for a further five years. It would be responsible for investigations of past violations, provision of remedies to persons injured, the promotion of reconciliation, and conflict prevention. Further details were left to a future non-constitutional instrument. The government's March 2006 proposal to establish a constitutional 'Human Rights Commission' to 'counter the large scale orchestration of alleged violations' and the 'falsification, exaggeration, orchestration, and stage-managing of human rights violations by detractors' was widely treated with derision.

[17] 'From Crisis to Human-centred Development' (Movement for Democratic Change, Harare, December 2003).

[18] 'In the event that those identified as being responsible . . . do not themselves, on a voluntary basis, offer to come before the Commission to tell their side of the story, the Commission may, at its discretion, [direct the matter for investigation for possible prosecution]': *MDC Policy 2008* (Movement for Democratic Change, Harare) 37.

[19] The communal 'right to know', the right to justice and a remedy, the right to reparations, and the 'right to non-recurrence': see discussion below.

that the culprits have been brought to justice in some way.' If anything, it is suggestive of a preference for criminal trials:

> '[A]ll victims will have an opportunity to assert their rights and receive fair and effective remedy, ensuring that the perpetrators stand trial and that the victims obtain reparations ... [this reflects] an obligation on the State to investigate, prosecute and punish the guilty.'

The proposed mandate of the commission includes 'to determine who was responsible for the incidents being considered, and to decide whether or not to recommend further investigations by an appropriate authority and possible prosecution.'[20]

In any event, this policy is of course subject to whatever political realities prevail in future. By May 2008, the MDC had made overtures to reassure in particular the defence and intelligence elements of the Mugabe regime's leadership and to guarantee their 'security'.[21] It is not clear whether this pledge consists of an undertaking to engineer a formal amnesty from any prosecution, or something more political by way of a guarantee not to pursue legal actions. As a result of the 2008 election stalemate and violence, the leader of the main MDC faction, Morgan Tsvangirai said that while he had long espoused the notion that Mugabe himself ought to be allowed to retire with dignity rather than face prosecution, that issue might need to be revisited given the events following the elections in March 2008.[22] The September 2008 agreement does not provide for any formal transitional justice mechanisms, providing tentatively in a section dealing with the promotion of equality, national healing, cohesion and unity by a new government, that the parties 'shall give consideration to the setting up of a mechanism to properly advise on what measures might be necessary and practicable to achieve national healing, cohesion and unity in respect of victims of pre and post independence political conflicts.'[23] While the political impasse continued at the time of

---

[20] MDC 2008 (n 18) 1, 36–38. The MDC policy appears to attempt—perhaps wisely—to structurally distance justice measures from the vexed issue of property losses, land seizures and land reform. The policy does not, however, mention a role for the international community in any justice process.
[21] 'Negotiating Zimbabwe's Transition' Africa Briefing No. 1 (International Crisis Group, Pretoria/Brussels, 21 May 2008) 4.
[22] Interview, BBC News 'Hardtalk', 18 April 2008. By May 2008, however, Mr Tsvangirai was again repeatedly speaking in terms of the need for a 'graceful and dignified exit' for President Mugabe. This position by Mr Tsvangirai has been overtaken somewhat by the September 2008 agreement between ZANU PF and the two MDC factions.
[23] See Article 7.1(c) of the Agreement (n 2). The agreement has been read among civil society actors and others as denying amnesty or immunity for perpetrators of political violence, or at the very least not openly providing for it. The agreement stipulates that the Government will 'apply the laws of the country fully and impartially in bringing all perpetrators of politically motivated violence to book' (Article 18(5)(i)); that 'while having due regard to the Constitution of Zimbabwe and the principles of the rule of law,' the prosecuting authorities will expedite the determination as to whether or not there is sufficient evidence to warrant the prosecution or keeping on remand of all persons accused of politically related offences arising out of or

writing, we note that there have been a range of discussions that have taken place since 2001 which have included a truth commission idea and, particularly most recently, have aimed to express that idea by reference to international expectations and/or international legal standards. It is within that political context that we situate our discussion about the desirability of a truth and reconciliation commission as a new Zimbabwe begins to take shape.

III. THE TRUTH COMMISSION PHENOMENON

What in particular commends a 'truth commission' approach to dealing with past injustices? In addition to the variety of approaches adopted in practice (discussed below), consideration of the intrinsic merits of truth commissions and the issues at stake in resorting to them provides, we would argue, relevant context within which any enquiry into the normative framework and 'minimum standards' of transition justice must be made. While some of what follows reveals discernible trends, it also underlies the complexity of arriving at appropriate and effective remedies. This suggests a difficulty with (and a need to avoid) becoming too prescriptive about what a state must or must not do in transitional justice settings.

In reaching or embedding a new political dispensation after systematic and large-scale human rights abuse, then, there exists a range of ways—'transitional justice options'—to deliberatively and formally deal with past injustices. 'Transitional justice' itself is now considered to be a vital component of prescriptions for modern 'peacebuilding', alongside disarmament, security sector reform, elections, and so on.[24] At the extreme respective ends of the

---

connected with the March and June 2008 elections (Article 18(5)(j)); for further comment see 'Some Preliminary Comments on the Agreement Compiled for the Research and Advocacy Unit' the South African Institute for Democracy (IDASA), 16 October 2008, available at http://www. kubatana.net/docs/demgg/analysis_of_zim_agreement_081016.pdf.

[24] D Mendlehoff, 'Truth-seeking, Truth-telling and Post-Conflict Peacebuilding: Curb the Enthusiasm?' (2004) 6 *International Studies Review* 355. The literature continues to grow. Commendable texts include: N Kritz (ed.), *Transitional Justice: How Emerging Democracies Reckon with Former Regimes* (US Institute of Peace, Washington DC, 1995 (3 volumes)) and Kritz's overview 'Where we are and How we got Here: an Overview of Developments in the Search for Justice and Reconciliation' in Henkin (ed) *The Legacy of Abuse: Confronting the Past, Facing the Future* (Aspen Institute, New York, 2002); J-P Lederach *Building Peace: Sustainable Reconciliation in Divided Societies* (US Institute of Peace, Washington DC, 1997); M Minow, *Between Vengeance and Forgiveness: Facing History after Genocide and Mass Violence* (Beacon Press, Boston, 1998); G Robertson, *Crimes Against Humanity: the Search for Global Justice* (Allen Lane, London, 1999); J MacAdams (ed), *Transitional Justice and the Rule of Law in New Democracies* (Notre Dame, Indiana, 2001); R Teitel, *Transitional Justice* (Oxford University Press, 2000); Rotberg & Thompson (eds), *Truth v Justice: The Morality of Truth Commissions* (Princeton University Press, 2000); E Daly and J Sarkin *Reconciliation in Divided Societies: Finding Common Ground* (University of Pennsylvania Press, Philadelphia, 2006); T Borer (ed), *Telling the Truths: Truth Telling and Peacebuilding in Post-Conflict Societies* (University of Notre Dame Press, 2006); T Govier, *Taking Wrongs Seriously: Acknowledgment, Reconciliation and the Politics of Sustainable Peace* (Humanity Books, 2008). For a recent overview, see R Teitel, 'Editorial Note: Transitional Justice Globalised' (2008) 2 *International Journal of*

'transitional justice options' range are either all-out criminal prosecutions of varying quality, or blanket amnesty with few questions asked and little attempt to find or explain the truth.[25] Most responses to large-scale violations tend—mainly for reasons of internal political expediency, but also as a result of international pressure—to adopt a position somewhere between the two extremes.

Truth commissions are one response resorted to increasingly in recent years. The term encompasses a broad range of possible institutions with different features and purposes. We adopt Hayner's understanding of the term to connote a certain kind of inquisitorial non-judicial body that normally displays the following characteristics: it focuses on the past; it investigates or receives information on a pattern of abuses over a certain or determinate period of time (rather than being general or focussing on a specific event); it is victim-focused; it is an ad hoc temporary body with a limited mandate, normally producing a report upon completion of its work; it is normally a State-sponsored body or emanates from and is authorized by the state.[26] Since 1974 numerous truth commissions have been established by States—with or without the assistance, encouragement or imposition of other states, the United Nations and other actors—either to support an ongoing peace process

Transitional Justice 1. For excellent resources see www.csvr.org.za (Centre for the Study of Violence and Reconciliation, Wits University) and www.itcj.org (International Centre for Transitional Justice); see also www.restorativejustice.org and www.ijr.org.za/transitionaljustice (Institute for Justice and Reconciliation, Cape Town); for a most extensive bibliography see the University of Wisconsin's 'Transitional Justice database project' www.polisci.wisc.edu/tjdb/bib.htm. We do not find it useful here to pursue whether the 'field' is a coherent one, has a future and is just getting going, or is already discredited as a unifying concept: Zachary Kaufman has opined that 'transitional justice is a broad term that [wrongly] attempts to unify under a single topic a vast array of activities (including inaction) that pursue different objectives and employ varying procedures': 'The Future of Transitional Justice' (2005) 1 *STAIR* 58–81, 77. We are cautious of the teleological prescriptiveness that might be seen to accompany formulas for effective transitional justice, and conscious that 'transitions' come in many forms: see too T Carothers 'The End of the Transition Paradigm' (2002) 12(1) *Journal of Democracy* 6. See also the discussion in L Bosire, *Overpromised, Underdelivered: Transitional Justice in Sub-Saharan Africa* (International Centre for Transitional Justice, New York, 2006) 8–9.

[25] J Dugard, 'Possible Conflicts of Jurisdiction with Truth Commissions', in Cassesse et al, *The Rome Statute of the International Criminal Court—A Commentary*, vol 1 (Oxford University Press, 2002) 693.

[26] P Hayner, *Unspeakable Truths: Facing the Challenge of Truth Commissions* (Routledge, New York, 2002) 14. Hayner's remains a most comprehensive comparative examination of truth commissions, and, like ours, many subsequent studies draw upon it. Sara Parker considers a truth commission to be 'a formal investigatory method implemented following some type of transition ... used to help societies come to terms with past abuses': S Parker, 'From Argentina to Zimbabwe: Chronicling the Emergence of an International Truth Commission Norm' Paper for the International Studies Association Annual Conference, 26–29 March 2008, San Francisco [copy with authors]. See also definitional issues discussed in M Freeman *Truth Commissions and Procedural Fairness* (Cambridge University Press, 2006), and 'The rule of law and transitional justice in conflict and post-conflict societies' Report of the Secretary-General (UN Doc. S/2004/616, August 2004), [50]: official, temporary, non-judicial fact-finding bodies investigating a pattern of human rights abuses; are victim-focussed and produce a report or recommendation.

or to promote democratic reforms and reconciliation in a post-conflict society.[27]

A number of broad factors commend the establishment of truth commissions as an element of a comprehensive approach to transitional justice: to help establish the truth, provide redress for victims, ensure accountability for perpetrators, identify and stimulate reforms and preventative effects, promote reconciliation, and create formal distance with the past.[28] The ordinary criminal courts in any country that has experienced civil conflict or oppressive rule are likely to be severely weakened if not entirely compromised.[29] Even if countries had strong legal institutions with sufficient resources, independence or credibility, sometimes the scale of collective violence in certain countries is so vast—there is such a degree of complicity by members of society generally—that it is impossible to conceive of attempting to prosecute all possible offenders. In any event, mere prosecutions, even if politically possible, do not necessarily achieve reconciliation or reduce tension.[30] A restorative justice approach may be more likely to.[31] (However, one ought to note that a restorative justice approach does not, properly speaking, discount the significance of criminal trials, which can as powerful a means of affirming the

---

[27] Hayner's 2002 study (*Unspeakable Truths*) identified 21 commissions. More have been created since: see the Centre for Transitional Justice at http://www.ictj.org. Parker's 2008 study (above) includes a table of over 30 commissions since 1982, and her research details evidence of demands for commissions in at least 10 other countries.

[28] E Daly, 'Truth Skepticism: An Inquiry into the Value of Truth in Times of Transition' (2008) 2 *International Journal of Transitional Justice* 23, 27.

[29] A Chapman and P Ball, 'The Truth of Truth Commissions: Comparative Lessons from Haiti, South Africa, and Guatemala' (2001) 23(1) *Human Rights Quarterly* 2. On the tensions between national courts and truth commissions, see generally W Schabas and S Darcy (eds), *Truth Commissions and Courts: the Tension Between Criminal Justice and the Search for Truth* (Springer, Berlin, 2005).

[30] Hayner, *Unspeakable Truths* (n 26) 12–14. By nature trials moreover 'paint an incomplete picture of the past': Bosire (n 24) 4; as Gerry Simpson has pointed out, war crimes trials in particular have long had a didactic, narrative, commemorative and educational and self-legitimating function (not always entirely consistent with their judicial purposes), but one which can readily distort history: 'Didactic and Dissident Histories in War Crimes Trials' (1997) 60 *Albany Law Review* 801, especially 824–6. A theme running through Govier's *Taking Wrongs Seriously* (n 24) is rejection of the notion that criminal trials, while important from a rule of law perspective, have utility in promoting reconciliation in a society: this perhaps both underestimates the significance of trials as a means of vindication for victims, and overestimates the significance of non-judicial communal relationship-building processes in building sustainable peace.

[31] For us, aspects of a restorative justice approach include responsiveness to community expectations, a recognition of the significance of locally-driven processes, and a need to focus on 'bottom-up' restorative processes, contrasted with attending primarily to processes involving only some elites (whether peacemakers, truth commissioners, prosecutors, or indicted persons). The overall focus is on the vindication of the victim, not the punishment of perpetrators. See van der Spuy, Parmentier and Dissel (eds), *Restorative Justice: Politics, Policies and Prospects* (Juta, Cape Town, 2007); J Braithwaite, *Restorative Justice and Responsive Regulation* (Oxford University Press, 2002); Biggar (n 4). We note this with a caution: the well-meaning promotion of some community-based rituals by external actors can amount to area-based exceptionalism: Tim Allen, 'Ritual (Ab)use? Problems with Traditional Justice in Northern Uganda' *Courting Conflict*, Chapter 6; see also in the same publication Nicholas Waddell and Phil Clark, 'Introduction', 10.

dignity of victims as the dialogic elements of reconciliation approaches. Trials are not merely backward-looking and may be essential to ensuring a sense of 'justice', avoiding self-help measures, and to deterring future abuses.)[32]

The most obvious commendation and objective of a truth commission is the attempt to establish 'the truth' about human rights abuses and to allow people in society to understand what has happened: that through an official truth body an accurate record of the country's past will be established and uncertain events will be clarified, and the silence and denial regarding human rights violations will be dealt with and the truth exposed.[33] In order to move toward the future, victims may need assurances about certain details about the past as well as recognition of their losses or pain.[34] Such processes can achieve a measure of symbolic closure through memory,[35] or a therapeutic and prin-cipled institutionalization of the memories of the abusive time,[36] to reach an

---

[32] H Jeong, *Peacebuilding in Postconflict Societies: Strategy and Process* (Lynne Reinner, Boulder, 2005) *Strategy and Process*, 165, 168–9.

[33] Hayner *Unspeakable Truths* (n 26) 25. Jeong has rightly pointed out that knowing 'the truth' of what actually took place is a necessary condition for forgiveness, but not a sufficient condition: *Strategy and Process*, 165; the same sceptical approach informs Daly's recent argu-ment (n 28) that without accountability, truth on its own merely produces injustice (34), while surveys of attitudes have shown that establishing the truth about an event is no guarantee that beliefs and attitudes will change upon being presented with that truth, indeed it may serve to hinder not promote reconciliation (37). In the same way, Pablo de Greiff points out that a suc-cessful process of truth-telling, trials, forgiveness formalities, etc, would not automatically mean that elements of society are reconciled: 'The Role of Apologies in National Reconciliation Processes: On Making Trustworthy Institutions Trusted' in Gibney & Howard-Hassman (eds), *The Age of Apology: Facing Up to the Past* (University of Pennsylvania Press, Philadelphia, 2007). Simon Chesterman also notes the distinction between acknowledgement and account-ability: *You, The People: The UN, Transitional Administration and State-Building* (Oxford University Press/International Peace Academy, 2004) ('Justice and Reconciliation: the Rule of Law in Post-Conflict Territories', Chapter 5) 157. More recently, (Daly n 28) has noted that 'the truth neither *is* nor *does* all that we expect of it'—it does not necessarily help victims, promote accountability or non-impunity, prevent future abuse, or ensure reconciliation.

[34] B Pouligny, 'Building Peace after Mass Crimes' (2002) 9(2) *International Peacekeeping* 202. This is not necessarily so that someone must be held to account: sometimes to know is enough. One argument for a more formal process after the conflict in Solomon Islands was that people were unable to concentrate on the future due to intense speculation, rumour and gossip on factual issues.

[35] B Hamber and R Wilson, 'Symbolic Closure through Memory: Reparation and Revenge in Post-Conflict Societies' (2002) 1(1) *Journal of Human Rights* 35. Rosalind Shaw has argued that the 'valorisation' of this kind of memory practice involving public recounts of violence is based on 'problematic assumptions about the purportedly universal benefits of verbally remembering violence': R Shaw 'Rethinking Truth & Reconciliation Commissions: Lessons from Sierra Leone' Special Report #135 (United States Institute of Peace, Washington DC, 2005) 7. Her view is that 'social forgetting' may be an equally valid strategy and in Sierra Leone was a cornerstone of established local processes of reintegration and healing and so held far more appeal than the truth commission approach. We note that Shaw in fact concedes that truth-telling may be effective in cases of covert, state-sponsored violence.

[36] See generally J Carroll & B Pasco, *Forgiving and Forgetting* (Life and Peace Institute, Uppsala, 2002). The emphasis is vividly captured in the name of the 'Recovery of Historical Memory' project in Guatemala: see Jeong, *Strategy and Process* (n 32) 185. See Naidu & Adonis 'History on their Own Terms: the Relevance of the Past' (Centre for the Study of Reconciliation and Violence (CSVR), Johannesburg, January 2007); see in general Southern African

Transitional Justice   87

institutionalized common memory, a national consensus on how the past is to be remembered and represented.[37] This is in contrast to denial and deliberate or non-deliberate forgetting (often perhaps a natural result of trauma and fatigue). The rationale behind formal public truth commissions is that deep wounds need to be cleaned and aired, not simply bound up and forgotten: out of sight is not out of collective mind.[38] One must 'bury the hatchet, not the past'.[39] Even if victims learn no new truth, the official acknowledgment of these abuses can be a vital factor in the processes of reconciliation and healing of individuals, groups, and the nation as a whole.[40] For many victims no new 'truth' will emerge, but formal acknowledgment of their truth can be vital in the shared healing process. This may also be what is meant by 'truth as acknowledgment' and 'recognition' as sufficient to sometimes comprise 'justice'.[41]

In addition to its truth-seeking and truth-recording function such a commission can be a platform for a range of processes intended to respond to the needs and interests of victims of human rights abuses, and to address perpetrators' responsibility. Peacebuilding and transitional justice have both structural and psycho-social dimensions. The psychological dimensions and needs

Reconciliation Project 'Memorialisation Bibliography' and 'Memorialisation and Reconciliation in Transitional Southern African Societies' (CSVR, Johannesburg, 2005); Naidu, 'The Ties that Bind: Strengthening the Links between Memorialisation and Transitional Justice' (2006) and 'Empowerment through Living Memory' (2004) (both CSVR, Johannesburg). On the troubled Indonesian province of Papua, where one proposed element of a new 'Special Autonomy' regime in 2001 was a truth and reconciliation commission, various indigenous Papuans have for some years asked for a process of 'pelurusan sejarah' (straightening of history): J Braithwaite et al, 'Peacebuilding Compared: Working Paper #1' (Australian National University, May 2008, draft; copy with authors) 31.

[37] Jeong, *Strategy and Process*, 158; also K Christie *The South African Truth Commission* (St Martin's Press, New York, 2000). One can concede that it is problematic to conceive of a commission's report being a single definitive impartial historical record or national memory expressing the experiences and truths of all actors, and optimistic to expect that such a single record might 'command agreement and heal social divisions': Shaw (n 35) 3. However, this view overlooks the relative significance of process over outcome; nor need a report purport to be definitive of 'the truth'—it can simply record various views and attempt some objectivity.

[38] This paragraph draws from the authors' joint newspaper opinion piece in *Business Day* (South Africa), 17 April 2008. Archbishop Desmond Tutu referred consistently to the imagery of opening, cleansing and balming of societal wounds throughout South Africa's Truth and Reconciliation (TRC) process.

[39] Terence McCaughey, 'Northern Ireland: Bury the Hatchet, not the Past' in Biggar (n 4): a new society cannot be built while mystery surrounds the fate of many people.

[40] Shaw has argued that 'nations do not have psyches that can be healed'—it is wrong to 'anthropomorphize' the nation as a suffering, feeling entity (see too T Borer, 'Reconciling South Africa or South Africans? Cautionary Notes from the TRC' (2004) 8 *African Studies Quarterly* 1) —and that 'ideas concerning the conciliatory and therapeutic efficacy of truth telling' are Western cultural products about memory and not necessarily applicable elsewhere: Shaw (n 35) 7. Truth-telling is not necessarily a complete therapy.

[41] A du Toit, 'The Moral Foundations of the South African Truth and Reconciliation Commission: Truth as Acknowledgment and Justice as Recognition' in Rotberg and Thompson (n 24).

are both individual and communal.[42] Such commissions can become the focal point for efforts going beyond the establishment of truth—efforts at *reparation*—by which is meant not merely financial or other economic or in-kind compensation, but broader notions of restitution, rehabilitation, satisfactions and guarantees of non-repetition.[43]

Truth commissions allow a forum for forgiveness to be given by the victim.[44] By not only learning facts and explanations but also telling their stories and receiving formal and communal recognition—including by the perpetrators—victims are afforded a chance to reclaim their dignity. At the same time, perpetrators are afforded a formal mechanism by which to renounce their violent deeds and to rejoin society in some fashion. In these ways it can be (part of) a joint national therapeutic or healing process, with a practical dividend for peace prospects. It can also help to focus on the wider patterns and causes of abuse and move away from attempting individual blame or guilt where this is unlikely to be constructive in the new society. Another important function that a truth commission can fulfil is to describe institutional responsibility for human rights abuses, and to outline the weaknesses in the institutional structures or existing laws that should be changed to prevent future abuses.[45] Ideally and relevantly, as Heinz Klug notes in relation to constitution-making, these processes and institutions provide a means (as they did in South Africa) to civilise political conflicts and channel the energies and tensions in a way that, done well, can reduce the potential for violence: debate about institutional design or practice structures the parameters of possible political action during the transition and its aftermath, and these institutions (constitutions, or here truth commissions) provide a site to receive the 'incompatible [justice or institutional] imaginations of local contestants'.[46]

---

[42] W Long & P Brecke, *War and Reconciliation: Reason and Emotion in Conflict Resolution* (MIT Press, Cambridge MA, 2003); R Fisher, 'Social-Psychological Processes in Interactive Conflict Analysis and Reconciliation' in H Jeong (ed), *Conflict Resolution: Dynamics, Process, Structure* (Ashgate, Aldershot, 2000); B Hamber, 'Does the Truth Heal? A Psychological Perspective on Political Strategies for Dealing with the Legacy of Political Violence' in Biggar (n 4) 131–150; see Jeong, *Strategy and Process*, 155, 159.

[43] Hayner's study (*Unspeakable Truths*) considers the variety of redress measures that might fall within the general term 'reparation'. For a comprehensive study of experiences in Southern Africa in developing official non-judicial reparation programmes for victims of human rights abuse, see Buford and van der Merwe, 'Reparations in Southern Africa' (n 12) and Hamber & Mofokeng, *From Rhetoric to Responsibility: Making Reparations to the Survivors of Past Political Violence* (CSVR, Johannesburg, 2000). See also 'Reparation' in *Reconciliation After Conflict: A Handbook* (n 13).

[44] There are perhaps conceptual problems with compelling victims to grant forgiveness, which ought to be a gift: J Braithwaite, *Restorative Justice and Responsive Regulation* (Oxford University Press, 2002) 15.

[45] Hayner *Unspeakable Truths*, 29.

[46] H Klug, *Constituting Democracy: Law, Globalism and South Africa's Political Reconstruction* (Cambridge University Press, 2000) 5–6. On the other hand, as discussed at n 51 below, as with Constitution-making, such commissions may foster division rather than cohesion, serving as a source of 'fragmentation and disintegration': W Murphy, 'Constitutions,

Transitional Justice   89

IV. SOME CAUTIONARY CONSIDERATIONS

The eventual goal of truth processes is normally the promotion of reconciliation and the reduction of tensions resulting from past violence. Our position
is generally in favour of truth commissions as a phenomenon on the premise
that history shows it is not usually sufficient or proper to simply leave past
injustices unaddressed and unresolved (it neither 'works' for peace nor is it
'right' for justice): some concerted, formal national attempt must be made to
account for past injustices and events, lest the alternative prevent members of
a society from moving forward in some fashion together. Trials are often
impossible or insufficient. Beneath the premise is an assumption that we think
is made out by experience but which may need to be tested, including empirically: that truth commissions and other explicit attempts to deal with the
past make an overall positive contribution to peacebuilding, or are an efficient,
effective, just, useful or legitimate way of dealing with widespread victimization and perpetration. In this regard, before considering the comparative
practice on various significant institutional design issues and international
legal parameters shaping these, we make the following ten cautionary remarks
about adopting a truth commission-type process at all. Apart from their intrinsic value, such considerations lend weight to our argument that given the
complexity and multiplicity of issues and legitimate choices facing a transitional regime, it will remain difficult to seek to prescribe—as a matter of
international law and practice—particular modes or features of a 'just' transitional order.

First of these cautions is that it is necessary (that is, it is both right and
prudent) to centre peacebuilding efforts in the will of the people.[47] It is quite
possible to conceive of a situation where the overwhelming view is that the
past ought simply to be left alone.[48] A deliberate decision not to pursue any
formalised process may also be one option. Some societies such as Spain after
General Franco simply drew a 'thick line' between past and present and
moved on, without any particular structural mechanisms for reconciling with
the past.[49] Secondly, a truth commission could be used as a political tool to
disproportionately allocate blame to one side, or a cosmetic exercise of mutual
'forgiveness' only by implicated or self-interested elites in pursuit of a
political deal and mutual immunity. Thirdly, given the emotive and highly

---

Constitutionalism and Democracy' in Greenberg et al (eds), *Constitutionalism & Democracy:
Transitions in a Contemporary World* (Oxford University Press, 1993).

[47] K Daglish and H Nasu, 'Towards a True Incarnation of the Rule of Law in War-torn
Territories: Centring Peacebuilding in the Will of the People' (2007) 54 *Netherlands
International Law Review* 81.

[48] Shaw's view is that despite pressure from NGOs and human rights activists for a truth
commission in Sierra Leone, most ordinary people preferred a 'forgive and forget' approach
(what she describes as deliberate social forgetting), out of fear of retaliation and reprisal and other
reasons: (n 35).

[49] Jeong *Strategy and Process* (n 32) 163; also Chesterman (n 33) 154.

contested subject matter, there is the risk that the commission could itself become a focus or forum of renewed conflict (both in settling on its design, during its process, or the tone of its report),[50] or antagonize those with residual power: influential but implicated persons upon whose cooperation the new, perhaps fragile, national unity depends. Fourth, a truth commission could be hugely distracting, draining and expensive at a time when other priorities exist.

Fifthly, every country situation is unique, 'reconciliation' in particular is something that needs to be defined within a specific cultural context,[51] and so a number of more general cautions need to be expressed in approaching foreign models and comparative experience. South Africa's experience has been hugely influential,[52] and is likely to be seen as apposite for Zimbabwe (perhaps without sufficient consideration of the many differences between these two neighbouring countries). However, no model of truth commission is ideal for all purposes, and in view of the historical, cultural, political and other differences that confront different regimes undergoing transition, certainly no model can be simply transposed directly from one situation to another.[53] The eventual model adopted will, if it is to be successful, need to be designed to

---

[50] This is one of the reasons why Mendlehoff suggests that we 'curb the enthusiasm' for truth commissions: (n 24). The UN handbook *Rule of Law Tools for Post-Conflict Societies: Truth Commissions* (Office of the High Commissioner for Human Rights, Geneva, 2006; (n 86) below notes (albeit only in conclusion, 36) that a commission can be a risky endeavour in a fragile transition. In *Taking Wrongs Seriously* (n 24), Trudy Govier consistently notes that a superficial or dishonest or forced truth and reconciliation process may not only be unsuccessful but even itself dangerous and produce effects opposite to those intended. Daly has observed that it is increasingly characteristic of transitional governments to be 'infatuated with the truth' ascribing it 'all manner of curative powers' and reaching for truth commissions in a 'headlong' fashion without pausing to consider alternatives or negative consequences: Daly 'Truth Skepticism' (n 28) 23–4. The considerable force of these arguments undermines the search for the normative 'neatness' implicitly sought by some commentators in relation to transitional justice.

[51] Jeong *Strategy and Process* 184.

[52] The literature it has generated including in terms of 'comparative models' is large. See recently K Emmanuel, 'Between Principle and Pragmatism in Transitional Justice: South Africa's TRC and Peace Building' ISS Paper # 156 (Institute for Security Studies, Pretoria, 2007) and the extensive bibliography therein. See generally A Boraine, *A Country Unmasked: Inside South Africa's Truth and Reconciliation Commission* (Oxford University Press, New York, 2000); Posel and Simpson (eds) *Commissioning the Past: Understanding South Africa's Truth and Reconciliation Commission* (Witwatersrand University Press, Johannesburg, 2002); S Garkawe, 'The South African Truth and Reconciliation Commission: a suitable model to enhance the role and rights of victims of gross violations of human rights? (2003) 27(2) Melbourne University Law Review 334; J Quinn and M Freeman, 'Lessons Learned: Practical Lessons Gleaned from Inside the Truth Commissions of Guatemala and South Africa' (2003) 25(4) Human Rights Quarterly 1117. For a critical appraisal of the South African TRC see Stuart Wilson, 'The Myth of Restorative Justice: Truth, Reconciliation and the Ethics of Amnesty' (2001) 17 South African Journal on Human Rights 531. The Institute for Justice and Reconciliation's paper 'Truth and Reconciliation in South Africa: Ten Years On' provides a realistic assessment of what a TRC can reasonably accomplish and provides an audit of the response of government and other agencies to the unfinished business of the TRC: www.ijr.org.za/publications/publications-v2-1/truth-and-reconciliatin-in-south-africa-10-years-on/.

[53] J Sarkin, 'The Necessity and Challenges of Establishing a Truth and Reconciliation Commission for Rwanda' (1999) 21 *Human Rights Quarterly* 767, 802.

respond to the particular needs and dynamics in Zimbabwe. A foreign model of institution might be legitimate and work well in a receiving country, provided that it is translated into local terms by the agency of local actors representative of the wider public.[54]

World Bank studies note that institutional designs have been most effective, unsurprisingly, when they meet needs 'in ways compatible with country conditions'. Significantly, 'supplying' institutions is not enough: demand for these needs to be created, people must want to use them.[55] As Davis has pointed out in relation to entrenching constitutionalism, institutional indigenisation enables such phenomena to reach and be reached by the grass-roots level.[56] Especially where external actors believe there to be certain model ways to build peace, we ought to bear in mind the warning given by Dezalay and Garth against the reproduction of global institutional 'prescriptions' of law or (in our case) quasi-legal institutions:

> Internationally-generated imports succeed only where the local situation allows them to be nationalised—made part of the indigenous structures and practices. Local histories determine what can be assimilated into local settings and how what is assimilated will affect long-standing local practices . . . while we tend to

---

[54] 'Modelling' as used in the social sciences describes the process by which one actor observes, interprets and copies the actions of another. It connotes more than mere imitation: rather it involves (or should involve) 'intelligent adaptation to ensure that the exotic plant can take root in native soil' B Opeskin, 'Australian Constitutional Law in a Global Era' in French, Lindell & Saunders (eds) *Reflections on the Australian Constitution* (Federation Press, Sydney, 2003) 176. We ought to be careful of the term 'exotic': while its courts and public institutions have been compromised, Zimbabwe is not to be conceived of as a 'noble savage' standing to benefit from the enlightenment of foreign institutional ideas; nor is it what Bhargava would call a 'symmetrically barbaric society' where there is no consensus on moral norms (R Bhargava, 'Restoring Decency to Barbaric Societies' in Rotberg & Thompson (n 24): agreed fundamental norms exist in Zimbabwean society and in its law (Chapter III of the *Constitution of Zimbabwe* 1979 (Bill of Rights), even if they have been breached and not practically enforceable for some time.

[55] The World Bank recommends that successful new institutions share these features: they complement what already exists; they innovate; they connect with 'users'; they are aware of competing institutions so that they remain oriented towards servicing needs: *World Development Report 2002* (Oxford University Press, New York, 2002).

[56] M Davis, 'East Asia after the Crisis: Human Rights, Constitutionalism and State Reform' (2004) 26(1) *Human Rights Quarterly* 126, 128; 145. In relation to interpreting the South African Bill of Rights, Currie and de Waal, *The New Constitutional and Administrative Law* Vol 1 (Juta, Cape Town, 2003) fn 24:

> While in South Africa we may look to the jurisprudence of . . . [other] constitutional democracies as a vast historical text from which to draw . . . , the principles of constitutionalism adopted by our courts will achieve acceptance only if they address local problems. It is the shaping of these principles in the context of applying them to local issues—in effect their hybridization—which will give them a unique South African character and life. *Our new experiment with constitutionalism will only bear fruit to the extent that these principles become ingrained into the hopes, dreams and practices of our society.* From there, they will become part of the global text from which others may [in turn] draw examples and arguments while simultaneously shaping them to meet their own circumstances.' [Emphasis added].

92   *International and Comparative Law Quarterly*

think of the rule of law as an international concept, law must be produced at the national level to make national sense.[57]

There is a related danger that in designing institutions such as truth commissions, too much emphasis is given to lawyers and experts, including foreign experts. In the constitution-making context, but in a relevant way to our topic, Shaw has asked whether we risk 'dangerously privileging law over politics, diverting constructive polity-building energies into blind alleys of discussion among technicians and experts about constitutional authority, sovereignty and legal rights which fail to illuminate ... fundamental questions of political acceptance and legitimacy'.[58]

A sixth caution is that we need to be conscious of the chronologies, prescriptions and formulae that international law and an international renewalist project may, even unconsciously, seek to impose on post-conflict societies: if actors in the international community suggest or require certain features based on international legal standards, what ideological preferences or structural dynamics does 'international law' contain for a particular society?[59] Seventhly, we ought to be aware of the danger of legitimizing the previous regime by effectively enabling its representational portrayal and perhaps redemption in an ordered, formal institutional process.[60] Eighthly, we see a risk, in particular in international expectations or responses to these, of a degree of ritualistic 'going through the motions',[61] or a situation whereby institutionalization becomes, paradoxically, a way of distancing society from the process and from its responsibilities, rather than a forum for engaging in these.[62]

---

[57] Y Dezalay & B Garth (eds), *Global Prescriptions: The Production, Exportation, and Importation of a New Legal Orthodoxy* (University of Michigan Press, 2002) 326. See also H Klug, 'Hybrid(ity) Rules: Creating Local Law in a Globalised World' in Dezalay & Garth, 276ff.

[58] 'Process, Responsibility and Inclusion in EU Constitutionalism: A Contribution to the Debate on a Constitutional Architecture' Constitutional Web Papers, No. 4, 2001 ([http://les1.man.ac.uk/conweb/]).

[59] S Marks 'Guarding the gate with two faces: international law and political reconstruction' (Symposium: The Rule of Law in the Era of Globalization) (1999) 6(2) *Indiana Journal of Global Legal Studies* 457.

[60] cf. R Wilson *The Politics of Truth and Reconciliation in South Africa: Legitimising the Apartheid State* (Cambridge University Press, 2001).

[61] Ritualism in this context is the application of institutionalised means for securing objectives in such an unreflective and automatic way that focus is lost on actually achieving those outcomes: Merton, *Social Theory and Social Structure* (Free Press, New York, 1968). In the context of truth commissions and for on another aspect of 'ritualism', see T Kelsall, 'Truth, Lies, Ritual: Preliminary Reflections on the Truth and Reconciliation Commission in Sierra Leone' (2005) 27(2) *Human Rights Quarterly* 361.

[62] Of course, many of these institutions are intended to be highly ritualistic and symbolic rather than attempting substantial individualised justice for perpetrators and individuals. It is conceivable that a traumatised society would prefer a ritualised, symbolic process at a distance than a very involved—but painful—process; for more discussion see M Humphrey 'From Victim to Victimhood: Truth Commissions and Trials as Rituals of Political Transition and Individual Healing' (2003) 14(2) *Australian Journal of Anthropology* 171.

Transitional Justice   93

Ninthly, and related to the danger of abuse by local elites, there is a risk that such institutions are cosmetic only, or are embarked upon for the wrong reasons as a primarily externally-driven or led agenda.[63] As Rudi Teitel has recently observed, compliance with the demands of international criminal tribunals and prescriptions for transitional justice has come to be seen as a path to political legitimacy for transitional states:[64] this might lead to taking decisions that are not in the best interests of resolving the actual problems facing that society, so jeopardising sustainable peace. 'Transitional justice options' ought not to be selected (or advised or imposed by donors or agencies) and embarked upon for reasons that have more to do with outsiders' expectations than what is needed—and wanted—on the ground. Before a truth commission is initiated in a particular setting, it ideally ought to be established whether such an exercise has popular support among ordinary persons (not just local or international NGOs or government elites).[65] For our argument the particular significance of this point is that as a result of the many complex decisions they face, it will prove difficult to discern normative content on transitional justice decisions by states.

Tenth and finally, what is possible by way of institutionalised response—how robust and intrusive and prosecutorial it might be, for example—is of course heavily dependent on what is politically feasible or wise according to the balance of political power at the time of the transition. This will vary from case to case,[66] and it is not only local issues that affect the justice options: foreign political pressure can be determinative.[67] A truth commission may represent a local political compromise, as criminal prosecutions would be too provocative or untenable given the residual power in elements of the previous incumbent regime (who may be part of a unity transitional government). Justice Goldstone has remarked that the South African process 'was a political decision. It wasn't taken for moral reasons or for reasons of justice. It was a political compromise between having Nuremberg-style trials on the one hand

---

[63] Parker (n 26) also notes (37) that some truth commissions might be manifestations more of an attempt to appease the international community than a considered, popular decision or response to domestic demand. Bosire (n 24) 3 has cautioned that unmet expectations of transitional justice efforts are partly due to a default resort to a legally and institutionally demanding understanding of transitional justice divorced from the reality of weak capacities. While critical of the 'infatuation' with truth commissions, Daly ought to acknowledge that the 'transition planners' to whom her related caution is directed are usually not just 'transitional governments' but international NGOs, donors, the UN and others: E Daly 'Truth Skepticism' (n 28) 23; 40–1.

[64] R Teitel, 'Transitional Justice Globalised' (n 24) 3.

[65] Shaw (n 35) 12. Notwithstanding the (sincere) keenness of some international civil society organisations, a truth commission is not something to be imposed upon a society according to some transitional justice formula, automatically as part of a conflict resolution 'first aid kit'. More recently Teitel used the term 'tool box' to make substantially the same point: (n 25) 4.

[66] See D Shea, *The South African Truth Commission: The Politics of Reconciliation* (United States Institute of Peace, Washington DC, 2000); on prosecution models, see G Bass, *Stay the Hand of Vengeance: The Politics of War Crimes Tribunals* (Princeton University Press, 2000).

[67] Parker (n 26) 3–5.

and forgetting on the other.'[68] By contrast, in Solomon Islands, and partly as a result of the relatively high level of political control and security influence that the intervening regional assistance mission could bring, the preference was to strengthen courts and pursue prosecutions, leaving reconciliation mechanisms to informal, church-based and community processes. The idea of a formal truth commission with the suggestion of amnesties was thought to send mixed messages about future responsibility for ethnic violence.[69] How and whether past injustices will be dealt with will largely be determined by the actual nature of any political transition in Zimbabwe. We are conscious that emphasising political realities can be something deployed by those acting in bad faith whose aim is to justify illegitimate transitional justice 'whitewash' strategies that fail to address victims' rights and needs. It nevertheless reinforces the difficulty in prescribing certain forms of transitional justice, that is, the difficulty of arriving at those standards in the first place.

Where there is a high level of awareness about the problem (accompanied by fatigue, political power imbalances, widespread communal implication, and the need to avoid creating a new venue of disputation), it is as least arguable, then, that Zimbabweans may feel that the best way to proceed is to 'leave the past alone'.[70] Most experience, as we argue, points the other way, especially where there are concerns about *who gets to decide how to proceed*. The often intense political pressure and the peace-seeking basis for 'justice compromises' again illustrates the difficulty of defining with any precision whether and how international law constrains a state's options in determining how to fulfil its general duty to act somehow to remedy human rights abuses within its jurisdiction.

---

[68] 'TRC preferable to trials' *Pretoria News* (18 August 1997), cited in A McDonald 'A right to truth, justice and a remedy for African victims of serious violations of international humanitarian law' (1999) 2 Law, Democracy and Development 139. Truth commissions are often—but not necessarily—the deliberate result of political compromise, rather than imposed by the dominant new regime. As Tomuschat points out, the 'background of a truth commission is invariably ... of stalemate in a political power play': C Tomuschat, 'Clarification Commission in Guatemala' (2001) 23 Human Rights Quarterly 233, 235. In the transition to democracy in South Africa, the white minority still wielded serious negotiating power, including through control of the police and military. In Chile and Argentina, the enduring influence and power of the military leadership meant that at least initially it was unthinkable to commence criminal actions against the main culprits. In El Salvador and in Guatemala, the commissions were components of the ceasefire and peace agreements where neither government nor rebels had suffered military defeat.

[69] Ho-Won Jeong observes that '[o]verall strategies of reconciliation are affected by political constraints and evolving intergroup relations in a postconflict society.' Imposing justice can have a disruptive potential and, for example, lead to military coups, so that it may be crucial 'not to provoke still-powerful elements in the armed forces that retain political veto power during a fragile democratic transition' so that for any process of truth-seeking 'the alignment of forces at the time of transition shapes the nature and degree of truth revealed': Strategy and Process (n 32) 155; 168–9; 185, and see this theme explored in A Rigby, *Justice and Reconciliation: After the Violence* (Lynne Reinner, Boulder, 2001).

[70] Victor de Waal's characterization of Zimbabwe's first decade after independence in 1980 is that it may have involved society as a whole deciding to simply move on, leaving the past behind: *The Politics of Reconciliation: Zimbabwe's First Decade* (David Philip, Cape Town, 1990) 45.

V. INTERNATIONAL LAW, MINIMUM STANDARDS AND A 'TRUTH COMMISSION NORM'

A new Zimbabwe Government will probably aim to appease international opinion. The MDC's 2008 Policy Statement notes that its justice strategy (including a truth commission) is intended to pre-empt criticism or alternative (international) remedies: '[n]othing can be gained by condoning violations of international law in our domestic law: victims will go above Zimbabwe's law and courts to international tribunals.'[71] The MDC's policy is said to be based on four international *legal* principles: the communal 'right to know', the right to justice and a remedy, the right to reparations, and the 'right to non-recurrence.' As noted above, while it does not expressly call for a truth commission, the September 2008 agreement records that the parties have considered the significance of taking measures to '*achieve national healing, cohesion and unity in respect of victims of pre and post independence political conflicts*' (emphasis added).

Aside from substantive international crimes which may have taken place in Zimbabwe (many of which are also violations of the Bill of Rights in Chapter III of the *Constitution of Zimbabwe* 1979), what international legal framework possibly informs, shapes or constrains the decision to pursue a truth-for-amnesty commission? We first consider the existence and content of the state's duty to afford a remedy for human rights violations, and the extent to which a concomitant of this might be a 'right to truth'; secondly, consideration is given to whether practice has led either to a minimum international standard for truth commissions' form and practice, or to a norm prescribing a truth commission process as a necessary component of a democratic transition from a violent past.

By its accession in 1991 to the *International Covenant on Civil and Political Rights* (ICCPR),[72] the Zimbabwean State has assumed the international obligation to afford an effective remedy to victims of human rights abuse (from whatever source). This amounts to a positive duty to investigate and to prosecute, bring to justice or take action against those responsible for serious violations of the rights provided for in that instrument; to provide victims with equal and effective access to justice; to provide appropriate remedies to victims; and to provide for (or at least facilitate) just and adequate reparations.[73] The State may also have a duty to provide protection

---

[71] MDC 2008 Policy (n 18) 1

[72] ICCPR 1966, GA Res. 2200A (XXI), UN Doc. A/6316, entered into force 23 March 1976—Zimbabwe acceded on 13 August 1991. Importantly it is also a party to the *African Charter on Human and Peoples' Rights* (the 'Banjul Charter') 1981, entered into force 21 October 1986—Zimbabwe ratified on 30 May 1986.

[73] Article 2 ICCPR; see also Article 8 of the *Universal Declaration of Human Rights* 1948 (GA Res. General Assembly Resolution 217A (III)); UN Human Rights Committee, 'General Comment No. 31 on Article 2 of the Covenant: The Nature of the General Legal Obligation Imposed on States Parties to the Covenant' (UN Doc. CCPR/C/74/CRP.4/Rev.6 (2004), [15], [16]; UN *Basic Principles and Guidelines on the Right to a Remedy and Reparation for Victims of Violations of International Human Rights and Humanitarian Law* (UN Commission on Human

and humanitarian assistance to internally displaced persons within its juris-diction.[74]

In the context of very widespread victimization, scarce resources and ca-pacity, and other competing considerations, it is suggested that the decision to establish a truth commission may be understood as a bona fide and sufficient attempt to fulfil the state's duties in this regard.[75] The second and third of the MDC's principles are clearly established in international law (a right to an effective remedy and to a form of reparation). Despite its unusual phraseol-ogy, the fourth (a 'right to non-recurrence') probably amounts to no more than the State's very well-established duty to promote human rights protection and prevent violations from whatever source. In relation to the first principle (the MDC's expression of an individual and communal 'right to know'), despite the trend for truth commissions in recent transitional arrangements, we are not sure of the solidity of arguments describing the alleged codification of a 'right to truth' in international law. While this has received some attention,[76] it is perhaps only one way of expressing the (well-established, perhaps expanding) duty on the State, referred to above, to at least initiate investigations into allegations of rights violations and attempt a reasonable remedy where ap-propriate.

At a more abstract level, some might argue that the form of truth commission that might be adopted is constrained normatively by what the

Rights, E/CN.4/Sub.2/1993/8; E/CN.4/1997/104); also (in relation to 'gross' violations), the *Basic Principles and Guidelines on the Right to a Remedy and Reparation for Victims of Gross Violations of International Human Rights Law and Serious Violations of International Humanitarian Law* adopted by the UN General Assembly on 16 December 2005 (A/Res/60/147). Under the 2005 *Basic Principles*, reparation should respond to the needs and wishes of the victims and be proportionate to the gravity of the violations and the resulting harm. It should include restitution, compensation, rehabilitation, satisfaction and guarantees of non-repetition. In addition to providing reparation to individuals, states should make adequate provision for collective re-parations for groups of victims and special measures should be taken to afford opportunities for self-development and advancement to groups who, as a result of human rights violations, were denied such opportunities.

[74] *UN Guiding Principles on Internal Displacement* (UN Doc. E/CN.4/1998/53/Add.2; 11 November 1998. In this respect, it is likely the Principles declare an international legal duty.

[75] The State's duty in respect of crimes of concern to the international community as a whole is considered below.

[76] See the positions expressed in 'Report of the Independent Expert: Update of Set of Principles to Combat Impunity' (E/CN.4/2005/102/) (Geneva, 2005) and 'Promotion and Protection of Human Rights: Study on the Right to Truth' (E/CN.4/2006/91) (OHCHR, Geneva, 2006). More study is necessary on the issue of sourcing support for the bindingness of rules from the practice and publications of influential intergovernmental agencies such as the OHCHR. The state duty to investigate alleged disappearances declared in the famous *Velasquez Rodriguez* case (Inter-American Court of Human Rights) (1989) 28 ILM 291 is one of the bases relied on in a recent overview expressing support for the existence of 'a right to truth': Parker (n 26) 22–25. Apart from the awkwardness of conceiving of a right to 'truth', we do not think that the sources of Art 2(3) ICCPR or *Velasquez* amount, as such, to an internationally enforceable 'right to truth': it is a duty to genuinely investigate and attempt to remedy human rights abuses, and no more precise content can be placed on it. For European practice, see A Mowbray 'Duties of Investigation Under the European Convention on Human Rights' (2002) 51 ICLQ 437.

Transitional Justice 97

international community would deem to be a 'respectable' form of process. A constitution-making analogy is instructive: Currie and de Waal, for example, have expressed the view that the diversity of constitutional alternatives before 1989 gave way to increased uniformity, with liberal constitutional principles becoming a prerequisite for 'international constitutional respectability'.[77] Klug too argued that during the 1990s it became possible to identify 'a thin, yet significant, international political culture, which is shaping the outer parameters of feasible modes of government.'[78] If the analogy could be applied to truth commissions and other temporary bodies, and although it is more likely to be a matter of political recognition than legal consequence, it could be argued that the quality of process (the sincerity of the effort, the extent to which it gives effect to internationally recognized rights, fulfils the State's duty to act on rights abuses and afford an effective remedy, the independence of the institution, and so on) and the legitimacy of the regime that sponsors it, can indicate whether a particular commission is accorded international 'respectability'.

Parker has recently expressed the view that an emerging international norm in relation to truth commissions can be discerned through both the practice and approval of States and of international organizations, and through the opinions of advocates, activists, and writers who consider such institutions to be necessary components of internationally acceptable and respectable transitions.[79] The implication of Parker's analysis is not just that commissions are coming to be required to display certain characteristics or features in order to pass legal muster as 'valid' institutions; it is that there is an emerging norm requiring a truth commission as a feature of a legitimate post-conflict transition. Parker's argument, couched mainly in international relations theory, seems directed more to the emergence of a political norm than one of 'hard' international law.[80] One question in determining the normative force to be attributed to a transitional State's decision to erect a truth commission is

[77] Currie & De Waal (n 56) 24.

[78] Klug (n 46) 6. The corollary of such comments ties into wider debate, beyond the scope of this paper, on whether an emerging norm of a right to democratic governance exists in international law (such as the work of Thomas Franck) or the more controversial claim attributed to Francis Fukuyama as to whether western liberal democracy is now recognised as the 'final form' of government.

[79] Parker (n 26). In support of the norm's crystallisation, her work chronicles the patterns of recommendation, praise and adoption of truth commissions, for example in UN-sponsored peace agreements or by agencies of the UN and international NGOs. We think it is misconceived to posit a norm on these bases alone. See also E Newman, 'Transitional Justice: the Impact of Transnational Norms and the United Nations' in Newman & Schnabel (eds) *Recovering from Civil Conflict* (Crown House, London, 2001).

[80] At other points, however, it is clearly asserted as a legal norm: Parker's conclusion not only confuses two bodies of law, but goes too far. She argues that 'not only does the truth commission mechanism agree with international principles of human rights law, but are in fact demanded by international humanitarian law itself' (25). The praise and practice (mainly of NGOs) narrated by Parker cannot be said to amount to a norm that a truth commission is an obligatory part of transitional justice.

whether this is done as a result of a legal conviction that it is bound to adopt such a strategy, or whether it is simply responding to local or international social and political demands. The practice of transnational NGO networks (and the uptake and response to their output) can contribute to norm development.[81] However, the mere fact that there is uniformity in guidelines, handbooks and other resources (for example, recommending a certain form of truth commission) is not itself indicative of a norm: many international transitional justice NGOs are entrepreneurial, self-interest is often at place their advocacy of 'minimum standards' surely needs to be seen in this light.

Perhaps supporting Parker's argument, and while not all 'transitional' situations are 'post-conflict' situations, some have argued that any new or emerging 'post-conflict law' would include justice and reconciliation models for criminal responsibility, as based on recent practice.[82] Related to such arguments is the question of whether the UN's practice and policies, which take place against the backdrop of overarching legal principles, have themselves contributed to the development of a normative or legal framework for the guidance and regulation of future UN involvement in post-conflict situations, including in relation to transitional justice options.[83] In our view, the merits and prevalence of truth commissions does not mean that a transition which forsakes such an institution has breached any norm. Provided the core of the Article 2(3) ICCPR duty is met, it is more likely that the politics of institution-making remain eclectic so that States have a range of alternatives in terms of transitional justice strategies.[84] Where the issue is likely to matter is in relation to the external or global validity of any amnesties provided by a national commission, which we return to below.

VI. A ZIMBABWEAN TRUTH COMMISSION: ESTABLISHMENT, MANDATE AND PROCESS

The reader will be conscious that, subject to the various cautions expressed above about the utility or appropriateness of comparative models and

---

[81] M Keck and M Sikkink, *Activists Beyond Borders: Advocacy Networks in International Politics* (Cornell University Press, Ithaca, 1998).

[82] C Stahn, '"Jus ad Bellum", "Jus in Bello" . . . "Jus Post Bellum"? Rethinking the Conception of the Law of Armed Force' (2006) 17 European Journal of International Law 921, 938–41. The difficulty in characterising very diverse political situations as 'transitional' or 'post-conflict' is, we would add, one consideration undermining the supposed normative conclusions to be drawn.

[83] N White & D Klaasen (eds), *The United Nations, Human Rights and Post-Conflict Situations* (Juris/Manchester University Press, 2005) 1, 3; the argument appears to be that since the UN with its 'unique claims to universal competence in human rights' has 'to a large degree' responsibility for setting the standards in this area, its practice can be the basis of new normative frameworks. See also Newman (n 79) 31. And see too R Cryer, 'Post-Conflict Accountability: a Matter of Judgment, Practice or Principle?' in N White & D Klaasen (eds), *The UN, Human Rights and Post-Conflict Situations* (Manchester University Press/Juris, 2005) 281–286 on the significance to be placed on the practice, which he chronicles, of the UN in negotiating peace agreements and it policy on amnesties.

[84] Klug (n 46) 23 (in relation to constitutional forms adopted by new or transitional states).

experiences (and other risks of a truth commission process), we are favourably disposed to these institutions as a form of practical but principled[85] compromise in transitional justice settings, partly on the empirical basis that they have assisted other societies faced with similar dilemmas. There are lessons to be learned from other experiences in relation to the various challenges that Zimbabweans might confront should they attempt to create a truth commission in future.[86] What follows is an attempt to briefly survey some comparative practices of States in establishing and carrying on national truth commission processes. We have selected ten design and operational features to illustrate that a diverse range of practices and procedures have been adopted. This survey will reveal that provided the commission represents a genuine attempt to provide a remedy (in fulfilment of the general duty discussed), it is really only in relation to the grant or purported grant of amnesties for serious crimes of concern to the international community as a whole that international normative considerations become apparent. As we discuss below, whether any grant of amnesty is recognized in international or foreign forums is partly dependent on the nature and quality of the process that gave rise to it, and (in turn) the legitimacy of the regime which set that process in place. That is, an essentially political assessment (locally and internationally) as to the independence, good faith and comprehensiveness of a commission is likely to be important to any legal issues arising about whether the state has discharged its remedial duty, or about the validity of amnesties granted.

First, the presence or absence of international support or even pressure leading to a commission or involved in its operation does not necessarily affect a commission's legitimacy. By contrast, international sponsorship may greatly assist a local commission's credibility, profile, perceived independence, as well as its funding and skills-base.[87] Secondly, the degree of genuine

---

[85] Cf Emmanuel (n 52).

[86] A number of tools and resources exist: see for example *Reconciliation after Violent Conflict* (International Institute for Democracy and Elections, Stockholm, 2003); D Orentlicher, *Report of the Independent Expert: Update of the Set of Principles to Combat Impunity* E/CN.4/2005/102 (United Nations, Geneva, 2005); *Rule of Law Tools for Post-Conflict Societies: Truth Commissions* (Office of the High Commissioner for Human Rights, Geneva, 2006); Amnesty International, *Truth, Justice and Reparation: Establishing an Effective Truth Commission* (London, 2007). See also generally the resources pooled at www.ictj.org (the International Centre for Transitional Justice, New York). For a comparative overview of different processes, see www.truthcommission.org (Harvard law school & the European Centre for Common Ground). See also Hayner, *Unspeakable Truths*, Chapters 4 & 5, and also P Hayner, 'Fifteen Truth Commissions—1974 to 1994' (1994) 16 *Human Rights Quarterly* 597. Some of these issues are canvassed by one of the authors in 2002: M du Plessis, 'Truth and Reconciliation Processes: Lessons for Zimbabwe?' Report No. 44 (South African Institute of International Affairs, Pretoria, 2002).

[87] International civil society organizations may play a very important role. See generally K Kumar (ed), *Rebuilding Societies after Civil War: Critical Roles for International Assistance* (Lynne Reinner, Boulder, 1997), and for a case study, McPherson, 'Supporting Post-Conflict Reconciliation: An Assessment of International Assistance to South Africa's Truth Commission (CSVR, Johannesburg, 2001); Cf J Braithwaite (n 44) 187 (outside peacemakers can seldom

participation of reputable local NGOs in designing and operating the commission is likely to shape perceptions of the standing and merit of the institution.[88] Thirdly, the degree of (perceived) operational independence from
other arms of government is likely to be significant for judgments on the
commission's legitimacy.[89] Fourthly, and directly related to capacity for independence but also of obvious practical importance, are issues of funding: a
successful and legitimate process requires genuine commitments in the form
of sufficient resources to investigate, research, conduct hearings, and so on.[90]
Fifthly, the funding question becomes more complicated in practice if it is
envisaged that the commission not only fund its own operations, but also be
responsible for distributing any form of monetary compensation for some
victims which may be envisaged.[91] On one view, the new government will
have inherited, in effect, certain liabilities against the State, some of which
may have been acted upon (by instituting civil claims). Issues might arise of
deprivation of property if the new order decides to attempt to retrospectively
immunise itself from already instituted civil (delict or tort-based) suits; the
international right to an effective remedy might be triggered. But there is no
clear duty to afford *monetary* compensation to victims. There is very little
practice on which to identify a normative trend.[92] Moreover, one is unlikely to
develop since there are both practical considerations (limited resources and
management of payment schemes in a weak governance scenario) and issues
of principle: to what extent is monetary compensation appropriate, especially

deliver the sort of engagement required at community level). There are many examples of commissions receiving external funding.

[88] International Centre for Transitional Justice *Truth Commissions and NGOs: the Essential
Relationship* (ICTJ, New York, 2004). Aside from advice, support, counselling and other activities, raising public awareness of the proposals for a truth commission or of the commission's work
once established or completed is an important role for local civil society.

[89] The ideal is of an institution 'free of direct influence or control by the government, including in the interpretation of its written mandate . . . , in developing its operating methodology
for research and public outreach, and in shaping its report and recommendations' Hayner, *Fifteen
Truth Commissions* (n 87) 179. One factor in favour of stronger international involvement in such
an institution is the influence a strong external actor can bring to bear, through conditionality and
other controls, or even 'hybrid' structures with expatriate impartial staff, in both ensuring operational independence and the perception of such independence.

[90] Financially under-resourced truth commissions have failed: Hayner, *Unspeakable Truths*,
69, 224. Throughout its operation the Guatemalan commissioners were constantly diverting their
energy away from the work of the truth commission and towards attempts to raise money from
networks within the international community: Tomuschat (n 68) 248.

[91] A truth commission's work may involve indirect financial consequences if, for example, it
recommends certain institutional and legal reforms or human rights training for security services,
refers matters for prosecution, proposes monuments and symbolic measures, or communal reparation in the form of development projects, or recommends the establishment of various bodies
to oversee and resolve land and property disputes.

[92] The South African TRC was empowered to make smaller 'Urgent Interim Reparation'
payments to victims (or their families) in urgent need, and 'Individual Reparation Grants' for up
to six years to 'eligible' victims. 22,000 eligible victims were identified during its proceedings,
and eventually a one-off payment of R30,000 was given to such persons from the specially
constituted President's Fund.

Transitional Justice   101

in cases of widespread victimization?[93] In Zimbabwe's own case, public compensation schemes have in the past been heavily subject to abuse and looting.[94] The *Breaking the Silence* report expressed the view in relation to the 1980s violence that individual compensation in Zimbabwe was not a feasible option, and this view may remain dominant. Given the practical need to ensure the integrity of any truth commission, and the critical economic situation, it would be very difficult to argue that the duty on the Zimbabwean State to afford redress included monetary compensation to victims.[95] There is no principle of international law and scant practice to suggest that, where other reparation measures are attempted, lack of monetary compensation is unacceptable.

Sixthly, the mandate of the commission may be significant to its political and normative acceptability. But commissions have been established in a wide variety of ways, the majority by presidential decree (Argentina, Chile, Haiti, Sri Lanka, Chad, Uganda), some by peace accord (El Salvador, Guatemala), and others created as a statutory body by the national legislature (South Africa).[96] Written mandates for truth commissions often have restricted terms of reference that reflect the political compromises agreed upon in the transition negotiations. Argentina, Uruguay and Sri Lanka's commissions were restricted by their mandate to consider only disappearances; the Uruguayan commission as a result missed the majority of human rights violations (such as torture and illegal detention) that had taken place during the military regime.[97] It is important that the terms of reference for any proposed commission in Zimbabwe be sufficiently broad to allow investigation into all forms of serious rights abuses, preferably leaving it to the commission to decide the most appropriate cases or practices to investigate.[98] The El Salvador commission's terms of reference, for example, left the mandate relatively open, requiring only that the commission should report on 'serious acts of violence ... whose impact on society urgently demands that the public should know the truth'.[99] A similarly flexible mandate would allow a fuller picture of the truth to emerge in Zimbabwe and would allow an investigation of a wider range of

---

[93] There is perhaps a tendency in the literature to focus on psychological aspects of communal 'healing', while glossing over the real needs victims may have for specific medical treatment and rehabilitation.

[94] See discussion in relation to the Zimbabwe context in the earlier section (n 13 above).

[95] Specific attention will be needed to the place of existing pension and compensation mechanisms which may be subject to legitimate claims preceding the recent crisis. A Zimbabwe commission might make recommendations but leave service provision to a range of other government and civil bodies.

[96] For a comprehensive list of the ways in which truth commissions have come to be established, see Hayner *Unspeakable Truths*, Appendix 1.

[97] Hayner *Unspeakable Truths* 72.

[98] Hayner *Fifteen Truth Commissions* 636.

[99] Hayner *Unspeakable Truths* 73. See too the South African TRC's mandate which called for investigation of 'gross violations of human rights, including the violations which were part of a systematic pattern of abuse'.

issues necessary for the achievement of reconciliation.[100] The variety of mandates and bases for mandates again reveals the lack of clear practice of the sort that might accrue some sort of normative weight in giving any content to the duty to afford a remedy.

Seventhly, it goes almost without saying that the empirical legitimacy of the commission—its ability to be accepted by the population as a credible body capable of finding some 'objective' truths—generally depends on the stature and reputation and ability of its senior members.[101] The merits of a 'hybrid' commission, including some foreign members, can be quite apparent in terms of both substance (skills) and form (local confidence).[102] The manner of appointing commissioners will be significant, although it is likely to be heavily influenced by the political power balances at the time. In recent years several commissions have adopted processes that have ensured transparency and public participation.[103] The South African model illustrates that it is possible to make some parts of the appointment process visible (for example, public interviews).[104] In South Africa, an Act of Parliament created the commission as an independent investigative body. A selection committee was formed, including representatives of local human rights NGOs, which then called for nominations from the public, and compiled a shortlist from which President

---

[100] Note, however, criticisms directed at the *overly* broad mandate of the Guatemalan Clarification Commission which was required to investigate 'the' human rights violations— textually meaning 'all' relevant human rights violations committed during twenty years of different dictatorships, provided they were linked to the armed confrontation. This overburdened the commission: Tomuschat (n 68) 239–240. The Nigerian equivalent's mandate to consider 'human rights violations or abuses' was understood very broadly: in its first few weeks of work 90 per cent of the 10,000 submissions pertained to labour disputes. The commission adjusted itself to focus on 'gross violations of human rights only': Hayner, *Unspeakable Truths* 69. One issue in Zimbabwe will be a mandate that includes human rights abuses associated with land invasions and displacement, without dragging the commission into the politics of land redistribution as they then stand.

[101] Sarkin (n 53) 804. Considerations also include the extent to which commissioners are seen to be representative of a range of perspectives, racial, ethnic and other backgrounds Hayner, *Fifteen Truth Commissions* 654. While institutional independence is significant, it is not out of the question to include political party actors. In Chile, eight commissioners were appointed from both sides: Sarkin (n 54) 806; Hayner *Unspeakable Truths* 35. This may be a political necessity, despite the ideal of non-partisanship. South Africa's Promotion of National Unity and Reconciliation Act 1995 provided commissioners should be 'fit and proper persons who are impartial and *who do not have a high political profile*' (emphasis added). However, it may be unavoidable that political party representatives are included—at least they are engaged.

[102] Both the Cambodian and Sierra Leone courts have been 'hybrid courts' involving local and foreign judges. See generally L Dickinson, 'The Promise of Hybrid Courts' (2003) 97(2) American Journal of International Law 295. In Chile, Argentina, and South Africa all the commissioners were nationals of their respective countries. However, El Salvador had all foreign commissioners (two Latin American and one American) and Guatemala had a mixture. It is unlikely that exclusively foreign commissioners would be acceptable in any Zimbabwean commission, and there are good reasons for including nationals.

[103] Sarkin (n 54) 806; Hayner, *Unspeakable Truths* 216.

[104] J Sarkin, 'The Trials and Tribulations of the South African Truth and Reconciliation Commission' (1996) 12 South African Journal on Human Rights 617, 621.

Mandela chose the Commission.[105] International actors can bolster legitimacy of this stage and help build confidence among the various actors. There has been great variety in terms of the professional backgrounds of commissioners,[106] the staffing size of the commission, and so on.[107]

An eighth area of consideration is that of timing of a truth commission. Here while a long delay might undermine the 'effectiveness' of any remedy, the considerations are almost entirely practical as well as dependent upon political imperatives. Experience shows that often the quicker the commission is set up and begins its work, while the window of opportunity and local and international political momentum is strong, the better.[108] On the other hand, a drawn-out design process can increase public awareness and legitimacy: there is no point establishing a wonderful new institution if nobody knows about it or uses it.[109] The 18 months spent designing the South African Truth and Reconciliation Commission after the democratic elections of April 1994, allowing broad input, political buy-in and nuanced legislative development might be seen as critical to the international recognition afforded to its outcomes overall. A second timing issue relates to the duration of a commission's mandate: a long, drawn-out process could still be fairly cosmetic. The majority of truth commissions have had very limited time to complete their work, usually between six months and a year to complete all investigation and to submit a report.[110] More recent commissions have worked for longer (almost five years in total for the South African TRC). Hayner suggests that one to two-and-a-half years is probably optimal.[111] On the other hand, it will take time for people to learn about, let alone trust and engage with such an

---

[105] A similar process was followed in Sierra Leone where the Special Representative of the UN Secretary General was appointed as selection co-ordinator and was directed to call for nominations from the public.

[106] There are strong arguments for having a range of professions, beyond the legal profession: see Hayner, *Unspeakable Truths* 217.

[107] In terms of staffing numbers, experiences again vary. Whereas Latin American commissions have enjoyed relatively large staff complements (Chile and Argentina had approximately sixty full time staff members each), others have had to do with very few personnel. Sarkin (n 53) 814. South Africa's TRC had the highest staff complement to date, with around three hundred staff between 1996 and 1998: Hayner *Unspeakable Truths* 218.

[108] Hayner *Unspeakable Truths* 221; also Hayner *Fifteen Truth Commissions* 640.

[109] Hayner points out that at this early stage a truth commission can also have the 'secondary effect of holding off pressure for immediate reforms and other measures of accountability, giving the government time to take stock, plan, and strengthen institutions as necessary to further its other transitional justice initiatives' Hayner, *Unspeakable Truths* 221.

[110] The Argentine, Chilean and Salvadoran Commissions were established very quickly by decree and had only nine months to generate an authoritative account.

[111] Hayner, *Unspeakable Truths* 222: to ensure that the commission works efficaciously towards its deadline, to enable healing to begin swiftly, and to ensure that a report (and its recommendations) is published while there is still buy-in to the reconciliation process. The Ugandan commission (narrated by Hayner) demonstrates the dangers: set up in 1986, the Commission of Inquiry in Uganda was given no time limit. It took over nine years before it finished, and by then had lost the support and interest of the public, and failed to produce the cathartic effect expected of the work of a commission.

institution.[112] Reconciliation and trust-building is a long-term process, of which any formal institution is only a part. Depending on the extent of public awareness-raising that is possible before it starts its work, and funding availability, any Zimbabwean commission might run for about two years. A more nuanced and possibly effective strategy would be for a permanent body but with a gradually narrowing mandate that looks later on at broader and historical issues too.[113]

A third, more controversial timing question, related to mandate and resource availability, concerns which periods of history a commission may be expected to study: how far back does 'the past' go?[114] In relation to the particular dynamics of the Zimbabwe situation this is likely to be a problematic issue, for while common sense, practicality and limited funds might suggest that the violence that has marked political repression since 2000 ought to be the primary focus of any commission, there will be various interest groups for whom the present is not explicable without a process that engages with the period 1980–2000 (in particular the *gukurahundi* period), before that with Rhodesia 1965–1979, and indeed going back to European settlement in 1890. The Rhodesian period is less suited to a truth commission than the 1980s since much more is known about the abuses that took place before 1980—even if those issues are not 'resolved'. There are a number of reasons why a future commission is unlikely to focus on the Rhodesian era directly.[115] One thing that may be considered relevant from the Rhodesian conflict was that it set in motion the pattern of non-inquisition and amnesty that has continued to this day. Structural and particular abuses during the Rhodesian era and the culture of impunity created are no doubt likely to form the backdrop to any future commission's report (and surviving Rhodesian or colonial era legislation may be the subject of recommendations for reform), but will not be considered further here.

---

[112] Whereas a formal institution needs to establish public trust and awareness in quite a short time, whereas local, women's and Church groups have long been familiar to the community (and are likely to still be operating long after a truth commission has wrapped up). Judicial and quasi-judicial mechanisms are not likely to be sufficient to reconstruct the moral order: other needs on the cultural, the social, the psychological, and spiritual levels may be called for: E Kiss, 'Moral Ambition within and beyond Political Constraints: Reflections on Restorative Justice' in Rotberg & Thompson (eds) (n 24).

[113] One idea is that the gradually narrowing mandate and budget enables the commission to ultimately run as a self-funding national attraction, by way of a museum. We are grateful to Professor John Braithwaite for this idea.

[114] Sarkin (n 53) 811–812.

[115] We think these reasons include the lapse of time; the legal barriers resulting from a succession of amnesties including under the Indemnity and Compensation Act 1975, the Amnesty Ordinance 1979, and the Amnesty (General Pardon) Act 1980 (Ch 9); the fact that the amnesty resulted from a compromise that effectively ended a decade-long civil war; the fact that a broad and largely effective political reconciliation process was set in motion at the time in 1980; the need to limit and focus any commission's mandate and workload; and the fact that the state abuses cannot be attributed to the Mugabe regime, whereas those from 1980 onwards can.

As mentioned earlier, a more difficult question is whether the 1980s *gukurahundi* and State violence in Matabeleland issue is the subject of any formal national process. Many civil claims against the State will now fall outside the limitations period for instituting these. It is impossible to say that any 'effective remedy' has been provided. This period in Zimbabwe's past is arguably unresolved and 'unprocessed' and represents a possible future source of civil disunity.[116] It may be that it is a subject-matter best left until greater political stability ensures that this fault-line will not be re-opened in a way that leads to ethnic division and disorder in any transitional Zimbabwe. It may be possible—and from the perspective of international legal duties acceptable— that a mandate is devised that preoccupies the commission with the post-2000 State violence, but which endeavours at a later date, and on a more broad level, to uncover some of the unknown facts of Zimbabwe's often violent past and offer a form of account and redress as appropriate or possible.

A ninth issue would be the various difficult questions of methodology re- garding, for example, how any Zimbabwean commission will gather evidence, due process rules and procedures, the level of proof relied upon to reach conclusions, confidentiality issues, and so on. Here there is some rather more solid normative background relating to internationally recognised rights to due process,[117] although practice has varied widely. In the Latin American countries, most of the hearings of those truth commissions were behind closed doors, whereas in South Africa hearings were public (with high levels of media coverage). The latter approach increases public appreciation of such commissions' work (in terms of allaying concerns about bias or cover-up) and prevents continued denial by sectors of society. Including in relation to the intended cathartic and therapeutic dimensions of publicly acknowledged processes,[118] public hearings importantly shift the focus from a mere *product* (a report), to the *process* itself.[119] In terms of procedure, it is to be expected that victims have a central role.[120] While it may be preferable for any

---

[116] In legal terms, it is this period that arguably witnessed the most serious crimes including possible crimes against humanity (systematic attacks on a civilian population during an internal armed conflict). On the other hand, Part IV of the 1997 *Breaking the Silence* report, while not a judicial verdict, accepted the view that the effect of the grant of amnesties is immunity from prosecution, and this view has not been challenged in any legal forum to date.

[117] See for instance article 14 of the ICCPR. For comprehensive treatment, see M Freeman, *Truth Commissions and Procedural Fairness* (n 24).

[118] Hayner, *Unspeakable Truths* 134. By contrast see Shaw's views that this is a peculiarly 'Western', 'Freudian' concept and not necessarily of application in some African countries: (n 36).

[119] Hayner, *Unspeakable Truths* 225. Sarkin (n 53) 817.

[120] The process of course also has huge significance for perpetrators, and part of the aim of any such process is to provide a forum for their rehabilitation, expression of contrition, moral recon- stitution and what Jeong calls 'the recovery of their own humanity' (*Strategy and Process* (n 33) 156). A commission may not have the resources or capacity for counselling services for those who testify. Community organizations, traditional healers, church structures, extended families and friends, and support groups may need to fill the breach: see Amoah & Greenbaum, 'Has Everything been Done? The Nature of Assistance to Victims of Past Political Atrocities in

Zimbabwean commission to follow the example of the South African, Argentine and Salvadoran commissions and undertake its own investigations rather than more passively relying on testimony and reports,[121] there are many political, resource and other considerations, and unsurprisingly this is not a trait universally discernable in such bodies. However, if it is to represent a comprehensive attempt (and part of 'an effective remedy'), a commission should at least aim to carry out an in-depth analysis of a fair number of violations so that it can document the types of violations that have been paradigmatic of the period.[122]

A tenth issue is the production of a report and recommendations by a truth commission. While the focus of a commission should be its process (which is itself a means of promoting reconciliation) interim and/or final reports can be very significant. To receive recognition and ultimately to fulfil its function, the report needs to be made readily available to the public, in publicly digestible form, and attempt 'closure' while not artificially cutting off debate. The final report is a formal attempt at capturing broadly 'the truth'—an overall acknowledgment of, attribution of responsibility for, and attempted redress of the abuses that occurred within the state.[123] A useful incidental function for a truth commission usually captured in any report, and one factor in

Southern Africa' and 'Resources on Services for Victims of Political Violence in Southern Africa' (Report and Bibliography for the Southern African Reconciliation Project) (CSVR, Johannesburg, 2005). Publication of the report and the termination of a commission's mandate is of course not likely to be—nor likely to purport to be—the 'end' of efforts at reconciliation, counselling, and other processes: see for example Kayser 'Interventions after the TRC: Reconciliation, Advocacy, Healing' (CSVR, Johannesburg, 2001).

[121] To this end, although commissions do not formally conduct criminal proceedings, they have increasingly taken on prosecutorial powers. For example, the South African TRC was authorised to subpoena witnesses, and more recently the Sierra Leone TRC was vested with far-reaching subpoena and search and seizure powers, although it did not make use of these extensively: see C Stahn, 'Accommodating Individual Criminal Responsibility and National Reconciliation: The UN Truth Commission for East Timor' (2001) 95 American Journal of International Law 955; see also Hayner, *Unspeakable Truths* 107–108. In Chile the commission did not carry out its own investigations despite its broad mandate, a feature viewed as a serious shortcoming: Sarkin (n 54) 816.

[122] Sarkin (n 53) 817. Due to its short mandate, the El Salvador commission conducted in-depth investigations of selected cases chosen as representative of typical victims, perpetrators, and types of abuse over the historical period of study. The South African approach was to attempt a more thorough engagement, rather than a typology: Hayner, *Unspeakable Truths* 73.

[123] While objective truth may be a difficult concept, and the official version likely to be contested, there is an inherent element of symbolism involved. Daly (n 28) 24, 28 criticises the attempt to promise or deliver 'a single unit of truth' or 'single ... authoritative record': the truth is inherently elusive, not monolithic, subjective, cannot 'be described by a single, elegant narrative'. Of course the report will not and should not in a pluralist democracy be 'the last word on the history of a country for all' (29). However, we think that it is likely that a population will appreciate the unscientific, symbolic and representational nature of the exercise. Daly also focuses unduly on the written report of a commission (see especially 26–7, 33), whereas surely it is its *process* which can be more significant in fulfilling its functions.

Transitional Justice 107

considering the overall seriousness of the attempt, can be forward-looking recommendations for law reform and other measures aimed at reducing the prevalence of conditions that enabled abuse to be unchecked and unremedied for so long.[124]

What this survey of issues reveals is the complexity and plurality of issues involved in the design and conduct of a formal truth, justice and reconciliation institution. It ought to be clear that the diversity of past practice and the range of competing considerations that require attention are likely to preclude any attempt to identify a standardization with normative consequences. While one is most reluctant to endorse multiple tiers of human rights standards by reference to resource availability—this can be abused as a convenient argument for inaction on human rights—it is unrealistic to overlook the fact that what is possible in the form, mandate, duration, etc of a transitional justice strategy (prosecution, truth commission, or other) is dependent on context, including resources.[125] Political contexts are idiosyncratic: there are a number of valid reasons for national authorities to prefer amnesty-for-truth to prosecution, for example. It is not just the politics of institution-making that remain eclectic: the legal framework within which to operate would appear to remain broad and largely non-prescriptive. Provided a bona fide attempt is made to provide an effective remedy as possible for the thousands of victims, and to 'take action' on the perpetrators in some way (including processing them through truth commission testimony), and unless internationally recognized due process rights are infringed, for example in the process of transmission of a person's case from truth commission to criminal prosecution, it is only really on the question of the grant of amnesty for crimes which may be of interest to the international community as a whole that international normative issues arise for truth commissions. We now turn to this issue.

---

[124] Recent commissions have provided extensive recommendations for reforms across many sectors of government and public life, including proposals for human rights training and education. The El Salvadoran TRC's recommendations ran to over fifteen pages, the South African TRC's recommendations 45 pages, and Chile's over 45 pages: Hayner, *Unspeakable Truths* 167. See also M Ensalaco, 'Truth Commissions for Chile and El Salvador: A Report and Assessment' (1994) 16 Human Rights Quarterly 656, 666–670. The recommendations on law reform and institutional change of the El Salvador commission were its greatest legacy: R Mani, *Beyond Retribution: Seeking Justice in the Shadows of War* (2002) 102. We think this last function is particularly important since one dilemma of a strongly independent commission may be that it sets the accountability of the state at a further remove.

[125] See Cryer (n 83) 269–271, who notes that decisions on post-conflict justice options, and what constitutes a sufficient investigation, must be sensitive to context: European Convention standards may not be appropriate to Zimbabwe; Cryer selects two reasons: other priorities, and the likeliness of a weak prosecutorial and judicial system making it difficult to prosecute offenders *en masse* (therefore, making the decision to establish a truth commission reasonable).

VII. QUESTIONS OF AMNESTY

Amnesty from prosecution is often the main incentive for agreeing to peace in the first place, and for cooperating and revealing the truth.[126] Subject to some important qualifications, it is surely a legitimate option in transitional societies—and may be a political necessity.[127] Recent prominent commissions such as the South African TRC and that in Timor-Leste have been accorded the power to grant amnesty.[128] The power to afford immunity from prosecution for a cooperative and forthcoming individual in a truth process sets up something of a tension between restorative justice ideals and traditional retributive justice principles and imperatives.[129] However, these imperatives can be reconciled. For one thing, truth commissions can be complementary to prosecutions.[130]

The Timorese model is of particular interest because of the example it offers to Zimbabwe on this question. In Timor's commission, individuals were

---

[126] See *Azapo v President of the Republic of South Africa* 1996 (4) SA 671 (CC), 681–685 (constitutionality of amnesty provisions of the statute establishing the TRC):

> Most of the acts of brutality and torture which have taken place have occurred during an era in which neither the law which permitted the incarceration or persons or the investigation of crimes, nor the methods and the culture which informed such investigations were easily open to public investigation, verification and correction. Much of what transpired in this shameful period is shrouded in secrecy and not easily capable of objective demonstration and proof. ... That truth, which the victims of repression seek so desperately to know is, in the circumstances, much more likely to be forthcoming if those responsible for such monstrous misdeeds are encouraged to disclose the whole truth with the incentive that they will not receive the punishment which they undoubtedly deserve if they do. Without that incentive there is nothing to encourage such persons to make the disclosure and to reveal the truth ...

[127] See generally P van Zyl, 'Justice without Punishment: Guaranteeing Human Rights in Transitional Societies' in Villa-Vicencio and Verwoerd (eds), *Looking Back—Reaching Forward: Reflections on the Truth and Reconciliation Commission of South Africa* (University of Cape Town Press, 2000). Indeed, international law has long acknowledged the place of amnesty. Notwithstanding that the *Geneva Conventions* regime is partly intended to prevent impunity, Article 4 of Additional Protocol II calls on states after the conclusion of internal conflicts to grant 'the broadest amnesty possible' to participants.

[128] On the South African TRC's amnesty process, see A McDonald, 'A right to truth, justice and a remedy for African victims of serious violations of international humanitarian law' (1999) 2 Law, Democracy and Development 139, 164–170; Hayner *Unspeakable Truths*, 98ff. On the amnesty process in East Timor, see Stahn (n 121) 962–965. As discussed below, South Africa purported to grant amnesty for international crimes, whereas the Timorese commission was unable to formally grant amnesty for international crimes.

[129] See L McGregor, 'Individual Accountability in South Africa: Cultural Optimum or Political Façade?' (2001) 95 American Journal of International Law 32, 37; S Wilson 'The Myth of Restorative Justice: Truth Reconciliation and the Ethics of Amnesty' (2001) 17 South African Journal on Human Rights 531, 542–545.

[130] Where amnesty is not appropriate, there is in principle no reason why related information cannot be provided to prosecutors in the criminal justice system to pursue should they chose to do so according to existing criteria. See in this regard Hayner, *Unspeakable Truths*, Ch 7; also C Lerche, 'Truth Commissions and National Reconciliation: Some Reflections on Theory and Practice' (2000) 7(1) Peace and Conflict Studies 1.

entitled to apply for amnesty by making full disclosure of their acts and by providing an association of their acts 'with the political conflicts of East Timor'.[131] The grant of immunity was limited to less serious offences, and made dependent on the performance of a visible act of remorse serving the interests of the people affected by the original offence.[132] This act may have involved community service, reparation, a public apology, and/or other acts of contrition. This Timor-style public contrition process facilitates community reintegration of low-level perpetrators and would be most apposite in particular to 'Border Gezi', 'Green Bomber' and other youth militia in Zimbabwe: given their large numbers, age and possibility of some duress involved in their participation in criminal acts, they can hardly all be prosecuted and are likely to be in need of serious rehabilitation and diversion into constructive ends. In addition to a symbolic act of contrition, a form of community or national service could be envisaged.[133] This reconciliation and rehabilitation procedure could be used to good effect to deal with certain less serious acts directed against persons and property in respect of land invasions in recent years.[134]

As a matter of the State's international legal obligations, it is not clear whether it is under a clear duty to prosecute and punish certain crimes, or may elect to deal with them through other means (such as amnesty). It may depend on whether the duty is actually to 'prosecute' and 'punish' or merely to 'take action against' or in respect of perpetrators, or even more broadly, a duty to ensure a process of 'justice'. That is, it may be that the duty is better expressed as a duty to investigate and to thereafter make a bona fide and considered decision and possibly take action against the perpetrator. In this case a possible position is that truth commissions (and other national-level processes) which may not result in any criminal trial and which may grant amnesty are either an acceptable form of 'punishment' (if that is the duty) or can fulfil the duty to investigate and take action against perpetrators.[135] The duty to take action relates to all human rights abuses (Article 2(3) ICCPR): a genuine truth commission process mainly without prosecutions may fulfil this, as it represents a form of providing justice. The problematic issue is in relation to amnesty and non-prosecution for abuses that are also international crimes.

---

[131] UNTAET Regulation 2001/10 (13 July 2001): this would preclude any criminal prosecution.

[132] Stahn (n 121) 963. Care must be taken to afford the perpetrator some dignity and redemption—it may be dangerous to institutionalize humiliation.

[133] Since 1992 Zimbabwean law has recognised a 'community service' alternative to prison.

[134] Arguably, a separate mechanism would need to be established for land claims issues. On overlaps between reconciliation and the land issue, see E McCandless, 'The Case of Land in Zimbabwe: cause of conflict, foundation of peace' www.restorativejustice.org/resources/world/africa3/africa/zimbabwe.

[135] See D Dyzenhaus, *Judging Judges, Judging Ourselves: Truth, Reconciliation and the Apartheid Legal Order* (Hart Publishing, Oxford, 1998) 28–33; also van Zyl (n 127) ('Justice without Punishment').

No 'all-encompassing' duty to prosecute can be discerned in international law: there is still room for movement.[136] For example, it remains an open question whether a duty to prosecute exists in relation to war crimes in an internal conflict. Arguably, it is still open to States to grant amnesty for international crimes without violating a rule of international law,[137] although it seems this will be a legally invalid act in respect of purported amnesties for the crimes of genocide, torture, and 'grave breaches' of the 1949 Geneva Conventions.[138] There appears to be a growing legal consensus that if granted, no purported amnesty for certain international crimes would be recognized as having any effect in international law, for example in providing immunity to any later international prosecution.[139] The Preamble of the Rome Statute of the International Criminal Court, while binding only in respect of parties to it, confirms this trend when it declares that 'it is the duty of every State to exercise criminal jurisdiction over those responsible for international crimes.'

In attempting to shape any future Zimbabwean truth commission process by reference to international standards, then, one issue might be whether only some amnesties 'count' internationally. The position appears to be that no

---

[136] R Cryer (n 83) 288.

[137] For a comprehensive consideration, see A O'Shea, *Amnesty for Crime in International Law and Practice* (Kluwer, The Hague, 2002). For discussion in favour of a general duty on states to prosecute and punish past crimes see for example D Orentlicher, 'Settling Accounts: The Duty to Prosecute Human Rights Violations of a Prior Regime' (1991) 100 Yale LJ 2537; N Roht-Arriaza, 'State Responsibility to Investigate and Prosecute Grave Human Rights Violations in International Law' (1990) 78(2) California Law Review 449; Dugard (n 25) 697 and the authorities cited therein. Much of the debate about the legality of amnesties is still—at least for now— somewhat academic: Hayner makes the important point that 'even where international law clearly requires prosecution of those accused of rights crimes, serious prosecutorial action against perpetrators is still uncommon and many blanket amnesties remain in force' (*Unspeakable Truths*, 90).

[138] Dugard (n 25) 699. The duty on a state to extradite or prosecute individuals for torture or genocide may be a matter of customary international law: *Prosecutor v Furundzija* (ICTY) IT-95-17/1-T, [156]ff. See too W Schabas, 'The Relationship between Truth Commissions and International Courts: the case of Sierra Leone' (2003) 25 Human Rights Quarterly 3, 1035.

[139] See generally Jeong, *Strategy and Process*, 166; J Gavron, 'Amnesties in the light of Developments in International Law and the Establishment of the ICC' (2002) 51 ICLQ 91. The United Nations Secretary General's view is that UN-endorsed peace agreements can never grant amnesties for genocide, war crimes, crimes against humanity, or gross violations of human rights. Amnesties purportedly given for such offences will not be considered a bar before UN-established or assisted courts: UNSG Report (n 24) [21]; Cryer has demonstrated that by 1999 the UN would not be party to peace deal that included an amnesty for international crimes (n 83) 284. A number of international and other tribunals have refused to recognize amnesties for grave breaches of human rights: *Furundzija* (ICTY Trial Chamber, 10 December 1998), *Barrios Altos* (Inter-American Court on Human Rights, Vol. 75 (Series C), 27 November 1998), [39]–[41] and various cases in the Special Court for Sierra Leone in relation to the Lomé Accord amnesty. The House of Lords in *Pinochet* can be understood to have overwhelmingly rejected the argument that Chile's decision to grant amnesty (immunity from prosecution) as part of its peace process ought to be respected by another court: *R v Bow Street Magistrates Court; ex parte Pinochet Ugarte (3)* [1998] 4 All ER 897. Unlike an acquittal in another forum, there is no rule of law preventing a national court from disregarding an amnesty granted elsewhere, provided it has jurisdiction.

Transitional Justice 111

clear rules can be enunciated to distinguish (from the perspective of international law) between permissible and impermissible amnesties, but 'international recognition might be accorded where amnesty has been granted as part of a truth and reconciliation inquiry and each person granted amnesty has been obliged to make full disclosure of his or her criminal acts as a precondition of amnesty and the acts were politically motivated.'[140] It is arguable that provided a national transitional justice process was legitimate (a bona fide attempt to resolve past injustices at a national level, taken by a democratically-elected government) and included a number of safeguards, international deference might be given to the process, since in such cases the afflicted State concerned is itself best placed to decide what measures may be most conducive for the facilitation of reconciliation at the national level; it is something calling for a judgment falling substantially within the domain of those entrusted with the difficult issues of such transitions.[141] Particularly if the South African experience is given weight, Zimbabwe would not necessarily breach international law if, facing difficult political compromises to avoid catastrophic civil war, after a formal process it granted amnesty to (or simply did not prosecute) those allegedly responsible for international crimes. Whether or not a subsequent international or foreign tribunal with jurisdiction would be bound to recognise any immunity as a result is a related but separate issue to whether the mere grant of such amnesty violates an international duty.

It would now be politically difficult—if not yet clearly legally impossible—for any future Zimbabwean commission to purport to grant amnesty for the international crimes of torture, crimes against humanity or genocide (to the extent that there are Zimbabwean officials who may be guilty of such crimes). The South African TRC was opened to criticism on these grounds,[142] but was the result of serious and principled domestic deliberation on the consequences of not prosecuting certain international crimes and its amnesties have not been

---

[140] J Dugard, 'Possible Conflicts of Jurisdiction with Truth Commissions' (n 25) 700. As such, the blanket amnesty in Chile passed by the regime prior to the establishment of the commission may not meet the required standard, while the South African amnesties granted by a quasi-judicial amnesty committee functioning as part of a TRC process established by a democratically elected government, may well do so. See too Mani (n 124) 112–113.

[141] *AZAPO v President of the Republic of South Africa* (1996) 4 SA 671, (cc) [20], [31], [42]–[45]. The Court's use of 'entrusted' highlights how a decision taken by a politically illegitimate regime might not receive the same political deference or (which might in amount to the same thing) international legal recognition. Cryer argues (n 83) 274–7, 289) that this 'national deference' argument not only is open to abuse by complicit or self-interested national authorities, but also insufficiently takes into account the international community's legitimate interests. Local amnesties for non-international crimes are easier to defer to: the only question is whether the ICCPR Art. 2(3) duty is met).

[142] For a critical reflection on the South African TRC in this respect, see J Dugard, 'Retrospective Justice: International Law and the South African Model', 269ff, in J McAdams (ed), *Transitional Justice and the Rule of Law in New Democracies* (1997; n 24 above); also C Jenkins, 'After the Dry White Season: The Dilemmas of Reparation and Reconstruction in South Africa' (2000) 16 South African Journal on Human Rights 421.

legally challenged elsewhere.[143] There exists an unresolved tension between international principle and the (occasional) legitimate local need to afford amnesty even for very serious crimes. This tension would remain even if there was a clear norm against national amnesty for international crimes. Retaining the aura and integrity of international prohibitions is vital, but imposing a clear duty to prosecute might put unworkable strain on societies seeking a political compromise to avert or end conflict. There exists a dilemma whether to recognise a clear, 'bright line' norm (knowing it will not be met, often for understandable reasons), or whether the content of the norm retains some leeway and a margin of appreciation to States. The latter option might, perhaps paradoxically, have the benefit of retaining the integrity of international prohibitions.

VIII. THE INTERNATIONAL CRIMINAL COURT: ANY IMPLICATIONS?

It is relevant in discussing prospects for transitional justice in Zimbabwe, in particular the possible role and functions of a truth commission, to briefly address whether international or foreign criminal tribunals might in any way overlap with any truth commission's subject matter. First, possibly overlapping with any future truth commission's work is always the prospect of prosecutions by foreign national courts applying received international law, of Zimbabwean offenders for crimes in Zimbabwe but who come within that court's jurisdiction. In 2003, for example, efforts were made to bring such an action in Canada against Zimbabwean leaders, while more recently in May 2008 the names of 18 Zimbabwe security officials along with allegations of their responsibility for torture were forwarded to South African prosecutors in terms of its national legislation implementing international criminal acts.[144] Should a criminal prosecution be instituted by a State under its domestic legislation, a national amnesty does not have an extraterritorial effect and while in practice certain types of amnesty have been recognized abroad, there

---

[143] The pursuit of justice for such crimes has long been a selective and irregular process: see Gerry Simpson's historical overview of war crimes trials: (n 30). While the Timorese truth commission could not grant immunity to persons who had committed a 'serious criminal offence', including the international crimes of genocide, crimes against humanity, war crimes, and torture: Stahn (n 121) 957–958, for a range of reasons including local peace exigencies not all persons known to have committed such acts were prosecuted.

[144] This referral to the National Prosecuting Authority of South Africa by the Southern Africa Litigation Centre was for possible action should the accused be found within South African jurisdiction: *Legalbrief Africa*, Issue 279, 5 May 2008. The South African legislation is The Implementation of the Rome Statute of the International Criminal Court Act 2002: see further Max du Plessis 'Bringing the International Criminal Court Home' (2003) 1 South African Journal of Criminal Justice 1. An attempt to invoke the Act was made in September 2002 while Robert Mugabe was attending an international conference in Johannesburg, while in January 2004 a United Kingdom national sought an order against President Mugabe from a London magistrates court on torture charges. For an overview of this avenue see J Charney, 'International Criminal Law and the Role of Domestic Courts' (2001) 95 American Journal of International Law 120.

is no mandatory rule of international law requiring States' courts to recognise an amnesty granted by another State.[145] While the possibility of national-level prosecution (and certainly any ongoing or completed prosecutions at the time) ought to be factored into considerations of 'transitional justice' options, and might impact on a future commission's work, this topic is otherwise beyond the scope of this paper.

Secondly, since at least 2003, a number of actors including the International Bar Association have called for the ICC to examine the Zimbabwe situation.[146] Two issues arise here: the possibility of ICC investigations in relation to Zimbabwe (before or after transition); and the effect, under the ICC system, of any proposed amnesty granted by a future Zimbabwean truth commission. There are two main reasons why the ICC might not be involved in any transitional justice issue in Zimbabwe. First, the Court has limited subject matter and temporal jurisdiction.[147] Secondly, while a Party can refer a situation to the Court (or the prosecutor initiate an independent investigation), the alleged crimes must have been committed by nationals of a Party or have taken place in a Party's territory.[148] Zimbabwe is not (at this time) a party to the *Rome Statute*. A possible source of ICC jurisdiction in Zimbabwe would be the Court's ability to have jurisdiction conferred upon it including where it otherwise lacks jurisdiction, by virtue of the UN Security Council's power to refer country situations to the Court acting under Chapter VII of the Charter of the United Nations (read with article 13(b) of the Rome Statute of the International Criminal Court). If the situation in Zimbabwe were to deteriorate significantly, or there was a pronounced inability or unwillingness of Zimbabwean authorities to act in respect of certain allegations, with a concomitant impact on regional peace and security, it is possible that the Security Council may receive a request for an ICC referral on this matter.

---

[145] Dugard, *Conflicts of Jurisdiction* (n 25) 699. The exercise of that discretion might be mainly contingent on the quality of amnesty process that the state had followed, which no doubt inherently involves a political judgment about the democratic legitimacy of the regime sponsoring the amnesty.

[146] Mark Ellis, International Bar Association, 7 March 2003 (IBA Press Release); see *Legalbrief Africa*, 7 March 2003. The August 2003 Zimbabwe civil society symposium's Declaration appeared to support the use of ICC mechanisms by any new government.

[147] It would be a jurisdictional threshold question whether the level and kinds of violence perpetrated by certain individuals in Zimbabwe might trigger the International Criminal Court's subject-matter jurisdiction, including whether they could be considered part of an intentional widespread or systematic attack directed against a civilian population; and the Court has jurisdiction only in relation to crimes committed on or after 1 July 2002.

[148] See articles 12, 13 and 14 of the Rome Statute of the International Criminal Court; see also P Kirsch and D Robinson, 'Trigger Mechanisms' in A Cassese et al (eds), *The Rome Statute of the International Criminal Court: A Commentary*, vol 1 (Oxford University Press, 2002). Zimbabwe signed the Rome Statute on 17 July 1998, but has not ratified it. A future government in Zimbabwe could, in terms of Article 12(3) of the Rome Statute (with 11(2)), make an ad hoc acceptance of the exercise of jurisdiction by the Court over its nationals or crimes committed on its territory; see also H-P Kaul, 'Preconditions to the Exercise of Jurisdiction', in Cassese et al.

If Zimbabwe in future accepts the Court's jurisdiction over specific crimes for the period that it was not a party to the Statute (or a Zimbabwean otherwise comes before the Court), and if a truth commission purports to grant amnesties to individuals responsible for serious human rights abuses, the question might arise whether such national amnesties would constitute a bar to ICC prosecution. The Rome Statute is silent on amnesty.[149] National amnesties in Zimbabwe would not per se prevent prosecution before the ICC. However, the prosecutor can probably indirectly recognise a national amnesty by declining to initiate a prosecution 'in the interests of justice.'[150] Should a Zimbabwean commission (or other process) that emanates from a recognised legitimate regime elect for compelling reasons to provide amnesties, the prosecutor might respect that position.

Given the limited jurisdiction of the ICC, and other concerns about the appropriateness of an international prosecution strategy in a future Zimbabwe,[151] the issue might not unduly complicate the process of any truth

---

[149] Commentators argue that this is because the Rome Statute was never drafted with the intention of allowing amnesty to be raised as a defence: Dugard, *Conflicts of Jurisdiction with Truth Commissions* 700–701; cf D Majzub, 'Peace or Justice? Amnesties and the International Criminal Court' (2002) 3 *Melbourne Journal of International Law* 251. How the ICC should deal with national level amnesties was put aside during negotiations on the Rome Statute, as there seemed no prospect of a consensus: J Holmes, 'The Principle of Complementarity' in Lee (ed), *The ICC: The Making of the Rome Statute* (Kluwer, The Hague, 1999) 60. Cases would be inadmissible before the ICC if they had already been subject to a criminal proceeding. While Article 17 of the Rome Statute refers to 'investigation' it seems clear that a truth commission investigation before a non-judicial body (granting amnesty) would not be sufficient to amount to a prior proceeding (requiring inadmissibility): the use of 'investigation' is tied to criminal proceedings since one will not be genuine where it is inconsistent with an intent to bring the person concerned to justice—a bona fide prosecution trajectory is what is contemplated: see Chesterman (n 33) 164; also Cryer (n 83) 277; Dugard, *Conflicts of Jurisdiction* (n 25) 701–2. The prosecutor's discretion is very wide and it is not clear how pardons and amnesties would fall to be treated: see generally J Dugard, 'Dealing with Crimes of a Past Regime: Is Amnesty Still an Option?' (2000) 12 Leiden Journal of International Law 1001.

[150] A 'genuine' amnesty (see discussion at n 140 above) might be recognised in appropriate circumstances. Article 53(2)(c) of the Rome Statute allows the Prosecutor to refuse prosecution where, after investigation, he concludes that 'a prosecution is not in the interests of justice, taking into account all the circumstances'; see too Dugard, *Conflicts of Jurisdiction* 702; also Cryer (n 83) 278. The prosecutor would no doubt consider the quality of the truth commission's process (and of the bona fides and legitimacy of the regime sponsoring it), the nature of the offence, and the terms of disclosure on which amnesty was granted. The ICC scheme is not so blunt or automatic or insensitive to local realities that local imperatives for restorative justice cannot be accommodated. On the other hand, as Cryer has noted (278–281) these decisions are taken at an international level, and are out of the hands of the national authorities; the public interest of the 'international community' can be a veil for national self-interest of others: 283. See too the section 'Prosecutorial Discretion and the Interests of Justice' in Siels and Weirda, *The International Criminal Court and Conflict Mediation* (n 5) 12. William Schabas has also noted that a genuine but non-judicial effort at accountability, falling short of prosecution, might 'have the practical effect of convincing the Prosecutor to set priorities elsewhere': *An Introduction to the International Criminal Court* (2nd edn, Cambridge University Press, 2004) 87.

[151] John Braithwaite has cautioned against 'select [international] trials of demonized individuals that exonerate the collective and that may jeopardize responsive regulation to protect the vulnerable', and how selective prosecution sends the signal that whoever is not charged is innocent: (n 44) 204.

commission that is established. Provided we do not see mere deals between elites, the world might need to drop calls for strong punitive measures and learn to live with a local political compromise that works for all Zimbabweans themselves. As Chesterman has said, '[a] central problem in this respect is that commentators with an international perspective often view such internal transitions through the lens of international criminal law: either the wrongdoers are held accountable, or they enjoy impunity.'[152] As our discussion and the experience of recent truth commissions illustrates, it is possible and may be necessary to have a more nuanced and practicable approach.

IX. CONCLUSION

The literature on truth commissions is vast (and growing), and the general consensus is that they are less inimical to reconciliation than trials, may provide relatively more comprehensive accounts of past facts, patterns, causes and consequences of human rights abuses than trials (and certainly blanket amnesties) permit, that they more readily promote healing and victim-centred processes, and that through their proposals for reforms they can make valuable contributions to the future democracy of their countries. The 'singularity' of truth commissions—one-off, limited purpose and lifespan institutions carrying for this reason a 'never again' message—commends them as a highly visible and powerful mechanism to break with past troubles.[153] At the same time, formal processes such as truth commissions can catalyse but are only one part of wider social processes. The features of a Zimbabwean commission will necessarily reflect the political compromises and stresses that often accompany a transition from autocracy to democracy. There needs to be a public participatory dimension to the justice design process: one risk will be that political actors might by consensus opportunistically 'drop' the issue of transitional justice as 'too hard'.

We should not be taken to be arguing a 'soft' approach in this paper: if the political control exists in a future democratic Zimbabwe, there ought to be every effort to prosecute and punish in particular those principally responsible for ordering and carrying out the appalling abuses witnessed in that country. However, a truth and reconciliation commission would be a valuable collateral strategy. Also, not only do formal justice mechanisms require a modicum of stability, there may need to be some privileging of 'peace' over 'justice' in the way those involved in negotiation, design and conduct of a transitional justice process choose to deal with past abuses. In appropriate circumstances (such as to avoid further bloodshed), a locally made

---

[152] Chesterman (n 33) 156.
[153] This characteristic of 'singularity' is rightly emphasised by Iliff (n 13).

compromise can sometimes be understood as a principled and morally relevant choice, not simply a pragmatic one.[154]

Along with the 'emerging normativity of global transitional justice', there is
more generally a call politically and intellectually for 'more law' or a greater
legalization of transitional justice issues, what Teitel recently perceived as a
demand 'for more judicialisation and tribunalisation.'[155] The focus ought not
to be blindly on 'a truth commission' or its forms, but on what process and
strategy best secures justice, reconciliation and repair in society. That is, a
responsive, reflexive approach that seeks to identify important problems and
fix them (including in consultation with those most affected and by reference
to a consideration of needs), not one predetermined by certain choices of
institutional forms or aimed at imposing the 'right' solution.[156] It is important
to articulate and identify the problem that needs to be addressed as regards
justice and reconciliation issues in transitional settings, and to design the institutional responses accordingly.[157]

International law would appear to set some minimum standards in particular
in relation to the core duty of a State to provide remedial measures for human
rights abuse and in relation to the international validity of national amnesties
for certain crimes. Certainly, the 'impunity gap' remains. However, if the
normative framework is evolving, as we think it is, there must be some space
for national measures taken bona fide in the interests of securing a peaceful
and legitimate transition to democracy, and attempts to describe a normative
minimum standard framework for truth commissions and other transitional
justice measures must, we think, accord a margin of appreciation to states
in determining how best to proceed with these very difficult issues. This is
especially so where the decision to pursue a particular track is that of an
internationally recognized and democratically elected regime, and taken after
a considered process where competing imperatives exist.

It is by no means clear what international legal requirements attend issues at
stake in truth commissions, but what would seem clear is that attempts to foist
upon States particular formulae for dealing with transitional justice might in
fact prevent the incremental growth of a stronger normative underpinning
to transitional justice mechanisms. States undertaking transitions are
likely to resist narrower limits to their options for local solutions (although
a high degree of international intervention in their peace process may
compel it). While minimum standards can be identified, unrealistic demands
are unlikely to attract the State support or response necessary for norm

---

[154] Compare Gutmann and Thompson's view that political stability is not itself a moral good
unless it is necessary to the promotion of future justice: 'The Moral Foundations of Truth
Commission' in Rotberg and Thompson (n 24) 23.
[155] R Teitel, 'Transitional Justice Globalised' (n 24) 2.
[156] See Sparrow, *The Regulatory Craft: Controlling Risks, Solving Problems, and Managing
Compliance* (Brookings Institute, Washington DC, 2000).
[157] Braithwaite (n 44) preface.

Transitional Justice   117

accretion.[158] On the other hand, if such States do respond to purported international requirements (for example, on the advice of expatriate international lawyers), this might set too high a standard and so distort what is actually required in their particular situation in terms of an acceptable resolution: it is easy to imagine a scenario whereby a belief in an international obligation to prosecute at all costs could seriously undo a fragile peace. If international law is 'the law of peace'[159] we ought to bear such issues in mind when considering the delicacies of transition in a deeply fractured state such as Zimbabwe.

The real challenge will be to adopt a sophisticated approach to addressing past human rights tragedies that draws the best from previous commissions in Africa and elsewhere, allows for a response to the core international crimes which are of concern to the international community as a whole, but which meets the practical political and social realities of the particular transition process.

---

[158] Local exigencies mean that detailed transitional justice prescriptions are unlikely to attract the practice and recognition necessary for international legal normativity. See also Cryer (n 83) 269.

[159] Public international law courses at the University of Cambridge have traditionally been offered by the formal title of 'the Law of Peace'.

[2]

COURTS AND DEMOCRACY IN POSTCONFLICT TRANSITIONS: A SOCIAL SCIENTIST'S PERSPECTIVE ON THE AFRICAN CASE

By Jennifer Widner [*]

A "second liberation" swept the African continent beginning in 1989. In many places, multiparty elections and a measured optimism gained ground. Yet during the 1990s, the spirit of moderation and tolerance typical of the early independence movements began to fray. The recent armed conflicts of Central and West Africa and the columns of refugees crossing borders have served as a blunt reminder of the fragility of many of the continent's democratic experiments.

In this new era, law plays a central, visible, yet delicate role in many peace settlements and democratic transitions, from South Africa to Ghana. Africa's courts have been challenged to provide the kinds of basic dispute resolution that lie at the core of what it means to be a "government." At the same time, African judges are mindful of Learned Hand's caution in *The Spirit of Liberty*, taped above a secretary's desk in Uganda. "Liberty lies in the hearts of men and women," Hand wrote. "[W]hen it dies there, no constitution, no law, no court can save it; no constitution, no law, no court can even do much to help it."[1] The success of a postconflict transition will depend, in part, on the role of courts in sustaining a spirit of liberty and tolerance in their societies.

Acting on Hand's challenge, my remarks will offer a social scientist's view of the role of courts in achieving peace and building new democracies. Because the language of the rule of law is now so much in vogue, observers too often tend to assume that courts can easily promote peace and democratic change in postconflict regimes, without looking closely at the grounds for such optimism. Empirically, in Africa courts have played a range of roles. In some cases, they have figured prominently in the settlement of conflict and the move to multiparty systems. In others, their importance is less evident.

This inquiry has three parts. The first section focuses on the significance of courts and conflict resolution in the immediate aftermath of war. The second section sketches the prophylactic role that courts and law can play in abating conflict in Africa's zones of relative peace and prosperity. The third part concentrates on the relationship between courts in promoting democratic transitions more generally. In particular, it examines three objectives people usually have in mind in the aftermath of conflict: the restoration of order and security, access to justice, and the integrity of impartial forums in settling ordinary disputes. The lesson is one of caution in placing too much faith in law and courts in postconflict transitions or in expecting quick results.

I. COURTS AND PEACE IN POSTCONFLICT SETTINGS

In recent years, international policy has often stressed the importance of courts in bringing an end to civil conflicts. Convincing combatants to lay down their arms may require a credible promise to punish war criminals or human rights abusers, and the rejection of any claim to impunity. Most of the successful interventions in internal conflicts by the United Nations and the United States have involved not just military operations, but also heavy reliance on civil-

---

[*] Associate Professor of Political Science, University of Michigan.
[1] The quotation is from Judge Hand's speech on May 21, 1944, at a ceremony in Central Park, New York City, to swear in 150,000 naturalized citizens. LEARNED HAND, THE SPIRIT OF LIBERTY 190 (Irving Dilliard ed., 3d ed. 1960).

affairs units to help rebuild police forces and judiciaries. Addressing disputes between claimants from hostile communities and rebuilding court systems can be an important first step in restoring divided societies and states.

Yet deep division can also render courts ineffective. After severe conflict or when extremism flourishes, people may be unwilling to accept judgments against men whose bloody boldness had been welcomed, or to respect sentences that do not treat wartime circumstances as extenuating. Victimized communities may not be willing to tolerate the release of detainees still under suspicion. Many postconflict settings are marked by additional concerns. Courts may be understaffed or lack resources. Limited access and delay often result, rendering the judiciary weak or delegitimizing it altogether. Moreover, national courts may not be able to provide the kinds of services central to the restoration of order. One may have to look both to indigenous methods of dispute resolution and to international forums.

The Role of Local Forums in Postconflict Transitions

In the immediate aftermath of conflict, one of the most important steps is to rebuild neighborhood forums for dispute resolution. These usually stress mediation or arbitration. Without such informal venues, the capacity of any formal judicial system is likely to be overwhelmed. Local forums can help to fill the gap while new judges and lawyers are trained, and gutted courthouses rebuilt. Otherwise, former combatants and traumatized civilians will probably turn away from fledgling institutions, and even resume the resolution of differences on the street. The cultural milieu of most African societies strengthens the legitimacy of local forums. Even in the continent's most stable countries, customary courts or community courts play significant roles. For example, among citizens of Botswana, the African country that has performed the best over the past forty years, most people surveyed think customary courts are effective in resolving ordinary disputes fairly and quickly.[2] Throughout the continent, as in many other parts of the world, neighbors and neighborhood forums remain important pillars of order without which state courts would be overburdened and unable to function effectively.

One of the main aims at the end of a civil war is to convince people to settle, to plant food crops, and to participate in productive economic activity. Inevitably, land disputes, differences of opinion about the identity of rightful heirs, stock-theft cases, and petty criminal matters ensue. Most of these kinds of cases are effectively and quickly resolved in neighborhood forums, which are more accessible and less expensive than state courts and whose personnel are better acquainted with local conditions.

The experiences of postconflict Uganda in 1985, parts of Somalia, and early postconflict Rwanda highlight neighborhood dispute resolution as an important first step. After Yoweri Museveni waged a successful rebel struggle and came to power in Uganda, he promised to restore the justice system. As one of his first measures, he created "resistance council courts" (later called "local council courts") at the village level. Staffed by elected representatives of a village or community, these courts heard disputes much as elders and chiefs had in the prewar era. The courts were given jurisdiction to hear petty disputes and were considered important because they embodied a forum that was accessible, inexpensive, and easily understood. The judges had no special training. The parties had no legal representation. Mediation and arbitration often featured in these courts, although appeal to the regular state courts could be sought by those who felt the local court had erred in a judgment.

For most ordinary purposes, especially in a period when state courts were unable to project themselves effectively in many rural areas, the resistance courts functioned reasonably well. The World Bank expected a surge in land disputes but found that these grassroots forums had taken care of the problem, at least initially. Ten years after their inception, the resistance council

---

[2] *See* Jennifer Widner, Public Attitudes Surveys, Botswana and Uganda (1995–1996) (on file with author).

courts were considered by most people in the central and southern districts of the country to be effective and fair in resolving everyday kinds of problems.[3]

As time passed, disputants exercised the right to appeal to a restored system of Ugandan state courts more frequently. The performance of the resistance council forums was undeniably uneven, and sometimes violated important legal norms. Joe Oloka-Onyango, a law professor at Makerere University, found that some resistance council courts ignored the law and showed bias, charged fees even though they were supposed to be free, and were not responsive to women's interests.[4] New professional judges grew concerned that the resistance courts sometimes handled more serious matters that properly belonged in courts of judicature. The neighborhood forums kept inadequate records, which required the state courts to hear cases on appeal *de novo*, and the ambiguous relationship between the formal judiciary and these local systems was fraught with tension. Yet there could be little doubt that the resistance council courts contributed importantly to an early (if imperfect) restoration of the rule of law in much of the country.

In Somalia, the successful restoration of order in conflict zones after the international intervention of 1992–1993 also relied on neighborhood forums. Australian peacekeepers sought to reestablish a local police force and community courts in the areas they entered. They recruited police personnel by asking elders to propose names; then investigated these candidates and made appointments. The Australians also tried to identify former judges acceptable to community members and enticed them to resume their roles. They rebuilt neighborhood police stations, courts, and a small prison. People quickly began to gather in these locations to have disputes heard and to obtain advice. Order materialized in these areas much more quickly than in others.[5]

In Rwanda, communities developed a similar response to the need for dispute resolution. The *gacaca*, or village courts, while initially destroyed by the conflict, quickly enjoyed a resurgence in many areas. Instead of returning to the old patterns of habitation in scattered huts, each owned by a nuclear family, members of extended families and their friends often sought to live close together in newly formed "villages" of their own design. The changes in residence patterns created a need for new gacaca committees. The voluntary character of the resettlement meant that members of these new communities trusted each other enough to make election an acceptable means of selecting members, and the number of gacaca rapidly increased.

Even in litigious societies, people resolve most disputes without reference to courts, and often without explicit reference to law. This background condition makes it possible for courts to do their jobs effectively. An orientation toward law as a reference point and toward the courts as a provider of impartial hearings remains important, but there is a great risk of overburdening these institutions if people cannot negotiate most of their differences in other ways. The ineffectiveness that can arise from overuse may undermine judicial legitimacy and lead people to turn away from law altogether or to take the law into their own hands. Restoring forums such as the resistance council courts in Uganda, the neighborhood courts in Somalia, and the gacaca in Rwanda establishes a foundation for the successful reconstruction of the rule of law.

The Role of State Courts

Reestablishing the state courts and the judiciary proper constitutes a second important part of postconflict transitions. People want an effective forum to hear criminal cases against "outsiders"—persons who have no kin to monitor and control their activities. They want impartial hearings of major civil disputes. As time passes and the value of land increases with the resump-

[3] *See id.*

[4] JOHN-JEAN BARYA & JOE OLOKA-ONYANGO, POPULAR JUSTICE AND RESISTANCE COMMITTEE COURTS IN UGANDA, *passim* (Kampala, Uganda, 1994).

[5] For one account, see Martin R. Ganzglass, *The Restoration of the Somali Justice System, in* LEARNING FROM SOMALIA: THE LESSONS OF ARMED HUMANITARIAN INTERVENTION 20 (Walter Clarke & Jeffrey Herbst eds., 1997).

tion of productive economic activity, the possibility of appealing land disputes from neighborhood courts becomes more and more important.

The success of the formal legal process is a joint effect of improvement in several different government services. The actual and perceived fairness of court procedures depends on the behavior and training of personnel not controlled by the judiciary, such as the police and prosecutors in criminal cases, and land boards and surveyors in land disputes. Rebuilding a judicial system is a more complicated and costly endeavor than first meets the eye.

Even in Africa's stable countries, police forces and prosecutors usually suffer from poor training and meager funding. Inquiries frequently fall short of accepted standards. In remote areas, the police often fail to investigate for lack of transportation to the crime scene, and the evidence goes stale. Prosecutors are usually new recruits, fresh out of undergraduate law programs.

Judges are caught in a difficult bind. If they dismiss cases on the grounds that a police investigation was flawed or the prosecution erred, they face popular ire. Community members generally have an idea who the troublemakers are, and express outrage at the release of alleged offenders, eroding the legitimacy of the courts. Mindful of this problem, judges sometimes take steps to help the prosecution make its case, reasoning that the government is less prepared and more poorly financed than the defense; they may even try to collect evidence on their own. In view of the common-law tradition of adversarial development of evidence and opposing arguments by the parties, these steps can make the judicial process appear partisan and executive-minded.

Thus, the ability of courts to help secure community peace after a conflict materializes only with increased capacity in several different services. Unfortunately, although many international donors find assistance to the courts attractive, rebuilding police forces and prosecutors' offices is much more difficult to sell. Nor do these kinds of expenditures win a new government unmitigated goodwill. Some rights abuses will occur, no matter what training is provided, and the government inevitably suffers the taint. Yet restoring the courts as a focus of dispute resolution—and creating a sense that the law is a source of security—will not succeed without more effective policing and prosecution.

The Role of International Tribunals

Confronting war crimes after a conflict shows that the community finds these abuses wholly unacceptable.[6] But the decision to prosecute carries various dangers in postconflict settings where the courts lack capacity. In the absence of trained police investigators, capable prosecutors, and experienced judges, trying to punish offenders through the courts may produce delay, challenge due process, or result in dismissals on technical grounds that many ordinary people think unfair. These circumstances may create the potential for a symbiotic relationship between international courts and fledgling domestic judiciaries.

The case of Rwanda demonstrates the advantages and disadvantages of international involvement in war crimes prosecutions. In Rwanda, the government has pursued the prosecution of war crimes through a two-track system. Initially, at the same time that the International Criminal Tribunal for Rwanda heard cases, others were channeled to the ordinary courts. In 1996 the Rwandan legislature established a special chamber in the national court system to hear these matters.[7]

The early troubles that afflicted Rwanda's domestic prosecution of war crimes help to illuminate why international tribunals are potentially useful. First, fear-inspired delay was an immediate problem after the conflict ended. Especially outside the Rwandan capital city of Kigali, magistrates, prosecutors, court clerks, and witnesses worried that their lives would be endangered if they took part in genocide prosecutions in national courts. Over three hundred survivors,

---

[6] The use of truth and reconciliation commissions will not always be an acceptable alternative to local parties.
[7] *See* Organic Law on the Organization of Prosecutions for Offences Constituting the Crime of Genocide or Crimes Against Humanity Committed Since 1 October 1990, Law No. 8/96, RWANDA OFF. GAZ., Aug., 30, 1996.

scheduled to testify as witnesses, were murdered between 1994 and 1997, and paralysis set in. Without security, officials and citizens feared to take the steps required to build the rule of law.

A shortage of personnel also affected prosecutions. Only twenty-six judicial police inspectors, the officials needed to carry out investigations, were left in service after the genocide. With thirteen hundred new prisoners arrested each week (during the initial months) and an average of three days of basic investigation necessary for each case, over seven hundred judicial police were required to keep up with the caseload. Delays in investigations led to the loss and destruction of evidence and inability to prosecute. Similarly, at the end of the conflict, only sixteen practicing attorneys remained in Rwanda, hardly enough to represent even those accused of the most serious charge of genocide; and defendants restricted the pool further by accepting only Hutu lawyers as trial counsel. The few available magistrates often needed special training to handle genocide cases.

Finally, domestic prosecution was hampered by the same kinds of problems that plague courts in many parts of the continent. No paper was available, so prosecutors had to buy it out of pocket. There was also no transportation or clerical support, and judicial personnel often had difficulty finding places to live.

The impossibility of prosecuting all those under remand became evident immediately. The slowness of the judicial process meant that at the January 1998 rate of disposition (three hundred trials per year), it would take four hundred years to process the estimated 127,000 cases.

The international community contemplated two remedies. One was to borrow foreign judges and lawyers who could help handle the load. But Rwandan law contained no provision for permitting foreign magistrates to judge cases, and the government did not favor permitting foreigners to do so, although it tolerated their presence as advisers. Most of the proceedings took place in Kinyarwanda, where reliable interpreters and translators were in short supply. People also worried about the effects that pay disparities between local and foreign magistrates would have on the attempt to rebuild the Rwandan judiciary.[8]

Any use of international defense counsel risked the popular perception that high-powered lawyers from rich countries had come to the rescue of the perpetrators of genocide, at the expense of the victims. The Belgian organization, Avocats sans Frontières, enlisted voluntary counsel. But a representative of the Association of the Bar of the City of New York and the American Bar Association argued against such participation. "[W]e would not wish," said Robert Van Lierop,

> to be perceived by citizens of Rwanda . . . as experienced . . . lawyers from a developed country . . . defending those against whom accusations of participating in genocide have been made. This is particularly true given the world's failure to act to stop the genocide when it started . . . and given the additional fact that the prosecution is operating under the severe handicap of having few lawyers, little experience, and extremely scarce material resources.[9]

The alternative was to train a large cadre of new Rwandan investigators, lawyers, and magistrates. Assistance provided by Citizens' Network, a Belgian NGO, helped prepare many more judicial police, although investigative capacity remained inadequate. Juristes sans Frontières, a French NGO, and the International Centre for Human Rights and Democratic Development of Montreal provided intensive courses. USAID and CIDA supported legal education for new judges at Halifax.[10]

Although these interventions assisted domestic prosecutions, congestion and delay remained a problem, and other difficulties began to materialize. An initial American suggestion

---

[8] *See* Leonardo Neher, Ana Maria Linares, Laurel Rose, & Paul Mathieu, Rwanda Rule of Law Design: Four Week Interim Report, Report prepared for USAID by ARD/MSI (1995).

[9] Robert F. Van Lierop, *Rwanda Evaluation: Report and Recommendations*, 31 INT'L LAW. 887, pt. VIII, Recommendations (1997).

[10] On the problem of obtaining defense counsel for defendants in national court trials, see Mark Drumbl, *Rule of Law Amid Lawlessness: Counseling the Accused in Rwanda's Domestic Genocide Trials*, 29 COLUM. HUM. RTS. L. REV. 545 (1998); LAWYERS COMMITTEE FOR HUMAN RIGHTS, PROSECUTING GENOCIDE IN RWANDA: THE ICTR AND NATIONAL TRIALS (July 1997), *obtainable from* <http://www.lchr.org/pubs/rwanda.htm>.

that plea bargaining be used to help identify the instigators of the violence and to remove the cases of lesser offenders from the dockets was never fully implemented.[11] Another, later, scheme promised expedited processing and reduced sentences in exchange for an admission of guilt, including details of the crime and identification of others involved, as well as an expression of remorse.[12]

The plea-bargaining and confessions programs faced several obstacles. In the early years, only 20 percent of defendants pleaded guilty. Prisoners were not informed about the terms of the program. Some circulated rumors that those who participated would receive the death penalty. No separate prison was established for prisoners who had pleaded guilty and given information. Commingled with defendants who had yet to stand trial, potential plea-bargain participants feared that if they confessed and gave information, other inmates would carry out reprisals. Indeed, considerable evidence indicates that the instigators of the carefully planned genocide[13] reestablished their authority in the prisons and threatened less culpable defendants (accused of serious assaults or crimes against property) so as to prevent confessions. Internal leaders also propagated the myth that prisoners were only temporarily incarcerated—that they could anticipate release through a coup or general amnesty.

Under these circumstances, there was considerable potential for the International Criminal Tribunal for Rwanda, established by the United Nations in 1994,[14] to alleviate the burdens of the local justice system. Removing the most powerful and high-ranking accused from the prisons could increase the probability of confessions. International jurisdiction for the prosecution of priority cases could also prevent the undue diversion of resources from other pressing court business and lessen local vulnerability to attacks from militia remnants or angry citizens.

Nonetheless, problems remained. For example, the Rwandan government wanted to prosecute defendants for genocide, not just murder, yet no law against genocide as such existed on the books in Rwanda. Though Rwanda had ratified the international convention on genocide, the parliament first had to pass legislation to make genocide a national crime. Some observers worried that doing so after the conflict would amount to an *ex post facto* law, challenging norms central to the very notion of the rule of law. (International lawyers might argue, however, that the status of genocide as an international crime meant that the principle *nulla poene sine lege* would not be violated.)

The International Tribunal has provided limited relief as well because of its own operational difficulties. While the Tribunal, sitting in Arusha, Tanzania, has obtained guilty pleas from a few top-level defendants,[15] it has failed to handle its caseload expeditiously, and has been impeded by poor administration.[16] Moreover, the International Tribunal's maximum sentence

[11] *See* Madeline H. Morris, *The Trials of Concurrent Jurisdiction: The Case of Rwanda*, 7 DUKE J. INT'L L. 349 (1997); *see also* José Alvarez, *Crimes of State/Crimes of Hate: Lessons from Rwanda*, 24 YALE J. INT'L L. 365 (1999).

[12] USAID, Assessment of Means of Expediting the Genocide Caseload in Rwanda (ms., Feb. 1998).

[13] See ALISON DES FORGES, "LEAVE NONE TO TELL THE STORY" (Human Rights Watch 1999), GÉRARD PRUNIER, THE RWANDA CRISIS: HISTORY OF A GENOCIDE (1995), and AFRICAN RIGHTS, RWANDA: DEATH, DESPAIR AND DEFIANCE (rev. ed. Aug. 1995), on the bureaucratic organization of the Rwanda genocide.

[14] Statute of the International Criminal Tribunal for the Prosecution of Persons Responsible for Genocide and Other Serious Violations of International Humanitarian Law Committed in the Territory of Rwanda and Rwandan Citizens Responsible for Genocide and Other Such Violations Committed in the Territory of Neighbouring States, Between 1 January 1994 and 31 December 1994, SC Res. 955, annex, UN SCOR, 49th Sess., Res. & Dec., at 15, UN Doc. S/INF/50 (1994), *reprinted in* 33 ILM 1602 (1994), *obtainable from* <http://www.ictr.org>.

[15] *See, e.g.*, Prosecutor v. Akayesu, Judgment, No. ICTR-96-4-T (Sept. 2, 1998), *reprinted in* 37 ILM 1399 (1998); Prosecutor v. Kambanda, Judgment and Sentence, No. ICTR-97-23-S (Sept. 4, 1998), *reprinted in* 37 ILM 1411 (1998). ICTR decisions are available online at <http://www.ictr.org>.

[16] *See* Office of Internal Oversight Services, Report on the Audit and Investigation of the International Criminal Tribunal for Rwanda, UN Doc. A/51/789, annex (Feb. 6, 1997), <http://www.un.org/Depts/oios/reports/a51789/ictrtit.htm>; Office of Internal Oversight Services, Report on the Follow-up to the 1997 Audit and Investigation of the International Criminal Tribunal for Rwanda, UN Doc. A/52/784, annex (Feb. 6, 1998), <http://www.un.org/Depts/oios/reports/a52_784.htm>; *see also* Report of the Expert Group to Conduct a Review of the Effective Operation and Functioning of the International Criminal Tribunal for the Former Yugoslavia and the International Criminal Tribunal for Rwanda, *in* Identical Letters Dated 17 November 1999 from the Secretary-General Addressed to the President of the General Assembly and to the Chairman of the Advisory Committee on Administrative and Budgetary Questions, UN Doc. A/54/634 (1999).

is life imprisonment, while Rwandan national courts can impose the death penalty. This disparity has led some to question the legitimacy of the scheme.

The bottom line is that in postconflict situations, a hobbled judiciary may exercise limited influence over the prospects for peace. Its influence may strengthen with time, but only in conjunction with neighborhood mediation or arbitration, more effective police services, and a carefully negotiated relationship to an international tribunal, which bears the burden of hearing war-crimes cases.

Little hard empirical evidence can be adduced to ground claims about the relative contribution of the state courts or law in general to postconflict reconstruction. In South Africa in the early 1990s, the judiciary attracted a remarkable level of trust from all parties. As a result, it could help stabilize a potentially volatile situation by certifying that the draft constitution conformed with the principles that peace negotiators had earlier set out.[17] But more common are situations in which judiciaries have lost credibility and capacity. In these settings, the state courts proper become significant actors only several years after conflict has ended.

II. The Role of Courts in Reconstructing Trust

Where conflict is not so severe and an orientation toward law can already be found, courts can sometimes help prevent the spread of armed conflict or its resumption. In Africa, a range of problems can increase the risk of renewed group conflict, including disagreements about the rightful heirs to positions as chief or king, the legitimacy of elections, and contending claims to land. Settling these disputes through individualized adjudication lessens the chance that contestants will resort to violence or seek to press their claims through group coalitions that spread instability. Disputes are less likely to be seen in all-or-nothing terms, and the very process of involvement in adjudication constitutes a civic education in productive means of settling differences. The success of courts in this process depends in part on the character of the substantive law, the persuasiveness and transparency of judges' reasoning, and the preexisting respect that the courts may attract, as well as features of the underlying situation.

Court action on vigilantism is one kind of action that can yield potential benefits. Even in stable and newly prosperous parts of Africa, state institutions often have very limited reach. Taking a matter to the police and then to a judge is expensive and time-consuming, frequently requiring difficult travel. Those seeking police assistance must often pay for fuel for the police to visit a crime scene, and courts sometimes ask litigants to reimburse them for the paper needed to create a file and preserve the official record. Self-help beckons as a tempting solution to problems of order on Africa's frontiers. As "outsider crime" increases (crime committed by people not from the community), so, often, does vigilantism. Such self-help often leads to the further disorder of protection rackets, harassment of people who are unpopular because of their age or origin, and intensification of the strains that set communities on edge and breed division.

In eastern Africa, a surge of cattle rustling, poaching, and other kinds of outsider crime spurred an increase in vigilantism in rural areas during the 1980s and 1990s. Young men from the affected communities organized to provide defense and to round up suspected thieves. In some instances, they even received financial or rhetorical support from governments that were unable to extend effective police protection. But often these groups passed and executed judgment on suspects without anything resembling a fair hearing, rather than turning suspects over to the regular police and courts. Human rights abuses committed by these vigilante groups also mounted. Under these circumstances, vigilantism could easily lead to intercommunal violence,

[17] Certification of the Constitution of the Republic of South Africa, No. CCT 23/96 (CC Sept. 6, 1996) (finding some provisions of the proposed constitution unacceptable) <http://www.polity.org.za/govdocs/constitution/cert.html>; Certification of the Amended Text of the Constitution of the Republic of South Africa, No. 37/96 (CC Dec. 4, 1996) (deciding that the amended text did comply with the Constitutional Principles) <http://www.concourt.gov.za/judgments/1996/const2.html>.

when the different cultural heritages of victims and suspects could give disputes an ethnic tinge and trigger retaliation.

In Tanzania, legislative action gave these groups extensive summary powers. However, individuals who suffered injury from them brought constitutional challenges and won restrictions on the role these "traditional armies" could play. Although the government did not immediately execute the courts' decisions that limited the armies' activities, the cases helped begin a public discussion of the dangers that vigilante groups could pose and the appropriate limits on their activity.[18]

A second example of the prophylactic effect courts may have on the outbreak or renewal of intercommunal violence centers on witchcraft. Many parts of Africa witnessed an upsurge of witchcraft cases in the late 1980s and 1990s—a time when livelihoods were threatened by instability and shortages of critical resources, particularly arable land. No systematic data are available to confirm the magnitude of the trend, but we can gain some sense of the scale of the phenomenon from newspaper reports and editorials, the impressions of lawyers and judges, and even popular anecdote. In Tanzania, the Ministry of Home Affairs recorded that between 1970 and 1984, 3,333 witchcraft-related incidents occurred, and 3,692 people died.[19] Other outbreaks of witchcraft scares took place in settings as diverse as Cameroon and Zimbabwe, and even within the internecine conflict of the antiapartheid movement in South Africa. Witchcraft accusations are a familiar technique to attack people perceived as weak or marginal, or, less often, troublemakers. The spread of such accusations can lead to community paranoia and mistrust, and a cascading chain of attacks.

The courts of eastern and southern Africa have attempted to put a brake on witchcraft scares by placing strict limits on the admissibility of "fear of witchcraft" as a defense to murder. They have limited admissible evidence as well, ruling out the subjective claim of "spectral evidence" as a basis for witchcraft allegations. To use fear of witchcraft as a justification for violence, the defendant must show that he acted in the heat of passion and that an ordinary person would have believed that the victim's actions constituted an act of witchcraft designed to produce harm. Once familiar to westerners, who endured their own struggles to control witchcraft in an earlier era, the laws and standards are used by the courts to reduce the opportunistic use of witchcraft allegations, which may provoke further community violence. When courts loosen these standards, and especially when they allow spectral evidence, retaliatory practices tend to proliferate and the judiciary itself may be pressured to become a forum for pursuing witchcraft suspects. Anecdotal evidence of this pattern surfaced in Cameroon, where the law contained fewer evidentiary restrictions and a flood of witchcraft allegations disrupted communities.[20]

A third sphere of judicial activity that may reduce ethnic clashes is the adoption of court-based mediation of serious neighborhood disputes. Although customary forums in Africa have stressed mediation of disputes, until recently most state courts did not offer forms of alternative dispute resolution. The increasing acceptance of alternative dispute resolution internationally has spurred local innovation, and an expanding number of African courts now permit and encourage mediation of selected types of cases. A Nigerian experiment has brought community leaders to court to help sort out neighborhood disputes. In Tanzania, communities have asked judges to help resolve group differences. One judge relates the story of an especially intractable conflict that neither elders nor religious leaders had succeeded in resolving. The judge was able to bring the parties together and settle the dispute. With a bit of weariness he remarked, "The people said they were so pleased that they would start to bring all of their problems to the

[18] Ngegwe s/o Sangija & Three Others v. Republic, Crim. App. No. 72 (Mwanza High Ct., Tanz. 1987); Maingu v. Mtongori & Nine Others, Civ. No. 16 (Mwanza High Ct., Tanz. 1988).

[19] *See* Simeon Mesaki, *Witch-Killing in Sukumaland*, *in* WITCHCRAFT IN CONTEMPORARY TANZANIA 47, 52 (Ray Abrahams ed., 1994).

[20] *See, e.g.*, Daniel D. N. Nsereko, *Witchcraft as a Criminal Defence, from Uganda to Canada and Back*, 24 MANITOBA L. J. 38 (1996); Cyprian F. Fisiy & Peter Geschiere, *Judges and Witches, or How Is the State to Deal with Witchcraft?* 118 CAHIERS D'ÉTUDES AFRICAINES 135 (1990).

court!"[21] The fear and hatred felt by members of one ethnic group toward members of another—for example, the fear of Hutu that Tutsi migrants would come to take their land—may be mitigated if the courts are seen as effective arbiters and mediators of disputes over vital matters. The availability of mediation gives the courts wider purchase, settling disputes even when there is no dispositive law to govern the matter.

III. SUSTAINING DEMOCRATIC REGIMES IN POSTCONFLICT TRANSITIONS

The establishment of democratic political structures is the main strategy for sharing power in postconflict transitions.[22] Although some scholars have written about the special problems of democracy in African states, democratic governance for postconflict regimes still conventionally enjoys the highest public legitimacy.[23] That legitimacy, under appropriate circumstances, can translate into stability.

In postconflict transitions, courts can enhance the levels of public contestation and inclusiveness of participation in political processes, as well as help to implement democracy as a set of everyday practices. The most direct impact on democratic culture may reside in reviewing the administration of elections. This extends from the counting of ballots to the fairness of campaign practices. Inability to handle challenges expeditiously can undermine the legitimacy of new governments and sow the seeds of deep division. Courts have leveled the playing field among contenders for public power by upholding rules that support free and fair elections.

African courts have shaped democratic transitions in other ways, too. Some decisions enhance freedom of speech. For example, in *Retrofit (Pvt.) Ltd. v. Minister of Information, Posts, and Telecommunications,*[24] the Zimbabwe Constitutional Court struck down a government telecommunications monopoly, in part on the ground that it impeded freedom of speech. Judges in South Africa, Uganda, and Tanzania have helped to draft new multiparty constitutions, as have some of their counterparts in other countries.

Yet the influence of courts in stabilizing postconflict democracies is not always straightforward. A social scientist may offer several observations about the causal relationships between courts and postconflict democracy in developing countries, based on the experience of African countries.

The Importance of a "Critical Juncture"

First, the capacity of courts to intervene depends on other actors. Changes in public attitudes toward the assertion of legal rights, in the willingness of incumbents to allow judicial decision making to go forward, and in the behavior of the legal community are necessary conditions for court involvement in democratization.

This confluence of events, or "critical juncture," began to develop in Africa during the mid-to-late 1980s. People started to make increasing use of the courts in many countries, filing more cases each year, and this attitude toward litigation is likely to spread from private questions to public questions. Although there are no broad cross-national studies of the use of courts in Africa, surveys conducted in Botswana, Uganda, and Tanzania in 1996 showed that a surprisingly large number of households took disputes to court for a hearing. Ordinary commu-

---

[21] Interview with Judge John Mroso, High Court of Tanzania, Arusha (Aug. 1995). Thus, gradually and often informally, African judiciaries are developing community programs similar to those of American courts, helping inhabitants settle neighborhood disputes outside the context of lawsuits.

[22] *See, e.g.,* Samuel H. Barnes, *The Contribution of Democracy to Rebuilding Postconflict Societies,* 95 AJIL 86 (2001).

[23] *See, e.g.,* Boutros Boutros-Ghali, Supplement to Reports on Democratization (Agenda for Democratization), UN Doc. A/51/761, annex (1996); *OAU Summit Closes with Calls for Democracy, Dignity,* Agence France-Presse, July 14, 1999 (OAU Secretary-General Salim A. Salim stating that future coup leaders "shouldn't expect to be invited" to the next summit), *available in* LEXIS, News Group File, Most Recent Two Years; African Charter on Human and Peoples' Rights, June 27, 1981, 21 ILM 58 (1982) (adopted by 18th Assembly of Heads of State and Government of the Organization of African Unity), <http://www1.umn.edu/humanrts/instree/z1afchar.htm> and <http://www.unhcr.ch/refworld/refworld/legal/instrume/women/afr_e.htm>.

[24] Retrofit (Pvt.) Ltd. v. Minister of Information, Posts, and Telecommunications, 1963 (3) BCLR 394 (ZS), 1995 SACLR LEXIS *307 (Dec. 18, 1995).

nity conflicts were usually taken to local councils or customary forums for resolution,[25] but the surveys showed surprisingly heavy use of magistrates courts as well.[26] Governments also gave courts more latitude. For a variety of reasons—the need to curb corruption, an effort to differentiate a new government from an arbitrary and abusive predecessor, and donor pressure— several heads of state granted judiciaries more autonomy and refrained from actions that visibly interfered with judicial independence.

At the same time, judicial attitudes began to alter. Greater contact with other members of the legal profession at international meetings and the acquisition of new technologies made it possible for judges to share decisions and acquire copies of international standards, helping to diminish an "executive-minded" predisposition to favor the government in disputes.

"Signaling"

Courts that play a central role in postconflict transitions also make heavy use of signaling devices. Judges usually have found a way to signal their receptiveness to new kinds of cases or new lines of argument in their decisions. But they have experimented with other approaches as well.

Many countries in Africa entertain advisory opinions from the judiciary and allow judges to serve on national commissions. In the early stages of democratic transitions in Africa, senior judges have served on commissions charged with writing a constitution—for example, judges participated in South Africa's constitutional transition, both in the drafting and, later, in the unusual certification process used to review the draft of the final document.[27] Justice Benjamin Odoki in Uganda presided over the redrafting of his country's constitution. And former Chief Justice Francis Nyalali of Tanzania chaired efforts to determine whether or not his country would move to a multiparty system. Both acknowledged the difficulties and the risks. For instance, Nyalali worried that people would have a hard time separating his role as chair of the commission from his role as head of the court. If the final document was unsatisfactory, the court would attract some of the blame. "But if we succeeded," he commented, "the image of the judiciary would be greatly improved."[28]

Influence Subject to Constraints

The ability of African courts to stabilize postconflict democracy is constrained by substantive law and by scarcity of resources.

If lawyers sometimes magnify the importance of courts to outcomes like peace and democracy, social scientists are often oblivious to the constraints that legal rules impose. Courts do not have unlimited latitude to narrow the application of harsh legislation, declare practices unconstitutional, or apply the standards of regional and international documents as domestic law. The ability of African courts to decide cases in ways that promote and stabilize democracy depends on the wording of constitutions and laws, on the status of international treaties and conventions under domestic law, and on local precedent.

---

[25] For fledgling institutions, there are times when the better part of valor is to limit the scope of activity. The willingness of citizens to place faith in the courts to resolve disputes impartially is partly a function of performance. When the risks of ineffectiveness run high, finding alternative ways of hearing disputes may be better than overburdening a system that has to play a very important role over the long term and that must gradually gain people's trust.

[26] In Tanzania, a World Bank survey found that 6–8% of residents had used the magistrates courts in the previous year. Contemporaneous surveys in Uganda and Botswana asked whether a member of the household had appeared as a party to a case in the magistrates courts during the previous five years. Overall, 14% had done so, and 45% had in areas with frequent land disputes. *See* UNITED REPUBLIC OF TANZANIA, PRESIDENTIAL COMMISSION OF INQUIRY AGAINST CORRUPTION, SERVICE DELIVERY SURVEY: CORRUPTION IN THE POLICE, JUDICIARY, REVENUE AND LANDS SERVICE 11 (World Bank/CIET International, Dar es Salaam, July 1996); *see also* Widner, *supra* note 2.

[27] *See* Certification of the Constitution of the Republic of South Africa, *supra* note 17; Certification of the Amended Text of the Constitution of the Republic of South Africa, *supra* note 17.

[28] Interview with Justice Francis L. Nyalali, Dar es Salaam, Tanzania (May 29, 1996).

Many African constitutions offer relatively weak protection of civil and political liberties, although the newer documents generally are stronger than those they replaced. Like the African Charter on Human and Peoples' Rights, they contain many limitations clauses and claw-back provisions. African constitutions afford some grounding for decisions stabilizing democracy, but they are not generally as fertile in this regard as constitutions in many other parts of the world.

Statutory law is also problematic. For example, the persistence of seditious libel laws provides a basis for limiting political criticism. "Societies acts" provide a vehicle for controlling freedom of association. And rules lowering the evidentiary showing that prosecutors must produce at preliminary hearings can open the judicial system to abuse—allowing governments to hold people in jail without sufficient grounds and afterwards decline to prosecute the case at trial, in most instances after having caused serious financial and other injury.

The second major constraint is financial. Courts rarely have adequate funds to carry out their operations. Usually, the courts can claim 1 percent or less of government budgets, and public budgets are small to begin with. Many new economic programs place countries on cash-accounting standards with cash budgets that must balance each month. These restrictions aggravate the problem of limited resources by creating uncertainty about the release of funds from the treasury.

Law reports lapsed in many parts of Africa in the 1980s and 1990s. Many governments also gave up the publication of statutes, and this lacuna has meant that magistrates and judges, especially at the lower levels, are put to rely on informal sources such as old university notes for their knowledge of the law, with predictable results. Although these materials are now becoming available again, their absence has impeded the courts' effectiveness and ability to develop a national or regional jurisprudence supportive of democracy.

These kinds of constraints limit the perceived effectiveness and fairness of the courts, and in turn may lessen popular willingness to resort to the law instead of the streets for dispute resolution.

Reciprocal Effects

The ability of the courts to influence public life may expand as other political openings occur. In most parts of the world, independent national courts have grown up slowly and haltingly, often in tandem with the expansion of competitive markets and democracy. The elements of this trio have rarely appeared all at once, but each has tended to reinforce the others by creating mutually supportive constituencies. For instance, over time, opposition political party leaders will favor independent judiciaries to safeguard civil and political liberties and to ensure impartial adjudication of election disputes. Likewise, entrepreneurs in competitive-market systems often come to believe that their investments depend on impartial enforcement of rules to preserve competition and protect contracts. Interest groups may also want impartial judicial resolution of disputes, hoping that principles of vested rights and *non ex post facto* will dissuade each new legislative session from overturning the laws its predecessor enacted.[29]

On the ground, one finds considerable evidence of reciprocal relationships and feedback effects. The effort to build judicial independence and to support decisions promoting civil liberties has corresponded in eastern and southern Africa with greater interest in markets and democracy. In many places, members of the bar, organized in law societies, have started to play watchdog roles and act as lobbies for independent courts and human rights, but they often do so after political space has already opened up. The existence of even a small space for comment and criticism has emboldened African lawyers, who in turn have begun to bring more civil and human rights cases to court. Their initiative accordingly reinforces the authority of the courts as important elements of the institutional landscape and creates more room for stronger action.

---

[29] *See* William M. Landes & Richard A. Posner, *The Independent Judiciary in an Interest-Group Perspective*, 18 J.L. & ECON. 875 (1975).

This kind of reciprocal causality works within court chambers, too. The former chief justice of Tanzania observed that "[c]ourage among judicial officers is [easier] to nurture and develop in a multi-party democracy than under a one party regime."[30] When judges see a surge of public support—and notice that the potential for retaliation (by other branches of government or by powerful litigants) has been limited by public opinion and international scrutiny—it becomes easier for the courts to act independently and to explore untried lines of interpretation. Institutions can shape character and vice versa.

Expectations About Courts and Democratic Transitions

If the relationship between courts and postconflict transitions to democracy has these features, what does it bode for the future? What kinds of expectations does it generate?

We can build on our several conclusions. Courts and law are likely to become more effective after a "critical juncture," a confluence of events that causes the executive to delegate more authority to the courts and changes people's willingness to take cases to judges for resolution. Where judges successfully signal their openness to certain types of cases and to democratic norms and practices, possibly through participation in constitution drafting, courts can become stronger players in transitions to democracy.

At the same time, much variation will remain in the degree to which actual court decisions and the judicial process promote democratic norms. Resource constraints and the characteristics of the substantive law will continue to create diversity in the roles courts play, as well as in the content of decisions. But postconflict democracy and the role of the courts can gradually reinforce each other, growing stronger over time.

IV. CONCLUSION

Appropriate methods of dispute resolution are important to postconflict reconstruction and democratic stabilization. Indigenous and local methods of mediation and arbitration can quell the violence of local disputes and prevent the escalation of intercommunal strife. The role of a formal court system can also be enhanced over time, as a way of opening democratic space and resolving weightier controversies, including the monitoring of elections. Most bilateral aid programs now include assistance to judiciaries because policymakers have chosen to act on these hunches. But the relationship between courts and postconflict stabilization is not always straightforward. The attitudes of other social actors, the efficacy of courts in signaling their ambitions for intervention, the character of the substantive law, and the way resources are mobilized will shape the kinds of contributions courts can make. Considered use of international tribunals can ease the pressures on fledgling court systems in dangerous postconflict situations, preserving their ability to function effectively in the future.

[30] Francis L. Nyalali, Keynote speech delivered at a seminar organized by the Commonwealth Judicial Education Institute for judges in East and Central Africa, Sheraton Hotel, Kampala, Uganda (Feb. 26, 1996) (on file with author).

[3]

Legal, Judicial and Administrative Reforms in Post-Conflict Societies: Beyond the Rule of Law Template

Richard Sannerholm*

Abstract

A common position adopted by the international community is that establishing the rule of law after violent internal conflict is an essential prerequisite in the transition from war to peace. In practical terms, this often translates into projects and programmes directed at the criminal justice sector. Rarely is rule of law acknowledged in relation to administrative law, public governance and economic management. This has several negative effects, particularly in societies where public mismanagement, bad economic governance and corruption run high, and especially if one considers these issues as constituting a large part of the reason for state 'failure'. But, a new trend is now vaguely discernible in the practice of the international actors involved in rebuilding war-shattered societies that gives priority to the rule of law in relation to public sector reform. Liberia provides, in this regard, an illustrative example through the agreement between the Transitional National Government of Liberia and donor agencies, where international experts will have co-signing authority over a number of budgetary issues, and where national judicial institutions will be strengthened in order to combat arbitrary governance and corruption.

1. The Role of Law in Post-Conflict Reconstruction

It has become a credo in the field of statebuilding[1] that for societies to manage the transition from conflict to durable peace, they must establish the rule of law.[2] Thus, in the rebuilding process of so-called 'failed states',[3] rule of law promotion has become a popular reform activity including activities such as, reviewing and

---

* Doctoral candidate in law at the University of Örebro, Sweden. E-mail: richard.sannerholm@bsr.oru.se. I would like to thank Vivienne O'Connor for invaluable comments and support. I would also like to thank Katarina Månsson, Daniel Lindvall and Maria Eriksson for reading earlier drafts of this article.

[1] Statebuilding is distinct from the more traditional crisis management forms of preventive diplomacy, peacemaking, peacekeeping and peacebuilding, see *Report of the Panel on United Nations Peace Operations*, UN Doc. A/55/305-S/2000/809, 21 August 2000; R. Caplan, *International Governance of War-Torn Territories* (2005); S. Chesterman, *You the People: The United Nations, Transitional Administration, and State-Building* (2004).

[2] See *Rule of law and Transitional Justice in Conflict and Post-conflict Societies* UN Doc. S/2004/616, 23 August 2004.

[3] The concept of 'failed states' was first popularised by G. Helman and S. R. Ratner, 'Saving Failed States', (1993) Winter *Foreign Policy*, Issue 89. The concept represents a security perspective on states in crisis. The perspective from the development community

66   *Richard Sannerholm*

vetting criminal laws in light of international human rights standards; training of judges and other legal professionals; supporting the formation of police forces and establishing human rights commissions and truth and reconciliation tribunals.[4] As some commentators sarcastically remarked in a recent study, rule of law is like apple pie and ice cream, it is a concept that no one can dislike.[5] This 'rule of law template' or 'justice triad' approach is promoted in a wide variety of different post-conflict situations from Afghanistan to Kosovo, Liberia and Haiti.[6]

But, there is a contestant to the title of the most popular reform activity. This alternative to the standard menu says that in order to successfully address root causes to a conflict, one need also to focus on rule of law in relation to other areas, in particular to governance and economic management. Stripped to its essentials, this argument implies that it might be equally important to review the laws on public procurement as it is to review penal codes, and equally important as creating a human rights commission is the establishment of an independent prosecutorial office with a mandate to investigate charges of corruption.

While this argument flies in the face of the popular perception that the greatest need in post-conflict societies is the implementation and protection of civil and political rights, and while it lacks the high-flying and symbolic traits of the present rule of law menu, it is quite logically constructed. What is more, it is all about rule of law and human rights promotion.[7] The alternative perspective views conflict as a development problem, and that without getting the economy back on track and without providing the basic means necessary for people to sustain themselves financially, conflict is never far away. In situations where the government misuses public resources, where the executive power curtails the judiciary, and where embezzlement and corruption is high, where water rights and land rights are hotly contested, rule of law has an important role to play.[8]

is wider in scope. The World Bank talks of 'Low Income Countries Under Stress', and the Organisation for Economic Co-operation and Development uses the term 'difficult partnerships', focusing on crisis as a development problem. [Is there a need for a reference here]

[4] For an overview of United Nations missions with rule of law components, see S. N. Carlson, 'Legal and Judicial Rule of Law Work in Multi-Dimensional Peacekeeping Operations: Lessons Learned Study', *UN Peacekeeping Best Practice Unit*, March 2006.

[5] J. Stromseth, D. Wippman and R. Brooks, *Can Might Make Rights? Building the Rule of Law After Military Interventions* (2006).

[6] A number of scholars refer to the present effort of promoting the rule of law as a template, menu, or orthodoxy. See T. Carothers, 'The Problem of Knowledge', in T. Carothers, (ed.) *Promoting the Rule of Law: In Search of Knowledge* (2006) and J. Stromseth *et al., op. cit.,* fn. 5.

[7] See the discussion in S. C. Agbakwa, 'A Path Least Taken: Economic and Social rights and the Prospects of Conflict Prevention and Peacebuilding in Africa', (2003) 47 *Journal of African Law*, 38–64.

[8] Sudan is an evocative case in point. The *Comprehensive Peace Agreement* (CPA) signed in 2005 is severely undermined by the executive power, despite several safeguards built into the agreement. The President has issued decrees undermining the legislative power of the National assembly, including decrees proposing to give the police and armed forces greater powers but with limited accountability. See International Crisis Group,

A counter-argument to this 'rule of law and development perspective' is that in the immediate situation after conflict, the rule of law menu represents urgent measures needed in order to guarantee peace, order and stability. This is correct, but directing legal and judicial assistance to governance and economic management should not follow long after.

This article will argue that there is a need to pay greater attention to rule of law in relation to issues such as governance and economic management, and that failure to do so may severely undermine the sustainability of other statebuilding reforms.

In order to set the stage for this article's central argument, Part 2 will provide an overview of the cause of crisis states while Part 3 will examine some of the implications of conflict for the legal and administrative sector. Part 4 will analyse the rule of law template in statebuilding, focusing on how the concept of rule of law is used by international actors. In Part 5, three critical capacities of the rule of law template will be analysed: law reform, judicial reform and human rights and police. This is followed by a discussion of a governance and economic management programme in Liberia in Part 6, as an alternative to the 'one-size-fits-all' approach currently dominating the agenda of rule of law and statebuilding entrepreneurs.

The primary focus in this article centres on volatile and crisis state situations. The defeatist question posed by Martin Doornbos, 'when starting from scratch, where does one begin' [9] to the case of statebuilding in Somalia, can serve as a geographical and conceptual denominator, and the same can be said of Robert Jackson's unconventional suggestion that certain states should be advertised by public notice on large signboards at all border entrances bearing the words: 'Warning: this country can be dangerous to your health.'[10]

2. A Crisis Anatomy

Understanding the anatomy of crisis situations is far from an academic interest; it holds great bearing on the quality of the response of the international community. As shown by Cater, how conflicts are understood greatly influences the strategies of the UN and other donors.[11]

Finding root causes to conflict was a much debated issue throughout the 1990s between proponents of a perspective which placed economic incentives as the main cause, and those who claimed that various forms of deprivations of justice and violations of human rights, authoritarian regimes, etc. were to blame.

'Sudan's Comprehensive Peace Agreement: The Long Road Ahead', *Africa Report No. 106*, 31 March 2006, 6.

[9] M. Doornbos, 'Somalia: Alternative Scenarios for Political Reconstruction' (2002) *African Affairs* 101 at 102.

[10] R. Jackson, *The Global Covenant: Human Conduct in a World of States* (2003) 295.

[11] C. Cater, 'The Political Economy of Armed Conflict and UN Intervention: Rethinking the Critical Cases of Africa' in K. Ballentine and J. Sherman, *The Political Economy of Armed Conflict: Beyond Greed and Grievances* (2003) 40 et. seq.

68   *Richard Sannerholm*

The international community has tended to depart from the perception that conflict is primarily caused by a deprivation of justice, meaning a lack or abuse of civil and political rights and the existence of an autocratic regime where political participation is non-existent.[12]

According to the 'justice-seeking' perspective, conflicts and crisis situations occur because people pursue certain grievances against the state, and when there are no adequate mechanisms and institutions in place for seeking redress, crisis looms nearby.

This 'justice seeking' approach is clearly illustrated in the report of the UN Secretary-General, *Rule of law and Transitional Justice in Conflict and Post-conflict Societies*, where it is said that past experience has demonstrated that the consolidation of peace as well as the maintenance of peace in the long term, cannot be achieved unless 'the population is confident that redress for grievances can be obtained through legitimate structures for the peaceful settlement of disputes and the fair administration of justice'.[13]

The report also holds that '. . . the heightened vulnerability of minorities, women, children, prisoners and detainees, displaced persons, refugees and others, which is evident in all conflict and post-conflict situations, brings an element of urgency to the imperative of the rule of law.[14] Rule of law is seen as a remedy for widespread insecurity.

While this perspective rightly posits human rights abuses at the centre of conflict and at the centre of the international response, it is intrinsically narrow in scope and generally excludes deprivation of social and economic rights. The justice-seeking approach tends to equate insecurity with violation of physical integrity rights. But, insecurity is much more than violations of civil and political rights. In a report from the World Bank called *Voices of the Poor: Crying Out for Change*, based on extensive world-wide interviews, eight factors of insecurity were listed: insecurities of work and livelihood; natural and human-made disasters; crime and violence; persecution by the police and lack of justice; civil conflict and war; macropolicy shocks and stresses; social vulnerability; health, illness and death.[15]

A broader perception of insecurity is also given by the Truth and Reconciliation Commission in Sierra Leone, which concludes that a number of factors are at play in a crisis situation. The Commission noted that it was years of bad governance, endemic corruption and the denial of basic human rights that created the conditions that made conflict inevitable. The Commission also observed that

---

[12]   R. Rotberg, 'Failed States in a World of Terror', (2002) *Foreign Affairs* 81 at 130 'in the last phase of failure, the state's legitimacy crumbles. Lacking meaningful or realistic democratic means of redress, protesters take to the streets or mobilise along ethnic, religious, or linguistic lines'.

[13]   *Op. cit.,* fn. 2, para. 2.

[14]   *Ibid.*

[15]   D. Narayan, R. Chambers, M. K. Shah and P. Petesch, *Voices of the Poor: Crying Out for Change* (2000) 151.

many of these causes are still not adequately addressed 'they are potential causes of conflict, if they remain unaddressed.'[16]

There are scholars who argue that objective grievances, such as human rights violations, have nothing, or very little to do with conflict and crisis.[17] Instead, they suggest that economic factors such as a high concentration of natural resources provide incentives for looting and predatory economic behaviour and, that rebel groups seek not to redress grievances, but enrichment, and that this causes conflict to erupt. The economic perspective is a very one-sided take-on conflict that pays little attention to the state as an actor, and it is difficult to explain the conflicts in Rwanda and Somalia as a struggle over coffee rentals and cows.[18] Nevertheless, the economic perspective does manage to bring attention to the fact that weak economic governance and widespread poverty, typical development problems, are central features among the root causes of conflict.

Objective grievances should not be disregarded as part of the explanatory power of conflicts but they should be viewed from a more comprehensive perspective. A number of objective grievances in post-conflict societies relate to physical integrity rights, however, a large part also concerns the right to water, land and adequate housing. Therefore, the role of economic, social and cultural rights, or rather the deprivation of these rights, should be more clearly acknowledged in the international rule of law response.[19] This entails recognition that 'resource misallocation, economic mismanagement, corruption, poor fiscal policies, and structural adjustment policies' can have negative effects on a society, and if left unaddressed, can cause the eruption of violent conflict. [20] As noted in the Report of the Secretary-General's High-level Panel on Threats, Challenges and Change, 'corruption, illicit trade and money-laundering contribute to state weakness, impede economic growth and undermine democracy. These activities thus create a permissive environment for civil conflict'.[21]

---

[16] Report of the Sierra Leone Truth and Reconciliation Commission, 'Witness to the Truth', Vol. 2, para. 37.

[17] See P. Collier and A. Hoeffler who analyse economic factors and link the existence of natural resources (such as oil, timber and diamonds) and a high level of commodity export to the probability of civil war based on a utility argument where a high concentration of natural resources provides an incentive for looting and predatory economic behaviour. P.Collier and A.Hoeffler, 'On Economic Causes of Civil War', Oxford Economic Papers (1998) 50; 'Justice Seeking and Loot-Seeking in Civil War' (1999); and 'Greed and Grievances in Civil War' (2001).

[18] For a critique of the 'loot-seeking' perspective, see K. Ballentine and J. Sherman (eds.), The Political Economy of Armed Conflict: Beyond Greed and Grievances (2003).

[19] See, e.g. Task Force Report on State Failure 'Phase III' 20 September 2000, p. vii 'as is true for other types of state failure, lower levels of material well-being are associated with a greater risk of ethnic war. We found that countries with worse-than-average infant mortality faced roughly double the odds of an outbreak of ethnic war.'

[20] Op. cit., fn. 7, p. 43.

[21] Report of the High-level Panel on Threats, Challenges and Change: A More Secure World: Our Shared Responsibility UN Doc. A/59/565, 2 December 2004, para. 23.

70   *Richard Sannerholm*

While this perspective – claiming that root causes to a conflict may consist in equal part of a lack of employment, education, widespread poverty and human insecurity as well as a lack of the right to vote – have not been ignored in the broader realm of statebuilding, it has been ignored by the 'rule of law menu'. Issues concerning the protection of social and economic rights and control of the executive power are generally left out of the statebuilding and rule of law equation.[22]

The UN High Commissioner for Human Rights observed in a report from early 2005 on Sierra Leone that progress in the area of human rights had been lopsided in favour of civil and political rights. Few improvements were registered in the area of economic, social and cultural rights, and from all indications, Sierra Leone was unlikely to meet the Millennium Development Goals in any of the areas.[23] The Secretary-General made a similar observation and noted that increasing respect for civil and political rights in Sierra Leone continued, but progress in the area of social and economic rights remained slow and cumbersome.[24]

For the planning and preparation of post-conflict statebuilding interventions with a substantial rule of law component, the multifaceted anatomy of crisis situations – the mixing of justice, economic and social conflicts – requires a holistic approach.

3. The Impact of Conflict on the Legal and Administrative Systems

The legal and administrative system is often the part of the state which is most vulnerable to conflict.[25] One striking feature is the high level of destruction of official buildings, particularly court houses, police stations, correctional centres and prisons; a level of destruction which seems endemic in crisis situations.[26] William G. O'Neill paints a tragic picture from Kosovo in 1999 following the withdrawal of the Serbian armed forces, and describes the situation as if '. . .

---

[22] This is in contradiction to the problems on the ground. If one looks to the annual reports of the Ombudspersons in Kosovo and Bosnia and Herzegovina, a large part of the complaints received concerns social and economic rights. See, *e.g.* '*Fourth Annual Report*' of the Ombudsperson in Kosovo.

[23] *Situation of Human Rights in Sierra Leone* UN Doc. E/CN.4 2005/113, 2 February 2005, para. 33.

[24] *Twenty-fifth Report of the Secretary-General on the United Nations Mission in Sierra Leone* UN Doc. S/2005/273, 26 April 2005, paras. 44–45.

[25] As concerns implications of crisis, a distinction can be made between international and national legal implications. Here, the national implications will be discussed, but it is worth noting that on the international level crisis situations entail a host of difficulties relating to a loss of *de facto* legal capacity to enter into new international agreements and treaties. For further discussion of international legal implications, see R. Koskenmäki, 'Legal Implications Resulting from State Failure in Light of the Case of Somalia', (2004) 73 *Nordic Journal of International Law*, 1–36.

[26] See H. Strohmeyer, 'Collapse and Reconstruction of a Judicial System: The United Nations Mission in Kosovo and East Timor', (2001) 95 *The American Journal of International Law*, 46–63.

Rule of Law Reforms in Post-Conflict Societies 71

a plague of heavily armed locusts had swept through, scouring the grounds for anything valuable and leaving broken windows and ripped-out electrical sockets in their wake.'[27]

This is not unique for Kosovo. A World Bank Joint Assessment Mission to East Timor, following the post-election violence, reported that over 70% of all administrative buildings were either fully or partially destroyed, and almost all office equipment and movable property was completely destroyed.[28] The fact that official records and court files are destroyed means, for example, that land, housing and property rights may be hard to legally identify. This, in turn, creates insecurity and prohibits local productivity and economic growth, further complicated by the return of refugees and internally displaced persons.[29] Widespread destruction makes the legal and administrative system of a war-torn society 'ahistorical'.[30]

In many cases, the legal and administrative system also suffers from a lack of independence due to an entrenched tradition of executive interference. This was recorded by the group of UN experts assessing the legal sector in Liberia in 2003 in relation to the establishment of a UN peace operation

> . . . public confidence in the judiciary is extremely low. Salaries and benefits . . . have not been paid for 17 months, providing an easy justification for acceptance of bribes and favours . . . Courts were extremely reluctant to rule against the government and 'telephone justice' was said to be common. By all accounts, Taylor's domination of the judiciary was far-reaching and extreme.[31]

Weakness in the administrative system is often a salient feature of post-war societies. The administrative legal framework tends to be unclear with overlapping jurisdictions between various agencies, leaving room for discretion or creating administrative inertia. This also means that the regulation of property rights, social services and the issuing of licences and permits for commercial activity

---

[27] W. G. O'Neil, *Kosovo: An Unfinished Peace* (2002) 75.

[28] World Bank, *'Joint Assessment Mission Report'* (1999) para. 15. See also *Report of the Secretary-General on the Situation in East Timor*, UN Doc. S/1999/1024, October 4, 1999, paras. 11–13.

[29] See A. Hurwitz, K. Studdard and R. Williams, 'Housing, Land and Conflict Management: Identifying Policy Options for Rule of Law Programming', *International Peace Academy, Policy Report*, October 2005.

[30] This is illustrated in the European Commission financial audits of state-owned enterprises and other revenue generating agencies in Liberia. In relation to, for example, Liberia Petroleum Refining Company, the financial audit observed that most of the records and official documents had been destroyed which made it difficult to determine the revenue generating potential, sort out concessions and contracts, as well as installing measures to curtail corruption in the company. 'Liberia Petroleum Refining Company' (2004) Volume 1 *Executive Report*.

[31] UN DPKO *Liberia: Legal and Judicial Planning Assessment and Concept of Operations*, 19 September 2003 (on file with author).

72   *Richard Sannerholm*

takes a hard toll, creating legal and administrative barriers for people struggling to return to some sort of normality.

In post-war societies, the previous law in force is often challenged and fiercely contested, as evident in Somalia and Kosovo. When the Special Representative of the Secretary-General in Somalia declared the criminal laws in force prior to the establishment of the UN mission to be applicable it provoked vigorous protests from the legal community in northern Somalia who perceived the penal code to be tainted by the former regime of Siad Barre.[32] Similarly, when the UN transitional administrator for Kosovo declared that the laws in force prior to the establishment of the UN mission should continue to apply, *mutatis mutandis*, several Kosovo-albanian judges refused to apply the law.[33]

In this regard, the current effort of developing model criminal codes for potential use in peace operations should be noted as a positive improvement of rule of law promotion practice. While the effort originally followed the recommendation in the Report of the Panel on United Nations Peace Operations, where a form of 'justice package' was suggested in order to more effectively address the issue of applicable law, the project has evolved and has the potential for more long-term use in criminal law reform.[34] The model codes encompass a Model Criminal Code, Model Code of Criminal Procedure, Model Detention Act and a Model Police Act. The drafting process has followed an inclusive and comprehensive approach involving consultations with legal practitioners and scholars across the globe.[35]

Related to this phenomenon is the emergence of parallel justice systems, as a response to a perceived bias in the formal justice system, or because of the weak function of formal law. Following the crisis in Somalia, customary law and Islamic law, Sharia, emerged and has since become a consolidated normative system in rural areas while the formal justice system applies only to the urban sector, at best.[36] A similar development has taken place in Sierra Leone. As noted in a recent assessment by the World Bank, the justice sector only serves the urban elite, the resources available to the sector are abysmal, and the general perception of the justice system is in general negative. In the countryside, people increasingly

---

[32] M. Ganzglass, 'The Restoration of the Somali Justice System', in W. Clarke and J. Herbst (eds.), *Learning from Somalia: The Lessons of Armed Humanitarian Intervention* (1997) at 28.

[33] SC Res. 1244 UN SCOR, 4011th mtg., UN Doc. S/RES/1244, 10 June 1999 and UNMIK Regulation 1999/1. See also Strohmeyer, *op. cit.*, fn. 26.

[34] *Report of the Panel on United Nations Peace Operations, op. cit.*, fn. 1, para. 83.

[35] See, V. O'Connor, 'Traversing the Rocky Road of Law Reform in Conflict and Post Conflict States: Model Codes for Post Conflict Criminal Justice as a Tool of Assistance', (2005) 16 *Criminal Law Forum*, 231–255.

[36] Somalia has three parallel legal systems: the Islamic law (SHARIA) customary law (XEER) and the formal state law. R. Haglund and R. Sannerholm, '*Comparative Law and Legal Development: Report of a Workshop Held in Garrowe, Puntland*' (Örebro University, 2003) on file with the author.

resort to customary and informal extra-judicial mechanisms for settling disputes and arranging their affairs.[37]

Finally, crisis states share, together with the rest of the community of developing countries, the general problems of severely constrained human and material resources, politicisation of the justice system; several laws that are not applied, lack of educated and adequately trained legal professionals, and a low level of access to justice. In times of conflict and prolonged insecurity, these characteristics become more acute problems. A low access to justice becomes no access to justice, several laws not applied turn into laws not applied at all, and a politicisation of the justice system, rule *by* law and not rule *of* law, eventually becomes rule by the gun.

Considering the fact that conflict is caused by a number of intertwined factors (from human rights abuses to widespread corruption) and considering that conflict creates a rule of law deficit in both the legal and administrative sectors, it is rather surprising that the majority of rule of law programmes and projects implemented in post-war societies has a tendency to focus almost exclusively on criminal justice, while neglecting the broader role played by law in a reconstruction process.

4. The Model Rule of Law in Statebuilding

Do we really need to discuss the rule of law? Is it not enough to act on the basis of 'I know it when I see it?' There are two compelling reasons for why a discussion and examination of the concept of rule of law in post-conflict statebuilding is warranted, indeed one could even say, urgently needed.

The first one is simply that if the international community is to continue to promote the rule of law as part of a reconstruction strategy, there should be some clear indications as to what, more precisely, is meant by the rule of law, beyond references to general goods such as human rights and democracy. Scholars and practitioners alike frequently criticise 'rule of law promoters' for lacking a precise definition of what, exactly, they are promoting.[38] Not knowing what to promote, yet still doing it, leads to confusion, contradictory results and a conflict of values, the argument goes.[39]

---

[37] Legal Vice Presidency, World Bank, '*Sierra Leone: Legal and Judicial Sector Assessment*', May 2004, 4.

[38] M. Rosenfeld, 'The Rule of Law and the Legitimacy of Constitutional Democracy' (2001) 74 *S. Cal. L. Rev.* at 1308 arguing that while there is no consensus of what the rule of law stand for there is reasonable consensus for what it stands against; G. P. Fletcher, *Basic Concepts of Legal Thought* (1996) 12 '*we are never quite sure what we mean by 'rule of law*'; and J. Shklar, 'Political Theory and the Rule of Law' in A. C. Hutchinson and P. Monahan, (eds.) *The Rule of Law: Ideal or Ideology* (1987) at 1 saying that rule of law may very well have become meaningless because of '*ideological abuse and over-use*'.

[39] R. Kleinfeld, 'Competing Definitions of the Rule of Law' in Carothers, *op. cit.*, fn. 6. p. 32 '*read any set of articles discussing the rule of law, and the concept emerges looking like the proverbial blind man's elephant – a trunk to one person, a tail to another.*'

74   *Richard Sannerholm*

Secondly, it is not only that discussing the rule of law will enhance the quality of communication between donor agencies involved in promoting the concept, and between the donor community and recipient states, which makes an examination of the concept warranted, it is also the fact that the rule of law sometimes has legal consequences. The EU in its external relations under the Cotonou agreement has included the rule of law as one criterion which the partner countries need to fulfil. Actions in violation of the rule of law can thus result in certain measures such as withholding funds and freezing assets. In order for these measures to be implemented in the event of a breach of agreement there must be a rather specific understanding of what the rule of law is.

But it is not at all clear what the rule of law means, what the concept includes, or in this context, what the rule of law does for socio-political and socio-economic development.[40] Instead, the axiom frequently referred to – that rule of law is necessary for economic development and democracy – is not, when held up to close light 'as axiomatic as it may first appear'.[41] Furthermore, the assumed causal link between enhanced rule of law and increased human rights protection is shaky, at best.[42] Instead it seems as if the rule of law is promoted on the basis of rather general assumptions and loose theoretical grounds.[43]

One way of approaching rule of law is to see it as a way of organising the state, how the state's relationship to its citizens should best be regulated, and how the relationship between the citizens should be regulated.[44] The rule of law, writes Susan Rose-Ackerman, has two fundamentally different aspects; 'the first sets legal limits, both civil and criminal, on private interactions. The second imposes limits on the political regime'.[45] In a somewhat scaled-down version, the rule of law could be presented as constituted by a set of principles: legality, legal certainty,

---

[40] First, it should be noted that rule of law has originated in two different legal 'families'. We have the Continental-European concept of 'Rechtsstaat' and the Common-law concept of 'rule of law'. Furthermore, rule of law is often within the academic discourse separated into a material and a formal connotation, where the former emphasises the formal procedures of the legal system without giving much attention to the substance, contrary to the latter where not merely the formal requirements should be fulfilled but also some form of political morality in terms of 'just', 'equitable' and 'fair' laws. For further reading, to name but a few, see, F. A. Hayek, *The Road to Serfdom* (1986); J. Raz, *The Authority of Law: Essays on Law and Morality* (Oxford University Press: New York, 1979); I. Shapiro (ed.), *The Rule of Law* (1994); B. Tamanaha, *On the Rule of Law: History, Politics, Theory* (2004); J. M. Maravall and A. Przeworski, *Democracy and the Rule of Law* (2003).

[41] Carothers, *op. cit.*, fn. 6, p. 17.

[42] See R. Peerenboom, 'Rule of Law and Human Rights: What's the Relationship?' (2005) *36 Georgetown Journal of International Law*, 36:1.

[43] Rule of law assistance is not a field, according to Carothers, 'if one considers a requirement for such a designation to include a well-grounded rationale, a clear understanding of the essential problem, a proven analytical method and an understanding of results achieved'. *Op. cit.*, fn. 6, p. 28.

[44] S. Rose-Ackerman, 'Establishing the Rule of Law', in Rotberg (ed.), *When States Fail: Causes and Consequences* (2004) 183.

[45] *Ibid.*, p. 182.

separation of powers and equality before the law with the primary purposes of protecting against arbitrary rule and guiding human conduct.[46] But this minimal or modest conception has scant support among international agencies, where emphasis tends to be placed on the rule of law as a concept intertwined with human rights, justice and democracy.[47]

The Secretary-General has attempted to establish a common rule of law definition, which will guide the work of the UN's various agencies, programmes and departments. Rule of law, it is said:

> . . . refers to a principle of governance in which all persons, institutions and entities, public and private, including the State itself, are accountable to laws that are publicly promulgated, equally enforced and independently adjudicated and which are consistent with international human rights norms and standards. It requires as well, measures to ensure adherence to the principles of supremacy of law, equality before the law, accountability to the law, fairness in the application of the law, separation of powers, participation in decision-making, legal certainty, avoidance of arbitrariness and procedural and legal transparency.[48]

This definition integrates both procedural (formal) and substantive (material) principles.[49] In addition, the definition also advocates for rule of law as an essential part of good governance through the reference to accountability, transparency and participation in decision making.[50] This definition will, without doubt, gain support and approval among many of the various actors involved in rule of law promotion, in the sense that it represents the general idea of rule of law as

---

[46] See, e.g. J. Raz, *The Authority of Law: Essays on Law and Morality* (1979); O. Kirchheimer, 'The Rechtsstaat as Magic Wall' in F. S. Burin and K. L. Shell (eds.), *Politics, Law, and Social Change: Selected Essays of Otto Kirchheimer* (1969); and R. H. Fallon 'The Rule of Law' as a Concept in Constitutional Discourse' (1997) *97 Colum. L. Rev.* 97:1.

[47] See, e.g. the Organisation for Cooperation and Security in Europe (OSCE) stating more than a decade ago in the seminal document Conference on Security and Cooperation in Europe that rule of law 'does not mean merely a formal legality which assumes regularity and consistency in the achievement and enforcement of democratic order, but justice based on the recognition and full acceptance of the supreme value of the human personality and guaranteed by institutions providing a framework for its fullest expression.' *Copenhagen Meeting of the Conference of the Human Dimension of the OCSE*, (1990) 1 (2).

[48] *Op. cit.,* fn. 2, para. 6.

[49] As a contrast, see the World Bank's definition saying that the rule of law prevails where: 'the government is itself bound by the law; every person is treated equally under the law; the human dignity of each individual is recognised and protected by law; and justice is accessible to all'. The Legal Vice Presidency, World Bank, *'Legal and Judicial Reform: Strategic Directions'* (2004) 1.

[50] See the Human Rights Commission's definition of good governance in Resolution 2000/64, 66th meeting, 26 April, 2000.

76 *Richard Sannerholm*

something good, something linked to democracy, something linked to human rights, and something linked to good governance.

But all good things do not go together, and it is evident that rule of law, following this definition, will be painstakingly difficult to operationalise and implement in post-conflict societies. High ambitions and soaring expectations are at the heart of the problem with the rule of law menu – too many 'goods' have been associated with rule of law that it is difficult to define, in concrete terms, what it will take to realise them.

What rule of law reformers have done to a large extent is modelled the rule of law menu based on their own national experiences and tried to mimic the conditions in their own legal contexts. Rwanda is a case in point. Following the post-genocide intervention the international community focused on a number of training programmes for the few remaining legal professionals in the fledging justice sector. Most of the international experts, however, came from common law backgrounds with little or no understanding of Rwanda's legal tradition, which is a mix of French and Belgian civil law which effectively hindered much of the rule of law reforms carried out. [51]

The rule of law menu tends to look like a checklist of what institutions it is assumed that rule of law needs in order to exist instead of asking the most basic question of why the rule of law is needed in the first place.[52] Moreover, the international promotion of rule of law has a strong tilt towards the function of regulating the relationship *between* citizens; rule of law has come to be equated with law and order, security, and low levels of crime, and the concept of security sector reform is sometimes used interchangeably with rule of law reform.[53] There is also a strong moral and political imperative to focus on human rights in relation

[51] C. Mburu, 'Challenges Facing Legal and Judicial Reform in Post-Conflict Environments: Case Study from Rwanda and Sierra Leone' *World Bank Conference on Empowerment, Security and Opportunity Through Law and Justice*, July 8–12, 2001, 29

[52] See generally, Kleinfeld, *op. cit.*, fn. 39.

[53] See *Making Standards Work: Fifty Years of Standard-setting in Crime Prevention and Criminal Justice*, Eleventh United Nations Congress on Crime Prevention and Criminal Justice, UN Doc. A/CONF.203/8, 1 April 2005, '. . . policing interventions in post-conflict societies should be viewed as an integral part of the rule-of-law continuum, coupled with parallel interventions in other components of the criminal justice system such as the judiciary and penal systems', para. 42. See also *A More Secure World, op. cit.*, fn. 21, paras. 229–230. The writing in this field has expanded rapidly. Presented here are some of the contributions that describe the present rule of law paradigm. M. Plunkett, 'Rebuilding the Rule of Law', in W. Maley, C. Sampford, and R. Thakur, *From Civil Strife to Civil Society: Civil and Military Responsibility in Disrupted States* (2003) 207–228; F. M. Lorenz, 'Civil-Military Cooperation in restoring the Rule of Law: Case Studies from Mogadishu to Mitrovica', in M. C. Bassiouni, *Post-Conflict Justice*, (2002) 829–849; R. Huang, 'Securing the Rule of Law: Assessing International Strategies for Post-Conflict Criminal Justice', *International Peace Academy*, Policy Paper, November 2005; and Center for Strategic and International Studies and the Association of the United States Army, 'Post-Conflict Reconstruction: Task Framework', May 2002; and Stromseth et. al., *op. cit.*, fn. 5.

to rule of law and, most actors identify rule of law as primarily a system for the protection of civil and political rights.

The rule of law template's preoccupation with criminal justice and human rights is a stark contrast to lessons learned from governance reforms and development aid in post-conflict reconstruction, where emphasis is placed on supporting war-torn societies' ability to perform certain limited functions such as protecting people from harm and to provide an economic framework in which people are capable to support themselves.[54] The more modest, but also more practically attuned policy of governance reforms in post-conflict societies is most clearly expressed by the UK's Department for International Development (DfID) and its 'good enough governance' strategy.[55] This strategy focuses on the main causes of instability, the main capacities of the state, and the accountability and legitimacy of the state, while avoiding reforms that are too ambitious for the implementation capacity of the post-conflict society.[56]

An illustrative example of how rule of law is equated primarily with law and order and human rights is the United Nations Development Programme (UNDP) project in Somalia, 'Role of Law and Security Programme' (ROLS), established in 1997.[57] The 'rule of law component' has three focal areas, the judiciary, law enforcement and human rights. These three elements, it is said, constitute a holistic and integrated approach to strengthening the emergence of rule of law in Somalia 'working by supporting the development of a transparent and independent judicial system that respects human rights and serves the people in a just and equitable manner'.[58] While lack of access to justice is a real problem in Somalia, in particular for vulnerable groups, land rights and grazing rights are other major problems from a subsistence perspective, while obstruction of justice by war-lords turned self-appointed local 'administrators' is an even greater problem. The case of Somalia highlights the fact that not all work to reform the legal sector should be labelled as rule of law reform, irrespective of whatever epithet donor agencies use.[59]

The dilemma with the discourse on rule of law in post-conflict societies is that while the present paradigm makes a correct assessment of the needs in post-conflict societies, it is also off the mark. War-torn societies are in need of justice triad reconstruction featuring criminal law reform, judges educated in gender sensitivity and an adequately trained police, yet there is also a need to expand the rule of law focus and bridge security and development perspectives,

---

[54] See *e.g.* 'OECD-DAC Principles for Good International Engagement in Fragile States' *OECD-DAC Draft Paper*, DCD 8/Rev2 (2005).

[55] DfID 'Why we need to work more effectively in fragile states' (January 2005). <http://www.dfid.gov.uk/pubs/files/fragilestates-paper.pdf> accessed 2006-03-23

[56] *Ibid.*, p. 20.

[57] UNDP, 'Role of Law and Security (ROLS) Programme' (2003). (On file with the author.)

[58] *Ibid.*, p. 1.

[59] Kleinfeld, *op. cit.*, fn. 39, p. 50ff, discussing the problems of a purely institutional approach to rule of law reform.

78   *Richard Sannerholm*

and it is necessary to focus more clearly on rule of law as a way of imposing both legal limits on the state and for enhancing law's capacity to actually guide human conduct to create an enabling environment for recovery.

This means that rule of law could be seen as encompassing much more than the present focus. Besides reforming the judiciary, bar associations, constitutions and the criminal law system, in order to remedy violations of civil and political rights, it could also encompass administrative and commercial law reform and activities to fight corruption to redress economic and social rights and ensure the principle of legality. The predominant focus on criminal justice and the judiciary is, as one commentator has put it, analogous to what the public health field would look like if it mainly focused on urban hospitals and the doctors staffing them, and ignored health nurses and other health workers.[60] Focusing on only one sector of the legal and administrative system tends to create a 'dualistic development of the justice system'[61] where investments in criminal justice and the judiciary gain momentum while corruption, administrative inertia and a low level of access become the norm in other sectors.

5. Three Critical Capacities: Reforming Laws, Enhancing Adjudicative Capacities and Supporting Law Enforcement and Human Rights Protection

The international community has identified institutional reform and law reform as the central components for a post-conflict statebuilding strategy. The institutions most often considered for reform, in a roughly descending order of importance, are the judiciary, police, national human rights commissions, correctional centres and prisons, and other agencies and departments of the state. In the following sections, three critical capacities of the present rule of law template – reforming laws, enhancing adjudication, and human rights protection and police reform – will be examined. These three broad categories exemplify the content of the current rule of law template, and some of the main methods of implementation.

The issue of both law reform and institutional building has frequently been approached as a technical or practical problem translated into refurbishing courthouses or importing 'good laws'. But the problem lies elsewhere. As noted by the Secretary-General in relation to Sierra Leone, courthouses and prison facilities have been built or renovated throughout the country, but 'progress has been slow in addressing such problems as undue delays in the trial and adjudication of cases and the lack of judicial personnel'.[62] Any type of externally promoted rule of law reform is, above all, a matter of enhancing capacity and changing behaviour, and as such, is more political than legal-technical in nature.

---

[60] S. Golub, 'A House Without a Foundation' in Carothers, *op. cit.*, fn. 6, p. 106.
[61] G. O'Donnell, 'Why the Rule of Law Matters', (2004) 15 *Journal of Democracy* 40.
[62] *Op. cit.*, fn. 24, para. 21.

A. Reforming Laws

Law reform has been one of the top priorities in justice system reconstruction in post-war states.[63] Law reform means providing technical assistance and legal advisory services to governments, assisting them in ratifying or acceding to international conventions, and assisting legislatures in drafting new legislation. Predominately, the reform efforts relate to criminal law reform, criminal procedure law reform, the legal framework for the judiciary and constitution making. Laws relating to citizenship and elections are also frequently adopted in the initial stages of post-conflict reconstruction.

International human rights standards and instruments play a pivotal role in law reform from two perspectives. First of all, human rights treaties are often used as a model for a review and overall assessment of the legal framework and, secondly, the United Nations often push hard for the signing and accession to international human rights treaties.[64] As a result, there is an interaction and integration of international standards on human rights into the national legal system during a short period of time.

International human rights law, in addition to United Nations norms and standards[65] is perceived to be 'a solid basis for guidance' and offers both 'orientation and inspiration, as well as an appropriate framework for establishing and re-establishing and strengthening criminal justice systems'.[66] In the same vein,

---

[63] As noted by Strohmeyer, *op. cit.*, fn. 26, p. 58, all other legal and judicial reform activities were surpassed by the need to establish a basic legal framework.

[64] Liberia is a good example. With the support of the United Nations, Liberia signed in 2004, the *Optional Protocol to the Covenant on Civil and Political Rights*; the *Optional Protocol to the Convention on the Elimination of All Forms of Discrimination; and; the International Convention on the Protection of the Rights of All Migrant Workers and Members of their Families*. Liberia also acceded to the following international instruments, *inter alia: Convention Against Torture and Other Cruel, Inhumane or Degrading Treatment or Punishment*; the *Convention on the Reduction of Statelessness; the United Nations Convention Against Transnational Organised Crime*; the *Protocol to Prevent, Suppress and Punish Trafficking in Persons, Especially Women and Children*, the *Protocol Against the Smuggling of Migrants by Land, Sea and Air*; the *Protocol Against the Illicit Manufacturing of and Trafficking in Firearms, their Parts and Components and Ammunition*; the *Basel Convention on the Control of Transboundary Movements of Hazardous Wastes and their Disposal*; and the *Rotterdam Convention on the Prior Informed Consent Procedure for Certain Hazardous Chemicals and Pesticides in International Trade*. See *Fifth Progress Report on the United Nations Mission in Liberia* UN Doc. S/2004/972, 17 December 2004.

[65] See, *e.g. United Nations Basic Principles on the Independence of the Judiciary* Adopted by the Seventh United Nations Congress on the Prevention of Crime and the Treatment of Offenders held at Milan from 26 August to 6 September 1985 and endorsed by General Assembly resolutions 40/32, 29 November 1985 and 40/146, 13 December 1985. See also UN training and instructions manuals, *United Nations Criminal Justice Standards for Peace-keeping Police* (1994); *Manual on the Effective Prevention and investigation of Extralegal, Arbitrary and Summary Executions* (1991) and the *Guidelines for the Conduct of United Nations Inquiries into Allegations of Massacres* (1995).

[66] *Op. cit.*, fn. 53, para. 43.

the Secretary-General has argued that international norms and standards bring a legitimacy that cannot be said to attach to the export of national standards.[67] The UN has also assisted in drafting national plans of action for the protection of human rights in the Democratic Republic of the Congo,[68] Sierra Leone[69] and Liberia.[70]

It is in this context, however, interesting to observe that ratification of human rights treaties and conventions does not seem to imply a stronger protection of human rights, and that it may even be perilous in the short-term period. Post-conflict societies are under an immense pressure to conform to international standards while they at the same time experience serious difficulties of providing basic services.[71]

In crisis states, the first priority is to determine the applicable legal framework. When the UN has assumed an administrative responsibility and exercised executive powers, as in Kosovo and East Timor, the laws in force at the time of the establishment of the respective UN missions were decided to apply, *mutatis mutandis*, insofar they did not conflict with human rights standards.[72] A problem with this approach is that it is rarely supported with instructions of how to assess the compatibility of existing national laws with international human rights. In Kosovo, it was left to the judges to interpret, with the consequence that judges poorly trained in human rights had to interpret 'the penal code or the criminal procedure code through the lens of international human rights instruments . . .'.[73]

Similarly, in Afghanistan, according to the Agreement on Provisional Arrangements in Afghanistan Pending the Re-establishment of Permanent Government Institutions, it was decided that the constitution of 1964 and the existing laws and regulations should continue to apply as long as they did not conflict with the agreement or international treaties to which Afghanistan is a party.[74] Nothing is said, however, about how the interpretation of a conflict of laws should be made, or what the competent authority would be.

Several UN missions in Africa have seen major investment in law reform. While described as 'assistance' to national governments, compared to executive powers in Kosovo and East Timor, and while the issue of law reform has been approached

---

[67] *Op. cit.*, fn. 2, para. 5.

[68] *Report of the Secretary-General on the United Nations Preliminary Deployment in the Democratic Republic of the Congo*, UN Doc. S/1999/790, 15 July 1999, para. 33.

[69] *Op. cit.*, fn. 24, p. 16.

[70] Seventh *Progress Report of the Secretary-General on the United Nations Mission in Liberia*, UN Doc. S/2005/291, 16 June 2005, para 62.

[71] See O. Hathaway, 'Do Human Rights Treaties Make a Difference?' (2001–2002) *111 Yale L. J.* 1935 and C. Keith, 'The United Nations International Covenant on Civil and Political Rights: Does it Make a Difference?', (1999) 36 *J. Peace Research* 95–118.

[72] See UNTAET Regulation 1999/1, Section 3.

[73] *Op. cit.*, fn. 26, p. 59.

[74] *Agreement on Provisional Arrangements in Afghanistan Pending the Re-establishment of Permanent Government Institutions*, Section II (1).

Rule of Law Reforms in Post-Conflict Societies   81

differently in the various missions, the result is that a substantial volume of new laws are drafted under the auspices of international actors.

This is a rarely recognised and discussed aspect of the international involvement in Africa. It reveals a built-in tension in the work of the international community and UN in particular, between policy decisions that reforms should be based on the local context and take local ownership seriously, while the reality for all practical reasons sometimes makes this an unworkable approach. The missions established in Sierra Leone or Liberia, for example, have not been given executive powers. However, the guise of 'assistance' should not steer away from the fact that laws are initiated, drafted and promoted by international experts, with continuing international aid as a levier.

As an example, in the DRC, the UN mission was charged with assisting in the re-establishment of a state based on the rule of law, which led to the establishment of a Joint-Commission with the Transitional Government on essential legislation, including post-transitional constitutional drafting.[75] Similarly in Liberia, the UN assisted the Ministry of Justice in reviewing and redrafting of laws relating to rape, human trafficking, juries and the financial autonomy of the judiciary.[76]

The focus on law reform in post-conflict societies illustrates a tendency of the international community to invest in high-profile areas where tangible results are easily measured. While this is laudable, it should not overshadow the principal problem in all post-conflict and developing countries, namely that of implementation and enforcement and of making laws accessible to the general population.

B. Enhancing Adjudicative Capacity

Next to law reform, strengthening the judicial system is a core objective for peace- and statebuilders. The goal is often presented as one of increasing the professionalism and independence of the judiciary, and to train and capacity-build judges in international human rights law. While judicial reform primarily focuses on the judiciary, this sector of reform also includes assistance to bar associations, public defender programme and prosecutorial services. Judicial reform is said to be one of the most difficult reform areas in which to measure swift progress and change.[77]

A first concern, however, is to address the general lack of qualified personnel. According to a recent assessment of the justice sector in Liberia, only three of the 130 magistrates are lawyers, and out of 300 justices of the peace, whose sole

---

[75] *Third Special Report of the Secretary-General on the United Nations Organisation Mission in the Democratic Republic of the Congo*, UN Doc S/2004/650, 16 August 2004, paras 25–26.

[76] *Op. cit.*, fn. 70, para. 49.

[77] T. Hammarberg and P. Gavian, 'Introduction', in A. H. Henkin (ed.), *Honouring Human Rights: From Peace to Justice* (1998) 11.

82 *Richard Sannerholm*

qualification is literacy, more than half are illiterate.[78] Burundi is another tragic case. Prior to the establishment of a UN mission, the Secretary-General reported that there were only 60 defence lawyers available in the country, most of them located in the capital.[79]

The difficulty of finding legal professionals to serve on the bench has been a problem in all of the recent UN missions in Africa, and it inevitably involves trade-offs on formal requirements and practical experience in the appointment process in order to rectify the judicial deficit. The lack of judges and magistrates not only results in a backlog of cases and prolonged times of detention but also means a total lack of access to justice, particularly in rural areas. In some cases, this problem has been approached by establishing mobile courts as a quick-impact project to deal with the most pressing matters of justice[80] or as in Liberia where the UN established a Case Flow Management Committee to address the issue of pre-trial detainees held for long periods of time.[81]

In Somalia, the UNDP, under the ROLS programme, has engaged in rebuilding the judiciary for nearly 10 years. While several of the reform activities relate to the physical reconstruction including printers, registers, law books and the establishment of an official gazette, much of the judicial reform has also been based on extensive training and 'retraining' of judges through a series of workshops.[82]

It is important to note that the problem with qualified personnel is not isolated to the courts. In a number of countries certain administrative agencies and quasi-judicial bodies are vested with adjudicative powers in commercial and administrative matters. Failure to include this aspect of state services when promoting rule of law can have negative long-term effects. In Sierra Leone, a deficit in regional administrators and other public officials in certain parts of the country resulted in UN personnel acting as *de facto* administrators in providing basic services, although it is not at all clear that this fell squarely within the mandate of the peace operation.[83]

Another element of judicial reform is judicial monitoring by international legal experts, or simply giving advice to courts in particularly sensitive matters. In Côte d'Ivoire, the Rule of Law Unit within United Nations Operation in Côte d'Ivoire provided advice to the local judiciary on issues concerning death in custody,

---

[78] International Crisis Group, 'Liberia: Resurrecting the Justice System', *Africa Report No. 107*, 6 April 2006, 1

[79] *Report of the Secretary-General on Burundi* UN Doc. S/2004/210, 16 March 2004, para. 37.

[80] *Fourth progress report of the Secretary-General on the United Nations Operation in Cote d'Ivoire*, S/2005/186, 18 March 2005, para. 43. This was also done in Kosovo. See the early OSCE report *'Observations and Recommendations of the OSCE Legal System Monitoring Section'* 7 November 1999.

[81] *Sixth progress report of the Secretary-General on the United Nations Mission in Liberia*, UN Doc. S/2005/177, 17 March 2005, para. 36.

[82] See, Judiciary Component in ROLS (2003), *op. cit.,* fn. 57.

[83] Peacekeeping Best Practice Unit, Lessons *Learned From United Nations Peacekeeping in Sierra Leone*, September 2003, 18.

torture or ill treatment, and arbitrary killings where the security forces had been involved. This measure is adopted as a way of strengthening the independence of the judiciary in a short-term build-up phase.[84]

An interesting aspect of judicial reform is that it rarely includes a focus on legal education and support to law schools. In both Liberia and Somalia, the UN mentions briefly the need for supporting legal education; however, the primary focus is on continuing legal training. While quickly finding, training and appointing judges are necessary measures in the short-term period, it does not address a long-term deficit. Furthermore, judicial reform represents to some extent an overzealous belief in judges' inclination to change. In post-conflict situations, where the judiciary sometimes benefit from a lack of supervision and a legal 'chaos', they are not always part of the solution but part of the problem.[85]

Past experiences caution against high expectations on speedy institutional change in the judiciary. Even when judicial reform has received support and commitment from the 'host' state and key actors, there is often a limited capacity to 'absorb' aid in any form due to weakness in the overall state administration. Furthermore, without effective public administration, tax collection and auditing of state funds, corruption flourishes, and even the best-designed institution-building programme within the rule of law template will have difficulties with sustainability.[86] This lack of 'absorptive capacity' fundamentally impedes the sustainability of reform – in any sector.

C. Law Enforcement and Human Rights Protection

Nearly all recently established missions include a police reform component.[87] Reforms in this area usually focus on increasing the number of police officers – as in the DRC where the UN mission, in co-operation with the Ministry of the Interior, has managed to train and deploy 6,000 police officers during 2004–2005 – or of training police officers in human rights and 'democratic policing', restructuring police forces, or reviewing the legal framework governing police work. Another aspect of police reform is 'training of trainers'. In Burundi the UN mission, United Nations Operation in Burundi, established police training centres and during 2004–2005 trained 160 police trainers, in addition to training in investigating and forensic techniques.[88]

---

[84] *Fifth progress report of the Secretary-General on the United Nations Operation in Côte d'Ivoire*, UN doc. S/2005/398, 17 June 2005, para. 46.

[85] See, Kleinfeld, *op. cit.* fn. 39f discussing the built-in tensions in legal and judicial reform.

[86] *Op. cit.*, fn. 77, p. 9.

[87] For a brief review of post-conflict police reform, see Call, 'Challenges in Police Reform: Promoting Effectiveness and Accountability', *International Peace Academy, Policy Report* (2003) and T. H. Tor and E. B. Eide, *Peacebuilding and Police Reform* (2000). UN civilian police units under the Department of Peacekeeping Operations is the principal actor in police reform.

[88] *Fourth report of the Secretary-General on the United Nations Operation in Burundi*, UN doc S/2005/328, 19 May, 2005, para. 25–26.

84 *Richard Sannerholm*

The major challenge in any police reform is to facilitate a change of 'culture and ethos'.[89] Several police forces in post-conflict societies have been part of a repressive regime, and they often suffer from mistrust and lack of confidence from the society in which they operate. In this respect, ensuring that adequate accountability mechanisms are in place is a crucial reform component, along with an appropriate screening and vetting process for those seeking to enrol following disarmament, demobilisation and re-integration activities.[90]

As concerns human rights, one frequently promoted and established institution is national human rights commissions.[91] While their mandate varies in relation to the different context, they are generally set up to monitor the human rights situation, carry out investigation and at times receive complaints from citizens, acting as a sort of ombudsperson institution. This is illustrated in the mandate for the Commission established in Afghanistan under the Bonn Agreement, whose responsibilities include human rights monitoring, investigation of violations of human rights, and the development of domestic human rights institutions.[92] Human rights commissions have also been established or planned for, with the assistance of the UN, in Liberia, DRC, and Burundi.

In Sierra Leone, a Human Rights Commission was established in 2004.[93] While it follows the general functions of other Commissions established, it has retained a rather wide set of powers, among others, the right to enforce the attendance of witnesses and examining them on oath, compel the production of documents, the power to issue orders to enforce its decisions, and to refer to the High Court for contempt an individual who refuses to comply with a decision.[94] Although an important step in creating a formalised national capacity to address human rights issues, the results have been modest in terms of effectively promoting and defending human rights.[95]

A large part of the human rights promotion under rule of law takes the form of training. A good example is the workshop organised by the UN in the DRC where 130 lawyers and magistrates were 'informed' about the Convention on the Elimination of All Forms of Discrimination Against Women in order to 'help ensure that the rights of women are effectively promoted and protected by the Congolese courts.'[96] While an important aspect of institution-building, it is unclear what the effect of training programmes has in the long-term perspective, and it is

---

[89] O'Neill, 'Police Reform in Post-conflict Societies: What We Know and What We Still Need to Know', *International Peace Academy, Policy Paper*, April 2005, 2.

[90] Call, *op. cit.*, fn. 87, p. 5.

[91] Generally following the *UN Principles Relating to the Status of National Institutions for the Promotion and Protection of Human Rights* (annex) Commission on Human Rights, 52nd meeting, March 3, 1992 Session, E/CN.4/1992/84. See also, *op. cit.*, fn. 2, para. 31.

[92] *Agreement on Provisional Arrangements in Afghanistan*, Section III C (6).

[93] *The Human Rights Commission of Sierra Leone Act*, No. 9, 26 August 2004.

[94] *Ibid.*, 8 (1) a–c.

[95] *Op. cit.*, fn. 77, p. 13.

[96] *Twentieth Report of the Secretary-General on the United Nations Mission in the Democratic Republic of the Congo*, UN Doc. S/2005(832), 28 December 2005, para. 45.

not altogether clear what it actually means in situations where judges continue to work unpaid, or where executive interference in the judiciary is still strong.

Finally, much of the human rights approach in statebuilding also includes efforts to build civil society institutions. This means supporting coalition building and enhancing the capacity of local human rights groups. An evocative case in point is from Côte d'Ivoire where the UN Mission, with funding from the Office of the High Commission for Human Rights, started a programme to strengthen national human rights groups and their capacity in raising the awareness of human rights among the population.[97] A similar approach was taken in Sierra Leone.[98] The UN agencies in co-operation with the Government of Sierra Leone also launched a nationwide consultation campaign in 2004 with the ambition to formulate national legislation for the implementation of the Convention on the Elimination of All forms of Discrimination Against Women, in addition to training of some 3,587 members of the civil society. The end-result of these activities is presented as a way to 'provide these groups with grounded knowledge of human rights principles as part of a gradual handover of the responsibility to monitor, promote and report on the human rights situation in Sierra Leone'.[99]

The focus on 'bottom-up' approaches such as the enhancement of civil society is laudable. Besides the fact that it is necessary in order to 'plant' reforms in the society, it also provides incentives for national ownership and participation in decision-making. However, as with the training of legal professionals, it remains unclear what effect building human rights advocacy groups will have in the long-term.

6. Alternatives to the Rule of Law Template: Beyond Criminal Justice

Although not yet clearly formulated in policy, there is a tendency among the actors of the international community predominantly involved in rebuilding crisis states to move beyond the narrow rule of law template and also include governance and economic management issues.[100] International assistance to Liberia illustrates, in this regard, an interesting example of this emerging paradigmatic shift.[101]

---

[97] *Seventh Progress Report of the Secretary-General on the United Nations Operation in Côte d'Ivoire*, UN Doc.,S/2006/2, 3 January 2006, para 32.

[98] *Op. cit.,* fn. 83, p. 56.

[99] *Op. cit.,* fn. 23, para. 65.

[100] See, for example, the comprehensive reform of Iraq's commercial law undertaken by the Coalition Provisional Authority (CPA) in just over a year of administration. T. W. Kassinger and D. J. Williams, 'Commercial Law Reform Issues in the Reconstruction of Iraq', (2004–05) 33 *Ga. J. Int'l & Comp. L.* 217.

[101] For two good descriptions of the crisis and conflict in Liberia see, F. Aboagye and A. M. S. Bah (eds.), *A Tortuous Road to Peace: The Dynamics of Regional, UN and International Humanitarian Interventions in Liberia* (2005) and A. Adebajo, *Liberia's Civil War: Nigeria, Economic and Regional Security in West Africa* (2002).

86   *Richard Sannerholm*

The present international involvement in Liberia is based on the resolution adopted by the Security Council in 2003,[102] following the signing of *Accra Comprehensive Peace Agreement* (ACPA) which was facilitated by the Economic Community of West African States (ECOWAS).[103] Among other reform activities, ACPA called for a restructuring of the Liberian police force,[104] establishment of an independent national commission on human rights[105] and a *Truth and Reconciliation Commission*,[106] and the reorganisation of the *National Elections Commission*.[107] The agreement also called for the establishment of a *Governance Reform Commission*,[108] with the objective of securing good governance in Liberia and a *Contract and Monopolies Commission*[109] (neither with executive authority nor enforcement capacities) for supervising all budgetary and other financial handling of the transitional government.

For nearly 3 years the international community has invested heavily in rule of law reforms in Liberia. It stands to be argued that after the international assistance to legal and judicial reform activities in Kosovo and East Timor, Liberia is the one place where the rule of law menu has received the strongest attention.

Nevertheless, and notwithstanding the creation of a special rule of law component within United Nations Mission in Liberia (UNMIL) (comprising a *Legal and Judicial System Support Division, Corrections Unit, Civil Affairs Section, Civil Police Mission, Human Rights Protection Service* and a *Gender Office*), the most basic and essential component of rule of law – ensuring a law abiding state – has failed to take root. One explanation is simply that it has never really been the primary focus of international assistance to Liberia.[110]

---

[102]   SC Res. 1509, UNSCOR, 4830th mtg., S/RES/1509, (19 September 2003). The resolution stipulates that UNMIL should, in regard to rule of law, 'assist the transitional government in conjunction with ECOWAS and other international partners in developing a strategy to consolidate governmental institutions, including a national legal framework and judicial and correctional institutions' para. 3 (q).

[103]   *Comprehensive Peace agreement Between the Government of Liberia and the Liberians United For Reconciliation and Democracy (LURD) and theMovement for Democracy in Liberia (MODEL) and Political Parties*, Accra, 18 August 2003, (hereinafter, ACPA). The Liberian Reconstruction Conference in 2003, which produced the *Results Focused Transitional Framework* also included a focus on governance and good economic management.

[104]   ACPA, Article VIII.

[105]   *Ibid.,* Article XII (2a).

[106]   *Ibid.,* Article XIII.

[107]   *Ibid.,* Article XVIII (2a).

[108]   *Ibid.,* Article XVI.

[109]   *Ibid.,* Article XVII.

[110]   This could be seen as a consequence of the absence of a broader strategy for post-conflict reconstruction on behalf of the UN peace operation in place in Liberia. See, R. Dwan & L. Bailey Liberia's Governance and Economic Management Assistance Programme (GEMAP): How it came into being, what it is and what we might learn from the process, A Joint review by the Department of Peacekeeping Operations' Peacekeeping Best Practices Section and the World Bank's Fragile States

Rule of Law Reforms in Post-Conflict Societies 87

The rule of law reforms implemented are more focused on high-profile areas such as ensuring women's rights, training judges in human rights sensitivity, and ensuring the rights of juvenile offenders. They are generally not concerned with how the emerging state in Liberia should be organised, or how the relationship between the state and citizens should best be regulated, outside the realm of criminal justice and civil and political rights.

The lack of a strategy for legal, judicial and administrative reforms aimed at securing the principle of legality in the transitional government, and for ensuring transparency, good governance and accountability mechanisms has severely undermined the peace process. [111]

In 2004, the European Commission and ECOWAS conducted financial audits and investigations into several state-owned enterprises and other revenue generating agencies. Based on the results of the audits the European Commission concluded that 'theft and fraud within the transitional government were so great that they were sabotaging any possibility for durable peacebuilding'.[112] The audits met resistance, in particular, the investigation by ECOWAS on allegations of corruption in state-owned enterprises, and several members of the Transitional National Government of Liberia attempted to obstruct the investigations.[113] The Liberian Institute for Certified Accountants filed a writ of prohibition to the Supreme Court, in order to restrain public officials from co-operating with ECOWAS and the EC.[114] The Supreme Court, however, refused the writ after civil society groups filed an *amicus* brief on behalf of the investigations.[115] Previous pressure from the international donor community had resulted in the formation of a *Task Force on Corruption* and a *Cash Management Committee*.[116] The Security Council had on several occasions, acting under Chapter VII of the UN Charter, adopted resolutions for the freezing of assets and supervision of the trade of diamonds, but with limited results.[117] Similarly, the European Council

---

Group, April 2006, p. 9 <http://siteresources.worldbank.org/INTLICUS/Resources/DPKOWBGEMAPFINAL.pdf>

[111] See International Crisis Group, 'Liberia's Elections: Necessary but Not Sufficient', *Africa Report No. 98*, September 2005, 7 at 15, noting that 'petty corruption manifests itself at the most ordinary level in Liberia' and that reform is needed of all levels of the state bureaucracy.

[112] The audits involved the following revenue generating agencies: Liberia Petroleum Refining Company; Forestry Development Agency; National Port Authority; Roberts International Airport; Bureau of Maritime Affairs; and Central Bank of Liberia. See also the report of UNDP, '*The Dimensions of Corruption in Post-War Liberia: Rebuilding the Pillars of Integrity and Strengthening Capacities*' (2006).

[113] *Report of the Secretary-General pursuant to Security Council resolution 1579 (2004) regarding Liberia*, UN doc S/2005/376, 7 June 2005, para. 36.

[114] *Op. cit.*, fn. 70, para. 8.

[115] *Op. cit.*, fn. 110, p. 5.

[116] *Op. cit.*, fn. 81, para. 4.

[117] See, SC Res.1521, UNSCOR, 4890th mtg., S/RES/1521 (22 December 2003); SC Res. 1532, UNSCOR, 4925th mtg., S/RES/1532 (12 March 2004); and SC Res. 1607, UNSCOR, 5208th mtg., S/RES/1607 (21 June 2005).

88   *Richard Sannerholm*

adopted certain measures against Liberia already in 2003 following reports that the government of Liberia failed to live up to the criteria of human rights protection, rule of law and good governance as stipulated in the *Cotonou Agreement*.[118] None of these measures, however, were sufficient in tackling the rule of law deficit within the transitional government.

As a response, a congregation of donors known as the *International Contact Group for Liberia* (ICGL) proposed a *Governance and Economic Management Assistance Program* (GEMAP).[119] This agreement, signed between the *Transitional National Government of Liberia* (TNGL) and the ICGL on 9 September 2005, represents an intrusive and radical form of international control and supervision over a number of economic and governance issues. It can be seen as a new form of statebuilding, where substantial focus is placed on rule of law within a broader context of public sector and economic management reform.

The main objective of the agreement is to improve governance and enhance transparency and accountability, by targeting revenue collection, expenditure controls and government procurement practices. These issues played a central role before and during the civil war. 'Bad' economic governance and lack of accountability eroded the capacity of the Liberian state and fuelled violent competition over lucrative natural resources.

GEMAP includes six components: financial management and accountability; improving budgeting and expenditure management; improving procurement practices and granting of concessions; establishing effective processes to control corruption; supporting key institutions; and capacity building.[120] The implementation of the agreement is the responsibility of the *Economic Governance Steering Committee* (EGSC) which consists of representatives from the Liberian government, civil society and international donors. The steering committee is chaired by the Head of State of Liberia.

In the following text, aspects of procurement practices, the fight against corruption, support to key institutions and progress and challenges under the first year of implementation will be discussed.

---

[118] *Council Decision of 25 August 2003 adopting measures concerning Liberia under Article 96 of the ACP-EC Partnership Agreement* (2003/631/EC). The adoption of certain measures was lifted in 2006 through Council Decision (2006/450/EC).

[119] Communiqué, Meeting of the International Partners on Economic Governance, *Follow-up to Liberia's Results Focused Transition Framework Annual Technical Meeting*, 11 May 2005. *Governance and Economic Management Assistance Program* done at Monrovia on 9 September [hereinafter, GEMAP]. In the preamble it is said the ICGL 'share serious concerns regarding Liberia's economic governance' and that 'after more than 18 months of intensive technical and policy advice and non budgetary financial support aimed at strengthening capacity, and following a strong initial start to address these areas, there is still widespread weak fiscal management . . .', 1. GEMAP will run for 36 months, unless the completion Point under the Enhanced Highly Indebted Poor Countries Initiative has not been reached.

[120] *GEMAP* pp. 1–4.

A. *Improving Procurement Practices and Granting of Concessions*

A striking feature of GEMAP is that several components call for the deployment of international experts with binding co-signature authority. No major transactions can take place without being examined by both a Liberian manager and an international counterpart.[121] For example, under the financial management and accountability component, an international expert will have co-signing authority over matters relating to banking and for ensuring that internal controls and audits are carried out according to established rules.[122] International experts will also have co-signing authority on financial management practices in various state owned enterprises. ECOWAS originally proposed that international judges would be brought in to sit on the Liberian bench. This was rejected by the TNGL as being too intrusive and sovereignty offensive, and the proposal was withdrawn.[123]

The reform of the procurement practices and granting of concessions has to be viewed in light of the fact that Liberia is not a poor country; on the contrary it is rich in natural resources such as timber and diamonds. But, through endemic mismanagement and bad governance, substantial portions of Liberia's resources have been lost. Subsequently, this component of GEMAP calls for increasing the transparency in public procurement by making it mandatory to list bidding parties, install open and competitive bidding and to publish results of public tenders.[124] Concessions in the past have not been subject to external control, and have fallen short of both national laws and international standards on public procurement.[125]

A procurement law has been passed and came into effect on 1 January 2006. Liberia will also join the *Kimberly Process Certification Scheme* and the *Extractive Industries Initiative* (EITI).[126] Reforming the procurement and concessions practices, and reviewing the legislation in this area, is a necessary strategy in order to guarantee that public assets are not used in political contests or for personal gains. A *Contract and Concession Review Committee* has also been established with a mandate to review contracts entered into by the TNGL between October 2003 and January 2006. The objective is to see if contracts have been written in accordance with the economic interest of the people based on four

---

[121] This has been put in place in the following institutions: Ministry of Finance; Central Bank of Liberia; Bureau of Budget; Ministry of Lands, Mines and Energy; National Port Authority; Robert's International Airport; Liberia Petroleum Refinery Cooperation; and the Forestry Development Agency.

[122] *GEMAP* p. 3. It is stressed throughout the agreement that the use of international experts is an interim measure, and that sustainability in reforms can only be achieved through national ownership and capacity.

[123] *Op. cit.,* fn. 111, p. 14.

[124] GEMAP, p. 4.

[125] See *e.g. World Trade Organisation, Agreement on Public Procurement,* Annex 4 Plurilateral Trade Agreements, The Uruguay Round Agreements, Marrakech 1994.

[126] The Kimberly Process Certification Scheme was created in 2002 and consists of 45 states and organisations who have met the minimum standards of the certification scheme which includes internal controls and certification of all shipments of rough diamonds. See <www.kimberlyprocess.com.>

90   *Richard Sannerholm*

principles; the method of procurement; the appropriateness of the contracts; the performance of the contracts and; their economic value.[127]

B. Establishing Effective Processes to Control Corruption

The Liberian justice system has been severely damaged by the long civil war. One fundamental implication resulting from Charles Taylor's rule is rampant corruption in the judiciary and frequent executive interference. Thus, the possibility of accountability mechanisms, judicial review and means of redress against government actions has been limited, at best.

GEMAP proposes in this regard, the establishment of an effective and independent *Anti-Corruption Commission* to assist in the investigation of fraud and corruption and other economic crimes.[128] The Commission, consisting of both Liberian and international experts, will have full prosecutorial powers. In addition, an independent prosecutor will be installed to work on corruption charges, and international technical assistance will be provided to enhance the investigative capacity of the prosecutorial office.[129]

The Commission is mandated to investigate cases brought before it by any person or group, including donor organisations who suspect that their funds and assistance programmes have not been properly used by the government. This measure will require the passing of appropriate legislation on the *Anti-corruption Commission*, the independent prosecutor as well as a review of the existing legal framework on corruption and economic crimes in Liberia.[130]

The international influence is notable in the anti-corruption strategy and 'international legal experts will support and advise the Liberian judiciary in the dispensation of justice, particularly in cases of corruption' in a form of 'co-location programme' where international judges sit with national judges.[131] This falls short of the original proposal by ECOWAS to let international judges dispense justice, but nevertheless represents an intrusive initiative. It can also be discussed what level of *de facto* discretion and independence the Liberian judges will have in relation to international experts 'advising' on the adjudication of high-profile cases.

From a rule of law perspective, this component carries significant weight and importance. Past experience has shown that disregard for the law, and a personalisation of power, is a major impediment on the quality of governance in Liberia, and a constant source of conflict. If holding public office is equated with

---

[127] Economic Governance Steering Committee *'Status Report Year 1'*, December 2006, 8.

[128] GEMAP, p. 4.

[129] *Ibid.*, p. 13. This is a stark contrast to the previous Anti-Corruption Agency established under ACPA, Executive Order No. 6 in June 2005, where no prosecutorial powers were included.

[130] See e.g. the *United Nations Convention Against Corruption*, General Assembly, UN Doc. Resolution A/58/422 (31 October 2003).

[131] GEMAP, p. 14.

massive personal enrichment, with few judicial checks and balances, or few taken seriously, violent competition for political power is never far away. Strengthening the general oversight system including substantial law reform is a considerable move forward in the direction of securing rule of law.

In September 2006, Liberia ratified the UN *Convention against Corruption* and the *African Union Convention on the Prevention and Combating of Corruption*. The conventions provide valuable strategies and instruments which could assist in the anti-corruption strategies under GEMAP. Furthermore, a *Memorandum of Understanding* has been signed between state-owned enterprises and commercial banks in Liberia on measures for the allocation of revenues in openly monitored and specified accounts.

C. Supporting Key Institutions

When it comes to supporting key institutions, the central focus is the *Central Bank*, the *General Auditing Office* and the *Governance Reform Commission*, the latter established under ACPA.

Regarding the *Central Bank*, GEMAP strives to secure the independence provided the Bank in the *New Financial Institutions Act* of 1999 and the *Central Bank of Liberia Act* of 1999. GEMAP also calls for a submission to the Legislative Assembly of a revised act establishing and securing the independence of the *General Auditing Office* independence.

The *Governance Reform Commission*, according to the agreement, will be strengthened along the lines of the ACPA, so that it may function as an Ombudsman, receiving complaints from citizens. The mandate also includes a review of the existing programme of good governance and the development of public sector reform.[132] This measure is important from a rule of law perspective, allowing for citizens to file complaints and address grievances in relation to administrative agencies, and can function as a complement to the *Anti-Corruption Commission*.[133]

The support to key institutions is interlocked with the capacity-building measures provided for by the agreement. Among the primary institutions to receive support under the GEMAP is the judiciary, but capacity building also extends to the civil service, with the need for training of civil servants and development of codes of conduct to strengthen the integrity system in Liberia.

---

[132] ACPA, Article XVI.

[133] A management study by the European Commission undertaken in 2006 proposed the creation of a new body (Good Governance Commission) as a continuation of the Governance Reform Commission. The new body would have the overall responsibility of overseeing the implementation of governance reforms in Liberia. See 'Management Study to Design a Secretariat, Commission or Body Responsible for Leading Good Governance Initiatives and Monitoring Recommended Reform Measures in Liberia' Short Term Consultancy funded by the European Union (ACP LBR 03) *Final Report*, May 2006.

92 *Richard Sannerholm*

D. *Progress under GEMAP and Challenges Ahead*

While the implementation of the agreement has gained momentum and seen some tangible progress, particularly in relation to improved fiscal discipline and increased revenues during 2006, several challenges remain.[134] One overarching challenge is to more closely link GEMAP with other rule of law programmes and projects carried out, principally with the reforms undertaken by UNMIL. As it stands now, UNMIL continues to co-ordinate overall rule of law programmes, and GEMAP has not been incorporated in a more comprehensive rule of law strategy of the UN.

Another challenge relates to the central dilemma of all internationally supported reform programmes: how to ensure sustainability once external support withdraws. The ICGL must balance the need for international supervision and control with local ownership and influence in the programme. The real test for GEMAP is for the Liberian state to continue with reforms, practices and standards after the completion of the agreement.

Finally, the agreement is only nineteen pages long. Considering the extensive scope which GEMAP now covers, much of the details are left to on-going negotiations as the implementation is carried out. With several important measures pending, such as drafting new laws to support the integrity system and the adaptation of the legal framework to the UN and AU conventions against corruption, GEMAP faces an important challenge of communication in order to reach the standards of good governance intrinsic in the agreement. Making the implementation process transparent, inclusive and open to criticism is important from the perspective of legitimacy and national ownership. In light of this, the agreement stands to gain from co-ordinating with UNMIL's overall rule of law reforms in reaching a broader audience considering UNMIL's public outreach activities and extensive training programmes of legal professionals.

7. Conclusion

The present rule of law template is not sufficiently broad to deal with post-conflict reconstruction. While the rule of law template shows progress in the creation of security and law and order, and in the protection of civil and political rights, it has fallen short in ensuring the principle of rule of law in relation to other sectors of the state. The result is widespread corruption and embezzlement of state assets, not just in Liberia but also in Sierra Leone, Burundi and other war-torn societies. This severely undermines states' capacity to implement pro-poor polices and address the deprivation of economic and social rights and is in the long run a threat to sustainable peace. In addition, a system of rule of law requires constant attention and is essentially very expensive to maintain. Failing to direct rule of law reforms to the issue of governance and economic management is therefore inherently

---

[134] EGSC *Status Report: Year 1*, December 2006, 11.

counter-productive. The legal sector cannot be sustained by international aid and assistance.

GEMAP can be seen as a reaction to the failure of the rule of law template to address root causes to conflict and issues, which continues to cause instability. The agreement manages to draw attention to the fact that rule of law promotion cannot follow a pre-fixed institutional template, but that any rule of law strategy must be context specific and holistic in its perception of problems and challenges.

There are, however, several difficulties with the agreement from the perspective of sovereignty that should be acknowledged, in particular, the intrusive measures of providing international experts with a co-signing authority.[135] The International Crisis Group has stressed that the agreement is *sui generis* and should not be seen as a template for other crisis states. The level of 'failure' and the fact that Liberia is resource-rich makes it a unique situation. This is a solid point to make. Nevertheless, it should not exclude the possibility of 'recycling' the general ideas and principles behind the programme. This seems to be the opinion held by the UN, and the Secretary-General has expressed the possibility of using a similar approach in Burundi.[136]

GEMAP manages to bridge security and development perspectives, with rule of law as the nexus. While criminal law reform and human rights promotion should continue to play a central role in the rule of law menu, these efforts should be situated within a broader governance reform strategy.

[135] *Op. cit.,* fn. 111, p. 12ff.
[136] *Op. cit.,* fn. 89, para. 51.

Part II
Europe

[4]

THE GOVERNANCE OF KOSOVO: SECURITY COUNCIL RESOLUTION 1244 AND THE ESTABLISHMENT AND FUNCTIONING OF EULEX

*By Erika de Wet**

I. BACKGROUND

On February 4, 2008, shortly before Kosovo's controversial unilateral secession from Serbia on February 17 of that year,[1] the Council of the European Union (EU) adopted a Joint Action creating the European Union Rule of Law Mission in Kosovo/EULEX (hereinafter EULEX), the largest and most important mission thus far undertaken within the common European foreign and defense policy.[2] Although EULEX is first and foremost a European undertaking, it is also strongly backed by the United States, which agreed to shoulder 25 percent of the operating costs while the remaining costs would be shared by European and other states.[3] In October 2008, the U.S. Department of State further agreed to provide EULEX with eighty police officers and up to eight judges and prosecutors.[4]

EULEX was intended to substitute for the rule-of-law functions of the United Nations Mission in Kosovo (UNMIK), which was created for an open-ended period of time by Security Council Resolution 1244 (1999) under Chapter VII of the United Nations Charter. That resolution effectively transferred all legislative, executive, and judicial matters to the special

---

* Professor of International Constitutional Law, University of Amsterdam; and Extraordinary Professor, North-West University, Potchefstroom campus, and University of Pretoria, South Africa. This contribution forms part of a project of the Netherlands Organization for Scientific Research on the implications of hierarchy in international law for the coherence and legitimacy of international decision making. The author benefited from discussions with Professor Niels Blokker, Mr. Ricardo Gosalbo Bono, Dr. Frederik Naert, Mr. Surya Sinha, and Professor Rüdiger Wolfrum.

[1] *Kosovo Declaration of Independence* (Feb. 17, 2008), 47 ILM 461 (2008), *available at* <http://www.assembly-kosova.org/common/docs/declaration_indipendence.pdf>; Christopher J. Borgen, *Kosovo's Declaration of Independence: Self-Determination, Secession and Recognition,* ASIL INSIGHTS, Feb. 29, 2008, *at* <http://www.asil.org>. The position of the United Nations with respect to the status of Kosovo is one of strict neutrality. By November 2008, Kosovo had been recognized by fifty-two states. Report of the Secretary-General on the United Nations Interim Administration Mission in Kosovo, para. 2, UN Doc. S/2008/692 (Nov. 24, 2008) [hereinafter Nov. S-G Report]; *see also* Daniel Fried, Signing of European Union Rule of Law Mission (EULEX) Agreement (Oct. 22, 2008), *at* <http://2001-2009.state.gov/p/eur/rls/rm/111171.htm>.

[2] Council of the European Union [EU Council], Council Joint Action 2008/124/CFSP, 2008 O.J. (L 42) 92 [hereinafter Joint Action]; *see also* Daniel Fried, Kosovo: The Balkans' Moment of Truth? (Mar. 4, 2008) (testimony before the Senate Committee on Foreign Relations), *at* <http://2001-2009.state.gov/p/eur/rls/rm/101722.htm>.

[3] Article 13 of the Joint Action, *supra* note 2, explicitly provides for the participation of third states in EULEX.

[4] Fried, *supra* note 2.

84   THE AMERICAN JOURNAL OF INTERNATIONAL LAW   [Vol. 103:83

representative of the United Nations secretary-general for Kosovo (the special representative).[5] However, although the final say in all areas of governance was vested in the special representative, the execution of many such functions was delegated to other organizations, notably the Organization for Security and Cooperation in Europe (OSCE), the United Nations High Commissioner for Refugees (UNHCR), and the European Union.

UNMIK itself was primarily responsible for restoring the health, educational, and other public services; exercising police functions in the short term and developing the Kosovar Police Service in the long term; and rebuilding the judicial and correctional system (Pillar I).[6] The OSCE undertook the tasks of promoting democratization and human rights, as well as capacity building in these areas (Pillar II).[7] UNHCR assumed responsibility for the coordination of humanitarian assistance to the many displaced Kosovars (Pillar III). Finally, the European Union took charge of economic reconstruction, including the coordination of international financial assistance and the reorganization of trade, currency, and banking matters (Pillar IV).[8]

The nature and scope of the civil administration that had to be undertaken in Kosovo therefore implied that even though the special representative formally had the last word in relation to all matters of governance, in practice he relied heavily on the support and cooperation of various states and international organizations.[9] Over time, the different organizations had to adjust their roles to the changes that were taking place on the ground. For example, whereas traditional peace-building and security efforts and the facilitation of the return of large numbers of Kosovar Albanian refugees constituted the main priority in the early years, the administration of justice later became a top priority.[10]

Moreover, since 2001 and in particular since 2004, UNMIK has systematically transferred powers to local institutions, which has led to a scaling down of its international personnel. It is within this context of changing circumstances that the participation of the European Union and the United States in EULEX should be considered, as they have argued that these changed circumstances require a different type of mission, one that is supportive rather than executive in nature.[11] Closer scrutiny reveals, however, that the creation of EULEX raised several questions of law and policy.

II. CONTROVERSIES PERTAINING TO THE EULEX MANDATE

A main point of controversy concerned whether the EULEX mandate was reconcilable with Security Council Resolution 1244. Since UNMIK was still in place at the time EULEX was created, the question arose in particular whether Resolution 1244 allowed for the introduction

---

[5] SC Res. 1244, paras. 5–6, 10–11 & Annex 2, paras. 3, 5 (June 10, 1999).

[6] Michael J. Matheson, *United Nations Governance of Postconflict Societies*, 95 AJIL 76, 79 (2001).

[7] *Id.* at 79; *see also* Tom Perriello & Marieke Wierda, *Lessons from the Deployment of International Judges and Prosecutors in Kosovo* 9 (International Center for Transitional Justice, Apr. 2006), *at* <http://www.ictj.org/en/news/pubs/index.html>.

[8] Matheson, *supra* note 6, at 80.

[9] *Id.* at 79.

[10] Hansjörg Strohmeyer, *Collapse and Reconstruction of a Judicial System: The United Nations Missions in Kosovo and East Timor*, 95 AJIL 46, 47 (2001).

[11] Neth. Parl., 2d Chamber, Inzet Nederlandse Politie en Koninklijke Marechaussee bij Internationale Civiele Politie-Operaties [Letter of the Ministers of Foreign Affairs, Defense, Internal Affairs, and Justice to the Second Chamber of the Dutch Parliament], Kamerstukken II, 2007/08, Doc. 27476, No. 8, at 3 (Mar. 20, 2008), *at* <http://ikregeer.nl/static/pdf/KST116780.pdf>.

of EULEX alongside UNMIK and, if so, how these two missions were to operate in practice given the potential overlaps in their mandates.[12] The matter was further complicated by the positions of the Kosovar government and the representatives of the Serb minority, whose cooperation is also necessary for the smooth functioning of UNMIK and EULEX.[13]

Whether EULEX was authorized by Resolution 1244 was hotly disputed within the Security Council itself. On the one hand, no one disputed that the resolution remains in force until the Security Council decides otherwise.[14] On the other hand, it was disputed whether it indeed provided a basis for the introduction of EULEX alongside UNMIK. Whereas the EU member states and the United States took the position that EULEX was grounded in Resolution 1244, Russia maintained that it was linked to Kosovo's (illegal) declaration of independence and was not covered by any Security Council mandate.[15]

Initially, the supporters of EULEX firmly believed that most states (including Russia and Serbia) would acquiesce in its existence and that the transfer of responsibilities from UNMIK to EULEX would be completed by June 15, 2008, the date that the new Kosovar Constitution was slated to enter into force.[16] By May 2008, however, EU officials acknowledged that their optimism in this regard had been premature.[17] In addition to encountering logistical and recruitment delays,[18] EULEX had not succeeded in securing broader international support for its mandate.[19] In the Security Council Russia persisted in questioning its legality, and several EU members still refused to recognize Kosovo.[20] This group included larger member states such as Spain, which indicated reluctance to cooperate with EULEX in the face of the persistent legal uncertainties surrounding its mandate.[21]

On the ground EULEX was hindered by the refusal of the Serb-controlled territories to recognize its authority while accepting that of UNMIK, which meant that EULEX had to work through UNMIK if it wanted to play any role in those areas.[22] At the same time, UNMIK would

[12] The issue of coordinating the coexisting mandates is taken up in the text preceding and following note 67 *infra*.

[13] Nov. S-G Report, *supra* note 1, para. 21.

[14] Report of the Secretary-General on the United Nations Interim Administration Mission in Kosovo, para. 291, UN Doc. S/2008/211 (Mar. 28, 2008) [hereinafter Mar. S-G Report]; Report of the Secretary-General on the United Nations Interim Administration Mission in Kosovo, paras. 14, 20, UN Doc. S/2008/354 (June 12, 2008) [hereinafter June S-G Report]; Neth. Parl., 2d Chamber, Inzet Nederlandse Politie en Koninklijke Marechaussee bij Internationale Civiele Politie-Operaties [Responses by the Ministers of Foreign Affairs and Defense to Questions of the Standing Commission of Foreign Affairs of the Second Chamber of the Dutch Parliament], Kamerstukken II, 2007/08, Doc. 27476, No. 9, at 2 (May 15, 2008), *at* <http://ikregeer.nl/document/KST118346>.

[15] EurActiv, *EU Kosovo Mission up in the Air*, EURACTIV, Apr. 16, 2008, *at* <http://www.euractiv.com>.

[16] During debates in the Dutch Parliament, the government indicated that the negative attitude of Russia would have no direct effect on the deployment of EULEX. In making this prediction, the Dutch government proved to be overconfident. *See* Kamerstukken II, *supra* note 14, at 2.

[17] Patrick Moore, *Analysis: Are UN, EU Part of the Problem in Kosovo?* RADIO FREE EUROPE RADIO LIBERTY, May 28, 2008, *at* <http://www.rferl.org>.

[18] By May 15, 2008, only three hundred officials had been deployed. *See* Kamerstukken II, *supra* note 14, at 2.

[19] June S-G Report, *supra* note 14, para. 4.

[20] By December 2008, Cyprus, Greece, Romania, Slovakia, and Spain still refused to recognize Kosovo.

[21] *See* EurActiv, *supra* note 15; Petra de Koning, *Russen Voorspellen Nieuw Geweld: Kosovo Patstelling Rond Rol Europese Missie in Onafhankelijkheid* [Russians Predicting New Violence: Kosovo Deadlock Concerning the Role of the European Mission After Independence], NRC HANDELSBLAD, June 12, 2008, at 7, *available at* <http://archief.nrc.nl/index.php/2008/Juni/12/Overig/07/> (by subscription).

[22] Nov. S-G Report, *supra* note 1, para. 4; *see also* André Cunha, *EULEX Inside UNMIK, Too Late?* (Apr. 23, 2008), *at* <http://www.osservatoriobalcani.org/article/articleview/9463/1/216>; Moore, *supra* note 17.

86   THE AMERICAN JOURNAL OF INTERNATIONAL LAW   [Vol. 103:83

effectively be removed from its civil administration tasks by the new Kosovar Constitution.[23] The Kosovar government had also adopted legislation reclaiming competence for this pillar, in particular in relation to publicly owned enterprises.[24] In essence, therefore, UNMIK and EULEX were confronted with a situation in which the Kosovar Albanian government preferred to terminate the UNMIK presence in favor of EULEX and the Serbian minority preferred the exact opposite.

These realities on the ground, combined with the legal challenges to EULEX, necessitated a compromise solution acceptable to all parties—the European Union, the United States, and the Kosovar Albanian government, on the one hand, and Russia, Serbia, and the Kosovar Serbian minority, on the other—before EULEX could become operational. Accordingly, in mid-June 2008, the secretary-general proposed that the operational role of EULEX, "under the overall authority" of the UN special representative, be enhanced in a manner conforming with the framework provided for in Resolution 1244.[25] But differences between the parties as to exactly what this proposal would imply in practice prevented the deployment and functioning of EULEX for several months. By the end of November, the Security Council unanimously accepted a report in which all the protagonists (with the exception of the Kosovar government) claimed to have reached a more concrete agreement on the six controversial areas of police, justice, customs, transportation and infrastructure, boundaries, and Serbian patrimony. As a result, EULEX's deployment, which by this time amounted to fewer than five hundred of the planned two thousand personnel, could be accelerated.[26]

The following analysis will explore some of the legal and practical ramifications of these events. It explores, in particular, the conditions under which Resolution 1244 provides for the establishment of civil administrations, as well as whether the initial establishment of EULEX conforms (and is likely to remain in conformity) with these criteria. In doing so, the analysis also examines some of the practical challenges that may confront the tandem existence of UNMIK and EULEX as they execute their respective mandates.

III. RECONCILING EULEX WITH RESOLUTION 1244

The Legal Basis of Chapter VII Mandates for Civil Administration

When analyzing the legal basis of mandates for civil administration under Chapter VII of the Charter, one can distinguish three scenarios: mandates for civil administration by the United Nations itself; those for civil administration by (an) individual member state(s); and those for civil administration by a regional organization.

---

[23] June S-G Report, *supra* note 14, para. 7.

[24] Nov. S-G Report, *supra* note 1, Annex 1, para. 1; *see also* June S-G Report, *supra* note 14, para. 9.

[25] June S-G Report, *supra* note 14, paras. 12–13, 16.

[26] By February 2008, UNMIK had reduced its police personnel from a peak of 3300 persons in 2001 to just under 1500. The remaining United Nations staff members amounted to 462. About UNMIK, *at* <http://www.unmikonline.org/intro.htm>. *See also* Ian Bancroft, *Confusion in Kosovo*, GUARDIAN.CO.UK, Nov. 17, 2008, *at* <http://www.guardian.co.uk>; European Union, European Security and Defense Policy, EULEX KOSOVO: EU Rule of Law Mission for Kosovo, Doc. EULEX/03 (Oct. 2008), *attached to* EU Council, Joint Press Statement by the United States of America and the European Union on US Participation in the EULEX Mission in Kosovo, No. 14619/08 (Presse 295) (Oct. 22, 2008).

As for the first scenario, by now the Security Council is widely acknowledged to have the power to establish a civil administration under the auspices of the United Nations on the basis of its implied powers under Chapter VII of the Charter. The implied power to establish a civil administration flows from the Security Council's express powers in Article 41 to take nonmilitary measures for the maintenance or restoration of international peace and security.[27] Since these civil administrations involve the delegation of Security Council powers to the UN secretary-general in the form of a special representative, Article 98 of the Charter constitutes a further basis for the delegation of powers.[28] The creation of UNMIK in Resolution 1244[29] was a manifestation of the Security Council's implied powers in accordance with Articles 41 and 98 of the Charter.

Second, the Security Council also has the power under Chapter VII of the Charter to authorize individual states to implement a civil administration. This was notably the case after the invasion of Iraq in March 2003, when the Security Council authorized the United States and the United Kingdom (the Authority) to conduct the civil administration of Iraq.[30] The authorization in that case stemmed from the Security Council's implied powers flowing from Article 41 together with Article 48(1) of the Charter. The latter article allows the Security Council to determine whether the decisions on the maintenance of international peace and security shall be taken by all the members of the United Nations or only some of them.

Furthermore, the Charter enables the Security Council to authorize regional organizations to administer a territory. Article 53(1) provides that the Security Council "shall, where appropriate, utilize regional arrangements or agencies for enforcement action under its authority."[31] When Article 53 comes into play as a basis for enforcement action, the question of what constitutes a "regional organization" arises.[32] In accordance with Article 52(1), a regional organization has the task of achieving the peaceful settlement of disputes within its own region.[33] The term "regional" implies a distinctive feature about the members of the organization, which is generally understood to be of a geographic nature.[34] It can relate either to the region from which all the member states come, or to the region in which the organization will operate, or a combination of these factors.[35] According to these criteria, the European Union, which is

[27] This line of argument was also followed with respect to the establishment of the International Criminal Tribunal for the Former Yugoslavia in *Prosecutor v. Tadić*, Appeal on Jurisdiction, No. IT–94–1–AR72 (Oct. 2, 1995), *available at* <http://www.icty.org>.

[28] UN CHARTER Art. 98. The first sentence of Article 98 reads as follows: "The Secretary-General shall act in that capacity in all meetings of the General Assembly, of the Security Council, of the Economic and Social Council, and of the Trusteeship Council, and shall perform such other functions as are entrusted to him by these organs."

[29] SC Res. 1244, *supra* note 5, paras. 5–6 & Annex 2, paras. 3–4.

[30] SC Res. 1483, paras. 4, 8 (May 22, 2003).

[31] *See* CHRISTIAN WALTER, VEREINTE NATIONEN UND REGIONALORGANISATIONEN: EINE UNTERSUCHUNG ZU KAPITEL VIII DER SATZUNG DER VEREINTEN NATIONEN 276 (1996); *see also* ERIKA DE WET, THE CHAPTER VII POWERS OF THE UNITED NATIONS SECURITY COUNCIL 291–93 (2004).

[32] WALTER, *supra* note 31, at 276.

[33] Ige F. Dekker & Eric P. J. Myjer, *Air Strikes on Bosnian Positions: Is NATO Also Legally the Proper Instrument of the UN?* 9 LEIDEN J. INT'L L. 411, 413 (1996); *see also* WALTER, *supra* note 31, at 276.

[34] WALTER, *supra* note 31, at 40.

[35] *Id.* at 40–41. The distinctive geographic factor can also be accompanied by cultural and historical ties such as those between the members of the British Commonwealth.

88   THE AMERICAN JOURNAL OF INTERNATIONAL LAW   [Vol. 103:83

aimed at regional integration, qualifies as a regional organization,[36] as do the Organization of American States and the League of Arab States.[37]

In addition to explicitly creating the United Nations civil administration that would become known as UNMIK and be controlled by a special representative,[38] Resolution 1244, in its paragraph 10, authorizes the secretary-general to establish a civil administration "with the assistance of relevant international organizations." This paragraph vests the secretary-general with the power to administer the territory, and authorizes him to (re)delegate certain functions of civil administration to other international organizations such as the European Union. As mentioned at the outset, this authority included the delegation of institution building to the OSCE, humanitarian relief to the UNHCR, and economic reconstruction to the European Union.

Scrutiny of the EULEX mandate reveals that it was not authorized by the Security Council, even though paragraph 1 of the preamble to the EU Council's Joint Action creating EULEX expressly refers to paragraph 10 of Resolution 1244. This reference affirms that the European Union considered the latter to be the basis for the creation of EULEX.[39] However, it glosses over the fact that EULEX was created at the initiative of the European Union itself. At the time of its creation, the secretary-general merely acknowledged receipt of the letter of Javier Solana, the high representative for the Common Foreign and Security Policy of the European Union (hereinafter the high representative), without issuing any formal response.[40] Some European Union member states nonetheless argued that the secretary-general had implicitly authorized EULEX by acknowledging that the evolving reality in Kosovo was likely to have significant operational implications for UNMIK.[41]

At the time, however, this position was probably no more than an acknowledgment of a fait accompli brought about by the European Union and the United States, rather than an implicit authorization. The first explicit indication of an attempt to transfer power from UNMIK to EULEX appeared in the report of June 12, 2008, in which the secretary-general declared his intention to enhance the operational role of the European Union pertaining to the rule of law under the overall authority of the United Nations.[42]

As this report was never endorsed by the Security Council because of disagreement over the way EULEX was to be deployed, it is questionable whether this attempt by the secretary-general conformed with Resolution 1244. The secretary-general seemed to assume that it fell within

---

[36] Although the legal personality of the European Union was not explicitly provided for in the founding treaties, it developed through practice. HENRY G. SCHERMERS & NIELS M. BLOKKER, INTERNATIONAL INSTITUTIONAL LAW 992 (2003); *see also* Treaty of Lisbon Amending the Treaty on European Union and the Treaty Establishing the European Community, Art. 46A, Dec. 13, 2007, 2007 O.J. (C 306) 1, *available at* <http://www.eurlex.europa.eu>.

[37] For a discussion on whether Article 41, combined with Article 48 of the UN Charter, can serve as an alternative basis for territorial administration by regional organizations, see WALTER, *supra* note 31, at 277.

[38] SC Res. 1244, *supra* note 5, paras. 5–6 & Annex 2, paras. 3, 5.

[39] Joint Action, *supra* note 2.

[40] Secretary-General in Security Council Statement Says UN Aim in Kosovo Stable Political, Security Situation, Protection of Population, Minorities, UN Press Release SG/SM/11426–SC/9253 (Feb. 18, 2008); *see also* Kamerstukken II, *supra* note 14, at 2.

[41] Kamerstukken II, *supra* note 14, at 2; *see also* Mar. S-G Report, *supra* note 14, paras. 30, 32.

[42] June S-G Report, *supra* note 14, para. 16 & Annex 1. On August 18, 2008, the special representative of the UN secretary-general and representatives of EULEX signed a technical arrangement on the handover of UNMIK assets to EULEX. Technical Arrangement Signed: UN and EU Agree on Handover of Assets Between UNMIK and EULEX, EULEX KOSOVO Press Release 1/2008 (Aug. 19, 2008), *available at* <http://www.eulex-kosovo.eu>.

his competence to delegate powers to EULEX, regardless of whether the Security Council had endorsed such action. For example, in his report of July 15, 2008, he noted that in light of the inability of the Security Council to provide guidance, he had instructed his special representative to move forward with the reconfiguration of UNMIK.[43] Nevertheless, this position remains highly controversial,[44] as in the past the secretary-general had consistently sought explicit endorsement by the Security Council of acts resulting in the transfer of governance-related competences from UNMIK to other actors.

These actions included, inter alia, the holding of the November 2001 elections, which constituted a basis for the establishment of institutions of self-government;[45] the inauguration of the Kosovar Assembly the following year;[46] and the subsequent transfer of competences to the so-called provisional institutions of self-government.[47] This consistent practice can be interpreted as an acknowledgment by the secretary-general that any reconfiguration of the mandate for civil administration resulting in a transfer of governance powers from UNMIK to other entities requires the explicit approval of the Security Council as a collective entity, including that of its five permanent members.

The Security Council explicitly endorsed the UNMIK reconfiguration only after the secretary-general's report of November 24, 2008, through the adoption of a Presidential Statement on November 26, 2008, which welcomed the cooperation between the United Nations and other international actors within the framework of Security Council Resolution 1244.[48] In essence, therefore, EULEX was legalized under Resolution 1244 ex post facto, namely, as of this latter date.[49]

Since a very limited number of EULEX personnel had been deployed before this time and EULEX became operational only in early December 2008, the initial absence of a legal basis for the EULEX mandate did not have any immediate practical consequences. Nonetheless, this analysis will illustrate that the continued legality of the EULEX mandate also depends on two additional factors: how the mandate is exercised and, in particular, whether all stakeholders accept the overriding executive authority of the special representative as long as Resolution 1244 remains in effect.

Corrective Oversight of Mandates for Civil Administration

When the Security Council authorizes a civil administration, it delegates binding powers to other entities such as the secretary-general and, through him, his special representative. For such a delegation to remain legal, the Security Council must retain overall control of the

---

[43] Report of the Secretary-General on the United Nations Interim Administration Mission in Kosovo, para. 3, UN Doc. S/2008/458 (July 15, 2008) [hereinafter July S-G Report]; *see also* June S-G Report, *supra* note 14, para. 19; *id.*, Annex 1, Letter Dated 12 June 2008 from the Secretary-General to His Excellency, Mr. Boris Tadić.

[44] *See* UN Doc. S/PV.5917, at 5, 17, 19 (June 20, 2008). While the secretary-general's position attracted support from the United Kingdom, *id.* at 17, and the United States, *id.* at 19, it was criticized by Serbia, *id.* at 5.

[45] Statement by the President of the Security Council, UN Doc. S/PRST/2001/27 (Oct. 5, 2001).

[46] Statement by the President of the Security Council, UN Doc. S/PRST/2002/4 (Feb. 13, 2002).

[47] Statement by the President of the Security Council, UN Doc. S/PRST/2003/1 (Feb. 6, 2003).

[48] Statement by the President of the Security Council, UN Doc. S/PRST/2008/44 (Nov. 26, 2008).

[49] Nov. S-G Report, *supra* note 1, para. 50; *see also* June S-G Report, *supra* note 14, para. 16 & Annex 1.

authorized mandate.[50] Delegation of the ultimate control of the exercise of such power would amount to an abdication of authority that would undermine the centralized nature of the binding powers that the Security Council may employ in the interest of international peace and security.[51] Delegation of extensive discretionary decision-making power to the civil administration to facilitate day-to-day governance must therefore not result in the relinquishment of overall control by the Security Council.

To retain overall control, the Security Council must be able to exercise corrective oversight of the execution of the mandate throughout its duration, meaning that the Council may override the decisions of those acting on its behalf.[52] Similarly, when the Security Council authorizes the secretary-general and his special representative under Chapter VII to (re)delegate certain functions of civil administration to other international organizations such as the European Union, they, too, will retain overriding power within the parameters of the original Security Council mandate. Such is the case in Kosovo, where Resolution 1244 explicitly requested that the secretary-general appoint a special representative to oversee the civil administration.[53] Consequently, the special representative would have the power to override any decision taken by EULEX, whether with respect to the appointment of personnel, the exercise of its functions, or otherwise.

Closer scrutiny of the command structure of EULEX reveals that at the time of its creation, it did not contain any formal recognition of the overriding powers of the special representative (or even of the Security Council itself). Instead, it provided for a chain of command that exclusively involved EU bodies and its overall authority resided in the EU high representative.[54] This position changed formally in July 2008, when High Representative Javier Solana confirmed that EULEX would function under the overall authority of the United Nations and would provide the secretary-general with all necessary reports.[55] In practice, regular reporting to the Security Council and/or the secretary-general has become a standard feature of all delegated

[50] This requirement was confirmed in relation to the delegation of military mandates in the *Behrami* decision of the European Court of Human Rights. Behrami & Behrami v. France; Saramati v. France, Joint App. Nos. 71412/01 & 78166/01, Admissibility Decision, para. 132 (May 31, 2007), *available at* <http://echr.coe.int/echr/en/hudoc>.

[51] DANESH SAROOSHI, THE UNITED NATIONS AND THE DEVELOPMENT OF COLLECTIVE SECURITY: THE DELEGATION BY THE UN SECURITY COUNCIL OF ITS CHAPTER VII POWERS 5, 33 (1999).

[52] For a discussion of the power of the delegator to override decisions of the delegate, see Case 9/56, Meroni & Co., Industrie Metallurgiche, SpA v. High Auth. of Eur. Coal & Steel Cmty., 1958 ECR 133. The underlying principles in this case, although developed in the context of EU law, were also affirmed in relation to United Nations mandates, *see Behrami & Behrami, supra* note 50, para. 132. *See also* DE WET, *supra* note 31, at 267–68; Niels M. Blokker, *Is the Authorization Authorized? Powers and Practice of the United Nations Security Council to Authorize the Use of Force by 'Coalitions of the Able and Willing,'* 11 EUR. J. INT'L L. 541, 553 (2000).

[53] SC Res. 1244, *supra* note 5, para. 6. See also the statement by the United Kingdom in UN Doc. S/PV.6025, at 19 (Nov. 26, 2008), that the executive authority of the special representative was not derived from Resolution 1244, but from the subsequent constitutional framework, which is not correct. This interpretation ignores not only the wording of the resolution, but also the fact that the constitutional framework was itself a product of an executive act of the special representative, namely, UNMIK Regulation 2001/9, On a Constitutional Framework for Provisional Self-Government in Kosovo, UN Doc. UNMIK/REG/2001/9 (May 15, 2001), *available at* <http://www.unmikonline.org>.

[54] Joint Action, *supra* note 2, Art. 7; EU Council, Javier Solana, EU High Representative for the CFSP, Welcomes the Appointments of Pieter Feith as EU Special Representative in Kosovo and Yves de Kermabon as Head of Mission of EULEX KOSOVO, Doc. S060/08 (Feb. 16, 2008); *see also* Kamerstukken II, *supra* note 14, at 7.

[55] EU Council, Summary of the Intervention of Javier Solana, EU High Representative for the Common Foreign and Security Policy Before the Meeting of International Organisations Active on the Ground in Kosovo (EU, NATO, UN, OSCE), Doc. S257/08 (July 18, 2008).

mandates of a civil or military nature and symbolizes the acceptance of the Security Council as the authorizing source of the mandate.[56]

Yet, even though reporting constitutes an important formal element of acceptance of UN authority, the actual behavior of EULEX will ultimately be decisive in determining whether it has indeed embraced the overall authority of the United Nations over the exercise of its mandate. Specifically, EULEX must accept that it is in coexistence with UNMIK (as opposed to being a substitute for it) and must execute its rule-of-law mandate in a manner that does not conflict with the oversight role that the special representative retains in Kosovo.

UNMIK's rule-of-law responsibilities (Pillar I) were primarily directed at restoring the criminal justice system and creating an independent and multiethnic local judiciary.[57] On the one hand, these tasks included the recruitment of international prosecutors and judges for dealing with serious (international) crimes and cases where ethnic bias was a major concern.[58] On the other hand, the tasks involved general judicial development, such as the recruitment and training of local prosecutors and judges, and oversight of the judiciary.[59] In the context of Pillar I, UNMIK also established an international civilian police force responsible for interim law enforcement functions. Simultaneously, it engaged in the establishment of the local Kosovar police department and, with the support of the OSCE, has participated in the recruitment and training of local police officers.[60]

As regards both the judiciary and the police, UNMIK has systematically transferred extensive responsibilities to local institutions. Nonetheless, in accordance with the authority vested in him by Resolution 1244, the special representative retains the power to change, repeal, or suspend laws that are incompatible with the mandate, aims, or purposes of UNMIK.[61] Thus, as long as Resolution 1244 remains in place, the special representative formally has the power to annul legislation by the Kosovar government, including any that pertains to the judiciary and the police.[62]

Resolution 1244 further implies that the special representative can override any decision taken by EULEX in those areas where it takes over rule-of-law functions of UNMIK. Given the opposition of the Serbian minority to the deployment of EULEX, in practice UNMIK and EULEX will exist alongside each other.[63] EULEX will oversee the institutions dominated by Kosovar Albanians,[64] and UNMIK will be directly involved in monitoring those in the Serbian-dominated areas of the territory. Like the UNMIK staff, the EULEX personnel will have certain

---

[56] Security Council Resolution 1244, *supra* note 5, para. 20, requested that the secretary-general report regularly to the Council on the implementation of the civil and military presences authorized by this resolution.

[57] Perriello & Wierda, *supra* note 7.

[58] HUMAN RIGHTS WATCH, NO. 4(D), 2006, NOT ON THE AGENDA: THE CONTINUING FAILURE TO ADDRESS ACCOUNTABILITY ON KOSOVO POST-MARCH 2004, at 6, *available at* <http://www.hrw.org/en/reports/2006/05/29/not-agenda-0>.

[59] *Id.* at 6.

[60] *Id.* at 38; Perriello & Wierda, *supra* note 7, at 9.

[61] UNMIK Regulation 1999/1, On the Authority of the Interim Administration in Kosovo, UN Doc. UNMIK/REG/1/1999 §§1–2 (July 23, 1999), *available at* <http://www.unmikonline.org>; *see also* Report of the Secretary-General on the United Nations Interim Administration Mission in Kosovo 39, UN Doc. S/1999/779 (July 12, 1999).

[62] Formally speaking, the special representative could also nullify the 2008 KUSHTETUTA E KOSOVËS [Constitution of Kosovo], *available at* <http://www.kushtetutakosoves.info>. However, in practice this is not likely to happen.

[63] Nov. S-G Report, *supra* note 1, paras. 21, 25; *see also* Bancroft, *supra* note 26.

[64] Nov. S-G Report, *supra* note 1, para. 52.

92   THE AMERICAN JOURNAL OF INTERNATIONAL LAW   [Vol. 103:83

corrective and executive competences in critical situations that the Kosovar police are incapable of handling or where human rights violations require intervention—notably, when it comes to such matters as organized crime, war crimes, financial crime, witness protection, and the prevention of riots.[65]

This coexistence, together with the fact that EULEX will exercise functions very similar to those of UNMIK, suggests that divergent or conflicting approaches to the rule-of-law mandate could arise.[66] The challenges facing EULEX and UNMIK can be illustrated by some of the difficulties facing the Kosovo criminal justice system, as well as by the potentially divergent approaches of these missions to their international responsibility for violations of international law.

Restoring the Criminal Justice System in Cooperation with Local Actors

Some of the pertinent challenges facing the Kosovar criminal justice system include the lack of coordination between local and international prosecutors and judges, deficient witness protection, and insufficient oversight of the local judiciary and police force. In practice, interaction between national and international prosecutors and judges has remained limited, as the international prosecutors and judges tend to focus only on serious (international) crimes and are physically separated from their local counterparts in terms of work space. The resulting lack of coordination has exacerbated the differences in standards of professional conduct between local and international staff, as well as the difficulties faced by local prosecutors because of inadequate staff and heavy caseloads.[67]

Witness protection, currently the responsibility of special units in the Kosovar police force, has proven to be very challenging in a society consisting of small communities and extensive family networks. The risk of exposure and intimidation is aggravated by long pretrial waiting periods and ineffective prosecution of persons interfering with witnesses.[68] Police officers remain especially reluctant to act as witnesses in court proceedings out of fear of intimidation.[69]

Oversight of the judiciary at the ground level rests with local institutions such as the Kosovar Ministry of Justice, while the Kosovar police force has operational control over policing responsibilities in Kosovo. Limited effective oversight, however, is actually exercised.[70] Similarly, the transfer of the so-called Professional Standards Unit to the Kosovar Police Service in 2005 has

---

[65] Kamerstukken II, *supra* note 11, at 4. In addition, EULEX had to oversee the implementation of the 2007 "Ahtisaari Plan," which Kosovo accepted unilaterally upon independence. This plan contained, inter alia, safeguards for minorities, a program for the decentralization of government, constitutional guarantees for all citizens, and measures for the protection and promotion of cultural heritage. Report of the Special Envoy of the Secretary-General on Kosovo's Future Status, UN Doc. S/2007/168, paras. 1–3 (Mar. 26, 2007). The status of the Ahtisaari Plan is uncertain in light of the compromise reached in December 2008 in accordance with which EULEX will function within the status-neutral framework of UNMIK.

[66] An estimated fourteen hundred EULEX police officers, forty judges, twenty prosecutors, and seventy prison workers are to be deployed throughout Kosovo. Joint Action, *supra* note 2, Art. 3(b); Kamerstukken II, *supra* note 14, at 4; *see also* Kamerstukken II, *supra* note 11, at 4.

[67] HUMAN RIGHTS WATCH, *supra* note 58, at 11.

[68] *Id.* at 38; *see also* July S-G Report, *supra* note 43, Annex 1, para. 25.

[69] HUMAN RIGHTS WATCH, *supra* note 58, at 38.

[70] *Id.* at 9.

not resulted in effective oversight of police misconduct. Obtaining information about the status of investigations into misconduct by police officers remains very difficult.[71]

Addressing these concerns in a manner that results in a well-functioning and well-supervised judiciary and police service that apply the same standards of policing and criminal justice throughout the territory will require major efforts of coordination between UNMIK and EULEX.[72] In addition, it will require intensive collaboration between these institutions and the Kosovar Ministry of Justice, the Kosovar Police Service, and those in charge of the local institutions in the Serbian-controlled areas.

However, as indicated above, the Kosovar Albanian government is rejecting the prolonged presence of UNMIK in the territory despite having paid lip service to Resolution 1244 in the Declaration of Independence.[73] It is therefore questionable whether the Kosovar government will be willing to cooperate extensively with the UNMIK authorities for any extended period, or to accept that the special representative can still override any of its decisions. Similarly, it remains doubtful whether the Kosovar government will cooperate with Serbian-dominated local authorities who are supported by UNMIK. Furthermore, that government's willingness to cooperate with EULEX may diminish over time if the latter is perceived as being too deferential to UNMIK, which could occur if EULEX attempts to give proper effect to Resolution 1244 by accepting the special representative's overall authority over the rule-of-law mission.

For their part, Kosovar Serbs have refused to participate in any Kosovar institutions, including the police and the judiciary, since the Declaration of Independence, and do not accept the Kosovar officials' exercise of authority.[74] As a result, inter alia, the courthouse of Mitrovicë closed down temporarily and is currently manned by a skeleton staff of international prosecutors and judges dealing solely with urgent criminal cases.[75] Since only UNMIK law is applied in the Mitrovicë courthouse (and not that adopted by the new Kosovar government), substantive law in the territory is already fragmented.[76] The Kosovar Serb community also remains opposed to the deployment of EULEX in its municipalities. This reluctance to cooperate with either the Kosovar authorities or EULEX might also spill over into a similar reluctance to cooperate with UNMIK, were it to be perceived as being too accommodating to the needs of EULEX and the Kosovar Albanians.

These challenges may additionally have consequences for the medium- and long-term existence of EULEX, which was initially created for two years.[77] If the Kosovar Albanian government perceives it as being too close to UNMIK, it may cease to condone EULEX's presence in the territory and frustrate its mandate, even if the Security Council endorses an extension of the mandate. On the other hand, an overly close alliance between EULEX and the Kosovar government may alienate Security Council members such as Russia and thwart the endorsement

---

[71] *Id.* at 44.

[72] Nov. S-G Report, *supra* note 1, para. 51. It will also involve the cooperation of the OSCE, which will remain involved in institution building in the territory. *See* HUMAN RIGHTS WATCH, *supra* note 58, at 48, 67.

[73] Nov. S-G Report, *supra* note 1, para. 52.

[74] June S-G Report, *supra* note 14, para. 5.

[75] Nov. S-G Report, *supra* note 1, para. 8. In Zubin Potok, the municipal and minor offenses courts are not operational at all, while the court liaison office of the Kosovo Ministry of Justice—which facilitates legal aid for Kosovar Serbs—is functioning at a minimal level because of security concerns.

[76] Some Serb-dominated municipalities also apply the Serbian law of self-governance. *See* Nov. S-G Report, *supra* note 1, para. 4.

[77] Joint Action, *supra* note 2, para. 20; *see also* Kamerstukken II, *supra* note 11, at 7.

94 THE AMERICAN JOURNAL OF INTERNATIONAL LAW [Vol. 103:83

of any extension of the mandate by the Council. If EULEX remains in Kosovo at the request of the Kosovar Albanian government under those circumstances, its authority would no longer be based on Resolution 1244, making the execution of its mandate on the territory a violation of that resolution.

In essence, therefore, efforts by UNMIK and EULEX to coordinate their rule-of-law practices and policies may alienate the respective local communities they are representing. But cooperating too closely with their respective local communities may alienate them from one another and lead to a de facto violation of Resolution 1244 if EULEX contravenes the will of the special representative in the execution of its mandate. In addition, by cooperating too closely with local communities, the missions may further the perception of de facto partition of the territory along ethnic lines.[78]

Coordinating the International Responsibility of UNMIK and EULEX

The focus of UNMIK and EULEX cannot be exclusively local; they will also have to devise a coherent policy of international responsibility. It goes without saying that the credibility of missions directed at developing the rule of law would be severely undermined if the main protagonists did not accept responsibility in a consistent fashion for their own violations of international law. There is a concrete risk that UNMIK and EULEX will take divergent approaches in this regard. When endorsing the reconfiguration of UNMIK, the UN secretary-general explicitly limited the international responsibility of the United Nations for violations of international law to the extent of its effective operational control.[79] Thus, with respect to operations such as EULEX where the effective control lies with the European Union, the United Nations will not accept international responsibility.

This position is a direct response to the *Behrami* decision of the European Court of Human Rights whose highly questionable reasoning—if consistently applied—could result in the attribution of international responsibility for the conduct of EULEX to the United Nations.[80] In this decision, the European Court attributed the actions of both UNMIK and the NATO Kosovo Force (KFOR) exclusively to the United Nations because their actions were authorized by Resolution 1244. In doing so, the Court did not acknowledge the effective control of certain member states over KFOR's actions as a criterion for the attribution of responsibility for potential human rights violations but, instead, relied on the criterion of overall control of the Security Council.

Although an extensive analysis of the European Court's reasoning falls outside the scope of this essay,[81] it is noteworthy that, in relying on the above delegation model to come to its conclusion, the Court interpreted that model too narrowly. It does not necessarily imply that the actions of KFOR must be attributed exclusively to the United Nations. Instead, the model acknowledges that the overall control exercised by the Security Council over KFOR's mandate

---

[78] *Im Versuchslabor Kosovo beginnt eine weitere Etappe*, N[EUE]Z[ÜRICHER]Z[EITUNG] ONLINE, Nov. 28, 2008, *at* <http://www.nzz.ch>.

[79] June S-G Report, *supra* note 14, para. 16.

[80] Behrami & Behrami v. France, *supra* note 50.

[81] For an analysis of this decision, see Pierre Bodeau-Livinec, Gionata P. Buzzini, & Santiago Villalpando, Case Report: Agim Behrami & Bekir Behrami v. France; Ruzhdi Saramati v. France, Germany & Norway, *in* 102 AJIL 323 (2008). *See also* K. M. Larsen, *Attribution of Conduct in Peace Operations: The "Ultimate Authority and Control" Test*, 19 EUR. J. INT'L L. 509 (2008).

allows for effective, day-to-day control by (the member states of) KFOR on the ground.[82] Therefore, if one regards attribution of responsibility and delegation of powers as two sides of the same coin (which the Court seemed to do), the attribution of responsibility should reflect awareness of the fact that (the member states of) KFOR exercised effective control in Kosovo at the time that the alleged human rights violations occurred. This view suggests that responsibility for human rights violations should be attributed first and foremost to (the member states of) KFOR, as opposed to the United Nations.[83]

This position is supported by United Nations practice, as the organization has never before accepted responsibility for violations of international law by troops acting on its overall authority but under unified command and control (as with KFOR). The secretary-general's statement in June 2008 that the United Nations would accept international responsibility in Kosovo only for actions under its effective control underscores that the United Nations has no intention of changing this practice. The statement also amounts to a rejection of the European Court's reasoning in the *Behrami* decision.[84]

If EULEX and its member states nonetheless tried to shield themselves behind the *Behrami* decision, an accountability vacuum would result, as both the European Union and the member states would then be absolving themselves of responsibility in a situation where no other entity would be likely to take responsibility.[85] Consequently, it is crucial for the European Union, as a subject of international law, to accept international responsibility for operations undertaken under its effective control in the context of EULEX.[86] In addition, UNMIK and EULEX should agree on addressing issues of international responsibility in an integrated and comprehensive manner to prevent the introduction of divergent practice and standards in Kosovo in this regard.

IV. CONCLUSION

The evolution of the mandate for civil administration in Kosovo illustrates the difficulties that arise in the face of an open-ended mandate for civil administration under Chapter VII of the Charter,[87] because of which any formal amendment necessitated by changing circumstances on the ground requires a subsequent Chapter VII resolution. In such a case, amendment can be prevented by the (threat of the) exercise of a reverse veto by any of the permanent members, even when a majority of the Security Council (including a majority of the permanent members) favor an amended mandate.

---

[82] DE WET, *supra* note 31, at 265.

[83] Fredrik Naert, *Accountability for Violations of Human Rights Law by EU Forces*, *in* THE EUROPEAN UNION AND CRISIS MANAGEMENT: POLICY AND LEGAL ASPECTS 375, 379 (S. Blockmans ed., 2008).

[84] In any event, the United Nations is not bound by a decision of the European Court, as it is not a party to the Convention for the Protection of Human Rights and Fundamental Freedoms, Nov. 4, 1950, Europ. TS No. 5, 213 UNTS 221.

[85] The matter might be different if in future Kosovo became a party to the European Convention on Human Rights and the issue of extraterritorial application did not arise. *See* Behrami & Behrami v. France, *supra* note 50, para. 150; *see also* Bosphorus Hava Yollari Turizm ve Ticaret Anonim Şirketi v. Ireland, 2005–VI Eur. Ct. H.R. 107, *available at* <http://echr.coe.int/echr/en/hudoc>.

[86] Naert, *supra* note 83, at 379.

[87] SC Res. 1244, *supra* note 5, paras. 5–6.

Under these circumstances, those pressing for change can be expected to attempt to facilitate it by (re)interpreting the existing legal framework (in this instance Resolution 1244). The success of the attempt will ultimately depend on the strength of the legal reasoning and political power exercised by those attempting to legitimate their actions in this manner. At the time of EULEX's creation, the protagonists seemed to have underestimated the importance of sound legal reasoning for the success of the mission, while simultaneously overestimating their ability to persuade opponents through political means. Persistent doubts within the United Nations membership about the legality of the EULEX mandate delayed the deployment of the mission for almost ten months and undermined its credibility before the mandate took effect.

Although the Security Council's endorsement of EULEX under overall United Nations control in November 2008 provided an ex post facto legal basis for the mandate, its long-term legality will depend on whether EULEX exercises its mandate in a manner that is compatible with the wishes of the special representative. The main resistance to the acceptance of the overriding power of the special representative in this regard is unlikely to come from within EULEX itself but, rather, from the local stakeholders whose interests it represents, the Kosovar government. The widespread opposition among Kosovar Albanians to the compromise solution that placed EULEX under the United Nations umbrella has the potential to undermine any good-faith attempts by EULEX and UNMIK to coordinate their rule-of-law activities.

Ironically, this obstacle to the functioning of EULEX seems to have resulted, at least in part, from the support of Kosovo's powerful Western allies for its maximalist stance throughout the negotiations over the territory's final status.[88] With the wisdom of hindsight, this approach can be termed short-sighted to the extent that it underestimated the political strength of the key stakeholders who opposed independence and their ability to thwart an interpretation of Resolution 1244 that would facilitate the replacement of UNMIK by EULEX.

In the absence of willingness on the part of all stakeholders to engage in dialogue and compromise, EULEX is unlikely to be able to exercise its mandate in accordance with Resolution 1244 for the duration of its mission, or to cooperate on a par with UNMIK in developing a coherent rule-of-law strategy for the territory as a whole. These circumstances, in turn, may undermine the viability of the EULEX mission beyond its initial two-year mandate and, by implication, that of the governance of Kosovo as a unified territory.

[88] Bancroft, *supra* note 26.

[5]

PEACEKEEPING AND PROSECUTORIAL POLICY: LESSONS FROM KOSOVO

By Gregory L. Naarden and Jeffrey B. Locke[*]

The international community has increasingly recognized the importance of criminal justice reform programs in postconflict reconstruction in the Balkans, Africa, and Asia.[1] In these societies, where crime and political violence are deeply connected, civil unrest undermines efforts to establish stable governing institutions, and weak criminal justice institutions ensure that this destabilizing spiral will continue.[2] Reform programs identify and address weaknesses of justice institutions through training and technical assistance, and international prosecutors (IPs) are brought in when local prosecutors are unable or unwilling to handle sensitive cases.

Defining the role of IPs has been a challenge for those overseeing the peace-building process. Separating the roles of IPs and domestic prosecutors requires balancing the urgent need to prosecute dangerous criminals and the longer-term need to ensure that local authorities can effectively carry out their official functions. To achieve this balance, international prosecutorial assistance programs must be devised with three categories of consideration in mind: analysis of the forms of crime that fundamentally hinder the peace-building process; design of a temporary structure that narrowly focuses IP efforts on those forms of crime; and reform of legislation so that prosecutors are empowered to fight crime aggressively in accordance with established international standards.

The experience of Kosovo is an extreme example of the challenges facing international administrators in a postconflict criminal justice system.[3] In the void left by retreating Serb forces in June 1999, the United Nations Interim Administration Mission in Kosovo (UNMIK) had to reconstruct justice institutions and simultaneously address widespread violence and the growing influence of organized criminal gangs. UNMIK established a Department of Justice (DOJ), appointed an international director of justice to run the DOJ, and vested IPs with the authority to prosecute in domestic courts.[4] UNMIK's initial strategy, however, lacked an overall vision for effectively fighting crime over the course of the peace-building process.

Recognizing the limitations of UNMIK's initial efforts, the UNMIK director of justice established a Criminal Division within the DOJ in March 2003.[5] The Criminal Division brought all IPs into a single hierarchical structure, headed by a chief international prosecutor. The new structure allowed senior justice officials to identify criminals who threatened the peace-building process, direct and set priorities for investigations into these individuals, and establish institutional capacity to fight destabilizing crime aggressively in the future.

[*] Foreign Service Officer, U.S. Department of State; and formerly Legal Officer, Department of Justice, United Nations Interim Administration Mission in Kosovo (UNMIK), respectively. The authors served in the UNMIK Department of Justice and directly participated in the events described in this Note. The views expressed herein are exclusively those of the authors, and do not reflect an official position of the United Nations or the United States government. The authors would like to thank Paul E. Coffey, Param-Preet Singh, Ioan Tudorache, and J. Clint Williamson for their invaluable guidance in reviewing the information contained in this Note.

[1] See Hansjörg Strohmeyer, *Collapse and Reconstruction of a Judicial System: The United Nations Missions in Kosovo and East Timor*, 95 AJIL 46 (2001); INTERNATIONAL CRISIS GROUP [ICG], COURTING DISASTER: THE MISRULE OF LAW IN BOSNIA & HERZEGOVINA 8–11 (ICG Balkans Report No. 127, 2002), *available at* <http://www.crisisweb.org/>; ICG, REBUILDING LIBERIA: PROSPECTS AND PERILS 24 (ICG Africa Report No. 75, 2004), *available at id.*

[2] See, e.g., The Missing Priority: Post-Conflict Security and the Rule of Law (Dec. 2003) (report prepared for the Office of Counterterrorism, U.S. National Security Council) (on file with authors) [hereinafter The Missing Priority].

[3] See MICHAEL E. HARTMANN, INTERNATIONAL JUDGES AND PROSECUTORS IN KOSOVO: A NEW MODEL FOR POST-CONFLICT PEACEKEEPING (U.S. Institute of Peace Special Report No. 112, 2003), *available at* <http://www.usip.org/pubs/specialreports/sr112.html>.

[4] UNMIK Regulation 2000/6, On the Appointment and Removal from Office of International Judges and International Prosecutors (Feb. 15, 2000); UNMIK Regulation 2000/34, Amending UNMIK Regulation 2000/6 On the Appointment and Removal from Office of International Judges and International Prosecutors (May 27, 2000); UNMIK Regulation 2000/64, On Assignment of International Judges/Prosecutors and/or Change of Venue (Dec. 15, 2000). UNMIK regulations are available online at <http://www.unmikonline.org>.

[5] Memorandum from Director of the Department of Justice to All DOJ Staff Members, Criminal Division (Mar. 14, 2003) (on file with authors).

728   THE AMERICAN JOURNAL OF INTERNATIONAL LAW   [Vol. 98:727

This article posits the Criminal Division as a model for structuring international efforts in postconflict prosecutorial programs. Part I briefly reviews UNMIK's mandate in the prosecutorial sector. Part II discusses the challenges facing the criminal justice system in Kosovo, identifying the types of crime that should be given priority to ensure international security, as well as the inherent weaknesses of postconflict law enforcement institutions. Part III examines the Criminal Division, including its hierarchical organization, jurisdiction, relationship to police units, and use of intelligence. Part IV describes the criminal legislative reforms that are essential to the work of the Criminal Division. Part V offers some concluding remarks.

I. UNMIK'S MANDATE AND THE INTRODUCTION OF INTERNATIONAL PROSECUTORS

The Security Council authorized the international administration of Kosovo on June 10, 1999, when it passed Resolution 1244. UNMIK was established as the civilian interim administration,[6] in which the special representative of the UN secretary-general (SRSG), as the head of UNMIK, exercised sole executive and legislative authority.[7] Under his mandate to maintain law and order, the SRSG wielded executive control over all aspects of law enforcement, including the power to appoint law enforcement and justice officials.

Recognizing the urgent need to contain widespread violence, Resolution 1244 authorized the deployment of both an international police force to work side by side with a newly established local police force,[8] and an international security force, KFOR,[9] to assist in ensuring public order.[10] No consensus was reached, however, on the needs of the justice sector, and no provisions dealt explicitly with IPs. Nevertheless, by early 2000 the SRSG and the international community realized that local prosecutors were not capable of leading an aggressive effort to prosecute criminals who were fundamentally jeopardizing the peace-building process. Local prosecutors who had been barred or purged from official positions under the regime of Slobodan Milošević lacked basic skills, could not carry out their duties objectively because of ethnically motivated bias, or were subject to threats or intimidation by high-profile figures or notorious defendants.[11]

The SRSG addressed this situation through his legislative authority. Under UNMIK Regulation 2000/6, issued on February 15, 2000, UNMIK placed an IP in the domestic prosecutorial service.[12] It soon became apparent that international justice personnel had to be deployed on a more widespread basis, which led the SRSG to issue UNMIK Regulation 2000/64 on December 15, 2000, giving UNMIK the ability to place IPs in the Office of the Public Prosecutor of Kosovo and each of the five district prosecutorial services in the province.[13] UNMIK steadily increased the number of IPs over the ensuing years, recruiting primarily from jurisdictions in North America, Europe, and Asia, and it maintained a complement of ten to fifteen IPs between 2003 and 2004.[14]

While UNMIK regulations serve as the legal basis for introducing IPs into Kosovo, they do not specify the role that IPs are intended to play. The division of labor between IPs and local prosecutors, as well as the supervision of IPs, was left ambiguous until 2003, an indication that UNMIK's justice program was more akin to plugging holes than to mounting a comprehensive

---

[6] SC Res. 1244, para. 11 (June 10, 1999), 38 ILM 1451 (1999) (outlining the scope of UNMIK's authority).

[7] UNMIK Regulation 1999/1 (July 25, 1999).

[8] SC Res. 1244, *supra* note 6, para. 11(i).

[9] KFOR is the NATO-led military presence in Kosovo.

[10] SC Res. 1244, *supra* note 6, para. 9(d).

[11] HARTMANN, *supra* note 3, at 6–7.

[12] UNMIK Regulation 2000/6, *supra* note 4. For a more detailed discussion, see HARTMANN, *supra* note 3.

[13] UNMIK Regulation 2000/64, *supra* note 4. International prosecutors were placed in the five district prosecutor's offices (Prishtina, Peja, Gjilan, Mitrovica, and Prizren), and the Office of the Public Prosecutor of Kosovo. Competencies of local prosecutors are outlined in the Law on Public Prosecutor Office, OFFICIAL GAZETTE No. 32/76, 1988 (Kosovo).

[14] The number fluctuates constantly because IPs sign six-month renewable contracts, and generally leave after one or two years. Because of UN hiring regulations, vacant slots remain unfilled for several months.

strategy to fight crime. No consensus evaluation was made of the actual capacity of local prosecution services to handle cases generally, and IPs often used their discretion to take on cases that could have been handled by local prosecutors.[15] IPs often had a negative impact on the institutional development of local prosecutorial services, as the decision by an IP to assume a case frustrated an opportunity to "test" the hypothesis that local prosecutors were unable or unwilling to take on that case. In many instances, local prosecutors expressed bewilderment or resentment at an IP's apparent belief that a local prosecutor could not handle a case.

IPs new to Kosovo did not have the background for a full evaluation of the unique and complex issues confronting the Kosovar criminal justice system. IPs generally acquired a regional outlook, based on the region in which they were located, and did not enjoy regular access to those with a provincewide view of the crime situation. Individual IPs had their own conception of the IP's role, and used their discretion accordingly. This situation led to disparities of charges in different jurisdictions, disparities in caseloads among prosecutors, and lack of uniformity regarding the types of cases selected by IPs.[16]

Despite these problems, it has always been widely agreed that IPs must be involved in the justice effort in Kosovo. The ability to investigate and prosecute dangerous crime figures lay at the heart of ensuring peace and security, and local prosecutors and police did not have this ability. The process of transferring executive authority from the United Nations to local officials began in 2001, when the SRSG promulgated the Constitutional Framework for Provisional Self-Government in Kosovo. Over a two-year period, the majority of governance functions has been returned to Kosovar institutions, and the United Nations has correspondingly downsized its operations. However, recognizing the importance of the justice sector in supporting this handover of power, the SRSG reserved plenary control over police and justice functions to internationals under the constitutional framework.[17]

II. DESTABILIZING CRIME AND POSTCONFLICT LAW ENFORCEMENT IN KOSOVO

The haphazard manner in which IPs were introduced into Kosovo limited their ability to prosecute those who posed an immediate threat to peace building. Implementing the much-needed more structured approach to crime fighting required an analysis of the circumstances facing the IPs: the types of crime that were destabilizing the peace-building process in Kosovo, and the capacity of Kosovar law enforcement institutions to investigate these crimes.

Types of Crime Destabilizing Peace Building

The initial emergency period after June 1999 featured a high incidence of crime, including looting and ethnic murders.[18] While order was restored to Kosovo within a relatively short time, accusations of ethnically motivated crimes, the growth of organized criminal gangs, the continued presence of extremist organizations, and the flourishing of corruption threatened domestic and regional security. Dealing with these fundamental types of crime and their destabilizing effect

---

[15] For example, the Criminal Division reviewed the caseload of an IP in preparation for his departure from UNMIK in June 2003. Of twenty-six cases that he had taken on, thirteen were handed back to local prosecutors because there was no justifiable reason for IP involvement. In these thirteen cases, Kosovo Albanians were accused of common crimes, and none of the suspects was involved in major organized crime or extremism. The charges included giving a false statement, vehicle registration fraud, and low-level smuggling. The Criminal Division found that local prosecutors were willing and able to deal with such cases.

[16] For example, in February 2003, one IP in Prizren had taken on four cases, and another IP in Peja had taken on twenty-six cases. All of the Prizren IP's cases involved high-ranking crime figures, and charges included war crimes, attempted murder of a judge, and terrorism. The Peja IP's caseload was more varied, and few of his cases involved serious crimes or high-ranking crime figures.

[17] UNMIK Regulation 2001/9, On a Constitutional Framework for Provisional Self-Government in Kosovo, ch. 8 (May 15, 2001).

[18] ICG, STARTING FROM SCRATCH IN KOSOVO: THE HONEYMOON IS OVER 2–5 (ICG Balkans Report No. 83, 1999), available at <http://www.crisisweb.org/>.

730   THE AMERICAN JOURNAL OF INTERNATIONAL LAW   [Vol. 98:727

on the postconflict government is a primary justification for the continued UN presence in Kosovo.

Investigating ethnically motivated crimes involves issues basic to the conflict between the Albanian and Serb populations. Both sides use the ethnic issue to manipulate public opinion and pursue political aims. The authorities in Belgrade and Prishtina spread accusations of ethnic violence to undermine UN efforts to implement a lasting peace settlement.[19] War crimes prosecutions of Serbs fuel charges of bias by Belgrade, whereas failure to prosecute Serbs has given Albanians fuel to stir up anti-Belgrade sentiment. War crimes prosecutions of members of the Kosovo Liberation Army (KLA), many of whom are revered as heroes by Albanians,[20] provoke resentment in the Albanian community, whereas failure to prosecute such individuals leads to criticism from Belgrade.[21] These types of cases go to the heart of the causes of the conflict, and often generate protests and violence.

The growth of organized criminal gangs involved in narcotics trafficking, weapons dealing, trafficking in human beings, and racketeering constitutes a significant destabilizing threat to Kosovo and Europe.[22] Organized crime figures exert an undue degree of influence on the provisional institutions of self-government, local business people, and the population at large.[23] The influence of Kosovar Albanian organized crime figures spreads from Turkey to Scandinavia, and investigating them requires a considerable outlay of resources from law enforcement authorities throughout the region.[24]

Extremist organizations incite ethnic Albanians in Kosovo, Serbia-Montenegro, Albania, and the Former Yugoslav Republic of Macedonia to violence against domestic authorities and the United Nations. These organizations, which nominally profess a Greater Albania, are used to cloak involvement in organized crime, including such activities as extortion and weapons trafficking. While these organizations do not enjoy wide popular support, their attempts to cause violent disruptive incidents are aimed at intimidating international and local officials, as well as the general population.[25]

Corruption jeopardizes the viability of self-government in Kosovo. Even though local officials have been given executive authority gradually, substantial corruption can be found at all levels of government. Kosovars must often bribe officials to receive basic administrative services, and the officials' willingness to accept kickbacks facilitates the commission of organized crime.[26]

---

[19] *See* ICG, KOSOVO'S ETHNIC DILEMMA: THE NEED FOR A CIVIC CONTRACT 4–14 (ICG Balkans Report No. 143, 2003), *available at* <http://www.crisisweb.org/>. In one case involving the murder on December 22, 2002, of a Serb resident of Cernica village (Gjilan/Gnjilane), statements of village residents led police investigators to suspect two Kosovo Albanians, which resulted in their arrest. An international prosecutor ultimately withdrew from prosecuting the Albanians because of lack of evidence and has instead found sufficient evidence to investigate a Serb resident of the village. Public Prosecutor v. Dervishi and Sylejmani, Withdrawal of Prosecution, Gjilan/Gnjilane District Prosecution No. PP 225/2002 (June 25, 2003). The ethnic riots in mid-March 2004 were sparked by accusations that an Albanian had shot a Serb in Čaklavica, and that Serbs had chased a group of Kosovo Albanian children into a river in Mitrovica. Investigations into each of these incidents have failed to reveal suspects, much less an ethnic motive.

[20] See, for example, the prosecutions against former KLA Llap zone commander Rrustem Mustafa and former high-ranking members of the Dukagjini Command unit. Prosecutor v. Latif Gashi et al., C.C. No. 425/2001 (Dist. Ct. Prishtina July 16, 2003); Prosecutor v. Idriz Balaj et al. [Dukagjini Case], C.C. No. 190/02 (Dist. Ct. Peja sitting in Prishtina, Dec. 17, 2002).

[21] *See generally* HARTMANN, *supra* note 3, Phase One: International Police but Kosovan Judges and Prosecutors, at 3–7.

[22] EUROPOL, 2003 EUROPEAN UNION ORGANISED CRIME REPORT 14–15.

[23] *See generally* HARTMANN, *supra* note 3, at 3–7; The Missing Priority, *supra* note 2, at 34–36.

[24] *See* Prosecutor v. Qamil Shabani et al., Request for Investigation and Imposition of Detention, No. HEP 273/04 (Dist. Ct. Prishtina Mar. 29, 2004). In this case, the prosecution and the police worked together in a six-month investigation that included numerous wiretaps; the development of relationships with law enforcement authorities in Germany, Serbia, Turkey, and other countries; and extensive expenditures for day-to-day operations from translations to guaranteeing secrecy.

[25] Extremist organizations attempted to use explosive devices to disrupt public order in March 2003 at the Kosovo-Serbia boundary line, and in April 2003 at a bridge near Mitrovica. Both attempts failed.

[26] For example, widespread corruption in vehicle registration centers facilitates a thriving trade in cars stolen throughout Europe.

Corruption jeopardizes the financial viability of the provisional institutions of self-government, and hinders the development of effective, legitimate, and transparent public institutions.[27]

Inherent Limitations to Law Enforcement

The forms of crime discussed above have a particularly detrimental effect on the peace-building process, but the ability to prosecute individuals who engage in such crimes depends on the capacity of law enforcement institutions to investigate them. Kosovar law enforcement institutions are constrained by at least six factors inherent in the postconflict environment.

First, the general chaos brought about by the conflict and the UN occupation has made it difficult to implement a coherent crime-fighting strategy. When NATO occupied Kosovo in June 1999, the police force and judicial system imposed under the Milošević regime collapsed. Initial efforts at criminal justice reform were of an emergency nature, to identify individuals who could serve as judges and prosecutors, and quickly begin addressing the growing number of serious crimes.[28]

Second, the UNMIK police are plagued by numerous structural problems.[29] The Kosovo police force consists of approximately eight thousand officers, including both international civilian police officers (CIVPOL) and local officers from the Kosovo Police Force (KPS). The police force as a whole is disorganized, and many key units cannot coordinate effectively with each other. Among the KPS ranks, and to a lesser extent the CIVPOL ranks, only a limited number of police officers have the technical and analytical ability to pursue complex and coordinated investigations. Among the CIVPOL ranks, a high degree of regular turnover in police units undermines the continuity of long-term, complex investigations. Furthermore, CIVPOL officers come from many different countries and different professional backgrounds and are not trained properly when they arrive in Kosovo. These limitations necessitate close cooperation with prosecutors, to ensure that key investigations continue efficiently and that police officers remain informed of legal procedures and developments.

Third, considerable resources must be diverted from the fight against crime to develop local institutions.[30] Kosovar law enforcement officers, prosecutors, and judges were excluded from official life under Milošević, and their abilities have either atrophied or been stunted for a decade. Local officials who take on important political or organized crime figures do so at great personal risk. The perspectives of many local participants in the criminal justice system continue to be colored by ethnic bias or bitterness left over from the Milošević regime.

Fourth, gathering reliable intelligence takes time, and building an intelligence network is incompatible with the short time horizons contemplated by UNMIK's mission mandate. Obtaining reliable intelligence is crucial in the early stages of investigations, especially those involving organized criminal gangs. Such intelligence—whether from confidential informants or other sources—may form the basis for applying for investigative measures, such as search warrants and wiretaps, or identifying important criminal figures. It takes a major investment of resources for law enforcement officials to build up networks of informants, assess the reliability of intelligence, and refine the information for use in criminal proceedings. In Kosovo, there was little reliable preexisting intelligence on organized criminal gangs operating before and after the NATO intervention. The intelligence gathered by the Serb authorities was unusable or lost.[31]

---

[27] UNMIK has cited controlling corruption as an important goal, as evidenced by the formation of a Financial Investigation Unit (composed of investigators from the Italian Guardia di Finanza); the issuance of UNMIK Regulation 2003/17, On the Promulgation of a Law Adopted by the Assembly of Kosovo on Public Financial Management and Accountability (May 12, 2003); and the issuance of UNMIK Regulation 2004/2, On the Deterrence of Money Laundering and Related Criminal Offences (Feb. 5, 2004).

[28] Strohmeyer, *supra* note 1, at 48–50, 51–56.

[29] These contentions are based upon the authors' personal experiences in conducting investigations with the UNMIK police.

[30] ICG, FINDING THE BALANCE: THE SCALES OF JUSTICE IN KOSOVO 11, 14–16 (ICG Balkans Report No. 134, 2002), *available at* <http://www.crisisweb.org/>.

[31] This is the assessment of informant handlers in the Kosovo Organized Crime Bureau.

732   THE AMERICAN JOURNAL OF INTERNATIONAL LAW   [Vol. 98:727

Fifth, the prosecution services have been forced to handle cases in which exigent security considerations had led security or law enforcement forces to make an arrest before completing a criminal investigation. In such situations, the evidence implicates suspects in criminality but is either weak and/or undeveloped. When KFOR obtains the information,[32] however, it implicates the suspect in a high degree of criminal activity that is aimed at derailing the peace process. A prosecutor is then handed a case where the suspect is generally recognized as a threat to security, but the prosecutor must work backwards to develop the case. The prosecutor must determine whether there are sufficient grounds to bring charges after the arrest, knowing that it will be difficult to collect evidence now that the suspect and his associates are aware that a criminal investigation is taking place.[33]

Sixth, conditions elsewhere, particularly in southeastern Europe, can profoundly affect the investigation of major crime in Kosovo. Albania has become a safe haven for many people wanted in Kosovo,[34] and investigations of human-trafficking rings and organized criminal gangs require a high degree of cooperation from law enforcement and justice officials from most of the countries lying between Turkey and Germany.

III. THE CRIMINAL DIVISION

The nature of criminal justice in Kosovo puts an unduly complicated burden on the prosecutorial services. On the one hand, they face an urgent need to prosecute those who engage in crimes that threaten postconflict reconstruction. On the other hand, the law enforcement situation places constraints on prosecutors that do not exist (or at least do not exist so acutely) in developed criminal justice systems. Under these circumstances, the purposes of international involvement in postconflict prosecutorial efforts must be narrowly tailored to address issues that are fundamental to the postconflict reconstruction.

The director of the Department of Justice established the Criminal Division in March 2003 to accomplish this goal.[35] Five aspects are essential to the mission of the division: hierarchical organization of prosecutors, definition of subject matter jurisdiction, provincewide jurisdiction, a direct relationship with police units, and access to intelligence.

Centralized Hierarchical Organization

The hallmark of the Criminal Division is supervision of prosecutions. The chief international prosecutor, who heads the Criminal Division, supervises all IPs and is vested with the authority to approve or deny all measures taken by them.[36] Operationally, once the police make an allegation against a suspect, an IP drafts a Case Initiation Report outlining the nature of the crime,

---

[32] For more on the use of KFOR intelligence, see Elizabeth Abraham, *The Sins of the Savior: Holding the United Nations Accountable to International Human Rights Standards for Executive Order Detentions in Its Mission in Kosovo*, 52 AM. U. L. REV. 1291, 1321–31 (2003).

[33] A particularly good example is the case against the former Albanian insurgent leader Shefqet Musliu. KFOR suspected Musliu of extremist activities in Kosovo, and the Serb authorities suspected him of extremist activities in southern Serbia. KFOR detained Musliu and turned him over to civilian police authorities in Kosovo in July 2003. While Musliu was probably involved in a variety of criminal activities, law enforcement authorities had not collected evidence that would lead to a particularly effective prosecution prior to his KFOR arrest. *See* Prosecutor v. Shefqet Musliu, Indictment, No. PP 107/03 (Dist. Ct. Gjilan/Gnjilane Dec. 9, 2003).

[34] In recent months, cooperation between Kosovo law enforcement authorities and the law enforcement authorities in Albania has increased. The Albanian police recently arrested and transferred Florim Ejupi, who was accused of killing eleven Serbs in a bus bombing in February 2001.

[35] For a similar discussion of the systematic approach taken by the U.S. Department of Justice's Organized Crime and Racketeering Section, see Paul E. Coffey, *The Selection, Analysis, and Approval of Federal RICO Prosecutions*, 65 NOTRE DAME L. REV. 1035 (1990).

[36] This hierarchical structure was outlined in UNMIK draft Regulation 2003/XX, On the Supervision of International Prosecutors (July 2003) (on file with authors). The draft regulation was never enacted, however, because of an internal conflict between the DOJ and the Office of Legal Affairs. The elements of the draft regulation were nevertheless implemented by the DOJ.

the identity and background of the suspect(s), and an initial assessment of the evidence gathered.[37] This report allows the head of the Criminal Division to evaluate the importance of the case and to engage in a dialogue with the IP on how to proceed. The head of the division reviews all subsequent measures undertaken by the IP in pursuing the case, and the IP must obtain the consent of the head of the division prior to filing an indictment or appeal.

The head of the Criminal Division also maintains a central case-tracking system, enabling him to monitor developments in all cases. Thanks to the tracking system, the chief international prosecutor can analyze the impact of IPs in prosecuting particular types of crimes and more effectively coordinate proceedings in different jurisdictions.

A Legal Unit, consisting of a group of junior lawyers, maintains regular operational contact with the main police units, particularly the Kosovo Organized Crime Bureau, the Counter-Terrorism Task Force, the Central Criminal Investigative Unit, and the Trafficking in Persons Investigative Unit.[38] The junior lawyers keep the head of the Criminal Division apprised of preliminary police investigations that may ultimately require an IP's participation. The Legal Unit is also a conduit for resolving extraterritorial legal issues. The junior lawyers identify issues in ongoing investigations or prosecutions that may require action by foreign authorities, and maintain contacts with INTERPOL and justice officials to ensure that international legal assistance is requested and obtained.

In practice, this hierarchical structure ensures a standard level of quality of prosecutions. Applications for search warrants and other investigative measures meet basic legal requirements.[39] Cases based on weak evidence do not proceed beyond the investigative stage, because the head of the Criminal Division makes the tactical decision not to undertake proceedings that lack a reasonable chance of conviction.[40] Resources are focused on the important cases.[41]

The major weaknesses of this structure are that it is composed exclusively of IPs, and that it runs parallel to domestic prosecutorial services. Only a limited number of qualified foreign prosecutors are able or willing to work in Kosovo, especially for an appreciable period of time. Nevertheless, the Criminal Division's method of supervising prosecutions is a workable, temporary structure that is ideally suited to postconflict reconstruction, which is conducted with thin prosecutorial resources and in conditions of acutely destabilizing crime.[42]

Subject Matter Jurisdiction

The resources of this structured group of prosecutors must be focused on the forms of crime that are particularly destabilizing. Given the prevalence of organized crime, corruption, and extremism in Kosovo, prosecutors must concentrate on criminal associations, financial crimes, and serious ethnic crimes. Ideally, such a cadre of prosecutors would be organized in a specialized unit, whose mandate was clearly defined by an administrative directive.

[37] Interoffice Memorandum from Director of DOJ to All International Prosecutors, Case Initiation Report (Mar. 25, 2003) (on file with authors).

[38] International CIVPOL officers have headed each of these units and held the key investigative positions. The units have also included some KPS officers who actively participate in investigations.

[39] For example, IPs supervise applications pursuant to UNMIK Regulation 2002/6, On Covert and Technical Measures of Surveillance, as the statute contains vague standards for obtaining and implementing judicial orders for wiretapping. For more on Regulation 2002/6, see note 81 *infra* and corresponding text.

[40] *See, e.g.*, Prosecutor v. Ruzhdi Saramati, No. AP–KZ 76/2002 (Sup. Ct. Oct. 9, 2002). The Supreme Court quashed a murder conviction and remanded the case for retrial. Despite the IP's intention to move forward, there was no hope of obtaining evidence to support a conviction on retrial, and the prosecution was withdrawn.

[41] In early 2004, IPs brought cases against prominent public officials and important organized crime figures for war crimes and narcotics trafficking. Prosecutor v. Qamil Shabani et al., Request for Investigation and Imposition of Detention, No. HEP 273/04 (Dist. Ct. Prishtina Mar. 29, 2004); Prosecutor v. Selim Krasniqi et al., Request for the Conduct of Investigations, No. HEP 26/2004 (Dist. Ct. Prizren Feb. 17, 2004).

[42] There are plans to incorporate this structure into the domestic prosecutorial services by establishing the Kosovo Special Prosecutor's Office, which will consist of specially trained Kosovo prosecutors who function along the lines of those in the Criminal Division. As of October 2004, the office remained in the planning stages.

However, plans to create a specialized chamber with a mandate geared to specific crimes in Kosovo were rejected[43] in favor of placing IPs directly into the existing domestic prosecutorial system. In the absence of legislation defining the role of IPs, the Criminal Division maintains an internal policy on the types of cases warranting IP involvement. It is generally understood that IPs should give top priority to cases involving serious ethnically motivated crimes, war crimes, prominent organized crime rings, terrorism, and corruption.[44] The chief international prosecutor implements this policy on a discretionary basis, relying on information provided by IPs in the Case Initiation Reports and additional information obtained by junior lawyers from the police or military, in making decisions about which cases IPs should assume.[45]

As no operating instructions or directives have formalized this policy, a certain degree of flexibility can be exercised in implementing it. This flexibility allows IPs to handle certain types of urgent investigations or prosecutions. For example, an IP can take on a case against an individual known to be a high-ranking organized crime figure, even when the case in question does not involve organized crime. Furthermore, an IP can handle a case involving sensitive issues that were not initially envisioned when IPs were brought to Kosovo, such as criminal cases against UNMIK personnel.[46]

This flexible internal policy, however, suffers from numerous flaws. Diverting resources from the core caseload to smaller, yet significant, issues limits the overall ability of the Criminal Division to investigate and prosecute cases with a direct nexus to the goals of the mission. For example, from late 2003 to mid-2004, IPs undertook the prosecution of approximately eight cases involving prison violence and escapes.[47] While the problems in the prison system required urgent action, in no way was it evident that local prosecutors could not effectively handle such cases. The problems of the prison system were the "problem of the day," and IP involvement was a quick fix that diverted resources from more fundamental types of cases.[48]

In light of these issues, subject matter jurisdiction should have been delineated more clearly.[49] While specific provisions would have limited the flexibility in the use of IPs, they would have guaranteed from the outset that IPs would participate only in cases with a direct nexus to the overall goals of the mission.

---

[43] For example, the plans to create the Kosovo War and Ethnic Crimes Court were scuttled. See the discussion in David Marshall & Shelley Inglis, *The Disempowerment of Human Rights–Based Justice in the United Nations Mission in Kosovo*, 16 HARV. HUM. RTS. J. 95, 130 (2003).

[44] The criteria are set out in §4.1 of draft Administrative Direction 2003/XX, Implementing UNMIK Regulation No. 2003/XX On the Supervision of International Prosecutors (July 2003). The administrative direction was not officially put into effect because of the impasse reached regarding the regulation of IP supervision. The principles of the draft administrative direction, however, were put into effect in practice.

[45] The factors in using this discretion are spelled out in §4.2 of draft Administrative Direction 2003/XX, *supra* note 44.

[46] From 2002 to 2003, the secretary-general has waived the immunity of numerous international staff hired by the United Nations to allow for investigations and prosecutions to proceed within the domestic court system. These suspects are prosecuted by international prosecutors with international judges as triers of fact. IPs have prosecuted international police officers for manslaughter, murder, and abuse of office. Prosecutor v. John Atanga, No. C.C. 13/03 (Dist. Ct. Prishtina Feb. 3, 2003); Prosecutor v. Sherif Abd Elaziz, No. Pr. 70/02 (Dist. Ct. Peja Nov. 12, 2002); Prosecutor v. Martin Almer, No. P128/2003 (Orahovac Mun. Ct. Oct. 7, 2003). In some cases in which immunity has been waived, the international suspected of a crime has been dismissed or the case is still in the investigative stages.

[47] UNMIK officials thought that if IPs assumed these prosecutions, UNMIK would send a strong message to the prison population in response to rising prison violence. In all but one case, the defendants were not high-level criminals.

[48] Other examples abound. In early 2004, IPs were asked to intervene in debt collection cases for KEK, the Kosovo electric company. UNMIK leaders thought it was important to "send a message" on issues related to revenue for the Kosovo Consolidated Budget, and arbitrarily determined that IP participation in these low-level criminal cases was necessary. However, local prosecutors had already prosecuted numerous persons for stealing electricity and there was no indication that the local prosecutors were not effective.

[49] This should have been done along the lines proposed in the draft Regulation and Administrative Direction on the Supervision of International Prosecutors, *supra* note 44.

Provincewide Jurisdiction

Specialized subject matter jurisdiction should be accompanied by broad geographical jurisdiction. In Kosovo, the preconflict legislation divided public prosecution services into five districts, and placed these services under the nominal supervision of the Office of the Public Prosecutor of Kosovo.[50] After the establishment of UNMIK, IPs, like their local counterparts, practiced in regional jurisdictions, although UNMIK Regulation 2000/64 allowed the SRSG to assign IPs to a case outside their region on an exceptional basis.[51] Enforcing these strict jurisdictional limitations spread the limited number of IPs thinly across a province with only two million inhabitants.

This arrangement limited UNMIK's ability to use IPs effectively. Coordinating with the police and court officials became difficult when cases involved crimes committed in multiple jurisdictions. When the situation in one district became exceptionally calm, the IPs in that district either remained idle or took on insignificant cases to keep busy. Conversely, when the situation in a district became intense, special arrangements had to be made on a case-by-case basis, which was not always possible. Something as simple as an IP's vacation generated massive amounts of bureaucratic activity simply to ensure that another IP could cover a case in his or her absence, which hindered the ability of the DOJ to conduct proceedings efficiently.[52]

In the spring of 2003, UNMIK appointed all IPs to all jurisdictions in Kosovo. While nominally occupying offices in one of Kosovo's five District Prosecutor's Offices, IPs may, at the discretion of the chief international prosecutor, take on cases throughout the province. Vesting IPs with provincewide jurisdiction equips the chief international prosecutor with greater flexibility to implement an effective crime-fighting strategy, primarily for logistical reasons.

Connections to the Police

A main aspect of the Criminal Division's structure is the institutionalized relationship with the police. The division established a practice of having investigators in the key police units immediately contact Criminal Division lawyers on all legal matters and on any major case. This arrangement ensures that the Criminal Division can supervise important investigations, identify complicated legal issues early in the investigation, make certain that the police collect evidence efficiently and lawfully, and determine whether IP involvement is necessary at the initial stages of a case.

Such direct supervision is required because of the difficulty of acquiring evidence, such as finding witnesses willing to come forward, and the need to order invasive investigative measures. These hindrances are compounded by the inherent limitations of law enforcement institutions, as described above in part II. Prosecuting crimes that fundamentally affect postconflict reconstruction, such as organized crime, requires an anticipatory investigative approach to identify key players and uncover organized criminal structures. The evidence necessary to prosecute these types of cases generally consists of material obtained through the use of covert measures, such as wiretapping, the use of confidential informants, undercover operations, and surveillance. Strategic planning, and obtaining all necessary judicial orders, requires a police-prosecutor relationship that is close and coordinated at the earliest stages of the investigation.

Prior to the establishment of the Criminal Division, the ad hoc relationship between IPs and the police limited the DOJ's capacity to prosecute major crime figures. An example of the way

---

[50] Law on Public Prosecutor Office, *supra* note 13.

[51] In such situations, the SRSG invoked provisions pursuant to UNMIK Regulation 2000/64, *supra* note 4, to permit IPs to act in another jurisdiction.

[52] For example, the Supreme Court reversed and remanded a case in which twelve individuals were convicted of possessing a large number of weapons simply because an IP appeared once at trial without the requisite authorization from the SRSG. Prosecutor v. Saqip Ibrahimi et al., No. AP 303/2001 (Sup. Ct. Mar. 18, 2002). On retrial, a district court panel convicted the suspects again, largely along the same lines as the first trial panel. To have appeared one day in court, the IP from a different district would have had to receive special permission from the SRSG pursuant to UNMIK Regulation 2000/64.

736   THE AMERICAN JOURNAL OF INTERNATIONAL LAW   [Vol. 98:727

the institutionalized relationship between police and prosecution can lead to concrete results was the arrest of Qamil Shabani, a notorious organized crime figure who ran a heroin-smuggling operation throughout Europe. While extensive investigations in Switzerland and Germany produced evidence of Shabani's criminality, the police in Kosovo made little progress between 2001 and 2003. When the Criminal Division was formed, however, the police investigation intensified. Division lawyers provided guidance on wiretapping, surveillance, and international legal assistance, and between September 2003 and March 2004, sufficient evidence was gathered to arrest Shabani and several others involved in his narcotics ring.[53]

The institutionalized participation of international prosecutors and junior lawyers from the Criminal Division at the early stages of police investigations ensures higher quality preliminary investigations, and increases the capacity of the law enforcement institutions to fight destabilizing crime.

Access to Intelligence

The Criminal Division gains access to information obtained by foreign intelligence agencies by maintaining a close relationship with the DOJ Sensitive Information Operations Unit. The unit consists of lawyers with NATO security clearance who have been seconded to the DOJ by NATO member states.[54] These lawyers establish liaison with military intelligence officers and the police to identify individuals whose criminal activity threatens the safety and security of Kosovo.

KFOR relies on intelligence gathered by NATO members in carrying out its mandate under UN Security Resolution 1244.[55] In some instances, information used by KFOR is relevant to criminal investigations, for example, to corroborate information obtained by the police or to identify individuals who should be investigated by law enforcement authorities. Accordingly, civilian use of such intelligence is appropriate in limited circumstances.[56] The presence of foreign military intelligence units in Kosovo helps to overcome the absence of police intelligence networks, and enhances the UN capacity to anticipate threats to peace and security.

Lawyers in the Sensitive Information Operations Unit review intelligence gathered by the military and then request that certain information be declassified for use by the Criminal Division. An IP will use such information to support applications for search warrants or other judicial orders within the confines of existing law. This framework for applying intelligence to criminal proceedings increases the basis on which the Criminal Division sets priorities and the ability of IPs to prosecute important crime figures.

The second lesson of UNMIK's experience in Kosovo is that, in the early stages of postconflict reconstruction, supervisory authorities must put a structure in place that ensures that resources are effectively focused on fighting destabilizing forms of crime. The five fundamental aspects of the Criminal Division serve as a framework for such a structure.

---

[53] Prosecutor v. Qamil Shabani et al., *supra* note 24.

[54] The United Nations cannot issue security clearances. Accordingly, IPs do not have access to intelligence information unless it is declassified.

[55] Paragraph 9 of Resolution 1244, *supra* note 6, reads:

> the responsibilities of the international security presence to be deployed and acting in Kosovo will include . . . [e]stablishing a secure environment in which refugees and displaced persons can return home in safety, the international civil presence can operate, a transitional administration can be established, and humanitarian aid can be delivered; . . . [and] [s]upporting, as appropriate, and coordinating closely with the work of the international civil presence.

[56] The United Nations has recognized that the reluctance to use intelligence in peacekeeping has "not served it well." UNITED NATIONS DEPARTMENT OF PEACEKEEPING OPERATIONS, LESSONS LEARNED UNIT, COMPREHENSIVE REPORT ON LESSONS LEARNED FROM UNITED NATIONS ASSISTANCE MISSION FOR RWANDA (UNAMIR): OCTOBER 1993–APRIL 1996, at 4 (1996), *available at* < http://www.un.org/Depts/dpko/lessons/UNAMIR.pdf>. However, the potential for abuse should be noted. Intelligence in this context has a very limited role—to support efforts at investigating individuals by lawful means.

IV. PROSECUTORIAL TOOLS

Structural reforms were not the sole aspect of UNMIK's criminal justice program. Since 1999 the SRSG has used his legislative authority to amend the preconflict criminal and criminal procedure codes to include basic substantive and procedural provisions that allow prosecutors to carry out their functions more effectively.[57] The SRSG was bound by law to see that these legislative amendments met international human rights standards.[58]

Substantive Provisions on Criminal Associations

The preconflict criminal law of Kosovo generally punished direct participation in criminal acts. Accordingly, UNMIK did not need to amend provisions applicable to violent ethnic crime, war crimes, and corruption so as to facilitate such prosecutions. However, the law lacked strong provisions relating to criminal associations, which hindered prosecutors and law enforcement officials in investigating and prosecuting organized crime and extremism.

UNMIK introduced definitions of specific types of criminal associations, facilitating the prosecution and investigation of indirect participants such as leaders, members, associates, and supporters of organized criminal gangs. The new provisions were drafted to balance the need to prosecute with the obligation to respect international human rights standards. Such law is essential given the need to investigate the members of criminal organizations who cannot be "caught in the act" of committing a crime because they insulate themselves from the act itself.

Regulation of organized crime. The UNMIK Regulation on Measures Against Organized Crime[59] defines and criminalizes associations that are joined with criminal intent, and follows draft provisions annexed to the United Nations Convention Against Transnational Organized Crime.[60] Under the regulation, an organized crime is "the commission of a 'serious crime' by a 'structured group' in order to obtain, directly or indirectly, a financial or other material benefit."[61] Section 2 of the regulation sentences members of the organized crime group to five to fifteen years of imprisonment, leaders of the group to seven to twenty years of imprisonment, and those who aid or abet the group to four to seven years of imprisonment. These penalties are to be served consecutively with those imposed for the commission of the underlying crime(s).

The preconflict criminal law punished leaders and members of criminal associations,[62] but the relevant provisions were rarely used to investigate or prosecute them and violations did not significantly increase the maximum sentences for the underlying crimes. Under the provision on leading a criminal association, the maximum term of imprisonment was five years; the maximum

---

[57] On April 6, 2004, a new provisional criminal procedure code and a provisional criminal code entered into force in Kosovo. This Note, however, makes reference to the legislation in effect prior to 1999 (the preconflict legislation), and the period between July 1999 and April 2004. The preconflict legislation consisted of the Kosovo criminal law, Serbian criminal law, the criminal law of the Socialist Federal Republic of Yugoslavia (SFRY), and the SFRY criminal procedure code. All provisions discussed were incorporated into the new codes, and all cases cited were initiated prior to April 2004.

[58] UNMIK Regulation 1999/24, On the Applicable Law in Kosovo (Dec. 12, 1999).

[59] UNMIK Regulation 2001/22, On Measures Against Organized Crime (Sept. 20, 2001). International human rights covenants, like the European Convention on Human Rights, are part of the applicable law in Kosovo. UNMIK Regulation 1999/24, *supra* note 58.

[60] United Nations Convention Against Transnational Organized Crime, GA Res. 55/25, Annex I (Nov. 15, 2000), *available at* <http://www.un.org/documents>.

[61] UNMIK Regulation 2001/22, *supra* note 22, §1(a). In section 1(b) a "serious crime" is defined as "conduct constituting an offence punishable by a maximum deprivation of liberty of at least four years." Section 1(c) defines a "structured group" as

     a group of three or more persons that:

         (i) exists for a period of time and acts in concert with the aim of committing one or more serious crimes;
         (ii) is not randomly formed for the immediate commission of an offence; and
         (iii) does not need to have formally defined roles for its members, continuity of its membership or a developed structure.

[62] SFRY CRIM. CODE Art. 26; Serbian CRIM. CODE Art. 227.

738   THE AMERICAN JOURNAL OF INTERNATIONAL LAW   [Vol. 98:727

term for membership was one year.[63] Under the preconflict provision on joint criminal enterprise, the maximum sentence was the maximum allowed for the underlying criminal act.[64] Moreover, no specific provisions dealt with aiding or abetting criminal organizations, and the elements of a structured group and intent were not spelled out statutorily.

The UNMIK Regulation on Measures Against Organized Crime made prosecutions of organized crime more viable by dramatically increasing the penalties for all forms of participation and clarifying the specific elements of the crime.[65] Such substantive changes were necessary in view of the degree of influence organized crime figures exert throughout the province. These criminals are often linked—directly or indirectly—with those involved in terrorist or extremist activities, and their influence extends beyond the province. Organized crime rings in Kosovo engage in various forms of criminality, including narcotics trafficking, extortion, smuggling, and human trafficking, and a significant portion of the province's economic system is based on organized crime.[66]

Regulation against terrorism. The UNMIK Regulation on the Prohibition of Terrorism and Related Offences broadly defines the act of terrorism to take into account the diverse range of activities involving regional extremist groups.[67] The regulation authorizes prosecution of persons who participate in terrorist organizations, which includes providing, soliciting, collecting, or concealing funds for purposes of terrorism,[68] and those who recruit persons for terrorist acts, train or receive training for purposes of terrorism, belong to a terrorist organization, or are leaders of a terrorist organization. The regulation also holds a person criminally responsible if he possessed credible information about the planning or commission of a terrorist act when it was possible to mitigate its effect or prevent the act and did not inform law enforcement authorities.

Under the preconflict terrorism statute, a prosecutor could charge only individuals who were directly implicated in a specific act of terrorism.[69] Proceedings could move forward only on the suspicion that the individual had caused "an explosion, fire, or [taken] some other generally dangerous action out of hostile motives," or had committed "an act of violence which may create a feeling of personal insecurity in citizens or in a group of citizens."[70] Even proceeding under theories of incitement, complicity, or aiding and abetting, a prosecutor would have to relate the conduct to participation in an underlying criminal act.

The broader UNMIK terrorism regulation calls for proceedings against those who directly participated in the act, but it also facilitates investigations into other members of the organization.[71] Giving police and prosecutors wider latitude in investigations helps them to prevent

---

[63] Serbian CRIM. CODE Art. 227.

[64] SFRY CRIM. CODE Art. 26.

[65] In February 2004, the Prishtina district court convicted a defendant of possession of sixteen kilograms of heroin with intent to distribute, organized crime, and illegal gun possession. The combined sentence was eleven years: five years for intent to distribute the narcotics, five years for organized crime, and one year for gun possession. Under the preconflict code, the defendant could not have been sentenced consecutively, pursuant to Article 48 of the SFRY criminal law. Prosecutor v. Islam Haxha et al., No. PP 563/2003 (Dist. Ct. Prishtina Feb. 9, 2004). In the case cited *supra* note 24, the maximum sentence for Qamil Shabani, who headed a major heroin-smuggling ring, is thirty years with a seven-year mandatory minimum. The maximum sentence under the preconflict code would have been fifteen years with a one-year minimum.

[66] EUROPOL, *supra* note 22; The Missing Priority, *supra* note 4.

[67] UNMIK Regulation 2001/12, On the Prohibition of Terrorism and Related Offences (June 14, 2001). Section 1(a) of the regulation includes in the list of terrorist acts murder, grave bodily injury, hostage taking, kidnapping, unlawful detention, poisoning of food or water, causing general danger, destroying or damaging public utilities, making or procuring weapons or instruments, unlawful possession of weapons or exploding substances, endangering internationally protected persons, hijacking of aircraft, jeopardizing the safety of an aircraft's flight, unauthorized acquisition or use of nuclear materials, and jeopardizing safety by the use of nuclear materials.

[68] Suppression of the financing of terrorism is the subject of an international convention. International Convention for the Suppression of the Financing of Terrorism, GA Res. 54/109, annex (Dec. 9, 1999), *available at* <http://www.un.org/documents>.

[69] SFRY CRIM. CODE Art. 125.

[70] *Id.*

[71] *See, e.g.,* Prosecutor v. Xhavit Morina et al., Indictment, No. PP 37/2003 (Dist. Ct. Prishtina Oct. 20, 2003) (Xhavit Morina prosecuted for terrorist acts and for being a leader of a terrorist organization); Prosecutor v. Ilmi

terrorist acts, and to arrest and prosecute terrorists. Such statutory reforms were necessary given the influence of extremist organizations in the region. For example, the Armata Kombetari Shqiptare (AKSH), or Albanian National Army (ANA),[72] has been identified as an extremist group that engages in terrorism in Kosovo, the Former Yugoslav Republic of Macedonia, Serbia, and Albania.[73] The AKSH General Regulations state that its objective is the "continuation of the fight for freedom in parts of divided Albanian territories, by a force from the motherland of Albania."[74]

The AKSH has established a command structure and is served by fund-raisers, members, and recruiters. The UNMIK terrorism regulation recognizes that acts of terrorism are often part of a bigger plan, and that those who directly commit the acts are usually foot soldiers. Merely prosecuting the foot soldiers has little effect on curbing the activities of the organization as a whole. IPs have undertaken prosecutions against approximately fifteen persons for varying levels of participation in terrorism. None of these cases could have been brought prior to the introduction of the UNMIK terrorism regulation.

Trafficking in human beings. The UNMIK Regulation on the Prohibition of Trafficking in Persons in Kosovo creates the crime of trafficking in human beings, and follows the draft provisions annexed to the United Nations Convention Against Transnational Organized Crime.[75] Under the regulation, trafficking is the

> recruitment, transportation, transfer, harbouring or receipt of persons, by means of the threat or use of force or other forms of coercion, of abduction, of fraud, of deception, of the abuse of power or of a position of vulnerability or of the giving or receiving of payments or benefits to achieve the consent of a person having control over another person, for the purpose of exploitation.[76]

Those who engage in trafficking, organize groups of people for the purpose of engaging in trafficking, or negligently facilitate trafficking are punishable by imprisonment ranging from six months to twenty years.[77] Additionally, the regulation punishes those who withhold travel documents while acting as an employer or agent, and those who procure sexual services from someone knowing that she is a victim of trafficking.

The preconflict code lacked provisions relating to this form of crime. Trafficking was not specifically defined in the criminal code, and other criminal provisions were insufficient to support investigations and prosecutions of traffickers. Kosovo's ambiguous status led to uncertainty regarding immigration provisions, and in the absence of a visa regime, prosecuting illegal transport of others across the border was difficult.[78] The criminal charge of intermediation in the exercise of prostitution[79] did not contemplate that a multitude of individuals, by force or deception, would facilitate the procurement of women or girls. Even if a prosecutor could secure a conviction for either of these offenses, the maximum punishment would have been five years of imprisonment.

Abazi and Tasim Zymeri, Indictment, No. PP 532/03 (Dist. Ct. Prishtina Sept. 30, 2003) (prosecuted for unlawful weapons possession); Prosecutor v. Naser Azemi and Gazmend Zeqiri, Amended Indictment, No. PP 178/02 (Dist. Ct. Gjilan Apr. 8, 2003) (prosecuted for being leaders of a terrorist organization); Prosecutor v. Nevzat Halili and Ismet Kryeziu, Amended Indictment, No. PP 734/2002 (Dist. Ct. Prishtina Apr. 2, 2003) (prosecuted for being leaders of a terrorist organization).

[72] The AKSH (or ANA) must be distinguished from the Kosovo Liberation Army, which disbanded in 1999. There is no direct link between the two, although some AKSH members may have belonged to the KLA.

[73] AKSH was declared a terrorist group by UNMIK Administrative Directive 2003/9, Implementing UNMIK Regulation 2001/12 (Apr. 17, 2003); *see also* ICG, SOUTHERN SERBIA'S FRAGILE PEACE 6–9 (ICG Europe Report No. 152, 2003), *available at* <http://www.crisisweb.org/>.

[74] The AKSH General Regulations are available online (in Albanian) at the AKSH Web site, <http://www.geocities.com/shqiponja2001al/letra.htm> (trans. in text by UNMIK translator).

[75] UN Convention Against Transnational Organized Crime, *supra* note 60, Annex 2, Protocol to Prevent, Suppress and Punish Trafficking in Persons, Especially Women and Children.

[76] UNMIK Regulation 2001/4, On the Prohibition of Trafficking in Persons in Kosovo §1.1(a) (Jan. 12, 2001).

[77] *Id.* §2.

[78] SFRY CRIM. CODE Art. 249(2).

[79] *Id.*, Art. 251.

740   THE AMERICAN JOURNAL OF INTERNATIONAL LAW   [Vol. 98:727

The UNMIK regulation addresses trafficking by specifically defining the crime, and by assessing criminal liability for all aspects of a trafficking ring. Such a measure was necessary because of the influence of those involved in human trafficking in the Balkans, which has grown exponentially since the outbreak of hostilities in the 1990s.[80]

Procedural Provisions on Collecting and Preserving Evidence

In addition to amending substantive provisions of the criminal law to facilitate the prosecution of criminal associations, UNMIK amended the criminal procedure code to increase the capacity to collect and preserve evidence. While the amendments to the criminal law strengthened existing provisions, the amendments to the procedure code gave prosecutors, both local and international, and the police capacities that had not previously existed. The need for the amendments was evidenced by the ease with which criminals could conceal their activities and intimidate witnesses or victims. Regulations on gathering evidence, protecting witnesses, and using police statements at trial assist prosecutors and law enforcement officials in developing cases against those involved in all forms of criminal associations.

Gathering evidence: covert measures. The UNMIK Regulation on Covert and Technical Measures of Surveillance and Investigation[81] specifies the conditions under which a prosecutor or judge can authorize law enforcement to undertake invasive investigative measures without the knowledge of one or more of the suspects. The UNMIK regulation conforms with the standards of the European Convention on Human Rights (ECHR), as the covert measures are prescribed by law and the covert measure ordered must be necessary and proportionate to the information being sought and a person's right to privacy.[82] By showing a grounded suspicion that an individual or individuals have committed a serious crime, prosecutors can order or request photographic or video surveillance in a public or private place, covert monitoring of conversations in a public or private place, search of postal items, interception of telecommunications, interception of communications by a computer network, use of tracking or positioning devices, a simulated purchase of an item, an undercover operation, a simulated corruption offense, metering of telephone calls, or disclosure of financial data.[83]

Prior to the introduction of the covert measures regulation, prosecutors relied on general provisions of the criminal procedure code that broadly outlined police investigative powers.[84] The absence of provisions authorizing the police to take invasive investigative measures did not permit vigorous collection of evidence against those who went to great lengths to conceal their criminal activity.

Authorizing such investigative techniques is a particularly useful tool in prosecuting organized criminal gangs and public officials who engage in corruption. In such situations, it is unlikely that any witnesses will come forward.[85] Often, the most compelling evidence of organized crime or membership in an organized crime ring is obtained through covert interceptions of telecommunications. In Kosovo, the police and prosecutors have effectively used intercepted

---

[80] *See* INTERNATIONAL ORGANIZATION FOR MIGRATION, VICTIMS OF TRAFFICKING IN THE BALKANS: A STUDY OF TRAFFICKING IN WOMEN AND CHILDREN FOR SEXUAL EXPLOITATION IN, THROUGH AND FROM THE BALKAN REGION (2001), *available at* <http://www.iom.int>.

[81] UNMIK Regulation 2002/6, On Covert and Technical Measures of Surveillance and Investigation (Mar. 18, 2002), *amended by* UNMIK Regs. 2003/5 and 2004/6.

[82] P. G. and J. H. v. United Kingdom, 2001–IX Eur. Ct. H.R. 195; Khan v. United Kingdom, 2000–V Eur. Ct. H.R. 279.

[83] UNMIK Regulation 2002/6, *supra* note 81, §1.

[84] Articles 151 and 155 of the law on criminal procedure gave the police and the prosecutor broad investigative powers but did not define what was needed legally for different investigative actions.

[85] Witnesses fail to do so either because they are beneficiaries of corruption or because organized crime rings are able to intimidate them with impunity.

telecommunications as supporting evidence in numerous cases, and in a few cases most of the evidence comes from the interception of telecommunications.[86]

Witness protection. Under the UNMIK Regulation on the Protection of Injured Parties and Witnesses in Criminal Proceedings,[87] a judge can order a wide variety of measures to protect the identities of witnesses.[88] The regulation, which complies with ECHR standards, balances the need to protect the safety of a witness with the right of a suspect to confront his accuser.[89] The scope of measures that can be ordered ranges from nondisclosure of personal data, to the giving of testimony in a separate room or by closed-circuit television, or in exceptional circumstances to shielding the identity of a witness from the defendant. Ordering anonymity is an extreme case and an anonymous witness alone cannot be the sole witness in establishing guilt, which conforms with ECHR jurisprudence.[90]

Under the preconflict procedure code, there was no statutory basis for granting witness protection. Prosecutors required the measures permitted under the UNMIK regulation because individuals implicating high-profile politicians, public officials, or organized crime figures endanger themselves from the moment they make themselves known to the police.[91] Pervasive witness tampering and intimidation have deterred many witnesses from coming forward, and have led to changes in testimony, jeopardizing important prosecutions. Threats against witnesses, attacks on witnesses, and murders of key witnesses have partly undermined the criminal justice system in Kosovo since the war.[92]

Protective measures under the regulation have had limited effect, particularly since Kosovo is such a small jurisdiction. Relocation, a potentially effective measure, is permissible under the regulation, but there are practical limitations.[93] Safe houses are only temporary solutions, and permanent relocation within the province is not viewed as a feasible solution.[94] The only effective form of witness protection is relocation to another country, which depends on the agreement of foreign governments.[95] Nonetheless, protective measures have enabled many individuals to come forward in high-profile cases.[96]

Witness statements as evidence. The UNMIK Regulation on the Use in Criminal Proceedings of Written Records of Interviews Conducted by Law Enforcement Authorities allows statements given to the police to be used as evidence at trial under certain circumstances, so as to establish guilt.[97] Given the degree of witness intimidation, and the possibility that witnesses will disappear

---

[86] Prosecutor v. Driton Hasani et al., Indictment, No. PP 979/03 (Dist. Ct. Prishtina June 28, 2004); Prosecutor v. Hasan Shala et al., Indictment, No. PP 925/03 (Dist. Ct. Prishtina May 28, 2004); Prosecutor v. Qamil Shabani et al., Decision to Conduct Investigations, No. HEP 273/04 (Dist. Ct. Prishtina Mar. 29, 2004); Prosecutor v. Shpend Gashi, Indictment, No. PP 860/03 (Dist. Ct. Prishtina Jan. 26, 2004).

[87] UNMIK Regulation 2001/20, On the Protection of Injured Parties and Witnesses in Criminal Proceedings (Sept. 20, 2001), *amended by* UNMIK Regulation 2002/01 (Jan. 24, 2002).

[88] Section 3.1 lists possible measures but does not restrict the prosecutor or judge from creating new measures that are not listed, as it states that "[t]he Court may order such protective measures as it considers necessary, including but not limited to . . . ."

[89] *See* Van Mechelen v. Netherlands, 1997–III Eur. Ct. H.R. 691; Doorson v. Netherlands, 1996–II Eur. Ct. H.R. 446.

[90] *See* cases cited *supra* note 89.

[91] The preamble to the regulation, in explaining the reasons for its drafting, specifically states, "Recognizing that the intimidation of injured parties and witnesses severely undermines efforts to effectively investigate and prosecute serious crimes in Kosovo . . . ." UNMIK Regulation 2001/20, *supra* note 87, pmbl.

[92] OSCE MISSION IN KOSOVO, REVIEW OF THE CRIMINAL JUSTICE SYSTEM (MARCH 2002–APRIL 2003): PROTECTION OF WITNESSES IN THE CRIMINAL JUSTICE SYSTEM 10–28 (2003), *available at* <http://www.osce.org/kosovo>.

[93] *Id.* at 19. The main practical limitation is that most foreign states are unwilling to help relocate witnesses.

[94] *Id.* at 19–21.

[95] Foreign governments have been unwilling to accept witnesses from Kosovo, and protected witnesses remain in the safe house for many months. This creates further limitations, as protection cannot be offered to prospective witnesses because of lack of space in the safe house.

[96] *See* Prosecutor v. Selim Krasniqi et al., *supra* note 41. An international investigating judge granted protective measures that allowed several witnesses to come forward in a war crimes case involving ten former KLA officers accused of running a detention camp.

[97] UNMIK Regulation 2002/7, On the Use in Criminal Proceedings of Written Records of Interviews Conducted by Law Enforcement Authorities (Mar. 28, 2002).

742   THE AMERICAN JOURNAL OF INTERNATIONAL LAW   [Vol. 98:727

or change their testimony, witness testimony must be preserved as evidence as early as possible in the investigative process. The regulation balances this need against the right of suspects to confront their accuser, which is mandated by the ECHR.[98] To use prior witness statements, the prosecutor or the judge, *ex proprio motu*, can make a motion to admit such a statement to the court to prove a fact in question. After the motion, the court must determine if admitting the statement would violate the defendant's right to confront the accused and the defendant's right to a fair trial.

Under the preconflict law, witness statements were admissible as evidence only when given before a judge during the course of proceedings, and prior witness statements could be used at trial in lieu of live testimony only under a narrow set of circumstances.[99] For the most part, the preconflict procedure code did not envision changes in testimony by witnesses as a result of threats or intimidation. Essentially, a suspect could have undermined an investigation by uncovering the identity of a witness and intimidating him before he testified at trial.

The UNMIK regulation is a powerful tool for law enforcement authorities. The ability to use police statements, under certain circumstances, as evidence at trial mitigates the effect of witness intimidation.

Capacity to Prosecute Strategically

The UNMIK Regulation on Co-operative Witnesses[100] vests prosecutors with a certain degree of discretion to grant immunity to persons who are accused of a crime but have information helpful to law enforcement. The discretion of the prosecutor in Kosovo is set out in section 2.5 of the regulation, under which, on the motion of a prosecutor, a judge may order "that there shall be no initiation or continuation of criminal proceedings against the Co-operative Witness for the criminal offence specified in the order and that no punishment shall be imposed for the offence so specified." A prosecutor may request full immunity if a judge determines that a suspect or defendant will give evidence in court that is likely to prevent further criminal acts or lead to the finding of truth in a criminal proceeding or a successful prosecution of another suspect.[101]

Under the preconflict procedure code, Kosovo was a mandatory prosecution jurisdiction,[102] where prosecutors were obliged to prosecute on the highest charge supported by the evidence.[103] Prosecutors could not offer a plea agreement to defendants who decided to testify against their coconspirators.

The UNMIK regulation does not offer more comprehensive prosecutorial discretion, which is often vital in efficiently prosecuting serious crimes. For example, it does not allow for plea bargaining or a discretionary rejection of prosecution. Nonetheless, the regulation does provide a key tool to prosecutors, who must often rely on minor players of serious crimes to help guarantee the successful prosecution of major players of serious crimes.

Such legislative reforms are crucial to postconflict reconstruction and they must be implemented as a package concurrently with a prosecutorial structure.

---

[98] *Id.*, section 3 includes safeguards that must be met before a statement can be used by the court in criminal proceedings.

[99] Articles 83 and 333 of the SFRY law on criminal procedure provided for limited instances in which a court could accept records of prior testimony when the witness could not appear. The testimony could be read into the trial record only if the witness had died, become mentally ill, could not be found, or could not appear because of age or illness.

[100] UNMIK Regulation 2001/21, On Co-operative Witnesses (Sept. 20, 2001).

[101] *Id.* §1(b).

[102] Article 18 of the law on criminal procedure states that "[t]he public prosecutor shall undertake the criminal prosecution if there is evidence that a criminal act which is prosecuted *ex officio* has been committed."

[103] There were very limited exceptions: for example, in minor cases where the maximum sentence was less than one year.

V. CONCLUSION

The UNMIK experience in Kosovo has been a test case of the viability of including an international prosecutorial component in transitional criminal justice systems. The United Nations missed an opportunity by failing to implement a strategically conceived and coordinated justice policy at the outset of the peace-building process. Nevertheless, UNMIK's experience is instructive for the future. In future postconflict reconstruction missions, the criminal justice environment should be evaluated before international prosecutors are introduced into the jurisdiction. Specifically, the supervising authorities must make a coherent analysis of the forms of crime that fundamentally affect the peace process, and a realistic assessment of the ability of law enforcement institutions to deal with those crimes. On the basis of this evaluation, the supervising authority should implement a temporary structure that reconciles the urgent need to address destabilizing crime with the inherent limitations of postconflict law enforcement agencies. Finally, the supervising authority must augment the effectiveness of this temporary structure with supporting legislation.

This form of international involvement can conceivably be implemented in several different ways. First, in the context of UN peacekeeping missions, the Department of Peacekeeping Operations (DPKO) can integrate an UNMIK DOJ-style Criminal Division into its operations, recruiting prosecutors as it does other civilians. The weaknesses of this approach, however, are that the United Nations has not succeeded in recruiting significant numbers of truly qualified justice experts; DPKO does not have the authority to give security clearances for intelligence, unlike member states; and delays in the UN procurement system hamper the acquisition of staff and equipment in a timely manner.

Second, the DOJ Criminal Division model can be implemented under the auspices of a DPKO mission but with considerable input from member states. In this situation, member states would second prosecutors, support staff, and equipment to a DPKO mission. The weakness of this approach is that success depends on the seriousness with which the contributing member states look upon the prosecutorial unit within the DPKO mission.

Third, the DOJ Criminal Division model can be implemented outside the auspices of a DPKO mission by a foreign authority that has pledged to assist the justice sector unilaterally, by a coalition of foreign authorities who have pledged such assistance, or by a transitional domestic authority. These kinds of scenario may arise when a territory is in transition, but the threat to international security has not led the Security Council to authorize a peacekeeping mission.

The final question relating to the Criminal Division model is how to turn the duties assumed by IPs back to local officials. Although this process is still in the early stages in Kosovo, the overriding goal is clearly to ensure that UNMIK's reforms become institutionalized within the domestic system. UNMIK's efforts will be evaluated by the degree to which local prosecutors are able or willing to assume controversial and significant cases in the absence of international assistance.

Regardless of the nature of international participation, the DOJ Criminal Division constitutes a workable model for a transitional prosecutorial service in a postconflict reconstruction mission.

[6]

The Disempowerment of Human Rights–Based Justice in the United Nations Mission in Kosovo*

David Marshall**

Shelley Inglis***

INTRODUCTION

In 1999, the overall mandate provided to the United Nations Interim Administration Mission in Kosovo ("UNMIK") and the Kosovo Force ("KFOR") was unprecedented in its complexity and magnitude.[1] KFOR, led by the North Atlantic Treaty Organization ("NATO"), and numbering between 40,000 and 50,000 troops, was responsible for ensuring peace and a secure environment throughout Kosovo. UNMIK had to govern an entire province and reestablish a functioning public sector in the midst of substantial destruction, communal devastation, and the exodus of the former regime. The number of tasks necessary to achieve this mandate was overwhelming, and included the development of a civil service, the establishment of all social services, and the reconstruction and operation of public utilities and roads, airports, and public transportation. Furthermore, UNMIK had to encourage economic growth through the establishment of a banking system and the formulation of budgetary, currency, and taxation policies. Essential to the ultimate success of the mission was also the development of a public broadcasting system, the support of independent media and civil society, and the cultivation of a political system in which political parties could flourish and peacefully cooperate. Most vitally, however, the UN needed a legal basis and a criminal justice system that could foster respect for the rule of law so that all activities could be carried out and sus-

* Opinions expressed in this Article are solely those of the authors and do not represent the views of any organizations or governments with which the authors have been or are associated. Significant portions of this Article reflect the authors' respective experiences while working in Kosovo.

** Senior Advisor to the International Cooperation Group, Department of Justice, Canada; Chief, Legal Systems Monitoring Section, Human Rights and Rule of Law Division, OSCE Mission in Kosovo, 2000–2001; Regional Rule of Law Advisor, OSCE, 1999.

*** Attorney, The Children's Law Center; Legal Advisor, Legal Systems Monitoring Section and Victim Advocacy and Support Section, Human Rights and Rule of Law Division, OSCE Mission in Kosovo, 2000–2002; Amnesty International Researcher, 1999.

1. See generally Michael J. Matheson, United Nations Governance of Postconflict Societies, 95 AM. J. INT'L L. 76 (2001).

tained. As a guarantor of democracy, UNMIK had to establish a governing administration and justice system premised on respect for the rule of law and the protection of human rights.

These immense tasks notwithstanding, there have been considerable achievements. With the implementation of the Constitutional Framework in 2001, and free and fair elections in November of that year, some democratic institutions have begun to take hold.[2] Political parties of all colors are flourishing and a degree of peace and security now exists for the vast majority of Kosovo Albanians, and to some degree, Kosovo Serbs and other minorities. There has been substantial improvement in the province's infrastructure, including roads, hospitals, and schools. But an effective and successful democratic transition also requires a coherent approach to criminal justice reform. Moreover, ensuring that respect for human rights takes hold, both in legal institutions and the populace at large, requires a continuous and coherent engagement by the international community. In this respect, UNMIK has failed. Indeed, the failure is so profound that it puts at risk the transition as a whole.

The mission failed to clearly establish the supremacy of international human rights standards as the framework within which UNMIK and KFOR should determine the extent and quality of their actions. By virtue of the UN's having placed all executive and legislative powers in UNMIK, the structure of the mission itself involves inherent tensions with democratic governance. In fact, UNMIK's and KFOR's executive actions have clearly contravened human rights standards but remained beyond any legal challenge. In this Article, we detail violations by UNMIK and KFOR of the right to liberty and the broader fair trial rights as set out in the International Covenant on Civil and Political Rights ("ICCPR")[3] and the European Convention on Human Rights and Fundamental Freedoms ("ECHR").[4]

UNMIK's legislative power has been used without the articulation of broad policy goals or any consistent, transparent, or inclusive process. In addition to the lack of judicial review of UNMIK's actions, policies regarding the establishment of the judiciary have led to concerns about its independence. In particular, the assertion of immunity for the acts of KFOR and UNMIK, even those actions taken in their official capacity, has resulted in a lack of any effective remedy for human rights violations in Kosovo.

Capitulating to political pressure to rebuild the justice sector quickly, UNMIK failed to develop any coherent strategy for the justice sector, including for war crimes cases. It opted instead for a dithering approach that proved catastrophic for defendants and victims alike, particularly Kosovo

---

2. UNMIK/REG/2001/9 (On a Constitutional Framework for Provisional Self-Government in Kosovo), 15 May 2001. All regulations are available at http://www.unmikonline.org/regulations/index.htm.

3. International Covenant on Civil and Political Rights, Mar. 23, 1976, 999 U.N.T.S. 171.

4. European Convention for the Protection of Human Rights and Fundamental Freedoms, Sept. 3, 1953, 213 U.N.T.S. 222.

Serbs. The mission failed to provide any pre-entry training on applicable law, a necessity for appointees who had not worked in the legal realm for more than ten years. This was compounded by a lack of foresight to provide the courts with the necessary tools to effectively prosecute crimes.

In announcing the creation in 1999 of a domestic war crimes court with a majority of international judges, UNMIK acknowledged the risk of judicial bias in the trials of Kosovo Serbs. But in the nine months between the announcement of its creation and its rejection, UNMIK took no steps to intervene and halt the investigation, indictment, and trials of alleged war criminals before Kosovo Albanian trial panels. The initial deployment of international judges and prosecutors was random and incoherent. These international actors, most without any criminal or humanitarian law experience, would be appointed to some, but not all, war crimes cases. Their presence in the early trials had little impact, as they were consistently outvoted by local judges. The ensuing convictions would eventually be reversed on appeal, but significant damage had been done to UNMIK's attempt to foster reconciliation and engender respect for the rule of law.

The founding documents of the mission made explicit the key role to be played by the human rights components (the international governmental organizations tasked with overseeing the mission's compliance with human rights) within the mission. These components met with considerable obstacles in fulfilling their mandates. Despite efforts to point out human rights concerns and to recommend ways to alleviate them, primary actors within UNMIK often failed to take corrective action. One of the most egregious examples of the marginalization of the human rights components was the UN's failure to engage them in the review of pending legislation for human rights compliance. As a result, critical legislation promulgated by UNMIK remains in violation of internationally recognized human rights standards.

National "ownership" is a key component for a successful transitional process. Effectively transforming society requires a real engagement with the local populace. But as the mission in Kosovo progressed, consultation on substantive issues in the areas of criminal justice and human rights was nearly nonexistent. Critical laws that introduced international judges and prosecutors and expanded domestic law were not adequately explained to local legal actors, and once promulgated, no attempt was made to engage the local population with the reasoning behind such decisions. It was almost three years into the mission before all regulations were translated into the local language. The result is a local population disillusioned and cynical about human rights rhetoric and disengaged from legal institutions. Rather than exemplifying transparency, adherence to the rule of law, and fairness, UNMIK and KFOR have demonstrated a disregard for international human rights and, as a result, have severely damaged the development of these principles in Kosovo.

I. BACKGROUND

A. *The Kosovo Crisis*

In 1989, the Yugoslav and Serbian governments revoked Kosovo's status as an autonomous province, stripping it of the entitlement to self-government under the Yugoslav Constitution and rendering it an integral part of the Republic of Serbia. This move marked the beginning of ten years of violations by Serb and Yugoslav authorities of the rights of Kosovo Albanians, who constituted the overwhelming majority of the population of Kosovo. The revocation of Kosovo's autonomy was also perceived to be the initial step toward the disintegration of the Federal Republic of Yugoslavia ("FRY") and the wars in Croatia and Bosnia and Herzegovina.[5]

With the imposition of Serbian law and authority in Kosovo, Kosovo self-government was dismantled; many Kosovo Albanians were forced from their positions of employment and from participation in most sectors of society, including public institutions, labor organizations, and governmental organs. Serbian curriculum and language were imposed at all levels of schooling, and Kosovo Albanians left the education system in large numbers as a result. Almost all Kosovo Albanians left the judiciary and law enforcement agencies and the Serbian authorities discontinued the administration of the Judicial Bar exam. Some Kosovo Albanians continued to practice in the legal system as defense lawyers representing accused Albanians in politically motivated proceedings. As a consequence of the disenfranchisement, Kosovo Albanians created parallel structures to govern and school themselves and undertook measures of passive resistance to the Serbian regime.[6]

At the end of 1995, the war in Bosnia came to an end, but the human rights issues in Kosovo were not addressed. During the 1990s, the Kosovo Liberation Army ("KLA") was created with the aim of using violence to overthrow the Serbian regime. In 1998, fighting between the Serb regime and the KLA intensified, and international engagement with Yugoslavia and Serbia resulted in the establishment in November 1999 of the Kosovo Verification Mission in Kosovo, implemented by the Organization for Security and Cooperation in Europe ("OSCE").[7] International pressure to peacefully resolve the simmering conflict in Kosovo culminated in peace talks in France and the comprehensive plan for Kosovo, the Rambouillet Agreement,[8] which Slobodan Milošević refused to sign in March 1999.

---

5. For a review of the rise to power of Slobodan Milošević in Serbia and the role of Kosovo politics, see LAURA SILBER & ALLAN LITTLE, YUGOSLAVIA: DEATH OF A NATION (1997).

6. For a comprehensive review of the history of the Kosovo Albanians, see NOEL MALCOLM, KOSOVO: A SHORT HISTORY (1999).

7. For perspectives on the role of the OSCE and Kosovo Verification Mission deployments to Kosovo within the larger framework of European peacekeeping, see Jan Wouters & Frederik Naert, *How Effective is the European Security Architecture? Lessons from Bosnia and Kosovo*, 50 INT'L & COMP. L.Q. 540, 558 (2001).

8. Interim Agreement for Peace and Self-Government in Kosovo, February 23, 1999, F.Rep.Yugoslavia-Rep.Serb.-Kosovo, *available at* http://www.usofficepristina.usia.co.at/doc1.htm. The Rambouillet Agreement

Without an explicit mandate from the United Nations, NATO began bombing Kosovo and Serbia on March 24, 1999. The Serbian regime and Yugoslav army orchestrated a widespread campaign to "ethnically cleanse" Kosovo of the Albanian community. This resulted in thousands of civilian deaths, significant numbers of rapes and other forms of torture, extensive burning and pillaging of communities, and the expulsion of approximately 800,000 persons from their homes.[9] The bombing campaign ended in June with the signing of the Military Technical Agreement, whereby the Yugoslav and Serbian forces were to withdraw, and the promulgation of Resolution 1244/1999 by the United Nations Security Council ("UNSC") on June 10, 1999.[10]

B. UNMIK and KFOR Mandate

Resolution 1244 authorized "the deployment in Kosovo, under United Nations auspices, of international civil and security presences."[11] Responsibilities of the security presence included, *inter alia,* establishing a safe environment for the return of refugees and displaced persons, ensuring public safety and order until the international civilian presence could take responsibility for this task, and supporting the work of the international civilian presence. Resolution 1244 mandated that the international civilian presence provide an interim administration for Kosovo "under which the people of Kosovo can enjoy substantial autonomy within the Federal Republic of Yugoslavia, and which will provide transitional administration while establishing and overseeing the development of provisional democratic self-governing institutions" and protecting and promoting human rights.[12]

UNMIK was established under Resolution 1244. The Secretary General ("SG") of the United Nations declared that "all legislative and executive powers, including the administration of the judiciary would be vested in UNMIK" and exercised by the Special Representative of the Secretary General ("SRSG").[13] These powers included the promulgation of legislation in the form of regulations and the authority to "change, repeal, or suspend existing laws to the extent necessary."[14]

---

laid out a framework for peaceful intervention in Kosovo to ensure the rights of Kosovars would be protected.

9 *See Report of the Secretary-General on the United Nations Interim Administration Mission in Kosovo*, U.N. SCOR, 54th Sess. ¶ 8, U.N. Doc. S/1999/779 (1999) [hereinafter *Report of the Secretary-General*]. *See also* Org. for Sec. & Cooperation in Eur., Kosovo/Kosova: As Seen, As Told: An Analysis of the Human Rights Findings of the OSCE Kosovo Verification Mission October 1998 to June 1999: Part One (1999), *at* http://www.osce.org/kosovo/documents/reports/hr/part1.

10. S.C. Res. 1244, U.N. SCOR, 54th Sess., 4011th mtg., U.N. Doc. S/RES/508 (1999) [hereinafter Resolution 1244].

11. *Id.* ¶ 5

12. *Id.* ¶ 10.

13. *See Report of the Secretary-General, supra* note 9, ¶¶ 35, 39.

14. *Id.* ¶ 39.

The complex structure of the mission included four components, called Pillars, each led by a Deputy Representative. A Principal Deputy ("PDSRSG") would assist the SRSG in managing the mission and ensure a coordinated approach among the Pillars.[15] Pillar I, led by the United Nations High Commissioner for Refugees ("UNHCR"), was charged with providing humanitarian aid and facilitating the return of refugees and internally displaced persons. Pillar II, led by the United Nations, was responsible for establishing the civil administration, which included the police force and the establishment of the judiciary and penal system. Pillar III, the Institution Building pillar, led by the OSCE, was to develop civil society and human rights institutions, media, and political parties. The considerable responsibility to plan and implement economic reconstruction went to the European Union in Pillar IV. In spring 2001, a new Pillar I was established called the Police and Justice Pillar.[16]

With the establishment of UNMIK, the SRSG created a forum for local consultation called the Kosovo Transitional Council. In 2000, the SRSG established a civilian administration with Departments, including the Administrative Department of Judicial Affairs ("DJA"), led by international and national co-heads. In November 2000, local municipal elections were held and locally administered municipalities were structured. The Departments on the national level, excluding the DJA, which was transformed into a solely international entity under Pillar I, remained in place until the creation of the Constitutional Framework, which established an Assembly, a President, and a Prime Minister with ten Kosovo government ministries. Kosovo-wide elections were held in November 2001, leading finally to the establishment of the Provisional Interim Kosovo Government in March 2002.

C. *The Emergency Judicial System ("EJS")*

On 28 June 1999, the SRSG issued an emergency decree establishing the Joint Advisory Council on Provisional Judicial Appointment.[17] The main mandate of the Joint Advisory Council consisted of recommending the pro-

---

15. *Id.* ¶ 45.

16. *See UNMIK at a Glance, at* http://www.unmikonline.org/intro.htm. This Pillar was created to ensure the integration and coordination of these two functions. It includes the local Kosovo Police Force, the local judiciary, and the local corrections service. This Pillar remained in UNMIK despite the establishment of the local provisional Kosovar administration, thereby leaving the Kosovar authorities with no competency over these governmental functions.

17. UNMIK Emergency Decree 1999/1, 28 June 1999 (providing legal basis for the establishment of the Joint Advisory Council); UNMIK Emergency Decree 1999/2, 28 June 1999 (appointing members of the Joint Advisory Council). *See also* Org. for Sec. & Cooperation in Eur., Observations and Recommendations of the OSCE Legal Systems Monitoring Section: Report Two—The Development of the Kosovo Judicial System (1999), *at* http://www.osce.org/kosovo/documents/reports/justice/report2.htm [hereinafter *OSCE LSMS: Report 2*]. The Joint Advisory Council was composed of three internationals and four local Kosovo members: one Kosovo Serb, two Kosovo Albanian, and one Kosovo Muslim (Bosniak).

visional appointment of judges and public prosecutors in the EJS for a three-month renewable period. EJS judges and prosecutors were appointed in three of the five regions of Kosovo.[18] In the other two regions, and with the assistance of the OSCE, judges and prosecutors, including one Kosovo Serb, traveled by helicopter to conduct bail hearings of persons arrested by KFOR. In some regions, EJS judges began conducting investigative hearings into alleged war crimes committed by Kosovo Serbs and Roma.

Though UNMIK's official policy goal was to establish a multi-ethnic society, due to the increasing violence and paucity of security for minority communities, it became impossible to convince the few Kosovo Serb judges who had remained to participate in the EJS.[19] In due course, between September 1999 and December 1999, most Kosovo Serb judges and prosecutors moved to Serbia, where many took up new judicial posts. The judicial vacuum from June 1999 to December 1999 resulted in a significant increase in serious criminal activity, including an apparent orchestrated campaign to kill the remaining Kosovo Serbs and any alleged collaborators.[20] UNMIK police were understaffed and domestic courts were not fully functioning.

At this time, there was a consensus within UNMIK that it might be necessary to declare a state of emergency. Although such a declaration would have resulted in the derogation of certain human rights for a limited period of time, there was broad agreement among the human rights components that, given the circumstances, it was appropriate. Periods of detention could be extended (as they eventually were), international judges and prosecutors could be brought in for limited periods to preside over issues of arrest and detention, and an intensive legal educational training program could be instituted. UNMIK demurred and opted to forge ahead with plans to start the regular judicial system within a matter of months.

On July 25, 1999, the SRSG approved UNMIK Regulation 1999/1, which provided that the law applicable in Kosovo was the law in force prior to the NATO intervention on March 24, 1999.[21] Members of the ethnic Albanian legal community resented and resisted this determination because they considered it offensive to reinstate the laws of the repressive Milošević regime, and they willingly disregarded the applicable law in the conduct of trials.[22] In response, in December 1999, the SRSG promulgated Regulation 1999/24,[23] which repealed Regulation 1999/1 and reinstated the laws applicable in 1989.

---

18. The five regions were Pristina, Mitrovica, Gnjilane, Pec, and Prizren.

19. *See OSCE LSMS: Report 2, supra* note 17.

20. *See* ORG. FOR SEC. & COOPERATION IN EUR., KOSOVO/KOSOVA: AS SEEN, AS TOLD: PART TWO (1999), *at* http://www.osce.org/kosovo/documents/reports/hr/part2/.

21. UNMIK/REG/1999/1 (On the Authority of the Interim Administration in Kosovo), 25 July 1999, *amended by* UNMIK/REG/2000/54, 27 Sept. 2000, and UNMIK/REG/1999/25, 12 Dec. 1999.

22. *See OSCE LSMS: Report 2, supra* note 17.

23. UNMIK/REG/1999/24 (On the Law Applicable in Kosovo), 12 Dec. 1999, *amended by* UNMIK/REG/2000/59, 27 Oct. 2000.

D. *Establishment of the Regular Judicial System*

UNMIK Regulation 1999/7 established the Advisory Judicial Commission ("AJC") to recommend candidates for judicial and prosecutorial appointment on a permanent basis.[24] Significant efforts, early on, to recruit minorities into the judiciary were without success.[25] Among the 354 judges (professional and lay) and public prosecutors sworn into district courts between January and March 2000, there was not a single Kosovo Serb.[26] The most recent Report of the Secretary General on UNMIK states that there are 341 local judges and prosecutors, including 319 Kosovo Albanians, four Kosovo Serbs, seven Turks, nine Bosniaks, and two Roma. As regards international judicial actors, there are twelve international judges and twelve international prosecutors.[27] The regular judicial system is comprised of the minor-offense court system, municipal courts, district courts, and the Kosovo Supreme Court.[28]

Other than judicial appointments, the AJC was also empowered to investigate judicial misconduct and to make recommendations to the SRSG.[29] The SRSG did not renew the AJC mandate and in April 2001 promulgated Regulation 2001/8 establishing the Kosovo Judicial and Prosecutorial Council, composed of nine members, the majority of whom are internationals.[30]

II. The Legal Framework

Despite the significant emphasis placed on international human rights standards as the basis for the mission's authority, no clear legal framework has been established in which both UNMIK and KFOR could be expected to function. The role of international human rights law in this regard has never been fully clarified. Although the Constitutional Framework clarifies the direct applicability of international human rights standards in Kosovo, it does not address human rights protection vis-à-vis UNMIK.

Within this legal vacuum, UNMIK and KFOR have violated international human rights principles, most notably by detaining individuals in

---

24. UNMIK/REG/1999/7 (On Appointment and Removal From Offices of Judges and Prosecutors), 7 Sept. 1999, *amended by* UNMIK/REG/2000/57, 6 Oct. 2000.

25. *See OSCE LSMS: Report 2, supra* note 17.

26. Interview with DJA official, in Pristina, Kosovo (Mar. 2000).

27. *Report of the Secretary-General on the United Nations Interim Administration Mission in Kosovo,* U.N. SCOR, 57th Sess., ¶ 26, U.N. Doc. S/2002/1126 (2002).

28. The minor-offense courts have jurisdiction over offenses punishable by a fine or imprisonment of no longer than sixty days. The jurisdiction of the municipal court covers offenses with sentences of up to five years imprisonment. The trial panel consists of three judges, two lay and one professional. District courts have jurisdiction over offenses that carry sentences of more than five years. The trial panel consists of five judges, three lay and two professional. There are no lay judges serving on the Kosovo Supreme Court.

29. In its first twelve months, the AJC failed to undertake any investigations, notwithstanding allegations of judicial bias against minorities.

30. UNMIK/REG/2001/8 (On the Establishment of the Kosovo Judicial and Prosecutorial Council), 6 Apr. 2001.

contravention of judicial orders of release and without any mechanisms for detainees to challenge their detentions. With regard to KFOR, the question of whether it is bound even by the applicable law has never been clearly answered and has led to KFOR's possessing seemingly unchallengeable authority.

The conflation of UNMIK's powers has provided room for executive abuse of authority, including the promulgation of legislation intended to usurp the judicial function and ensure the success of the executive agenda. There has been a failure to develop any legislative process, including ensuring meaningful consultation with local actors and transparency. The lack of a process has resulted in ineffective laws, often not implemented, and has created serious obstacles to the ability of the courts to apply the law.

Without clear guidance on human rights and concrete limitations on state power, the judiciary has been unable or unwilling to use its authority to ensure the enforcement of international human rights standards. The lack of institutional guarantees of independence, particularly in regard to international participation in the judiciary, has created concerns over the real independence of the judiciary under UNMIK. Immunity for UNMIK and KFOR actions and the failure to develop the judiciary to forcefully fulfill its role as the third branch of democratic government has negatively impacted the role of the courts in Kosovo as guarantors of the rule of law and human rights.

A. The Role of International Human Rights Law

In the Secretary General's Report of July 12, 1999, which detailed the authority and competencies of the mission, the SG interpreted UNMIK's obligation under Resolution 1244 to protect and promote human rights as requiring it to be guided by internationally recognized human rights standards *as the basis for the exercise of its authority*.[31] UNMIK's authority is almost absolute because all executive and legislative power is vested in the SRSG. The SG further directed that persons holding public office or undertaking such duties shall observe internationally recognized human rights standards in exercising their functions and shall not discriminate against any persons on any grounds, and that the laws should be implemented only to the extent that they conform to international human rights standards.

1. UNMIK Regulations

The first UNMIK law, Regulation 1999/1[32] On the Authority of the Interim Administration in Kosovo (later amended in Regulation 1999/25[33]), mirrored, in part, the provisions declared by the SG. It made domestic law applicable only in so far as it was compatible with human rights standards,

---

31. *See Report of the Secretary-General, supra* note 9, ¶ 42.
32. UNMIK/REG/1999/1, *supra* note 21.
33. UNMIK/REG/1999/25, *supra* note 21.

and required all persons undertaking public duties or holding public office to observe internationally recognized human rights standards in the course of their functions. Moreover, it mandated non-discrimination in the implementation of public duties and official functions. However, the Regulation was silent as to the implications of these provisions. It did not state unequivocally that international human rights standards were to be directly applicable in Kosovo. Furthermore, it did not provide that such standards are the basis for UNMIK's authority, i.e., that they form the framework within which the mission, including the exercise of UNMIK executive and legislative authority and the judiciary, should function.

This ambiguity regarding Kosovo's governing principles is significant. Without a clear framework set out in the applicable law for the realization of rights and a mechanism for the restraint of excessive state power, the disproportionate authority concentrated in the SRSG could go unchallenged. The obligation to uphold internationally recognized standards and not to discriminate could be rendered meaningless because there would be no framework within which to enforce them. UNMIK's power could be used arbitrarily and unfairly, without accountability, transparency, or predictability— in contravention of the meaning of justice and the rule of law.

In light of this, human rights and rule-of-law advocates and experts argued that human rights norms were the framework within which the international presence and its local counterparts must function. This contention was based on the presumed intentions of the UNSC in Resolution 1244 and the SG's report. Human rights groups and institutions argued that the United Nations, when acting as a governing power, was obligated to uphold the same standards that it had itself created to ensure the rights of the people vis-à-vis their governments.[34] Bound by the human rights provisions of the Charter on which it was founded, the UN has a special responsibility to set the standard for human rights protection for governments when the UN itself is acting as a governing power. More formalistic positions on the issue were based on the fact that the FRY was a signatory to the ICCPR, among other human rights documents, and the United Nations, as an "occupying" force within the FRY, was obligated to ensure those rights.[35] Regardless of the basis for these various legal arguments, advocates urged that, in order to sustain the legitimacy of the mission itself, the SRSG only exercise his authority to the extent that it conformed to international human rights law and that he declare that such standards applied to him and his administration.

---

34. *See* LEGAL SYS. MONITORING SECTION, ORG. FOR SEC. & COOPERATION IN EUR., REVIEW OF THE CRIMINAL JUSTICE SYSTEM IN KOSOVO 19 (Feb.–July 2000), *at* http://www.osce.org/kosovo/documents/reports/justice [hereinafter *OSCE LSMS July 2000 Rev.*].

35. Despite its legal validity, the irony of the argument cannot be ignored. *See* AMNESTY INT'L, SETTING THE STANDARD? UNMIK AND KFOR'S RESPONSE TO THE VIOLENCE IN MITROVICA 4–5 (2000).

Advocates also took the position that international human rights standards applied to KFOR. There are multiple bases for this position. As a force established under UN auspices, KFOR is obligated to observe UN standards and to act in accordance with the UN Charter. As with UNMIK, the FRY's obligations should extend to KFOR. It was also argued that the jurisprudence of the European Court of Human Rights suggests that states that have ratified the ECHR may have the obligation to act in accordance with it even when taking action outside of their territory.[36] Although the arguments regarding KFOR and human rights standards are complicated, advocates contended that, at a minimum, when KFOR undertook law enforcement activities, it was required to uphold the same standards as bound the UN civilian administration.

The fairly opaque references to international human rights law and its relevance within the patchwork of the applicable law in Regulation 1999/1[37] and Regulation 1999/24[38] caused years of debate and tension within the international presence in Kosovo. Since the beginning of the mission, human rights and rule-of-law advocates have argued that, not only is the UN bound by international human rights standards, but that these regulations, despite their vagueness, made international human rights law applicable in Kosovo. As a result, all acts of the judiciary as well as those of the executive and the legislature would be held to these standards. In monitoring the establishment of the judiciary and law enforcement, the OSCE observed that the gaps in the founding Regulations created significant confusion on the part of the local judiciary concerning the role of international human rights law in the applicable law.[39] Moreover, it was clear that there was no mutual understanding of the status of the standards within the international components of the mission itself. As a result, the OSCE recommended in September 2000 that the SRSG clarify the status of international law by legislating its direct applicability and supremacy.[40] Such action was never taken.

Notwithstanding UNMIK's unwillingness to expressly declare that human rights standards did not apply to its authority, many inside the mission argued that adherence to such standards was not possible in light of the obstacles UNMIK faced. Although in the initial phases some human rights advocates had argued that the SRSG should declare a state of emergency and derogate from those standards,[41] in March 2001, the SG pronounced that "there has been considerable progress in the implementation of UNMIK's mandate. The emergency phase is largely over."[42] As the mission grew, the

---

36. See id. at 5; Loiziduo v. Turkey, 20 Eur. Ct. H.R. ¶ 52 (1996).

37. UNMIK/REG/1999/1, supra note 21.

38. UNMIK/REG/1999/24, supra note 23.

39. See OSCE LSMS July 2000 Rev., supra note 34, at 15–20.

40. Id. at 22.

41. See WILLIAM G. O'NEILL, KOSOVO: AN UNFINISHED PEACE 78 (2002).

42. Report of the Secretary-General on the United Nations Interim Administration Mission in Kosovo, U.N.

resistance to recognizing human rights law as a binding framework for UNMIK authority appeared to increase in the face of enhanced security and the development of the judiciary.

Just before the March 2001 SG's report, an internal UNMIK document from the PDSRSG's office argued that the mission was confronted with a choice between ensuring human rights and establishing security.[43] In essence, the document asserted that human rights protection was the primary obstacle to security. This document was prepared to justify the use of the SRSG's executive power in violation of human rights principles. The fact that such a position was held by those at the highest levels of UNMIK reflected a fundamental lack of understanding of the reasoning behind the principles of human rights law. In response to the paper, the OSCE noted that this stance, if accepted, would undermine the entire premise for the existence of human rights doctrine. It argued that "[s]eeking to place limitations upon applicable international human rights laws is unlikely to resolve the problems in the judicial system, nor effectively address existing security concerns. Creating a comprehensive, co-ordinated and clearly planned strategy to address the immediate and long-term needs of the justice system, whilst guaranteeing due process, continues to represent a critical challenge for UNMIK."[44]

Within the mission, there was no disagreement that UNMIK would need to make difficult policy choices regarding the implementation of its mandate and that some actions would not strictly adhere to human rights standards. Indeed, human rights laws are standards that require interpretation and are consistently taking shape as jurisprudence develops. However, UNMIK never took steps to formally recognize its obligations by legislating the supremacy of human rights standards, and did not consistently work towards adherence to them by establishing and respecting mechanisms to ensure compliance. Rather, it knowingly and blatantly violated them.

2. *The Constitutional Framework*

Kosovo lacked a constitution, the conventional mechanism for guaranteeing rights and limiting state power, until the end of 2001. In transitional justice systems, the creation of a new constitutional framework or the novel interpretation of older constitutions is one of the major forces of change in a newly emerging democratic state.[45] Although the 1974 Constitution of the Socialist Federal Republic of Yugoslavia and the corresponding Kosovo pro-

---

SCOR, 56th Sess., ¶ 62, U.N. Doc. S/2001/218 (2001).

43. Org. for Sec. & Cooperation in Eur., A Blueprint for Ensuring Security and Establishing the Rule of Law in Kosovo (on file with authors).

44. Legal Sys. Monitoring Section, Org. for Sec. & Cooperation in Eur., Review of the Criminal Justice System in Kosovo 7 (Sept. 2000–Feb. 2001), *at* http://www.osce.org/kosovo/documents/reports/justice [hereinafter *OSCE LSMS Feb. 2001 Rev.*].

45. *See* Ruti G. Teitel, *Transitional Jurisprudence: The Role of Law in Political Transformation*, 106 Yale L.J. 2009 (1997).

vincial constitution were arguably applicable law, in practice they could not be applied by UNMIK. Even if there had been attempts to enforce parts of the old constitution, the lack of clarity as to the role of the Kosovo Supreme Court in light of the undeniable *de facto* limitation on the jurisdiction of the FRY Supreme Court in Kosovo was problematic. The early UN mission regulations did not address the status of these constitutions. Nor did they provide any illumination on the authority of the Supreme Court as the highest court in Kosovo, let alone the enforceability of human rights norms by such a court. In short, there was no constitutional basis for persons in Kosovo to seek the realization of fundamental principles of civil or human rights or for the judiciary to place limitations on executive or legislative authority in accordance with those principles.

In May 2001, the Constitutional Framework was promulgated, and in November, Kosovo-wide elections were held for the Provisional Institutions of Self-Government.[46] Although the Framework does provide for a democratically elected government with competencies in certain areas, other func tions inherent to a self-governing administration are left to international actors. UNMIK continues to solely control the areas of law enforcement and justice, both considered to be beyond the capacity of the locally elected government actors.[47] Although not expressly addressed in the Framework, it is understood within the mission that formulating legislation concerning law enforcement and criminal justice remains solely within the competencies of UNMIK. More broadly, the SRSG has retained all powers of executive and legislative authority to ensure the implementation of Resolution 1244.[48] These areas of "reserved powers," including an unfettered legislative veto, appear to be so far-reaching as to undermine the democratic legitimacy of the Framework itself. The most stark example of this so far has been the SRSG's appointment of judges and prosecutors without the approval of the Kosovo Assembly in violation of the Constitutional Framework.[49]

The Framework incorporates by reference and makes directly applicable in Kosovo the rights enumerated in the primary human rights documents, with a few notable exceptions, such as the Convention against Torture and other Cruel, Inhuman, or Degrading Treatment or Punishment.[50] The

---

46. UNMIK/REG/2001/9, *supra* note 2.

47. *See id.* ch. 8.

48. *Id.* chs. 12, 14.

49. *See UN Appoints Legal Figures in Kosovo without Assembly's Approval*, DEUTSCHE PRESSE AGENTUR, Dec. 13, 2002. The Assembly had requested more information regarding the backgrounds of the Serb candidates, particularly during the war and the Milošević regime. Twenty-one of the forty-two candidates are Serbs.

50. UNMIK/REG/2001/9, *supra* note 2 ch.14. The regulation made the following conventions applicable in Kosovo: the Universal Declaration on Human Rights; the European Convention for the Protection of Human Rights and Fundamental Freedoms and its Protocols; the International Covenant on Civil and Political Rights; the Convention on the Elimination of All Forms of Discrimination Against Women; the Convention on the Rights of the Child; the European Charter for Regional or Minority Languages; and the Council of Europe's Framework Convention for the Protection of National Minorities.

framework did clarify the direct applicability of international human rights standards in Kosovo, but did little to change the situation as advocates had perceived it. The Framework provides for the creation of a Special Chamber of the Supreme Court with jurisdiction to determine "whether any law adopted by the Assembly is incompatible with this Constitutional Framework;" to resolve disputes among the Provisional Institutions; and to resolve disputes regarding acts that infringe upon the independence of certain bodies and to determine which acts are covered by immunity. The Framework clearly allows for judicial review of administrative actions taken by the Provisional Government in line with the domestic administrative laws.[51]

However, in the Constitutional Framework, the Supreme Court and its Chamber appear to have no jurisdiction over actions taken by UNMIK. The document thus does not provide an answer to the question of human rights protection vis-à-vis UNMIK itself. This is especially problematic because UNMIK has retained sole administrative authority over justice and law enforcement, areas which are closely entwined with human rights guarantees. As a result, despite the creation of the Kosovo-wide government and a constitutional framework, the limitation on the authority of international organizations and the rights of Kosovars to seek review of and redress for alleged violations of their rights by UNMIK and KFOR remain unclear.

B. KFOR: The Military Presence

Resolution 1244 is the basis for the establishment of KFOR, the NATO-led international security presence in Kosovo, under a unified command structure controlled by the Commander of KFOR ("COMKFOR"). KFOR's responsibilities do not appear as broad and far-reaching as those delegated to the civilian authorities. Two of KFOR's eight responsibilities are specifically limited by the proviso that the responsibility ends when the civilian presence can take it over. The provision that gives KFOR the most expansive authority is the mandate to establish "a secure environment in which refugees and displaced persons can return home in safety, the international civil presence can operate, a transitional administration can be established, and humanitarian aid can be delivered."[52] Although this provision may have been intended to apply to the return of the Kosovo Albanians from refuge, it forms the basis for KFOR's substantial role in providing security for the ethnic minority communities, particularly the Kosovo Serbs, in postwar Kosovo.

Resolution 1244 makes the military and civilian presences distinct and apparently co-equal partners in the endeavor to establish a democratic Kosovo. The SRSG, as leader of the civil presence, must "coordinate closely with the international security presence to ensure that both presences oper-

---

51. *Supra* note 2, chs. 9.4.1–9.4.11.
52. Resolution 1244, *supra* note 10, ¶ 9c.

ate towards the same goals and in a mutually supportive manner,"[53] and the responsibilities of the security force explicitly include "[s]upporting, as appropriate, and coordinating closely with the work of the international civil presence."[54] However, this is the only official guidance on the intended relationship between the civil and security presences. There are no clear parameters to KFOR's authority. Although KFOR is established "under UN auspices," KFOR was not intended to be subject to the SRSG or the SG, and it did not have the command and control structure of other "Blue Helmet" missions. Despite the language of mutual cooperation and support between UNMIK and KFOR detailed in Resolution 1244, the practical implications of the interrelationship between the two, and the question of KFOR's ultimate authority, pose significant challenges to the protection of human rights in Kosovo.

1. The Applicable Law and the Law Enforcement Mandate

The question of limitations on KFOR's power arose early in Kosovo. It was clear that KFOR would need to take on considerable obligations in the area of law enforcement under its mandate of "[e]nsuring public safety and order until the international presence can take responsibility for this task."[55] The substantial vacuum in Kosovo required a tough approach from KFOR, and many, including human rights advocates, argued for more substantial involvement of KFOR in ensuring the rule of law.[56] As for KFOR's actions in law enforcement, during the initial stages of the mission it appeared that KFOR would be limited by the applicable law and international human rights standards. The Interim SRSG declared that law enforcement activities are a joint responsibility and, when conducted by KFOR and UNMIK police, they must be undertaken in line with international human rights standards.[57] This move indicated early on that the SRSG's power to legislate could bind KFOR, presuming that KFOR would act in accordance with the applicable law, and that human rights would also limit KFOR's authority at least in the areas of law enforcement.

As the justice system developed, the question of whether there were identifiable, predictable, and rights-based limits on KFOR's actions was not clarified but rather obscured. COMKFOR never clearly acknowledged that it was bound by international human rights law. Moreover, the question of whether the law in Kosovo applies to KFOR has not been resolved. UNMIK

---

53. *Id.* ¶ 6.

54. *Id.* ¶ 9f.

55. *Id.* ¶ 9d.

56. O'NEILL, *supra* note 41, at 105.

57. Sérgio Vieira De Mello (Special Representative of the Secretary General), Statement on the Right of KFOR to Apprehend and Detain Persons who are Suspected of Having Committed Offenses Against Public Safety and Order, July 4, 1999 [hereinafter Statement of the Interim SRSG]. *See also* Press Release, United Nations Interim Administration in Kosovo, UN Moves to Set Up Judicial System in Kosovo (July 1, 1999), *available at* http://www.unmikonline.org/archive.htm#1999.

itself has been inconsistent in its approach to KFOR, stating at times that it has no control over KFOR's actions but at the same time legislating, when convenient, in regards to KFOR. With the promulgation of regulations that explicitly addressed KFOR, it was understood that the SRSG could regulate KFOR and that it could be bound by the law. Regulation 2000/47 On the Status, Privileges and Immunities of KFOR and UNMIK and their Personnel in Kosovo stated that KFOR shall respect applicable law and regulations *in so far as* they do not conflict with the fulfillment of their mandate under Resolution 1244.[58] There are a host of particular regulations purportedly regulating KFOR and its powers.

However, the outcome of Regulation 2000/47, because of its failure to answer the question of KFOR's mandate under Resolution 1244, is that KFOR is bound by the law when it wants to be, but not when it does not. This is exemplified by the fact that regulations concerning basic human rights principles in the area of rule of law are considered not to apply to KFOR despite the fact that it is still involved in law enforcement. The most significant law in this regard is Regulation 2001/28 On the Rights of Persons Arrested by Law Enforcement Authorities, which took more than a year to promulgate and caused significant friction between the UN administration and the human rights components within the mission.[59] The regulation provides arrestees with certain basic human rights that were not within the FRY Code of Criminal Procedure. Unlike other regulations, the definition of law enforcement agencies does not include KFOR and therefore is arguably not applicable to KFOR even when it exercises its powers to arrest and detain. This undermines legal certainty and results in potential inconsistency of treatment under the law.

2. *Extra-Judicial Detention*

It is in the area of detention that the exercise of extraordinary authority of KFOR has generated the most attention. Fairly early on in the establishment of the judicial system, COMKFOR declared its authority to detain persons without any judicial review and to continue to detain persons despite a judicial decision to release the person from custody. KFOR argued that its mandate under Resolution 1244 provided it with such authority where such detention is necessary to address a "threat to KFOR" or under its mandate to provide "a safe and secure environment [for as long as] civilian authorities are unable or unwilling to take responsibility for the matter."[60]

58. UNMIK/REG/2000/47 (On the Status, Privileges and Immunities of KFOR and UNMIK and Their Personnel in Kosovo), 18 Aug. 2000.

59. UNMIK/REG/2001/28 (On the Rights of Persons Arrested by Law Enforcement Authorities), 11 Oct. 2001.

60. Statement of the Interim SRSG, *supra* note 57. *See also* AM. BAR ASS'N/CENT. EUROPEAN & EURASIAN LAW INITIATIVE, JUDICIAL REFORM INDEX FOR KOSOVO (Apr. 2002) at 16, *at* http://www.abanet.org/ceeli/publications/jri/home.html.

Within UNMIK, it was argued that the local judicial system could not be trusted to respond to ethnically motivated crime and that such extraordinary action would assist in establishing an environment based on the rule of law. Yet the first so-called COMKFOR detention arose in the case of Shaban Beqiri and Xhemal Sejdiu, who were ordered released by a judge on November 16, 1999, but detained by COMKFOR until July 25, 2000, when an international judge decided that only the courts had the authority to detain.[61] Despite this decision, that same month, COMKFOR detained Afrim Zeqiri, a murder suspect who had been released by an international investigating judge.[62] Even with internationals in the system, KFOR did not abide by judicial authority.

During the conflict in Southern Serbia and the war in Macedonia, COMKFOR detained hundreds of persons, including juveniles. These actions were allegedly based on KFOR's authority to maintain a secure environment rather than on its authority to ensure public safety and order. This distinction has always been difficult to understand, and neither KFOR nor UNMIK has made an attempt to clarify it through legislation or by consistency of actions. This has led to uncertainty in Kosovo about the scope of KFOR's authority.

Although KFOR did hand over some of these detainees to the judicial system, for the most part KFOR did not purport to be detaining people for suspected violations of the criminal law. In May 2001, the SRSG passed Regulation 2001/10 On the Prohibition of Unauthorized Border/Boundary Crossings, in a move intended to allow for criminal prosecution of these groups and to afford KFOR a legal basis for the detentions.[63] In addition, Regulation 2001/7 On the Authorization of Possession of Weapons in Kosovo, provided KFOR with another legal basis for detention of persons caught with unauthorized weapons.[64] Despite this, KFOR, for the most part, does not utilize the law or claim to be detaining individuals for the purposes of criminal proceedings. Instead, even today KFOR continues to argue that the legal system is ill-equipped to address illegal activity and has developed a parallel system for review of its own detentions.

Human rights advocates and components of the mission argued early on that COMKFOR detentions are in violation of human rights standards and constitute arbitrary and unlawful action. There is no judicial mechanism by which persons so detained can challenge their detention. Moreover, as the practice continued in the face of a continuously developing law enforcement

---

61. See OSCE LSMS July 2000 Rev., supra note 34.

62. In this case, despite KFOR's asserted independent authority, COMKFOR sought authorization from the SRSG to detain. KFOR and UNMIK have often been inconsistent regarding their relationship. At times, they use the purported authority of the SRSG to substantiate KFOR's actions and, at other times, claim that the SRSG has no control over KFOR's actions.

63. UNMIK/REG/2001/10 (On the Prohibition of Unauthorized Border/Boundary Crossings), 24 May 2001.

64. UNMIK/REG/2001/7 (On the Authorization of Possession of Weapons in Kosovo), 21 Feb. 2001.

and judicial system with international participation, reports have high-lighted that such action on the part of COMKFOR poses an unprecedented intrusion into the judicial function and undermines the rule of law. KFOR's establishment of parallel procedures falling short of standards of due process did nothing to assuage these concerns.

Despite ongoing criticism of KFOR on this issue, it has continued to hold persons in detention without any judicial process and continues to maintain that this is, in part, based on its law enforcement mandate until the civilian authority can take over. Even three years into the mission, KFOR appeared to be expanding its authority to detain persons outside of the justice system and refining its parallel system of review. KFOR's approach has arguably rendered meaningless the SG's condition on KFOR's authority in the area of public peace and order. Practically speaking, KFOR has boundless and un-fettered authority in Kosovo.

Regarding the actions of KFOR that breach international law, there is no remedy or process for review. Despite the recommendations of human rights advocates, there remains no clear mechanism through which persons can seek redress of alleged human rights abuses by KFOR. There has been a fail-ure of the human rights components of the mission, probably due to a lack of political will, to monitor the conduct of KFOR sufficiently, leaving it, in most cases, beyond public scrutiny. Most significantly in this regard, there is no oversight by the Ombudsperson Institution of KFOR. Although the Sec-retary General provided that the Ombudsperson Institution has jurisdiction over allegations of human rights abuses by any person or entity in Kosovo, the founding regulation, Regulation 2000/38 On the Establishment of the Ombudsperson Institution, did not provide it with the authority to investi-gate KFOR.[65] As a result, there is no human rights oversight of the actions of KFOR.

C. Executive Powers

The SRSG, as the head of UNMIK, was vested with all executive powers. Although the UNSC established the civilian presence for an initial twelve-month period, there were no temporal limitations on the mission other than a final political solution to the Kosovo situation. There is no clear indication of when such a solution will be found. The task of developing genuinely democratic institutions even on an interim basis may not be easily or quickly accomplished. For almost three years, UNMIK administered the province until it handed over a significant amount of authority to a newly created domestic, yet still provisional, government. In that period, UNMIK used its executive power to detain individuals in contravention of interna-tional human rights standards and without any possible mechanism for de-

---

65. UNMIK/REG/2000/38 (On the Establishment of the Ombudsperson Institution in Kosovo), 30 June 2000.

tainees to challenge their detention in the courts. As UNMIK had not only all executive powers but also all legislative powers, it was able to promulgate legislation to serve its agenda in individual cases or in reaction to unwanted situations and circumstances. These types of laws undercut the establishment of a society based on the rule of law and human rights.

1. Executive Detentions

The SRSG's assertion of an executive power to order detention has been one of the most controversial actions in the area of criminal justice and human rights taken by the mission. In the summer of 2000, the SRSG began detaining individuals despite their lawful release by the judicial authority. On August 18, 2000, the SRSG continued what had been a COMKFOR detention of a murder suspect, Afrim Zeqiri, despite the fact that his release was ordered by an international judge.[66] The action was unprecedented, and human rights advocates quickly pointed out the ways in which it contravened fundamental principles of human rights law. Human rights components of UNMIK underscored that the action not only jeopardized the authority and independence of the courts, but that the lack of a mechanism to challenge it deprived individuals so detained of any recourse.

In early 2001, the UN Office of the Legal Advisor in New York provided the SRSG with a test to follow when considering whether or not to order an executive detention. This guidance maintained that the executive order to detain could be used in a case where there was risk of judicial impropriety or misconduct. However, even where a majority-international judiciary adjudicated controversial cases, the SRSG would usurp the role of the judiciary and order detention.

On August 25, 2001, the SRSG promulgated Regulation 2001/18 On the Establishment of a Detention Review Commission for Extra-Judicial Detentions Based on Executive Orders, which was apparently designed to provide some review of, and add legitimacy to, the SRSG's orders to detain.[67] Prior to the promulgation of the regulation, the SRSG had ordered the detention of three Kosovo Albanians suspected of bombing a bus full of Serbs despite the fact that a majority-international panel had, on grounds of insufficient evidence, ordered their release. The Regulation was quickly deconstructed by the human rights components of the mission and the Commission was found not to meet the requirements of an independent and impartial tribunal established by law.[68] It became clear that the SRSG was using his legislative authority to usurp a decision of an independent and im-

---

66. See OSCE LSMS July 2000 Rev., supra note 34.

67. UNMIK/REG/2001/18 (On the Establishment of a Detention Review Commission for Extrajudicial Detentions Based on Executive Orders), 25 Aug. 2001.

68. See OMBUDSPERSON INSTITUTION IN KOSOVO, SPECIAL REPORT NO. 4 (Sept. 12, 2001), available at http://www.ombudspersonkosovo.org.

partial court by establishing an executive body to consider the legality of an executive action.

The Commission was convened in October 2001, when it confirmed the continued detention in the case of the three Kosovo Albanians. However, the suspects were released in December 2001 as a result of lack of evidence, and the Commission has never since been convened.

More than six persons have been subject to SRSG orders to detain at different times. It is noteworthy that in May 2002, Afrim Zeqiri, the first person to be detained by the SRSG, was acquitted on the basis of insufficient evidence, after almost two years in detention.[69]

2. Lack of Clear Delineation Between Branches of Government

The conflation of executive and legislative power has provided significant room for interference in the judicial realm. The promulgation of legislation establishing the Commission on Executive Detentions illustrates the lack of checks on executive power. Similarly, other legislation promulgated by UNMIK appears to be ad hoc, either intended to provide for a particular outcome in certain cases or to respond to isolated events. In early 2000, UNMIK passed its first law clearly in response to a particular situation. Regulation 2000/04 On the Prohibition Against Inciting to National, Racial, Religious or Ethnic Hatred, Discord or Intolerance signaled international outrage at local press coverage that alleged certain Kosovo Serbs were war criminals and provided identifying information.[70] This Regulation has never been utilized, though such press coverage has continued. There are other examples of this, such as Regulation 2001/10 On the Prohibition of Unauthorized Border/Boundary Crossing, which was created to address concerns of KFOR in regards to the movement of persons between Serbia and Kosovo during the uprising of Albanians in Southern Serbia.[71] It has rarely been applied and does little to clarify the real issues of who, and under what circumstances, can enter Kosovo.

In January 2001, Regulation 2001/2, amending Regulation 2000/06 On the Appointment and Removal from Office of International Judges and International Prosecutors, was passed to ensure that the international prosecutor in the case of Afrim Zeqiri could resurrect an abandoned prosecution.[72] It was clear that this provision was intended to apply solely to this particular case, as it could only be applied within thirty days from the date of the

---

69. UNMIK, *After Two Years in Prison, Afrim Zeqiri Found Innocent* (June 15, 2002), *available at* http://www.unmikonline.org/press/2002/mon/june/lmm150602.htm.

70. UNMIK/REG/2000/4 (On the Prohibition Against Inciting to National, Racial, Religious or Ethnic Hatred, Discord or Intolerance), 1 Feb. 2000.

71. UNMIK/REG/2001/10, *supra* note 63.

72. UNMIK/REG/2001/2 (On the Appointment and Removal from Office of International Judges and International Prosecutors), 12 Jan. 2001 (amending UNMIK/REG/2000/6). *See also* UNMIK, *supra* note 69.

promulgation of the regulation. Despite these legal maneuvers, Zeqiri was acquitted of all charges in spring 2002.[73]

Beyond the dubious nature of the procedure leading to the passage of these regulations, these laws rarely produced the expected results, either due to lack of enforcement or poor construction. Without a strong framework for balancing UNMIK authority, the executive was able to act recklessly and without regard for the way it could influence the development of democratic principles and practices in Kosovo.

D. Legislative Powers

In order to create a legal basis for the implementation of the UNMIK mandate, the SRSG was vested with legislative power, including the authority to change, appeal, or suspend any existing laws. Regulation 1999/1 codified this authority, and made the applicable law the regulations of the SRSG and the laws in effect prior to March 22, 1999, insofar as they conform with international human rights standards.[74] Under Regulation 1999/24, promulgated five months later, the applicable laws were those in effect prior to the revocation of Kosovo's autonomous status on March 22, 1989, insofar as they conform with international human rights standards.[75]

In 1999, the SRSG created the Joint Advisory Council on Legislative Matters ("JAC"), which was composed of local law professors and other legal actors, the Office of the Legal Advisor ("OLA"), the OSCE, the Council of Europe and American Bar Association Central European and Eurasian Law Initiative ("ABA/CEELI"). This consultative and collaborative body was intended to advise the SRSG on the applicable law and be the forum in which the legislative reform process would primarily take place. Although the UN never issued any regulations regarding its authority, it was assumed that all UNMIK regulations would be reviewed by the JAC and comments forwarded to the SRSG through the OLA. The local legal community's adverse reaction to the promulgation of Regulation 1999/1, which re-instituted the Serbian laws, exemplified the need for consultation with the local community.[76]

1. The Applicable Law

The challenge of determining what constitutes applicable law is overwhelming, not only to the international lawyers in the mission, but also to the local legal community. The problems are multifaceted and involve parsing out what the applicable law is, finding the laws in relevant languages,

---

73. UNMIK, *supra* note 69.

74. UNMIK/REG/1999/1, *supra* note 21.

75. UNMIK/REG/1999/24, *supra* note 23.

76. UNMIK/REG/1999/1, *supra* note 21. *See* Wendy S. Betts et al., *Special Feature: The Post-Conflict Transitional Administration of Kosovo and the Lessons Learned in Efforts to Establish a Judiciary and Rule of Law*, 22 MICH. J. INT'L L. 371, 374 (2001).

and deciding to what extent they should be applied and whether the laws, written in the 1970s and 1980s and based on a communist system, can realistically be applied in light of the establishment of UNMIK. It has been and continues to be a daunting task.

Although these issues arose initially in the context of the criminal justice arena, the question of applying the laws in the area of government administration has proven even more difficult. As a result, it is understandable that many of UNMIK's actions have not completely conformed with the pre-1989 legal regime. The problems that have resulted from the state of the applicable law require an independent analysis and are beyond the scope of this Article. However, it is necessary to highlight the obstacles UNMIK continues to face in negotiating an effective path to meaningful legislative reform and a state based on the rule of law.

The requirement that the domestic law be applied only to the extent that it conforms with international human rights standards proved too complicated for local actors to handle early on.[77] The international human rights components of the mission set about highlighting where the domestic criminal laws were incompatible and suggesting that the judiciary not apply them. The DJA was urged to formulate interpretative guidelines to the judiciary on ensuring compliance with international human rights standards in the implementation of local law. Court circulars were produced to achieve this goal, but they appeared to have little impact. For example, there was much attention given to the publication of a circular instructing judges on interpreting the criminal procedural code to provide counsel to persons who cannot afford one where justice requires.[78] Although published in 2001, it has rarely been used. Even in cases where possible trafficking victims were facing imprisonment, and the trafficking regulation provided for the right to defense counsel, courts often failed to appoint counsel to these women. In general, efforts to find mechanisms for the interpretation of local law according to international standards appeared fruitless. Even where the law was clear and could be applied in light of those standards, the local judiciary and UNMIK police had difficulties conforming their actions to the law or consistently applying the law. The questions of what the local law was and how it should be applied, particularly its application in light of international human rights norms, considerably hampered the functioning of the justice system.

It was acknowledged that a complete review and reform process, starting with the criminal laws, would be necessary. UNMIK almost immediately initiated this process within the framework of the JAC. Substantial resources were invested in the process by UNMIK, the OSCE, ABA/CEELI, and the Council of Europe. In particular, the Council of Europe dedicated international and regional experts to the task and financed trips by working group

---

77. Betts et al., *supra* note 76 at 383–84.
78. *See OSCE LSMS: Report 2, supra* note 17.

members to Strasbourg to consult directly with well-known experts. Most of the local input was provided by respected university professors of criminal law. In early 2000, the United Nations International Children's Emergency Fund ("UNICEF") and the OSCE also initiated a process of redrafting the criminal laws in regard to juveniles, and presented to the JAC a separate code for juveniles that incorporated international human rights principles.

As a result of UNMIK's placing a considerable amount of emphasis on the inadequacy of Kosovo's old laws, by 2001, the need for new laws to assist the system became a mantra of the local judiciary and legal community. The criminal penal and procedure laws were finalized in the fall of 2001 and sent to the SRSG for promulgation. Although the laws were not perfect, they were the result of a consultative process among local, regional, and international actors. At this time, the draft juvenile justice law, which had undergone a process of local consultation, was reconsidered in light of the draft penal and procedural framework, and more resources were invested in finalizing the juvenile justice code.

However, as of this writing, these laws have yet to be passed. In fact, many within the mission question whether there is the political will within UNMIK to implement the draft laws. Under UNMIK's interpretation of the Constitutional Framework, the Provisional Government Institutions do not have the authority to promulgate criminal laws. UNMIK has provided no explanation to members of the international community nor, more importantly, to the local community for the failure to promulgate the draft penal and criminal procedure and juvenile justice laws. There has been no other comprehensive legal reform project undertaken by UNMIK.

2. The Legislative Process

UNMIK was not created as a democratic administration and cannot be expected to possess the qualities of a democratically elected legislative branch. The foundational concepts of democratic legislatures such as legislative transparency, public commentary and awareness, accountability to the needs and expectations of constituencies, and constitutional or other limitations could not be inherent to the way in which UNMIK created laws. That said, one would expect a degree of accountability from the agency charged with holding governments worldwide to account. Yet few steps have been taken to formulate a process which involved these concepts.

As the mission developed, the number of legislative reform initiatives grew, and UNMIK did not craft a plan to ensure the effectiveness of the legislative process. The result was catastrophic. There was no oversight of who was drafting laws or how drafts impacted or related to each other and the preexisting law. The JAC became less and less relevant and OLA began to bypass the consultative process altogether. By February 2001, there was no systematic consultation with the JAC on regulations and the OLA maintained that legislation that was "interventionist," i.e., of political character, did not require local consultation.[79] Despite vocal protest from all members of the JAC, regulations were provided to the JAC as a token gesture. By the end of 2001, it was clear that what had begun as one of the only high-level forums for international and local consultation and cooperation on legal issues had become an empty shell. As with all other areas of development within the justice sector, UNMIK's consultation with local actors on legislative reform and on the legislative reform agenda diminished rather than expanded over time.

The result of UNMIK's legislative process, or lack thereof, was that many regulations involved the use of legal terminology unknown to the local legal community.[80] In some cases, therefore, international experts were unsure if certain regulations could really be applied. There was little, if any, guidance on the practical implementation of the regulations and there was no forethought given to the logistical and practical implications of passing new laws. The practical problems ranged from ensuring translation of the laws in local languages to dissemination to the judiciary. Until recently, a significant number of regulations had not been translated into the local languages.[81] The UN has ignored a recommendation from the OSCE that no law be passed without its being translated. In addition, the public was not informed about the state of the law or of legal reform initiatives, and there were no attempts to undertake public relations campaigns to increase awareness. The acute failure to address these issues continues to hamper the timely and effective implementation of the laws.

There is no doubt that the creation of an effective legislative process in this context raises complex and weighty issues and involves tremendous time, energy, and resources. UNMIK has been dealing with all other aspects of administering a province. However, initiating a process to address some of

---

79. *OSCE LSMS Feb. 2001 Rev., supra* note 44.

80. *See, e.g.,* UNMIK/REG/2000/4, *supra* note 70. This regulation demonstrates problems associated with the lack of an established legislative process. The drafting of the regulation was overseen by internationals with insufficient understanding of the local law. As a result, once promulgated, internationals (OSCE and the Kosovo Judicial Institute ["KJI"]) debated whether some of the provisions could really be applied in light of the law. KJI even developed a training plan which included a discussion about the inapplicability of some of the provisions. Additionally, the regulation did little to tie into the local penal law, which had provisions overlapping with the trafficking regulation. As the regulation reflected the most modern and sophisticated definition of trafficking, it was complex and understandably difficult for the local judiciary to apply. Not until the winter of 2002 were the judges and prosecutors offered useful materials explaining the elements of the complex crime of trafficking. Although promulgated fairly quickly, the regulation was not translated into Albanian and Serbian for some time, resulting in the application of the old laws. Even after translation and almost a year after it had been passed, many judges claimed that they had never received a copy of the regulation. Many of the provisions of the regulation have yet to be effectively applied. *See generally* LEGAL SYS. MONITORING SECTION, ORG. FOR SEC. & COOPERATION IN EUR., KOSOVO: REVIEW OF THE CRIMINAL JUSTICE SYSTEM 47 (Oct. 2001), *at* http://www.osce.org/kosovo/documents/reports/justice/criminal_justice3.pdf.

81. As of April 2002, no regulation promulgated in 2002 had been translated into the local languages. Of the forty-one regulations promulgated in 2001, only nineteen had been translated into Albanian and thirty-one into Serbian. Twenty-five of the twenty-six administrative directives had not been translated. By the end of 2002, all regulations had been translated. *See* Official Gazette of Regulations, *at* http://www.unmikonline.org/regulations/index.htm.

these problems would have made UNMIK a better legislature and the judicial system more effective. The lack of an appropriate legislative process has led to the creation and promulgation of legislation that cannot be applied effectively or at all, undermining the development of consistency and transparency in the application of the law. It has also resulted in legislation that does not conform to international human rights standards. However, there has appeared to be no will to undertake change. The most cynical explanation for UNMIK's inertia in facing the lack of an effective process may be an unwillingness to pay the price for such a process. UNMIK would no longer be able to create results-based legislation to fix individual cases or sacrifice human rights principles for perceived effectiveness of law enforcement.

The Constitutional Framework does little to provide legal certainty and clarity as to the legislative process because certain areas of lawmaking are presumed still to fall within UNMIK authority and all legislative acts are to be vetted by OLA and approved by the SRSG. Presumably, OLA can make unilateral changes to any laws suggested by the Assembly. As to regulations that impact criminal justice, whether there is any local consultation is still a question, as the JAC was officially disbanded in late 2002. Moreover, it is not clear who is involved in formulating and approving regulations that impact criminal justice or legal issues under the authority of the provisional government.

E. The Judiciary

UNMIK was tasked with establishing a multi-ethnic, independent, and impartial judiciary to ensure the rule of law. It was clear from the first days of the mission that in order to maintain public peace and order in postwar Kosovo the creation of a functioning judiciary needed to be one of UNMIK's primary objectives. It would underpin the ability of UNMIK to implement other aspects of its mandate.

Unlike the administrative and law enforcement authorities, only Kosovars were initially appointed to the judiciary and prosecution. The reasons underlying this decision are not clear. Within the first six months of the mission, however, discussion began about the need to include international actors in these bodies. The main impetus for this was concern about the capacity of the local, mainly Kosovo Albanian, judiciary to make impartial decisions in trials of persons alleged to have committed war crimes and other violations of international humanitarian law against members of their own community. In the early part of the mission, many argued for the inclusion of international actors to ensure impartial decisions in war crimes trials. Most commentators failed to foresee the more significant challenges that the judiciary would face as the sole independent branch of the UNMIK administration.

1. *Judicial Review of Executive and Legislative Authority*

The judiciary is the only part of UNMIK that could effectively balance the power of the SRSG. Many within UNMIK expected that when the SRSG abused his authority, the courts would consider the abuse and provide a remedy. This would involve judicial review of the lawfulness of legislation promulgated by the SRSG when raised in individual cases and, where warranted, interpreting the laws to ensure that they conform in practice to international human rights standards. Despite the lack of a clear mandate to the courts in this regard from UNMIK itself, human rights components of the mission maintained that the standards themselves required the courts to engage in judicial review as well.

The primary example in this regard has been the issue of *habeas corpus*—judicial review of the basis for detention. Despite consistent advocacy within UNMIK for a review of the detention process, there was no legislative response. It was argued that the Supreme Court of Kosovo should fill gaps in the domestic law to enable it to hear challenges to all detentions, particularly those of the SRSG, find that the powers exercised by the UN were in violation of international human rights standards as part of the applicable law, and order the release and compensation of the defendant. In a challenge to the executive detention of Afrim Zeqiri on this basis before the Supreme Court, the court demurred, deciding that the SRSG's action was an administrative one, and therefore needed to be reviewed according to administrative procedure.[82]

However, with the promulgation of Regulation 2000/47 On the Status, Privileges and Immunities of KFOR and UNMIK and their Personnel in Kosovo, UNMIK, in its capacity as the legislature, gave itself and its executive actions immunity from judicial process.[83] The impact of this immunity is illustrated by a well-known case in which a municipal court considered an individual's challenge to a decision of the municipality and decided in favor of the individual.[84] UNMIK's response was to instruct the court, through a letter, that its delegate was immune, rendering the court's decision unenforceable. The promulgation and exercise of such expansive immunity is in violation of international human rights standards and has rendered nonexistent the right of Kosovars to seek a remedy for violations of their fundamental rights.

The courts have declined to take an active role and act as a counterbalance to the power of the SRSG. Expectations that the local judiciary would grasp and interpret human rights principles, assert its authority over the SRSG, and provide a remedy may have been unrealistic in light of the *realpolitik* of the Kosovo community. UNMIK represents the international

---

82. *See* UNMIK, *supra* note 69.
83. UNMIK/REG/2000/47, *supra* note 58.
84. *See* Ombudsperson Institution in Kosovo, *Elife Murseli Against the United Nations Mission in Kosovo* (Dec. 10, 2001), *available at* http://www.ombudspersonkosovo.org/upd_04/murseli91201.doc.

community that came to assist the Kosovars in developing their own democratic autonomy, and KFOR was to protect Kosovo from the return of the Serb regime. However, even with the inclusion of international judges and prosecutors, the judiciary has mostly refused to take on executive and legislative power or to enforce international human rights law. In individual cases where courts have initiated their role in this regard, those decisions have not been respected.[85] Needless to say, UNMIK itself, despite being made aware of the ramifications of its assertion of immunity, has taken no action to demonstrate that it, too, is bound by the rule of law.

2. *Judicial Independence and Impartiality*

The independence and impartiality of the judiciary is the basis for its legitimacy in a democratic state. The way in which the judiciary and prosecution services have been established by UNMIK has caused concern regarding the independence of the courts. The ad hoc process for the introduction of internationals into the system has not achieved the goals that many advocates had hoped for. Rather, the process has created the potential for harm to the local community's perception of justice because of a seemingly parallel international court system with ties to the executive.

The lack of any meaningful disciplinary mechanism for judges raised concerns in early 2001 regarding the institutional independence of the judiciary. These were addressed in part by the creation of a Judicial Inspection Unit ("JIU") within DJA and the Kosovo Judicial and Prosecutorial Council ("KJPC") established by Regulation 2001/8.[86] The KJPC, which provides recommendations to the SRSG on the discipline and removal of local judges, has local as well as international involvement, including minority representation, and has begun to function effectively.[87] Local inspectors, accepting a difficult job, have been integrated into the JIU, although there are still too few. Recent reports indicate that the length of appointment of the local judiciary is being addressed, and current appointments will last until the end of the international mandate.[88]

The fact that the KJPC is only a consultative body and not truly independent from the executive, and that the SRSG has legislated for himself the power to remove local judges and prosecutors on his own motion, without any recommendation by the KJPC, is troubling. There is no way for a judge or prosecutor to challenge the KPJC's recommendation or the SRSG's decision. The JIU remains distant from the population because there is no clear

---

85. The case of Shaban Beqiri and Xhemal Sejdiu, discussed above, provides an example. *See OSCE LSMS July 2000 Rev., supra* note 34.

86. UNMIK/REG/2001/8, *supra* note 30.

87. *See* LEGAL SYS. MONITORING SECTION, ORG. FOR SEC. & COOPERATION IN EUR., KOSOVO: REVIEW OF THE CRIMINAL JUSTICE SYSTEM (Sept. 2001–Feb. 2002) *at* http://www.osce.org/kosovo/documents/reports/justice/criminal_justice4_eng.pdf (as of January 2002, the KJPC had adjudicated ten cases resulting in six removals, two reprimands and warnings, and two acquittals).

88. *See* AM. BAR ASS'N, *supra* note 60, at 4.

way for the public to address complaints to it and it remains within the increasingly internationalized DJA of Pillar I.

Positive steps towards ensuring the institutional independence of the local judiciary have been overshadowed by the establishment of an international judiciary without any institutional guarantees of independence. International judges and prosecutors are hired as UN employees and are subject to six-month renewable terms in office. There is no disciplinary mechanism by which complaints can be brought against them. The procedures of disqualification of judges for partiality do not apply to internationals. Although the OSCE has recommended that international judicial actors be subject to the same requirements of tenure, accountability, and discipline as the locals, including investigation by the JIU and the KPJC, the SRSG has taken no such action.[89]

The random allocation of cases is considered an important mechanism in ensuring the appearance as well as the reality of the courts' independence. Within the regular court system, the practice of discretionary allocation by the president of the court is being addressed to ensure random case assignment. However, there is no guarantee of the perception of independence regarding the appointment of international judges and prosecutors to cases; the international judges may select which cases they take and the executive may directly appoint them to individual cases under Regulation 2000/64 On the Assignment of International Judges/Prosecutors and/or Change of Venue.[90] There are no enforceable criteria for executive decisions about which cases have international judges and prosecutors or which individual judges and prosecutors get assigned. Ironically, the stated objective of the regulation, to ensure independence and impartiality, has garnered a perverse result. The lack of any mechanism to ensure a random assignment of judges to cases creates the perception that the executive may interfere at any time with any given case.

In addition to the institutional mechanisms that have allowed for room for executive interference into the judicial function, there have been concerns that the executive has interfered directly with the decisions of judges in specific cases. For example, in June 2000, in the case of an African international staff member of the International Organization for Migration "extradited" from Kenya and detained in Kosovo, the DJA, after meeting with the SRSG, was directly involved in attempting to guide the decision of the local investigating judge and control the nature of the information provided to the detainee's wife. Although there has been some anecdotal information published on this issue, little information has been disseminated about the extent of direct executive interference in judicial decisions in specific cases.[91]

---

89. *See id.* at 43.
90. UNMIK/REG/2000/64 (On the Assignment of International Judges/Prosecutors and/or Change of Venue), 15 Dec. 2000.
91. *See* AM. BAR ASS'N, *supra* note 60, at 30–31.

III. The Criminal Justice System

In 1999 UNMIK had to develop a justice system from scratch. UNMIK hired Kosovo Albanian judges and prosecutors who had not practiced law for ten years. UNMIK was also faced with a severely diminished law enforcement and forensic capability. However, the most pressing question was how to resolve the cases of Kosovo Serbian alleged war criminals arrested following the arrival of UNMIK. With the mission promoting the need for a multi-ethnic Kosovo, its approach to these sensitive cases could have proved pivotal in its attempts to reconcile the two communities as well as fostering respect for the rule of law.

Yet UNMIK produced no coherent strategy for the justice sector.[92] Its approach was short term, in that it was reactive rather than thoughtful and deliberative. In addition to this posture, UNMIK failed to take into account the chronic and systemic problems inherent in a legal system without a culture of due process rights. Most Kosovo Albanian lawyers were poorly skilled and had no understanding of human rights law or professional legal ethics.[93] Law enforcement and forensic tools were not effectively developed to assist the courts. Legal initiatives were not explained to local legal actors or the population at large. And UNMIK's approach to the war crimes cases was clearly lacking in strategic vision. Evidence of judicial bias against Kosovo Serbs, though publicly acknowledged by UNMIK, did not bring their trials to a halt, and the introduction of international judges and prosecutors initially proved futile due to a vague mandate and limited role.[94] The miscarriages of justice that followed would later be overturned, only fuelling tension between the ethnic communities. UNMIK's approach destroyed the opportunity for the courts to dispense justice fairly and effectively. This ultimately hampered the justice system's capacity to meet its obligations under international human rights law

A. Legal Systems Development

1. Training

In the period between 1989 and 1999, most former Kosovo Albanian judges and prosecutors were not afforded the benefit of using their legal skills or continuing their legal education. Equally troubling was the region's

---

92. For a similar UN approach to the war crimes cases in East Timor, see Suzannah Linton, *Prosecuting Atrocities at the District Court in Dili*, 2 Melb. J. Int'l L. 414 (2001).

93. *See* Org. for Sec. & Cooperation in Eur., Observations and Recommendations of the OSCE Legal Systems Monitoring Section: Report One—Material Needs of the Emergency Judicial System 49–54 (1999), *at* http://www.osce.org/kosovo/documents/reports/justice/report1.htm [hereinafter *OSCE LSMS: Report 1*].

94. *See id.* at 58; Legal Sys. Monitoring Section, Org. for Sec. & Cooperation in Eur., Kosovo's War Crimes Trials: A Review (2002), *at* http://www.osce.org/kosovo/documents/reports/human_rights/10_WarCrimesReport_eng.pdf [hereinafter *OSCE LSMS War Crimes Report*].

past disregard for international human rights law.[95] Prior to the arrival of UNMIK, the local judiciary had no exposure to these laws or to other modern European laws and procedures.

The political urgency to create some semblance of a legal system drove UNMIK to proceed with appointing judges and prosecutors without first establishing some form of legal training on the applicable law, legal ethics, and the role of human rights law and standards. The Kosovo Judicial Institute of the OSCE organized a two-day workshop for all legal professionals in November of 1999, but judges and prosecutors were not selected until December 1999. Between then and the end of January 2000, when the first court became operational, UNMIK provided no legal training.

In May 2000, judges and prosecutors received their first legal training at a joint Council of Europe/OSCE seminar on Articles 5 and 6 of the ECHR.[96] Similar training took place in September 2000, and induction training for newly appointed judges and public prosecutors took place in November 2000. In March 2001, KJI provided training on the FRY Criminal Procedure Code ("CPC") for both local and international judges and prosecutors, though most internationals did not attend.[97]

The legal training failed to improve the quality of judicial proceedings.[98] First, the training programs focused on European human rights law jurisprudence, an unknown field to local lawyers. Rather than being informed on the relevant international case law, Kosovo legal professionals needed instruction on applying such standards in the courtroom. In particular, judges needed to know how human rights law can be used to fill gaps in domestic law, such as the right to *habeas corpus*, or to void incompatible provisions in the domestic law, such as the failure to afford detainees a right to counsel on arrest.

Judges, prosecutors, and defenders also required training on basic legal skills, such as the questioning of witnesses, legal reasoning, the development of evidence, and the role of professional ethics. Inadequate questioning at the investigative stage can have a debilitating effect on the chances for obtaining a legally and factually sound verdict. Indeed, poorly drafted written verdicts, which fail to adequately summarize the facts or explain the legal elements of the crime, would in due course result in numerous reversals on appeal.

Finally, there was little follow-up to the Council of Europe/OSCE training, with few visits to courts by KJI or OSCE staff to assess where improvements were needed. Assessments were made pursuant to concerns raised in reports issued twice a year by the OSCE's Legal Systems Monitor-

---

95. *Report of the Secretary-General, supra* note 9.
96. *See OSCE LSMS Feb. 2001 Rev., supra* note 44, at 40.
97. *Id.*
98. For an exhaustive review of the chronic problems identified in the Kosovo criminal justice system, *see OSCE LSMS July 2000 Rev., supra* note 34; *OSCE LSMS Feb. 2001 Rev., supra* note 44.

ing Section ("LSMS"), an inadequate response to a critical part of the mission's goals. The OSCE, which was primarily responsible for legal training, failed to address these issues. The result was a transitional judicial regime that continued to apply laws that were incompatible with basic international human rights law.

2. KFOR

KFOR was mandated with responsibility for ensuring peace and security in the region, and prior to the arrival of UNMIK police, effected hundreds of arrests and detentions. Given its capacity, KFOR performed reasonably well in keeping the peace, but its peacekeeping role did not include criminal investigations, collection of evidence, or forensic analysis, and it is these functions that were needed most in the first six months. The failure to examine sites of alleged war crimes speedily and undertake general evidence gathering would come to debilitate the chances of success in the domestic war crimes and other trials.

3. Law Enforcement

Though KFOR deployed with rapid speed, the arrival of UNMIK police was slow and poorly organized. Its authorized strength was 4,781 within the first twelve months of the mission, but the number deployed was half that.[99] Some countries sent officers who spoke no English, and had no experience with criminal investigations or crowd control.[100] No deploying country provided pre-entry training on the applicable law, on international human rights standards, or on local culture. UNMIK police received copies of the OSCE compilation of applicable laws, but its distribution was as inconsistent as its application.

The domestic applicable law proved troublesome, most particularly for law enforcement from common law jurisdictions. The criminal procedure code did not provide for police warnings on arrest or during police interrogation. The code did not make reference to a right to counsel prior to being brought before an investigative judge. The domestic law states that comments made by a defendant in the course of an interrogation were not admissible in court, though, critically, other evidence that was subsequently developed through the interview often was.[101] UNMIK police officers took full advantage of this clear gap regarding the rights international law affords detainees: UNMIK police officers from the United States, for example, began administering polygraph tests to defendants. It would be two years be-

---

99. Interview with senior UNMIK police official, in Pristina, Kosovo (Sept. 2000).
100. Observations by the authors, in Pristina, Kosovo (Sept. 2000).
101. 1974 CRIMINAL PROCEDURE CODE, art. 83 (Fed. Republic of Yugoslavia) [hereinafter CPC].

fore UNMIK would promulgate a regulation that afforded detainees the right to counsel on arrest.[102]

The use of informers, police infiltration, or other surveillance techniques, common in both common law and civil law jurisdictions, were not utilized or developed in any coherent manner by UNMIK police. A reactive approach to law enforcement and a failure to develop a form of investigation that included a surveillance capacity further hindered the effective prosecution of criminal cases.

4. *Protection of Victims and Witnesses*

The participation, cooperation, and assurance of veracity on the part of victims and witnesses would be crucial to the functioning of the system as a whole, particularly in light of the lack of forensic evidence. Public reports dating from early 2000 raised this issue regarding war crimes trials and the perpetration of ethnically motivated crimes.[103] It was highlighted early on that victims and witnesses might fear reprisal for providing information to the police and that UNMIK police could not provide any safeguards. As the system developed, victim and witness testimony was often retracted, inconsistent, or modified during the course of the proceedings, leading to unreliable results in cases. The lack of services for victims and witnesses disproportionately affected those who were most vulnerable and disenfranchised in the community, such as female victims of sexual and domestic violence. There was a substantial need to undertake confidence-building measures to engender community trust in the system and to develop meaningful mechanisms to ensure victim services and safety. However, no steps were taken on this issue in the initial stages of developing the judiciary and law enforcement.

With the promulgation of Regulation 2001/4 On the Prohibition of Trafficking in Persons in Kosovo, some victim protections were instituted in regards to this important human rights problem.[104] However, no resources were put towards ensuring the enforcement of these provisions; they remain, for the most part, only aspirational at this writing. Even the practical issues of ensuring translation for victim witnesses in a language they understand has not been effectively addressed by DJA. In 2001, UNMIK police also created a witness protection program modeled on the United States approach.[105] This program is not integrated into the court system, fails to reflect the reality of the majority of crime in Kosovo, is totally without any local involvement, and is, therefore, likely unsustainable. Early recognition of and coherent planning for integrating access to justice and fair treatment

---

102. UNMIK/REG/2001/28, *supra* note 59.

103. *See* AMNESTY INT'L, FEDERAL REPUBLIC OF YUGOSLAVIA, KOSOVO: RECOMMENDATIONS TO UNMIK ON THE JUDICIAL SYSTEM (2000), *available at* http://www.web.amnesty.org/ai.nsf/index/EUR700062000.

104. UNMIK/REG/2001/4 (On the Prohibition of Trafficking in Persons in Kosovo), 12 Jan. 2001.

105. Interview with UNMIK police official, in Pristina, Kosovo (Summer 2001).

of victims, and corresponding protections for witnesses, could have greatly improved the effectiveness of the criminal justice system.

5. Forensics

Though there was much confusion over the applicable law and the role of international fair-trial standards, there was little doubt that UNMIK police were severely hampered in their investigative and forensic capabilities. In the critical period between June 1999 and December 1999, UNMIK police were without a "scenes of crimes" unit that would systematically collect forensic and other physical evidence. This remained the case for two years. Law enforcement was working with neither ballistics nor blood and fiber expertise. Forensic evidence collected, usually weapons or bullets, was sent to Bulgaria and sometimes Germany for forensic analysis. The few reports that did come back were cursory examinations of the evidence, often not more than one paragraph, and therefore lacked evidentiary weight. Defense counsel were in no position to challenge the reports' conclusions because there was no local expertise to call upon. Requesting the court to order the attendance of a foreign expert was unrealistic.[106]

This lack of forensic support proved most devastating in the war crimes and rape cases. In such cases, the existence and quality of medical and forensic evidence is often a crucial component. Though investigators from the International Criminal Tribunal for the former Yugoslavia ("ICTY") conducted extensive forensic examinations of sites critical to their investigations, no such approach was adopted by UNMIK police for the war crimes cases that would be tried locally. Ordinarily, this role would be within the exclusive domain of an investigative judge, who would direct police and forensic experts. But given the judicial vacuum that existed in 1999 and the inexperienced judges appointed in 2000, UNMIK was under an obligation to take the lead and provide the necessary tools to ensure that investigators, UNMIK police, and the judiciary all had the capacity to conduct sophisticated evidence collection. It did not do so. Two years into the mission there was still no dedicated facility for the examination of rape victims. Though rape kits had been provided to regional UNMIK police stations, no training was given as to their use.[107] Medical reports, if actually produced in court, were brief and lacking in sufficient detail.[108]

Due to logistical and financial constraints, Pristina-based doctors would not attend crime-scene investigations and would often refuse to testify in court. Without the cooperation of local doctors, and with little follow-up by UNMIK police and judicial officials or defenders, potentially critical forensic information did not reach the court. This endemic problem was high-

---

106. For a detailed look at cases affected by the lack of forensic capabilities, see *OSCE LSMS Feb. 2001 Rev.*, *supra* note 44, at 42

107. Interview with UNMIK police official, in Pristina, Kosovo (Spring 2001).

108. For further details on rape cases, see *OSCE LSMS Feb. 2001 Rev.*, *supra* note 44, at 44.

lighted in the Beqiri and Sopi case. More than a year after the indictment of two men for attempted murder, it emerged that the victim, mistakenly believed to be a Kosovo Serb, had been taken to the Pristina hospital, and had in fact died the following day. The hospital failed to provide this information to the police, the court, or defense counsel, and the legal actors did not follow up on the fate of the victim.[109]

The impact of the lack of such resources on the criminal justice system cannot be underestimated. In a period covering more than two years, the role played by forensic evidence and other investigatory techniques was nominal. Investigative judges and trial courts would come to rely on the witness testimony of the relevant parties involved, with no supporting or corroborative evidence. Given the likelihood of biased testimony in rape cases and inter-ethnic criminal trials, in particular the war crimes trials, the role of the international judges and prosecutors would be pivotal.

6. *International Judicial Actors*

In February 2000, Mitrovica (a city at the northern edge of Albanian-controlled areas and long a symbol of ethnic division) saw an explosion of violence that resulted in a number of deaths and injuries. Following these incidents and allegations of a judicial failure to investigate them, an international judge and prosecutor were appointed to the Mitrovica District Court. UNMIK Regulation 2000/34 extended to UNMIK the power to appoint international judges and prosecutors to all courts in Kosovo, but their introduction was ad hoc.[110] Although the regulation provided greater discretion in the use of international judges and prosecutors, their presence in war crimes investigations and trials was almost nonexistent.

Following criticism from the Kosovo Serb community and a pending hunger strike by Kosovo Serb inmates, in April 2000, UNMIK introduced one international judge into every trial panel.[111] But the steps taken proved inadequate because they failed to alleviate the perception or reality of ethnic bias: a trial panel consists of five decision makers, all of whom have a vote. DJA stated that this approach was driven by the lack of international judges, which was puzzling given the number of European states willing to provide significant judicial assistance.[112] Moreover, there was no reason why these trials could not be delayed pending the recruitment of new interna-

---

109. *OSCE LSMS Daily Reports* (on file with authors).

110. UNMIK/REG/2000/34 (On the Appointment and Removal from Office of International Judges and International Prosecutors), 27 May 2000 (amending UNMIK/REG/2000/6).

111. *OSCE LSMS July 2000 Rev.*, *supra* note 34, at 69.

112. *See, e.g.*, News Release, UK Foreign and Commonwealth Office, Foreign Secretary Reports on Talks With Kofi Annan (Mar. 14, 2000), *available at* http://www.britain.it/news/00mar/014c.htm. UK Foreign Secretary Robin Cook stated, "I would expect shortly to see at least a dozen, perhaps more, of the British legal profession working to help bring justice to Kosovo. The first should arrive before the end of next month."

tional judges. There was no call from the Kosovo Serb community or from defendants to expedite trials before majority ethnic Albanian trial panels.

Although the limited number of internationals posed a problem for UN-MIK, a more serious issue was identifying candidates with relevant expertise for these cases. Of the internationals that were appointed between 1999 and 2001, few had conducted trials involving serious criminal offenses and none had any practical experience in, or knowledge of, international humanitarian law. Indeed, one international judge's experience was exclusively in riparian rights. Furthermore, no attempts were made to provide pre-entry training on either humanitarian law or the FRY CPC. In September 2000, the ICTY held a training session in Kosovo on humanitarian law for both judges and prosecutors. The majority of international judges and prosecutors did not attend. The recruitment of adequately qualified international judges and prosecutors did not occur until 2001–2002.

The lack of adequate translators and low pay for local judges complicated the establishment of a working relationship between local and international judges. Even after pay increases, district court judges receive a yearly salary of approximately U.S. $5,000 compared to the approximately U.S. $100,000 paid to international judges.[113] International judges and prosecutors, who received round-the-clock armed protection, could often be seen moving through the region with a phalanx of bodyguards, staff, and vehicles. No such service was afforded local judges, more likely to be victims of violence and intimidation.

7. UNMIK Consultation with Local Judicial Officials

Following the appointment of judges and prosecutors to the regular courts in 1999, UNMIK did take steps to consult local judicial officials on a regular basis, predominantly in relation to administrative matters. Substantive legal initiatives or policy-related matters were rarely discussed with or disclosed to local officials. The most controversial of these initiatives were Regulation 1999/1[114] and Regulation 2000/64,[115] on the Authority of the Interim Administration in Kosovo and the Assignment of International Judges/ Prosecutors, respectively.

Primarily to address the concerns of judicial bias raised in the war crimes cases, Section 1 of Regulation 2000/64 grants to prosecutors, the accused, or defense counsel the right to petition the DJA for the assignment of an international prosecutor and a three-judge trial panel that consists of a majority of international judges where this is "necessary to ensure the independence and impartiality of the judiciary or the proper administration of justice."[116] In the absence of a petition, DJA may act on its own motion.

---

113. See AM. BAR ASS'N, supra note 60, at 20.
114. UNMIK/REG/1999/1, supra note 21.
115. UNMIK/REG/2000/64, supra note 90.
116. Id.

Prior to its promulgation, UNMIK made no attempt explain to local judges, politicians, or the general public the rationale behind the regulation. This resulted in widespread resentment throughout the ethnic Albanian community. In court, local judges refused to be recruited for the Regulation 64 panels and the Kosovo Supreme Court sent a letter to the SRSG stating that the regulation was a violation of international law. In the war crimes trial of Sava Matic, which was heard by a Regulation 64 panel, the third member of the trial panel, an ethnic Albanian, called a press conference and issued a public dissent to the acquittal of Matic.[117]

Adequate consultation prior to promulgation would probably have engendered some judicial support for Regulation 64, given that the local judiciary was generally supportive of the Kosovo War and Ethnic Crimes Court ("KWECC"), for which UNMIK did much advance work with local actors. The numbers of international judges and prosecutors has increased rather than decreased as local capacity has developed. The mentoring aspects of the international presence, cited as one of the reasons for their involvement, has been almost nonexistent. The use of substantial resources in developing an enhanced international judiciary indicates a lack of trust in and attention to the local judges and prosecutors and a dismissive attitude towards the long-term development of a local justice system.

With the creation of Pillar I and the Department of Justice in 2001, the exclusion of locals in the administration of justice increased. This move indicated that there was little faith or interest in building local capacity to administer justice fairly and effectively. Despite UNMIK's mandate to develop the capacity of the locals to administer democratic institutions, including the justice system, there is no Kosovar leadership in the DJA. The Ministry of Public Services within the Provisional Government has some authority regarding the logistical administration of the justice system. However, the attitude among internationals in UNMIK seems to be that this department will have no impact on substantive judicial policymaking.

Although some international control over the justice system should continue to ensure a balance of power between ethnic and regional interest groups, there should be enhanced efforts to ensure local decision making and capacity building. The decision regarding UNMIK's continued administration of law enforcement and the judiciary was never clearly explained within the mission, to the local legal community, or to the public whom the police and courts serve. But this failure to engage local legal actors is part of the broader problem of UNMIK's failure to foster respect for legal institutions and the rule of law.

---

117. *See Decision to Acquit Serb for Kosovo War Crimes Absurd*, AGENCE FRANCE-PRESSE, Jan. 30, 2001. Following a successful appeal by the public prosecutor, Matic was acquitted on retrial.

B. War Crimes Trials[118]

> Successor criminal trials are expected to lay the foundation of the transition by expressing disavowal of predecessor norms, yet for such trials to realize their normative potential, they must be prosecuted in the keeping with the full procedural legality associated with working democracies in ordinary times.[119]

Within six months of UNMIK's arrival, law enforcement had detained more than forty persons for war crimes-related offenses.[120] During this period there was much discussion among UN policymakers as to whether there should be an international judicial presence in these cases, but no policy was developed.[121] Though no official explanation was provided, UN officials have informally stated that the reasoning behind the decision to permit local courts to investigate such cases was to instill in the Kosovars a sense of local ownership in the justice system.[122]

There was some movement on the issue when, in December 1999, the SRSG announced publicly that UNMIK was creating a domestic court, KWECC, to try war criminals and ethnically motivated crime.[123] The catalyst for this decision was the growing anecdotal evidence from KFOR and OSCE human rights monitors that there was judicial bias against Kosovo Serbs and other minorities in judicial proceedings. The most striking example was the Momcilovic case.

1. The Momcilovic Case

In July 1999, one month after NATO's arrival, and at the height of ethnic tension, three members of the Momcilovic family, Kosovo Serbs, were arrested in relation to an inter-ethnic incident. Four ethnic Albanians asserted that they arrived at the Momcilovic home in order to have their car repaired, when, without reason, the Momcilovic family opened fire, killing two men and seriously injuring two others. The ethnic Albanians, who denied being in possession of weapons, were released from custody. The Momcilovics were indicted for murder, attempted murder, and weapons possession and ordered detained. One of the four ethnic Albanian males was indicted in relation to the attempted murder of a U.S. KFOR soldier during the exchange of gunfire.[124]

Found at the crime scene by U.S. KFOR was a video, which had recorded the salient parts of the gunfight. Although the videotape did not show the

---

118. See generally OSCE LSMS War Crimes Report, supra note 94.

119. Teitel, supra note 45, at 2037.

120. See OSCE LSMS July 2000 Rev., supra note 34, at 74.

121. Interview with official at the Office of the SRSG, in Pristina, Kosovo.

122. Interview with senior DJA official, in Pristina, Kosovo (Apr. 2001).

123. See OSCE LSMS July 2000 Rev., supra note 34, at 71.

124. Id. at 65; Org. for Sec. & Cooperation in Eur., Justice on Trial: The Momcilovic Case (Aug. 16, 2000) (unpublished manuscript) (on file with authors) [hereinafter Momcilovic].

killing of the two men, it did undermine the prosecution's case and support the defense's case of lawful self-defense by showing the arrival of the ethnic Albanians at the Momcilovic home, armed and attempting to break into the premises, followed by an exchange of gunfire.

Although aware of the video's existence, the local investigative judge and public prosecutor refused to watch the video or enter it into evidence. The FRY CPC obligates the court to ensure that the "subject matter is fully examined, that the truth is found . . . ."[125] Given that the video undermined the prosecution's case and supported the defense case of lawful self-defense, it was arguably admissible under the above provision.

Following an aborted first trial, and prior to the second trial, more than one year after arrest and detention, U.S. KFOR produced more than 100 pages of witness statements from U.S. soldiers present at the crime scene in 1999, in which they admitted to the killings and attempted murders for which the Momcilovics were indicted.[126] This delay was never explained. The statements also indicated that U.S. KFOR had destroyed the weapons and ammunition recovered from the crime scene and had not conducted autopsies. These revelations notwithstanding, the local prosecutor persisted. The ethnic-Albanian males, now prosecution witnesses, reasserted their earlier claim of being unarmed and acting innocently. The international judge, who was president of the trial panel, did not take steps to halt proceedings but did introduce the video. Three weeks later the Momcilovics were acquitted of murder and attempted murder, convicted of weapons possession, and sentenced to twelve months' custody.[127]

Partly as a result of the early evidence of bias exhibited in this case, UNMIK announced in December 1999 that the KWECC would be composed of a majority of international judges and prosecutors who would try war crimes cases. Both the local and international community, including human rights organizations, welcomed the announcement.[128] Pending the establishment of KWECC, in May 2000, the SRSG informed Kosovo Serb detainees that they would receive speedy trials before a mixed trial panel that included internationals and Serbs.[129] Such trial panels never materialized. In September 2000, and without public explanation, KWECC was abandoned. Despite acknowledging, in public statements accompanying the announcement of KWECC, the potential for judicial bias in war crimes cases, in the

---

125. CPC art. 292(2).

126. *GI's Testimony May Clear Serbs in an Albanian's Death*, N.Y. TIMES, July 25, 2000, at A3.

127. *See Momcilovic, supra* note 124. Following the trial, UNMIK took no steps to charge the prosecution witnesses with weapons possession, conspiracy to murder, or perjury. No steps were taken to investigate the local prosecutor for malicious prosecution or even an ethics violation, evidence of which appeared overwhelming. Moreover, the ethnic-Albanian male indicted in relation to the attempted murder of U.S. KFOR soldiers, who was released from custody in 1999, has yet to stand trial.

128. *See* AMNESTY INT'L, *supra* note 103. *See also Report of the Secretary-General on the United Nations Interim Administration Mission in Kosovo*, U.N. SCOR, 45th Sess., ¶ 60, U.N. Doc. S/2000/538 (2000).

129. *See* Press Release, United Nations, Kosovo Detainees Agree to End Hunger Strike (May 22, 2000), *available at* http://www.un.org/peace/kosovo/news/99/may00_4.htm#Anchor43.

nine months that preceded the September announcement, UNMIK took no steps to halt the war crimes investigations or trials of Kosovo Serbs by ethnic Albanians.

2. The War Crimes Investigations

In a civil law system, fact gathering in a criminal case is done at the investigative stage by the examining judge. In Kosovo, the newly appointed judges had limited experience in conducting criminal investigations and between 1999 and 2001 took few steps to investigate the war crimes cases they were assigned. Examination of witnesses was cursory and statements implicating a defendant were not adequately explored in order to determine if evidence needed to be confirmed, developed, or discarded. The failure to gather facts adequately at the investigative stage led to problems at trial, where witnesses would often expand on earlier testimony, leaving the trial panel to determine if a witness was exaggerating. Effective questioning at the investigative stage may have alleviated these problems.

The failure to investigate adequately prior to indictment was exacerbated by chronic delays in the judicial investigations. Regulation 1999/26 mandated that in serious cases detainees must be indicted within twelve months of arrest. This was an extension of the domestic law, which required an indictment within six months.[130] As the twelve-month deadline approached, all Kosovo Serb defendants were indicted. Delays in their indictments seemed to have had less to do with problems in collating evidence and more with taking revenge on an ethnic group. In one case, three brothers were arrested on October 7, 1999 and charged with war crimes.[131] Within a month of arrest, the examining judge ceased the investigation. There were no further developments in the case until October 2000, when, without explanation, the public prosecutor requested an extension of the investigation and detention, which was granted by a panel of judges that included an international judge. Because it was beyond twelve months, this extension order was in violation of Regulation 1999/26.[132] When the error was pointed out to DJA, the defendants were released and not re-arrested.[133]

According to the applicable law, a defendant can only be indicted if there is "sufficient evidence to warrant a reasonable suspicion" that the defendant had committed a crime.[134] The FRY CPC provides various safeguards to ensure that an insufficient investigation will not lead to an indictment, but will trigger either a request for further investigation or abandonment of the

---

130. UNMIK/REG/1999/26 (On the Extension of Periods of Pretrial Detention), 22 Dec. 1999, § 1.
131. OSCE LSMS Feb. 2001 Rev., supra note 44, at 79.
132. UNMIK/REG/1999/26, supra note 130.
133. OSCE LSMS Feb. 2001 Rev., supra note 44, at 79–80. DJA offered compensation to the defendants.
134. CPC art. 270.

case.[135] Prior to trial, the court also has the power to reject an indictment for insufficiency of evidence.[136] In cases concerning Kosovo Serb defendants, none of these safeguards seemed to apply. With little oversight by the international judges or prosecutors, and despite the lack of evidence, those Kosovo Serb defendants who had not escaped did in fact stand trial.[137]

3. Trial Panels

In November 1999, local courts began issuing war crimes-related indictments ranging from aggravated murder to genocide.[138] The trial of Milos Jokic, indicted for genocide, was the first such trial and took place in May 2000 before a majority-local trial panel and local prosecutor.[139] Jokic was convicted of war crimes and sentenced to twenty years' imprisonment. His appeal before a majority international panel succeeded on the grounds of insufficient evidence. He was retried before a Regulation 64 panel and acquitted.[140] The trial of Dragan Nikolic followed, but before an exclusively local panel and prosecutor.[141] He too was convicted and sentenced to twelve years' imprisonment. Nikolic's conviction was reversed on appeal, and he was acquitted on a retrial before an all-international trial panel.[142] Indictments and trial dates continued, with no effort by DJA to bring coherence to the situation. The makeup of Kosovo Serb defendants' trial panels appeared to be determined more by fate than reason. Those fortunate enough to have been overlooked by local judges setting trial dates or indicted after late 2000 could apply to be tried by a Regulation 64 panel.

But the use of Regulation 64 panels caused much friction within the Kosovo Serb community. This was primarily due to DJA's failure to ensure that *all* war crimes-related offenses qualified for an international prosecutor and majority international trial panel. DJA also failed to issue procedural guidelines setting out the basis on which the regulation would be administered. The end result was that some alleged war criminals successfully petitioned for Regulation 64 panels, while others would be tried before a majority-international panel and local prosecutor. While the participation of a local prosecutor as co-counsel with an international should be encouraged, evidence suggested that ethnic Albanians could not conduct such a prosecu-

---

135. CPC art. 174.

136. CPC art. 270(4).

137. *Mass Jail Break*, BBC WORLD NEWS, Sept. 3, 2000, *available at* http://news.bbc.co.uk/2/hi/world/europe/908620.stm. By September 2000, more than twenty Kosovo Serb detainees had escaped from UNMIK detention facilities.

138. *See OSCE LSMS War Crimes Report, supra* note 94, at 9.

139. *Id.* at 17.

140. *See* UNMIK, *Milos Jokic, Suspect of Genocide, Released Due to Lack of Evidence* (May 2, 2002), *available at* http://www.unmikonline.org/press/2002/mon/may/lmm050502.htm.

141. *See OSCE LSMS War Crimes Report, supra* note 94, at 12–13.

142. UNMIK, *Dragan Nikolic, Accused of Murder, Released by Gjilane Court* (Apr. 19, 2002), *available at* http://www.unmikonline.org/press/2002/mon/apr/lmm190402.htm.

tion fairly. Local prosecutors issued genocide indictments in four cases.[143] None were successfully prosecuted because, as either the trial or appellate court found, there was no evidence of genocide in these cases.

A few war crimes cases straddled the period of promulgation. This should not have barred DJA from intervening and suspending such cases, pending a Regulation 64 panel review, but they demurred. DJA took no steps to suspend, or to apply the regulation to, the trial of Momcilo Trajkovic, accused of committing one of the most serious war crimes in the region.[144] The trial began in November 2000 and continued until March 2001.[145] It was alleged that Trajkovic had ordered police forces allegedly under his control to commit widespread acts of murder, kidnapping, mistreatment, and expulsion. Trajkovic was also alleged to have collated lists of persons to be killed. During his trial, the local prosecutor introduced evidence of torture allegedly committed by the defendant in the 1980s.[146] This allegation did not form part of the indictment and appeared to prejudice the defendant's trial. In a case prosecuted by local counsel and before a majority local panel, Trajkovic was convicted and sentenced to twenty years' imprisonment. Before the Kosovo Supreme Court, the local prosecutor filed a request that the conviction be affirmed. The international prosecutor intervened and admitted trial error.[147] The appellate court reversed the conviction on the grounds that there was insufficient evidence.[148]

Because Regulation 64 was promulgated at such a late date, all those tried prior to its promulgation were convicted.[149] Between 2001 and 2002, the Kosovo Supreme Court, majority-international, reversed most of these convictions and ordered re-trials on the grounds that there was insufficient evidence to convict.[150]

4. Translations

Given the presence of international judges and prosecutors, adequate translation of witness testimony is critical. Trials involving internationals are conducted in three languages: English, Albanian, and Serbian. Because DJA had earlier failed to devise a strategy for these cases, no one had considered the question of professional translation, with the result that, when DJA appointed internationals to sit on cases, translators were chosen at random, either from court staff or the pool of DJA assistants. Due to the lack of translation equipment in 2000, translators would often sit with the interna-

---

143. *OSCE LSMS War Crimes Report*, *supra* note 94, at 34.
144. *See id.* at 24.
145. The Trajkovic case, like the other war crimes cases, was staggered so that trial dates would often consist of monthly hearings.
146. *See OSCE LSMS Feb. 2001 Rev.*, *supra* note 44, at 33.
147. *OSCE LSMS War Crimes Report*, *supra* note 94, at 24–25.
148. *Id.*
149. *See id.* at 54.
150. *Id.* at 48–49.

tional and convey testimony *sotto voce*. As a result, it was not possible for the legal parties to know whether the information being conveyed was accurate.

In due course, this approach was changed so that translated testimony could be heard in open court. It quickly became apparent that many of the translators failed to understand local dialects, in particular Kosovo Serb testimony (there was only one native Serb-speaking translator in the region). The result was a cacophony of voices attempting to determine the meaning of witness testimony. Eventually, translation equipment to facilitate simultaneous translation was retained, but problems persisted with the poor quality of translation and inadequate equipment that was either in insufficient quantity or failed to work because of electricity blackouts. These problems caused further delays to trials.

C. Fairness and Non-discrimination Generally

Although the prosecution of war crimes and other violations of humanitarian law is the *sine qua non* of fairness in transitional justice systems, it was clear from the beginning of the mission in Kosovo that, as with all other societies in transition, ethnic discrimination would not be the only major human rights issue encountered by the justice system. Discrimination or failure to appropriately address gender and juvenile justice and the mentally ill were quickly identified by parts of the international presence to be of vital importance to ensuring a fair criminal justice system. The cases facing the criminal justice system involving these groups were not negligible or extraordinary. From September 2000 to February 2001, the OSCE found that the number of serious criminal cases involving juveniles, excluding lower level crime, constituted twenty-three percent of all cases.[151] During that same six-month period, sexual violence cases constituted twelve percent of all completed cases.[152]

Efforts to concentrate on juvenile justice, spearheaded by UNICEF, led to the creation of a functioning task force and to training of the judiciary. The OSCE, in cooperation with UNMIK police and the International Organization for Migration, took the lead in tackling the issue of trafficking in women and other gender justice issues. Within the mental health field, a working group was established involving DJA's Penal Management section, doctors, and the OSCE. As a result, training, working groups, and draft legislation were implemented on many levels.

However, the overall impact of these initiatives, with the exception of the repatriation program for trafficking victims, has been questionable. One of the primary problems is that these areas, by their nature, are complex and must involve multi-sectoral policy and planning. It quickly became clear that there could be little change without a concerted effort across multiple

---

151. *OSCE LSMS Feb. 2001 Rev., supra* note 44, at 28.
152. *Id.* at 60.

fields and areas of responsibility. Despite the plethora of alternatives to detention in the law, without remedial programs for delinquent youth, juvenile judges had only so many options. Without services to address the medical and psychological needs of victims of domestic and sexual violence, these
women had little legal hope. Persons with mental illness require medical
treatment and deserve rights-based protections, even when they are alleged
perpetrators of crime or a threat to themselves or others. In essence, without
a functioning social services network and effective collaboration with criminal justice actors, the needs of these important groups in the criminal justice
system could not be addressed.

Despite the seriousness of the situation, there was minimal meaningful
involvement by DJA or the other top levels of the mission. The Administrative Department of Health and Social Welfare would, at times, participate in
the working groups and initiatives. However, the social welfare side of the
Department was severely under-staffed and under-resourced, particularly in
regards to these areas. These groups simply were not a priority. As a result,
when systematic change was necessary, there was no comprehensive approach
and little political will to ensure that the underlying issues would be tackled. With major international agencies struggling to identify solutions,
there were few avenues to reach the high levels of the mission. Even UNI-
CEF, with the mandate to advise the SRSG on child protection directly, had
trouble gaining access to and a response from the SRSG. Although substantial attempts were made by many organizations, they could not garner political support from the top levels of UNMIK. Consequently, the substantial
human and material resources invested in improving the responses to these
groups have not created meaningful change.

IV. HUMAN RIGHTS OVERSIGHT OF UNMIK

When the SG set out the objectives of the international presence in
Kosovo in two reports to the UNSC, they clustered around the theme of
fostering respect for the rule of law and for human rights.[153] Indeed, the SG
explicitly stated that a "culture" of human rights was to be infused into all
activities of the mission.[154] The human rights mandate was given, primarily,
to the OSCE, though other essential human rights-related components were
established.[155]

The mission began with international actors' sincere attempts to take
thoughtful approaches, based on human rights and rule-of-law principles.
But as the mission matured, compliance with human rights standards by
UNMIK and KFOR authorities declined, and the approach to criminal jus-

---

153. See Report of the Secretary-General, supra note 9; Report of the Secretary-General Pursuant to Paragraph
10 of Security Council Resolution 1244, U.N. Doc. S/1999/672 (1999) [hereinafter Report Pursuant to Paragraph 10].

154. See Report of the Secretary-General, supra note 9, ¶ 42.

155. See Report Pursuant to Paragraph 10, supra note 153.

tice became increasingly erratic. Executive detentions increased in use despite the presence of an international judiciary, consultation with local actors was rendered nearly obsolete, and the OSCE became increasingly irrelevant. As a part of its mandate, the OSCE was obligated to publicly report on the mission's compliance with human rights standards. Such reporting, privately considered too critical in UN circles, led to its marginalization.

The SG mandated the creation of an independent Ombudsperson Institution to investigate and publicly report on human rights abuses by UNMIK and all public entities in Kosovo.[156] Highly critical of the administration, the Institution was often ignored by the authorities. Similarly, the human rights components within the UN itself were ostracized. The Senior Human Rights Advisor to the SRSG left and was not replaced, and the SRSG's Office of Human Rights and Community Affairs was stripped of its human rights advisory role. Despite the clear mandate from the SG that this office ensure that legislation conformed to human rights standards, it, as well as the other components, was not consistently engaged in the formulation of legislation. The vigorous human rights mechanisms envisioned in the SG's report failed to fulfill their mandates, did not effectively engage the local population, and set a poor precedent for the role of human rights protections in future peacekeeping missions.

A. The Human Rights Mandate

The SG, in a report dated July 12, 1999, assigned the lead role of institution building within UNMIK to the OSCE and stated that one of its tasks would be human rights monitoring and capacity building.[157] The Report instructed UNMIK to develop coordinated mechanisms in order to facilitate monitoring of the respect for human rights and to "embed a culture of human rights in all areas of activity."[158] Specifically:

> UNMIK will have a core of human rights monitors and advisors who will have *unhindered access* to all parts of Kosovo to investigate human rights abuses and ensure that human rights protection and promotion concerns are addressed through the overall activities of the mission. Human rights monitors will . . . report their findings to the [Deputy Special Representative for Institution-Building]. The findings of human rights monitors will be made public . . . and will be shared . . . with United Nations human rights mechanisms[.] UNMIK will provide a coordinated reporting and response capacity.[159]

---

156. *See Report of the Secretary-General, supra* note 9.
157. *See id.*
158. *Id.* ¶ 42.
159. *Id.* ¶ 87. Emphasis added.

In a Letter of Agreement between the UN and the OSCE, it was agreed that the OSCE would develop mechanisms to ensure that the courts and other judicial structures operate in accordance with international human rights standards.[160] Though the OSCE had the human rights mandate, there were other human rights–related components to the mission.

The SG's report required that, as a part of the SRSG's executive office, a Senior Human Rights Adviser "ensure a proactive approach on human rights in all UNMIK activities and ensure the compatibility of regulations issued by UNMIK with international human rights standards."[161] The SRSG's Office of Human Rights and Community Affairs ("OHRCA") was charged with advising the SRSG on human rights and minority-related issues. There was a Senior Human Rights Adviser from the initial stages of the mission until around March 2000. Thereafter, OHRCA was without the leadership of an experienced human rights lawyer. Within the UN administration, the OSCE established the Administrative Department for Democratic Government and Civil Society, which has been transformed into the Prime Minis ter's Office of Good Governance, Human Rights, and Gender under the local government structure.[162]

OLA has exclusive authority to draft legislation, and yet it does not have a dedicated post for a human rights lawyer. Since 1999, OLA has not had an experienced human rights or criminal justice lawyer on staff. UNMIK police had a position for a human rights advisor to the Police Commissioner, which was filled and active from September 2000 until November 2001. Though not a component of the mission, the UN Office of the High Commissioner for Human Rights ("OHCHR") had a presence, and under their general mandate an obligation to monitor and report on human rights compliance.

The SG's July 1999 report further recognized that "a strong system of human rights protection offers accessible and timely mechanisms for the independent review, redress and appeal of non-judicial actions," and required that an Ombudsperson Institution be established as an independent body with jurisdiction over allegations of human rights abuses by "any person or entity in Kosovo."[163] The Ombudsperson was obligated to conduct investigations and make recommendations to authorities, including those "on the compatibility of domestic laws and regulations with recognized international standards."[164] The Ombudsperson was required to provide regular reports to the SRSG and make its findings public.[165]

---

160. Letter from UN Department of Peacekeeping Operations to Knut Vollebaek, OSCE Chairman-in-Office (July 19, 1999).

161. *Id.*

162. UNMIK/REG/2000/40 (On the Establishment of the Administrative Department for Democratic Government and Civil Society), 10 July 2000.

163. *Report of the Secretary-General, supra* note 9, ¶ 89–90.

164. *Id.* ¶ 90.

165. *Id.*

B. *Legal Monitoring*

Monitoring of the judicial system and correctional service fell to the OSCE's Legal Systems Monitoring Section, the largest legal systems monitoring mechanism in any OSCE mission, and one of the largest in any peacekeeping mission in the UN's history. It was mandated to report on systemic violations of international law and gross violations of fair trial standards in individual cases. In March 2000, UNMIK formally recognized this monitoring role by promulgating a regulation that recognized the OSCE's responsibility "for the independent monitoring of the judicial system and correctional service."[166]

LSMS primarily focused on war crimes cases, ethnically motivated crime, detention, the treatment of juveniles and the mentally ill, and victims of sexual violence. From October 2000, LSMS began issuing periodic public reports highlighting systemic human rights violations and abuses in individual cases.[167] Such reports were issued pursuant to the mandate to support UNMIK in the development of the judiciary and correctional service.

C. *The Marginalization of the Human Rights Mandate*

In 1999, human rights policy was often coordinated among the OSCE, OHCHR, UNMIK Police representatives, and OHRCA. Local actors were also, at times, consulted. For example, the JAC, which was comprised of members of the local legal and political community, was often involved in the review of draft legislation. In December 1999, a large Human Rights Conference of international experts and local human rights activists from all sectors of Kosovo society was held.[168] However, as time went on, the international human rights components of the mission, particularly the OSCE, did little to engage the local human rights community effectively on a policy level. Although working group initiatives did involve some local NGOs, few real connections and genuine working relationships were established with prominent Kosovo human rights groups. As with other parts of UN-MIK, the human rights components also trivialized the local community and the importance of its sense of ownership and input.

The UN–OSCE agreements notwithstanding, LSMS monitors faced much opposition from court officials and correctional staff, both local and international. The central dispute related to the degree of access that should be afforded the monitors. LSMS considered "unhindered access" to mean access to all court records and detainees, albeit on a confidential basis. The OSCE took the view that monitoring under the mandate required an exhaustive analysis of cases that could not be achieved by simply watching trials because human

166. UNMIK/REG/2000/15 (On the Establishment of the Administrative Department of Justice), 21 Mar. 2000.

167. *See, e.g., OSCE LSMS July 2000 Rev., supra* note 34.

168. O'NEILL, *supra* note 41, at 130–31.

rights abuses in the context of the criminal justice system begin on arrest. Judicial officials considered access to court hearings sufficient under the mandate. DJA failed to intervene, claiming that to do so would interfere with the independence of the courts. Two years following the creation of LSMS, an agreement was reached with DJA under which monitors would be given broad access to relevant legal materials.

However, even after an agreement on access was reached, monitors again faced obstruction in 2002. International judicial officials attempted to restrict access of human rights monitors to investigatory hearings and information in cases of internationals charged with criminal conduct. In addition, when the OSCE began to introduce more coherent monitoring of law enforcement and security personnel, similar restrictions occurred. There has been little consistent and effective monitoring of the law enforcement agencies and their actions.

Questions of access and the nature of public reporting of institutional failings resulted in much friction among DJA, UNMIK police, and the OSCE. Identifying areas in need of judicial reform in a public document appeared to irk senior UN officials. Although publicly the mission appeared to welcome such self-scrutiny, internally what were intended as constructive critical insights into a developing justice system were taken as personal slights.

Since late 2000, OLA and DJA have been developing human rights and criminal justice policy often without any discussion with the human rights components of the mission, though consultation with UNMIK police and KFOR has taken place. The exclusion of the OSCE, in particular, appeared to be in reaction to its comments on critical criminal justice issues. Rather than seek an accommodation, OLA and DJA excluded the OSCE from the relevant working groups and failed to keep them informed of substantive developments.

Since March 2000, OHRCA has been crippled by the lack of a Senior Human Rights Advisor and as a result has had little impact on the development of policy in this area. In fact, the UN eventually abolished this human rights advisory component in the summer of 2001, resulting in the lack of any human rights input at the SRSG level. Similarly, OHCHR faded from view. Despite its global human rights mandate, it was unable to alter the course of UNMIK human rights policy.

It took considerable time and resources to develop the Ombudsperson Institution, which set about fulfilling its mandate in 2000.[169] The Institution has published numerous reports and investigated a significant number of cases. The Second Annual Report, covering 2001–2002 and published July 10, 2002, provides insight into the apparent disregard by UNMIK of the Institution's mandate.[170] The bitter report gives a list of all the various ac-

169. UNMIK/REG/2000/38, *supra* note 65.
170. OMBUDSPERSON INSTITUTION IN KOSOVO, SECOND ANNUAL REPORT 2001–2002 (2002),

tions taken by the Institution, and details the response, or lack thereof, from UNMIK. The response of the PDSRSG to the report was equally acrid and defensive, denying that UNMIK has responsibilities as a surrogate state and providing rosy responses to questions concerning the reality of human rights protection in Kosovo.[171] This litany exposes a rift between UNMIK and the Institution and provides a gloomy picture of UNMIK's respect for human rights mechanisms.

The strongest indications of the marginalization of the human rights mandate in Kosovo and of the decrease in attention to human rights are the recent Reports of the Secretary General on UNMIK to the Security Council. Unlike initial reports about the mission, reports in 2002 do not even mention the state of protection of human rights and compliance with standards in Kosovo, but rather focus on law and order and the increasing use of international judges and prosecutors.[172] These lie in stark contrast to the emphasis placed on respect for rule of law and human rights protection in the founding documents of the mission.

D. *Legislative Compliance with Human Rights Standards*

The failure of OLA to consult the relevant human rights experts in the mission and to ensure that draft regulations are vetted for human rights compliance resulted in regulations that violate basic human rights standards. Regulation 1999/26 amends the domestic law and empowers a court to extend pre-trial custody to twelve months in serious cases (the domestic law permits six months).[173] The practice of pre-trial detention pursuant to that regulation is in violation of Article 5(3) and (4) of the ECHR and Article 9(3) and (4) of the ICCPR in that the regulation fails to make adequate provision for the periodic review of the extension of custody time limits throughout the period of detention covered by the regulation. The regulation also fails to provide the detainee the right to initiate a review of an order for detention. At no stage is the detainee entitled to challenge the reasons for detention provided by either the investigative judge or the public prosecutor. During the drafting of this regulation, the Senior Human Rights Advisor to the SRSG, according to his mandate, made known to the OLA that this regulation, if promulgated, would not comply with international

---

available at http://www.ombudspersonkosovo.org/doc/specreps/Final2AnnualReport200210-07-02English.htm.

171. Response from PDRSG, Ombudsperson's Second Annual Report 2001–2002: Responses to Errors of Judgment and Fact (on file with authors).

172. *See Report of the Secretary-General on the United Nations Interim Administration Mission in Kosovo,* U.N. SCOR, 57th Sess., U.N. Doc. S/2002/436 (2002); *Report of the Secretary-General on the United Nations Interim Administration Mission in Kosovo,* U.N. SCOR, 57th Sess., U.N. Doc. S/2002/779 (2002); *Report of the Secretary-General on the United Nations Interim Administration Mission in Kosovo,* U.N. SCOR, 57th Sess., U.N. Doc. S/2002/1126 (2002). The reports include captions about tackling crime and violence, combating terrorism and organized crime and building law enforcement and judicial capacity.

173. UNMIK/REG/1999/26, *supra* note 132.

human rights standards.[174] However, OLA refused to follow the recommendations of the Advisor. Thereafter, human rights advocates both inside and outside the mission publicly criticized UNMIK for promulgating legislation in violation of their mandate from the SG, but the regulation was not amended or repealed.

In addition to Regulation 1999/26, other regulations, in particular Regulation 2000/47 On the Status, Privileges and Immunities of KFOR and UNMIK and their Personnel in Kosovo,[175] Regulation 2001/17 On the Registration of Contracts for the Sale of Real Property in Specific Geographical Areas of Kosovo,[176] and Regulation 2001/18 On the Establishment of a Detention Review Commission for Extra-judicial Detentions Based on Executive Orders,[177] have been scrutinized and found to violate fundamental principles of human rights by the human rights components of the mission, in particular the Ombudsperson Institution.[178]

In April 2001, a final draft regulation written by OLA relating to a detainee's right to counsel included a provision stating that counsel can be present during the interrogation of a detainee but "shall remain silent."[179] It was disclosed to DJA and an international prosecutor but no attempt was made to clear the draft with the relevant human rights experts or law enforcement officials. The result was a final draft regulation in a critical field that was in breach of basic international human rights standards.[180] The controversial provision was eventually deleted from the promulgated regulation, although other troubling provisions remain.[181]

In February 2001, the OSCE recommended that a human rights vetting mechanism be established to ensure the conformity of new regulations with human rights norms. Despite this, it was not until summer 2002 that the UN initiated a mechanism to ensure that draft legislation was in compliance with international human rights standards. The Human Rights Oversight Committee was established with terms of reference that include the power "to consider and agree on actions and policy to ensure respect for human rights by all UNMIK Pillars."[182] The Committee, comprised of the heads of

---

174. *See* O'NEILL, *supra* note 41, at 78.

175. UNMIK/REG/2000/47, *supra* note 58.

176. UNMIK/REG/2001/17 (On the Registration of Contracts for the Sale of Real Property in Specific Geographical Areas of Kosovo), 22 Aug. 2001.

177. UNMIK/REG/2001/18, *supra* note 67.

178. *See generally* Ombudsperson Institution in Kosovo, Special Reports, *available at* http://www.ombudspersonkosovo.org.

179. OLA, *Final Draft: On the Rights of Persons Arrested by Law Enforcement Authorities* (Apr. 2000) (draft regulation).

180. International standards and case law recognize the right to the *assistance* of counsel during detention, interrogation, and preliminary investigations. Silent counsel is, in effect, no counsel. *See* Eighth United Nations Congress on the Prevention of Crime and the Treatment of Offenders, *Basic Principles on the Role of Lawyers*, ¶¶ 1, 6, 17, U.N. Doc. A/CONF.144/28/Rev.1 (1990).

181. *See* UNMIK/REG/2001/28, *supra* note 59.

182. Human Rights Oversight Committee, Terms of Reference (internal document) (on file with authors).

the Pillars, is to be advised by the Inter-Pillar Working Group on Human Rights, an amalgam of components to the mission that include the OSCE, DJA, UNMIK police, KFOR, OLA, UN Office of the Political Advisor, and OHCHR. There is no local participation. As of late 2002, no attempts have been made to review current UNMIK legislation for human rights compliance. Indeed, whether this new mechanism will ensure that future laws comply with international human rights standards will depend upon the degree of human rights law expertise present and to what extent the OLA drafters respect the Committee's advice.

CONCLUSION: IMPLICATIONS FOR TRANSITIONAL JUSTICE

Establishing a *de facto* government and a new justice system is an enormous and complex task, made more difficult when the new regime is confronting serious societal wounds. Transitions from repressive regimes to democracies based on the rule of law and respect for human rights are not achieved in a matter of months. In a very short time and under difficult circumstances, UNMIK accomplished a degree of security, stability, and democracy. Despite these achievements, the international intervention in postwar Kosovo has provided some sobering lessons in the area of criminal justice and human rights from which future peace-building missions should learn.

Peace-building missions need to be premised on the recognition that developing a justice system based on the rule of law and human rights is the key to a successful democratic transition. International administrations must be structured to limit the amount of power vested in the transitional administrator and ensure a more sophisticated system of checks and balances. In peace-building missions that require some degree of autocratic decision making, meaningful efforts need to be made to ensure that actions do not undermine fundamental principles of democratic governance. Such missions should function within a clear legal framework, which if not rooted in a constitution, at a minimum has at its core international human rights standards. Regardless of the nature of the executive power, whether local or international, such a framework must be applicable to all authorities, including the security component. In this regard, it must be made explicit that security forces, particularly when undertaking civilian functions, are obligated to conform their actions to the law.

In order to guarantee the enforcement of the framework, an independent court system must fulfill its role as a check on excessive state power and the protector of fundamental rights. Crucial to cultivating a strong, independent court system is the creation of a zealous and innovative Supreme Court, which may require the cooperation of international and local judicial actors. Institutional mechanisms for ensuring the independence and impartiality of the judiciary must be implemented as soon as practicable. Peace-building authorities must respect and follow judicial decisions, notwithstanding disagreement with them. Actions that violate fundamental rights, even though well intentioned, risk jeopardizing the mission's goals. The use of arbitrary detentions by the executive and the rejection of lawful court orders set a precedent that the UN may come to deeply regret because such moves undermine the democratic objective of developing an independent and strong judiciary.

Transitional regimes require a reformation of the law. In instances where a legal vacuum exists, a semblance of process needs to be established despite the apparent urgency of the situation on the ground. In addition, there needs to be a short- and a long-term vision brought to the creation of a legislative reform agenda. The legislative process must include transparency, consultation, and public engagement. The public must be made clearly aware of what the law is and the reasoning behind its promulgation. Initially a mechanism must be developed for a timely dissemination of the law to the relevant actors and to the public. No law should be implemented until this process has occurred. Once the process is determined, peace-building authorities must adhere to it, even in the face of significant challenges. The combination of a short- and long-term agenda and adherence to an established and transparent process that engages the local population will ultimately result in more effective and just laws.

It must be accepted that peace and order, even in a *de facto* state of emergency, can be achieved concurrently with respect for the protection of basic human rights. Peace-building missions require both external and internal human rights mechanisms. The mission in Kosovo as envisioned was exemplary in this regard. But the reality proved that such mechanisms may be disregarded and made irrelevant. The failure to ensure a meaningful presence of criminal justice and human rights experts during the creation of policy and drafting of legislation can result in irregular policy decisions and unlawful regulations. Those responsible for the development of peace-building missions must ensure that key human rights positions are filled by those with the relevant expertise and are provided the political support for tackling the difficult issues that will arise. In addition to a more engaged OHCHR, the UN Department of Peacekeeping Operations should contain a human rights component to provide field missions with support and expertise.

In situations in which the international community is engaged in rebuilding post-conflict societies that have a history of internal discord, there must be a substantial international presence of judges and prosecutors early on. In particular, in cases that most challenge the capacity of local legal actors, such as war crimes-related offences, judicial investigations must be conducted by internationals, and the composition of the trial panel must be majority-international. Having said this, it is critical that local legal actors be engaged in this process as well. For example, local prosecutors should co-chair war crimes prosecutions.

Peace-building missions must ensure that those selected as international judicial actors are competent for such high-profile posts. Pre-entry legal training on relevant provisions of the domestic law and international human rights standards is essential. International judicial actors must be independent and impartial and subject to investigation, discipline, and removal from office. The use of international judicial actors must be well planned and must coincide with increasing local capacity. It is imperative that the inclusion of international judicial actors not result in the creation of a parallel justice system with ties to the political agenda of the peace-building mission.

Most critically, future peace-building missions must ensure that a coordinated and thoughtful approach to developing a criminal justice sector is adopted. Such a strategy must be premised on a broad and comprehensive assessment of all of the critical components and an effective justice process that is beyond merely the courts. A holistic approach would include assessing the needs of law enforcement agencies, medical and forensic expertise, and legal services. In addition, consideration has to be given to the development of victims services, witness protection, and a network of social services to meet the needs of particular groups such the victims of sexual violence, juveniles, and the mentally ill. This requires a synergy of all relevant actors in the field, one that engages law enforcement, judicial officials, defenders, legislative and policy experts, and human rights advocates.

Finally, future peace-building strategies must involve the genuine participation of the local community. Failure to consult relevant local actors in policy and legislative developments can immeasurably detract from a mission's goals. Simultaneously, effectively transforming society requires a real engagement with the local populace. Consultation on critical issues and dissemination of information to the public must be substantive and genuine. Justice sector reform requires that the international community not only take into account local experiences, wishes, and expectations but also allow such values to shape the development of the justice system.

Part III
Legal Frameworks
and the Rule of Law

[7]

PROMOTING THE RULE OF LAW ABROAD

The Problem of Knowledge

Thomas Carothers

EXECUTIVE SUMMARY

Although the current rule-of-law promotion field is still expanding as it approaches the end of its second decade, it still faces a lack of knowledge at many levels of conception, operation, and evaluation. There is a surprising amount of uncertainty, for example, about the twin rationales of rule-of-law promotion—that promoting the rule of law will contribute to economic development and democratization. There is also uncertainty about what the essence of the rule of law actually is—whether it primarily resides in certain institutional configurations or in more diffuse normative structures. Rule-of-law promoters are also short of knowledge about how the rule of law develops in societies and how such development can be stimulated beyond simplistic efforts to copy institutional forms. And the question of what kinds of larger societal effects will result from specific changes in rule-of-law institutions is also still open. Although aid institutions engaged in rule-of-law assistance do attempt some "lessons learned" exercises, many of the lessons produced are superficial and even those are often not really learned. Several substantial obstacles to greater knowledge accumulation in this field persist, including the complexity of the task of promoting the rule of law, the particularity of legal systems, the unwillingness of aid organizations to invest sufficient resources in evaluations, and the tendency of both academics and lawyers not to pursue systematic empirical research on rule-of-law aid programs. Whether rule-of-law aid is on the path to becoming a well-grounded field of international assistance remains uncertain.

WHEN RULE-OF-LAW AID PRACTITIONERS gather among themselves to reflect on their work, they often express contradictory thoughts. On the one hand they talk with enthusiasm and interest about what they do, believing that the field of rule-of-law assistance is extremely important. Many feel it is at the cutting edge of international efforts to promote both development and democracy abroad. On the other hand, when pressed, they admit that the base of knowledge from which they are operating is startlingly thin. As a colleague who has been closely involved in rule-of-law work in Latin America for many years said to me recently, "we know how to do a lot of things, but deep down we don't really know what we are doing." Though some practitioners harbor no doubts and promote the rule of law abroad with a great sense of confidence, most persons working in the field openly recognize and lament the fact that little really has been learned about rule-of-law assistance relative to the extensive amount of on-the-ground activity.

This fact raises an interesting puzzle. The current rule-of-law promotion field—which started in the mid-1980s in Latin America and now extends to many regions, including Eastern Europe, the former Soviet Union, Asia, and sub-Saharan Africa—is already older than its precursor was, the law and development movement of the 1960s and early 1970s, when that earlier movement ran out of steam and closed down. The law and development movement died out above all because of a too-obvious gap between its ambitions and its achievements. Yet the current rule-of-law field—which has some important similarities to but also differences from the law and development movement—is still expanding as it approaches the end of its second decade, despite an apparent lack of knowledge at many levels of conception, operation, and evaluation.

The answer to the puzzle may lie not so much in differences between the substance of the two movements—though those differences are real—than in differing contexts. The law and development movement was launched in the optimistic days of the early 1960s when hopes for democracy and development were high for the newly decolonized states of Africa and Asia, and for the developing world as a whole. Yet as the law and development movement unfolded, that broader context of optimism deteriorated quickly. Democratic experiments failed in many parts of the developing world in the 1960s and the broader hope for rapid developmental gains ran into contrary realities in many countries. By the end of that decade, the modernization paradigm on which U.S. foreign aid of the 1960s, including the law and development movement, had been based was already in serious doubt and a pessimistic assessment of foreign aid caused much retooling and retraction.

In contrast, the optimistic context of the crucial early years of the current rule-of-law aid movement—the heady period of the end of the Cold War—has held up somewhat longer. Though simplistic thinking about the ease and naturalness of the many dual transitions around the world to democracy and market economics has met with many disappointments, the international aid community has not (yet) experienced a major disillusionment with the underlying assumptions about aid for democracy and market economics from which the rule-of-law aid movement operates.

6 PROMOTING THE RULE OF LAW ABROAD

It may be then that a still-favorable, though increasingly shaky context holds together the rule-of-law assistance movement. This should not prevent us, however, from pushing at this question about knowledge: What is the problem of knowledge that aid practitioners allude to in private? What is it that practitioners do not know that they feel they should know as they engage in rule-of-law promotion projects around the world? What about the many "lessons learned" that are dutifully reported in institutional documents? And to the extent there really is a problem of knowledge, what causes it and what might ameliorate it?

SELF-EVIDENT BUT UNCERTAIN RATIONALES

The problem of knowledge in rule-of-law promotion can be considered as a series of deficits at various analytic levels, descending in generality. To start with, there is a surprising amount of uncertainty about the basic rationale for rule-of-law promotion. Aid agencies prescribe rule-of-law programs to cure a remarkably wide array of ailments in developing and post-communist countries, from corruption and surging crime to lagging foreign investment and growth. At the core of this burgeoning belief in the value of rule-of-law work are two controlling axioms: The rule of law is necessary for economic development and necessary for democracy. When held up to a close light, however, neither of these propositions is as axiomatic as it may at first appear.

It has become a new credo in the development field that if developing and post-communist countries wish to succeed economically they must develop the rule of law. One form of this economic rationale for rule-of-law work focuses on foreign investment: If a country does not have the rule of law, the argument goes, it will not be able to attract substantial amounts of foreign investment and therefore will not be able to finance development. Leaving aside the first question of whether foreign investment is really always a requirement for development (since it is not clear, for example, that the economic success of a number of the major Western economies, such as the American and Japanese economies, was based on substantial amounts of inward foreign investment), there is a notable lack of proof that a country must have a settled, well-functioning rule of law to attract investment. The argument has an undeniable common sense appeal—investors will want predictability, security, and the like. Yet the case of China flies squarely in the face of the argument—the largest recipient of foreign direct investment in the developing world happens to be a country notorious for its lack of Western-style rule of law. It is clear that what draws investors into China is the possibility of making money either in the near or long term. Weak rule of law is perhaps one negative factor they weigh in their decision of whether to invest, but it is by no means determinative. A recent study of the rule of law and foreign investment in post-communist countries points to a similar conclusion. Weak rule of law is not a major factor in determining investment flows, and the more important causal relationship may be in the reverse direction: The presence of at least certain types of foreign investors may contribute to the development of the rule of law through their demands for legal reforms.[1]

A broader form of the argument about the relationship between the rule of law and economic development emphasizes an array of rule-of-law components—such as the need for legal predictability, the enforcement of contracts, and property rights—as necessary for the functioning of a modern market economy. Again the appeal of this argument is obvious and probably contains elements of truth. But as Frank Upham has argued in a study of the supposed relationship between an idealized apolitical, rule-based system of law and the economic development of the United States and Japan, the relationship is by no means as clear-cut as many might hope.[2] Similarly, a review by Rick Messick of studies that attempt to find causal relationships between judicial reform and development notes that "the relationship is probably better modeled as a series of on-and-off connections, or of couplings and decouplings," in other words the causal arrows go both directions and sometimes do not appear at all.[3] It is not possible here to survey all the literature on what is in fact an extremely complex, multifaceted question about the relationship of the rule of law and economic development. The central point is that simplistic assertions such as have become common among aid agencies to the effect that "the rule of law" grosso modo is necessary for development are at best badly oversimplified and probably misleading in many ways. The case of China again points to some of the shortcomings of the assertion. Many countries being told that they must have Western style of rule of law before they can achieve significant economic growth look with envy at China's sustained economic growth of the past twenty years and wonder why the prescription did not apply there.

Things are similarly murky on the political side of the core rationale. Unquestionably the rule of law is intimately connected with liberal democracy. A foundation of civil and political rights rooted in a functioning legal system is crucial to democracy. But again, the idea that specific improvements in the rule of law are necessary to achieve democracy is dangerously simplistic. Democracy often, in fact usually, co-exists with substantial shortcomings in the rule of law. In quite a few countries that are considered well-established Western democracies—and that hold themselves out to developing and post-communist countries as examples of the sorts of political systems that those countries should emulate—one finds various shortcomings: (1) court systems that are substantially overrun with cases to the point where justice is delayed on a regular basis; (2) substantial groups of people, usually minorities, are discriminated against and unable to find adequate remedies within the civil legal system; (3) the criminal law system chronically mistreats selected groups of people, again, usually minorities; and (4) top politicians often manage to abuse the law with impunity, and political corruption is common.

Of course one can interpret this to mean that because of the deficiencies in the rule of law these countries are imperfect democracies. This is true enough, but the point is that they are widely accepted in the international community as established democracies. Yet their aid agencies are telling officials in the developing and post-communist world that well-functioning rule of law is a kind of tripwire for democracy. It would be much more accurate to say that the rule of law and democracy are closely intertwined but that major shortcomings in the rule of law often exist within reasonably democratic political systems. Countries struggling to become democratic do not face a dramatic choice of "no rule of law, no democracy" but rather a series of smaller, more complicated choices about what elements of their legal systems they wish to try to improve with the expectation of achieving what political benefits.

In short, the axiomatic quality of the two core rationales of the current wave of rule-of-law assistance efforts—that the rule of law is necessary for economic development and democracy—is misleading when used as a mechanistic, causal imperative by the aid community. Rule-of-law aid practitioners can probably prescribe rule-of-law programs with a safe belief that these initiatives may well be helpful to both economic development and democratization, but they really do not know to what extent there are direct causal connections at work and whether similar resources directed elsewhere might produce greater effect on economic and political conditions.

8   PROMOTING THE RULE OF LAW ABROAD

THE ELUSIVE ESSENCE

Rule-of-law aid providers seem confident that they know what the rule of law looks like in practice. Stated in shorthand form, they want to see law applied fairly, uniformly, and efficiently throughout the society in question, to both public officials as well as ordinary citizens, and to have law protect various rights that ensure the autonomy of the individual in the face of state power in both the political and economic spheres. Their outlook on the rule of law can certainly be criticized for its narrowness. They do not have much interest in non-Western forms of law, in traditional systems of justice, or, in the case of some American rule-of-law experts, even in civil law. But it is important to go beyond that fairly obvious weakness to a different aspect of the problem of knowledge: Rule-of-law aid practitioners know what the rule of law is supposed to look like in practice, but they are less certain what the essence of the rule of law is.

By their nature as practitioners intent on producing tangible, even measurable changes in other societies, rule-of-law aid specialists need to concretize the appealing but inevitably somewhat diffuse concept of "the rule of law." In the broader field of democracy assistance, the pattern has been for democracy promoters to translate the overarching idea of democracy into an institutional checklist or template that they can pursue through a series of specific aid intiatives.[4] Similarly, rule-of-law promoters tend to translate the rule of law into an institutional checklist, with primary emphasis on the judiciary.

The emphasis on judiciaries is widespread in the rule-of-law field, with the terms *judicial reform* and *rule-of-law reform* often used interchangeably. The emphasis derives from the fact that most rule-of-law promotion specialists are lawyers and when lawyers think about what seems to be the nerve center of the rule of law they think about the core institutions of law enforcement.

Yet it is by no means clear that courts are the essence of a rule-of-law system in a country. Only a small percentage of citizens in most Western rule-of-law systems ever have direct contact with courts. In a certain sense courts play a role late in the legal process—it might well be argued that the making of laws is the most generative part of a rule-of-law system. Yet rule-of-law programs have not much focused on legislatures or the role of executive branch agencies in law-making processes. The question of which institutions are most germane to the establishment of the rule of law in a country is actually quite complex and difficult. Yet for the last ten to fifteen years, rule-of-law programs have given dominant attention to judiciaries, without much examination of whether such a focus is really the right one.

The uncertainty goes beyond the question of "which institutions?" Indeed, doubt exists about whether it is useful to conceive of and attempt to act upon rule-of-law development in primarily institutional terms. Clearly law is not just the sum of courts, legislatures, police, prosecutors, and other formal institutions with some direct connection to law. Law is also a normative system that resides in the minds of the citizens of a society. As rule-of-law providers seek to affect the rule of law in a country, it is not clear if they should focus on institution-building or instead try to intervene in ways that would affect how citizens understand, use, and value law. To take a simple example, many rule-of-law programs focus on improving a country's courts and police on the assumption that this is the most direct route to improve compliance with law in the country. Yet some research shows that compliance with law depends most heavily on the perceived fairness and legitimacy of the laws, characteristics that are not established primarily by the courts but by other means, such as the political process. An effort to improve compliance thus might more fruitfully take a completely different approach.

In sum, the question of where the essence of the rule of law actually resides and therefore what should be the focal point of efforts to improve the rule of law remains notably unsettled. Rule-of-law practitioners have been following an institutional approach, concentrating on judiciaries, more out of instinct than well-researched knowledge.

HOW DOES CHANGE OCCUR?

Even if we leave aside the problem of where the essence of the rule of law resides and accept the institutionalist approach that has become the norm, we see that rule-of-law aid providers face a problem of knowledge with regard to the very basic question of how change in systems actually occurs. Aid providers know what endpoint they would like to help countries achieve—the Western-style, rule-oriented systems they know from their own countries. Yet, they do not really know how countries that do not have such systems attain them. That is to say they do not know what the process of change consists of and how it might be brought about.

In launching and implementing the many rule-of-law programs of recent years, rule-of-law aid specialists have blurred this lack of knowledge by following what has been the approach to achieving change in the broader field of democracy assistance: attempting to reproduce institutional endpoints. This consists of diagnosing the shortcomings in selected institutions—that is, determining in what ways selected institutions do not resemble their counterparts in countries that donors believe embody successful rule of law—and then attempting to modify or reshape those institutions to fit the desired model. If a court lacks access to legal materials, then those legal materials should be provided. If case management in the courts is dysfunctional, it should be brought up to Western standards. If a criminal procedure law lacks adequate protections for detainees, it should be rewritten. The basic idea is that if the institutions can be changed to fit the models, the rule of law will emerge.

This breathtakingly mechanistic approach to rule-of-law development—a country achieves the rule of law by reshaping its key institutions to match those of countries that are considered to have the rule of law—quickly ran into deeply embedded resistance to change in many countries. The wave of judicial and police reform efforts in many Latin American countries sponsored by the United States in the second half of the 1980s, for example, initially bounced off institutions that had deep-seated reasons, whether good or bad, for being the way they were and little inclination to accept the reformist ideas brought from the outside.

The sobering experience with the early wave of efforts to promote institutional change produced two responses in the rule-of-law aid community. The first was a great deal of attention to what quickly came to be called "will to reform."[5] The new wisdom held that absent sufficient will to reform on the part of key host country officials, efforts to reform judiciaries, police, and other key institutions would be futile. It was up to rule-of-law aid providers to find and support "change agents" in the institutions, with the predominant assumption being that such agents would reside in the leadership of the institutions in question.

The sudden focus on will to reform was a way of restating the problem of how change occurs—aid providers should not presume change will naturally occur once institutions are introduced to the right way of doing things. Instead, change will occur when some of the key people inside the system want it to occur and those persons are given enabling assistance that allows them to carry out their will.

Though taken within the rule-of-law aid community as a crucial new insight, the focus on will to reform was a smaller step forward than it initially appeared. Major questions abound, still unanswered. For example, how does will to reform develop? Can it be generated and if so how? Should we assume that institutions change through gradualist reform processes willed by persons inside the system? Does public pressure play a major role? What about abrupt, drastic change provoked by persons outside the institutions who are dissatisfied with their function or who have their own goals about what institutions to have?

The other response to the initial wave of disappointments was the introduction within the rule-of-law aid community of the concepts of incentives and interests. After bouncing off a number of reform-resistant institutions, rule-of-law aid providers began saying that it was necessary to understand the underlying interests of institutional actors and to try to reshape the incentives to which these actors responded. This represented progress and allowed some analytic insights, which while rather basic were at least better than completely technocratic approaches. Aid providers began confronting the unpleasant fact, for example, that poorly performing judicial systems in many countries served the interests of powerful actors in various ways (for example, not serving as a means of justice for poor persons seeking to uphold land claims) and that the persons in those systems had no incentives to change their ways and had some significant incentives not to. But it was hard to go beyond new insights to new methods to produce change. Realizing that incentive structures are distorted is one thing; doing something about it is another. To some extent, casting the problem of change in terms of interests and incentives has ended up being more a restatement of lack of knowledge about how change occurs than an answer to it.

WHAT EFFECTS WILL CHANGE HAVE?

Although rule-of-law aid providers lack knowledge about what might produce broad-scale change in the role and function of law in a society that seems to lack the rule of law, they nevertheless do succeed in helping produce change in some specific areas. When they do, however, they often do not really know what effects those changes will have on the overall development of the rule of law in the country.

Consider several examples. A focus of many judicial reform programs has been to speed up the processing of cases by slow, inefficient courts. Such programs highlight administrative reforms, usually featuring the much-favored tool of case-tracking software. The aid providers' assumption is that efficient processing of cases is one small but vital element of the rule of law and improving that processing will improve the rule of law. Yet even in this well-defined, circumscribed area there is a surprising amount of uncertainty. For example, it is possible that if the processing of cases speeds up in a country where justice has long been quite poorly served, the number of cases filed with the courts might skyrocket, clogging the courts anew and effectively negating the reform achieved. Or, if the system has significant unfairness built into it, such as political bias or control, does increasing the speed of cases through the system actually represent a gain for the rule of law? This question arose vividly in Egypt in the second half of the 1990s where the United States devoted significant resources to helping the Egyptian judiciary improve its case management and speed up its processing of cases.

Another example concerns the spillover effects of improvement in one part of the system to other parts. A key belief animating some programs of commercial law reform in authoritarian or semi-authoritarian contexts is that if international aid efforts can help improve the quality of justice on commercial matters, this will augment justice in other domains and thus represent a kind of stealth method of promoting the rule of law in a broader political sense. The Western aid organizations supporting rule-of-law reforms in China and Vietnam regularly invoke this argument. It is of great appeal to donors who on the one hand seek to pave the way for business reforms that will facilitate commerce but on the other hand want to defend themselves against charges that they are assisting authoritarian regimes. Though attractive, the argument is not grounded in any systematic research and represents a typical example in the rule-of-law world of an appealing hypothesis that is repeated enough times until it takes on the quality of a received truth.

One more example concerns means of increasing judicial independence. Rule-of-law aid providers have given considerable attention to trying to find ways to increase judicial independence in Latin America and now are tackling the issue in other regions. Believing that one of the stumbling blocks is the hold on the process of judicial selection and promotion by politicized, corrupted ministries of justice, they have pushed for and supported efforts to establish semi-autonomous judicial councils to take over these functions. The idea has common sense appeal, but despite an accumulating record of experience there has been little effort to date to examine in any systematic fashion whether the various new judicial councils have improved the situation. The first such study indicates that the results are not impressive.[6] Anecdotal evidence from Argentina and other countries suggests that as often happens with institutional solutions to deeper problems, the underlying maladies of the original institutions end up crossing over and infecting the new institutions.

These are just several of many possible examples that indicate that even when aid programs are able to facilitate fairly specific changes in relevant institutions, it is rarely clear what the longer-term effects of those changes are on the overall development of the rule of law in the country in question.

LIMITATIONS OF LESSONS LEARNED

In analyzing the levels and extent of the problem of knowledge in the field of rule-of-law assistance, I do not mean to imply that no learning is taking place. Aid practitioners, especially those who are close to the field efforts and have extensive experience in projects in at least several countries, often accumulate considerable knowledge about how to go about promoting the rule of law. Yet the knowledge tends to stay within the minds of individual practitioners and not get systematized or incorporated by the sponsoring institutions.

Aid institutions do seek to come up with "lessons learned" and to present them in official reports as evidence that they are taking seriously the need to reflect critically on their own work. Yet most of the lessons learned presented in such reports are not especially useful. Often they are too general or obvious, or both. Among the most common lessons learned, for example, are "programs must be shaped to fit the local environment" and "law reformers should not simply import laws from other countries." The fact that staggeringly obvious lessons of this type are put forward by institutions as lessons learned is an unfortunate commentary on the weakness of many of the aid efforts.

12 PROMOTING THE RULE OF LAW ABROAD

There is also the persistent problem of lessons learned not actually being learned. Experienced practitioners have consistently pointed, for example, to the fact that judicial training, while understandably appealing to aid agencies, is usually rife with shortcomings and rarely does much good.[7] Yet addicted to the relative ease of creating such programs and their common sense appeal, aid organizations persist in making judicial training one of the most common forms of rule-of-law assistance. Similarly, it has become painfully clear on countless occasions that trying to promote the rule of law by simply rewriting another country's laws on the basis of Western models achieves very little, given problems with laws not adapted to the local environment, the lack of capacity to implement or enforce the laws, and the lack of public understanding of them. Yet externally supported law reform efforts in many countries, especially those efforts relating to the commercial domain, often continue to be simplistic exercises of law copying. The problem of reforms being blocked by underlying interests and incentives turns out not only to apply to institutions in the aid-recipient countries but to the aid agencies themselves.

OBSTACLES TO KNOWLEDGE

Confronted with the lack of systematic, well-grounded knowledge about how external aid can be used to promote the rule of law in other countries, aid officials have usually responded by arguing that the field is relatively young and still in the early stage of learning. As the years pass, however, this explanation is losing force. If one takes together the law and development movement and the current rule-of-law promotion field, over thirty years of activity are now under the bridge, surely enough time for real learning to take place. It is apparent therefore that some embedded obstacles to the accumulation of knowledge exist below the surface. At least five can be identified at a quick glance.

First, there is the unavoidable fact that the rule of law is an area of great conceptual and practical complexity. Understanding how law functions in a society, the roles it plays, and how it can change is extremely difficult, especially in societies that are not well understood by aid providers from many points of view. Foreign aid providers have found it hard enough to develop effective ways of analyzing and acting upon much more delimited challenges, such as increasing the supply of potable drinking water or vaccinations in poor societies. Grasping the problem of the shortcomings of law throughout the developing and post-communist worlds is an enormous intellectual and practical challenge.

Related to this is a second problem—the tremendous particularity of the legal systems, or perhaps better stated, the functioning of law, in the countries of Latin America, Asia, Africa, Eastern Europe, and the former Soviet Union where rule-of-law promoters are at work. A rule-of-law aid provider traveling to Guyana, Yemen, Madagascar, or some other country to set up an assistance project is faced with the daunting challenge of understanding the realities of law in that particular society. He or she is unlikely to be able to draw much up-to-date, detailed, comprehensive, and insightful information about the problem because the availability of such knowledge tends to be highly sporadic. Even to the extent that some such information exists, drawing the connection between it and the question of "what to do?" is akin to stringing a very long, thin line between two distant points.

The third obstacle is that aid organizations have proven themselves to be ill-adept at the task of generating and accumulating the sort of knowledge that would help fill the gap. They profess great interest in lessons learned but tend not to devote many resources to serious reflection and research on their own efforts.[8] They are by nature forward-looking organizations, aimed at the next project or problem. Personnel tend to change positions regularly, undermining the building up of institutional knowledge. They are criticized by others if they are seen as devoting too much time to study and not enough to action. And they work in a context of broader doubt about the value of aid, which has led to a tremendous set of conscious and unconscious defensive walls being built up around their activities, including rule-of-law work.

Fourth, if aid organizations are themselves not sponsoring the kind of applied policy research that would build knowledge in the rule-of-law promotion domain, neither are political science departments or law schools. This kind of research is eminently applied in nature and thus tends not to attract scholars, who have few professional incentives to tackle questions that arise from and relate to aid activities. Remarkably little writing has come out of the academy about the burgeoning field of rule-of-law promotion in the last twenty years. And only a small part of that existing literature is written by scholars who have had significant contact with actual aid programs.

A fifth obstacle is the fact that many lawyers—who tend to dominate the operational side of rule of law aid—are not oriented toward the empirical research necessary for organized knowledge accumulation. They often have relatively formalistic views of legal change and are slow to take up the developmental, process-oriented issues that have come to inform work in other areas of socioeconomic or sociopolitical change. Also, lawyers working on rule-of-law aid programs sometimes feel in tension with the aid organizations of which they are part. They are a minority legal subculture in organizations unfamiliar with and often not wholly comfortable with legal development work. This leads the rule-of-law aid practitioners to feel they lack the space necessary for searching studies of rule-of-law aid and to be wary of other development specialists attempting to raise hard questions about this work.

WHEN IS A FIELD A FIELD?

The rapidly growing field of rule-of-law assistance is operating from a disturbingly thin base of knowledge at every level—with respect to the core rationale of the work, the question of where the essence of the rule of law actually resides in different societies, how change in the rule of law occurs, and what the real effects are of changes that are produced. The lessons learned to date have for the most part not been impressive and often do not actually seem to be learned. The obstacles to the accumulation of knowledge are serious and range from institutional shortcomings of the main aid actors to deeper intellectual challenges about how to fathom the complexity of law itself.

Thus far the field of rule-of-law assistance has expanded less because of the tangible successes of such work than because of the irresistible apparent connection of the rule of law with the underlying goals of market economics and democracy that now constitute the dual foundation of contemporary international aid. With a recognizable set of activities that make up the rule-of-law assistance domain (primarily judicial reform, criminal law reform, commercial law reform, legal education work, and alternative dispute resolution), a growing body of professional specialists, and a consistent place on the international aid agenda, rule-of-law assistance has taken on the character of a coherent field of aid. Yet it is not yet a field if one considers a requirement for such a designation to include a

14 **PROMOTING THE RULE OF LAW ABROAD**

well-grounded rationale, a clear understanding of the essential problem, a proven analytic method, and an understanding of results achieved. Doubtless many types of work with law in developing and post-communist countries are valuable and should be part of the international community's engagement with these countries. However, whether rule-of-law promotion is in fact an established field of international aid or is even on the road to becoming one remains uncertain.

NOTES

1. See John Hewko, "Foreign Direct Investment: Does the Rule of Law Matter?" Carnegie Endowment Working Paper no. 26 (Washington, D.C.: Carnegie Endowment for International Peace, April 2002).

2. See Frank Upham, "Mythmaking in the Rule of Law Orthodoxy," Carnegie Endowment Working Paper no. 30 (Washington, D.C.: Carnegie Endowment for International Peace, September 2002).

3. Rick Messick, "Judicial Reform and Economic Development: A Survey of the Issues," *The World Bank Research Observer*, vol. 14, no. 1 (February 1999), pp. 117–36.

4. On the democracy template, see Thomas Carothers, *Aiding Democracy Abroad: The Learning Curve* (Washington, D.C.: Carnegie Endowment for International Peace, 1999), ch. 5.

5. The first major shift to a focus on will to reform came after a review in the early 1990s by the U.S. Agency for International Development (USAID) of its own rule-of-law programs. See Harry Blair and Gary Hansen, *Weighing in on the Scales of Justice: Strategic Approaches for Donor-Supported Rule of Law Programs*, USAID Program and Operations Assessment Report no. 7 (Washington, D.C.: USAID, 1994).

6. See Linn Hammergren, "Do Judicial Councils Further Judicial Reform? Lessons from Latin America," Carnegie Endowment Working Paper no. 28 (Washington, D.C.: Carnegie Endowment for International Peace, June 2002).

7. See, for example, the critical analysis of judicial training programs in Linn Hammergen, *Judicial Training and Justice Reform* (Washington, D.C.: USAID Center for Democracy and Governance, August 1998).

8. One noteworthy exception is the study of legal and judicial reform by Linn Hammergren, sponsored by USAID and released as four papers in 1998.

[8]

COLLAPSE AND RECONSTRUCTION OF A JUDICIAL SYSTEM: THE UNITED NATIONS MISSIONS IN KOSOVO AND EAST TIMOR

*By Hansjörg Strohmeyer**

Within the span of only a few months in 1999, the United Nations was faced with one of the greatest challenges in its recent history: to serve as an interim government in Kosovo and East Timor.

In Kosovo, in response to massive attacks on the Kosovar Albanian population, including orchestrated and wide-scale "ethnic cleansing," the North Atlantic Treaty Organization (NATO) conducted an eleven-week air campaign against Yugoslav and Serbian security forces and paramilitary groups.[1] The campaign resulted in the agreement of the Federal Republic of Yugoslavia to withdraw all Yugoslav and Serbian security forces from the territory. On June 10, 1999, one day after the suspension of NATO's air strikes, the United Nations Security Council adopted Resolution 1244 (1999), establishing the United Nations Interim Administration in Kosovo (UNMIK).

Only three months later, in the aftermath of the UN-organized "popular consultation" in which the overwhelming majority of East Timorese had voted for independence, the Security Council created the International Force for East Timor (INTERFET),[2] to halt the violent campaign of killing, burning, and looting that had been waged by heavily armed militia supporting the integration of East Timor into Indonesia, at times with the support of the Indonesian security forces. Following INTERFET's successful restoration of peace and security to the half-island, the Security Council adopted Resolution 1272 (1999) on October 25, 1999, establishing the United Nations Transitional Administration in East Timor (UNTAET).

The scope of the challenges and responsibilities deriving from these mandates was unprecedented in United Nations peacekeeping operations. Both resolutions vested the United Nations with a comprehensive mandate, in effect empowering it to exercise all legislative and executive authority in Kosovo and East Timor and to take responsibility for the

* Hansjörg Strohmeyer is a judge in Düsseldorf, Germany, and a policy adviser in the United Nations Office for the Coordination of Humanitarian Affairs. From October 1999 to February 2000, he was the acting principal legal adviser to the United Nations Transitional Administration in East Timor and then served as deputy principal legal adviser to the mission until June 2000. From June to August 1999, he served as the legal adviser to the special representative of the Secretary-General in Kosovo. The author wishes to thank Fatemeh Ziai for her assistance in the preparation of this article. The views expressed in the article are entirely those of the author in his personal capacity and do not necessarily reflect the views of the United Nations.

[1] The conflict between Serbian military and police forces and Kosovar Albanian forces had flared up in the course of 1998, leaving over 1,500 Kosovar Albanians dead and approximately 400,000 expelled from their homes. The deteriorating situation led the NATO Council to authorize activation orders for air strikes on October 13, 1998. On March 24, 1999, NATO actually began "Operation Allied Force," following the refusal of the Federal Republic of Yugoslavia to sign the Rambouillet accords. The two-round negotiation of the accords in February and March 1999 had been facilitated by the contact group for the Balkans (France, Germany, Russia, Italy, the United Kingdom, and the United States) and was aimed at reinstating substantive autonomy and self-government in Kosovo. The representatives of the Kosovar Albanian community signed the accords.

[2] SC Res. 1264 (Sept. 15, 1999). On August 30, 1999, some 98% of East Timorese voters had gone to the polls and decided, by a margin of 21.5% to 78.5%, to reject autonomy for East Timor, proposed by the Republic of Indonesia, and to begin, instead, a process of transition toward independence. Following Indonesia's failure to control the security situation in East Timor, as guaranteed in the political agreements leading up to the popular consultation of August 30, 1999, the Security Council established INTERFET. *See also* Agreement on the Question of East Timor, May 5, 1999, Indon.-Port., Agreement Regarding Security Arrangements, May 5, 1999, UN-Indon.-Port., UN Doc. S/1999/513, Anns. I, III, respectively.

administration of justice,[3] the third branch of government. The latter alone was an enormous task, which essentially required the complete re-creation of the judiciary. In addition, however, each mission had to rebuild the entire public sector, including the reconstruction and operation of public utilities, ports, airports, and a public transport system; establish a functioning civil service, requiring the selection and payment of civil servants; create a network of social services, including employment offices and health care; rehabilitate and maintain road systems; ensure the provision of primary, secondary, and higher education; create the necessary conditions for economic development, including the establishment of a banking system, the formulation of budgetary and currency policies, the attraction of foreign investment, and the establishment of a comprehensive tax, customs, and levies scheme; and develop public-broadcasting and mass-media capabilities.

Above all, the United Nations needed to create a legal framework within which these activities could be carried out. The legislative powers granted by the Security Council could not be exercised until each mission took steps to draft, promulgate, and enforce a range of United Nations regulations,[4] which would have the force of law in the administered territories. This daunting task was further complicated by the fact that, in both Kosovo and East Timor, the armed interventions had led to the withdrawal, in their entirety, of the political and administrative cadres that had previously governed the territories, including the security and law enforcement apparatus.

The initial operational strategy of both missions instinctively gave priority to traditional peace-building efforts, including ensuring peace and security in the territory to be administered and facilitating the return of hundreds of thousands of refugees. The experiences of both Kosovo and East Timor have proven, however, that from the outset the administration of justice must be counted among the top priorities of such an operation. Indeed, while emergency humanitarian assistance, physical rebuilding, and political negotiations are being carried out in postconflict situations, criminal activity does not cease; in fact, it often flourishes. Moreover, evidence of violations of international humanitarian and human rights law can be destroyed, while the perpetrators of serious crimes remain at large. The failure to address past and ongoing violations promptly and effectively, and to create a sense of law and order, can impede the broader objectives of the operation. At the same time, the United Nations civil police forces, which were entrusted in both undertakings with law enforcement, cannot do so in a meaningful way in the absence of a functioning judiciary.

Thus, it is essential that such missions, commonly referred to as "nation-building" operations, function within a framework of law and order, and that they be enabled, from the

---

[3] *See* SC Res. 1244, para. 11(a), (b), (i) (June 10, 1999), 38 ILM 1451 (1999) ("[p]romoting the establishment . . . of substantial autonomy and self-government in Kosovo"; "[p]erforming basic civilian administrative functions where and as long as required"; and "[m]aintaining civil law and order"); SC Res. 1272, para. 1 (Oct. 25, 1999), 39 ILM 240 (2000) ("establish . . . a United Nations Transitional Administration in East Timor (UNTAET), which will be endowed with overall responsibility for the administration of East Timor and will be empowered to exercise all legislative and executive authority, including the administration of justice"); *see also* UNMIK Regulation 1999/1, §1.1 (July 25, 1999) ("All legislative and executive authority with respect to Kosovo, including the administration of the judiciary, is vested in UNMIK and is exercised by the Special Representative of the Secretary-General"); UNTAET Regulation 1999/1, §1.1 (Nov. 27, 1999) ("All legislative and executive authority with respect to East Timor, including the administration of the judiciary, is vested in UNTAET and is exercised by the Transitional Administrator"). All the regulations promulgated by UNMIK and UNTAET are available online at <http://www.un.org/peace/kosovo/pages/regulations> and <http://www.un.org/peace/etimor/untaetR/UntaetR.htm>.

[4] The United Nations, which traditionally promotes international law, was actually mandated, both in Kosovo and in East Timor, to legislate and create new law in areas that normally fall within the competence of a national legislature. By promulgating UN regulations that have the status of laws and supersede any other law on the regulated matter at issue, the head of the UN mission, in effect, becomes the exclusive legislator of the administered territory. *See* SC Res. 1272, *supra* note 3, para. 6 (stating that "the Transitional Administrator . . . will . . . have the power to enact new laws and regulations and to amend, suspend or repeal existing ones"). As the experience in Cambodia has shown, many of these regulations remain in force even after the completion of the UN transitional administration, or serve as a blueprint for subsequent national legislation.

earliest stages, to carry out minimal judicial and prosecutorial functions, including arrests, detention, investigations, and fair trials. Moreover, the effective reconstruction of the justice sector requires a coherent approach that places equal emphasis on all its elements: police, prosecution, judiciary, and the correctional system.

Nevertheless, taking on the administration of justice in Kosovo and East Timor was no simple task, even if based on a comprehensive mandate. How can a justice system be administered when there is no system left to be administered; when the personnel needed to carry out judicial tasks have departed or are tainted by their perceived affiliation with the previous regime; when the courthouses and related facilities have been destroyed, looted, or even mined; and when the laws to be applied are politically charged and no longer acceptable to the population and the new political classes?

I. THE SITUATION UPON ARRIVAL

To understand fully the daunting tasks awaiting the United Nations upon its arrival in Priština and Dili, respectively, one has to look more closely at the circumstances that prevailed in the early days of each mission.

Kosovo

The situation encountered by the first UNMIK officials to arrive in Kosovo on June 13, 1999, was devastating: as a result of the systematic cleansing of the Kosovar Albanian population by the Yugoslav and Serbian security forces, the majority of Kosovo's population had been expelled and was living in refugee camps abroad.[5] Soon after the arrival of the United Nations, however, the refugees started to return from Macedonia and Albania at a historically unprecedented scale and speed. Those returning to the abandoned, and in many cases burned and looted, towns and villages of Kosovo[6] were often highly traumatized—not only by the months of violence preceding the deployment of the UN mission, but also by the decades of oppression and discrimination they had suffered under Serbian rule. By June 25, 1999, the number of spontaneous returns had reached 300,000, with some 50,000 refugees crossing into Kosovo every day, by car, by tractor, and on foot. Only two weeks later, by July 8, more than 650,000 refugees had returned to the territory, creating a tense humanitarian and security situation. In need of immediate housing and material support, an increasing number of returnees resorted to violence and intimidation as a means of retrieving some semblance of their previous lives. Looting, arson, forced expropriation of apartments belonging to Serbs and other non-Albanian minorities, and, in some cases, killing and abduction of non-Albanians became daily phenomena.[7] Moreover, organized crime, including smuggling, drug trafficking, and trafficking in women, soon flourished. It was apparent, within the first few days, that the previous law enforcement and judicial system in Kosovo had collapsed.[8] Criminal gangs competing for control of the scarce re-

[5] At the end of the Kosovo conflict, out of a population estimated at 1.7 million, almost half (800,000) had sought refuge abroad, mainly in neighboring Albania, the former Yugoslav Republic of Macedonia, and Montenegro. In addition, an estimated 500,000 people were internally displaced within Kosovo. *See* Report of the Secretary-General on the United Nations Interim Administration Mission in Kosovo, UN Doc. S/1999/779, para. 8 (July 12, 1999), <http://www.un.org/Docs/sc/reports/1999/s1999779.htm> [hereinafter Secretary-General's Kosovo Report].

[6] According to a preliminary survey of 141 villages by the United Nations High Commissioner for Refugees, 64% of homes were severely damaged or destroyed, and household waste and human remains had contaminated 40% of the water resources. *See Chronology UN Interim Administration in Kosovo (UNMIK), 8 July* [1999] <http://www.un.org/peace/kosovo/news/kos30day.htm>.

[7] *See* HUMAN RIGHTS WATCH, FEDERAL REPUBLIC OF YUGOSLAVIA: ABUSES AGAINST SERBS AND ROMA IN THE NEW KOSOVO (HRW Report, No. 10(D), 1999).

[8] *See* Matthew Kaminski, *UN Struggles with a Legal Vacuum in Kosovo; Team Improvises in Effort to Build a Civil Structure*, WALL ST. J., Aug. 4, 1999, at A14.

sources immediately started to exploit the emerging void.[9] In addition, the Kosovo Liberation Army (KLA)[10] returned and rapidly penetrated the entire territory of Kosovo, often installing its own administrative structures—parallel to those of the United Nations—and urging Serbs to leave.[11]

Besides establishing a civilian administration, Security Council Resolution 1244 had created the Kosovo Force (KFOR), an international force composed of NATO troops that was charged with ensuring "public safety and order until the international civil presence can take responsibility for this task."[12] In response to the rising security concerns and pursuant to its mandate, KFOR started to carry out large-scale arrests to restore public peace and order to the territory. In just two weeks, this policy led to a backlog of more than two hundred detainees, many of them held for such serious criminal offenses as arson, violent assaults, and murder, but also for grave violations of international humanitarian and human rights law.[13] In view of the gravity of these offenses, and the possible effect of their prosecution and trial on the peace and reconciliation process in Kosovo, UN personnel considered it particularly important to observe fair-trial standards to the maximum extent possible. Using the code of criminal procedure of the Federal Republic of Yugoslavia as its basis, but applying those laws within the framework of recognized international human rights standards,[14] UNMIK strove to accord initial judicial hearings to detainees within seventy-two hours of their arrest, and to determine whether or not to detain them and commence investigations. In addition, UNMIK had to ensure that detainees were provided with sufficiently qualified defense counsel. The fact that most of the detainees would accept defense counsel only from their own ethnic group did not make the task any easier.

This emergency situation made it imperative for UNMIK to turn its immediate attention to the reestablishment of the core functions of the Kosovo judiciary.[15] KFOR itself was neither ordered nor prepared to exercise these functions, which, according to Resolution 1244, was a civilian task falling under the mandate of UNMIK.

Nevertheless, the conditions for accomplishing this task were not favorable. As a result of the policy of gross, government-sanctioned discrimination, applied with particular vigor since 1989,[16] virtually no Kosovar Albanians remained in the civil service. Most severely

---

[9] *See* Secretary-General's Kosovo Report, *supra* note 5, para. 6.

[10] The KLA (also known under its Albanian acronym UCK for Ushtria Clirimtare e Kosoves) was the main military organization fighting for the liberation of Kosovo from Serbian rule. Its origins go back as far as 1996. Only in November 1997, however, did UCK members identify themselves for the first time to the public.

[11] By early July, approximately 58,000 members of ethnic minorities in Kosovo, mainly Serbs, had left the territory and registered for assistance with the Yugoslav Red Cross. See further LAWYERS COMMITTEE FOR HUMAN RIGHTS, KOSOVO: PROTECTION AND PEACE-BUILDING: PROTECTION OF REFUGEES, RETURNEES, INTERNALLY DISPLACED PERSONS, AND MINORITIES 2 (1999).

[12] SC Res. 1244, *supra* note 3, para. 9(d). "Operation Joint Guardian" commenced on June 12, 1999.

[13] *See Controversy Erupts as Kosovo Judges Sworn in*, SHAPE News Morning Update, July 1, 1999 <http://www.fas.org/man/dod-101/ops/docs99/mu010799.htm>.

[14] *See* European Convention for the Protection of Human Rights and Fundamental Freedoms, Nov. 4, 1950, Art. 5(3), 213 UNTS 221: ("Everyone . . . shall be brought promptly before a judge or officer authorized by law to exercise judicial power . . ."). The term "promptly" represents a stringent standard. In Brogan v. United Kingdom, 145 Eur. Ct. H.R. (ser. A) at 28–30, paras. 49–53 (1988), *obtainable from* <http://www.echr.coe.int/eng/Judgments.htm>, the European Court of Human Rights held that four days and six hours was too long a period to meet this standard. *See also* International Covenant on Civil and Political Rights, Dec. 16, 1966, Art. 9(3), 999 UNTS 171.

[15] UN Secretary-General Kofi Annan was quoted as saying: "The security problem in Kosovo is largely a result of the absence of law-and-order institutions . . . ." *See* John J. Goldman, *Kosovo Tense But Getting More Stable, UN Reports*, L.A. TIMES, July 14, 1999, at A12.

[16] In February 1989, ethnic Albanians held widespread strikes in Kosovo, a province of the Republic of Serbia, to protest proposed constitutional amendments to the Serbian constitution aimed at limiting the province's autonomy status. The federal authorities of Yugoslavia imposed "special measures"—a de facto state of emergency—and sent troops into the province. On March 23, 1989, the constitutional changes were approved, effectively giving Serbia control over Kosovo's police and judiciary. In July 1990, following a resolution approved by 114 Kosovar Albanian delegates to Kosovo's assembly declaring the territory "an equal and independent entity within the

affected was the judicial sector: politically and ethnically motivated appointments, removals, and training had led to a judiciary in which only 30 out of 756 judges and prosecutors were Kosovar Albanian.[17] The exodus of the non-Albanian population of Kosovo, among them many of the Serb and Montenegrin lawyers who had administered Kosovo's justice system for the last decade, had accelerated the total collapse of the judicial system. The few judicial officials who decided to stay behind were considered to be representatives of the previous regime and soon faced death threats.

East Timor

As difficult as the situation was in Kosovo, the United Nations faced even greater challenges in East Timor.[18] UNTAET staff members will never be able to forget the panorama of devastation that awaited them upon their arrival in East Timor: most public and many private buildings ruined and smoldering in the midst of what had once been towns and villages, now all but abandoned by their former inhabitants, cut off from transport and communication, and lacking a governmental superstructure. Immediately after the popular consultation of August 30, 1999, heavily armed groups and forces sympathetic to the integration of East Timor into Indonesia had conducted a "scorched earth" campaign in which they had burned and looted entire towns and villages, attacked and killed at random in the streets, and forcibly "evacuated" or kidnapped people to the western half of the island, which was still part of Indonesia. In response, thousands of East Timorese had abandoned their homes, fleeing into the mountains of central East Timor or across the border into West Timor.[19] Many East Timorese towns and villages had turned into ghost cities in which virtually all houses, apartment buildings, and shops were demolished.

The preexisting judicial infrastructure in East Timor was virtually destroyed. Most court buildings had been torched and looted,[20] and all court equipment, furniture, registers, records, archives, and—indispensable to legal practice—law books, case files, and other legal resources dislocated or burned. In addition, all judges, prosecutors, lawyers, and many judicial support staff who were perceived as being members de facto of the administrative and intellectual privileged classes, or who had been publicly sympathetic to the Indonesian regime, had fled East Timor after the results of the popular consultation were announced. Fewer than ten lawyers were estimated to have remained, and these were believed to be so inexperienced as to be unequal to the task of serving in a new East Timorese justice system.

In this situation, it quickly became apparent to UNTAET officials that a justice system in East Timor, including the necessary regulatory framework, first had to be *built*—and built within the shortest possible time—before it could be *administered*, as called for in Security Council Resolution 1272.[21]

framework of the Yugoslav federation," Serbian authorities abolished both the assembly and the government of Kosovo, closed down the only Albanian daily, and took over the state-owned television and radio stations. *See* NOEL MALCOLM, KOSOVO, A SHORT HISTORY 346 (Harper Perennial 1999) (1998).

[17] *See* Secretary-General's Kosovo Report, *supra* note 5, para. 66.

[18] *See* James Traub, *Inventing East Timor*, FOREIGN AFF., July/Aug. 2000, at 74, 82–83.

[19] To date, the exact number of refugees and internally displaced persons in East Timor in October 1999 has not been definitely established. It has been estimated, however, that more than one-third of East Timor's pre–September 1999 population of some 800,000 was at least temporarily dislocated. According to UNTAET sources, a total of 162,444 refugees had returned to East Timor from abroad by May 31, 2000. In addition, tens of thousands of people who had temporarily left their homes and escaped to safer locations in the mountainous regions of East Timor had returned to their places of origin.

[20] According to the World Bank–sponsored Joint Assessment Mission to East Timor, over 70% of all administrative (i.e., government) buildings were partially or completely destroyed, and almost all office equipment and consumable materials totally destroyed. WORLD BANK, JOINT ASSESSMENT MISSION REPORT 4, para. 15 (Dec. 17, 1999), *obtainable from* <http://www.wbln0018.worldbank.org/eap/eap.nsf>; *see also* Report of the Secretary-General on the Situation in East Timor, UN Doc. S/1999/1024, paras. 11–13 (Oct. 4, 1999).

[21] *See* Hansjörg Strohmeyer, *Building a New Judiciary for East Timor: Challenges of a Fledgling Nation*, 11 CRIM. L.F. 259 (2000).

Most pressing was the need for a mechanism to review the arrests and detentions that had been carried out by the Australian-led INTERFET.[22] At the same time, the United Nations civil police force was faced with a growing number of ordinary crimes, including such serious offenses as violent assault, rape, and murder. INTERFET had established a temporary arrest and detention system that was run by military personnel but was neither mandated nor equipped to try, convict, or sentence criminal offenders.[23] Because of the scheduled gradual withdrawal of INTERFET from East Timor, beginning in December 1999, and the scarcity of immediately deployable international lawyers, UNTAET needed to install a civilian mechanism that, if nothing else, would provide the minimum judicial functions required upon arrest and detention.

The enormous task of rebuilding a judicial system had to be carried out in the initial stages of both missions, when the operation had a very small staff, logistics and a communications infrastructure were just being set up, mass media to support activities such as the search for qualified lawyers were not yet available, and construction materials for the building or refurbishment of destroyed judicial facilities and prisons were an extremely scarce commodity.[24] In addition, the lack of sufficient numbers of domestic translators—a problem common to most United Nations missions—affected cooperation with the local population in virtually all sectors of civil administration, but most tangibly in law enforcement.[25]

II. IMMEDIATE MEASURES

It was against this backdrop that the United Nations missions in Kosovo and East Timor began their respective efforts to plan, design, and put in place initial arrangements aimed at addressing urgent needs and serving as the nucleus for a future judiciary in each territory. The enormity of the task, and the extent to which it would mirror the obstacles being experienced in the political, economic, and humanitarian sectors of each mission, soon became evident.

Appointment of Judges and Prosecutors

In any legal system, the appointment of judges and prosecutors is a complex and multilayered effort. Despite the United Nations' comprehensive mandate and the urgent need to fill judicial positions as swiftly as possible, political considerations prevented the heads of the two missions from simply appointing candidates of their choosing. In view of the political and symbolic significance of such appointments in a postcrisis situation and the United Nations' desire to act in sharp contrast to the flagrant politicization of judicial appointments that had characterized the previous regimes, it was essential to proceed in a transparent and professional manner that would give legitimacy to the undertaking. First, capable candidates

---

[22] *See* SC Res. 1264, *supra* note 2. The INTERFET-run Forced Detention Center delivered over 25 detainees into the custody of the UNTAET civilian police and the East Timorese judiciary on January 14, 2000. Many of these detainees had been arrested by or handed over to INTERFET on charges of serious violations of international humanitarian and human rights law committed during the postballot violence.

[23] Based on its mandate to restore peace and security in East Timor, the Australian INTERFET contingent had created a temporary detention system. Individuals apprehended by INTERFET were held in the Forced Detention Center and granted an initial hearing by an INTERFET legal adviser within 24 hours. If not released, they were transferred, within 96 hours, to the Detention Management Unit for review of the detention order. The Detention Management Unit consisted of four additional INTERFET legal advisers (one reviewing officer, one prosecutorial officer, one defending officer, and one visiting officer) who reported to the commander of INTERFET on a daily basis. In addition, the International Committee of the Red Cross, the UN High Commissioner for Refugees, and family members were granted regular visits to ensure adherence to generally accepted prison standards.

[24] In Kosovo, since the Serb withdrawal was still ongoing and the public buildings subsequently required extensive de-mining and cleanup efforts, the de facto headquarters of UNMIK in the first two weeks was located in the residential building that had served as the living quarters of the initial UN staff since their arrival on June 13, 1999.

[25] See further *infra* note 41.

had to be identified; next, selections had to be made in accordance with objective and verifiable criteria and merit, but also in mind of the need for political or ethnic balance; and finally, the entire process had to be transparent and based on a sound legislative framework.

In both Kosovo and East Timor, the establishment of independent judicial commissions became the primary mechanism for the selection of judges and prosecutors and served as an important safeguard for the establishment of an independent and impartial judiciary.[26] The commissions were designed as autonomous bodies; they were to receive applications from persons with a law degree, at a minimum. The commission would then select candidates for judicial or prosecutorial office on the basis of merit and, eventually, make recommendations on appointments to the head of the UN mission. The East Timorese commission was also entrusted with drawing up codes of ethics for judges and prosecutors and acting as a disciplinary body to review complaints of misconduct.

Both commissions were to include local and international legal experts. In Kosovo, the Joint Advisory Council on Judicial Appointments,[27] later succeeded by the Advisory Judicial Commission,[28] was set up only two weeks after the arrival of the first UNMIK staff members. It initially comprised seven lawyers, including two Kosovar Albanians, one Bosniak (Muslim Slav), and one Serb, all of whom had extensive previous experience in the administration of justice in Kosovo, and three international lawyers from different international organizations. In East Timor, the Transitional Judicial Service Commission was a five-member body that included three East Timorese and two international experts, and was chaired by an East Timorese of "high moral standing."[29] The United Nations deemed it essential to recruit the majority of the commission members among local experts and to empower them to overrule the international members so as to build a strong sense of ownership over the new judiciaries and to inject as much domestic expertise as possible into the process. Over time, the international membership of the commissions was expected to be phased out, but a suitable mechanism would meanwhile have taken root through which future local governments could make nonpartisan judicial appointments.

Whereas the East Timorese leadership endorsed the composition of the Transitional Judicial Service Commission,[30] the appointment of the commission members in Kosovo prompted a more controversial reaction among UNMIK's local interlocutors, in particular representatives of the KLA. One of the Kosovar Albanian experts, who had been the last president of Kosovo's abolished Supreme Court, was considered to stand for the old Yugoslav order and was criticized for his involvement in the trials of Kosovo Albanian leaders in the aftermath of the 1989 strikes.[31] The Serb member was evicted from his apartment after only a few days in office. He then joined the general Serb exodus to Serbia proper and was threatened with death if he returned. For his part, the Bosniak member was immediately accused of having collaborated with the previous Serb-dominated regime in Kosovo. These reactions were perhaps to be expected, given the political turmoil taking place in

---

[26] *See* AMNESTY INTERNATIONAL, AMNESTY INTERNATIONAL'S 16 RECOMMENDATIONS TO THE PARTIES AT RAMBOUILLET, para. III (AI Index No. EUR 70/08/99, 1999).

[27] *See* UNMIK Emergency Decree 1999/1 (June 28, 1999).

[28] *See* UNMIK Regulation 1999/7 (Sept. 7, 1999). According to section 2.1 of this regulation, the composition of the commission was changed to eight local and three international lawyers, of different ethnicity and reflecting varied legal expertise.

[29] *See* UNTAET Regulation 1999/3, §2 (Dec. 3, 1999). The current chairman of the commission is Bishop Dom Basilio de Nascimento from the diocese of Baucau.

[30] The membership of the Transitional Judicial Service Commission was determined by the UN transitional administrator, in concert with the National Consultative Council (NCC). The NCC was the supreme body established by UNTAET to provide a consultative mechanism to ensure the participation of the East Timorese people in the decision-making process during the transitional administration in East Timor. The council consisted of 15 members, 11 of them East Timorese, appointed by the transitional administrator. In October 2000, the NCC was expanded into a 33-member body, in effect serving as the nucleus of an East Timorese parliament. *See* UNTAET Regulation 1999/2 on the Establishment of a National Consultative Council (Dec. 2, 1999).

[31] On the strikes, see *supra* note 16.

Kosovo and the clear divisions being created along ethnic lines. At the same time, as described in greater detail below, the efforts to achieve ethnic balance in accordance with the mission's stated policy,[32] coupled with the dearth of lawyers from which to draw in the setup phase of the mission, made it difficult to avoid such an outcome.

While obstacles such as these posed serious challenges to the missions' efforts to build new judicial systems in both territories, perhaps the greatest difficulty lay in identifying candidates who had the necessary professional experience and were also politically acceptable to the general public.

In Kosovo, from the outset the declared goal of the United Nations administration was to establish a judiciary that reflected the various ethnic communities.[33] Clearly, no reconciliation efforts, including the prosecution and trial of individuals suspected of grave violations of international humanitarian and human rights law, could succeed without an ethnically and politically independent and impartial judicial system that enjoyed the confidence of the population. As a practical matter, however, many Kosovar Albanian lawyers had belonged to the persecuted intellectual classes and had thus either gone underground or taken refuge abroad in the weeks and months preceding the deployment of UNMIK. Most of those who remained were considered to be collaborators with the previous regime. Even an immediate cross-organizational effort in neighboring Macedonia and Albania to screen refugee camps for lawyers did not yield the hoped-for results. Over the next few months, the time-consuming search for qualified legal personnel was taken up by the regional offices in Kosovo of the United Nations and the Organization for Security and Co-operation in Europe (OSCE),[34] which operated by word of mouth, district by district, networking through the few remaining lawyers and seeking nominations from the KLA and the Democratic League of Kosovo, Kosovo's main political forces at the time. Only gradually were a number of sufficiently qualified lawyers identified.

On June 30, 1999, two weeks after the arrival of the first UNMIK staff in Priština, the search had already yielded its initial results: the head of the United Nations mission was able to appoint nine judges and prosecutors, among them three Serb jurists, on the basis of recommendations of the Joint Advisory Council. They served as mobile units with jurisdiction throughout the territory of Kosovo. By mid-July, these judges and prosecutors had conducted hearings on 249 detainees in all of Kosovo's five districts, releasing 112. The initial appointments were controversial because of a perceived overrepresentation of Serb lawyers.[35] Nevertheless, by July 24, 1999, as the mission had gradually identified more lawyers, the number of UNMIK-appointed judges and prosecutors had risen to twenty-eight,[36] comprising twenty-one Kosovar Albanians, four Serbs, one Roma, one member of the Turkish community in Kosovo, and one Bosniak.

Although less complex politically, the task of identifying candidates for judicial or prosecutorial office in East Timor was equally herculean. The exodus of all Indonesian and pro-Indonesian lawyers, judges, and prosecutors, as well as many law clerks and secretaries, had left East Timor with a huge void in experienced legal personnel.[37] Under Indonesian rule, no East Timorese lawyers had been appointed to judicial or prosecutorial office. As a result,

---

[32] *See* SC Res. 1244, *supra* note 3, para. 10 ("to ensure conditions for a peaceful and normal life for all inhabitants of Kosovo"); *see also* Secretary-General's Kosovo Report, *supra* note 5, paras. 40, 66.

[33] *See* Secretary-General's Kosovo Report, *supra* note 5, para. 66 ("There is an urgent need to build genuine rule of law in Kosovo, including through the immediate re-establishment of an independent, impartial and multi-ethnic judiciary.").

[34] The OSCE mission in Kosovo forms one of the four integral components of UNMIK and is responsible for matters relating to institution- and democracy-building, and human rights in Kosovo.

[35] The nine judges and prosecutors included five Kosovar Albanians, three Serbs, and one ethnic Turk. *See Controversy Erupts as Kosovo Judges Sworn in, supra* note 13.

[36] *See* UNMIK Press Release, July 24, 1999, UN Doc. UNMIK/PR/18; *see also* LAWYERS COMMITTEE FOR HUMAN RIGHTS, *supra* note 11, at 5.

[37] The Australian Section of the International Commission of Jurists (ICJ) supported this assessment. *See* ICJ, REPORT ON VISIT TO EAST TIMOR FOR EAST TIMOR PROJECT COMMITTEE MARCH 2000 (2000).

there were no jurists left in East Timor with any relevant experience in the administration of justice or the practical application of law. Thus, immediately upon its arrival in Dili, UNTAET began the process, through word of mouth and with the support of its local staff and civil-society groups, of identifying lawyers, law graduates, and law students. In the absence of a functioning broadcasting network, INTERFET volunteered to drop leaflets from airplanes throughout the territory, calling for legally qualified East Timorese to contact any UNTAET or INTERFET office or outpost. Only a week later, an initial group of seventeen jurists had been identified. In their first meetings, the lawyers sat on the ground outside the former governor's headquarters, since the departing Indonesian security forces and pro-integration militias had left behind no chairs or other furniture in the looted and burned court buildings.

Within two months, over sixty East Timorese jurists had formally applied for judicial or prosecutorial office. All the applicants had completed law school—mostly in Indonesian universities—and were enthusiastic about the opportunity to play a historic role in the first criminal and civil trials of a free East Timor. They also took pride in being part of a judicial system that would strive to respect the rule of law and encourage, rather than inhibit, the professional participation of East Timorese. After a rigorous interview and selection process, conducted by the previously established Transitional Judicial Service Commission,[38] the transitional administrator appointed the first-ever East Timorese judges and prosecutors on January 7, 2000.[39] Further appointments have since followed. However, only a few of these jurists had any practical legal experience, some in law firms and legal aid organizations in Java and other parts of the Indonesian archipelago, and others as paralegals with Timorese human rights organizations and resistance groups; none had ever served as a judge or prosecutor.

In both missions, the rationale for the rapid appointment of local judges and prosecutors was based on numerous similar considerations. The most critical reason, as noted above with regard to East Timor, was the territories' lack, soon after the establishment of the missions, of a review mechanism for those who had been arrested and detained by KFOR and INTERFET. Neither the United Nations nor the international community at large was able, on such short notice, to deploy an adequate number of international lawyers with enough knowledge of the legal traditions of the administered territories.[40] In addition, the political sensitivity to the euphoria and excitement that had followed international intervention in both Kosovo and East Timor required accommodating the general expectation that the international community would demonstrate an immediate commitment to domestic involvement in democratic institution building, especially in the legal sector. Hopes for self-determination and self-government meant that the appointment of local judges—an unprecedented move, for example in East Timor, that was unknown even under Portuguese colonial rule—took on enormous symbolic significance. Moreover, both missions considered that the immediate involvement of local lawyers would avoid, or at least minimize, any disruptive effect on the judiciary once the limited international funds earmarked for financing international lawyers inevitably dwindled and forced their withdrawal. Finally, the experience of other United Nations missions has shown that the appointment of international lawyers leads to a myriad of practical concerns that would have overburdened the

---

[38] *See* UNTAET Regulation 1999/3 on the Establishment of a Transitional Judicial Service Commission (Dec. 3, 1999).

[39] The appointments on January 7, 2000, included eight judges and two prosecutors. Their swearing-in ceremony, held in the still-devastated shell of the courthouse in Dili, was an emotional experience for both the East Timorese and the internationals involved. Before some 100 members of the general East Timorese public and numerous representatives of the international community, UNTAET Transitional Administrator Sergio Vieira de Mello took the oath from each appointee and handed each one a black robe.

[40] Since the legal systems in both Kosovo and East Timor were based on civil law, potential international judges and prosecutors were required to have sufficient practical experience in the administration of justice in a civil-law system to be immediately operational. Moreover, those lawyers had to be proficient in English—the working language of the missions—and able to make a longer-term commitment.

missions in their setup phases, such as the costly requirements of translating laws, files, transcripts, and even the daily conversations between local and international lawyers,[11] as well as the enormous time and expense of familiarizing international lawyers with the local and regional legal systems.

Legal Assistance

The scarcity of experienced legal personnel affected the legal-assistance sector as well. Neither Kosovo nor East Timor boasted a developed legal aid system before the United Nations arrived in its territory. Faced with the high number of arrests carried out in the first weeks of the missions, the United Nations was impelled to live up to the due-process and fair-trial standards it itself had promoted for more than fifty years, and to ensure the provision of adequate legal counsel to the detainees. This was particularly important since many of those arrested belonged to certain ethnic or political groups or, in some cases, were suspected of grave violations of international humanitarian and human rights law, which made their cases politically sensitive.

In Kosovo, UNMIK identified lawyers of different ethnic backgrounds who were qualified and willing to serve as defense counsel in such cases, and it provided each detainee with a list of their names. The enormous number of detainees, however, by far exceeded the number of available lawyers. In East Timor, section 27 of UNTAET Regulation 2000/11 of March 6, 2000, expressly recognized the basic right to legal representation and the obligation to ensure effective and equal access to lawyers. Consequently, UNTAET set up the nucleus of an UNTAET-financed public-defender system; but owing to the scarcity of experienced lawyers, UNTAET identified only a relatively small pool of defenders.

Legal Training

The dearth of experienced lawyers placed a particular burden on the United Nations to ensure that adequate legal and judicial training programs were immediately put in place, so that the few available jurists, including the newly appointed judges and prosecutors, would be prepared, as soon as possible, to discharge their much-needed functions.

In East Timor, unlike other contexts in which the international community has supported judicial training programs, it soon became clear that professional legal training would need to extend beyond technical assistance: legal training was a pivotal element in building and empowering local judicial ranks and in creating a stable legal system. Such training had to focus not only on conveying legal and practical skills but, equally important, on fostering appreciation of the crucial role of the judiciary in society and the benefits of a culture of law. In a society that had never before experienced respect for the rule of law, and in which the law was widely perceived as yet another instrument for wielding authority and control over the individual, the meaning of independence and impartiality of the judiciary had to be imparted gradually.

To lay the foundation for comprehensive practical and theoretical training upon which the new East Timorese judiciary could be built, UNTAET developed a three-tiered approach consisting of (1) a series of one-week, compulsory "quick impact" training courses for judges, prosecutors, and public defenders prior to their appointment to office; (2) mandatory ongoing training for judges, prosecutors, and public defenders upon their appointment

---

[11] Extensive involvement of international lawyers would inevitably have led to the need for translation of every court session and every court-produced and legal document, the interpretation of every communication with other lawyers, and, more important, the creation of an extensive translation apparatus for plaintiffs and defendants. Also, in East Timor in particular, it has proven to be virtually impossible to deploy a sufficient number of international jurists with a civil-law background who are able to make a minimum commitment of six months to one year in East Timor and, ideally, have some knowledge of the applicable law and traditions of East Timor.

to office; and (3) a "mentoring scheme," in which a pool of experienced international legal practitioners who were familiar with civil-law systems would serve as "shadow" judges, prosecutors, and public defenders without actually exercising judicial power. This was essentially an interim approach; the mission recognized that it would ultimately be necessary to establish a judicial training center that functioned independently of the government and that afforded an important role in defining the curriculum to the East Timorese themselves.[42] However, its extremely stretched resources, and difficulties in recruiting a sufficient number of experienced trainers and mentors with a background in civil law, prevented the United Nations, at least at the outset, from fulfilling its objective of providing the newly appointed judges, prosecutors, and public defenders with sufficient legal training and assistance.

The need for judicial training also surfaced similar attention in Kosovo, although it was less dramatic because of the availability of a larger number of lawyers with practical experience in the administration of justice. The Secretary-General of the United Nations reported on July 12, 1999, that "it will be important to provide immediate 'quick start' training programmes in domestic and international law for those Kosovo Albanian lawyers who were trained during the time of the 'parallel institutions' or were banned from practising their profession."[43]

Nevertheless, the issue of training had to be tackled carefully. Bearing in mind the long legal tradition of the former Yugoslavia, many of the lawyers educated in Yugoslav universities considered the emphasis on professional training to be somewhat patronizing. For their part, Kosovar Albanian lawyers, particularly those schooled during the decade of "parallel institutions,"[44] reacted extremely cautiously to the notion of training for fear that the inadequacy of their experience and skills might disqualify them for judicial office or, yet again, provide an advantage to those who had "collaborated" with the previous regime. More readily accepted was the notion of training in international legal instruments, including the European Convention on the Protection of Human Rights and Fundamental Freedoms and the 1966 International Covenant on Civil and Political Rights, so as to ensure that, in conformity with UNMIK Regulation 1999/1, judicial officials observed internationally recognized human rights standards.[45]

UNMIK's plans to start legal training courses and create a judicial training center were severely hampered by a vigorous debate on the applicable law in Kosovo. Although Regulation 1999/1 provided that the laws previously in effect in Kosovo—that is, the currently appli-

---

[42] Supported by the New Zealand Institute of Judicial Studies, UNTAET has been developing plans to establish a Judicial Studies Board (JSB) since January 2000, in order to institutionalize judicial training and education. The JSB was intended to comprise seven members, four of whom would be East Timorese jurists, who would identify and set priorities regarding training needs, coordinate donor assistance on legal training, and promote judicial excellence, including awareness of the social context of law.

[43] Secretary-General's Kosovo Report, *supra* note 5, para. 69 (also stating that "[g]enerally, newly appointed judges should receive continuous training, particularly in the area of the law and application of international instruments on human rights").

[44] Following the abolition of Kosovo's autonomy status in 1989 and the subsequent closing of ethnic Albanian institutions in the territory, the Kosovar Albanian population established a system of so-called parallel institutions, essentially the creatures of a separate republic, among others in the educational sector, that were intended to continue Kosovo's self-government and to maintain a distinct Albanian culture and identity outside the official Serb- or Yugoslav-dominated institutions. With the closing of the Albanian wing of the law faculty of the University of Priština in 1991, the Kosovar Albanian teaching staff and students were forced to find shelter in private homes and buildings so as to continue a distinct legal education for those students. Despite the lack of governmental funding and severe practical difficulties—for example, all literature was kept in the libraries of the Serb faculty building, which was barred to Kosovar Albanians—the Faculty of Law, like all other faculties of the University of Priština, maintained its struggle to provide adequate education throughout the period of Serb administration of Kosovo. See further MALCOLM, *supra* note 16, at 348–49.

[45] UNMIK Regulation 1999/1, *supra* note 3, §2, which states:

In exercising their functions, all persons undertaking public duties or holding public office in Kosovo shall observe internationally recognized human rights standards and shall not discriminate against any person on any ground such as sex, race, color, language[,] religion, political or other opinion, national, ethnic or social origin, association with a national community, property, birth or other status.

cable laws of Serbia and the Federal Republic of Yugoslavia—were to be applied, political representatives of the Kosovar Albanians demanded a return to the legal system that had existed before the abolition of Kosovo's autonomy status in 1989.[46] This debate significantly delayed the mission's ability to carry out the urgently needed quick-impact training.

Reconstruction of the Physical Infrastructure

Both Kosovo and East Timor had just emerged from violent and highly destructive conflicts, which had heavily damaged their physical infrastructure. As a result, one of the most crucial steps in rebuilding their judicial systems was the physical reconstruction of the judicial infrastructure, including court buildings and offices.

In Kosovo, virtually all public buildings, including the courts, had to be cleared of mines and booby traps before they could be reclaimed for public purposes. In the course of the conflict, files had been dislocated, official forms and stationery had been destroyed, and valuable office equipment had been appropriated by the withdrawing security apparatus. The situation was so grave that the first UN-appointed judges and prosecutors had to bring their own dated typewriters to the initial hearings to be able to draft decisions and court records.

In East Timor, the situation was far worse: it was estimated that between 60 and 80 percent of all public and private buildings had been destroyed in the violence of September 1999.[47] As noted above, the destruction encompassed most court buildings and their office equipment and legal resources.

Step by step, UNTAET had to start rebuilding courthouses, police stations, and prisons. The first judges to be sworn in were required to work in smoke-blackened chambers and courtrooms that were devoid of furniture—much less computers and other apparatus—and nearly bereft of legal texts. None of the buildings had electricity or running water, since even the wiring and pipes had been stripped by the withdrawing Indonesian army and militia forces. Basic stationery and office equipment had to be provided out of UNTAET's own supplies, and official forms and stamps had to be re-created. More significantly, UNTAET struggled, on a daily basis, to identify and collect copies of the laws that, in accordance with its Regulation 1999/1, formed the applicable body of law. Sometimes UNTAET staff members were able to retrieve copies of law books from the ruins of official buildings, but mostly they sought donations from private law firms and law schools in Indonesia and Australia. The support of the Australian legal profession for UNTAET's efforts in this respect was exemplary,[48] the donations extending beyond law texts to include robes for the new judges and prosecutors and folding chairs for the court building in Dili.

The Correctional System

The correctional facilities met with the same fate as most of the other buildings and infrastructure during the violence in Kosovo and East Timor. The identification of suitable facilities in which to hold those apprehended and arrested by the international forces and the United Nations civil police thus became one of the most dramatic challenges faced by both missions.

In Kosovo, the withdrawing Yugoslav security forces had emptied all the prisons and "transferred" the inmates, among them many political prisoners of Kosovar Albanian origin, to unknown locations in Serbia proper. Moreover, many prisons had been damaged or destroyed and the guards had fled with the withdrawing forces. As a result, the hundreds of individuals detained in the first few weeks had to be held in makeshift military facilities,

---

[46] For more detail, see the section "Legal Framework" *infra* p. 58.

[47] *See supra* note 20 and corresponding text.

[48] In January 2000, Australian Legal Resources International appealed to the Australian legal profession, on behalf of UNTAET and through the Law Council of Australia, for law texts, courtroom furniture, computers, and judges' robes. The response was overwhelming.

which usually consisted of army tents in KFOR camps that were guarded by military officers who had no experience in the administration of prisons and international standards on the detention of civilians.

In East Timor, the situation was even worse. Not only had all the prison guards left during the exodus of the Indonesian security forces, but also all prison facilities had been burned and rendered unusable.[49] The limited capacities of the makeshift detention center inherited by the United Nations from INTERFET had been stretched to the maximum, leaving no more space for detainees and ordinary criminals. Consequently, the United Nations had to limit the number of arrests. At times, UN civil police officers were even forced to release suspects who had been arrested for serious criminal offenses so that they could detain returning militia members implicated in the commission of grave violations of international humanitarian and human rights law in the violence of August and September 1999. The failure to arrest such individuals would have been unacceptable in the eyes of both the general public and its political leadership.

The inadequacy of the interim facilities and the fact that the UN civil police were neither trained nor equipped to carry out the functions of prison wardens made it clear that the United Nations urgently had to reconstruct suitable facilities, identify experienced international wardens, and develop local capacities. These essential tasks were made difficult, however, by the reluctance of donors to fund, whether directly or indirectly, the reconstruction or erection of prison facilities, and of United Nations member states to provide contingents of prison personnel.

Legal Framework

All of these challenges were surpassed by the need to establish a basic legal framework for the judiciary in each territory. Judicial appointments, legal training, and the performance of judicial, prosecutorial, and other legal functions, all depended on the existence of a clear body of applicable law. Neither in Kosovo nor in East Timor did the previous legislation constitute a sufficient legal basis for the establishment of an independent and effective judiciary. Thus, in both territories the United Nations first had to draft regulations indicating which previously existing laws still applied, or setting forth entirely new laws, before it could establish the corresponding judicial and other public institutions.[50]

In their Regulation 1999/1, both UNMIK and UNTAET had decided in effect that the laws that had applied in each United Nations–administered territory prior to the adoption of Security Council Resolutions 1244 and 1272, respectively, would apply, *mutatis mutandis,* insofar as they conformed with internationally recognized human rights standards and did not conflict with the Security Council's mandate to each mission or any subsequent regulation promulgated by the mission.[51] This decision was made solely for practical reasons: first, to avoid a legal vacuum in the initial phase of the transitional administration and, second, to avoid the need for local lawyers, virtually all of whom had obtained their law degrees at domestic universities, to be introduced to an entirely foreign legal system.

Especially in Kosovo, this decision prompted vigorous protest by local politicians and the legal community. The Yugoslav criminal laws, in particular, were considered to have been one of the most potent tools of a decade-long policy of discrimination against and repres-

[49] On this subject, see the findings of Human Rights Watch, Unfinished Business: Justice for East Timor, Press Backgrounder (Aug. 2000).
[50] *See* UNMIK Regulations 1999/1, *supra* note 3; 1999/2 (Aug. 12); 1999/5 (Sept. 4); 1999/6 (Sept. 7); 1999/7 (Sept. 7) (replacing UNMIK Emergency Decree 1999/1); *see also* UNTAET Regulations 1999/1, *supra* note 3; 1999/3, *supra* note 29; 2000/11 (Mar. 6); 2000/14 (May 10); 2000/15 (June 6); 2000/16 (June 6).
[51] *See* UNMIK Regulation 1999/1 and UNTAET Regulation 1999/1, *supra* note 3, §§2, 3. The wording of section 3.1 of UNTAET Regulation 1999/1 (the factual statement "the laws applied" is used rather than "the applicable laws") carefully avoids the retroactive legitimation of the Indonesian occupation in East Timor.

sion of the Kosovar Albanian population.[52] The political representatives of the Kosovar Albanian community thus threatened to cease cooperating with the United Nations, and newly appointed judges and prosecutors resigned from office, demanding an immediate return to the laws applicable in Kosovo before the revocation of its autonomy status within Serbia. This demand was made primarily for political reasons, since these laws were by no means more democratic than the Yugoslav criminal laws. On December 12, 1999, UNMIK finally promulgated a regulation providing that the law in force in Kosovo prior to March 22, 1989, would serve as the applicable law for the duration of the UN administration, effectively superseding the relevant provisions in UNMIK Regulation 1999/1.[53]

In practice, moreover, the formula laid out in UNMIK and UNTAET Regulations 1999/1 proved to be rather difficult to apply in both Kosovo and East Timor, because it did not actually spell out the laws or specifically identify the elements that were inconsistent with internationally recognized human rights standards. Rather, it required the lawyers, many of whom were inexperienced, to engage in the complex task of interpreting the penal code or the criminal procedure code through the lens of international human rights instruments, applying those provisions that met international standards, while disregarding those that did not, and substituting for the latter the appropriate standard under international law. The difficulties that can arise are obvious. For example, whereas determining that a provision allowing twenty or more days of detention without a judicial hearing[54] violates international human rights standards is relatively easy, consistently defining the standard that should apply instead under such a provision is much more difficult. In both territories, only a few local lawyers were even familiar with the practical application of international human rights norms, which aggravated the situation.

Yet another challenge faced by both missions was to obtain, from the government that had just withdrawn, all the legislation constituting the applicable body of law and to translate these rules so that international experts could assist their local colleagues in the practical application of the formula contained in section 3 of UNMIK and UNTAET Regulations 1999/1, requiring consistency with international standards.

Thus, in practice, the formula introduced by the United Nations administrations in Kosovo and East Timor, which was aimed at avoiding a legal vacuum and ensuring that the laws applied conformed with international standards from the outset, led to considerable legal and political difficulties. In consequence, both United Nations missions ultimately had to conduct comprehensive reviews of all the legislation that was pivotal to the establishment of an independent and impartial judiciary, and the law-and-order sector more generally, and amend or supersede these laws as necessary through subsequent UN regulations. In the meantime, however, the United Nations civil police and the judiciary had to apply the existing legislation on a daily basis, trying their best, but struggling to do so in accordance with the requirements of UNMIK and UNTAET Regulations 1999/1.

III. CONCLUSION

The establishment of a functioning governmental structure, including the re-creation of the judicial branch, from "ground zero" is a daunting task. In recent years, the United Nations has been entrusted with providing assistance to the legal and judicial systems of several countries in postconflict situations, including, most recently, Cambodia, Haiti, and

---

[52] *See* Kaminski, *supra* note 8.

[53] According to section 1.1 of UNMIK Regulation 1999/24 (Dec. 12, 1999), "[t]he law applicable in Kosovo shall be: a. The regulations promulgated by the Special Representative of the Secretary-General and subsidiary instruments issued thereunder; and b. The law in force in Kosovo on 22 March 1989." According to section 3, "[t]he present regulation shall be deemed to have entered into force as of 10 June 1999."

[54] *See* REPUBLIC OF INDONESIA, DEPARTMENT OF INFORMATION, LAW-BOOK ON THE CODE OF CRIMINAL PROCEDURE Arts. 20, 24 (n.d.) (Act No. 8/1981).

Bosnia and Herzegovina. Nowhere other than Kosovo and East Timor, however, did this task require the establishment of a coherent judicial and legal system for an entire territory virtually from scratch.

The experiences of the United Nations in Kosovo and East Timor have shown that the reestablishment, at a minimum, of basic judicial functions—comprising all segments of the justice sector—must be among a mission's top priorities from the earliest stages of deployment. Indeed, the absence of a functioning judicial system can adversely affect both the short- and the long-term objectives of the peace-building effort, including the restoration of political stability necessary for the development of democratic institutions, the establishment of an atmosphere of confidence necessary for the return of refugees, the latitude to provide humanitarian assistance, the implementation of development and reconstruction programs, and the creation of an environment friendly to foreign investment and economic development. The lack of adequate law enforcement and the failure to remove criminal offenders can inevitably affect both the authority of the mission and the local population's willingness to respect the rule of law. In the worst of cases, such an atmosphere can push self-proclaimed vigilante forces to take law enforcement into their own hands and resort to illegal detention, which can threaten the safety and security of the local population and the international staff. Finally, a functioning judicial system can positively affect reconciliation and confidence-building efforts within often highly traumatized postcrisis societies, not least because it can bring to justice those responsible for grave violations of international humanitarian and human rights law.

The United Nations' most recent experiences in transitional administration demonstrate that justice, and law enforcement more broadly, must be seen as effective from the first days of an operation. The inability to react swiftly to crime and public unrest, particularly in postconflict situations when criminal activity tends to increase, and the failure to detain and convict suspected criminals promptly and fairly, can quickly erode the public's confidence in the United Nations. In Kosovo, a total of 14,878 criminal offenses were reported from January to August 2000 alone; over the same period 3,734 people were arrested.[55] Thus, the establishment of effective judicial institutions can be critical to the long-term success of a mission and the sustainability of its governance and democratic-institution-building efforts.

Given the current prevalence of intrastate conflicts and the likelihood that such conflicts will lead to the emergence of autonomous regions or independent states in the future, the United Nations may be asked to establish a transitional administration for other situations, which will inevitably include the creation of a judicial system. The enormous difficulties encountered in Kosovo and East Timor in this respect have shown that the United Nations and the international community at large must enhance their rapid-response and coordination capacities so that the necessary attention and resources can be directed to this key area of civil administration. While international civilian policing resides at the core of prototypical peacekeeping operations, this element cannot be focused on at the expense, or without due consideration, of the other elements of a functioning law enforcement and judicial system.

In addition to early and sensible mission planning, involving representatives of the local legal profession, and committing the necessary financial and human resources, implementing the following recommendations would further enhance the United Nations' capacity to build or reconstruct postcrisis judicial systems.

1. Establishment of judicial ad hoc arrangements. A law enforcement vacuum in the early days of a mission should be avoided by establishing ad hoc judicial arrangements to facilitate the detention and subsequent judicial hearings on individuals who are apprehended on crim-

---

[55] *See* INTERNATIONAL CRISIS GROUP, KOSOVO REPORT CARD 31, 44 (ICG Balkans Report No. 100, 2000) (stating that the criminal offenses "included 172 murders, 116 kidnappings, 160 attempted murders, and 220 grievous assaults").

inal charges. The UN experience in both Kosovo and East Timor demonstrates that, where there has been a complete breakdown of the judicial sector, the quick deployment of units of military lawyers, as part of either a United Nations peacekeeping force or a regional military arrangement such as KFOR and INTERFET, can fill the vacuum until the United Nations is staffed and able to take over what is ultimately a civilian responsibility.[56]

The advantage of such an arrangement would be that military lawyers, who would make up an integral part of the peacekeeping force, could be rapidly deployed together with the troops. In contrast, civilian United Nations staff, many of whom must go through a lengthier recruitment process, cannot be immediately deployed. In this emergency phase, military lawyers would have to be in a position to execute legal functions, including arrest, detention, prosecution, and initial adjudication, immediately, without engaging in the time-consuming task of assembling and familiarizing themselves with local laws. Thus, as a practical matter, they would all have to come from the same country and to apply the laws in force in that country.[57] It would be understood, however, that such military arrangements would remain in place only for a limited and clearly defined period of time, until responsibility could be handed over to an adequately functioning civilian body. Moreover, any such arrangements would have to accord strictly with internationally recognized human rights and other relevant legal standards.[58]

Intuitively, one would hesitate to involve military actors in this sensitive area of civil administration, but in the absence of sufficient and immediately deployable civilian resources, it may be the only appropriate response to avoid the emergence of a law enforcement vacuum. The experiences in both Kosovo and East Timor have proved that the emergence of such a vacuum can ultimately be more detrimental to the objective of developing an independent judicial system and effectively protecting a population's human rights than the establishment of a temporary military-run judiciary.

The establishment of ad hoc military arrangements for a transitional period would provide the United Nations with the time and space to devise the appropriate legal system for the duration of the transitional administration and to take the necessary steps toward building the foundation for a truly independent judicial branch. Such a system would help the mission avoid the sense of urgency that could drive it to fill judicial positions with individuals who might turn out not to enjoy the general acceptance of the local population and its leadership, as happened in Kosovo, or to grapple early on with the practical problems posed by the lack of experienced lawyers, as happened in East Timor. Moreover, this approach would permit the United Nations to carry out a proper assessment of the available human and physical resources, possibly including the screening of applicants for serious violations of international law, to give due consideration to existing political and cultural sensitivities, and to provide initial legal training as necessary.

2. Formation of a standby network of international lawyers. Regardless of the institution of ad hoc military arrangements, the United Nations must enhance its own capacity to establish a functioning judiciary as rapidly as possible, by ensuring that the fundamental task of judiciary building is part of its emergency first-phase response. It is thus imperative for the

---

[56] Compared to the improvised policy in Kosovo, the existence in East Timor of the INTERFET-sponsored Detention Management Unit, *see supra* note 23, until early January 2000 allowed UNTAET at least to engage in more in-depth planning of the future judicial system and to carry out the difficult search for East Timorese jurists.

[57] Ideally, they would apply the set of interim rules on criminal procedure and substantive criminal law referred to in the fourth recommendation at p. 62 *infra*.

[58] The United Nations' Model Agreement with member states that contribute personnel and equipment to peacekeeping operations includes the following standard provision: "[The United Nations peacekeeping operation] shall observe and respect the principles and spirit of the general international conventions applicable to the conduct of military personnel." *See* Daphna Shraga & Ralph Zacklin, *The Applicability of International Humanitarian Law to United Nations Peace-Keeping Operations: Conceptual, Legal and Practical Issues, in* INTERNATIONAL COMMITTEE OF THE RED CROSS, SYMPOSIUM ON HUMANITARIAN ACTION AND PEACE-KEEPING OPERATIONS 39, 44 (Umesh Palwankar ed., 1994).

United Nations to develop a standby network (as opposed to a costly standing capacity) of experienced and qualified international jurists that can be activated at any given time. In view of the significant practical differences between the common-law and civil-law systems, experts in both systems should be recruited in sufficient numbers to ensure that they can adequately respond to the specific needs of the territory to be administered. Since quick deployment is crucial to the effectiveness and credibility of an operation in its early stages, the United Nations should create a network based on standby agreements with member states, agencies, and academic institutions to facilitate the mobilization of these jurists on short notice, within a few days, if required. If provided with ongoing training in international legal and human rights standards, and updated information on international instruments and judicial developments, the members of this network would eventually constitute a sufficient number of qualified international lawyers, who could work as trainers, mentors, judges, and prosecutors.

　　3. *Immediate reconstruction of the correctional system.* In view of the enormous difficulties experienced in both Kosovo and East Timor in this sector, urgent priority must be given to the immediate establishment of an adequate prison infrastructure. A functioning correctional system is not only complementary, but also inextricably linked, to the creation of a functioning law enforcement mechanism. Despite the reluctance of many donors to finance correctional facilities, such a mechanism cannot be established without sufficient and quickly disbursable funding for immediate reconstruction efforts. Thus, the United Nations must make a concerted effort to convince donor countries that funding for this crucial task must be incorporated, from the outset, in the consolidated budget for the activities of a transitional administration, and based on assessed rather than voluntary contributions. In this connection, the United Nations should not fail to include a sufficient number of professional international prison guards and wardens in its mission planning and budgeting.

　　4. *Creation of an immediately applicable legal framework.* The availability of an immediately applicable legal framework is an important prerequisite for the building of judicial institutions. Capacities within and outside the United Nations must thus be identified for quickly drafting new legislation in accordance with internationally recognized standards and with due consideration to the legal traditions (i.e., civil law or common law) of the territory at issue. To facilitate this effort, the United Nations must develop standby arrangements with partner agencies such as the World Bank, the International Monetary Fund, and the Council of Europe, as well as with universities and nongovernmental organizations. Particularly in the setup phase of a mission, and at its request, these agencies could prepare initial drafts that would subsequently be finalized by the United Nations in concert with local lawyers. Significantly, such arrangements would promote early cooperation, without requiring lengthy assessment and approval procedures in advance.

　　In this regard, a body of law-enforcement-related legislation should be developed as part of a "quick-start package" for United Nations–administered territories. Readily applicable criminal procedure and criminal codes, as well as a code regulating the activities of the police, have proved to be essential to the unimpeded functioning of the UN civil police component of peace-building missions. First of all, the UN civil police need to act with legal certainty and in accordance with clearly spelled-out legal provisions so as to carry out their daily law enforcement activities effectively and without fear of breaching the law. Second, the civil police need a clear legal framework in which to train the future local police force in democratic policing. Third, newly appointed judges, prosecutors, and lawyers must be clear as to what the applicable law is in order to execute their functions. Thus, as an indispensable initial step, the United Nations must draft a set of interim rules of criminal procedure and substantive criminal law in core areas of police activity, including arrest/detention and searches/seizures. In the long term, the United Nations could promote the development of a model criminal procedure code that would be used by all UN missions that are mandated to rebuild a legal system, including the temporary ad hoc military arrangements referred to above. In areas other than criminal law, UN regulations from previous missions could serve as model regulations where applicable.

5. Prioritization of legal training. The international community must play an active role in providing adequate professional training to newly appointed lawyers, judges, and prosecutors so that the judiciary will be equipped with the highest level of technical competence, will be strongly committed to the principles of judicial independence, and as an institution will respect human rights and understand how to protect these rights in its day-to-day work.

Professional legal training in complex postcrisis situations such as those in Kosovo and East Timor extends beyond technical assistance. It is a pivotal element of capacity building and empowerment for the creation of a stable legal system. For example, given the lack of East Timorese experience in the administration of justice, the United Nations should ideally have been in a position immediately on deployment to provide quick-impact training and mentoring programs on core issues such as pretrial standards, the conduct of hearings, and the drafting of detention orders. For, in addition to enhancing appreciation of the judiciary's role in society, such training would also advance the concept of an independent and impartial judiciary as protecting rights and freedoms, rather than as serving as an instrument of repression, power, or control. However, the necessary training and mentoring programs for local lawyers cannot be implemented unless sufficient financial and human resources are obtained. The initial establishment of a comprehensive database, including reference to potential providers of judicial training and their programs, would help to ensure a quicker response in this regard.

None of the above recommendations is intended to provide the final answer on how best to build a judiciary from scratch, since every postcrisis situation is unique and requires an adapted response. The international community will have to accept that such a process requires its commitment and that of the United Nations system from the very start and, even then, is bound to experience serious setbacks. Yet careful consideration of how an independent and operational judicial system can enhance the long-term objectives for the territory to be administered maximizes the chances that the United Nations will succeed in creating a secure environment and guiding a postconflict society toward political stability, economic recovery, and reconciliation.

[9]

United Nations Reform and Supporting the Rule of Law in Post-Conflict Societies

David Tolbert*
with
Andrew Solomon**

I. Introduction and Overview

The reform of the United Nations ("U.N.") is a priority both for the organization itself and for its member states. In recent years, a multitude of reports exploring the future path of the organization and its role in a troubled world have been published.[1] While all of these documents stress the importance of reforming the U.N., questions remain as to how reforms will be implemented and what impact they will have.

One area that is repeatedly mentioned both in terms of U.N. reform and the future role of the organization is in building the "rule of law" in developing countries in general and post-conflict societies in particular. This Article discusses what is meant by the "rule of law" and which aspects of the rule of law are relevant to the U.N.'s current and future work. This Article also explores how the organization can use its resources and expertise, in coordination with other actors, to help build the rule of law in societies devastated by armed conflict.

While post-conflict societies differ from each other in significant respects, they all encounter common problems, including addressing crimes committed

* Deputy Prosecutor, International Criminal Tribunal for the former Yugoslavia [hereinafter ICTY]. Executive Director, American Bar Association Central European and Eurasian Law Initiative [hereinafter ABA-CEELI], 2000–2003. Deputy Registrar, Chef de Cabinet to the President and Senior Legal Adviser, ICTY, 1996–2000, and Chief, General Legal Division, United Nations Relief and Works Agency, 1993–1996. The views expressed are those of the Author alone and not those of the United Nations or the ICTY. The Author would like to thank Aude Rimailho for her valuable assistance in the preparation of this Article. The Author also thanks Erik Sayler.

** Director of Research and Outreach Programs, American Society of International Law. Co-director of Research and Special Projects, ABA/CEELI, 2002–2004. Mr. Solomon contributed the Parts on the Role of Bench and Bar, Legal Education and Training, and Other Primary Actors.

1. *See, e.g.*, The Secretary-General, *Report of the Secretary-General: In larger freedom: towards development, security and human rights for all*, U.N. GAOR, 59th Sess., U.N. Doc. A/59/2005 (Mar. 21, 2005) [hereinafter *In larger freedom*]; The Secretary-General's High Level Panel on Threats, Challenges, and Change, *Report of the Secretary-General's High-level Panel on Threats, Challenges and Change: A more secure world: our shared responsibility*, U.N. GAOR, 59th Sess., U.N. Doc. A/59/565 (Dec. 2, 2005), *available at* http://www.un.org/secureworld [hereinafter *High Level Panel Report*]; The Secretary-General, *Report of the Secretary-General: Road map towards the implementation of the United Nations Millennium Declaration*, U.N. GAOR, 56th Sess., U.N. Doc. A/56/326 (Sept. 6, 2001).

during the conflict, reestablishing a functioning government, and healing residual animosities and divisions within the society. In addition to post-conflict issues, these societies must also address problems such as poverty, corruption, and the lack of a legal infrastructure—problems that confront other underdeveloped countries. One should be careful not to create a false dichotomy between traditional rule of law development work and efforts to build the rule of law in post-conflict societies. In fact, many of the strategies employed in the former are also relevant to the latter.

This Article first addresses what is meant by the "rule of law" and, more fundamentally, what can be done to help develop it in post-conflict societies. In order to give effect to the rule of law, these societies must address the crimes committed during the conflict, create sound legal infrastructure, and build functioning institutions. We next address what role the U.N. can most effectively play in fostering this process. This discussion focuses on the proposals of the Secretary-General's High Level Panel on Threats, Challenges and Change ("the Panel"),[2] which aimed to make recommendations for change and serve as the blueprint for U.N. reform.

One of the principal institutional weaknesses identified by the Panel is that the U.N. lacks the capacity to address adequately the needs of countries in transition from war to peace. The Panel makes a number of proposals to address this issue, including the establishment of a Peacebuilding Commission supported by the Peacebuilding Support Office ("PSO") and the Rule of Law Assistance Unit ("RLAU").[3] An important component of this effort to increase the U.N.'s capacity to support and assist countries in the transition from war to peace is rule of law assistance.

In view of these proposed reforms, we discuss and examine these new institutions. We will focus particularly on the RLAU, which is slated to play the key role in pushing forward the rule of law agenda in post-conflict societies. During the course of this discussion, it is important to take into account other actors with which the U.N. cooperates and to outline the respective roles played by the U.N. and its partners. Finally, in an effort to determine how the U.N. system as a whole might evolve to more effectively support the development of the rule of law in these societies, we explore the connection between these efforts and U.N. reform more broadly.

II. Defining and Applying the Rule of Law

A. *What Is the Rule of Law? Which Rule of Law?*

The phrase "the rule of law" is found in most discussions regarding post-conflict societies, and those about the work of the U.N. generally. Indeed, the rule of law is seen by many to be of primary importance in post-conflict societies. For example, Lord Ashdown, then High Representative for Bosnia-

---

2. *High Level Panel Report, supra* note 1, ¶¶ 261–269.
3. *Id.*

Herzegovina, noted: "In hindsight, we should have put the establishment of the rule of law first, for everything else depends on it: a functioning economy, a free and fair political system, the development of civil society, public confidence in the police and the courts."[4] This view is widely shared by governments and non-governmental actors alike.[5]

Despite the ubiquity of its usage and the importance of the idea, the rule of law, much like the concepts of "justice" or "transitional justice," is endowed with "a multiplicity of definitions and understandings . . . even among the [U.N.'s] closest partners in the field."[6] There are a number of approaches to defining the rule of law or at least identifying the principal elements that constitute the concept. For example, the Secretary-General has defined it in these terms:

> The rule of law is a concept at the very heart of the Organization's mission. It refers to a principle of governance in which all persons, institutions and entities, public and private, including the State itself, are accountable to laws that are publicly promulgated, equally enforced and independently adjudicated, and which are consistent with international human rights norms and standards. It requires, as well, measures to ensure adherence to the principles of supremacy of law, equality before the law, accountability to the law, fairness in the application of the law, separation of powers, participation in decision-making, legal certainty, avoidance of arbitrariness and procedural and legal transparency.[7]

This is a good "black letter" definition of the rule of law because it covers the principal elements that lawyers expect in terms of how the law is created and applied. However, an important element is missing from any such definition. As Gerhard Casper puts it, "the rule of law is not a recipe for detailed institutional design. [It is] an interconnected cluster of values."[8]

Casper articulates a number of approaches to defining the rule of law, ranging from a minimalist approach whereby the rule of law is simply a set of rules administered by an independent judiciary, to the idea that the rule

---

4. Paddy Ashdown, *What I Learned in Bosnia*, N.Y. TIMES, Oct. 28, 2002, at A2.

5. Sir Emyr Jones Parry, U.K. Permanent Representative to the U.N., Address to the International Security and Global Issues Research Group and the David Davies Memorial Institute Seminar (Nov. 10, 2004) (transcript available at http://www.ukun.org/articles_show.asp?SarticleType=17&Article_ID=813) ("This view of the critical importance of justice and the rule of law both pre– and post-conflict is not one held only by a few western democratic governments . . . the [U.N.] Secretariat, NGOs and academics are all agreed.").

6. The Secretary-General, *Report of the Secretary-General: The Rule of Law and Transitional Justice in Conflict and Post-Conflict Societies*, ¶ 5, U.N. Doc. S/2004/616 (Aug. 23, 2004) [hereinafter *Rule of Law Report*].

7. *Id.*, ¶ 6. *See also* Thomas Carothers, *The Rule of Law Revival*, 77 FOREIGN AFF. 95 (1998).

8. Gerhard Casper, Rule of Law? Whose Law? Keynote Address, 2003 CEELI Award Ceremony and Luncheon, San Francisco, Cal. (Aug. 9, 2003) *quoting* Martin Krygier, INTERNATIONAL ENCYCLOPEDIA OF THE SOCIAL & BEHAVIORAL SCIENCES 13404 (Smelser & Baltes eds., 2001), *available at* http://iis-db.stanford.edu/pubs/20677/Rule_of_Law.pdf.

of law is a set of substantive rules requiring a democratic political system.[9] Given these various approaches, "the concept of the rule law is a fairly empty vessel whose content, depending on legal cultures and historical conditions, can differ considerably and, therefore, can give rise to vast disagreements and, indeed, conflicts."[10] One can easily see how differences in the various approaches might lead to conflict. For example, in Iraq there has been considerable debate regarding the extent to which *Shari'a* law, as opposed to secular approaches, should be incorporated into the Iraqi constitution and legal system.[11]

In view of these various approaches and possible differences in definition, Casper also indicates that there are several universalist approaches to the rule of law.[12] Of these, he notes that public international law, which primarily derives "its authority from agreement, consensus, and custom among nation states," at least with respect to human rights law "is, if not considered binding worldwide, then at least highly authoritative."[13] Almost all countries have acceded to the United Nations Charter and an overwhelming majority of states are parties to the International Covenant on Civil and Political Rights and the International Covenant on Economic, Social and Cultural Rights.[14]

Thus, while countries with different legal systems have varied approaches to both procedural and substantive law, there is widespread agreement on the essential elements of the rule of law, as distilled in international human rights law.[15] These include basic due process rights—such as the right to counsel, the right of an accused person to know the charges against him or her, and the presumption of innocence—as well as a number of other civil rights including freedom of religion, freedom of expression, and freedom of association.[16] Given the widespread acceptance of these human rights norms, they serve as a reference point from which to answer the question of what is meant by "the rule of law." Of course, this is only a partial answer to the question of the substantive norms that societies must adopt and implement before they are said to have established the rule of law. International human rights law only establishes the minimum procedural and substantive legal

---

9. *Id.*; *see generally* Agnes Hurwitz & Kaysie Studdard, Policy Paper, International Peace Academy, Rule of Law Programs in Peace Operations 3 (Aug. 2005), http://www.ipacademy.org/Programs/Research/ProgReseSecDev_Pub.htm.

10. Casper, *supra* note 8.

11. *Q&A: Wrangling Over Iraq's Constitution*, N.Y. TIMES, July 27, 2005.

12. Casper, *supra* note 8 (identifying three principal strands of the universalist approach: divine law, natural law and public international law).

13. *Id.*

14. *See* International Covenant on Civil and Political Rights, Dec. 16, 1966, 999 U.N.T.S. 171 [hereinafter ICCPR]; International Covenant on Economic, Social, and Cultural Rights, Dec. 16, 1966, 993 U.N.T.S. 3.

15. Casper describes it in this way:

 [W]e take the nation states by their word when it comes to their basic commitment to the rule of law and to human rights. Given the overwhelming international agreement, virtual consensus, concerning fundamental rights and rule of law, we should assume that the burden of proof has shifted to those countries that would deny the rule of law in principle.

Casper, *supra* note 8.

16. *See* ICCPR, *supra* note 14, arts. 14, 18, 19, 21, 22.

guarantees; it does not define the substance of other laws to be adopted. More importantly, the almost universal formal adoption by states of these human rights norms does not guarantee that they will be implemented. Indeed, it is clear that in some countries these rights are honored sporadically at best. Finally, as we have discussed above, the rule of law is not simply a bundle of rules, but rather a "cluster of values."

In sum, there exists a set of rules—international human rights norms—that establish the minimum of what must be in place before a state or society can move toward the rule of law. This approach also addresses, at least at the theoretical level, issues that arose in the law and development movement[17] of the 1960s. That movement has been criticized, *inter alia*, as a form of neo-colonialism for its efforts to transplant legal norms from North America to developing countries.[18] Defining the rule of law in terms of widely accepted international norms therefore allows for the emergence of the concept of the rule of law at an international level without the taint of undue Western influence.

We now move from the essential legal norms to a discussion of how these norms can be given effect in a post-conflict society. In particular, we explore how, in societies devastated by conflict and destruction, the norms established by widely accepted human rights instruments move from the printed page to enforcement in courts and legal processes. We also explore the role of a reformed U.N. in that process.

B. A Framework for Supporting the Rule of Law in a Post-Conflict Society

1. Addressing the Past: Holding Those Responsible to Account

Addressing the past is, initially, the most pressing issue in a post-conflict society. To do so in an effective manner requires that individuals who have committed serious crimes during the conflict be held accountable through a mechanism that delivers justice to victims and punishment to perpetrators. This is a particularly difficult task when there is an absence of trust between different ethnic communities or political groupings and no functioning judicial system. Given the U.N.'s unique mandate to promote peace and security, it has a critically important task in helping to establish appropriate mechanisms to address the crimes of the past without reigniting the prior conflict.

---

17. Thomas Carothers describes the law and development movement in the following terms:
> Programs emphasized legal education, particularly the goal of trying to recast methods of teaching law in developing countries in the image of the American Socratic, case-oriented methods . . . [and] encouraged lawyers and legal educators in developing countries to treat the law as an activist instrument of progressive social change.

THOMAS CAROTHERS, AIDING DEMOCRACY ABROAD: THE LEARNING CURVE 24 (1999).

18. *See* Varda Hussain, *Note, Sustaining Judicial Rescues: The Role of Outreach and Capacity-Building Efforts in War Crimes Tribunals*, 45 VA. J. INT'L L. 547, 551–58 (2005).

The process of holding accountable those responsible for serious violations of international humanitarian law[19] is a recent development. One might believe that in the past, these crimes were seemingly forgotten as societies tried simply to "move on." However, one need only examine the continuing debate over the slaughter of Armenians at the beginning of the twentieth century,[20] the ongoing attempts to hold military and political leaders accountable in South American countries decades after atrocities were committed,[21] and the repeated cycles of violence in the Balkans[22] to conclude that societies have consistently demanded some form of justice for mass crimes.[23] The basis of the rule of law is that no person, no matter his or her position, is above the law. There can be little hope for a society that continues to be governed by those who have committed mass crimes with impunity. Thus, without some accountability for such crimes, there can be no basis for a post-conflict society to establish the rule of law.

Of course, there are some who argue that justice and peace sometimes conflict, in that the leaders of a country, no matter how tainted by "war crimes," may be essential to negotiating peace. If this argument were correct, attempts to impose justice could undermine efforts to establish peace.[24] However, while there are legitimate debates to be had on the timing of justice initiatives, this argument creates a false choice between peace and justice, at the expense of the rule of law. A peace arrangement that leaves in place leaders who have committed crimes is simply buying time until the seeds sown by those crimes

---

19. International Humanitarian Law is a set of rules which seeks to protect people who have not participated, or who are no longer participating, in hostilities. It also restricts the methods and means of warfare. *See, e.g.*, Convention with Respect to the Laws and Customs of War on Land, July 29, 1899, 32 Stat. 1803, T.S. 403; Convention Respecting the Law and Customs of War on Land, Oct. 18, 1907, 36 Stat. 2277, T.S. 539; the four Geneva Conventions of Aug. 12, 1949 [hereinafter Geneva Conventions]; the Convention on the Prevention and Punishment of the Crime of Genocide, *opened for signature* Dec. 9, 1948, 102 Stat. 3045, 78 U.N.T.S. 277 *(entered into force* Jan. 12, 1951). The Geneva Conventions include Geneva Convention for the Amelioration of the Condition of the Wounded and Sick in Armed Forces in the Field, Aug. 12, 1949, 6 U.S.T. 3114, 75 U.N.T.S. 31; Geneva Convention for the Amelioration of the Condition of Wounded, Sick, and Shipwrecked Members of Armed Forces at Sea, Aug. 12, 1949, 6 U.S.T. 3217, 75 U.N.T.S. 85; Geneva Convention Relative to the Treatment of Prisoners of War, Aug. 12, 1949, 6 U.S.T. 3316, 75 U.N.T.S. 135; Geneva Convention Relative to the Protection of Civilian Persons of Time of War, Aug. 12, 1949, 6 U.S.T. 6516, 75 U.N.T.S. 287. The Geneva Conventions were supplemented by the Protocol Additional to the Geneva Conventions of 12 August 1949, and Relating to the Protection of Victims of International Armed Conflicts, Aug. 15, 1977, U.N. Doc. A/32/144; Protocol Additional to the Geneva Conventions of 12 August 1949, and Relating to the Protection of Victims of Non-International Armed Conflicts, Aug. 15, 1977, U.N. Doc. A/32/144.

20. *See, e.g.*, Bertil Duner, *What Can Be Done About Historical Atrocities? The Armenian Case*, 8 INT'L J. HUM. RTS. 217 (2004).

21. *See, e.g.*, Roseann M. Latore, *Coming Out of the Dark: Achieving Justice for Victims of Human Rights Violations by South American Military Regimes*, 25 B.C. INT'L & COMP. L. REV. 419 (2002).

22. *See generally* MISHA GLENNY, THE BALKANS 1804–1999: NATIONALISM, WAR AND THE GREAT POWERS (1999).

23. *See, e.g.*, 1 TRANSITIONAL JUSTICE: GENERAL CONSIDERATIONS xxii (Neil J. Kritz ed., United States Institute of Peace Press 1995) ("[T]here is a growing consensus that, at least for the most heinous violations of human rights and international humanitarian law, a sweeping amnesty is impermissible.").

24. *See, e.g.*, Judge Hisashi Owada, *Some Reflections on Justice in a Globalizing World*, 97 AM. SOC'Y INT'L L. PROC. 181 (2003).

undermine that society again. Failure to address past crimes thus hinders the restructuring of a post-conflict society because it disregards the rule of law.

While acknowledging that post-conflict situations are highly complex, it is worth noting the example of post-war Germany, where considerable efforts were made to address past crimes through both international and domestic trials, setting the stage for a society based on the rule of law.[25] On the other hand, in the former Yugoslavia, the failure to address the past, including crimes committed during World War II, has been cited as one of the causes of the eruption of violence in the 1990s.[26]

The next challenge in terms of accountability is the manner in which to hold individuals responsible in a fragile post-conflict society. Following the trials at the end of World War II, there were very few developments in terms of international mechanisms to hold individuals accountable for such crimes.[27] During this time, international norms, established by the Geneva Conventions and subsequent protocols, the Genocide Convention, and a plethora of other normative treaties,[28] have developed and have been widely adopted. However, with the exception of certain domestic prosecutions, most notably the Eichmann trial,[29] these laws were largely not enforced.

This lacuna has begun to be addressed over the past two decades, in a variety of ways.[30] For example, South Africa and many Latin American countries have wrestled with histories where state officials committed extensive human rights abuses including torture, murder and "disappearances."[31] The response to these crimes has been varied, with at least thirty countries, including South Africa and a number of Latin America states, pursuing truth and reconciliation commissions.[32] While the approach differed in the various countries, these were usually non-judicial mechanisms[33] in which testimony and other evi-

---

25. *See generally* 2 TRANSITIONAL JUSTICE: COUNTRY STUDIES 1–69 (Neil J. Kritz ed., United States Institute of Peace Press 1995) (discussing post-Nazi Germany).

26. *See generally* TIM JUDAH, THE SERBS: HISTORY, MYTH AND THE DESTRUCTION OF YUGOSLAVIA (1997) (analyzing Serbian history, politics and war).

27. *See* Cherif Bassiouni, *From Versailles to Rwanda in Seventy-Five Years: The Need to Establish a Permanent International Criminal Court*, 10 HARV. HUM. RTS. J. 11, 13–39 (1997).

28. *E.g.*, Convention against Torture and Other Cruel, Inhuman or Degrading Treatment or Punishment, Dec. 10, 1984, 660 U.N.T.S. 195 (*entered into force* June 26, 1987).

29. *See* Att'y Gen. of Israel v. Adolf Eichmann, 36 I.L.R. 5 (Isr. D.C., Jerusalem, Dec. 12, 1961), aff'd, 36 I.L.R.277 (Isr. S. Ct., May 29, 1962). *See also* HANNAH ARENDT, EICHMANN IN JERUSALEM: A REPORT ON THE BANALITY OF EVIL (Faber and Faber 1963).

30. In a somewhat related development, in the post-1989 era a number of Eastern European countries introduced lustration laws, which provided for excluding certain persons from participating in public life and were used for screening and "prosecuting" former communist leaders, candidates for office and selected public employees. These laws were adopted in Germany, Bulgaria, Hungary, Albania, Romania, and certain former Soviet Republics. *See, e.g.*, Act from 5 July 1996 on Civil Service, Dz.U.96.89.402 (Poland).

31. *See* Declaration on the Protection of All Persons from Enforced Disappearances, G.A.Res. 47/133, 47 U.N. GAOR Supp. (No. 49), at 207, U.N. Doc. A/47/49 (Dec. 18, 1992).

32. *Rule of Law Report, supra* note 6, ¶ 26.

33. In South Africa, there was a judicial effect in that amnesty was granted in exchange for truthful testimony. *See* Rosemary Nagy, *Violence, Amnesty and Transitional Law: "Private" Acts and "Public" Truth in South Africa*, 1 AFR. J. LEGAL STUD. 1 (2004).

dence was considered, a record establishing the facts relating to the conflict was created to the extent possible, and victims were permitted to tell their stories in an official forum.[34] These non-judicial proceedings accord with the basic human rights notion that victims should know the truth about crimes committed against them and their loved ones.[35] This right to know was initially articulated by the U.N. Human Rights Commission in its *Set of Principles for the Protection and Promotion of Human Rights through Action to Combat Impunity*, and has been widely recognized in international judicial rulings.[36] These include decisions by the U.N. Human Rights Committee, acting under the International Covenant for Civil and Political Rights, as well as in the case law of the Inter-American Court of Human Rights and the European Court of Human Rights.[37]

International judicial mechanisms to hold individuals accountable for serious violations of international humanitarian law recently emerged for the first time since the Nuremburg and Tokyo trials with the creation of the International Tribunal for the former Yugoslavia ("ICTY") in 1993. This was soon followed by the establishment of the International Criminal Tribunal for Rwanda ("ICTR"). These two ad hoc tribunals, so-named due to their limited subject matter, temporal, and territorial jurisdictions,[38] have a number of achievements to date. They were each created by the U.N. Security Council acting under Chapter VII of the U.N. Charter. They thus have an international legal basis and avoid the label of "victor's justice,"[39] one commonly attached to their Nuremburg and Tokyo predecessors which were established by the victorious Allies.

These tribunals have established a comprehensive body of law, both substantive and procedural, which has helped to break the historical pattern of impunity in the post–World War II era. They have been widely viewed as conducting fair trials,[40] providing a measure of justice to victims, and re-

34. *See* Elizabeth Stanley, *Truth Commissions and the Recognition of State Crime*, 45 BRIT. J. CRIMINOLOGY 582 (2005).

35. *See* U.N. Hum. Rts. Comm'n, *Independent Study on Best Practices, including recommendations, to Assist States in Strengthening Their Domestic Capacity to Combat All Aspects of Impunity*, U.N. Doc. E/CN.4/2004/88 (Feb. 27, 2004) *(prepared by* Prof. Diane Orentlicher) [hereinafter *Independent Study*].

36. U.N. Econ. & Soc. Council, Comm'n on Human Rights, *Updated Set of Principles for the protection and promotion of human rights through action to combat impunity*, § II(A), U.N. Doc. E/CN.4/2005/102/Add.1 (Feb. 8, 2005).

37. *Independent Study, supra* note 35, § II(A) (discussing the right to know and surveying the jurisprudence recognizing that right).

38. Statute of the ICTY, May 25, 1993, 32 I.L.M. 1203; Statute of the International Criminal Tribunal for Rwanda, Nov. 8, 1994, 33 I.L.M. 1598.

39. *See* Hervé Ascensio, *La Justice Pénale Internationale de Nuremberg à La Haye* [International Criminal Justice from Nuremberg to The Hague], *in* LA JUSTICE PÉNALE INTERNATIONALE 29–44 (Simone Gaboriau et al. eds., Presses Universitaires de Limoges, 2002). *See also* Kenneth Anderson, *Humanitarian Inviolability in Crisis: The Meaning of Impartiality and Neutrality for U.N. and NGO Agencies Following the 2003–2004 Afghanistan and Iraq Conflicts*, 17 HARV. HUM. RTS. J. 41, 65–67 (defending the idea of "victor's justice").

40. Erik Møse, *Impact of Human Rights Conventions on the Two ad hoc Tribunals*, *in* HUMAN RIGHTS AND CRIMINAL JUSTICE FOR THE DOWNTRODDEN: ESSAYS IN HONOUR OF ASBJØRN EIDE 179, 191–93

moving war criminals from the seats of power and thus "clearing the ground" for more responsible government. The long-term deterrent impact of the tribunals is unclear, but overall they have accomplished much under difficult circumstances,[41] not the least by putting the respective leaders of the Federal Republic of Yugoslavia (Milosevic) and Rwanda (Kambanda) on trial.

The ad hoc tribunals do, however, have their critics.[42] Some claim that their limited jurisdictions, which allow for the trial of human rights violators from Rwanda and Yugoslavia but not from stronger countries, undermine their legitimacy.[43] This argument, however, appears to have lost much of its force with the advent of the International Criminal Court ("ICC"), which has a much broader mandate, and which would not have been possible without the ad hoc tribunals' trailblazing work. Moreover, while the critics have a point when they note the inequity of treatment from one country to the next, this hardly justifies not holding to account some perpetrators of mass atrocities simply because others cannot presently be held accountable.

Others claim that the tribunals are slow and too costly.[44] Though there is some merit to such claims, the slow pace and the high expense stems in part from the difficulties of establishing institutions situated outside the subject country and without the coercive powers typically available to other courts. Moreover, there are costs associated with translations, travel, U.N. bureaucracy, and the sheer difficulties of the cases. With respect to costs, the expense of the trials actually compares favorably with similarly complex trials in developed countries such as the United States.[45] A careful examination of the facts show that these tribunals have achieved much in very difficult circumstances and have had a positive impact on the rule of law both within their respective jurisdictions and beyond.

A more telling criticism is the lack of connection that these tribunals have with the countries over which they exercise jurisdiction.[46] Both tribunals have experienced difficulties explaining their records to the people in the former Yugoslavia and Rwanda, respectively, and have had little impact on the long-term development of legal infrastructure in these countries. While there were legitimate reasons for establishing the ad hoc tribunals outside their respective regions—it would have been impossible to establish the ICTY in war-torn Yugoslavia—nonetheless the physical separation created serious issues.

(Morten Bergsmo ed., 2003).

41. David Tolbert, *The International Criminal Tribunal for the Former Yugoslavia: Unforeseen Successes and Foreseeable Shortcomings*, 26 FLETCHER F. WORLD AFF. 7, 9 (2002), *available at* http://www.abanet.org/ceeli/publications/other_pubs/tolbert_fletcher_forum.pdf.

42. *See, e.g.*, Ralph Zacklin, *The Failures of the Ad Hoc Tribunals*, 2 J. INT'L CRIM. JUST. 541 (2004).

43. *See generally* Jose Alvarez, *Crimes of States/Crimes of Hate: Lessons from Rwanda*, 24 YALE J. INT'L L. 365 (1999) (discussing Rwandan genocide).

44. Zacklin, *supra* note 42.

45. *See generally* David Wippman, The Costs of International Justice (2006) (unpublished draft, on file with author) (comparing costs of international tribunals with costs of U.S. trials).

46. *See* Tolbert, *supra* note 41.

This explains in large measure the move toward different approaches when conflicts arose in Sierra Leone, East Timor, and Kosovo, and also the belated establishment of a tribunal to try the crimes committed by the Khmer Rouge in Cambodia in the 1970s.[47] In each of these cases, a "hybrid" or "mixed" court was established in-country, composed of international judges and prosecutors working together with their domestic counterparts.[48] The underlying premise is twofold: (1) by being located in the country, and to the extent possible also applying domestic law, justice is brought closer to the local population; (2) the mixture of international and domestic legal professionals allows for training and development of local judges and lawyers.

The hybrid courts are attractive in that they have a more direct impact on the population and on the development of legal professionals. On the other hand, it is simply not possible to try every high-level accused in-country, as the political and security situation may not allow it. There are also problems in attracting the appropriate international staff to countries decimated by conflict. Nonetheless, such hybrid courts and tribunals have an important role to play, both in delivering justice and in building local capacity through the mentoring of domestic judges and prosecutors.[49]

It is also worth noting that the Special Court for Sierra Leone[50] ("SCSL"), a hybrid court established by agreement between the U.N. and the Government of Sierra Leone, operated simultaneously alongside a truth and reconciliation commission. The Court has jurisdiction over individuals bearing "the greatest responsibility" for crimes committed during that conflict, while the Commission investigates and establishes a historical record of the conflict and promotes reconciliation.[51]

The ICC has taken into account the importance of domestic prosecutions of serious violations of international humanitarian law by adopting a "complementarity" regime as its jurisdictional basis.[52] Under this regime, the ICC cannot proceed unless the local authorities "cannot or will not" initiate a

---

47. *See* Jenia Iontcheva Turner, *Nationalizing International Criminal Law*, 41 STAN. J. INT'L L.1 (2005).

48. *See* Laura A. Dickinson, *Transitional Justice in Afghanistan: The Promise of Mixed Tribunals*, 31 DENV. J. INT'L L. & POL'Y 23, 26–39 (2002).

49. It is also possible for an international tribunal to transfer certain lower-level cases to domestic or hybrid courts, as is now occurring between the ICTY and courts and prosecutors in the countries of the former Yugoslavia. The state court in Bosnia-Herzegovina is a hybrid court. *See* The Secretary-General, *Report of the International Tribunal for the Prosecution of Persons Responsible for Serious Violations of International Humanitarian Law Committed in the Territory of the Former Yugoslavia since 1991*, ¶¶ 123–124, 138, 142–143, 174, U.N. Doc. A/60/267/S/2005/532 (Aug. 17, 2005).

50. Agreement Between the U.N. and the Government of Sierra Leone on the Establishment of a Special Court for Sierra Leone, U.N.–Sierra Leone, Jan. 16, 2002, U.N. Doc. S/RES/1315, *available at* http://www.specialcourt.org/documents/Agreement.htm.

51. The Secretary-General, *Eighth Report of the Secretary-General on the United Nations Mission in Sierra Leone*, ¶ 7, U.N. S/2000/1199 (Dec. 15, 2000). *See also* William A. Schabas, *The Relationship Between Truth Commissions and International Courts: The Case of Sierra Leone*, 25 HUM. RTS. Q. 1035 (2003) (discussing the various functions of the Truth and Reconciliation Commission in Sierra Leone).

52. Rome Statute of the International Criminal Court, art. 1, July 17, 1998, 37 I.L.M. 999, [hereinafter Rome Statute].

prosecution.[53] Thus, unlike the ad hoc tribunals which exercise primacy over local judicial authorities, the ICC attempts a partnership with domestic courts and acts only as a court of last resort. Moreover, states ratifying the ICC Statute are required to adopt the law as established by the ICC Statute. In this regard, the contribution of the ICC has been to establish clearly the current state of international humanitarian law and to require ratifying states to adopt it.[54]

There are, therefore, a number of approaches to dealing with crimes and other past events in a post-conflict society.[55] Truth commissions and local processes, such as *Gacaca*,[56] have a role to play in establishing the historical record of a conflict and providing a forum for victims. There are two further points to be made about these mechanisms. The first concerns instances where the truth and reconciliation process complements a criminal process, such as in the case of Sierra Leone or Rwanda. In Rwanda, the scale of the crimes and the number of perpetrators are too great for international or domestic courts to try each and every perpetrator. Similarly, in Sierra Leone, certain perpetrators may not be of an age suitable for prosecution.[57] In these cases, members of the senior political and/or military leadership "most responsible" are held accountable for mass crimes, while other perpetrators are dealt with through parallel mechanisms such as the truth commissions and local processes. Second, it is arguable that certain lower intensity conflicts might be better addressed by a truth and reconciliation commission. Nonetheless, we would strongly argue that this cannot be at the expense of justice: the principal perpetrators must be held to account in a criminal process.[58] Otherwise, the attempt to build the rule of law will begin on faulty footing and the society risks slipping back into conflict.

---

53. *Id.*, art. 17.

54. *See* Turner, *supra* note 47.

55. One development that runs counter to local prosecutions is the adoption of universal jurisdiction for certain international crimes. That is, a state can assert jurisdiction over certain crimes (e.g., crimes against humanity) on account of the nature of the crime without a factual nexus between the crime and that jurisdiction. Universal jurisdiction, however, seems to have hit its high water mark, and is now being approached more cautiously. In any event, it suffers from some of the drawbacks of the ad hoc tribunals, such as lack of connection to place of the crimes, without the legitimacy that the tribunals have derived from being U.N. organs. For these and other reasons, its role is likely to be limited. *See generally* MITSUE INAZUMI, UNIVERSAL JURISDICTION IN MODERN INTERNATIONAL LAW: EXPANSION OF NATIONAL JURISDICTION FOR PROSECUTING SERIOUS CRIMES UNDER INTERNATIONAL LAW 269 (2005).

56. *Gacaca* refers to a traditional Rwandan method of conflict resolution. When social norms were broken or disputes arose, meetings were convened between the aggrieved parties. Contemporary *Gacaca* jurisdictions deal not with local disputes but with genocide, and are a modified form of the traditional tribunals. *See* William A. Schabas, *Genocide Trials and Gacaca Courts*, 3 J. INT'L. CRIM. JUST. 879 (2005).

57. Ann Davison, *Child Soldiers: No Longer a Minor Incident*, 12 WILLAMETTE J. INT'L L. & DISP. RESOL. 124, 133–34 (2004).

58. *See* Jeanne M. Woods, *Reconciling Reconciliation*, 3 UCLA J. INT'L L. & FOREIGN AFF. 81, 103–04 (1998). It is noteworthy that the South African experience (where full amnesty was possible) had unique features, as illustrated by a South African delegate's comment on the Rule of Law Report: "We are the first to concede that our South African experience may not be applicable to other countries emerging from conflict and the lessons we have learned may not travel well." U.N. SCOR, 59th Sess., 5052d Mtg. at 13, U.N. Doc. S/PV/5052 (Oct. 6, 2004) [hereinafter 5052d Mtg.].

It appears that the world will not return to the approach of the post-war period when leaders committed atrocities with total impunity. What remains unclear is how accountability mechanisms will evolve. Despite their achievements, it is unlikely that there will be new ad hoc tribunals in the near future. Instead, the ICC and hybrid courts will likely come to play the central role in international judicial mechanisms. Because of its limited resources, the ICC will only be able to try the most serious crimes and the leaders of the highest level. Thus, other mechanisms, particularly hybrid courts of various types, will need to be established.

The United Nations will continue to play a key role in establishing these mechanisms. Although the ICC is not a U.N. organ, it was established under U.N. auspices and has a number of important links to the U.N., including the possibility of referrals by the U.N. Security Council,[59] as has now occurred with Darfur.[60] While a number of U.N. Member States, including Security Council members, have not ratified the ICC Statute and, in the case of the United States, actively oppose the ICC, the Darfur example illustrates that in certain cases the ICC will work on the basis of a U.N. mandate. Other international hybrid courts have been established primarily through the efforts of the U.N., either by agreement with the relevant state, as with the Extraordinary Chambers for Cambodia,[61] or under the auspices of U.N. Peacekeeping Operations, as in Kosovo and East Timor.[62]

The U.N.'s role in establishing these international and hybrid courts has been crucial, as no other organization has the legitimacy or the expertise to establish such courts. One need only compare the generally supportive response of the international legal community to the courts established by the U.N. with the critical response that the Iraqi Special Court has received from experts and nongovernmental organizations ("NGOs") alike, to see the credibility and legitimacy that the U.N. bestows upon a process.[63] Since the promotion of peacebuilding and the rule of law are both critical elements of a reformed U.N., the institution must use its credibility and experience to build upon its past work in these areas.

The ad hoc tribunals were created with little thought to their long-term effects and with an inadequate understanding of their relationships with the affected regions.[64] Though subsequent efforts like the SCSL have tried to

---

59. For referral of situations by the Security Council, see Rome Statute, *supra* note 52, art. 13(b). Pursuant to Art. 16 of the Statute, the Security Council can also defer investigations and prosecutions before the Court for a (renewable) period of twelve months. *Id.* art. 16.

60. S.C. Res. 1593, ¶ 1, U.N. Doc. S/RES/1593 (Mar. 31, 2005). Significantly, the United States abstained rather than vetoing this resolution, despite its opposition to the ICC.

61. G.A. Res. 57/228, U.N. Doc. A/RES/57/228 (May 13, 2003).

62. *See* S.C. Res. 1244 ¶ 5, U.N. Doc. S/RES/1244 (June 10, 1999) (approving the deployment of international civil and security presences in Kosovo); S.C. Res 1410, U.N. Doc. S/RES/1410 (May 17, 2002) (discussing the situation in East Timor).

63. *E.g.,* Cherif Bassiouni, *Post-Conflict Justice in Iraq: An Appraisal of the Iraqi Special Tribunal,* 38 CORNELL INT'L L.J. 327 (2005).

64. *See* Tolbert, *supra* note 41.

build on the lessons learned, they have done so unsystematically. It is therefore clear that there are a number of concrete and specific steps that can be
undertaken by the proposed RLAU to buttress accountability mechanisms and
support the rule of law in post-conflict societies. First, given the importance
of the ad hoc tribunals and the truth and reconciliation commissions,[65] the
RLAU should make it a priority to thoroughly study challenges to international justice efforts. What should be the relationship between international
or hybrid courts and truth and reconciliation commissions? What is the best
structure for these courts? What procedures should be adopted, and how can
the procedures and practices of existing international tribunals and hybrid
courts be adapted for the future? What has worked from a procedural point
of view? How might the ICC interact with a hybrid court? What legislative
mechanisms or legislation could be proposed to enhance international cooperation for these courts and tribunals, which have been hampered by the failure
of certain states to cooperate on arrests and other obligations? How can the
Security Council use its powers to be more supportive of these courts and
tribunals?

While many of these topics may be addressed by academics and other interested parties, the RLAU should systematize these studies, commissioning
special reports and research and establishing links with partner organizations.
The RLAU could also play a key role in identifying personnel for future courts.
New categories of lawyers and investigators have emerged in recent years
with the ad hoc tribunals and hybrid courts. There are now legal professionals with experience investigating, prosecuting, defending against, and judging international criminal charges. These individuals have valuable experience that can be used again in other locales. A systematic attempt must be
made to capture their knowledge and to call on them again.

2. Creating a Legal Framework: U.N. Transitional Administrations; Issues of Applicable Law

Basic governance ranks high on the list of problems that a post-conflict
society must address. Without a functioning government, the chaotic situation left by the conflict will invariably lead to human misery and instability
that may expand beyond a country's borders.[66] All post-conflict societies experience, to varying degrees, the breakdown of the institutions of governance.[67]
Thus, in almost all recent post-conflict situations, with the notable exception of Iraq, the U.N. Security Council has established U.N. transitional ad-

---

65. *In larger freedom, supra* note 1.

66. Also, it is clear from recent events—such as in the Democratic Republic of the Congo and Liberia—that instability caused by a collapse of basic governance can lead to regional instability. *See, e.g.,*
Jamie O'Connell, *Here Interest Meets Humanity: How to End the War and Support Reconstruction in Liberia, and
the Case for Modest American Leadership*, 17 HARV. HUM. RTS. J. 207 (2004).

67. *See, e.g.,* Mark A. Drumbl, *Rights, Culture and Crime: The Role of the Rule of Law for the Women of Afghanistan*, 42 COLUM. J. TRANSNAT'L L. 349, 351 (2004).

ministrations to provide a temporary governing authority[68] and has vested them with responsibility for rebuilding the justice system and re-establishing the rule of law. As putative governments, these transitional authorities are the key players in efforts to promote the rule of law in their respective countries.

Transitional authorities face many issues, including the provision of essentials such as adequate food and shelter.[69] However, with respect to governance, the critical issue to be addressed initially is what law is enforceable in the country. While institutional development is important, either a legal code or a set of rules adopted by a transparent process must first exist. This is particularly true in a country that has seen the manipulation of the law by a previous regime or one that has not yet developed legal norms.

Unfortunately, in many instances, the mandates of these transitional administrations have been unclear or hopelessly broad, making it difficult to interpret their authority and the legal framework within which they operate. As one commentator notes, "[Security Council] resolutions are often too vague or too ambiguous to provide secure guidance for post-conflict justice."[70] This is a problem that should be tackled through U.N. reform efforts. The failure to craft clear mandates no doubt arises in part due to the urgency of the conflict situation, but also because lessons from previous situations have not been adequately learned. There are important roles to be played by the new PSO and RLAU, which under the Panel's Report will play the key roles in supporting the Peacebuilding Commission and in implementing U.N. policy. The reform of U.N. transitional administrations is an important part of their work and thus the PSO and RLAU should consider it a priority to examine problems with the mandates in Kosovo, East Timor, and other transitional administrations, and develop model mandates that incorporate the lessons of the past. Naturally, these models will have to be adapted to the particular situation. Nonetheless, the availability of such models will put the Security Council in a better position to construct clearer mandates in the future.

Although a clear mandate is important for establishing the legal powers of a transitional administration, significant issues remain. Respective peacekeeping missions have made efforts to establish or identify the law applicable in their territory, but these efforts have largely been on an ad hoc and temporary basis. This situation leads to confusion regarding the applicable law and to the application of law not in conformity with relevant international human rights norms. Therefore, there is often no proper set of laws for a transi-

---

68. *See* Anna Roberts, *"Soldiering in Hope": United Nations Peacekeeping in Civil Wars*, 35 N.Y.U. J. INT'L L. & POL. 839 (2003).

69. These needs are essential human rights under the International Covenant of Economic, Social and Cultural Rights, *supra* note 14; however, post-conflict societies are not generally in a position to adjudicate these issues through legal systems, which are instead addressed through international relief and development agencies. *See, e.g.,* Ivan Simonovic, *Post–Conflict Peace-Building: The New Trends*, 31 INT'L J. LEGAL INFO. 251 (2003).

70. Carsten Stahn, *Justice Under Transitional Administration: Contours and Critique of a Paradigm*, 27 HOUS. J. INT'L L. 311, 320–24 (2005) (citing Kosovo and East Timor as prime examples); *see also* Hurwitz & Studdard, *supra* note 9, at 7.

[handwritten margin note: no aplicable law — East Timor]

tional authority or government to implement or build upon. This is sometimes referred to as the problem of "applicable law" and was alluded to in both the Secretary General's report on the rule of law in post-conflict societies ("Rule of Law Report") and the report of the Panel on United Nations Peace Operations.[71]

Although there are variations among jurisdictions, certain baseline norms of criminal law and procedure must be implemented for the rule of law to take root. If these basic elements are disregarded in the initial phase of a transitional administration, rule of law efforts will be hampered. Fortunately, certain steps are currently being taken to address the issue of "applicable law" which the U.N. can subsequently build upon. The University of Galway and the United States Institute of Peace have been working with international experts to develop transitional legal codes that "create a coherent legal framework" and which "draw upon lessons learned in past peace operations and are tailored for the specificities of a . . . post-conflict environment."[72] Moreover, they draw from various legal systems and therefore "represent[ ] a cross-cultural model inspired by a variety of the world's legal systems."[73]

These transitional codes contain laws covering such matters as the protection of witnesses, the treatment of victims, and other matters critical to hybrid or local courts dealing with past crimes. There is, therefore, a potentially significant supplementary role that transitional codes can play in supporting local "war crimes" prosecutions in either domestic or hybrid courts.

As of the time of writing, these transitional codes have yet to be made public. However, by providing a ready-made legal framework, such codes potentially represent an important step in assisting post-conflict societies to move toward the rule of law. The efficacy of these codes could be considerably enhanced if the U.N. were to endorse them after appropriate review. Moreover, these codes and other efforts to establish a legal framework in post-conflict societies will need to be regularly updated and adapted to the needs of each country to which they are applied. This seems a role well-suited to the RLAU, as it is in a position to give legitimacy to such codes and, through working with other parties, to update these efforts and ensure that they are adapted accordingly.

The adoption of transitional codes is important, but it must be followed by appropriate elections and the reform of the country's laws. Some such programs

[handwritten: Transitional codes]

71. Panel on United Nations Peace Operations, Aug. 21, 2000, *Report*, U.N. Doc A/55/305-S/2000/809, *available at* http://www.un.org/peace/reports/peace_operations/docs/a_55_305.pdf; Rule of Law Report, *supra* note 6.

72. *See* National University of Ireland, Galway, Model Codes for Post-Conflict Criminal Justice Project, http://www.nuigalaway.ie/human_rights/Projects/model_codes.html (providing a description of the transnational codes project) [Hereinafter Model Codes]. In addition, the U.N. Office on Drugs and Crime has been involved in reviewing a set of comprehensive draft model codes for post-conflict criminal justice; *see generally* Eleventh United Nations Congress on Crime Prevention and Criminal Justice, Bangkok, Thailand, Apr. 18–25, 2005, *Making standards work: fifty years of standard-setting in crime prevention and criminal justice*, *available at* http://daccessdds.un.org/doc/UNDOC/GEN/V05/813/56/PDF/V0581356.pdf?OpenElement.

73. Model Codes, *id.*

are already being implemented by various organizations. For example, the Organization for Security and Co-operation in Europe, the Carter Center, and a variety of other organizations currently monitor elections. Other groups, such as the National Democratic Institute, provide technical assistance for elections, political parties, and the democratic process. Although it is not necessary for the U.N. to further develop this form of technical expertise, it does need to continue to play a role in the timing and sequencing of elections, as elections held before a country is ready may be counter-productive.[74]

Legislative assistance programs are also needed because parliamentarians are often inexperienced and need training and guidance in their new roles. They may also be inclined to resort to counterproductive means. Some may even consider reigniting the embers of the previous conflict. Similarly, government officials frequently have little background experience for their new jobs and need training and support. However, it is notoriously difficult to have an impact in this area, in large part because of corruption and a lack of understanding of local factors.[75]

Numerous NGOs and donors are already involved in providing legislative assistance. The U.N., therefore, need not engage in additional programmatic efforts on this front, but it could serve a useful function by facilitating cooperation and planning between the implementers and by coordinating legislative assistance programs with other rule of law programming, as outlined below.

3. The Next Steps: Building Legal Institutions

The above discussion has focused on the building blocks of rule of law efforts in a post-conflict society: defining the rule of law, dealing with past crimes, and establishing a legal framework. The next analytical step is to examine the essential elements needed to breathe life into the rule of law: establishing an independent judiciary, a vibrant legal profession, and a robust system of legal education. The distinction between the two steps is somewhat artificial, as war crimes trials or related mechanisms will likely proceed alongside programs to support, for example, an independent judiciary. Furthermore, efforts to hold war criminals accountable for their actions can and should assist in other aims, such as developing the legal profession and the judiciary. However, for analytical purposes, the topics discussed below follow sequentially from the discussion above. It is true that other areas critical to the establishment of the rule of law are not addressed here, notably policing, law enforcement, and anti-corruption programs.[76] However, they are separate conceptually from the approach taken herein, which focuses on the legal

---

74. Carothers, *supra* note 17, at 123–55 ("It is true that a rush to elections is not always advisable in transitional countries.").

75. *Id.* at 177–87 ("If asked to name the area of democracy assistance that most often falls short of its goals, I would have to point to legislative assistance.").

76. *See, e.g.*, William Burke-White, *A Community of Courts: Towards a System of International Criminal Law Enforcement*, 24 MICH. J. INT'L L. 1 (2002).

norms and institutions necessary for the creation, interpretation, and application of the law, as opposed to its enforcement.

While the following subjects bear a closer relationship to the discipline of development[77] than the earlier discussion, and often apply not only to post-conflict societies but also to underdeveloped countries generally,[78] they are nonetheless essential for post-conflict societies. For example, it is axiomatic that without functioning courts and a judiciary system, there can be no rule of law. An independent judiciary is therefore at the heart of establishing the rule of law for a post-conflict society, just as it is for a developing country. Because developing and post-conflict societies often face similar obstacles, it would be unwise to make false distinctions between traditional rule of law development and specific rule of law efforts in societies recovering from conflict. At the same time, we must take into account the special problems that post-conflict societies face.

The key institutions needed for the protection of the rule of law are not difficult to identify. However, they are exceedingly hard to build or re-build. In doing so, the key challenge is not so much the question of court buildings and technology, or even the passage of relevant laws, but rather of changing the attitudes of legal professionals and society at large toward these essential institutions. Furthermore, programs must try to import a "cluster of values" that underlie the rule of law and not simply adhere to some rote definition of law. Outside assistance cannot impose these values. These groups must find ways to facilitate the development of the rule of law rather than impose it. Bearing this in mind, the discussion turns to the key institutions: the judiciary, the legal profession, and legal education.

C. The Role of the Bench and the Bar

Strengthening judicial independence is not merely a common focus of strategies for the promotion of the rule of law in post-conflict societies. Frequently, it is also the starting point for efforts to establish law and order and to ensure accountability for human rights abuses and war crimes. An independent judiciary is a central pillar of the rule of law and in many ways a guarantor of the fundamental human rights of individuals and groups. Moreover, an independent judiciary that administers justice and resolves disputes in a peaceful, predictable, and transparent manner enables good governance,

---

77. *See* Agnes Hurwitz, *Towards Enhanced Legitimacy of Rule of Law Programs Multidimensional Peace Operations*, Workshop paper at the European Society of International Law Forum on International Law (May 26–28, 2005), *available at* http://www.esil-sedi.org/english/pdf/Hurwitz.pdf ("[S]upport for rule of law institutions has been part of development policy for much longer than is usually acknowledged, hidden under the guise of public sector reforms or good governance and democratization.").

78. *See* Eric Jensen, *The Rule of Law and Judicial Reform: The Political Economy of Diverse Institutional Patterns and Reformers*, *in* BEYOND COMMON KNOWLEDGE: EMPIRICAL APPROACHES TO THE RULE OF LAW, at 336, 345–46 (Erik G. Jensen & Thomas C. Heller eds., 2003) (identifying three waves of law reform efforts: reform of administrative organs, the law and development movement, and current efforts, which include for the first time post-conflict societies).

economic development, and social equality.[79] The absence of an independent judiciary, capable of applying the law without discrimination and holding state authorities as well as individuals accountable for crimes and abuses of power, can threaten the success of other aspects of post-conflict reconstruction and reform. In this way, justice sector reforms that promote judicial independence defuse tensions that could otherwise reignite violence and give rise to authoritarian rule.

In 1985, the U.N. promulgated a concise set of universally recognized principles of judicial independence that describe the core elements essential to any modern judicial system. The United Nations Basic Principles on the Independence of the Judiciary ("BPIJ"),[80] was endorsed by the U.N. General Assembly in two resolutions.[81] The General Assembly thus affirmed the central role judges play in the administration of justice. It is imperative that post-conflict societies put into effect the structural safeguards and other guarantees discussed in the BPIJ, particularly those that facilitate the judiciary's independence from all other branches of government, most notably the executive branch. These safeguards include the constitutionalization of judicial independence, the prohibition of improper interference in judicial decision-making, the explicit recognition of jurisdiction over judicial matters, the authority to decide issues of statutory competence, and the right of judges to form associations to promote the interests of the profession and its independence. The BPIJ also outlines international standards on the qualifications, selection, and training of judges, imposes conditions of service and tenure, and creates standards for discipline, suspension, and removal of judges from the bench.

Considerable resources have been devoted to promoting judicial independence around the world in accordance with the international standards expressed in the BPIJ and similar documents.[82] Yet significant challenges remain. This is, in part, because in many post-conflict societies and countries with authoritarian legacies, the judiciary was often used to protect the parochial interests of ruling elites rather than the rights of the general population.

---

79. *See, e.g.*, Jeremy Pope, TRANSPARENCY INTERNATIONAL SOURCEBOOK 2000, Ch. 8, *available at* http://www.transparency.org/sourcebook/08.html (last visited Mar. 11, 2006) ("An independent, impartial and informed judiciary holds a central place in the realization of just, honest, open and an accountable government."). *See also* Denis Galligan, *Principal Institutions and Mechanisms of Accountability, in* COMPREHENSIVE LEGAL AND JUDICIAL DEVELOPMENT: TOWARDS AN AGENDA FOR A JUST AND EQUITABLE SOCIETY IN THE 21ST CENTURY 34 (Van Puymbroeck ed., 2001) ("Judicial supervision of the administration is an essential feature of a system of government and administration based on the rule of law.").

80. *See generally* Seventh U.N. Congress on the Prevention of Crime and the Treatment of Offenders, Aug. 26–Sept. 6, 1985, *Basic Principles on the Independence of the Judiciary, available at* http://www.unhchr.ch/html/menu3/b/h_comp50.htm.

81. *See* G.A. Res. 40/32, U.N. Doc. A/RES/40/32 (Nov. 29, 1985), *available at* http://www.un.org/documents/ga/res/40/a40r032.htm; *see also* G.A. Res. 40/146, U.N. Doc. A/RES/40/146 (Dec. 13, 1985), *available at* http://www.un.org/documents/ga/res/40/a40r146.htm.

82. *See, e.g.*, The Judicial Group of Strengthening Judicial Integrity, *The Bangalore Principles of Judicial Conduct* (Nov. 25–26, 2002), *available at* http://www.unodc.org/pdf/crime/corruption/judicial_group/Bangalore_principles.pdf.

Therefore, rule of law reform strategies in these transitional environments must continue to focus on promulgating and implementing constitutional and legislative frameworks that secure judicial powers. With some input in the selection process from the judiciary itself through judicial qualification commissions, judicial appointments should be made on the basis of objective criteria in order to foster the selection of independent, impartial, and well-qualified judges. Similarly, judges should be appointed for fixed terms that provide guaranteed tenure. Justice sector reform efforts should also seek to raise the qualifications of judges and judicial personnel through training, including the establishment of judicial training centers. Measures must be adopted to provide the judiciary with adequate resources and sufficient judicial personnel to manage caseloads and dispose of cases in a timely and efficient manner. Finally, efforts must be made to strengthen the role of judicial associations that promote the interests of the profession and encourage compliance with ethical standards.

These standards and procedures are particularly important in a post-conflict situation, where formerly warring groups do not trust one another to act in accordance with local professional practices. Therefore, it is important that reform-minded judges and those who reject nationalist or divisive approaches are aware of these standards and can use them appropriately. Much more could be done to support such judges through training on the BPIJ and other international standards. Moreover, the hybrid court model, discussed above in relation to war crimes cases, could also be utilized for other types of proceedings. In Bosnia-Herzegovina, this approach has been adopted with respect to organized crime cases, with international judges and prosecutors working alongside national judges,[83] just as it is done in war crimes cases and much like it was done in the Human Rights Chamber. The RLAU should evaluate the success of this endeavor and examine the possibilities of using international judges in other cases. In principle, nothing prohibits this approach, provided it can be shown to have substantial benefits.

An independent judiciary, widely considered *conditio sine qua non* of promoting the rule of law, is hardly the sole institutional requirement in this endeavor. Rule of law experts, local reformers, and other stakeholders rightly emphasize that an independent judiciary and mechanisms such as special tribunals and truth commissions are necessary in ensuring accountability for war crimes and human rights abuses in post-conflict societies.[84] However, focus on the judiciary must not come at the expense of establishing other institutions necessary for promoting, and perhaps more importantly sustaining, the

---

83. *See* High Representative's Decision Appointing an International Prosecutor for the "Organized Crime Chamber" (Feb. 24, 2005), http://www.ohr.int/decisions/judicialrdec/default.asp?content_id=34120.

84. Hansjorg Strohmeyer, *Collapse and Reconstruction of a Judicial System: The United Nations Missions in Kosovo and East Timor*, 95 AM. J. INT'L L. 46, 60 (2001) ("[A] functioning judicial system can positively affect reconciliation and confidence-building efforts within often highly traumatized post crises societies, not least because it can bring to justice those responsible for grave violations of international humanitarian and human rights law.").

rule of law in post-conflict societies. A more comprehensive approach to accomplishing these goals must take other institutions and legal professionals into account, most notably criminal defense lawyers and public defenders.

In addition to judges, lawyers are the main actors in a country's legal system and are an important means by which individuals or groups gain access to justice and resolve disputes in a peaceful and transparent fashion. According to the U.N. Basic Principles on the Role of Lawyers ("BPRL"), lawyers play a vital role in "furthering the ends of justice and the public interest."[85] An independent legal profession comprised of a cadre of well-trained and ethical lawyers can ensure due process and protect fundamental rights by pursuing the necessary remedies when these rights have been infringed upon. Thus, lawyers can facilitate the public's confidence in the fairness and efficacy of the legal system, which is essential not only to the formal and institutional development of the rule of law, but also to instilling the values that make up the informal aspects of the rule of law in a democratic society. Moreover, as members of the broader legal profession as a whole, lawyers can contribute to the law reform process and serve as advocates for judicial sector reform and judicial independence.

Like the BPIJ, the BPRL sets forth international standards for establishing and safeguarding the independence and status of lawyers. That document also articulates standards for ensuring effective access of all persons to the legal services that they provide, including legal aid for the indigent and other vulnerable segments of the population. The BPRL also stresses the importance of the freedom of expression and association for lawyers, and outlines certain guarantees—such as protection from intimidation and improper interference—that help ensure lawyers are able to effectively carry out their responsibilities.[86] In addition, these principles emphasize standards that lawyers and professional associations of lawyers should abide by in areas such as education and training, legal services and representation, ethics and discipline, and promotion of the interests of the profession itself. The BPRL was first adopted in 1990 by the Eighth U.N. Congress on the Prevention of Crime and the Treatment of Offenders, and was welcomed by a U.N. General Assembly resolution calling states "to take them into account within the framework of their national legislation and practice."[87]

The BPRL principles are not legally binding on members of the U.N. Rather, the document is an expression of the international community's view on the role of lawyers in a democratic, law-based society. The potential value of the BPRL is in providing guidance to state authorities, the legal profession, and civil society organizations in drafting laws on the legal profession—

---

85. Eighth U.N. Congress on the Prevention of Crime and the Treatment of Offenders, Aug. 27–Sept. 7, 1990, *Basic Principles on the Role of Lawyers*, ¶ 10, *available at* http://www.unhchr.ch/html/menu3/b/h_comp44.htm.

86. *Id.* ¶¶ 16–23.

87. U.N. G.A. Res. 45/166, ¶ 15, U.N. Doc. A/RES/45/166 (Dec. 18, 1990), *available at* http://www.un.org/documents/ga/res/40/a40r146.htm.

such as criminal and civil procedure codes, laws on advocates and lawyers, and standards on legal ethics—and ensuring the implementation of this legislative framework so that individuals have access to effective and affordable legal representation. Combined with the BPIJ, the BPRL can be used by internal and external actors alike to assess the progress toward the institutional development of the rule of law in emerging democracies and post-conflict societies. In both environments, the legal profession and lawyers often face considerable challenges in fulfilling their role in advancing the rule of law.

The unfortunate reality is that lawyers do not automatically enjoy the independence and status afforded to them by these international standards. Lawyers in many post-conflict societies, as well as those in former authoritarian countries, must first overcome structural impediments to the independence of their profession, including the existence of legislative frameworks that relegate the profession to a subservient position in a legal hierarchy dominated by the state prosecutor. In other instances, lawyers may be subject to excessive regulation in the form of licensing requirements and disciplinary rules overseen by the Ministry of Justice, as opposed to an independent national or regional bar association. Safeguards necessary to ensure effective legal representation and parity with the prosecution, including lawyer-client confidentiality and access to information, are often also absent. Moreover, it is not uncommon for lawyers to be harassed and intimidated when representing clients who have fallen out of favor with the authorities. In some cases, nonstate actors such as organized crime organizations, warlords, and ethnic-based militias can also improperly influence and corrupt lawyers.

Given the above discussion, it is not surprising that lawyers sometimes function more like cogs in a machine designed to protect state, political, tribal or other parochial interests rather than serving as zealous defenders of their clients and the law. The blame cannot be placed solely on state authorities such as the Ministry of Justice. In many cases, the legal profession has been ineffective or incapable of regulating itself and improving standards for the qualification, integrity, and effectiveness of its members. Another problem is that bar associations may split along ethnic lines. For example, in post-conflict Bosnia-Herzegovina, it was difficult to form bar associations that encompassed all three ethnic groups involved in the conflict. This difficulty was exacerbated by the political division of the country—pursuant to the Dayton Accords— into two entities, thus giving credence to those who opposed an integrated bar association.[88] In such cases, intervention through U.N. or other transitional authorities may be necessary. However, these issues are sometimes generational and progress may ultimately depend on the emergence of a next generation of lawyers less influenced by the passions and hatreds of the conflict.

---

88. Based on observations of one of the Authors from interactions and meetings with lawyers and bar association officials in the former Yugoslavia.

D. Legal Education and Training

The independence and status of legal professionals in post-conflict societies, much like in former authoritarian countries, are often undermined by the fact that many legal professionals, including both lawyers and judges, suffer from inadequate substantive knowledge, practical skills, and access to information required of the profession.[89] A law school graduate may possess a diploma, but this does not ensure that he or she has acquired the practical skills in legal research, writing, and reasoning, or the substantive knowledge of basic areas of domestic law required to perform his or her professional duties. Moreover, advanced training and continuing legal education for judges and lawyers is often lacking. As a result, familiarity with significant legal developments and specialized topics of law, including aspects of international human rights and humanitarian law, is particularly difficult to come by once someone enters the profession. If efforts to promote the rule of law in post-conflict societies are to succeed, judges and lawyers must be better prepared to practice law, to address the needs of society and their fellow citizens, and to promote the interests of the profession. Reforming legal education—both initial and advanced training—should therefore be a part of comprehensive rule of law promotion strategies.

Legal education reform is a complex undertaking, requiring the establishment of law school accreditation standards, the introduction of new courses into traditional curricula, and the improvement of teaching methods. This type of institutional reform requires considerable resources and is difficult even under optimal conditions. With international support and guidance, some progress is being made. However, in many fragile states seeking to overcome the legacies of authoritarian rule or armed conflict, legal education remains an ongoing challenge. One of the principal reasons is that legal education is largely unregulated by ministries of education and justice. As a result, there has been a proliferation of unaccredited law schools, many of which do not provide adequate education and training in the law. Also, many law schools continue to favor compulsory curricula comprised of courses in legal theory, constitutional law, civil law, and criminal law. There is now a slow experimentation with electives in areas such as international law, human rights, refugee law, gender issues, alternative dispute resolution, legal ethics, and other practice-oriented courses. But such experimentation is severely limited by insufficient resources and expertise. Lecture-based instruction also remains the norm, although legal clinics, moot court, and mock-trial activities are increasingly employed as means to increase the practical skills of students so that they are better prepared to enter the profession and to assume their responsibilities in rendering legal assistance and administering justice fairly and efficiently.

---

89. Mark Dietrich, *Three Foundations of the Rule of Law: Education, Advocacy, and Judicial Reform*, in LAW IN TRANSITION 57 (2002), *available at* http://www.ebrd.com/pubs/legal/5410.pdf. *See generally* Christopher P. M. Waters, *Post-Conflict Legal Education*, 10 J. CONFLICT & SECURITY L. 101, 101–19 (2005) (describing how armed conflict and war affect legal education).

III. U.N. REFORM AND THE RULE OF LAW IN POST-CONFLICT SOCIETIES

A. *The Challenges*

The difficulties in implementing the various programs discussed above should not be underestimated. As the Secretary-General has said: "Restoring the capacity and legitimacy of national institutions is a long-term undertaking."[90] Even in the context of less devastated countries, Thomas Carothers finds that "what stands out . . . is how difficult and often disappointing [rule of law assistance] work is."[91] In post-conflict societies with no functioning judiciary (or, in some cases, with complete lawlessness), there is often very little upon which the rule of law can be built.

Peacekeeping missions have faced daunting tasks in reestablishing order and basic infrastructure,[92] making mistakes and arguably undermining efforts to establish the rule of law. For example, the U.N. Mission in Kosovo ("UNMIK") has been criticized for failing to take "a coherent approach to criminal justice reform," leading to the conclusion that "the failure is so profound that it puts at risk the transition as a whole."[93] UNMIK has also struggled with the question of the applicable law for criminal matters, a process that continued for years.[94] Other criticisms include, *inter alia*, ill-conceived training for judges, inadequate measures to protect witnesses, and poor use of international judges and prosecutors.[95] Finally, UNMIK and other missions have been faulted for failing to consider adequately local sensibilities, thus imposing their will in a manner that some have characterized as violating human rights norms and thus undermining the rule of law.[96]

Whether the criticism of UNMIK and other transitional administrations[97] is fully justified can be debated. However, there has generally been a lack of coherent planning regarding the judicial sector in U.N. missions.[98] This is,

---

90. *Rule of Law Report, supra* note 6, ¶ 27.

91. Carothers, *supra* note 17, at 170.

92. For example, UNMIK was tasked with "govern[ing] an entire province and re-establish[ing] a functioning public sector in the midst of substantial destruction, communal devastation, and the exodus of the former regime." David Marshall & Shelley Inglis, *The Disempowerment of Human Rights–Based Justice in the United Nations Mission in Kosovo*, 16 HARV. HUM. RTS. J. 95, 95 (2003).

93. *Id.* at 96. This criticism is echoed in Stahn, *supra* note 70, at 327 ("The U.N. failed, however, to develop a coherent approach to justice in the first phase of its engagement in mission.").

94. Marshall & Inglis, *supra* note 92, at 115–17.

95. *Id.* at 116–46. Marshall and Inglis are critical of UNMIK's approach on a variety of other rule of law and human rights issues and conclude that "the international intervention in postwar Kosovo has provided some sobering lessons in the area of criminal justice and human rights from which peace-building missions should learn." *Id.* at 144. *See also* Wendy Betts, Scott Carlson & Gregory Gisvold, *The Post-conflict Transitional Administration of Kosovo and the Lessons-learned in Efforts to Establish a Judiciary and Rule of Law*, 22 MICH. J. INT'L L. 371 (2001) (providing an overview of efforts to establish the rule of law in post-conflict Kosovo).

96. Frederic Megret & Florian Hoffmann, *The U.N. as a Human Rights Violator? Some Reflections on the United Nations Changing Human Rights Responsibilities*, 25 HUM. RTS. Q. 314, 334–35 (2003).

97. Similar criticisms are made of other U.N. Missions. *See, e.g.*, Stahn, *supra* note 70, at 333–38 (discussing U.N. Missions in East Timor, Afghanistan, and Iraq).

98. *See* Hurwitz & Studdard, *supra* note 9, at 2–4.

to some extent, understandable given the inherent difficulties, but the poor planning also starkly highlights the lack of coherent strategies, coupled with an insufficient knowledge of local conditions. Some of these issues can be more readily addressed than others. For example, transitional codes can partly remedy the problem of applicable law. Other problems, such as the protection of witnesses, pose difficult challenges, but there is considerable experience at the ad hoc tribunals and in national systems that could be utilized to address these issues.[99] At a more fundamental level, the U.N. must address the lack of coherent prior planning in these missions, which has frequently led to improvisation. While it is difficult to foresee precisely where crises will arise, it is less difficult to identify recurrent issues. Future missions must also draw lessons from past experiences.

This lack of planning is hardly limited to the U.N. Mark Malloch Brown, then administrator of the U.N. Development Program, noted: "[C]ooperation among donors is too often the exception rather than the rule resulting in a failure to accumulate information and lessons learned . . . [with donors] often engaged in overlapping or contradictory projects . . . ."[100] Other examples abound[101] because the anarchic situation in a post-conflict society is often mirrored in a chaotic situation among the various donors and implementing groups. This is particularly true at the start-up phase of peacekeeping operations. At this stage, donors, NGOs, the World Bank, regional banks, private sector contractors, and the U.N. itself may all overlap on rule of law issues. The potential for duplication is immense. As one commentator puts it, "The issue of coordination or the lack thereof, is one of the most recurrent problems of post-conflict peacebuilding, from Guatemala to Cambodia to Sierra Leone . . . ."[102] At present there is no formal arrangement to provide a forum for addressing inter-organizational coordination.

There are also issues related to the design of programs intended to assist the development of the rule of law. These issues have been identified in various places, including the Rule of Law Report,[103] and they apply with equal force to both post-conflict societies and other developing countries. A particular problem is the issue of designing programs that fit local needs, rather than the adoption of a "cookie cutter" approach that uses a standard model regardless of the nature of conflict or the society in question. It is important to note that while programs obviously must take local conditions into account, prior experience can also lead to the development of models and approaches

---

99. *See, e.g.,* Andreea Vesa, *Protective Measures for Witnesses and the Rights of the Accused,* CEELI Discussion Papers Series (June 15, 2003), *available at* http://www.abanet.org/ceeli/publications/conceptpapers/icty_wit_prot.pdf (discussing the ICTY's experiences with witness protection measures, and its influence on international criminal law).

100. 5052d Mtg., *supra* note 58, at 4.

101. *See, e.g.,* Carothers *supra* note 17, at 165.

102. Hurwitz & Studdard, *supra* note 9, at 10.

103. *Rule of Law Report, supra* note 6, ¶¶ 8–10.

that apply to numerous places. Donors and experts should not be discouraged from drawing on previous experience.

There are also difficulties with the use of international experts, on whom many NGOs and governments rely. Such experts are sometimes seen as "parachuting" into a situation, giving their pre-packaged presentation, staying in the best hotels available, making little effort to speak the local language, and then leaving. While this is clearly a caricature and is belied by the many dedicated experts who have given valuable and unselfish service,[104] there are real reasons for concern. First, although international expertise is vital, it is important that the society feel that the process is "theirs" and not the property of outsiders. If the process is seen as primarily imposed or created by foreign donors and experts, the programs are unlikely to be successful. Moreover, if the expert is simply trying to "transplant" his or her system into another country, he can create confusion and can, in effect, undermine the rule of law. This was certainly one of the key problems with the law and development movement and continues to be an issue with some American and other Western NGOs.[105]

In other instances, attempts are made to revamp a country's law by moving from a civil law tradition to a common law system. This happened recently in Bosnia-Herzegovina,[106] with regard to criminal procedure. The result was that lawyers and judges must now deal both with the usual issues of a post-conflict society and also with learning new procedural law. While there are practices such as "telephone justice"—taking instructions from the party boss—that clearly need to be addressed, fundamental changes in existing legal systems should be approached warily. This does not mean that all changes in procedure should be avoided. A key strategy in the reform process must be to reform the laws, but not necessarily to change the underlying approach in that system. For example, in Russia, a number of important reforms were introduced to the criminal procedure code, shifting considerable powers from prosecutors to judges, without changing the system to an adversarial system.[107] The point to be stressed here is that experts must find ways to reform the system without introducing so much change that legal professionals are overwhelmed.

Another ongoing debate among organizations working in the rule of law arena involves "top down" versus "bottom up"[108] approaches. The "top down" model is characterized by reform of state institutions, with a focus on the judi-

104. See generally Louis Aucoin, The Role of International Experts in Constitution-Making, 5.1 GEO. J. INT'L AFF. 89 (2004), available at http://journal.georgetown.edu/Issues/ws04/ws04_le_aucoin.html.

105. Carothers, supra note 7.

106. See Helke Gramcko, Can US-Type Court Management Approaches Work in Civil Law Systems? Experiences From the Balkans and Beyond, 11(1) EUR. J. ON CRIM. L. POL'Y & RES. 97 (2005); The Human Rights Center and the International Human Rights Law Clinic, University of California, Berkeley, & the Centre for Human Rights, University of Sarajevo, Justice, Accountability, and Social Reconstruction: An Interview Study of Bosnian Judges and Prosecutors, 18 BERKELEY J. INT'L L. 102, 136–40 (2000).

107. See American Bar Association, Central European and Eurasian Law Initiative, CEELI in Russia (2005), http://www.abanet.org/ceeli/countries/russia/program.html.

108. See Carothers, supra note 17, at 157–251.

ciary, bar associations, prosecution services, legislatures, and related institutions. In contrast, the "bottom up" approach focuses on "civil society," broadly
defined as non-state and non-private business actors such as NGOs.[109] While
the scope of NGOs is broad, in the context of rule of law assistance they are
usually limited to such organizations as victims' groups, legal reform advocacy
groups, and groupings of lawyers such as women lawyers, young lawyers or law
students, and human rights advocates.

There are strong advocates for both approaches. The "bottom up" approach,
utilizing civil society actors, has arisen in part because of frustrations experienced in dealing with state institutions, which often employ individuals with
no interest in reform. The idea is that such civil society groups will pressure
the institutions to change and develop while younger individuals in these
groups gain valuable experience, perhaps eventually joining the institutions
and providing the impetus for reform. These civil society groups provide immense energy and commitment to change on a number of fronts including
women's rights, gender crimes and human trafficking, corruption, environmental issues, and human rights. These issues are important to the development of the rule of law, but are unlikely to have much traction in state institutions. Moreover, there is inherent value in having impassioned advocates
pushing on these issues.

In recent years, there has been more focus on and more funding available
for civil society groups, who nonetheless often struggle with long-term sustainability and impact. Others, such as victims' groups, may initially play an
important role in efforts to address war crimes but lose significance as time
passes. Compared to the "top down" approach, civil society efforts may have
a more indirect effect on the rule of law. However, in many instances the "top
down" approach may be difficult if the state institutions are themselves not
amenable to change or reform. The approach followed may depend on the
state of the particular country and its institutions. Thus, the debate between
the two approaches is a false choice in many respects, as elements of both
approaches may ultimately prove necessary. The relevant issues concern how
the two approaches may be utilized in a particular situation. Thus, it is important to examine how donors and others involved in reconstructing the
legal systems make their choices and interact with one another. Such coordination could address such common problems as multiple donors over-funding a
popular NGO at the expense of more pressing needs.

There are many difficult issues to be addressed in terms of rule of law assistance in a post-conflict or developing country. Many of those issues are
substantive, but there are also important methodological issues. These include

---

109. *See* Gordon White, *Civil Society, Democratization, and Development (I): Clearing the Analytical
Ground*, 1(3) DEMOCRATIZATION 379 (1994) (defining civil society as "an associational realm between
state and family populated by organizations which are separate from the state, enjoy autonomy in relation
to the state and are formed voluntarily by members of society to protect or extend their interests or values" (*quoted in* Carothers, *supra* note 17, at 209)).

planning for both the short-term and the long-term, coordinating between donors, reconciling approaches between different donors, addressing problems relating to the use of international experts, and ensuring that local solutions are not sidelined by the "one size fits all" approaches of some donors and assistance providers. The next questions concern which groups are providing different types of assistance and what role a reformed U.N. might play in addressing these difficult and complex issues.

B. The Other Primary Actors

As previously noted, numerous organizations and actors are engaged in rule of law promotion in post-conflict societies. In addition to various U.N. agencies, these include other international and multilateral organizations, donor governments, development banks and international financial institutions, and NGOs.[110] Increased international focus on rule of law promotion as an integral aspect of post-conflict reconstruction has spawned a virtual rule of law industry over the past two decades. Many actors, both public and private, now offer assistance to countries seeking to reform their legal and judicial systems by providing funding, resources, and technical expertise in drafting legislative frameworks and developing institutions to support rule of law programs. In addition to rebuilding the institutions of modern justice systems, these actors can also be instrumental in fostering the values and attitudes that make up a "rule of law culture" within a society, and in creating a demand for the rule of law at the political and grassroots levels.[111]

Individual governments, acting through their foreign assistance agencies, play a particularly significant role in rule of law promotion. This often takes the form of providing funding for legislative and institutional reforms. Organizations such as the United States Agency for International Development, the United Kingdom's Department for International Development, and the German Agency for Technical Assistance, also provide bilateral technical assistance aimed at improving legislative drafting, raising the qualifications of legal professionals and law enforcement, and introducing material resources and modern technologies for more efficient administration of justice.

Similar initiatives are pursued on a multilateral basis by international organizations and financial institutions, including the Organization for Security and Cooperation in Europe, the Council of Europe, the European Union, the Organization for Economic Cooperation and Development, the European Bank for Reconstruction and Development, the Asian Development Bank, the World Trade Organization, and the World Bank. Aside from funding rule of law pro-

---

110. Although the presence of many of these actors in a country often provides needed support and resources for rule of law promotion, it can also make for what has been referred to as a "circus atmosphere." *See* Mary Theisen & Eliot Goldberg, The Stanley Foundation, *Post Conflict Justice: The Role of the International Community* 7 (1997), *available at* http://www.stanleyfoundation.org/reports/Vantage97.pdf.

111. Ronald J. Daniles & Michael J. Trebilcock, *The Political Economy of Rule of Law Reform in Developing Countries*, 26 MICH. J. INT'L L. 99 (2004).

grams, these organizations are also able to focus the attention of local stake-holders and policy-makers on specific rule of law issues like combating corruption, strengthening alternative dispute resolution in both commercial and non-commercial matters, and improving access to justice for minorities and vulnerable segments of society. Through its Conflict Prevention and Reconstruction Union and the Post-Conflict Fund, the World Bank supports post-conflict reconstruction efforts of governments, NGOs, and U.N. agencies in dozens of countries such as Afghanistan, Cambodia, Kosovo, Sierra Leone, Timor-Leste, and the Palestinian Territories.

NGOs are also central to rule of law promotion efforts in post-conflict societies. Many of the day-to-day operational aspects of rule of law promotion are carried out by NGOs, which typically receive their funding from governments and international organizations. In contrast to their donors, which often operate through political and diplomatic channels, NGOs such as the American Bar Association Central European and Eurasian Law Initiative ("ABA/CEELI"), Freedom House, Transparency International, International Development Law Organization, and the International Center for Transitional Justice ("ICTJ"), mostly work on rule of law promotion and related activities at the grassroots or "bottom up" level. Some advocacy-oriented organizations use civic education programs, war crimes documentation, and "naming and shaming" campaigns to educate and mobilize the public in order to hold governments accountable for violating human rights. The ICTJ, for instance, has facilitated dialogue among civil society activists and supported public consultation initiatives on questions of justice and accountability in Afghanistan, Indonesia, and Sri Lanka. While there has been a tendency among NGOs to work in opposition to governments, it is increasingly common for NGOs to cooperate with public authorities in rule of law promotion and justice initiatives such as the establishment of truth and reconciliation commissions. However, most NGO activities still involve working with civil society organizations and fostering relationships with local stakeholders in order to build the capacity and sustainability of institutions like professional associations of lawyers and judges, law school faculties, judicial training centers, and civil society organizations.

Part of this work also involves diagnostic assessments of key aspects of the rule of law which can be used by civil society organizations and governments, as well as by the international donor community, to develop reform strategies and initiatives to promote the rule of law. For instance, ABA/CEELI has developed and implemented the Judicial Reform Index ("JRI") and the Legal Profession Reform Index ("LPRI") to assess judicial independence and the status and effectiveness of the defense bars in conflict-affected societies such as Kosovo, Bosnia, Macedonia, and Tajikistan.[112] Similarly, the International Legal Assistance Consortium ("ILAC") mobilizes teams of international experts in

---

112. *See generally* American Bar Association, Central European and Eurasian Law Initiative, http://www.abaceeli.org.

rule of law to assess post-conflict justice systems and to make recommendations to host governments and others on types of assistance that is needed to reestablish a functioning legal system and judiciary.[113] Following its 2003 assessment mission to Iraq, ILAC has provided trainings on international humanitarian and human rights law to Iraqi judges, prosecutors, and lawyers as part of its support for the justice sector in Iraq.

C. A New Role for the United Nations

The blueprint for U.N. reform has been established in the Report of the Secretary-General's High-level Panel on Threats, Challenges and Change ("the Report"). The Report notes that there is currently no place in the U.N. system "to assist countries in their transition from war to peace," and proposes a Peacebuilding Commission to take on that and related tasks.[114] In proposing this, the Report first described some of the organization's greatest strengths:

> The [U.N.'s] unique role in this area arises from its international legitimacy; the impartiality of its personnel; its ability to draw on personnel with broad cultural understanding and experience of a wider range of administrative systems, including the developing world; and its recent experience in organizing transitional administration and transitional authority operations.[115]

The Report proposes that the Commission, *inter alia*, assist transitions from war to peace and "marshal and sustain the efforts of the international community in post-conflict peacebuilding over whatever period may be necessary."[116]

To support the Commission, the Report has proposed that the PSO be established in the U.N. Secretariat, with a relatively small staff and an interagency advisory board, chaired, quite appropriately, by the Chair of the U.N. Development Group. The Report also makes reference to developing "a robust capacity-building mechanism for rule-of-law assistance."[117] Accordingly, the Secretary-General has indicated that the RLAU will be located in the PSO.[118] At the time of writing, few other details are publicly available about the plans for the RLAU. The comments that follow are, thus, somewhat speculative.[119]

---

113. ILAC is composed of over thirty organizations from around the world. These include member organizations such as the International Bar Association, International Commission of Jurists, the Union Internationale de Avocats, Inter-American Bar Association, Arab Lawyers Union, Pan African Lawyers Union, and the Conseil Consultatif de Bearreau Europeens. For more information on ILAC, see http://www.ilac.se.

114. *High Level Panel Report, supra* note 1, ¶ 261.

115. *Id.*

116. *Id.*, ¶ 264.

117. *Id.*, ¶ 177.

118. The Secretary-General, *Report of the Secretary-General: Strengthening the U.N. Crime Prevention and Criminal Justice Programme*, U.N. GAOR, 59th Sess., U.N. Doc. A/59/205.

119. *See* Hurwitz & Studdard, *supra* note 9, at 12 ("[RLAU] should be given a leading role in policy

The creation of the RLAU is to be welcomed, although given the enormity of the task it is disconcerting that the present plans call for a relatively small unit. In U.N. parlance, a "unit" generally includes around ten staff members. The Report envisions the entire PSO to be comprised of about twenty posts. Hopefully, with the high profile of peacebuilding and rule of law assistance both in the Report and in general discussions regarding U.N. reform, these resource issues will be given further consideration. If these critically important areas are under-resourced, there will be significant cause for concern with respect to the seriousness of the U.N.'s commitment to reform. Moreover, if staffing is limited, the U.N. is likely to continue in a more ancillary role in rule of law assistance, rather than the robust one envisaged by the Report.

Assuming sufficient resources are available, the U.N. is in a position to play a significantly enhanced role in rule of law support. It has, as the Report has identified, unique assets such as its neutrality, the geographical breadth and experience of its staff, and its international legitimacy. These are features that no government, donor, or NGO possesses. In addition to these factors, peacekeeping missions are conducted under U.N. auspices and, therefore, many of the transitional justice issues are already clearly within the U.N.'s portfolio. International and hybrid tribunals are the creation or partial creation of the U.N. The U.N. is thus also well-positioned to address issues relating to these tribunals and to provide them with support. The case for active U.N. involvement on these issues becomes even stronger once we consider other U.N. agencies with mandates covering human rights, development, and other post-conflict and development-related matters.

However, U.N. involvement also has certain disadvantages. The U.N. can be a highly bureaucratic organization that is difficult to mobilize and that suffers from political paralysis when its members do not work in harmony. Its "management culture" and internal accountability mechanisms have sometimes come under severe criticism.[120] Moreover, in certain circumstances, some of the greatest strengths of the U.N. can become weaknesses. For example, the diversity of its staff can sometimes lead to lack of focus and conflicting approaches that confuse the very domestic professionals that they are meant to assist.

With these assets and liabilities, what should be the strategic plan of the new PSO and the RLAU? One place to start is by assessing the lessons of the past and developing models which address the difficult issues that post-conflict societies face. This includes a thorough understanding of accountability mechanisms, including the ad hoc tribunals, hybrid tribunals, and truth commissions. Until these past efforts have been credibly assessed, future decisions

---

development and coordination of rule of law assistance, and should contribute to the U.N.'s adoption of a coherent strategic approach and a common methodology for sound analysis, planning and implementation.").

120. *See, e.g.*, Independent Inquiry Committee into the UN Oil-For-Food Programme, The Management of the UN Oil-For-Food Programme, Vol. 1 (2005), http://www.iic-offp.org/Mgmt_Report.htm.

on these critically important issues will be based merely on anecdotal evidence. That is hardly a recipe for success.

One of the significant problems facing transitional administrations and post-conflict societies is a lack of coordination between donors, implementers, and other parties. Since transitional administrations operate under a Security Council mandate, the RLAU is well-placed to engage in a planning process that rationalizes the strengths and abilities of the various actors—both national and international—working in rule of law and related arenas. This process would take place in two steps.

First, as part of its long-term planning goals, the RLAU must work with principal donor governments and NGOs to establish an overall blueprint for rule of law activities in post-conflict situations. This blueprint, which should draw on the knowledge of all concerned, can then serve as the basis for the much more rapid planning that occurs on the ground following a conflict. It is essential that transitional administrations have an office for rule of law matters which is closely connected to the RLAU. The ideal role of the U.N. would be to allow the various NGOs and donors to work effectively within a structure that seeks to avoid duplication and wasted effort. While NGOs and donors may not react well to a heavy-handed approach, experience has shown that there is also less duplication and waste in countries where there is at least informal coordination. In a post-conflict situation, the U.N., with a properly staffed office dealing specifically with these matters both in headquarters and in the field, should be able to help fill a void that might otherwise undermine their efforts. It is important to emphasize that the U.N. rule of law efforts must also be present in the field operation. If there is no field presence, the U.N. will lack the credibility or local knowledge to fulfill the task.

In addition to these practical issues, the RLAU must also carve out a role to address some of the difficulties plaguing rule of law providers. "The rule of law" is still frequently misunderstood, even by some of those engaged in the work itself. Thus, it is important to closely examine the current methods by which it is implemented. For example, the use of foreign experts is a mainstay of virtually every rule of law program, with foreign experts conducting training and research and making proposals about countries that they may know very little about. There has been much criticism, including in the Rule of Law Report, of the use of these experts. There have also been calls for a greater reliance on local expertise and solutions.[121] However, there is virtually no information, much less empirical evidence, on which to base these conclusions. Rule of law assistance has developed rapidly over the last decade and a number of questions regarding its implementation remain.

For example: what type of foreign expert is the most effective in terms of training, drafting legislation, and providing advice, and what types of training could make them more effective? How are experts received by post-conflict

---

121. *Rule of Law Report, supra* note 6, ¶ 13.

societies? How does the public perceive these programs? Which programs are most effective? There is some evidence that it is difficult to make an impact, but it is not clear which of the program is most effective. This kind of information can be obtained through public surveys and polling data. Accordingly, it makes sense to spend a small amount of resources to measure the impact prior programs have had on legal professionals and on the population as a whole. For example, Eric Stover has, in a somewhat different context, interviewed witnesses about their experiences at the ICTY and their perceptions of the Tribunal both before and after the experience.[122] His conclusions have been very useful in making adjustments to programs supporting victims and witnesses. While, at first glance, such proposals may appear unorthodox, there is much to be learned from the social sciences in this regard. The rule of law is too important to be left to guesswork and anecdotes.[123]

Consideration also needs to be given to the roles non-lawyers might play in rule of law assistance work. Mark Malloch Brown says that "rule of law is too important to be left to the lawyers."[124] Others have suggested that reliance on lawyers has led to "a conflation between rule of law and lawyers, and a realization that multidisciplinary teams" might be more adept at addressing issues of rule of law.[125] While the design of programs should certainly include experts in other fields, it is questionable whether non-lawyers could actually serve as implementers, since it may be difficult to obtain the necessary respect from judges and lawyers to be effective in these roles. However, these insights and proposals deserve close examination.

Two other areas identified by the Report in which the RLAU could play a useful role are in establishing best practices and in identifying expertise. In a field with many donors and assistance providers, a systematic approach to identify best practices among the sundry actors could achieve real benefits. While there have been exchanges between organizations regarding best practices, the Unit, if properly resourced, could serve as the convener for such discussions. Related to this is the need to identify experts both within and outside the U.N. system and to compile a roster of these experts. A database with pertinent information about these experts can allow for better selections to be made in the future, rather than relying on the informal contacts that have dominated past efforts. Specific attention should be given to ensuring that "new" experts from post-conflict societies—that is, professionals who have been on the domestic side of assistance programs and have developed their own expertise—are included in such a database. This involves a cultural shift for the U.N., as it

---

122. MY NEIGHBOR, MY ENEMY: JUSTICE AND COMMUNITY IN THE AFTERMATH OF MASS ATROCITY (Eric Stover & Harvey M. Weinstein eds., 2004).

123. Thomas Carothers, *Promoting the Rule of Law Abroad: The Problem of Knowledge* 9 (Carnegie Endowment, No. 34, 2003), http://www.carnegieendowment.org/publications/index.cfm?fa=view&id=1169 ("Rule-of-law practitioners have been . . . [working] more out of instinct than well-researched knowledge.").

124. 5052d Mtg., *supra* note 58.

125. Hurwitz & Studdard, *supra* note 9, at 9.

means that in-house expertise must be developed in order to identify the right trainers and experts. In this regard, the U.N. can learn from some of its NGO partners who often do a better job of identifying the best people for these tasks.

To facilitate the above steps and to show the U.N.'s renewed commitment to, and more active involvement in, supporting the rule of law, consideration should be given to convening a symposium or forum under U.N. auspices to address the issues noted above and to take stock of current efforts. This would give the U.N. the opportunity to test out these and other ideas and to begin to establish its new role. A second step would be to convene regular meetings of the donor governments, NGOs, and others involved in rule of law assistance work. Most of these groups are represented in New York or Washington and would probably welcome such regular interaction. More importantly, such regular coordination meetings should be replicated in the relevant field operations. The U.N. representative in these field operations could also serve a useful role by acting as a repository for information on best practices, quality of experts, and other matters so that this information is not lost through the inevitable shifting and departure of personnel.

Ultimately, whether these specific ideas are pursued by a reformed U.N. is less important than whether these new organs, particularly the RLAU, can think creatively. The challenges are immense and past efforts have often proved disappointing. Thus, the Unit should not only put forward practical proposals through increased coordination and expertise, but should also facilitate new thinking about these issues. In these efforts, it must work closely with other partners and make new relationships in the social sciences and in academia so that it can fulfill its new and expanded role.

IV. CONCLUDING REMARKS

Building the rule of law encompasses many issues, from defining the term to making it a reality. Despite the difficulties, even critics of rule of law efforts acknowledge its importance in societies moving from conflict to peace.[126] A variety of strategies and programs have been developed to assist in building legal institutions and to impart the "cluster of values" that lies at the heart of the rule of law. However, in light of the many difficult obstacles, these efforts are often only partially successful. It is clear that if any progress is to be made, certain key issues must be addressed. First, societies must deal with crimes of the past through any one of a variety of mechanisms, so long as it ensures that those most responsible are held criminally accountable in a transparent and legitimate process. The society must also establish a broad legal framework in which the rule of law can flourish. The next phase focuses on developing the legal institutions, including an independent judiciary, competent lawyers, and effective legal education. An active and vibrant civil society

---

126. *See* Carothers, *supra* note 123.

composed of domestic NGOs and activists is critical to reform both the relevant institutions and the attitudes of legal professionals and society at large.
As has been argued above, it is important that these strategies be understood
as complementary rather than as in competition with each other.

There is widespread agreement that rule of law assistance should focus on
these matters, but there is also considerable uncertainty regarding the effectiveness of the various strategies and techniques. This uncertainty is rooted in
the considerable knowledge gaps which remain in rule of law areas. This situation is accompanied by an often chaotic approach to rule of law programming
in field operations and a lack of planning and coordination by primary actors
such as donor governments, NGOs, private contractors, and international agencies. Until these issues are more effectively addressed, efforts to support the
rule of law will continue to face significant obstacles.

United Nations reform efforts create an opportunity to start to fill these
gaps and to strengthen rule of law efforts. If the Report's recommendations
are realized, the U.N. will be in a better position to provide the necessary
leadership. It is the only actor that has the credibility and legitimacy to provide the research and conceptual thinking to address some of the epistemo-
logical issues that confront this field, as well as to address practical coordination issues on the ground. Hopefully, these reforms will not be watered down,
leaving the U.N. under-resourced and overwhelmed in the face of immensely
difficult issues. There is an important role for a reformed U.N. to play, but there
must be the resources and the will to achieve these reforms. Otherwise, U.N.
reform will fail, leaving post-conflict societies in desperate, if not hopeless,
straits.

[10]

From Neo-Colonialism to a 'Light-Footprint Approach': Restoring Justice Systems

MATTEO TONDINI

The article analyses peacebuilding theories and methods, as applied to justice system reform in post-conflict scenarios. In this respect, the international authorities involved in the reconstruction process may traditionally choose between either a *dirigiste* or a consent-based approach, representing the essential terms of reference of past interventions. However, features common to most reconstruction missions, and relatively poor results, confirm the need for a change in the overall strategy. This requires international donors to focus more on the 'demand for justice' at local levels than on the traditional supply of financial and technical aid for reforms. The article stresses the need for effectively promoting the 'local ownership' of the reform process, without this expression being merely used by international actors as a political umbrella under which to protect themselves from potential failures.

> *Experience has shown that the number of UN agencies*
> *flying their flags in a country*
> *is not proportionate to the overall success achieved.*
> Lakhdar Brahimi[1]

The idea of justice in peacebuilding missions under the UN's aegis has always represented the cornerstone of the new social order in war-torn countries. International missions in Somalia, Bosnia, East Timor and Kosovo have been marked by the full participation of international officials in the policymaking process, acting as kinds of trustees. In consequence, these legal systems introduce new laws and codes that have the ring of authoritarianism and appear to be dropped in from on high. Most of these operations have seen the use of 'mixed' internationally–nationally staffed tribunals. Some have also been characterized by the establishment of courts composed of international judges in charge of the administration of a novel justice system, along with the imposition of human rights-inspired legal models derived from the idealistic character of military interventions that originated the civil reconstruction missions in the first place. For instance, in Rwanda, according to some scholars, the extensive engagement of international actors in justice system reform has created a 'donor-driven justice',[2] completely separated from the country's legal tradition. By contrast, the justice system in Afghanistan has been shaped according to a different perspective that consists mainly in paying due attention to the legal and judicial systems previously in place, leaving the restoration of the sector to be in charge of the Afghan government (at least formally), with international actors performing a limited coordination role. The UN labelled this strategy a 'light-footprint approach'.[3]

A limited role in the justice sector's reform has been also performed by the UN missions in the Democratic Republic of Congo (DRC), Haiti, Burundi and Liberia, while in Cambodia UNTAC withdrew after the enactment of statutory laws, with the implicit assent of the national authorities. In Sierra Leone, apart from the establishment of a special court to prosecute war crimes and crimes against humanity, the UN mission's advisory task focused more on advising the local government on police reform than on the restoration of a viable system of justice.[4]

Whatever the role of international agencies in reforming the legal systems of post-conflict countries, it has inevitably implied a form of cultural influence and/or imposition. Failures and limited accomplishments in establishing functioning legal and judicial systems have further led to the birth of peacebuilding theories and strategies, based on the lessons learned from previous interventions. However, such strategies raise further doubts about their utility and efficacy. In order to address such issues, this article analyses peacebuilding as applied to justice system reform. The first two sections consider the need for a balance between imposed and consensual solutions, and calls for a settlement of the political order before providing legal or judicial reforms. The third section illustrates the reasons for choosing a model of reform based on local consensus and how to successfully rely on it (considering the real 'demand for justice'). There then follows a tentative analysis of some common characteristics of peacebuilding operations, in which international authorities play a role in the reform of local systems of justice. It draws attention to the meagre goals achieved so far and suggests a change in the overall strategy, as stressed in the conclusion. This study does not take into account the Iraqi case, first because of the limited role played by international actors other than the United States, and second because continuing civil war in the country precludes relevant analysis.

Does Justice Follow a Political Order?

Legal reforms in territories recovering from conflicts do not usually follow the same rationale or present the same options. Each situation reveals unique and non-repeatable characteristics that prevent the implementation of a 'one-size-fits-all' formula. Relevant variables might include the security situation, the historical reasons for the armed conflict, and the starting level for the restoration – while the results of the reconstruction process may be deeply influenced by the strategic and operational choices of both local and international political actors. Naturally, the availability of economic resources (sustained by donor commitments) also plays a key role, although the efficacy of financial aid may be ruined by a high level of corruption. Afghanistan and Haiti, for example, are considered to be among the most corrupt countries in the world notwithstanding the international statebuilding missions in place.[5]

In addition, historically, the re-establishment of the judicial system in a country has mainly followed the foundation of a new political order, imposed at the end of a conflict. In other words, a stable and secure political order has always represented the *conditio 'sine qua non* of post-conflict reconstruction'.[6]

Therefore, in the absence of a secure environment, any efforts to promote national reconciliation as well as to establish a functioning justice system are doomed to fail.[7] However, recent examples, such as those in Iraq, Afghanistan (by military means alone) and to some extent, Kosovo and Timor Leste (through massive international political apparatus), show that this 'natural paradigm' has shifted towards a new model encompassing the use of external institutional design to shape a political order which has not yet taken root. As has been sharply argued, 'contemporary international intervention takes place in weak states, not conquered ones.'[8] This seems to be a successful option when the foundations of the new political system are solid and the renovation of the political class is effectively carried out, also by means of a peace agreement or a formal surrender. Nevertheless, it may turn into a debilitating factor when the authority in charge fails to prevail militarily over competing forces or otherwise is not accepted by a relevant part of the population. Some scholars note that such problems always occurred in the past: 'in Cambodia ... Bosnia, Angola, and Western Sahara ... the lines blurred between when the war ends and the peace begins', so that '[j]ustice officials [will] inevitably find themselves in a similarly grey area.'[9] A clear example of such a trend is offered by the reconstruction process in Afghanistan, where the limited accomplishments in the restoration of the justice sector are coupled with the stalemate in military operations.[10] Nonetheless, at a July 2007 Rome Conference on the Rule of Law in Afghanistan, both Afghan and international political leaders involved in the reconstruction of the justice sector replied to allegations of inefficiency by stating that the achievement of stability in the country is firmly anchored in the country's social and economic development, basically indicating that military operations and reconstruction need to move forward together.[11]

On the contrary, critics argue that this new credo in the Western-oriented 'rule of law', as the basic precondition to secure stability and democracy, may be deceptive. As pointed out by Thomas Carothers, 'the idea that specific improvements in the rule of law are necessary to achieve democracy is dangerously simplistic', as in Western countries '[d]emocracy often, in fact usually, co-exists with substantial shortcomings in the rule of law.'[12] This suggests that establishing the rule of law is not a panacea for solving political instability because '"Rule of law" regulation through the prioritization of law above the political sphere cannot compensate for, or overcome, the political problems involved in peace-building and post-war reconstruction.'[13] Conversely, relegating the political process behind restoration of the justice system would reverse the theory of rule of law as derived from the liberal democratic contract theory of consent and would probably encourage arbitrary rule-making by local political elites.[14]

The Unsolvable Dilemma: A Neo-Colonial or Consent-Based Approach?

It is often said that the theory and practice of UN post-conflict reconstruction has progressively shifted from a 'consent-based model', as in the missions in Namibia, Cambodia and El Salvador, towards a 'neo-colonial model', as in Somalia, Kosovo and Timor Leste. Eventually, the overall UN approach would return to looking minimalist with the recent UN Assistance Mission in Afghanistan (UNAMA). In this respect, the 'light-footprint approach' is the product of those past failures and excesses registered in the establishment of quasi-state administrative apparatus run by international authorities, which have deeply conditioned the reform of local state institutions according to foreign-imposed models. However, this clear-cut subdivision raises further issues. Generally, on the one hand, representing the history of peacekeeping operations as a progressive evolution, including tasks of increasing complexity, has been lately considered misleading and normatively unhelpful.[15] On the other hand, with regard to post-conflict justice reform, it has been noted that both the 'dirigiste' (i.e. neo-colonial) and the light-footprint models present a common feature, being the active and 'direct involvement of international actors in the restoration of justice and the rule of law'.[16] Some scholars also suppose that even the light-footprint approach merely represented a first step, justified by the circumstances of the case, towards the further establishment of a full administrative structure, modelled according to those in Kosovo or East Timor.[17]

The theorized neo-colonial approach would mainly develop in prearranging 'justice packages', ready to be deployed in case of need. The 'packages' should encompass both legal experts (trainers, attorneys and judges, clerks) and applicable norms (e.g. substantive and procedural model criminal codes), in order to fill vacuums in justice administration. The creation of such packages follows the recommendations contained in the 2000 Brahimi Report and the 2004 Report of the UN Secretary-General on Transitional Justice.[18] In trying to avoid risks of excessive external influence, experts suggest that national authorities should decide which part of this pre-drafted legislation should be included in their own legal systems.[19] While in theory this principle sounds fine, it still shirks the issue of local elite capacity to become genuinely autonomous from external influence in taking significant political decisions, and to be accountable to local populations rather than to foreign actors involved in the reconstruction process.[20] In this respect, academic debate is focused on the political role played by the newly established rule-of-law institutions, as well as the political nature of programmes supported by international actors.[21] Tensions between those who deem institutional design to be the core objective of the reconstruction process and those who lament the lack of dialogue between local and international actors, reflect the unresolved dilemma between imposition of foreign administrative templates and a true social contract. Indeed, on the one hand, reconstruction of the justice sector could be (realistically) led by international donors for pure national interest, being that of 'lawfully' securing the exploitation of the country's resources by 'leaven[ing] ...commercial courts with foreign judges'.[22] On the other hand, a limited use of 'pre-packaged' codes and standby personnel would be nonetheless indispensable, whereas in the case of the UN mission in Liberia the justice system has to be rebuilt from scratch.[23] Yet, the fact that, nowadays, projects aimed at drafting new applicable codes in peacekeeping operations are still financed[24] may raise doubts of whether this 'dirigiste' trend has been definitively abandoned. However, the real efficacy of choices based on lessons learned from previous operational scenarios is increasingly questioned, as admitted by the same UN Secretary-General in his 2004 report.[25] The problem appears irresolvable, since in practice every act of external institutional assistance to countries recovering from conflict implies a certain level of cultural influence.

Considering Local Consensus and Demand for Justice as Preconditions for Success

Willing to draft a model aimed at establishing functioning and reformed judicial institutions in post-conflict countries, scholars come to the self-evident approach of looking for consensus and political legitimacy from a double domestic and international perspective.[26] This practically means, on the one hand, that the foundation of the mission's mandate should lie on a firm legal basis, particularly including 'legitimate' international agreements and/or clear Security Council mandates, and, on the other hand, that such reforms should be accepted by the population to which they apply. In other words, the rule-of-law reforms should be aimed at securing the 'local ownership' of the reconstruction process, according to a 'social compact' between all the relevant stakeholders, including of course the local population.[27] With regard to this, it becomes fundamental to identify the relevant actors to be involved in the reconstruction process. As noted elsewhere, they may be grouped into three main categories: (1) the population (citizens, civil society and business community); (2) political authorities (political leadership – at both national and local level – and the civil service); and (3) justice and security sector institutions members.[28]

Arranging a 'social compact' for justice with the local population, in order to promote compliance with the law and general stability, would mean moving on from this 'rule-of-law orthodoxy', primarily based on the re-establishment of courts, towards a more balanced approach, which would comprise the 'legal empowerment' of a growing part of the population.[29] This should help in creating a reformist political process that would in turn lead to a more realistic establishment of the rule of law, potentially different from the original Western idea of *Rechtsstaat*. The UN itself has started to explore this approach by recommending the strengthening of community-based justice oriented towards informal justice mechanisms.[30] Besides, tribal justice is currently fostered in Afghanistan by a specific project run by the United Nations Development Programme (UNDP),[31] while traditional justice institutions have been successfully employed in the post-genocide reconciliation phase in Rwanda, through the so-called '*gacaca* courts'. However, it has to be stated that these informal justice mechanisms have been supported by international and national authorities primarily for practical reasons. For instance, by 2001, the Rwandan government estimated that it would take 200 years to try in state courts all the 100,000 individuals accused of participation in genocide.[32]

In economic language, the theory of peacebuilding, as applied to law reforms, should shift from concentrating on the supply of justice to the effective demand for justice. Research indicates that a demand for justice must exist so that the law formally in force is actually put into practice and policymakers and law professionals are responsive to it.[33] In addition, to be successfully 'transplanted' into the legal order concerned, the new body of law should adapt to the local conditions or contain principles already familiar to the local population. Such a policy in turn would probably strengthen the public demand for institutions to enforce the rule of law. On the contrary, if the new body of law was merely imposed (as in the case of colonization), the initial demand for using it would probably be weak, conditioning the effectiveness of the overall rule-of-law reform. However, relying excessively on local ownership is not without risks, because, even if this usually safeguards domestic culture against the dangers of external interference, it may still cause reduction in the level of individual rights protection if domestic policymakers are unwilling or unable to promote human rights protection or criminal prosecution.[34]

Common Features of Post-conflict Judicial System Reforms

A common feature of justice reform in post-conflict scenarios is the fragmented consolidation process of the legal systems concerned, which 'almost never conform to the technocratic ideal of rational sequences on which the indicator frameworks and strategic objectives of democracy promoters are built.'[35] This may prevent accurate assessment of the outcomes of any reconstruction process, because the performance metrics may be clogged by too many variables. However, some useful indicators may be identified in order to evaluate success in reconstruction: (1) serious crime rates (especially homicides and violent crimes); (2) other crime indicators (drug and human trafficking); (3) the level of political violence and insurgency; (4) perception of security.[36] Naturally, the effectiveness of justice reforms also rests on people's compliance with the law. Research shows that such compliance 'depends most heavily on the perceived fairness and legitimacy of the laws, characteristics that are not established primarily by the courts but by other means, such as the political process'.[37] However, the people's perception of the fairness of a single justice system stems from the level of expectations and other irrational elements. Nevertheless, it seems possible to draw up a few features common to the majority of justice system restorations in post-conflict situations: (1) a high level of destruction of judicial buildings with consequent missing official records (that implies problems, for example, in identifying property rights); (2) a domestic judicial system character-ized by the strong interference of local executive authorities (corruption and 'telephone justice'); (3) the law in force not being integrally consistent with international human rights standards and/or its validity being contested by the population; (4) the presence of a parallel/unofficial system of justice; (5) available human and material resources.[38]

Collapse of the Previous Justice System

As argued by a practitioner in 1999, '[e]stablishing the judicial system in East Timor entail[ed] building a system "from scratch"'.[39] Over 70 per cent of all administrative buildings were partially or completely destroyed, while most courts had been torched or looted, resulting in the loss of registers, records, archives and other legal resources. The first recruiting campaign for personnel to serve in the judicial administration was carried out by launching leaflets from an aeroplane throughout the region. The UN administration found that only about 70 Timorese citizens who still lived in the country had graduated from law school, while none of them had been practising law under the Indonesian control of the country.[40] Other sources confirm that the number of indigenous lawyers remaining after the referendum on independence was fewer than 10.[41] A similar situation has occurred in Kosovo, where the collapse of the law enforcement and the judicial system was pretty clear since the very beginning of the UN mission. To overcome the lack of buildings and personnel, a judicial mobile unit, comprising nine judges and prosecutors (including three Serbs), was initially established, and in three weeks the number had increased to 28.[42] In Afghanistan, the formal system of justice in place during the Taliban period (founded on both Islamic courts and tribal councils) collapsed with the fall of Kabul in late 2001. Judicial buildings were almost crumbling and correctional facilities were close to non-existent (excluding the Policharki complex, outside Kabul). In addition, since July 1964, no one had made a compilation of the applicable laws passed during the 30 years of turbulent history, since, due to past destruction, there was no complete set of the *Official Gazette* available for reference.

Insecurity and Judicial Corruption

The functionality of the justice system may be threatened by the security situation. In Kosovo, at the beginning of the UN mission, due to Milošević's post-1989 purge of administrative personnel, only 30 out of 756 judges and prosecutors were Kosovar Albanians. Following the return of Albanian refugees and displaced people, most of the Serbian magistrates moved back beyond the Serbian borders. The few who decided to stay were considered to be linked to the previous regime and immediately threatened, as were the members of the council in charge of initial judicial appointments.[43] As a consequence, local judges are reported to have often ruled in favour of Kosovar defendants even though the law supported the Serbian plaintiffs, for fear of reprisals. In Rwanda, over 300 survivors, who were also witnesses in genocide trials before state courts, were murdered between 1994 and 1997, paralysing the justice system.[44] A solution to the threat of reprisal has often been to staff local courts with international judges, thus creating different types of 'mixed courts'. Although, these courts are mainly employed in the transitional justice phase (as in the Special Court for Sierra Leone; the Special Panel in the Court of Dili, East Timor; the Extraordinary Chambers in the Courts of Cambodia; and the War Crimes Chamber of the Court of Bosnia and Herzegovina), international judges currently serve in the Kosovo judiciary under a two-track system. On the one hand, international judges are appointed to the regular courts; on the other hand, special internationalized panels are created for the most sensitive war crimes trials. Basically, international judges in Kosovo do not receive case assignments from the president of the court in which they sit, but from the UN administration's department of justice: thus, they act as a de facto parallel (i.e. special) jurisdiction.[45]

It is easy to imagine that corruption is another decisive factor that weakens the credibility of justice in post-war countries. According to the Corruption

Perception Index 2006, almost all the countries in which UN missions are in charge of the legal reforms taking place are among the most corrupt in the world, with Haiti being at the bottom of the list.[46] In Afghanistan, the judiciary is even considered by the population to be the most corrupt of state institutions.[47] In order to overcome any potential destabilizing factor, UN doctrine suggests vetting the bench and excluding individuals associated with past abuses.[48] However, vetting the judicial personnel for their impartiality or competence may entail an initial judicial vacuum or allegations of the system's politicization. In this respect, the administration of Brčko District in Bosnia, where international authorities required judicial personnel to resign and reapply through a more transparent procedure, may be taken as a model and a successful compromise.[49]

Reform of the Applicable Law

The applicable law is a recurring issue in peacebuilding operations. In the first instance, the domestic law formally in force may be seen by the population as an instrument of the previous regime and thus perceived as radically unfair or illegitimate, as in the case of Kosovo. Domestic law may also violate international human rights law provisions, as in the case of several Indonesian laws applied in Timor Leste, or be discriminatory against women, as in Haiti. Moreover, domestic law may be outdated and may not cover relevant crimes such as trafficking, money laundering and organized crime (as in the penal codes of Angola, dating back to 1886, and Haiti, dating back to 1925).[50] Eventually, the presence of parallel administrative bodies, as a reaction to the imposition of past tyrannical or colonial rule, may entail the spread of non-statutory customary law.

Whatever role they formally play in the sector's reconstruction, international actors often support the re-establishment of the legislative framework in force earlier than the previous regime, often for practical reasons. This has frequently accompanied the repeal of those provisions of law incompatible with human rights standards (and with the regulations issued by the UN administration where appropriate), as occurred during the UN missions in Kosovo, Timor Leste, Somalia and Afghanistan. In Kosovo, the UN administration decided on the law in force as of 1989 (the pre-Milošević era). In Timor Leste, at the very beginning of the intervention, the law in force remained provisionally that applied before the UN mission, even though a list of Indonesian laws – contrary to human rights – to be repealed was also published.[51]

Usually, domestic criminal law provisions are among the first to be abolished. In Somalia, the special representative of the UN Secretary-General declared that the 1962 Somali criminal code applied in the country, although specific *habeas corpus* provisions were added in order to make it compliant with human rights law. Eventually, the UN authorities assisted local delegates in the constitution-making process.[52] At the beginning of the international intervention in Afghanistan, according to the 'Bonn Agreement', the interim legal system in force was to consist of the 1964 'monarchical' constitution and of the full compilation of domestic laws and regulations passed since that time, unless in conflict with the constitution or the agreement. A former Italian magistrate also redrafted an interim criminal procedure code to be applied in Afghanistan, pending the enactment of a new code by the Afghan parliament.[53] On the other hand, the criminal procedure code was also redrafted in Brčko District. The new code was inspired by a party-driven approach, also abolishing the investigating judge and providing for the judge to play a more limited role.[54] Yet, the UN administration in Timor Leste repealed the Indonesian Criminal Procedure Code and enacted new Transitional Rules of Criminal Procedure, while the UN mission in Cambodia set forth new substantive and procedural criminal provisions to be applied during the transitional period.[55] The UN administration in Kosovo followed this trend by issuing a provisional criminal procedure code and a criminal code in 2003.

Parallel/Unofficial Justice Systems

As for the existence of unofficial systems in post-conflict operations, it can be acknowledged that in many developing countries customary systems operating outside the state administration 'are often the dominant form of regulation and dispute resolution, covering up to 90% of the population in parts of Africa.... Customary tenure covers 75% of land in most African countries, affecting 90% of land transactions in countries like Mozambique and Ghana.'[56] In 1999, customary law was reported to be widespread in the countryside of Timor Leste, while the role of traditional dispute-resolution mechanisms was defined by international officials as 'indispensable' for the stability of the country's justice system.[57] In Kosovo, the establishment of parallel judicial institutions by the Albanian population during the Milošević regime has been followed by the birth of parallel municipal courts – ruled by Kosovo Serbs – after the UN intervention. Two different non-statutory legal and judicial systems, that is, Islamic law and customary law (called 'Xeer'), still exist in Somalia. In particular, they represent a consolidated normative framework in rural areas. Traditional practice was often encouraged by the international authorities. For instance, the Australian forces used to identify former judges who were acceptable to local community members and to persuade them to resume their role in the 'neighbourhood forums'.[58] Similarly, in Afghanistan, councils of elders apply both customary and Islamic law, coupled with statutory courts in the provinces outside Kabul, and settle up to 80 per cent of cases.[59]

Human and Material Resources

Lack of financial and human resources for the restoration of the justice system is a common feature of reconstruction missions. In this respect, the re-establishment of a police service is often considered more important than the judicial system for short-term stability: this, for instance, was the case of the UN mission in Somalia.[60] However, it has been noted that obviously a successful strategy may not depart from both services being fully operational and working in partnership.[61] In this respect, in order to give a clear idea of the priorities of the international donors in Afghanistan, it might be noted that until early 2005, the justice sector had only received 2–4 per cent of the financial resources allocated to the entire security sector.[62] Lack of funds for the judicial system is also reported in the case of Sierra Leone, where the priority of police reform and the establishment of the special court for the prosecution of serious crimes committed during the conflict, have drawn financial resources away from the development of the justice system.[63] In Timor Leste, the shortage of both physical and financial resources is reported to have hampered even the functioning of the Special Crime Panels established within the Dili Court.[64]

Current Situation

The goals accomplished by peacebuilding missions in the re-establishment of justice do not appear encouraging. The situation in Africa is particularly critical. In the DRC, the status of lawyers' associations seems weak, and access to justice is seriously restricted for the majority of people. In several parts of the country, the military and civil justice systems are reported to be non-functioning. In August 2006, the president of the Congolese Military High Court denounced the ineffectiveness of the court system, the corruption and the lack of law reforms. Only 60 out of 180 courts supposedly in place actually exist, while only 30 seem to be actually functioning. Moreover, there is a wide gap (about half) in the number of judges required to sustain the system. Such inefficiencies, coupled with the population's lack of trust, have led the customary justice system to flourish.[65]

In Sierra Leone, functioning courts are currently concentrated in the capital, Freetown, together with most of the judges and attorneys (90 out of 100 practising lawyers in the country work in Freetown). Customary law is spread all over the remaining territory – to some extent fostered by the former British colonial regime.[66] According to the World Bank, 'approximately 85% of the population falls under the jurisdiction of customary law',[67] which is also sanctioned in the constitution. Integration between formal and informal systems of justice occurs within the statutory 'local courts', which apply local customary law and whose judges are appointed by local administrative leaders with the approval of the Ministry of Local Government and Community Development. Notwithstanding this, the population 'perceives the judicial system to be slow, ineffective and corrupt'.[68]

In Somalia, initially, the UN mission (UNOSOM II) achieved a limited success in reconstructing the Somali justice system. By March 1995, at the end of the UN mission's mandate, 11 appeal, 11 (out of 18) regional, and 46 (out of 92) district courts were operating in the country.[69] Currently, the UNDP is managing a Rule of Law and Security Programme (ROLS, originally established in 1997), although its activities appear to be concentrated in Somaliland, due to more stable political conditions. The programme's efficacy has yet to be assessed.

In Afghanistan, the judiciary is reported as being politicized and often staffed by corrupt officers. This lowers public confidence in the statutory law and facilitates the establishment of unofficial courts ruled by the Taliban.[70] The overall situation of the judicial sector in the country is relatively poor, as the reconstruction activities are hampered by the security situation on the ground. In addition, they have scarcely reached rural areas far from Kabul.[71] In Timor Leste, research by the Judicial Sector Monitoring Programme confirms that a high number of cases of sexual abuse or domestic violence are informally settled by village councils. Police sources admit that law enforcement officials often prefer to refer minor crimes to such forums instead of formally charging the suspects.[72]

The Cambodian justice system is reported as being in a 'catastrophic state',[73] while in Haiti the violent crime rates are among the highest in the world: the Organization of American States estimates that from September 2004 to April 2005 there have been about 600 murders, including 19 police officers.[74]

In Kosovo, the overall level of confidence in the judiciary is reported as being relatively low (30.8 per cent), although the public perception of results differs on the basis of ethnic origin. Corruption is considered to be the greatest challenge to the system, while undue political interference still conditions court rulings.[75] Although the crime rates were dramatic at the beginning of the mission (in the period from January to August 2000, international authorities reported 14,878 criminal offences and arrested 3,734 persons[76]), the number of violent crimes has progressively decreased in the first three years of reconstruction,[77] even if, in 2003, still one-third of the prisoners in Kosovar detention facilities (about 400) were accused of murder.[78] In 2003, 6,282 persons were convicted of criminal offences by municipal and district courts.[79] However, the judicial consequences of the March 2004 riots will probably leaven the crime statistics.

Concluding Remarks: The New Mantra of Local Ownership

The evidence available indicates the need for a change of course in the overall approach to the reform of justice in war-torn societies, as interventions tend to be largely ineffective. This can be due to the strategy adopted so far, although the reasons for the failure probably have to be sought in the fragmented reality of post-conflict interventions, with international actors often pursuing diverse and competing interests. On the contrary, every classification of peace operations on the basis of official mandates and functions, may be useful for theoretical studies, but may also be highly misleading. As regards the restoration of the justice sector, the theory does not take into account the *real* authority exercised by international actors. Indeed, to be scientifically valuable, research should quantitatively reveal the level of transfer of knowledge among all the international players involved (including hired consultants attached to local government institutions) and domestic authorities. On the other hand, a reliable study should qualitatively illustrate which international and domestic actors are engaged in the reconstruction process and also indicate the presence of resistance.[80] In this respect, even a 'light footprint' such as that in Afghanistan may very closely resemble more complex missions such as those in Timor Leste or Kosovo. This is the case when laws are officially passed by the Afghan parliament but are in fact drafted by 'independent' experts hired by foreign governments and cooperation agencies assigned to local institutions, while the latter are in turn pressured by international donors 'to cooperate'.

A genuine change could be simply summarized by the phrase 'promoting ownership beyond simply assessing it'.[81] Indeed, the tendency to affirm publicly the local ownership of state-building processes may represent a mere umbrella under which international actors protect themselves in case of failure. Morever, '[w]hen delays, obstacles, and drawbacks cannot be ignored any longer, they are blamed on the local actors.'[82] Ultimately, one can argue, this assumed 'light approach' in reconstruction, decided by international policymakers, is simply a result of their incapacity to impose order (even by military means) and, *a fortiori*, an acknowledgement of the weakness of the legal values 'exported' to countries recovering from conflicts. Perhaps, looking for the effective 'demand for justice' may represent the only way to influence successfully the legal culture of war-torn societies. However, once again, this may reflect the real aims of the international actors engaged in peace operations.

ACKNOWLEDGEMENT

A draft version of this article was presented at the 6th Pan-European Conference on International Relations, Turin, 12–15 September 2007, and appeared on the conference's website. Any views or opinions expressed are solely those of the author and do not necessarily represent those of the institution or the office in which the author is currently serving.

NOTES

1. Lakhdar Brahimi, speech at the 'Great Negotiator' Award Acceptance, Harvard Law School, 2 Oct. 2002, quoted in Jacob S. Kreilkamp, 'UN Postconflict Reconstruction', *New York University Journal of International Law and Politics*, Vol.35, No.3, 2003, pp.619–70, at p.665.
2. Barbara Oomen, 'Donor-Driven Justice and Its Discontents: The Case of Rwanda', *Development and Change*, Vol.36, No.5, 2005, pp.887–910, at p.894.
3. 'The Situation in Afghanistan and Its Implications for International Peace and Security', Report of the Secretary-General, 18 Mar. 2002, UN doc. A/56/875–S/2002/278, p.16.
4. Department of Peacekeeping Operations, *Lessons Learned from United Nations Peacekeeping Experiences in Sierra Leone*, United Nations, Sept. 2003, p.51, accessed at http://pbpu.unlb.org/pbpu/library/SL-LL%20Report.pdf.
5. Seth G. Jones, Jeremy M. Wilson, Andrew Rathmell and K. Jack Riley, *Establishing Law and Order After Conflict*, Santa Monica, CA: RAND, 2005, p.100.
6. CSIS and AUSA, *Play to Win: Final Report of the Bi-Partisan Commission on Post-Conflict Reconstruction*, Jan. 2003, p.7, accessed at www.reliefweb.int/rw/lib.nsf/db900SID/LGEL5JVD76/$FILE/csis-play-jan03.pdf?OpenElement.
7. Jane E. Stromseth, David Wippman and Rosa Brooks, *Can Might Make Rights?: Building the Rule of Law After Military Interventions*, New York: Cambridge University Press, p.134.
8. Roberto Belloni, 'Rethinking "Nation-Building": The Contradictions of the Neo-Wilsonian Approach to Democracy Promotion', *Whitehead Journal of Diplomacy and International Relations*, Vol.8, No.1, 2007, pp.97–109, at p.103.
9. Mark Plunkett, 'Reestablishing Law and Order in Peace-Maintenance', *Global Governance*, Vol.4, No.1, 1998, pp.61–79, at p.63.
10. Matteo Tondini, 'Rebuilding the System of Justice in Afghanistan: A Preliminary Assessment', *Journal of Intervention and Statebuilding*, Vol.1, No.3, 2007, pp.333–54.
11. Vincenzo Nigro, 'La Nato: "Niente alibi sull'Afghanistan"'['NATO: "No alibi in Afghanistan"'], *Repubblica* [Rome], 4 Jul. 2007, p.6.
12. Thomas Carothers, *Promoting the Rule of Law Abroad: The Problem of Knowledge*, Washington, DC: Carnegie, Jan. 2003, p.7, accessed at www.carnegieendowment.org/files/wp34.pdf.
13. David Chandler, 'Imposing the "Rule of Law": The Lessons of BiH for Peacebuilding in Iraq', *International Peacekeeping*, Vol.11, No.2, 2004, pp.312–33, at p.314.
14. David Chandler, 'Back to the Future? The Limits of Neo-Wilsonian Ideals of Exporting Democracy', *Review of International Studies*, Vol.32, No.3, 2006, pp.475–94, at p.483.
15. Ralph Wilde, 'Representing International Territorial Administration: A Critique of Some Approaches', *European Journal of International Law*, Vol.15, No.1, 2004, pp.71–96, at p.76.
16. Carsten Stahn, Justice under Transitional Administration: Contours and Critique of a Paradigm', *Houston Journal of International Law*, Vol.27, No.2, 2005, pp.311–44, at pp.314–15.
17. Brahimi (see n.1 above), p.664.

RESTORING JUSTICE SYSTEMS AFTER CONFLICTS 249

18. 'Comprehensive Review of the Whole Question of Peacekeeping Operations in All Their Aspects', Report of the Chairman of the Panel on United Nations Peace Operations, 21 Aug. 2000, UN doc., A/55/305–S/2000/809, p.14; 'The Rule of Law and Transitional Justice in Conflict and Post-Conflict Societies', Report of the Secretary-General, 3 Aug. 2004, UN doc., S/2004/616, p.11.
19. Reyko Huang, *Securing the Rule of Law: Assessing International Strategies for Post-Conflict Criminal Justice*, International Peace Academy policy paper, Nov. 2005, p.4, accessed at www.ipacademy.org/Programs/Research/ProgReseSecDev_Pub.htm.
20. On Afghanistan, see Jonathan Goodhand, 'Afghanistan in Central Asia', in Michael Pugh and Neil Cooper (eds), *War Economies in a Regional Context: Challenges of Transformation*, Boulder, CO: Lynne Rienner, pp.45–89, at p.76.
21. Agnes Hurwitz and Kaysie Studdard, *Rule of Law Programs in Peace Operations*, International Peace Academy policy paper, Aug. 2005, p.10, accessed at www.ipacademy.org/Programs/Research/ProgReseSecDev_Pub.htm.
22. Stephen Krasner, 'The Case for Shared Sovereignty', *Journal of Democracy*, Vol.16, No.1, 2005, pp.69–83, at p.80.
23. Vivienne O'Connor, 'Traversing the Rocky Road of Law Reform in Conflict and Post-Conflict States: Model Codes for Post Conflict Criminal Justice as a Tool of Assistance', *Criminal Law Forum*, Vol.16, Nos3–4, 2005, pp.231–55, at pp.231–2.
24. See in particular the 'Model Codes for Post-Conflict Criminal Justice Project', Irish Centre for Human Rights, Galway and United States Institute of Peace. Another example is represented by the Crisis Response Pool established by the Norwegian Ministry of Justice and the Police.
25. UNSG (report S/2004/616; see n.18 above), p.7.
26. Sally Morphet, 'Current International Civil Administration: The Need for Political Legitimacy', *International Peacekeeping*, Vol.9, No.2, 2002, pp.140–62.
27. Rama Mani, 'Balancing Peace with Justice in the Aftermath of Violent Conflict', *Development*, Vol.48, No.3, 2005, pp.25–34, at 33.
28. Annika S. Hansen and Sharon Wiharta, *The Transition to a Just Order – Establishing Local Ownership After Conflict*, Folke Bernadotte Academy research report, 2007, pp.5–6, accessed at www.folkebernadotteacademy.se/roach/The_Transition_to_a_Just_Order.do?pageId=235.
29. Stephen Golub, *Beyond Rule of Law Orthodoxy: The Legal Empowerment Alternative*, Washington, DC: Carnegie, Oct. 2003, p.37, accessed at www.carnegieendowment.org/files/wp41.pdf.
30. 'Uniting Our Strengths: Enhancing United Nations Support for the Rule of Law', Report of the Secretary-General, 14 Dec. 2006, UN doc., A/61/636–S/2006/980, p.13.
31. Matteo Tondini, 'The Role of Italy in Rebuilding the Judicial System in Afghanistan', *Revue de droit militaire et de droit de la guerre*, Vol.45, Nos1–2, 2006, pp.79–118, at p.100.
32. Leila Chirayath, Daniel Berkowitz, Katharina Pistor and Jean Francois Richard, *Customary Law and Policy Reform: Engaging with the Plurality of Justice Systems*, Washington, DC: World Bank, July 2005, p.19, accessed at http://siteresources.worldbank.org/INTWDR2006/Resources/477383-1118673432908/Customary_Law_and_Policy_Reform.pdf.
33. Daniel Berkowitz, Leila Chirayath, Caroline Sage and Michael Woolcock, 'The Transplant Effect', *American Journal of Comparative Law*, Vol.51, No.1, 2003, pp.163–204, at p.165.
34. Stahn (see n.16 above), pp.337–8.
35. Thomas Carothers, 'The End of the Transition Paradigm', *Journal of Democracy*, Vol.13, No.1, 2002, pp.5–21, at p.15.
36. Jones (see n.5 above), p.24.
37. Carothers (see n.12 above), pp.8–9.
38. Richard Sannerholm, 'Legal, Judicial and Administrative Reforms in Post-Conflict Societies: Beyond the Rule of Law Template', *Journal of Conflict and Security Law*, Vol.12, No.1, 2007, pp.65–94, at pp.70–1.
39. Hansjoerg Strohmeyer, 'Building a New Judiciary for East Timor: Challenges of a Fledgling Nation', *Criminal Law Forum*, Vol.11, No.3, 2000, pp.259–85, at p.266.
40. James Dobbins, Seth Jones, Keith Crane, Andrew Rathmell, Brett Steele, Richard Teltschik and Anga Timilsina, *The UN's Role in Nation-Building from the Congo to Iraq*, Santa Monica, CA: RAND, 2005, p.169.
41. Strohmeyer (see n.39 above), p.263.
42. Strohmeyer, 'Collapse and Reconstruction of a Judicial System: The United Nations Missions in Kosovo and East Timor', *American Journal of International Law*, Vol.95, No.1, 2001, pp.46–63, at pp.48, 53.
43. Ibid., pp.50–2.

44. Jennifer Widner, 'Courts and Democracy in Postconflict Transitions: A Social Scientist's Perspective on the African Case', *American Journal of International Law*, Vol.95, No.1, 2001, pp.64–75, at pp.67–8.
45. Tom Perriello and Marieke Wierda, *Lessons from the Deployment of International Judges and Prosecutors in Kosovo*, International Center for Transitional Justice, New York, Mar. 2006, p.15, accessed at www.ictj.org/static/Prosecutions/Kosovo.study.pdf.
46. Johann G. Lambsdorff, 'Corruption Perceptions Index 2006', in Transparency International, *Global Corruption Report 2007*, Cambridge: Cambridge University Press, 2007, pp.324–30.
47. Center for Policy and Human Development, *Afghanistan Human Development Report 2007*, Kabul, 2007, p.61.
48. UN Secretary-General (see n.30 above), pp.9,13.
49. Louis Aucoin, 'Building the Rule of Law and Establishing Accountability for Atrocities in the Aftermath of Conflict', *Whitehead Journal of Diplomacy and International Relations*, Vol.8, No.1, 2007, pp.33–49, at p.38.
50. O'Connor (see n.23 above), p.236.
51. Suzannah Linton, 'Rising from the Ashes: The Creation of a Viable Criminal Justice System in East Timor', *Melbourne University Law Review*, Vol.25, No.1, 2001, pp.122–80, at p.136.
52. Stahn, 'The United Nations Transitional Administrations in Kosovo and East Timor: A First Analysis', *Max Planck Yearbook of United Nations Law*, Vol.5, 2001, pp.105–83, at p.131.
53. Tondini (see n.31 above), pp.85,95.
54. Michael G. Karnavas, 'Creating the Legal Framework of the Brčko District of Bosnia and Herzegovina: A Model for the Region and Other Postconflict Countries', *American Journal of International Law*, Vol.97, No.1, 2003, pp.111–31, at p.122.
55. O'Connor (see n.23 above), p.240.
56. Chirayath (see n.32 above), p.3.
57. Strohmeyer, 'Policing the Peace: Post-Conflict Judicial System Reconstruction in East Timor', *University of New South Wales Law Journal*, Vol.24, No.1, 2001, pp.171–82, at p.179.
58. Widner (see n.44 above), p.66.
59. Center for Policy and Human Development (see n.48 above).
60. Michael J. Kelly, *Restoring and Maintaining Order in Complex Peace Operations: The Search for a Legal Framework*, The Hague: Kluwer, 1999, p.78.
61. Aucoin (see n.49 above), p.38.
62. Mark Sedra, 'Security Sector Reform in Afghanistan: The Slide Towards Expediency', *International Peacekeeping*, Vol.13, No.1, 2006, pp.94–110, at p.100.
63. Department of Peacekeeping Operations (see n.4 above), p.51.
64. Suzanne Katzenstein, 'Hybrid Tribunals: Searching for Justice in East Timor', *Harvard Human Rights Journal*, Vol.16, 2003, pp.245–78, at pp.263–4.
65. Eirin Mobekk, *MONUC: DDRRR, DDR, Military and Rule of Law Reform – Reducing Violence Against Women*, London: Action Aid, Oct. 2006, p.19, accessed at www.actionaid.org/assets/pdf%5CUN_DRC.pdf.
66. Stephen Golub, 'The "Other 90 Per Cent": How NGOs Combat Corruption in Non-Judicial Justice Systems', in Transparency International, *Global Corruption Report 2007*, Cambridge: Cambridge University Press, 2007, pp.129–37, at p.135.
67. Chirayath (see n.32 above), p.3.
68. International Crisis Group, *Sierra Leone: The State of Security and Governance*, Freetown/Brussels: Africa Report No.67, 2 Sept. 2003, p.21.
69. Kelly (see n.60 above), pp.77–8.
70. Ahmad N. Nadery, 'Peace or Justice? Transitional Justice in Afghanistan', *International Journal of Transitional Justice*, Vol.1, No.1, 2007, pp.173–9, at p.175.
71. See the data reported in Tondini (see n.10 above), p.337.
72. Celestine Nyamu-Musembi, 'Gender and Corruption in the Administration of Justice', in Transparency International, *Global Corruption Report 2007*, Cambridge: Cambridge University Press, 2007, pp.121–8, at p.126.
73. Suzannah Linton, 'Safeguarding the Independence and Impartiality of the Cambodian Extraordinary Chambers', *Journal of International Criminal Justice*, Vol.4, No.2, 2006, pp.327–41, at p.329.
74. Justice Studies Center of the Americas, *Report on Judicial Systems in the Americas 2006 –2007*, Jun. 2007, accessed at www.cejamericas.org/reporte.
75. SEESAC, *SALW Survey of Kosovo*, Belgrade, 2006, pp.47–8, accessed at www.seesac.org/reports/KOSOVO.pdf.

RESTORING JUSTICE SYSTEMS AFTER CONFLICTS 251

76. Strohmeyer, 'Making Multilateral Interventions Work: The U.N. and the Creation of Transitional Justice Systems in Kosovo and East Timor', *Fletcher Forum of World Affairs*, Vol.25, No.2, 2001, pp.107–28, at p.111.

77. Jeremy M. Wilson, 'Law and Order in an Emerging Democracy: Lessons from the Reconstruction of Kosovo's Police and Justice Systems', *Annals of the American Academy of Political and Social Science*, Vol.605, No.1, 2006, pp.152–77, at p.168.

78. Jones (see n.5 above), p.45.

79. OMIK, *Review of the Criminal Justice System: Crime, Detention and Punishment*, Pristina, Dec. 2004, p.49, accessed at www.osce.org/documents/mik/2004/12/3984_en.pdf.

80. Annika S. Hansen and Sharon Wiharta with Bjørn R. Claussen and Stian Kjeksrud, *The Transition to a Just Order – Establishing Local Ownership After Conflict: A Practitioners' Guide*, Folke Bernadotte Academy Research Report, 2007, p.25, accessed at www.folkebernadotte academy.se/roach/The_Transition_to_a_Just_Order.do?pageId=235.

81. Derick W. Brinkerhoff, 'Where There's a Will, There's a Way? Untangling Ownership and Political Will in Post-Conflict Stability and Reconstruction Operations', *Whitehead Journal of Diplomacy and International Relations*, Vol.8, No.1, 2007, pp.111–20, at p.118.

82. Belloni (see n.8 above), p.107.

[11]

Post-Conflict Peace-Building and Constitution-Making
Dr. Kirsti Samuels*

Peace-building accomplished through international intervention has had little success in achieving sustainable peace. In February of 2004, Haiti slipped back into chaos and despair, turning ten years of international and Haitian state-building efforts to dust. Liberia is in its second round of international intervention since returning to conflict in 2004 following UN supervised elections in 1997. There is daily violence in Iraq and ongoing instability in Afghanistan. Kosovo remains under UN administration, with an uncertain future and ongoing undercurrents of conflict.

Theories abound for the lack of success in peace-building. Some focus on operational limitations and the unintended negative consequences of international aid, while others focus on institutional lacunae.[1] Increasingly though, it is accepted that the most critical problems involve a lack of knowledge of how to rebuild states and an associated failure of state-building strategy.[2] This Article focuses on one of the key elements of post-conflict peace-

---

* PhD (Oxon), BCL (Oxon), LLB BSc (Syd), Associate, Head of the State Building Program, International Peace Academy, 777 UN Plaza, New York, NY 10017-3521. E-mail: samuels@ipacademy.org.

[1] The recent United Nations High-Level Panel on Threats, Challenges and Change highlighted the lack of a unit within the UN responsible for peace-building and advised the creation of a new body to fill this institutional lacuna. United Nations, *A More Secure World: Our Shared Responsibility*, Report of the Secretary-General's High-Level Panel on Threats, Challenges and Change, UN Doc A/59/565 at 69, ¶¶ 263–64 (2004).

[2] See, for example, Francis Fukuyama, *State-Building: Governance and World Order in the 21st Century* (Cornell 2004); Kirsti Samuels and Sebastian von Einsiedel, *The Future of UN State-Building: Strategic and Operational Challenges and the Legacy of Iraq*, Intl Peace Academy (2004), available online at <http://www.ipacademy.org/Publications/Publications.htm> (visited Oct 24, 2005); Roland Paris, *At War's End: Building Peace After Civil Conflict* (Cambridge 2004); Center for Strategic and International Studies and Association of the US Army, *Play to Win: Final Report of the Bi-Partisan Commission on Post-Conflict Reconstruction* (2003), available online at <http://www.csis.org/media/csis/pubs/playtowin.pdf> (visited Oct 24, 2005); Paul Collier, et al, *Breaking the Conflict Trap: Civil War and Development Policy*, World Bank Poly Research Rep (World Bank and Oxford 2003); Conflict, Security and Development Group, *A Review of Peace Operations: A Case for Change: East Timor* (King's College 2003), available online at <http://www.jsmp.minihub.org/

building: the role of constitution-making in the political and governance transition.

It is widely acknowledged that the provision of security is the sine qua non of peace-building, and increasingly that the building or rebuilding of public institutions is key to sustainability; however, the fact remains that a successful political and governance transition must form the core of any post-conflict peace-building mission. As we have observed in Liberia and Haiti over the last ten years, conflict cessation without modification of the political environment, even where state-building is undertaken through technical electoral assistance and institution- or capacity-building, is unlikely to succeed.[3] On average, more than 50 percent of states emerging from conflict return to conflict.[4] Moreover, a substantial proportion of transitions have resulted in weak or limited democracies.[5]

The design of a constitution and its constitution-making process can play an important role in the political and governance transition.[6] Constitution-making after conflict is an opportunity to create a common vision of the future of a state and a road map on how to get there. The constitution can be partly a peace agreement and partly a framework setting up the rules by which the new democracy will operate.

An ideal constitution-making process can accomplish several things. For example, it can drive the transformative process from conflict to peace, seek to transform the society from one that resorts to violence to one that resorts to political means to resolve conflict, and/or shape the governance framework that will regulate access to power and resources—all key reasons for conflict. It must also put in place mechanisms and institutions through which future conflict in the society can be managed without a return to violence.

Reports/otherresources/Peace4Timor_10_3_03.pdf> (visited Oct 24, 2005). See also Thomas M. Franck, *Collective Security and UN Reform: Between the Necessary and the Possible*, 6 Chi J Intl L 597 (2006); Michael J. Glennon, *Platonism, Adaptivism, and Illusion in UN Reform*, 6 Chi J Intl L 613 (2006); John C. Yoo, *Force Rules: UN Reform and Intervention*, 6 Chi J Intl L 641 (2006); William Maley, *Democratic Governance and Post-Conflict Transitions*, 6 Chi J Intl L 683 (2006); Seth G. Jones and James Dobbins, *The UN's Record in Nation Building*, 6 Chi J Intl L 703 (2006).

3   For a general discussion of these interventions, see Chetan Kumar, *Building Peace in Haiti*, IPA Occasional Paper (Lynne Rienner 1998); Adekeye Adebajo, *Building Peace in West Africa: Liberia, Sierra Leone, and Guinea-Bissau*, IPA Occasional Paper (Lynne Rienner 2002).

4   There is a 39 percent risk that peace will collapse within the first five years and a 32 percent risk that it will collapse in the next five years. Paul Collier and Anke Hoeffler, *Conflicts*, in Bjorn Lomborg, ed, *Global Crises, Global Solutions* (Cambridge 2004).

5   See Thomas Carothers, *The End of the Transition Paradigm*, 13 J Democracy 5, 13 (Jan 2002).

6   For the purposes of this Article, a constitution is defined as a system which establishes the fundamental rules and principles by which a state is governed. The constitution can be unwritten, or can be codified in one or more documents, such as a peace agreement.

I. THE CRITERIA FOR ASSESSMENT: DEMOCRACY AND PEACE

Democracy and peace are adopted in this Article as the two criteria by which the impact of constitutions should be assessed. For countries emerging from violent conflict or facing the threat of violent conflict, the importance of sustainable peace is self-evident. The importance of democracy requires a little more explanation. Despite the fact that transitions to democracy have been shown to be highly destabilizing and conflict prone,[7] and that democratization without careful understanding of the pressures on the society can create conflict in itself, democratization should still be considered the best governance structure for long-term conflict cessation.

In the immediate post-conflict environment, the adoption of a democratic regime can assist in the resolution of the struggle for power by providing an internationally accepted standard of who is entitled to govern. This standard is based on open and fair competition for power, structured around the popular vote.[8] Moreover, conflict-mediating structures and increased opportunities for participation should encourage non-violent resolution of conflicts.[9] As Jock Covey, Deputy Special Representative for the Secretary-General in Kosovo highlights, this is one of the key elements for the creation of sustainable peace.[10]

In the longer term, adoption of participatory democratic governance structures is best able to ensure peace and legitimacy. The evidence suggests that in established democracies, ethnopolitical groups are more likely to protest than rebel, minimizing internal violence.[11] Other studies have found that autocracies

---

7   Jack Snyder, *From Voting to Violence: Democratization and Nationalist Conflict* 352 (Norton 2000).

8   See Sunil Bastian and Robin Luckham, *Introduction: Can Democracy Be Designed?*, in Sunil Bastian and Robin Luckham, eds, *Can Democracy Be Designed?: The Politics of Institutional Choice in Conflict-Torn Societies* 1, 5 (Zed 2003). See also Ted Robert Gurr, *Peoples Versus States: Minorities at Risk in the New Century* 153 (US Institute of Peace 2000).

9   See Gurr, *Peoples Versus States* at 153 (cited in note 8). See, for example, Matthew Krain and Marissa Edson Myers, *Democracy and Civil War: A Note on the Democratic Peace Proposition* (1997), in Harvey Starr and Randolph Siverson, eds, 23 *International Interactions* 109, 114–15 (Gordon and Breach 2003), Christian A. Davenport, *"Constitutional Promises" and Repressive Reality: A Cross-National Time-Series Investigation into Why Political and Civil Liberties Are Suppressed*, 58 J Politics 627 (1996).

10 Covey states that peace will only become durable when parties seek to achieve their goals through peaceful means in a legitimate competition for power. Jock Covey, *Making a Viable Peace: Moderating Political Conflict*, in Jock Covey, Michael J. Dziedzic, and Leonard R. Hawley, eds, *The Quest for Viable Peace: International Intervention and Strategies for Conflict Transformation* 99, 114 (US Institute of Peace 2005).

11 Gurr, *Peoples Versus States* at 162 (cited in note 8). The Polity data set was used to compare data on ethnopolitical conflict in four categories of nations in 1985–1998: twenty-seven old democracies, thirty-three new democracies established between 1980 and 1994, thirty-two transitional regimes

Chicago Journal of International Law

are less stable (more prone to regime change) than democracies.[12] Thus, democracy is both the most stable and the least conflict-prone regime type.[13]

The importance of democratization is implicitly recognized, although it is often not explicitly stated, in the UN peace-building approach.[14] Nonetheless, in practice, the political and governance elements of state-building have proven particularly difficult. Even in those instances where security has been established, state-building has largely resulted in cosmetic political change and created weak, unstable, or even criminal states. In the former President of Liberia's words, "The state we produced turned out to be a criminal state, legitimized by elections."[15] As we saw in Liberia, the recreation of a predatory, shadow, or authoritarian state is likely to lead to a return to conflict.[16] This is

---

(mixture of autocratic and democratic features or had attempted a transition to democracy after 1970 and had not consolidated), and twenty-six autocracies. Id at 154.

12   Havard Hegre, et al, *Toward a Democratic Civil Peace? Democracy, Political Change, and Civil War*, 1816–1992, 95 Am Pol Sci Rev 33, 44 (2001). See also Christian A. Davenport, *Freedom under Fire: State Repression, Conflict and the Fragility of Domestic Democratic Peace* (2005), forthcoming paper from the ISA Convention on Dynamics of World Politics: *Capacity, Preferences, and Leadership* (Mar 2005).

13   Hegre, *Toward a Democratic Civil Peace?* at 44 (cited in note 12).

14   For instance, the official mandate for the United Nations Transitional Administration in East Timor ("UNTAET") stresses the need to "carry out its mandate effectively with a view to the development of local democratic institutions." Security Council Res No 1272, UN Doc S/RES/1272, ¶ 8 (1999). This was most clear in the later reports of the Secretary-General emphasizing that the holding of democratic elections was "no doubt, the most important, since it entails the establishment of a political system that is responsive to the citizens and a political leadership that is responsible in its decisions." United Nations, *Report of the Secretary-General on the United Nations: Transitional Administration in East Timor*, UN Doc S/2000/738, § VIII(69) (2000). Note also that the role of elections and democratization as an alternative to violence to produce a "just and durable settlement" of a conflict has been emphasized by the Security Council and Secretary-General. See, for example, Security Council Res No 745, UN Doc S/RES/745, preamble (1992) (Cambodia); Security Council Res No 957, UN Doc S/RES/957, ¶ 3 (1994) (Mozambique); Security Council Res No 1159, UN Doc S/RES/1159, ¶ 16 (1998) (Central African Republic); Security Council Res No 1497, UN Doc S/RES/1497, ¶ 12 (2003) (Liberia). See also Boutros Boutros-Gali, *An Agenda for Democratization*, UN Doc A/51/761 (1996); General Assembly Res No 50/185, UN Doc A/RES/50/185 (1996); United Nations, *Report of the Secretary-General: Support by the United Nations System of the Efforts of Governments to Promote and Consolidate New or Restored Democracies*, UN Doc A/51/512 (1996).

15   Interview with Dr. Amos Sawyer, former President of the Interim Government of National Unity in Liberia and Associate Director and Research Scholar in the Department of Political Science at Indiana University, in New York, NY (Mar 28, 2005) (on file with author).

16   Michael Bratton, *State Building and Democratization in Sub-Saharan Africa: Forwards, Backwards, or Together?*, Afrobarometer Working Paper No 43, 8 (2004), available online at <http://www.afrobarometer.org/AfropaperNo43.pdf> (visited Oct 25, 2005). This conclusion is also consistent with the finding of the State Failure Task Force that partial democracies are seven times more likely to fail than full democracies or autocracies. Jack A. Goldstone, et al, *State Failure Task Force Report: Phase III Findings* vi (Science Applications Intl 2000).

why a carefully designed and managed political and governance transition to democracy is integral to any state-building strategy.

II. THE ROLE OF PARTICIPATORY CONSTITUTIONAL PROCESSES

Initiating changes to the political culture of a society is one of the most difficult aspects of any post-conflict transition. It requires substantial changes to behavior as well as to expectations and norms. These sorts of societal changes require long-term strategies involving large segments of society. They require extensive education and sensitivity campaigns as well as dialogue and consensus-building within society. These more intangible aspects of peace-building are frequently overlooked in favor of more technical rebuilding and assistance. Nonetheless, they are essential to long-term change.

One opportunity for societal dialogue that arises in most UN managed peace-building is the adoption of a participatory constitution-making process. It is increasingly recognized that *how* constitutions are made, particularly following civil conflict or authoritarian rule, impacts the resulting state and its transition to democracy. The process of constitution-building can provide a forum for the negotiation of solutions to the divisive or contested issues that led to violence. It can also lead to the democratic education of the population, begin a process of healing and reconciliation through societal dialogue, and forge a new consensus vision of the future of the state.

Until recently, constitutional theory tended to focus on constitutions in stable political contexts rather than the importance of constitutions during periods of political change. A realist approach in political theory views constitutions as reflections of the balance of power at their time of drafting and thus does not consider them to have any particular role as agents of change or in transitions.[17] The idealist perspective recognizes their foundational role, and considers them to provide a break with the old regime and act as the foundation of the new political order.[18] However, it is "transitional constitutionalism," or "new constitutionalism," that best recognizes the multifaceted role of such

---

[17] For a general discussion, see Arend Lijphart, *Democracies: Patterns of Majoritarian and Consensus Government in Twenty-One Countries* (Yale 1984). See also Guillermo O'Donnell and Philippe C. Schmitter, *Transitions from Authoritarian Rule: Tentative Conclusions about Uncertain Democracies* (Johns Hopkins 1986).

[18] Bruce Ackerman, *The Future of Liberal Revolution* 61 (Yale 1992). See also Bruce Ackerman, *Constitutional Politics/Constitutional Law*, 99 Yale L J 453, 456 (1989).

constitutions.[19] As Tietel points out, constitutionalism is "inextricably enmeshed in transformative politics"—it codifies the prevailing consensus and also transforms it.[20] Constitution-making must be recognized as a process "or a forum for negotiation amid conflict and division."[21]

The content of a constitution, and the extent to which it sets up a democratic process rather than merely divides the spoils between political elites, will impact the state's chances of long-term peace and the quality of the democracy created. A recent study by the International Institute for Democracy and Electoral Assistance ("IDEA"), explored twelve cases of constitution-building undertaken during times of transition from civil conflict or authoritarian rule[22] and emphasized the complexity of these processes and the wide variety of factors that affect their outcome. Nonetheless, some interesting trends can be identified in the cases.[23]

In the study, the more representative and more inclusive constitution building processes resulted in constitutions favoring free and fair elections, greater political equality, more social justice provisions, human rights protections, and stronger accountability mechanisms.[24] In contrast, processes

---

19   The concept of "transitional constitutionalism" refers to constitutional developments that occur immediately after a period of substantial political change. See Ruti Teitel, *Post-Communist Constitutionalism: A Transitional Perspective*, 26 Colum Hum Rts L Rev 167, 168 (1994).

20   Ruti Teitel, *Transitional Jurisprudence: The Role of Law in Political Transformation*, 106 Yale L J 2009, 2076 (1997).

21   Vivien Hart, *Constitution-Making and the Transformation of Conflict*, 26 Peace & Change 153, 154 (2001).

22   Carolyn McCool, *The Role of Constitution-Building Processes in Democratization: Afghanistan Case Study* (Intl IDEA 2004); A.A. Mohamoud, *The Role of Constitution-Building Processes in Democratization: Bahrain Case Study* (Intl IDEA 2005); J. Esteban Montes and Tomás Vial, *The Role of Constitution-Building Processes in Democratization: Chile Case Study* (Intl IDEA 2005); Iván Marulanda, *The Role of Constitution-Building Processes in Democratization: Colombia Case Study* (Intl IDEA 2004); Randall Garrison, *The Role of Constitution-Building Processes in Democratization: East Timor Case Study* (Intl IDEA 2005); Jill Cottrell and Yash Ghai, *The Role of Constitution-Building Processes in Democratization: Fiji Case Study* (Intl IDEA 2004); Roddy Brett and Antonio Delgado, *The Role of Constitution-Building Processes in Democratization: Guatemala Case Study* (Intl IDEA 2004); Andrea Mezei, *The Role of Constitution-Building Processes in Democratization: Hungary Case Study* (Intl IDEA 2005); Edward Schneier, *The Role of Constitution-Building Processes in Democratization: Indonesia Case Study* (Intl IDEA 2005); Jill Cottrell and Yash Ghai, *The Role of Constitution-Building Processes in Democratization: Kenya Case Study* (Intl IDEA 2004); John Simpkins, *The Role of Constitution-Building Processes in Democratization: Nigeria Case Study* (External Perspective) (Intl IDEA 2004); Priscilla Yachat Ankut, *The Role of Constitution-Building Processes in Democratization: Rwanda Case Study* (Intl IDEA 2005). All case studies are available online at <http://www.idea.int/conflict/cbp> (visited Oct 24, 2005).

23   The Author participated in the study as an external consultant and prepared the final analytical study. These comments are derived from the Author's analysis of the case studies.

24   The cases of Kenya, Guatemala, and Colombia show that a participatory process can have a substantial impact on the content of the document produced. The broad participatory process in

dominated by one interest or faction tended to result in constitutions favoring that interest or entrenching power in the hands of certain groups.[25] Moreover, the more participatory processes initiated a dialogue and began a process of democratic education in societies that had not had political freedom or the chance to shape the governance of their state in the past.[26] The participatory processes seem to have empowered the people.

"Pacted"[27] democratic transitions in Latin American and Southern Europe show similar trends. While the pacted democracies in Venezuela, Colombia and Brazil did survive the authoritarianism of the 1960s and 1970s, they undermined social and economic equality and empowered actors for whom democracy was not a priority.[28] The experience in Spain, in contrast, was largely positive, resulting in a consolidated democracy.[29]

Encarnación has argued that the key difference between the two outcomes is the question of who participated in the bargaining cartel.[30] In Venezuela, Colombia, and Brazil the pact-making was elite-driven and secretive with few

---

Kenya resulted in the inclusion of provisions addressing issues of social and economic justice, as well as issues of corruption and the failure of political elites to act responsibly. See Cottrell and Ghai, *Kenya Case Study* at 26–27 (cited in note 22). In Colombia and Guatemala, the participatory and inclusive process resulted in strongly reformed constitutions that expressly provided rights to those groups who had not up to then gained political protection or recognition. See Marulanda, *Colombia Case Study* at 24–25 (cited in note 22); Brett and Delgado, *Guatemala Case Study* at 48 (cited in note 22).

[25] A draft written by one faction or one dominant interest results in a document that tends to be biased towards that interest. For instance, the 1980 Pinochet constitution in Chile sought to entrench a military control and exclude the left from political power. It resulted in years of oppressive dictatorship. See Montes and Vial, *Chile Case Study* at 5–9 (cited in note 22). The 1990 Fiji constitution sought to entrench military and indigenous Fijian power and has been the source of increasing tensions. See Cottrell and Ghai, *Fiji Case Study* at 8, 34 (cited in note 22). The Nigerian and Bahrain constitutions, which were imposed by authoritarian bodies, include provisions that dilute popular control of the legislature and the executive. See Simpkins, *Nigeria Case Study* at 2–3 (cited in note 22); Mohamoud, *Bahrain Case Study* at 20 (cited in note 22).

[26] Popular consultation certainly brought about public support for a Rwanda constitution, as it did in South Africa—another country with a highly participatory process. See Ankut, *Rwanda Case Study* at 17–18 (cited in note 22); Simpkins, *Nigeria Case Study* at 16 (cited in note 22). In contrast, the people have strongly rejected the constitutions in Nigeria and Bahrain, which were not at all participatory for the very reason that they were imposed on, rather than made by, the people. See Simpkins, *Nigeria Case Study* at 2–3; Mohamoud, *Bahrain Case Study* at 20–21 (cited in note 22).

[27] A political pact is defined as "an explicit, but not always publicly explicated or justified, agreement among a select set of actors which seeks to define (or, better, to redefine) rules governing the exercise of power on the basis of mutual guarantees for the 'vital interests' of those entering into it." O'Donnell and Schmitter, *Transitions from Authoritarian Rule* at 37 (cited in note 17).

[28] Id at 42.

[29] See Omar G. Encarnación, *Do Political Pacts Freeze Democracy?: Spanish and South American Lessons*, 28 W Eur Pol 182, 189 (2005).

[30] Id at 197.

Chicago Journal of International Law

powerful actors, including the outgoing regime, whereas in Spain the bargaining group included practically the whole "ideological spectrum."[31] Thus, negotiations that involve a small number of elite participants, seek to impose long-term power divisions, restrict the policy agenda, and limit government accountability to the broader population, should be avoided as they undermine the quality of the democracy created in the long-term.

The cases reviewed in the IDEA study also emphasized that frequently the conflicts resulted from, or were exacerbated by, stark elite-population divisions. Thus, any chance of long-term resolution of such conflicts would require the sort of dialogue and negotiation that was rendered possible by the participatory national dialogue processes. This is consistent with Hart's writings emphasizing that the people must be included in the search for solutions to conflict, rather than conflict resolution being a "division of the spoils" between factions. Hart points out that "[w]here conflict is essentially over governance by, and respect for, a diversity of people and peoples, those people and peoples must be heard in the process of constitution making."[32] Power is not "solely an inter-elite matter, and limited to purely geo-ethnic and institutional aspects."[33] For sustainable peace, the governance framework will have to be more inclusive and "build up broader stakes of participation in the peace-building process."[34]

The IDEA cases did not provide evidentiary support for the concern that participatory processes will have a divisive effect, or be dominated by radical extremist views, in highly divided societies or societies emerging from traumatic conflict. The participatory element did not increase divisions or provide warlords with greater power. In Afghanistan, for instance, the participation process was managed in a careful fashion to prevent the warlords or Islamic extremists from dominating the process. Nonetheless, such divisive impacts are a possibility if the participatory and consultative process is not carefully designed.

The use of more participatory and inclusive processes does appear to broaden the constitutional agenda and prevent the process from degenerating into a mere division of spoils between powerful players. However, at the same time, such constitutions tended to threaten the established power structures,

---

[31]   Id at 192. Spain adopted many different forms of pacts: a secret pact between Franco's democratic opposition that set up the democratic transition based on a series of compromises; followed after the elections of 1977 by policy-making pacts such as the Moncloa pact which addressed economic reform, salary regulation, and incorporated extensive redistributive policies. For a discussion of the different Spanish pacts, see id at 187–92.

[32]   Hart, *Constitution-Making* at 160 (cited in note 21).

[33]   J. 'Bayo Adekanye, *Power-Sharing in Multi-Ethnic Political Systems*, 29 Security Dialogue 25, 32 (1998).

[34]   Id at 33.

which frequently reacted by undermining them—amending them, preventing them from being adopted, or preventing their enforcement. Thus, a key challenge becomes how to address the opposing requirements of creating incentives for the powerful players to participate, without abdicating a genuine consultative process that fosters political dialogue and empowers the people. There is no simple answer to this dilemma, which requires careful weighing of the surrounding circumstances and options for implementation of the constitution, including the degree of outside enforcement capability and the degree of internal popular activism.

III. THE ROLE OF CONSTITUTIONAL ENGINEERING

Creating sustainable democratic institutions is a second key challenge in peace-building. The design of the constitution seeks both to create new democratic institutions and to assure their protection in the longer term. Unless they are carefully designed and implemented, democratic institutions can ferment conflict in sharply divided societies.[35] A poor governance framework will undermine the sustainability of the peace. It can exacerbate fault lines, divisions, and tensions in society; entrench conflict-generating electoral or governance models, or provide a basis for contesting the government.

In Haiti, for instance, the 1987 Constitution continues to undermine sustainable peace. The majoritarian structure has encouraged tyranny of the majority and reinforced Haiti's winner-takes-all political culture. Uncertainty in the constitutional provisions on elections has also provided a flash point for violence following the 2000 elections, the results of which were contested by the opposition. Moreover, the dissolution of the army was never constitutionally ratified and contributes to the ongoing instability and the former army members' sense of frustrated entitlement.[36]

Nonetheless, an appropriate governance framework may not be able to ensure sustainable peace and democracy. Any attempt to change basic system rules in society through constitutional or institutional reform faces considerable implementation challenges, including path-dependency, political transaction

---

[35] Frances Stewart and Meghan O'Sullivan, *Democracy, Conflict and Development—Three Cases*, in Gustav Ranis, Sheng-Cheng Hu, and Yun-Peng Chu, eds, 1 *The Political Economy of Comparative Development into the Twenty-First Century: Essays in Memory of John C.H. Fei* (Edward Elgar 1999); Bastian and Luckham, *Can Democracy Be Designed?* at 1 (cited in note 8).

[36] See Stephen Temple, *UN Troops Launch Offensive Against Former Haitian Soldiers as Country Prepares for Elections*, World Market Analysis (Mar 25, 2005); Jane Regan, *Haiti: Despised and Disbanded, a Blood-Stained Army Returns*, IPS-Inter Press Service (Sept 7, 2004).

costs, and inertia. Moreover, there is an emerging consensus that formal institutions will only be effective when they do not conflict with informal ones.[37]

Therefore, constitutional reform alone will not overcome long-entrenched informal and institutional practices unless there is substantial domestic support for the changes. When accompanied by appropriate incentives, the design of new rules can set a new agenda, change the rules of the game, and begin a process of reform; however, to do so they must be integrated with the sort of transformative societal processes discussed above.

IV. THE CHOICE OF CONSTITUTIONAL MODELS

The search for institutional structures that encourage moderate behavior is a crucial aspect of governance structures in post-conflict environments, and is widely viewed as a key to preventing the return to conflict. The pure majoritarian democratic model is generally considered unsuited to conflict-prone and highly divided societies.[38] As the Carnegie Commission on Preventing Deadly Conflict points out:

> [I]n societies with deep ethnic divisions and little experience with democratic government and the rule of law, strict majoritarian democracy can be self-defeating. Where ethnic identities are strong and national identity weak, populations may vote largely along ethnic lines. Domination by one ethnic group can lead to a tyranny of the majority.[39]

Incentives in the form of power-sharing structures and electoral rules have long been used to shape democracy to address division and to encourage moderation. These structures and rules generally take the form of variations on the consociational power-sharing and integrative governance models, which are the two main alternatives to the pure majoritarian democratic model. Consociational power-sharing involves power-sharing between cooperative but autonomous groups,[40] whereas integrative governance aims to transcend group

---

37   Adekanye, *Power-Sharing* at 29 (cited in note 33); Michael Bratton and Nicolas van de Walle, *Democratic Experiments in Africa: Regime Transitions in Comparative Perspective* (Cambridge 1997); Ian S. Spears, *Africa: The Limits of Power-Sharing* 13 J Democracy 123, 130 (July 2002).

38   Arend Lijphart, *Patterns of Democracy: Government Forms and Performance in Thirty-Six Countries* 32–33 (Yale 1999).

39   Carnegie Commission on Preventing Deadly Conflict, *Preventing Deadly Conflict: Final Report* 100 (Carnegie Commission 1997).

40   See Ulrich Schneckener, *Making Power-Sharing Work: Lessons from Successes and Failures in Ethnic Conflict Regulation*, 39 J Peace Research 203 (2002).

differences by encouraging groups to cooperate around common political goals.[41]

There remains much uncertainty surrounding the impact of different governance choices in post-conflict environments. This is partly because such governance structures involve a complex interaction between various institutions and processes and a particular historical and cultural environment. It is also the result of the highly polarized nature of the debate over consociationalism. As Timothy Frye points out, "one gets the sense that the original combatants have settled in for a long period of trench warfare."[42]

A. EXECUTIVE POWER-SHARING

A recent study by International Peace Academy ("IPA") provides some interesting insights into the medium-term impact of constitutional choices in conflict-prone environments.[43] The study focuses on how the constitutional rules and political institutions adopted in six countries following violent conflict impacted on the broader democratization process and peacefulness in each state.[44]

Putting aside the question of power-sharing during periods of transition immediately after conflict (when it is often the only option to stop the violence), the study investigates the impact of such structures in the medium-to-long-term.[45] Overall, the cases support the view that formal executive power-sharing[46] leads to a fragile peace, often without violence but also without reconciling the parties or addressing the underlying tensions. Moreover, while all societies investigated already had longstanding deep divisions, these appeared to have

---

[41] I adopt terminology from Robin Luckham, Anne Marie Goetz, and Mary Kaldor, *Democratic Institutions and Democratic Politics*, in Bastian and Luckham, eds, *Can Democracy Be Designed?* 14, 45 (cited in note 8).

[42] Timothy Frye, *Presidents, Parliaments and Democracy: Insights from the Post-Communist World*, in Andrew Reynolds, ed, *The Architecture of Democracy: Constitutional Design, Conflict Management, and Democracy* 81 (Oxford 2002).

[43] Kirsti Samuels, *State Building and the Consequences of Constitutional Choices in Conflict-Prone Environments: Bosnia and Herzegovina, Fiji, Lebanon, Northern Ireland, South Africa and Uganda* (IPA Policy Paper, forthcoming 2005) (on file with author).

[44] The six case studies that form the basis of that study were prepared for IPA by the following experts: Sumantra Bose, *Bosnia and Herzegovina Case Study for IPA*; Jill Cottrell and Yash Ghai, *Fiji Case Study for IPA*; Paul Salem, *Lebanon Case Study for IPA*; Adrian Guelke, *Northern Ireland Case Study for IPA*; Paul Graham, *South Africa Case Study for IPA*; Miria Matembe, *Uganda Case Study for IPA*. Case studies are on file with author; their publication is forthcoming.

[45] Samuels, *State Building and the Consequences of Constitutional Choices*, IPA Policy Paper (cited in note 43).

[46] Bosnia and Herzegovina, Lebanon, and Northern Ireland each adopted formal power-sharing to end civil conflict. Fiji adopted formal power-sharing to avoid civil conflict.

become even more entrenched and radicalized during the power-sharing phase. Voluntary power-sharing along non-ethnic lines,[47] in contrast, did achieve inclusive governments in the cases considered, and even seem to have lessened the ethnic divisions.

The cases highlight the fragility of a power-sharing government and the degree to which it is reliant on genuine commitment by the political leadership. A power-sharing government is vulnerable to collapse when parties pull out or threaten to do so. Working through consensus requires substantial commitment and compromise, which is difficult to achieve in highly divided societies.

Unsurprisingly, under these conditions the power-sharing governments have been repeatedly immobilized by the clauses intended to ensure moderation and consensus (for example, Lebanon, Northern Ireland, and Fiji).[48] In Lebanon, for instance, Salem points out that the "decision making is complex, slow and often paralyzed. Prime ministers that come in with a clear agenda find themselves unable to form a cabinet fully responsive to them nor to implement the policies they are proposing."[49]

In all of the cases where a power-sharing agreement was successfully implemented, it did provide an alternative to violent conflict (Lebanon, Northern Ireland, Bosnia Herzegovina, and South Africa). However, implementation has been a key difficulty. Such agreements generally represent none of the parties' preferred outcomes.[50] Moreover, there is a large trust deficit. As Bose points out in relation to Bosnia and Herzegovina, there is a "deep sense of injury, betrayal and distrust that continues to dominate mutual perceptions and relations between the Bosnian communities in the post-war phase."[51] The

---

[47]   South Africa and Uganda adopted voluntary inclusive government models.

[48]   In Fiji, the parties continually frustrate the intention of the agreement despite attempts by the courts to enforce the agreement. There has been a surge of nationalist single-ethnicity parties, and tension and violence continues to grow between the ethnic Fijian and the Indo-Fijian communities. See Bureau of Democracy, Human Rights, and Labor, US State Department, *Country Reports on Human Rights Practices: Fiji* (Mar 4, 2002), available online at <http://www.state.gov/g/drl/rls/hrrpt/2001/eap/8308.htm> (visited Oct 11, 2005). In Northern Ireland, even with outside intervention, the power-sharing government has repeatedly fallen apart, leading to a return to direct rule from London. See Encarta Online Encyclopedia, entry for "Ireland, Northern" (Microsoft 2005), available online at <http://encarta.msn.com/text_761571415__1/Northern_Ireland.html> (visited Oct 13, 2005).

[49]   Salem, *Lebanon Case Study for IPA* (cited in note 44).

[50]   In Bosnia and Herzegovina, for instance, partition was preferred by many, and in Northern Ireland half the population seeks integration with the UK while the other half seeks a united Ireland.

[51]   Bose, *Bosnia and Herzegovina Case Study for IPA* (cited in note 44).

presence of an outside state, which may be key to enforcement,[52] can also create tensions, however, as it did with respect to Syria's presence in Lebanon.

Moreover, the formalized divisions of power along identity or ethnic lines appear to entrench the ethnic and divisive positions that have fueled the conflict, rather than ameliorate them. While all societies investigated already had longstanding deep divisions, these appeared to become even more radicalized during the power-sharing phase. In Northern Ireland, Fiji, and Bosnia and Herzegovina there has been a distinct increase in support for more extreme political parties over more moderate parties since the adoption of power-sharing structures.[53]

South Africa (post-transition) and Uganda also adopted executive power-sharing, but with two key differences: the criterion was not ethnic, racial or religious, and inclusion was a voluntary decision by the dominant party. In South Africa, after the end of the formal power-sharing government during the period of transition, the African National Congress continued to run a power-sharing government on a voluntary basis. While the National Party left the official power-sharing transitional government to stand in opposition in 1996, it recently rejoined this voluntary government of national unity. In Uganda, a unique no-party inclusive government model was adopted by President Museveni after the war. Although the system has become less accommodating to divergent views in recent times, for a decade or more it provided a relatively effective inclusive government.

These voluntary power-sharing models were adopted without outside pressure and were backed up by domestic political commitment. In Uganda and South Africa, the system may have actually lessened the role of ethnicity in politics.[54] The voluntary nature of these agreements seems important as it

---

[52] In Bosnia and Herzegovina, the international community continues to play a central role in enforcing the agreement. Syria has been the dominant power-broker in Lebanon since the signing of the Taif agreement, and the UK has played that role in Northern Ireland.

[53] In Bosnia and Herzegovina the only significant party with a cross-national ideology is the Social Democratic Party ("SDP"), but even the SDP's support is largely mono-ethnic Bosnian. Bose, *Bosnia and Herzegovina Case Study for IPA* (cited in note 44). The electoral environment in Northern Ireland is dominated by sectarian politics, which is seemingly institutionalized by the requirement that members register as Unionist, Nationalist or Other, and the only cross-confessional party has decreasing support. Guelke, *Northern Ireland Case Study for IPA* (cited in note 44). In Fiji, even though the power-sharing is not formally ethnically based, the elections have favored the newly created more extreme nationalist and ethnically based parties. No cross-ethnic parties have been created and those that were cross-ethnic have split into their constituent parts. Cottrell and Ghai, *Fiji Case Study for IPA* (cited in note 44). Even in Lebanon, which has relied on power-sharing along confessional lines for close to a hundred years, the divisions remain as strong as ever.

[54] Graham, *South Africa Case Study for IPA* (cited in note 44); Matembe, *Uganda Case Study for IPA* (cited in note 44).

reflects a commitment by the political leaders to an inclusive government of national unity, whereas a formal executive power-sharing agreement is generally seen as an uncomfortable compromise by all parties.

B. ELECTORAL MODELS

In the post-conflict context, elections are highly divisive and can easily undermine the chance of building a sustainable democracy.[55] Reilly emphasizes the need to design the rules "in such a way as to promote moderate voices over extremist ones, and to facilitate intra-group as well as inter-group competition."[56] The aim must be to use the electoral process to transform the competition for political power.[57]

One of the major debates in this field has been whether a list proportional representational ("PR") model (where the proportion of votes a party receives is reflected in the number of seats it holds in parliament), a preferential model, such as the alternative vote ("AV") model (where electors rank the parties in order of preference and votes are allocated through these preferences until a winner emerges), or majoritarian model with fixed ethnic quotas, is best able to ensure the required moderation and representativeness.

Empirical studies have demonstrated greater voter participation in PR than in simple majoritarian electoral systems[58] and have showed that the difference in degree of satisfaction between winners and losers is smaller in consociational models than in simple majoritarian models.[59] Nonetheless, the impact of electoral systems in a particular political environment is complex, and no simple empirical link between PR systems and higher levels of political support among ethnic minorities can be established.[60]

55   Benjamin Reilly, *Democratic Validation*, in John Darby and Roger MacGinty, eds, *Contemporary Peacemaking Conflict, Violence, and Peace Processes* 174, 176 (Palgrave Macmillan 2003).

56   Id at 179.

57   In addition to electoral structure, the question of the timing of elections is often problematic. Early elections increase division and can entrench the warring parties as the dominant political players, while late elections can entrench the compromise interim solution and may fail to achieve any opening up of the political space, unless the interim process is carefully planned.

58   According to a study by Blais and Carty (1990) comparing over five hundred elections across twenty nations as noted in Pippa Norris, *Ballots Not Bullets: Testing Consociational Theories of Ethnic Conflict, Electoral Systems, and Democratization*, in Reynolds, ed, *The Architecture of Democracy* 206, 214 (cited in note 42).

59   According to a study by Anderson and Guillory (1997) comparing the satisfaction with democracy among consensual and majoritarian political systems in eleven EU member states. Id at 215.

60   Norris' study compares the political attitudes and behavior of a range of ethnic minorities to test the consociational proposition that PR systems are more effective at engendering support for the political system among ethnic minorities. She concludes that data from the 1996–1998 Comparative Study of Electoral Systems—comparing political attitudes and behavior among a

In the IPA study, the electoral systems in the six case studies ranged across "majoritarian with quotas" (Uganda, Lebanon), "preferential" (Northern Ireland, Fiji, Republika Skrska), and "list proportional representation" (South Africa, Bosnia Herzegovina).[61] A majoritarian model with fixed ethnic quotas was seen to encourage the election of moderates in sufficiently mixed districts, but not to do so in districts dominated by one ethnic group. In Lebanon, for instance, a candidate running for a Christian seat in a mixed district in Lebanon was also required to appeal to the Muslim community; however, in districts dominated by one ethnic group this moderating impact was not felt.[62] A disadvantage of the system was that the rigidity resulting from the fixed ethnic or religious quotas froze the divisions at the time the electoral system was adopted. In contrast, reserved seats for women, or other interest groups, appeared to encourage the participation of new actors in politics, but did so without entrenching ethnic or religious divides. In Uganda, for instance, such quotas[63] did not entrench religious or ethnic divisions, and in combination with the "no party" system, seem to have refocused the political discourse away from religion and ethnicity.

One of the more concerning results in the study was the unpredictability of the preferential voting models (such as the Single Transferable Vote ("STV"), or Alternative Vote ("AV")) that have been put forward as encouraging moderation and compromise across ethnic lines. The consociational list PR model, as Horowitz argues, places the focus on post-electoral coalitions, which in his view "no doubt entail compromise over the division of cabinet portfolios, but typically not compromise over divisive inter-ethnic issues."[64] It does not require candidate parties and coalitions to attract votes across group lines. In these case studies, however, there is little support for Horowitz's argument that preferential

---

diverse range of ethnic minorities in the US, UK, Australia, Taiwan, Ukraine, Lithuania, Poland, Romania, the Czech Republic, Spain, New Zealand and Israel—did not provide evidence for the proposition that PR party list systems engender higher levels of political support among ethnic minorities than majoritarian systems. Id at 233. Note that one of the weaknesses of the study is that it did not differentiate between levels of satisfaction in countries emerging from conflict and levels of satisfaction in states that have distinct minorities within them but have not suffered ethnic polarization or ethnic violence.

61 See IPA case studies (cited in note 44).

62 See Salem, *Lebanon Case Study for IPA* (cited in note 44). In practice, however, in Lebanon, elite collusion has led to the creation of pre-agreed lists, undermining electoral contest.

63 For background on the use of quotas in Uganda, see Sylvia Tamale, *Introducing Quotas in Africa: Discourse and Legal Reform in Uganda*, Intl Institute for Democracy and Electoral Assistance (Nov 2003), available online at <http://www.quotaproject.org/CS/CS_Uganda_Tamale-6-6-2004.pdf> (visited Oct 13, 2005).

64 Donald L. Horowitz, *Constitutional Design: Proposals Versus Processes*, in Reynolds, ed, *The Architecture of Democracy* at 15, 20, 22 (cited in note 42).

voting systems such as the AV better promote pre-electoral coalitions since they encourage compromise to attract voters across ethnic lines.[65]

In the cases considered, results were hard to anticipate, and in some cases the system actually funneled votes to more extreme parties. Northern Ireland adopted multi-member district STV, considered one of the most sophisticated electoral systems, which has both a proportional and preferential basis.[66] While the electoral results under STV were more moderate and balanced in comparison to a simple majoritarian model, the model had a somewhat unpredictable outcome in comparison to list PR.[67] Even facing the possible defeat of the Good Friday Agreement, pro-Agreement moderate politicians, such as David Trimble, still called on electors to vote for other anti-Agreement Unionist parties rather than the moderate pro-Agreement nationalist SDLP.[68]

Alternative Vote is considered to have the greatest moderating influence of the preferential electoral models. Fiji has adopted AV (although only twenty-five out of seventy-one seats are open seats—the remainder are allocated on the basis of ethnic quotas). It was initially hoped that AV would lead to the development of multi-racial parties or foster preference-deals among moderate parties, but, even the small proportion of open AV seats seem not to have favored moderation. In the 1999 elections, the AV system gave the Indian FLP party a majority of seats even though it only had 33 percent of first choice support. Under a PR system, the FLP would have had to govern with one of the other parties, either Fijian or moderate Indian. The electoral model, and the FLP's reluctance to make a power-sharing government work, may have contributed to the distrust by ethnic Fijians and the coup overthrowing it. In the 2001 elections, the AV system explicitly funneled votes towards more extreme parties.[69]

Republika Srpska's experience is similar. The OSCE (which is responsible for all party and election related matters in Bosnia and Herzegovina) experimented with AV for the 2000 presidential elections. In those elections the hard-line Serb candidate won a decisive victory, as the Bosnians refused to cross ethnic boundaries and gave their second preference to Bosnian parties that had no hope of winning rather than support moderate Serb parties. Additionally, the hard-line Serb parties campaigned on the basis that the electoral changes aimed to undermine them, which seemingly resulted in increased voter support.

---

65   Id at 20.

66   Peter Harris and Ben Reilly, eds, *Democracy and Deep-Rooted Conflict: Options for Negotiators* 198–99 (Intl IDEA 1998).

67   See Guelke, *Northern Ireland Case Study for IPA* (cited in note 44).

68   Id.

69   See Ghai, *Fiji Case Study for IPA* (cited in note 44).

According to Bose, the Serb voters realized the aim of the electoral changes and sought to defeat them. The OSCE changed the electoral system back to open list PR in 2002.[70]

A list PR model based on electoral support for parties (rather than for ethnic or religious groups) was seen to have the advantage of providing proportional representation of minorities in parliament, and seemed to provide the greatest opportunity for evolution towards a society less divided along ethnic or religious lines. For instance, the case author suggested that, in South Africa, factors such as class and geography are increasingly playing a role in elections.

Closed list PR models can place large influence in the hands of parties, and can undermine the relationship of accountability between the candidates and the voters. Open list PR systems, which allow voters to choose who on the list will be elected, as recently adopted in Bosnia and Herzegovina, ameliorate these difficulties. A key disadvantage of open list systems—that it can be difficult to implement agreements on women's participation—may be overcome through the use of reserved seats for women.

V. THE CHALLENGE OF IMPLEMENTATION AND MONITORING

Finally, it is worth discussing the challenges of implementation and monitoring of a governance structure in post-conflict environments. One key difficulty is the dominance of the executive in power-conflict environments. A climate of unregulated power will ultimately undermine the stability and legitimacy of the new state, and in immature democracies, the institutions that have been built are frequently too weak to hold governments accountable, which jeopardizes long-term stability.

The dominance of the executive is often exacerbated by the institutional weakness of parliament and the courts, which play a key role in overseeing and balancing the executive in established democracies. In East Timor, an extreme example, most parliamentarians have no experience in drafting legislation and do not read the language in which the laws are written.[71] Thus parliament is largely bypassed by the executive government. A drift towards authoritarianism will substantially undermine the quality of the democracy, increasing the risk of a return to conflict and may lead to the unraveling of much of the state-building effort.

The inadequacy of traditional checks and balances creates a dilemma for the international community. Clearly, when executive power has been

---

[70]   See Bose, *Bosnia and Herzegovina Case Study for IPA* (cited in note 44).

[71]   See Kirsti Samuels, *Assessing State-Building in Timor-Leste: Peacefulness and Quality of the Democracy at the Five-Year Mark* (IPA Policy Report, forthcoming 2005) (on file with author).

Chicago Journal of International Law

transferred to the domestic government, the international community has much less leverage. One approach could be to put economic and political pressure on the new government to abide by basic governance rules. Ashraf Ghani, one of the most inspired and resolute domestic counterparts in recent state-building missions and a key player in the Afghan transitional government, suggests that the best way to conceptualize the situation is that of a double compact: "A compact between rulers and their people and a compact between the government and the international community. And this must be framed in a context of a series of achievable benchmarks."[72]

One of the benchmarks could be the expectation that domestic government will abide by the constitution negotiated as part of the transition. Accordingly, the international community could take a more proactive approach to ensuring that any new government acts in accordance with its constitutional obligations.

International monitoring of elections is already widely accepted. The international community can also play a role in enforcement through the placing of international judges on the benches of constitutional courts. In Bosnia and Herzegovina, for instance, the Court includes three international judges appointed by the President of the European Court of Human Rights to avoid ethnic deadlock.[73] Other influences can derive from the requirements for joining economic organizations, or the use of aid policy conditionality.[74] In Europe, EU pressure and joining standards are considered to have played an important role in shaping the post-communist Eastern European states and encouraging the adoption of human rights standards.[75]

---

72   Ashraf Ghani, *The United Nations High-Level Panel on Threats, Challenges and Change: Assessing the Options and Exploring Reactions to the Report's Post-Conflict Peacebuilding Recommendations*, Speech at a meeting of the Center for Strategic and International Studies (Mar 10, 2005) (on file with author).

73   In Bosnia the nine member court has four members who are selected by the Federation House of Representatives and two members selected by the Republika Srpska National Assembly. To prevent ethnic deadlock in adjudication, the remaining three members of the court must be non-citizens, are selected by the President of the European Court of Human Rights "after consultation with the Presidency," and cannot be citizens of any neighboring country. Bosnia and Herzegovina Const, art VI, § 1. Two international judges sit on the East Timor Court of Appeal. See *Attacks on Justice 2002: East Timor*, Intl Commission of Jurists (Aug 27, 2002), available online at <http://www.icj.org/news.php3?id_article=2657&lang=enIMG/pdf/easttimor.pdf> (visited Oct 13, 2005).

74   This view is also supported in the article by Stewart and O'Sullivan, *Democracy, Conflict and Development* at 355 (cited in note 35).

75   Marina Ottaway, *Democratization and Ethnic Nationalism: African and Eastern European Experiences* (Overseas Development Council 1994). See also, Ekaterini Papagianni, *European Integration and Eastern European Nationalism: A Comparative Study of Minority Policies in Estonia, Latvia, Romania and Slovakia* (2003) (PhD Dissertation, Columbia University) (on file with author).

VI. CONCLUSION

The design of a constitution and constitution-making process is an integral part of the political and governance transition in peace-building. However, it is also a particularly difficult aspect, both because there is little understanding of the impact of constitutional processes and constitutional designs in post-conflict states, and because these decisions must be made in highly charged, divided, often violent environments. Moreover, as Rothchild points out, "the short-term security concerns of the bargaining parties may be at odds with the long-term institution-building needs of the society."[76]

In relation to constitution-making process, the more participatory and inclusive processes were seen to broaden the constitutional agenda and avoid the process degenerating into a mere division of spoils between powerful players. At the same time, such constitutions tended to threaten the established power structures. The key dilemma is therefore how to ensure both that the powerful players participate and are committed to the process, and yet also ensure that the process fosters political dialogue and empowers the people.

In relation to constitutional design, this Article has shown that there is an urgent need for the development of new approaches to executive power-sharing. The cases support the view that formal executive power-sharing leads to a fragile peace that is free of violence but does not affect underlying tensions. Power-sharing agreements were seen to be susceptible to deadlock and collapse, to require extensive international intervention, and to risk both entrenching and radicalizing underlying divisions. Yet there are few ready alternatives. If power-sharing can be achieved on a voluntary basis, this seems to produce a more effective inclusive government, although the majority party leadership required for such a model is rare.

This Article has also shown that the electoral model chosen can impact the outcome of elections, but the cases illustrate that designing electoral models to promote moderation or facilitate intra-ethnic compromise is not straightforward. A key concern results from the unpredictability of the preferential voting models, which have been put forward as encouraging moderation and compromise across ethnic lines. In the cases considered, results were difficult to anticipate, and in some cases the system actually funneled votes to more extreme parties.

Finally, this Article highlights the difficulties that arise from the likelihood that the courts and parliament, traditional checks and balances, will be

---

[76] Donald Rothchild, *Settlement Terms and Postagreement Stability*, in Stephen John Stedman, Donald Rothchild, and Elizabeth M. Cousens, eds, *Ending Civil Wars: The Implementation of Peace Agreements* 117–18 (Lynne Rienner 2002).

Chicago Journal of International Law

disproportionately weak in a post-conflict environment, and the need to develop alternative mechanisms of constitutional enforcement.

[12]

'Jus ad bellum', 'jus in bello' … 'jus post bellum'? – *Rethinking the Conception of the Law of Armed Force*

Carsten Stahn*

Abstract

The law of armed force is traditionally conceptualized in the categories of jus ad bellum and jus in bello. This dualist conception of armed force has its origin in the legal tradition of the inter war period. This essay revisits this approach. It argues that the increasing interweaving of the concepts of intervention, armed conflict and peace-making in contemporary practice make it necessary to complement the classical rules of jus ad bellum and in jus in bello with a third branch of the law, namely rules and principles governing peace-making after conflict. The idea of a tripartite conception of armed force, including the concept of justice after war ('jus post bellum') has a long-established tradition in moral philosophy and legal theory. This article argues that this historical concept deserves fresh attention from a legal perspective at a time when the contemporary rules of jus ad bellum and jus in bello are increasingly shaped by a normative conception of law and justice and a broadening notion of human security. Moreover, it identifies some of the legal rules and principles underlying a modern conception of 'just post bellum'.

1 Introduction

Since *Grotius' De Jure Belli ac Pacis*, the architecture of the international legal system has been founded upon a distinction between the states of war and peace. At the beginning of the 20th century, it was taken for granted that 'the law recognizes a state of peace and a state of war, but that it knows nothing of an intermediate

* Dr.jur., LL.M. (NYU), LL.M. (Köln–Paris), Associate Legal Officer. International Criminal Court, Visiting Fellow Leiden University. The views expressed in this article are those of the author alone and do not necessarily reflect the views of the International Criminal Court. This article is part of a broader research project of the author on '*jus post bellum*'. Email: Carsten.Stahn@icc-cpi.int.

922   *EJIL* 17 (2006), 921–943

state which is neither one thing nor the other'.[1] Today, this claim stands to be revisited.

Traces of the historic distinction between war and peace are still present in some distinct areas of law.[2] However, war and peace are no longer perceived as strict organizing frameworks for the categorization of rules of international law. The United Nations Charter has narrowed the grounds on which subjects of international law may legitimately resort to armed violence.[3] There are multiple situations in which (what was formerly called) 'the law of war' and the 'law of peace' apply simultaneously.[4] Moreover, the question of how to make peace in periods of transition following war has become one of the main preoccupations of international law and practice since 1945.[5] These developments raise some doubts as to whether some of the traditional understandings of international law still suffice to explain the complexities of contemporary international law.

Both the increase of interventions and the growing impact of international law on post-conflict peace make it particularly timely and pertinent to take a closer look at the architecture of the law of armed force. The current debate about the law of armed force is mostly focused on a discussion of the *status quo* of *jus ad bellum* and *jus in bello*[6] and the relationship between these two branches of law[7]. This essay seeks to offer a different perspective on the contemporary law of armed force, by suggesting a systemic rethinking of the categories of the law. It argues that some of the dilemmas of contemporary interventions may be attenuated by a fresh look at the past, namely a

---

[1]   See House of Lords, Lord MacNaghten, *Janson v Driefontein Consolidated Mines Ltd.* [1902] AC 484. Lassa Oppenheim's classical treatise on international law divided the entirety of the rules of international law into the categories of peace and war. See H. Lauterpacht (ed.), *Oppenheim's International Law* (6th edn., 1947), i (Peace) and ii ('War and Neutrality').

[2]   See, *inter alia*, the project of the ILC on the effects of armed conflict on the law of treaties. For a survey of the various reports of the Commission on this topic, see ILC, *Effects of armed conflicts on treaties*, available at http://untreaty.un.org/ilc/guide/1_10.htm.

[3]   See S. Neff, *War and the Law of Nations* (2005), at 315–356.

[4]   A good example is the parallel applicability of human rights law and international humanitarian law. See ICJ, *Legal Consequences of the Construction of a Wall in the Occupied Palestinian Territory*, Advisory Opinion of 9 July 2004 [2004] ICJ Rep 136, para. 106.

[5]   Multi-dimensional peacekeeping operations and modern interventions have gradually led to a departure from the notion of peace in the mere absence of violence ('negative peace'). This is, *inter alia*, reflected in the concept of collective 'responsibility to protect', which encompasses three dimensions of communitarian conflict management in cases of large-scale atrocities: preventive action, responsive action, and post-conflict engagement ('responsibility to prevent', 'responsibility to react', and 'responsibility to rebuild'). See paras. 138 and 139 of GA Res. 60/1 (2005 World Summit Outcome) of 24 Oct. 2005.

[6]   See among others Ratner, 'Jus ad Bellum and Jus in Bello after September 11', 96 *AJIL* (2002) 905; Lietzau, 'Old Laws, New Wars: Jus ad Bellum in an Age of Terrorism', 8 *Max Planck Yearbk UN L* (2005) 383.

[7]   See generally on this distinction Scelles, 'Jus in Bello, Jus ad Bellum', 6 *Nederlands Tijdschrift voor Internationaal Recht* (1959) 292; Kolb, 'Origins of the Twin Terms Jus ad Bellum/Jus in Bello', 320 *Int'l Rev of the Red Cross* (1997) 553. On the interplay see Canor, 'When Jus ad Bellum Meets Jus in Bello: the Occupier's Right of Self-defence Against Terrorism Stemming from Occupied Territories', 19 *Leiden J Int'l L* (2006) 129.

(re)turn to a tripartite conception of armed force based on three categories: *'jus ad bellum'*, *'jus in bello'* and *'jus post bellum'*.[8]

2 The Erosion of the Classical War–Peace Distinction

This exercise requires some reconsideration of formerly established groundwork. The starting point is the bipolar peace and war distinction. This classical distinction has its origin in 19th-century thinking when war and peace were conceived to be completely distinct legal regimes. War and peace were not only distinguished in temporal terms ('state of war'/'state of peace'), but were considered to be independent legal frameworks with mutually exclusive rules for wartime and peacetime.[9] This clear-cut distinction lost its *raison d'être* in the 20th century.[10] Three changes may be observed, in particular:

The gradual outlawry of war as a legal institution in the 20th century has removed one fundamental prerequisite of the classical peace/war dichotomy, namely the recognition of war as a legitimate category of law. War is no longer treated as a legally accepted paradigm, but as a factual event regulated by (different bodies of) law. It has thus become uncommon to treat war and peace as separate and diametrically opposed legal institutions and to theorize the rules of international law on the basis of this dialectical relationship.

Second, there is no (longer a) clear dividing line between war and peace.[11] The classical dichotomy of peace and war has lost part of its significance due to the shrinking number of inter-state wars after 1945 and the increasing preoccupation of international law with civil strife and internal armed violence.[12] International

---

[8]   To date, scholarship on the concept of *'jus post bellum'* has been rare. Where literature exists, it has mostly approached the topic from the angle of just war theory. See B. Orend, *War and International Justice, A Kantian Perspective* (2000), 57; ibid., *'Jus Post Bellum'*, 31 *J Social Philosophy* (2000) 117; ibid., *The Morality of War* (2006), at 160–190; Bass, 'Jus Post Bellum', 32 *Philosophy & Public Affairs* (2004) 384; and DiMeglio, 'The Evolution of the Just War Tradition: Defining Jus Post Bellum', 186 *Military L Rev* (2005) 116. The existing contributions on the subject differ considerably in content. For different treatments see Iasiello, 'Jus Post Bellum. The Moral Responsibilities of Victors in War', 57 *Naval War College Rev* (2004) 33; Boon, 'Legislative Reform in Post-conflict Zones: Jus Post Bellum and the Contemporary Occupant's Law-Making Powers', 50 *McGill LJ* (2005) 285; and the study by C. Schaller, *Peacebuilding und ius post bellum, Völkerrechtliche Rahmenbedingungen der Friedenskonsolidierung nach militärischen Interventionen* (2006), available at http://www.swp-berlin.org/de/common/get_document.php?id=1663# search=%22Schaller%20Jus%20Post %20Bellum%22. For a short analysis of *jus post bellum* as a legal concept see C. Stahn, *Jus Ad Bellum, Jus in Bello, Jus Post Bellum: Towards a Tripartite Conception of the Law of Armed Force*, ESIL Inaugural Conference Paper, available at www.esil-sedi.org/english/pdf/Stahn2.PDF.

[9]   War and peace were diametrically opposed concepts. It was assumed that a 'state of war' excluded the applicability of the law of peace. For an insightful discussion see Neff, *supra* note 3, at 177–196.

[10] See Wright, 'The Outlawry of War and the Law of War', 47 *AJIL* (1953) 356, at 365; H. Lauterpacht, 'The Limits of the Operation of the Law of War', 30 *British Yearbk Int'l L* (1953) 206, at 240.

[11] Some authors began to advocate the existence of a grey zone between war and peace in the 1940s. See Schwarzenberger, 'Jus Pacis, Ac belli?', 37 *AJIL* (1943) 460, at 470; Jessup, 'Should International Law Recognize an Intermediate Status Between War and Peace?', 48 *AJIL* (1954) 98.

[12] See Human Security Report, *The Changing Face of Global Violence* (2005), at 18 ('[i]n the last decade, 95% of armed conflicts have taken place within states, not between them').

924   *EJIL* 17 (2006), 921–943

practice has dealt with multiple situations which are neither 'declared wars' in the conventional sense, nor part of peacetime relations, such as threats to peace caused by repressive state policies. Moreover, international law comes into play in processes of transition from one stage to the other, namely in transitions from peace to war or in transitions from war to peace.[13] If one were to theorize this phenomenon, it would be more correct to speak of a tri-dimensional (rather than bipolar) system, covering the phases of conflict, peacetime relations and the transition from conflict to peace.

Third, it is becoming increasingly clear that some of the problems arising in the period of transition from conflict to peace cannot be addressed by a simple application of the 'law of peace' or the 'laws of war', but require 'situation-specific' adjustments, such as organizing frameworks and principles which are specifically geared towards the management of situations of transition between conflict and peace.[14]

3 Revisiting the Dualist Conception of the Law of Armed Force

This transformation is only partially reflected in the contemporary conception of the law of armed force. This body of law is based on a dualist conception of armed force

---

[13] Principles of the traditional 'law of peace' are increasingly applied to societies, which are not in a clear situation of war or peace, but are involved in a process of transition from conflict to peace (e.g. the gradual collapse of state structure).

[14] There appears to be a growing awareness that to end hostilities requires not only measures to terminate conflict (conflict termination), but active steps to build peace (peacemaking). This type of engagement has facilitated the application of norms of international law to situations of transition from conflict to peace, such as standards for transitional justice, elections, and democratization as well as property claims mechanisms, compensation regimes, and individual human rights procedures in (post-)conflict societies. Some of the rules and procedures applicable in situations from conflict to peace require deviations from commonly established norms in order to accommodate the specific tensions of societies in transition. Standards of democratic governance may have to be adjusted to a polity in transition. Caretaker governments, e.g., may be allowed to exercise governing authority without being formally legitimated through the holding of elections. Criminal proceedings may have to be focused on the prosecution of the 'most serious crimes' ('targeted accountability'). Property claims may have to be dealt with in specific mass claims procedures in order to facilitate a speedy reversion of the consequences of armed conflict and/or to facilitate minority returns. For examples in the cases of Bosnia and Herzegovina and Kosovo see Commission for Real Property Claims of Displaced Persons and Refugees (BiH), *End of Mandate Report (1996–2003)* (2004), at 3; OSCE Mission in Kosovo, Department of Human Rights and Rule of Law, *Property Rights in Kosovo 2002–2003* (2003). International military forces, which are traditionally bound by wartime obligations, have been forced to respect certain peacetime standards (such as *habeas corpus* guarantees), when exercising public authority in a post-conflict environment. See Parliamentary Assembly Res. 1417 (2005), *Protection of Human Rights in Kosovo*, available at http://assembly. coe.int/main.asp?Link=/documents/adoptedtext/ta05/eres1417.htm. See generally S. Chesterman, *You the People: The United Nations, Transitional Administration and State-building* (2004), at 126–152; R. Caplan, *International Governance of War-torn Territories* (2005), at 179–195. See also J. Dobbins *et al.*, *The UN's Role in Nation-building: From the Congo to Iraq* (2005).

which distinguishes the law of recourse to force (*jus ad bellum*) from the law govern-ing the conduct of hostilities (*jus in bello*).[15]

The distinction between *jus ad bellum* and *jus in bello* has a long tradition in the the-ory of warfare (*Vitoria*,[16] *Wolff*,[17] *Vattel*[18]). However, it found its place in positive law only at the time of the League of Nations, when the Kellogg-Briand Pact outlawed the absolute power to resort to war by its prohibition of aggressive war.[19]

The recognition of *jus ad bellum* and *jus in bello* as legal concepts has brought import-ant conceptual innovations *vis-à-vis* the legal thinking of the 19th century. It has not only changed the perception of war, but reaffirmed the indiscriminate application of the obligations of warring parties in the conduct in hostilities.[20] *Jus ad bellum* and *jus in bello* were declared to be distinct normative universes, in order to postulate the principle that all conflicts shall be fought humanely, irrespective of the cause of armed violence.[21]

However, the current architecture of the law of force continues to be shaped by cer-tain antinomies. Firstly, the distinction between the justification for the use of force and the *jus in bello* is not always as clear-cut and stringent as is sometimes claimed. While there is agreement that principles and entitlements under *jus in bello* (for instance, the requirements of necessity, proportionality and humanity and the privi-leges of combatants) should generally apply independently of the cause of armed con-flict,[22] there are cases in which findings under one body of law shape the applicability or interpretation of the other body of law.[23] Following the motivation of interventions in cases such as Iraq in 1991 and Kosovo in 1999, there has even been discussion

---

[15] For a general treatment see Yoram Dinstein, *War, Aggression and Self-Defence* (4th edn., 2005); and *ibid.*, *The Conduct of Hostilities under the Law of International Armed Conflict* (2004).

[16] In his *De indes et de iure belli relectiones*, Vitoria distinguished lawful motives of war from just limits in war. See Vitoria, *De iure belli relectiones* (1539), Nos. 15 ff and 34 ff. For an English translation see E. Nys (ed.), *De iure belli relectiones* (trans. J.B. Pate, 1917).

[17] See C. Wolff, *Jus gentium methodo scientifica pertractatum* (1749), at paras 888 ff.

[18] See E. Vattel, *Law of Nations* (1758), iii, chap. VIII.

[19] It appears in legal writing in the 1920s. Enriques used the term *jus ad bellum* in 1928. See Enriques, 'Considerazioni sulla teoria della guerra nel diritto internazionale', 20 *Rivista di diritto internazionale* (1928) 172. Later, Kunz took up the notion in an article pubished in 1934: see Kunz, 'Plus de lois de guerre?', 41 *Revue Générale de Droit International Public* (1934) 22. However, the breakthrough came only after the end of the Second World War, when the express distinction between *jus ad bellum* and *jus in bello* gained widespread acceptance in monographs: see, e.g., L. Kotzsch, *The Concept of War in Contempo-rary History and International Law* (1956), at 86 and 89.

[20] This is, *inter alia*, reflected in the preamble to Additional Protocol 1 to the Geneva Conventions which makes it clear that the provisions of the Protocol apply in all circumstances without distinction based on the 'nature or origin' of the underlying conflict.

[21] This is also reflected in the factors triggering the applicability of *jus in bello*. The 'state of war' doctrine pro-vided sovereigns with discretion to recognize the existence of a war in the legal sense. In the 20th century, this subject test was replaced by an objective requirement based on the factual character of a conflict.

[22] This appears to be the official position of the ICRC, according to which international humanitarian law 'addresses the reality of a conflict without considering the reasons for or legality of resorting to force': see ICRC, *International Humanitarian Law: Answers to your questions* (2002), at 14.

[23] The most prominent example of the nexus between *jus in bello* and *jus ad bellum* is the definition of armed conflict in Art. 1(4) of Additional Protocol I, which extends the applicability of the law governing inter-national armed conflicts to 'armed conflicts which people are fighting against colonial domination and

926   *EJIL* 17 (2006), 921–943

whether there should be a new normative dispensation, according to which egregious violations of *jus in bello* could be regarded as the trigger for rights under the *jus ad bellum*.[24]

Secondly, the dualist conception of the law of armed force carries an idea of exclusiveness which is increasingly anachronistic in the context of the growing diversification and application of international law in all spectrums of public life. The *jus ad bellum/jus in bello* narrative reflects, to some extent, the traditional dichotomy between war and peace. *Jus ad bellum* is traditionally perceived as the body of law which provides grounds justifying the transition from peace to armed force, while *jus in bello* is deemed to define 'the conduct and responsibilities of belligerent nations, neutral nations and individuals engaged in armed conflict in relation to each other and to protected persons'.[25] This understanding suggests that each of these two bodies of law contains its own specific and exclusive system of rules which comes into play in circumstances when the traditional rules of the 'law of peace' cease to be of adequate guidance. Such an assumption is misleading, because it is premised on the idea that the underlying period in time is governed by a specific body of law,[26] rather than by a multiplicity of subject-specific legal regimes originating from different sources of law.

Moreover, this dualist system, with its strict focus on the period of armed hostilities, is increasingly artificial since it fails to reflect the growing interrelation between armed violence and restoration of peace. A dualist conception of armed conflict based on the division between *jus ad bellum* and *jus in bello* presents a simplified account of the sequencing and categorization of human conduct throughout armed hostilities. The operation of both systems of rules (governing armed force) is centred on a specific period, namely the period from the outbreak of hostilities to conflict termination. This centralization is open to criticism because it is often impossible to draw a clear-cut distinction between the (continued) conduct of armed hostilities and a post-conflict setting. It also fails to reflect the growing impact of international law on the restoration of peace after conflict.

These findings make it necessary to revisit the classical dualist construction of the law of armed force (*jus ad bellum/jus in bello*) and to think about a broader conception of conflict, including the recognition of principles governing peace-making after war.

---

alien occupation and against racist regimes in the exercise of their right of self-determination'. It is occasionally argued that *jus in bello* and *jus ad belllum* constitute 'sometimes competing, sometimes complementary' bodies of law. See Berman, 'Privileging Combat? Contemporary Conflict and the Legal Construction of War', 43 *Columbia J Transnat'l L* (2004) 6.

[24] See ASIL, 100th Annual Meeting, *The Relationship Between Jus Ad Bellum and Jus In Bello: Past, Present, Future* (2007, forthcoming).

[25] See the definition of *jus in bello* in Wikipedia Encyclopedia, *Laws of War*, available at http://en.wikipedia.org/wiki/Jus_in_bello.

[26] This understanding was reflected in the legal tradition of the 19th century according to which the presence of a state of war precluded the application of all rules applicable in peacetime. See Neff, *supra* note 3, at 178.

A *Features of* jus ad bellum *and* jus in bello

One of the main achievements of the modern law of armed force is that it provides more than a mere framework outlawing armed violence or setting limitations on the conduct of armed forces.[27] Contemporary rules of armed force do not contain only prohibitions for states and armed forces; they channel armed violence and regulate the relations between different actors (military forces, civilians, ousted government) in situations of armed conflict. However, the classical concepts of *jus ad bellum* and *jus in bello* contain gaps with respect to the management of post-conflict relations.

Concepts such as individual criminal responsibility or the 'humanization' of the conduct of warfare[28] were far less developed at the time, when the current rules of *jus ad bellum* and *jus in bello* were originally conceived. The traditional rules of *jus in bello* are therefore only partially equipped to address the problems arising in the context of peacemaking and the transition from armed conflict to peace. The classical rationale of *jus in bello* is to limit the consequences of armed conflicts on non-combatants (including vulnerable groups such as the wounded, women and children), property and the environment. Accordingly, *jus in bello* provides only a fraction of principles governing the process of conflict termination, including capitulations and armistices.[29] Similarly, the principle of international criminal responsibility for the commission of serious crimes is only partially covered by the Geneva Law.[30]

Furthermore, gaps and structural ambiguities exist on at least three other levels: the temporal scope of application of the norms of international humanitarian law, the continuing uncertainty about the feasible scope of application of rules of international humanitarian law, and the difficulty to conduct exercises in state- or nation-building under the auspices of the law of occupation.

The norms of international humanitarian law, by definition, apply only to a limited extent to the period following the cessation of hostilities. Additional Protocol I provides that the application of the Geneva Conventions and the Protocol will cease 'on the general close of military operations'.[31] This moment is usually deemed to occur 'when the last shot has been fired'.[32] Only selected provisions apply after the 'cessation of active hostilities'. A 'post-conflict' duty, namely the obligation to repatriate, is

---

[27] See recently Berman, *supra* note 23, at 4–5.

[28] See Meron, 'The Humanization of Humanitarian Law', 94 *AJIL* (2000) 239. For a human-rights-based interpretation of the laws of war see, e.g., Martin, 'Using International Human Rights Law for Establishing a Unified Use of Force Rule in the Law of Armed Conflict', 64 *Saskatchewan L Rev* (2001) 347.

[29] See Arts 35–41 of the 1907 Hague Convention (IV) Respecting the Laws and Customs of War on Land.

[30] See, *inter alia*, the provisions on grave breaches of the Geneva Conventions. In its jurisprudence, the ICTY, found that crimes committed in non-international armed conflicts are punishable under customary international law, although 'common Article 3 of the Geneva Conventions contains no explicit reference to criminal liability for violation of its provisions': see ICTY, *Prosecutor v Tadic*, Decision on Defence Motion for Interlocutory Appeal on Jurisdiction, 2 Oct. 1995, at paras 128–132.

[31] See Additional Protocol I, Art, 3(b); See also Fourth Geneva Convention, Art. 6 which provides that the application of the convention shall cease 'on the close of military operations'.

[32] See *Final Record of the Diplomatic Conference of Geneva of 1949* (Berne: Federal Political Department, 1949, repr. 2005), ii–A, at 815. However, the protracted nature of modern conflicts and the involvement of potentially numerous armed groups and factions make it often difficult to determine a definitive

928   *EJIL* 17 (2006), 921–943

activated in a classical 'wartime' situation, namely before the close of military operations, which marks the date of the termination of 'armed conflict'. Moreover, parts of
the 'law of war', namely specific duties of the occupant under the laws of occupation,
continue to apply in a 'peacetime' situation, namely after the close of military operations.[33] The norms of international humanitarian law are therefore only to a limited
extent relevant to the broader process of building peace after conflict.

Secondly, there are doubts as to the extent to which it is desirable and feasible to
extend the applicability norms of '*jus in bello*' to the process of peace-making. Following the Bulletin of the Secretary-General on the observance of international humanitarian law by UN forces, there is widespread agreement that UN peacekeepers are
bound to observe 'fundamental principles and rules of international humanitarian
law', although the UN is not a party to the Hague or Geneva Conventions.[34] However,
it is unclear as to what extent international humanitarian law can and should be
used to regulate civilian activities undertaken by such actors in the aftermath of the
conflict, whether it be under the umbrella of occupation, the United Nations, or
within the framework of a multinational administration. In these situations, the
choices of international humanitarian law collide with other frameworks such as
international human rights law, which offers, in many ways, a more modern and a
more nuanced framework to address challenges of peace-building. International
human rights law regulates public authority directly from the perspective of individual and group rights (human rights, minority rights, self-determination), whereas
international humanitarian law continues to view public authority, at least partly,
through the lens of competing state interests.[35]

The law of occupation, the only branch of the *jus in bello* which deals explicitly with
post-conflict relations, is ill-suited to serve as a framework of administration.[36] Both
the Hague and the Geneva law are conceived of as legal frameworks to address temporary power-vacuums after conflict. Their focus lies on the maintenance of public
security and order and the protection of the interests of domestic actors. These
requirements force occupying powers to exercise restraint in the shaping of the law
and institutions of occupied territories.[37] The examples of post-war Germany and
Japan have shown that the needs and dynamics of processes of post-conflict

---

point in time at which the laws of war cease to operate: see Roberts, 'The End of Occupation: Iraq 2004',
54 *ICLQ* (2005) 27, at 34.

[33]   See Art. 6 of the Fourth Geneva Convention.

[34]   See United Nations, Secretary-General's Bulletin, ST/SGB/1999/13, 6 Aug. 1999, at para. 1. This position has been defended by the Institut de Droit International since the early 1970s. See Institut de Droit
International, 'Resolution, Conditions of Application of Humanitarian Rules of Armed Conflict to Hostilities in which United Nations Forces may be Engaged', 54(II) *Annuaire Institut de Droit International*
(1971) 465. See also generally M. Zwanenburg, *Accountability of Peace Support Operations* (2005).

[35]   See Mégret and Hoffmann, 'The UN as a Human Rights Violator? Some Reflections on the United Nations
Changing Human Rights Responsibilities', 25 *Human Rights Quarterly* (2003) 314.

[36]   For a discussion see Bhuta, 'The Antinomies of Transformative Occupation', 16 *EJIL* (2005) 740.

[37]   See Art. 43 of the Hague Regulations as well as Art. 47 of the Fourth Geneva Convention. Arts 64 and
65–70 of the Fourth Geneva Convention provide certain exceptions to the continuation of the previously
applicable law.

reconstruction are difficult to reconcile with the provisions of the law of occupation *stricto sensu*.[38]

The limitations of the law of occupation again became apparent in the case of the occupation of Iraq. In this case, the Security Council invented a new model of multi-lateral occupation,[39] which merged the structures of belligerent occupation with ele-ments of peace-making under Chapter VII, in order to facilitate reconstruction under the umbrella of collective security. This model produced more questions than answers. Security Council Resolution 1483 embodied some modern principles of international law into the framework of the occupation.[40] However, the reference of the Council to two parallel legal regimes, namely the continued application of the law of occupation on the one hand,[41] and principles of state-building on the other,[42] left the limits of reconstruction in a legal limbo.[43] Some measures of the Coalition Provi-sional Authority (CPA), such as the creation of the Iraqi Special Tribunal or the reform of the Iraqi private sector,[44] remained doubtful from a legal perspective.[45]

These examples confirm that the contemporary *jus ad bellum* and *jus in bello* are based on related, but partly distinct, rationales or foundations from the process of peacemaking.[46] It therefore makes some sense to argue that the period of transition from conflict deserves an autonomous legal space in the architecture of the law of armed force.

[38] For a critique of the *deballatio* doctrine see E. Benvenisti, *The International Law of Occupation* (2003), pref-ace and at 72–96.
[39] See also Benvenisti, 'The Security Council and the Law on Occupation: Resolution 1483 on Iraq in His-torical Perspective', 1 *Israel Defense Forces L Rev* (2003) 23, sect. III.
[40] The resolution reaffirmed, in particular, that post-war occupation does not entail a transfer of sover-eignty or title over the territory, but rather a mandate to build or restore domestic self-determination or self-government. Furthermore, as occupying powers, the US and the UK were bound to promote the wel-fare of the local population, including ensuring equal rights and justice, while being subjected to a rudi-mentary form of public accountability *via* their duty to report to the Security Council: *ibid.*
[41] SC Resolutions 1483 and 1511 recognized the occupation of Iraq but did not authorize it in a formal way. The Coalition Provisional Authority therefore remained bound by the Hague Regulations and the Geneva Conventions. This was set out in a letter dated 8 May 2003 in which the UK and the US stated that they would 'strictly abide by their obligations under international law, including those relating to the essential humanitarian needs of the people of Iraq'.
[42] Several responsibilities mentioned in SC Resolution 1483 went beyond the ordinary framework of the maintenance of law and order under the laws of occupation ('effective administration of the territory'; 'creation of conditions in which in which the Iraqi people can freely determine their own political future' (para. 4); establishment of 'national and local institutions for representative governance' (para. 8.c)).
[43] See also Zwanenburg, 'Existentialism in Iraq: Security Council Resolution 1483 and the Law of Occupa-tion', 86 *Int'l Rev of the Red Cross* (2004) 745, at 765–766.
[44] CPA Order No. 39 provided the basis for the privatization of the Iraqi economy, while permitting 100% foreign ownership in most sectors. Bids were limited to members of the 'coalition of the willing'.
[45] For a critical survey of the practice of the Coalition Provisional Authority in Iraq see Sassòli, 'Legislation and Maintenance of Public Order and Civil Life by Occupying Powers', 16 *EJIL* (2005) 694.
[46] The need for an autonomous set of criteria for *jus post bellum* under the just war doctrine has been stressed by Michael Walzer with respect to occupations: see Walzer, 'Just and Unjust Occupation', in M. Walzer, *Arguing About War* (2004), at 163. For a full discussion of the separation of *jus ad bellum, jus in bello,* and *jus post bellum* see Boon, *supra* note 8, at 292.

930   *EJIL* 17 (2006), 921–943

B *Inadequacies of a Dualist Conception of the Law of Armed Force*

Logically, the argument in favour of an extension of the categories of the law of armed force could have been made in the 1930s. However, the claim for recognition of a third branch of the law of armed force is particularly compelling at a time when the restoration of peace and justice in the (post-) conflict stage is conceived as the other side of the coin of intervention.

1 *Peacemaking as the Other Side of Intervention*

The case in favour of the regulation of peace-making is in part supported by a change of discourse about the justification of intervention. Traditionally, the use of military force was justified by the purpose of thwarting security threats or conquering foreign territories. The prohibition of the use of force and the revitalization of the collective security system have modified this picture. Today, interventions are often justified by a bundle of post-conflict oriented purposes, including, most notably, the defence of universal and communitarian values such as human rights, democracy or self-determination.[47] Increasingly, attempts are made to justify intervention on multiple grounds, which take into account the effects of the intervention on the post-conflict phase. In such circumstances, it is only logical that this phase be recognized in the equation of armed force.

This tendency is further reflected in contemporary practice. There are multiple initiatives to establish a link between the 'pre-' and the '(post-) conflict' phase. The most far-reaching proposition has been made by the International Commission on Intervention and State Sovereignty. In its report, *The Responsibility to Protect*, the Commission suggested a new conception of responsibility following intervention ('responsibility to rebuild'), noting that modern interventions cannot end after the cessation of military activities, but require ongoing engagement to prevent conflict.[48] Subsequently, this idea was taken up in slightly moderated form in the High-Level Panel Report on Threats, Challenges and Change,[49] the Report of the Secretary-General entitled 'In Larger Freedom: Towards Development, Security and Human Rights for All'[50] and in the Outcome Document of the 2005 Word Summit[51] which lays down certain basic principles concerning the meaning and scope of the international 'responsibility to protect'.[52] It can also be found in the mandate of the Peacebuilding Commission, which was created to address the challenge of helping countries with

---

[47] This is partly a result of the ever-widening interpretation of the notion of 'international peace and security' in the practice of the Security Council.

[48] See Report of the International Commission on Intervention and State Sovereignty, *The Responsibility to Protect* (Dec. 2001), para. 5.1.

[49] See Report of the UN High-level Panel on Threats, Challenges, and Change, *A More Secure World: Our Shared Responsibility* (2004), at paras 201–203.

[50] See Secretary-General, *In Larger Freedom, Towards Development, Security and Human Rights for All*, 21 Mar. 2005, at para. 135. The UN Secretary-General emphasized a similar need in his report, *The Rule of Law and Transitional Justice in Conflict and Post-conflict Societies*, 23 Aug. 2004, at para. 2.

[51] See GA Res. 60/1 (2005 World Summit Outcome) of 24 Oct. 2005.

[52] See *ibid.*, at paras. 138 and 139. For an analysis of the concept of 'responsibility to protect' see Stahn, 'Responsibility to Protect: Political Rhetoric or Emerging Legal Norm?', 101 *AJIL* (2007) (forthcoming).

the transition from war to lasting peace.[53] These steps indicate a growing link between the use of force and the restoration of peace.

2 From Morality to Legality

Traditionally, this link has been explained in moral terms. Proponents of the just war theory have used moral justifications to argue that a 'just war' requires 'a just peace'.[54] Similarly, '*jus post bellum*' was mostly theorized as a moral paradigm.[55] Recently, this line of reasoning was used in the context of modern interventions. It has been argued that humanitarian interventions create a certain moral responsibility to become engaged in reconstruction.[56] A similar argument has been made in the context of nation-building in Iraq.[57] Some scholars have taken the view that the coalition had an ethical responsibility to help rebuild Iraq, because it had been involved in promoting regime change. The collapse of law and order and domestic structures following the intervention, it is argued, created a moral duty for coalition members to stay in Iraq and a moral justification to exercise 'temporary political authority as trustee on behalf of the people governed, in much the same way that an elected government does'.[58] This experience has sparked calls for a better theorization of post-war justice 'for the sake of a more complete theory of just war'.[59]

These suggestions are useful, but they do not go far enough. A purely 'morality-driven' justification of post-conflict engagement does not suffice to explain the reality of contemporary practice. There are some indications that there is a legal connection between the 'pre-' and the 'post-conflict' phase. In contemporary practice, it is not enough to establish that the motives which lead up to the recourse to force pursue a lawful and commonly accepted purpose. The acceptability of an intervention is equally measured by its effects and implications after the use of armed force.

A legal connection between the use of force and post-conflict engagements may be construed in at least two ways. The performance of post-conflict engagements may either be a building block of the legality of liberal interventions or a means to render

---

[53] See GA Res. 60/1, *supra* note 51, at paras 97–105. For a survey see Stahn, 'Institutionalizing Brahimi's "Light Footprint": A Comment on the Role and Mandate of the Peacebuilding Commission', 2 *Int'l Organizations L Rev* (2005) 403.

[54] For a survey see M. Walzer, *Just and Unjust Wars: A Moral Argument with Historical Illustrations* (3rd edn., 2000); see also B. Orend, *Michael Walzer on War and Justice* (2000) and Stanford Encyclopedia of Philosophy, *War*, available at http://plato.stanford.edu/entries/war/.

[55] See Orend, 'Justice After War', 16 *J Ethics & Int'l Affairs* (2002) 43, at 44 ('a coherent set of plausible values to draw on while developing an account of just war settlement'). See also the definition of *jus post bellum* in the Stanford Encyclopedia of Philosophy, *supra* note 54. ('[J]us post bellum refers to justice during the third and final stage of war: that of war termination . . . There is little international law—save occupation law and perhaps the human rights treaties—and so we must turn the moral resources of just war theory').

[56] See Korhonen, '"Post" as Justification: International Law and Democracy-Building after Iraq', 4 *German LJ* (2003), No. 7. For a discussion of legality and morality in the context of Kosovo see also Krisch, 'Legality, Morality and the Dilemma of Humanitarian Intervention After Kosovo', 13 *EJIL* (2003) 323.

[57] See N. Feldman, *What We Owe Iraq: War and the Ethics of Nation-Building* (2004).

[58] *Ibid.*, at 3.

[59] See Bass, *supra* note 8, at 384. A similar argument is made by DiMeglio, *supra* note 8, at 162.

932   *EJIL* 17 (2006), 921–943

the consequences of an unauthorized use of force more acceptable in the international legal system.

The first type of argument has been made in connection with liberal interventions ('humanitarian intervention', 'democratic intervention') in general. Both humanitarian and democratic interventions are directly founded on the idea of peace-making through the restoration of human rights and standards of good governance.[60] It has therefore been argued that such interventions require states to take sustainable measures to implement the proclaimed goals of the use of force, including efforts to restore basic human rights and democratic governance in the post-intervention phase. This obligation is derived from the very requirements of liberal interventions and considerations of proportionality of the use of force.[61] Such uses of force, so goes the argument, are only permissible if the corresponding action is appropriate and capable of removing the threat that motivated the use of force (*'Verpflichtung zur Nachsorge'*).[62] The novelty of this approach lies in the fact that it derives certain (post-) conflict responsibilities from the very requirements of intervention,[63] instead of deducing such duties from the concept of responsibility for internationally wrongful acts (reparation, compensation).[64]

It is more difficult to establish a link between the use of force and post-conflict engagement in the context of unauthorized interventions. There is some ground to argue that the issue of the legality of the use of force and the conduct after intervention should be kept entirely apart in such cases.[65] However, one may witness a certain tendency in practice to invoke post-conflict engagement as a factor to validate

---

[60]   For arguments in this direction see Reka, 'UNMIK as International Governance within Post-Conflict Societies', *New Balkan Politics*, Issue 7/8, available only at http://www.newbalkanpolitics.org.mk/napis.asp?id=17&lang=English, sect. II ('[m]aybe the case of Kosovo could represent a contribution towards the new liberal doctrine for the "re-conceptualization of international law", by which the "transnational legal process thereby spurs internal acceptance of international human rights" principles').

[61]   The exercise of administering functions by UNMIK and KFOR in Kosovo has been regarded as a formal requirement of the legality of the humanitarian intervention itself, which is said to impose a post-conflict responsibility on the intervening actors (*'Verpflichtung zur Nachsorge'*): see P. Zygojannis, *Die Staatengemeinschaft und das Kosovo* (2002) at 125 ('[d]ie Verpflichtung des Intervenienten zur Nachsorge als Rechtsfolge durchgeführter humanitärer Intervention').

[62]   *Ibid.*

[63]   Note that this argument has recently been used by the High-Level Panel on Threats, Challenges, and Change in its list of criteria for the authorization of interventions by the Security Council. The Report of the High-Level Panel on Threats, Challenges, and Change linked the legitimacy of interventions to their capacity to meet 'the threat in question': see High-Level Panel, *supra* note 49, at para. 207.

[64]   See Arts 31 and 36 of the ILC Draft Articles on the Responsibility of States for Internationally Wrongful Acts, *Report of the ILC on the Work of its Fifty-third Session*, UN GAOR, 56th Sess., Supp. No. 10, at 43, UN Doc A/56/10 (2001).

[65]   In particular, a forcible regime change cannot be justified by the mere invocation of the law of occupation: see Chesterman, 'Occupation as Liberation: International Humanitarian Law and Regime Change', 18 *Ethics & Int'l Affairs* (2004) 51, at 56. For a lack of justification of *jus ad bellum* violations through *jus post bellum* see also Orend, *Morality of War, supra* note 8, at 195.

intervention or to respond benevolently to the *status quo* created by it.[66] Some interventions (Liberia, Sierra Leone, Kosovo, Afghanistan, Iraq) have drawn support from different scales of approval and legitimation, which vary according to the intent of the Security Council and the degree of UN engagement: *ex post facto* validation and mitigation. [67]

Both lines of thought confirm one common trend, namely a growing interweaving of the concepts of intervention and the restoration of peace. Some interventions appear to require subsequent (post-) conflict engagement, in order for their outcomes to be recognized as valid or acceptable. This finding lends support to the view that considerations of (post-) conflict peace should form part of the architecture of the law of armed force.

C *Historical Origins of a Tripartite Conception of Armed Force*

Calls for an expanded conception of the law of armed force are by no means novel. The plea for a tripartite conception of rules of armed conflict has some precedents in legal history. Several proponents of the 'just war' doctrine discussed post-conflict principles in their writings. Francisco Suarez, for example, argued in favour of extending the just war categories to a third period, namely the ending of justly

---

[66] For a broader examination see Franck, *Recourse to Force: State Action Against Threats and Armed Attacks* (2002), at 158–162. Such a technique was explicitly applied by the Council in the context of its retroactive endorsement of the unauthorized ECOMOG interventions in Liberia and Sierra Leone: see SC Res. 788 (1992) and SC Res. 1260 (1999). A similar argument was made in relation to the NATO action and subsequent UN involvement in Kosovo in 1999 in Operation Allied Force. Although the Council did not expressly validate NATO's intervention *ex post facto*, the adoption of Res. 1244 (1999) by the Security Council and the subsequent creation of UNMIK could be viewed as an implicit endorsement of NATO action. In the case of Operation Enduring Freedom, it was debated whether the intervention exceeded the parameters of Art. 51 and interfered with the Security Council's responsibilities under Chap. VII, at least insofar as it entailed the overthrow of the Taliban regime. See Frank and Rehman, 'Assessing the Legality of the Attacks by the International Coalition against Terrorism against Al Qaeda and the Taliban in Afghanistan: an Inquiry into the Self-defence Argument under Article 51 of the Charter', 67 *J Crim L* (2003) 415; Delbrück, 'The Fight Against Global Terrorism: Self-defence or Collective Security as Internal Police Action? Some Comments on the International Legal Implications of the "War Against Terrorism"', 44 *German Yearbk Int'l L* (2001) 9, at 21. In that respect, the operation drew some subsequent support from the acknowledgement of the effects of the use of force by the Council through the endorsement of the Bonn Agreement and the subsequent establishment of UNAMA: see SC Res. 1386 (2001). The reaction of the Council to the Iraq crisis may be interpreted as a case of application of the theory of mitigation. Security Council members refrained from acknowledging the (il)legality of Operation Iraqi Freedom, yet they absolved it from legal sanction. Faced with growing security gaps and the need to restore sovereign and democratic institutions in post-war Iraq, the Council decided, as the Secretary-General stated, to 'place the interests of the Iraqi people above all other considerations': see Secretary-General, Press Release SG/SM/8945, 16 Oct. 2003, available at http://www.un.org/News/Press/docs/2003/sgsm8945.doc.htm.

[67] Note that the Report of the High-Level Panel on Threats, Challenges, and Changes establishes criteria not only for the authorization, but also for the endorsement of the use of military force: see High-Level Panel, *supra* note 49, at para. 207.

declared and fought wars.[68] In his Disputation XIII on War (1621), Suarez distinguished three periods in his conception of a just war: 'its inception; its prosecution, before victory is gained; and the period after victory'. Furthermore, he formulated post-conflict principles based on necessity concerning war reparation, the fate of property rights after war and the treatment of the conquered state.[69]

A more refined account of the forms and conditions of conflict termination was given only four years later by Hugo Grotius, who secularized just war theory in his *De Jure Belli ac Pacis*.[70] Grotius placed war within the broader categories of justice and control.[71] Book Three of his work incorporates not only concrete principles on the lawfulness of the waging of war and permissible conduct in hostilities, but also rules on surrender,[72] calls for moderation in the acquisition of sovereignty,[73] guidelines on good faith between enemies,[74] rules for the interpretation of peace treaties[75] and indications 'in what manner the law of nations renders the property of subjects answerable for the debt of sovereigns'. Grotius concluded his work with 'admonitions on behalf of good faith and peace, postulating that even 'in war peace should always be kept in view'. However, overall, Grotius' work remained focused on the identification of principles concerning the period of hostilities itself.

Findings on the conduct of post-conflict relations may also be found in Vattel's *Droit des Gens, ou Principes de la Loi Naturelle* of 1758.[76] Vattel repudiated, in particular, Hobbes' conception of war as the natural state of man and dedicated Book IV of his law of nations to the restoration of peace 'and the obligation to cultivate it', which he derived from natural law.[77] Chapter II of Book IV dealt exclusively with peace treaties. It set out general principles concerning the formation, the effect, and the execution

---

[68]   See Suarez, 'The Three Theological Virtues, Disputation XIII', in J.B. Scott (ed.), *Classics of International Law* (1995), xx, at 836. See also Vitoria, *supra* note 16, De Indis, iii, at 60 ('Third Canon: When victory has been won and the war is over, the victory should be utilized with moderation and Christian humility, and . . . so far as possible should involve the offending state in the least degree of calamity and misfortune, the offending individuals being chastised with lawful limits').

[69]   However, his findings were deeply shaped by the scholastic tradition. Suarez endorsed, *inter alia*, a victor's right to just punishment of the conquered state and the entitlement of the victorious power to deprive citizens of the opponent of their goods and their liberty, if necessary for complete satisfaction: see Suarez, *supra* note 68, at 840 and 843.

[70]   See H. Grotius, *De Jure Belli ac Pacis* (trans. F.W. Kelsey), in J.B. Scott (ed.), *Classics of International Law* (1995), ii. See on Grotius and Just War Theory P. Haggenmacher, *Grotius et la Doctrine de la Guerre Juste* (1983).

[71]   See generally Kingsbury, 'A Grotian Tradition of Theory and Practice?: Grotius, Law, and Moral Skepticism in the Thought of Hedley Bull', 17 *Quinnipiac L Rev* (1997) 3.

[72]   See Grotius, *supra* note 70, Bk 3, at 739–740.

[73]   See *ibid.*, chap. XV, at 770.

[74]   See *ibid.*, chap. XIX, at 792.

[75]   See *ibid.*, chap. XX, at 808–819.

[76]   See E. de Vattel, *Le Droit des Gens, ou Principes de la Loi Naturelle, appliqués à la Conduite et aux Affaires des Nations et des Souverains* (1758), iii, English translation by C.G. Fenwick, 'The Law of Nations or the Principles of Natural Law Applied to the Conduct and to the Affairs of Nations and of Sovereigns', in J. B. Scott (ed.), *Classics of International Law*, Vattel, Text of 1758, Books I–IV (1995), at 15.

[77]   See Vattel, *supra* note 76, Bk IV, chap. I, at 343.

of peace treaties, which were designed to serve as guidelines for the conduct of sovereign actors.[78]

This thinking was later developed by Immanuel Kant, who may be counted as one of the conceptual founders of a tripartite conception of warfare.[79] Kant introduced the notion of 'right after war' (*'Recht nach dem Krieg'*) in his philosophy of law (*Science of Right*), which formed part of *The Metaphysics of Morals*.[80] Kant expressly divided the 'right of nations in relation to the state of war' into three different categories, namely '1. the right of going to war; 2. right during war; and 3. right after war, the object of which is to constrain the nations mutually to pass from this state of war and to found a common constitution establishing perpetual peace'.[81] Kant's ideas were novel, because he linked the rules of war to the broader perspective of eternal peace. He developed this thought in Article 6 of the Articles for Perpetual Peace Among States. He established an express connection between the rules of *jus in bello* and perpetual peace, stating that '[n]o state shall during war permit such acts of hostility which would make mutual confidence in the subsequent peace impossible', such as 'the employment of assassins, prisoners, breach of capitulation, and incitement to treason in the opposing state'.[82]

Kant's preoccupation with (just) war termination did not end here. Kant identified a number of parameters, according to which peace should be shaped. One of the central premises of his post-war theory, which may again be found in the 'Articles for Perpetual Peace' is that [n]o treaty of peace shall be considered valid as such, if it was made with a secret reservation of the material for a future war'.[83] Furthermore, he argued that the victor is not entitled to punish the vanquished or to seek compensation merely because of its military superiority. Kant emphasized that peace settlements must respect the sovereignty of the vanquished state and the self-determination of its people, foreshadowing thereby some of the key features of modern peace-making. [84]

4 A Modern Framework for an Old Idea

This holistic understanding of the use of armed force gains new relevance in a modern context.[85]

---

[78] See *ibid.*, at 346–361.

[79] See Orend, *War and International Justice, supra* note 8, at 57 and 63 (n. 22).

[80] Kant's *The Science of Right* was published in 1796, as the first part of his *Metaphysics of Morals (Die Metaphysik der Sitten)* (1797).

[81] See I. Kant, *The Science of Right, supra* note 80, at 53 (Nature and Division of the Right of Nations).

[82] See I. Kant, *Perpetual Peace* (1795), Sect. 1, Art. 6.

[83] *Ibid.*, Sect. 1, Art. 1.

[84] See Kant, *Science of Right, supra* note 80, at 58 (Right after War). A weakness of Kant's law after conflict is that he still relied on the notion of 'conquest' and neglected the concept of individual criminal responsibility. Similarly, he did not rule out the possibility that an 'unjust enemy' can be forced 'to accept a new constitution of a nature that is unlikely to encourage their warlike inclinations'.

[85] See also Stanford Encyclopedia of Philosophy, *supra* note 54, at 2.3. For a survey of the relevant literature see *supra* note 8.

936   *EJIL* 17 (2006), 921–943

A *From* 'jus post bellum' *to 'Rules and Principles of (Post-)conflict Peace'*

Of course, the classical conception of 'justice after war' cannot simply be transposed to a modern setting. Certain adjustments must be made, if the idea of '*jus post bellum*' is translated from a moral principle into a legal notion.

First, the concept of a fair and just peace must be decoupled from the historical understanding which associated fairness with the idea of justice in favour of the party which had fought a just and lawful war (being a war which was waged for the right reasons) and fought in an appropriate manner. Today, considerations of fair and just peace must be deemed to apply equally to all parties to a conflict. Thus, the principal justification for distinguishing *jus ad bellum* and *jus in bello* applies equally with respect to idea of '*jus post bellum*': parties must end a dispute in a fair and just fashion irrespective of the cause of the resort to force.[86] At the same time, principles of conflict termination apply independently of violations in the conduct of armed force.[87] Such violations may even strengthen the need for fair and just peace-making (accountability, compensation, rehabilitation).

Second, the applicability of principles of post-conflict peace can no longer depend exclusively on moral considerations, such as righteousness of waging war. The concept of a fair and just peace must be framed by reference to certain objective rules and standards that regulate guidelines for peace-making in the interest of people and individuals affected by conflict.[88]

Third, peace-making is not strictly aimed at a preservation or return to the legal *status quo ante*, but must take into account the idea of transforming the institutional and socio-economic conditions of polities under transition. In this sense, peace-making differs from the classical rationale of the law of occupation. The ultimate purpose of fair and just peace-making is to remove the causes of violence. This may require positive transformations of the domestic order of a society. In many cases, a fair and just peace settlement will ideally endeavour to achieve a higher level of human rights protection, accountability and good governance than in the period before the resort to armed force.

---

[86] See also Boon, *supra* note 8, at 290.

[87] Note also that *jus in bello* makes no distinction between lawful and unlawful combatants when determining duties under the law of occupation. The ICTY has clarified in its jurisprudence that the applicability of the law of occupation is based on factual considerations: see, *inter alia*, ICTY, Appeals Chamber, *Prosecutor v Tadic*, Case No. IT-94-1-A (1999), at para. 168.

[88] This has certain implications for the relationship between *jus ad bellum* and peacemaking. An illegal use of force does not automatically entail the illegality of all engagement in the post-conflict phase. For an insightful discussion see Schaller, *supra* note 8, at 15–18. For a different view see Orend, *Morality of War*, *supra* note 8, at 162 ('failure to meet *jus ad bellum* results in automatic failure to meet *jus in bello* and *jus post bellum*'). Measures taken by an intervening force after conflict are judged by their own standards. Similarly, violations of principles of conflict termination do not *per se* justify a return to armed violence. The question when it is justified to resort to armed force remains dictated by the rules on the recourse to force.

However, the classical rationale behind the notion of *jus post bellum*, namely the idea of regulating the ending of conflicts and easing the transition to peace through certain principles of behaviour, is highly relevant in the context of international law in the 21st century. It may be argued that the classical concepts of *jus ad bellum* and *jus in bello* are complemented by a specific set of rules and principles that seek to balance the interests of different stakeholders in transitions from conflict to peace. Under this construction, armed force must not only be lawful under the law on the recourse to force and in keeping with the rules of *jus in bello* but must also satisfy certain rules of (post-) conflict settlement.[89]

The regulation of substantive components of peace-making is not merely determined by the discretion and contractual liberty of the warring factions, but is governed by certain norms and standards of international law derived from different fields of law and legal practice.

Just a few examples suffice to illustrate this argument here. The formation of peace settlements is governed by Article 52 of the Vienna Convention on the Law of Treaties and considerations of procedural fairness; the limits of territorial dispute resolution are defined by the prohibition of annexation and the law of self-determination; the consequences of an act of aggression are *inter alia* determined by parameters of the law of state responsibility, Charter-based considerations of proportionality and human rights-based limitations on reparations;[90] the exercise of foreign governance over territory is limited by the principle of territorial sovereignty, the prohibition of 'trusteeship' (over UN members) under Article 78 of the Charter limits occupation law under the Fourth Geneva Convention, as well as the powers of the Security Council under the Charter; the law applicable in a territory in transition is determined by the law of state succession as well as certain provisions of human rights law (for instance, non-derogable human rights guarantees) and the laws of occupation; finally, the scope of individual criminal responsibility is defined by treaty-based and customary law-based prohibitions of international criminal law.

These norms may be said to be part of a broader regulatory framework ('post-conflict law'), which encompasses substantive legal rules and principles of procedural fairness governing transitions from conflict to peace.[91] These norms are in many cases partly codified, but entangled with or superseded by subsequent international practice. Moreover, they are complemented by legal principles or 'soft law', which are relevant to particular decisions or situations. Some norms (for instance, *jus cogens* prohibitions) constitute 'hard' law ('rules') [92]. They are applicable 'in an all-or-nothing

[89] See also in the context of just war theory Bass, *supra* note 8, at 389. For a proposed separation of *Jus post bellum* from *jus ad bellum* and *jus in bello* see also Boon, *supra* note 8, at 290–292 and Schaller, *supra* note 8, at 17–19.
[90] Note that the crime of aggression forms part of the jurisdiction of the International Criminal Court. However, the exercise of jurisdiction by the Court is contingent on the definition of the crime under Statute: see Art. 5(2) of the Rome Statute of the International Criminal Court, 17 July 1998.
[91] For a narrower vision of *jus post bellum* as a 'law of post-war reconstruction' see Boon, *supra* note 8, at 285.
[92] Sometimes, different legal provisions may conflict or compete with each other (e.g., duty to prosecute *v* duty of a state to protect the security of its people; right of individual of access to the Court *v* immunity of international organizations). Such conflicts may be solved by way of a distinction between 'rules' and 'principles': see R. Dworkin, *Taking Rights Seriously* (1978), at 24 ff.

938   *EJIL* 17 (2006), 921–943

fashion'.[93] Others are based on broader principles which may be balanced against each other, 'taking into account the relative weight of each'.[94]

B Sketches of Post-conflict Law

It would go beyond the framework of this contribution to present a conclusive account of rules and principles of post-conflict peace. However, six organizing rules and principles may be presented here by way of an example. These principles share some parallels with the parameters of just peace under the just war theory (right intention, legitimate authority for a peace settlement; discrimination and proportionality of the terms of peace),[95] without being identical to the latter. They may be derived from a comparative survey of international law and practice in the three major eras of peace settlements: namely 1919, 1945 and the post-Cold War era.

1 Fairness and Inclusiveness of Peace Settlements

Firstly, there is some evidence that the establishment of sustainable peace requires a collective bargaining process, involving a fair hearing of the interests of all parties to the conflict at the negotiating table.

At the time of the Treaty of Versailles, the terms of peace were essentially set by a bargaining process amongst the victors over the rights and obligations of the vanquished. Today, such conduct would conflict with certain standards of peace-making. Article 34 of the Vienna Convention on the Law of Treaties posits that a peace treaty does not bind states that did not consent to its terms. Accordingly, no single state and no group of states may unilaterally make binding determinations for a third state. Moreover, modern practice points towards a neutralization of interests in the bargaining process. If the defeated entity is not present at the negotiation of the peace settlement itself, its interests should be determined by a collective forum with third-party input.[96]

Similar considerations of fairness apply in favour of groups and minorities protected by international law by virtue of the right to self-determination and autonomy

---

[93] *Ibid.*

[94] *Ibid.*

[95] No common framework of *jus post bellum* principles has yet been established in the relevant literature. In his *War and International Justice, supra* note 8, at 232–233, Orend lists the following five principles: just cause, right intention, public declaration and legitimate authority, discrimination, and proportionality. A more elaborate list is offered by the same author in *Morality of War, supra* note 8, at 180–181.

[96] The peacemaking practice of the 1990s indicates that the neutralization of the bargaining process is one of the central parameters of peacemaking. In cases such as Iraq (SC Res. 687) and Kosovo (SC Res. 1244), the authors of the use of force had a say in shaping the content of post-conflict peace under the umbrella of collective security. The former FRY agreed on the principles contained in Annex II to Res. 1244 (1999) (resolution of the Kosovo crisis): see para. 9 of the preamble to SC Res. 1244 of 10 June 1999. The principles contained in Annex II set a framework for Res. 1244. Iraq participated, without voting, in the discussions on SC Res. 687 of 3 Apr. 1991. Moreover, SC Res. 687 contains several elements of consent: see paras 3 (demarcation of the boundary line between Iraq and Kuwait) and 33 (acceptance of a cease-fire). Furthermore, peace settlements such as the Dayton Accord or the Ethiopia–Eritrea agreement transmit the message that a State using force against another entity should be present when the terms of peace are negotiated.

rights. These groups may be represented by state entities in treaty negotiations. How-ever, they are entitled to an adequate representation of their collective interests in a constitutional settlement regulating their status.[97]

2 The Demise of the Concept of Punishment for Aggression

Secondly, international practice since 1945 indicates the replacement of the harsh concept of territorial punishment for purposes of deterrence by the more moderate techniques of state responsibility, disarmament and institutional security arrangements.[98]

International law has become hostile to the idea of 'punishing' an aggressor through the imposition or dictate of territorial changes in the post-conflict phase.[99] Territorial mutilations or compulsory transfers of populations of the kind that took place at the end of the Second World War would be ruled out today under the UN Charter and the 1949 Geneva Conventions.[100] Peace-makers are required to respect the territorial integrity of the vanquished state and the rights of its people.[101]

The only organ which could theoretically take punitive measures against states that have placed themselves outside the community of peace loving and law-abiding nations, is the Security Council. However, even the Council's authority under the Charter would hardly suffice to justify *permanent* transfers of territory against or with-out the will of a state for the purpose of deterring future aggression. Such action con-flicts with the limits of the Security Council under Article 24 of the Charter, including the recognition of territorial integrity and the principle of self-determination. More-over, less intrusive post-conflict measures, such as reparation, disarmament and adjudication of war crimes, are usually at hand and better suited to serve the purpose of peace-making which guides the exercise of powers by the Council under the Charter.

3 The Humanization of Reparations and Sanctions

A similar trend towards moderation in the treatment of an aggressor may be traced in the area of reparations.[102] Contemporary developments in international law point to the emergence of a rule that prohibits the indiscriminate punishment of a people through excessive reparation claims or sanctions.

Harsh financial loads may not only make a people accountable for misdeeds of an irresponsible regime, but amount to the collective punishment of an entire population.

---

[97] For a survey of institutional models see M. Suksi, *Constitutional Options for Self-determination: What Really Works?*, available only at http://www.tamilnation.org/selfdetermination/99suksi.htm.

[98] For a similar consideration see Bass, *supra* note 3, at 390–393.

[99] The Draft Articles of the International Law Commission on State Responsibility, *supra* note 64, refrain from approving any concept of punishment of a State for the commission of unlawful acts of force. They limit the consequences of internationally wrongful acts to the level of 'civil responsibility', according to which a State can obtain restitution, compensation, and satisfaction only for the harm suffered.

[100] Art. 49 of the Fourth Geneva Convention prohibits forcible transfers of population and deportation.

[101] This may be derived from Art. 2(1) of the UN Charter and the prohibition of annexation under inter-national law. See also GA Res. 2625 (XXV), Declaration on Principles of International Law concerning Friendly Relations and Co-operation among States in accordance with the Charter of the United Nations.

[102] For a similar argument with regard to the proportionality of reparations see Orend, *War and International Justice, supra* note 8, at 227–228; Bass, *supra* note 8, at 408–411.

940   *EJIL* 17 (2006), 921–943

One of the lessons emerging from the practice of peace treaties is that reparation and compensation claims must be assessed in light of the economic potential of the wrongdoing state and its implications for the population of the targeted state.[103]

This conclusion was drawn by the former Article 43(3) of the 1996 Draft Articles on State Responsibility, which stated that reparation shall 'in no case . . . result in depriving the population of a State of its own means of substance'. This claim receives additional support from the move to targeted sanctions under the collective security regime[104] and the rise of socio-economic human rights obligations preventing states or international actors from imposing economic liabilities on another state which would disable the later in ensuring minimum socio-economic standards (food, health care) *vis-à-vis* its own population. [105]

4 The Move from Collective Responsibility to Individual Responsibility

Similarly, there is a move from collective to individual responsibility.[106] This move is reflected in the crystallization of the principle of individual criminal responsibility. This principle prohibits collective punishment, that is, punishment of persons not for what they have done, but for the acts of others;[107] furthermore, it establishes the general rule that individuals are punished for their own wrongdoing, and not on behalf of the state.[108] This differentiation prevents a population from being held accountable for the misdeeds of its rulers and from being exposed to charges of collective guilt.

5 Towards a Combined Justice and Reconciliation Model

Fifthly, there is a trend towards accommodating post-conflict responsibility with the needs of peace in the area of criminal responsibility. This specific tension did not receive broad attention in historical peace settlements, partly because the concept of international criminal responsibility was less developed, and partly because peace settlements were less frequently dedicated to the resolution of the problems of civil wars. Today, it is at the heart of contemporary efforts of peace-making. Modern international practice, particularly in the context of United Nations peace-building,

---

[103] As noted by Professor Brownlie, 'experience has shown that victors can hardly expect to exact "adequate compensation" in reparations for large-scale aggression without violating the principles of humanity and good policy': see I. Brownlie, *International Law and the Use of Force by States* (1963), 153.

[104] The effectiveness of targeted sanctions was highlighted in the Report of the UN High Level Panel, *supra* note 49, which emphasized that the threat of sanctions 'can be a powerful means of deterrence and prevention', but specifically highlighted the utility of targeted sanctions in 'putting pressure on leaders and elites with minimum humanitarian consequences . . . and can be tailored to specific circumstances'. See also paras 106–108 of GA Res. 60/1 (2005 World Summit Outcome).

[105] See also the UK's comment on former Art. 43(3) of the ILC Draft Articles on State Responsibility, noting that reparation must not endanger international peace and security. See UN Doc A/CN.4/488.104.

[106] For a discussion of this problem under the angle of just war theory see Orend, *War and International Justice, supra* note 8, at 232.

[107] This principle is expressed in Art. 50 of the Annex to the 1907 Hague Convention No. IV. See also Art. 33 of the Fourth Geneva Civilian Convention which notes that '[c]ollective penalties and likewise all measures of intimidation . . . are prohibited'.

[108] The autonomy of individual responsibility from state responsibility is, in particular, expressed in the removal of official immunity from punishment for aggression, genocide, crimes against humanity, and war crimes. See Art. 27 of the Rome Statute, Art. 7(2) of the ICTY Statute, and Art. 6 of the ICTR Statute.

appears to move towards a model of targeted accountability in peace processes, which allows amnesties for less serious crimes and combines criminal justice with the establishment of truth and reconciliation mechanisms.[109]

6 People-centred Governance

Lastly, there is a shift of focus from state-centred mechanisms of organizing public power to 'people-based' (individual and/or group-based) techniques of political settlement. Peace-making, more than ever before, is tied to the ending of autocratic, undemocratic and oppressive regimes, and directed towards the ideal of 'popular sovereignty' held by individuals instead of states or elites. A procedural legal basis for this claim may be found in Article 21 of the Universal Declaration of Human Rights and Article 25 of the International Covenant on Civil and Political Rights. Moreover, a broader notion of internal self-determination has emerged since World War II, which links the protection of a people under international law to the enjoyment of institutional rights (such as autonomy of federalist structures) in the domestic legal system. Finally, human rights guarantees and procedures for holding governments accountable are increasingly part of a treaty-based or 'regional *acquis*', and therefore binding on successor states or regimes. [110]

These norms may be said to create, *inter alia*, a duty for domestic or international holders of public authority in situations of transition to institute political structures that embody mechanisms of accountability *vis-à-vis* the governed population and timelines to gradually transfer power from political elites to elected representatives.[111]

5 Conclusion

These few examples indicate that that there are certain macro-changes in the conception of peace-making. Modern practice displays a stark tendency to move from a statist and national-interest driven conception of conflict termination to a pluralist and problem-solving approach to peace-making, uniting affected parties, neutral actors and private stakeholders in their efforts to restore sustainable peace.[112] This process lends new support to an old postulate, namely the idea of (re-)connecting the concepts of *jus ad bellum* and *jus in bello* to considerations of fair and just peace-making (the former '*jus post bellum*').

The recognition of a tripartite conception of the law of armed force would serve several purposes. It would fill, first of all, a certain normative gap. At present, there is a

---

[109] For a full discussion see Robinson, 'Serving the Interests of Justice. Amnesties, Truth Commissions and the International Criminal Court', 14 *EJIL* (2003) 481; Stahn, 'United Nations Peacebuilding, Amnesties and Alternative Forms of Justice: A Change in Practice?, 84 *Int'l Rev of the Red Cross* (2002), 191; *ibid.*, 'Complementarity, Amnesties and Alternative Forms of Justice—Some Interpretative Guidelines for the ICC', 3 *J Int'l Criminal Justice* (2005) 695.

[110] See, e.g., Human Rights Committee. General Comment No. 26, which established the principle of automatic succession of States into obligations under human rights treaties.

[111] See also Boon, *supra* note 8, at 293–295.

[112] For an excellent survey of the transformation of the international legal system see Kingsbury, 'The International Legal Order', in P. Cane and M. Pushnet (eds), *Oxford Handbook of Legal Studies* (2003), at 271.

942   *EJIL* 17 (2006), 921–943

considerable degree of uncertainty about the applicable law, the interplay of different structural frameworks as well as the possible space for interaction between different legal orders and bodies of law (international law v. domestic law, human rights law v. law of occupation etc.) in a post-conflict environment. The articulation of a body of law after conflict would identify legal rules, which ought to be applied by international actors (unless an exception applies) and clarify specific legal principles,[113] which serve as guidance in making legal policy choices in situations of transition.

Secondly, the revival of a tripartite conception of armed force has a certain systemic function. It would build a bridge between the 'pre-' and the 'post'-conflict phase, which is lacking in the contemporary architecture of the law of armed force. The recognition of rules and principles of post-conflict peace would establish a closer link between the requirements of the use of force and post-conflict responsibilities in the context of intervention. Under a tripartite conception of the law of armed force, international actors might be forced to consider to a broader extent the impact of their decisions on the post-conflict phase, including modalities and institutional frameworks for peace-making, before making a determination whether to use force.[114]

Moreover, such rules and principles might allow a more nuanced assessment of the legality or legitimacy of the use of force.[115] This argument is particularly compelling in the context of humanitarian and democratic interventions. Such interventions would be judged not only by their purported goals, but by their implications and effects. Post-conflict law might provide the necessary parameters and benchmarks to determine whether the respective goals have been implemented in a fair and effective manner and in accordance with the law.

Finally, the development of post-conflict law may have certain implications for the contemporary *jus in bello*.[116] The move to a tripartite conception of the law of armed force would, in particular, avoid an overburdening of the obligations of the military and temper the concerns of those who argue that the contemporary *jus in bello* is not meant to serve as a surrogate framework for governance in peacetime situations,[117] while preserving the interests of peace-making. Considerations of fair and just peace

---

[113] Principles may be understood as 'optimization commands', which ought to be carried out to the greatest possible degree in the circumstances of an environment of transition.

[114] See also Orend, *Morality of War, supra* note 8, at 181 who speaks of the need for 'an ethical "exit strategy" from war' which deserves 'at least as much thought and efforts as the purely military exit strategy [which is] so much on the minds of policy planners and commanding officers'.

[115] The 2005 World Summit Outcome document omitted to define standards for the evaluation of interventions. However, the High-Level Panel suggested five basic criteria of legitimacy to be taken into account by the Security Council 'in considering whether to authorize or endorse the use of military force', namely: (a) *Seriousness of threat*, (b) *Proper purpose*, (c) *Last resort*, (d) *Proportional means*, (e) *Balance of consequences*: see High-Level Panel, *supra* note 49, at para. 207.

[116] For a brief discussion of the relationship between *jus post bellum* and *jus in bello* see Bass, *supra* note 8, at 386–387.

[117] For a study of this question see M. Kelly, *Restoring and Maintaining Order in Complex Peace Operations: The Search for a Legal Framework* (1999); *ibid.*, 'Iraq and the Law of Occupation: New Tests for an Old Law', 6 *Yearbk Int'l Humanitarian L* (2003) 127.

would be part of the equation of armed force, however not under *jus in bello* in the proper sense, but under the law after conflict. These principles would have an indirect impact on the phase of armed conflict itself. Parties to an armed conflict would operate under a general obligation to conduct hostilities in a manner which does not preclude a fair and just peace settlement in the post-conflict phase.

It is clear from this survey that some of the features of a tripartite conception of armed force (for instance, the interplay between *jus ad bellum*, *jus in bello* and '*jus post bellum*') require further thought. However, one fact is becoming increasingly evident: the development of rules and principles of post-conflict peace should form part of the agenda and the table of contents of international law in the 21st century.

[13]

PEACE AGREEMENTS: THEIR NATURE AND LEGAL STATUS

*By Christine Bell**

The last fifteen years have seen a proliferation of peace agreements. Some 50 percent of civil wars have terminated in peace agreements since 1990, more than in the previous two centuries combined, when only one in five resulted in negotiated settlement.[1] Numerically, these settlements amount to over three hundred peace agreements in some forty jurisdictions.[2] International standards have even begun to regulate peace agreements. United Nations guidelines, guidelines and recommendations of the secretary-general, and Security Council resolutions have all normatively addressed peace agreements: both the processes by which they are negotiated and their substance, particularly with relation to accountability for past human rights abuses.[3]

The rise of the peace agreement has four common threads. The end of the Cold War saw an increase both in violent conflict occurring mainly within state borders (although often with transnational dimensions), and in the international attention devoted to such conflict.[4] Second, a common approach to conflict resolution emerged that involved direct negotiations between governments and their armed opponents, who were treated for these purposes as equals.[5] This approach contrasted with earlier methods of noninterference or engaging primarily

---

* Professor of Public International Law, Transitional Justice Institute, University of Ulster. The author would like to thank Colm Campbell, Kathleen Cavanaugh, Christine Chinkin, John Darby, Shane Darcy, Jérémie Gilbert, Christopher McCrudden, Ian Martin, Fionnuala Ní Aoláin, Ursula O'Hare, Ruti Teitel, Colin Warbrick, and David Wippman for comments on earlier drafts; and also William Twining for earlier advice. The author also thanks Catherine O'Rourke for invaluable research assistance and comments; Joy Bell, Megan Fairlie, and Catherine Turner for proofreading; and John McNee and John McCann for assistance with Latin. Mistakes that remain are the author's own.

[1] TIMOTHY D. SISK, PEACEMAKING IN CIVIL WARS: OBSTACLES, OPTIONS, AND OPPORTUNITIES (Kroc Inst. Int'l Peace Stud., Occasional Paper Series No. 20:OP:2, 2001), *available at* <http://www.nd.edu>; *see also* A More Secure World: Our Shared Responsibility, Report of the High-Level Panel on Threats, Challenges and Change, UN Doc. A/59/565, ¶85 (2004), In Larger Freedom: Towards Development, Security and Human Rights for All, Report of the Secretary-General, UN Doc. A/59/2005 & annex, ¶108 (2005); *cf.* Peter Wallensteen & Margareta Sollenberg, *Armed Conflicts, Conflict Termination and Peace Agreements, 1989–96,* 34 J. PEACE RES. 339 (1997).

[2] CHRISTINE BELL, PEACE AGREEMENTS AND HUMAN RIGHTS, app. (2000). See also the increasing number of Web sites and publications dedicated to making the text of peace agreements available, for example, Conciliation Resources, <http://www.c-r.org>; U.S. Institute of Peace, <http://www.usip.org>; and INCORE: University of Ulster, <http://www.incore.ulst.ac.uk/services/cds/>.

[3] *See* Women, Peace and Security, Report of the Secretary-General, UN Doc. S/2004/814; SC Res. 1325 (Oct. 31, 2000); UN Press Release SG/SM/7257, Secretary-General Comments on Guidelines Given to Envoys (Dec. 10, 1999) (noting the issuance of guidelines addressing human rights and peace negotiations); UN Comm'n on Hum. Rts., Addendum: Updated Set of Principles for the Protection and Promotion of Human Rights Through Action to Combat Impunity, UN Doc. E/CN.4/2005/102/Add.1 [hereinafter Principles to Combat Impunity]; *see also* The Rule of Law and Transitional Justice in Conflict and Post-conflict Societies, Report of the Secretary-General, UN Doc. S/2004/616 (providing for a series of recommendations for negotiations, peace agreements, and Security Council mandates); Report of the Panel on United Nations Peace Operations [Brahimi Report], UN Doc. A/55/305–S/2000/809, ¶58 (providing for UN ability to put conditions on peace agreements in which it will be asked to be involved); *cf.* A More Secure World, *supra* note 1, ¶¶103, 226–28, 264; In Larger Freedom, *supra* note 1, *passim.*

[4] INTERNATIONAL LAW AND ETHNIC CONFLICT (David Wippman ed., 1998); Patrick M. Regan, *Conditions of Successful Third-Party Intervention in Intrastate Conflicts,* 40 J. CONFLICT RESOL. 336 (1996).

[5] Christopher Clapham, *Rwanda: The Perils of Peacemaking,* 35 J. PEACE RES. 193, 194 (1998) (arguing that a new notion of "standing" emerged after the Cold War, which required that all parties to the conflict be recognized as valid participants in any peacemaking process).

374   THE AMERICAN JOURNAL OF INTERNATIONAL LAW   [Vol. 100:373

with states, often through regional frameworks.[6] Third, this method resulted in a common approach to settlement design that linked cease-fires to agreement on new political and legal arrangements for holding and exercising power. Fourth, hard-gained settlement terms were formally documented in written, signed, and publicly available agreements, involving both domestic and international participation.

While the events of September 11, 2001, appear to have accelerated a renewed focus on interstate conflict, surprisingly perhaps, the widespread use of peace agreements has quietly continued and even found new contexts.[7] Peace agreements have become relevant to attempts to reconstruct societies in the wake of interstate conflict, as evidenced by the situations in Kosovo, Afghanistan, and Iraq. Here, the interstate use of force has led to international involvement in internal state building. This project has required the forging of accords between conflicted groups through a process of constitution making as negotiated agreement.

Despite the prevalence of documents that could be described as peace agreements, and the emergence of legal standards addressing them as a category, the term "peace agreement" remains largely undefined and unexplored. The label is often attached to documented agreements between parties to a violent internal conflict to establish a cease-fire together with new political and legal structures.[8] A decade and a half of post–Cold War practice has given rise to a growing scholarship on peace agreements, particularly in the social science and conflict resolution fields. However, this literature has paid little attention to the role of the peace agreement as a binding document. Social scientists and conflict resolution analysts have examined what makes peace agreements succeed or fail. They have tried to isolate the different elements of settlements, so as to test empirically and through case studies the extent to which they reduce conflict.[9] This research, in its design and results, treats peace agreements as a group but tends to accord a limited role to the related questions of how an agreement is worded and whether or not it is a legal document. It focuses on the prime factors affecting compliance as the dynamics of third-party interventions;[10] the structural characteristics of conflict processes, such as the role of "ripeness" and economics;[11] changing regional and/or systemic power relationships and balances;[12] and the range of issues covered by the agreement (with some attention to settlement design).[13] Legal literature, in contrast, has produced detailed

---

[6] *See* MALCOLM N. SHAW, INTERNATIONAL LAW 1036–39 (5th ed. 2003) (on noninterference). For an example of a regional framework that focused on the state and required disarming of armed opposition groups as a precursor to direct negotiations, see Agreement for Procedure on Establishing Firm and Lasting Peace in Central America, Aug. 7, 1987, Costa Rica–El Sal.–Guat.–Hond.–Nicar., UN Doc. A/42/521–S/19085, annex (1987), 26 ILM 1166 (1987).

[7] See peace agreement Web sites cited *supra* note 2.

[8] BELL, *supra* note 2, at 6.

[9] *See generally* ENDING CIVIL WARS: THE IMPLEMENTATION OF PEACE AGREEMENTS (Stephen John Stedman, Donald Rothchild, & Elizabeth M. Cousens eds., 2002); FEN OSLER HAMPSON, NURTURING PEACE: WHY PEACE SETTLEMENTS SUCCEED OR FAIL (1996) (for overviews of the field).

[10] *See, e.g.*, Kristian Skrede Gleditsch & Kyle Beardsley, *Nosy Neighbors: Third-Party Actors in Central American Conflicts*, 48 J. CONFLICT RESOL. 379 (2004); Regan, *supra* note 4; Stephen John Stedman & Donald Rothchild, *Peace Operations: From Short-Term to Long-Term Commitment*, 3 INT'L PEACEKEEPING 17, 25 (1996) (giving some limited attention to the clarity of a peace agreement); Barbara Walter, *The Critical Barrier to Civil War Settlement*, 51 INT'L ORG. 335 (1997).

[11] *See, e.g.*, I. WILLIAM ZARTMAN, RIPE FOR RESOLUTION (1985); WORLD BANK, CONFLICT PREVENTION AND RECONSTRUCTION UNIT, BREAKING THE CONFLICT TRAP: CIVIL WAR AND DEVELOPMENT POLICY 83 (2003), *available at* <http://www-wds.worldbank.org/>.

[12] *See, e.g.*, James D. Fearon & David D. Laitin, *Ethnicity, Insurgency, and Civil War*, 97 AM. POL. SCI. REV. 75 (2003).

[13] *See, e.g.*, VIRGINIA PAGE FORTNA, PEACE TIME: CEASE-FIRE AGREEMENTS AND THE DURABILITY OF PEACE (2004); LOUIS KRIESBERG, CONSTRUCTIVE CONFLICTS: FROM ESCALATION TO RESOLUTION 283–84 (1998); Dorina A. Bekoe, *Toward a Theory of Peace Agreement Implementation: The Case of Liberia*, 38 J. ASIAN & AFR. STUD. 256 (2003); Ulrich Schneckener, *Making Power-Sharing Work: Lessons from Successes and*

appraisals of the terms, structure, and legal nature of specific agreements[14] but little sustained analysis of peace agreements per se.[15]

Each position is worth challenging. As regards legal literature, the scale of the phenomenon of peace agreements; the emerging body of standards dealing with them as a group; and a range of common practices relating to their negotiation, design, content, and implementation—all point to a set of documents with common legal features. As regards social science literature, the sidelining of the legal attributes of peace agreements with respect to compliance or implementation flies in the face of even the most nuanced accounts of why law might matter. Further insight into compliance is useful, given that research suggests that nearly half of all peace agreements break down within five years, and more within a ten-year period, while many of the remainder enter a "no war, no peace" limbo whose evaluation is difficult.[16]

This article explores the role of peace agreements in peace processes from a legal perspective. In particular, it examines when and how peace agreements emerge in peace processes (part I), and the extent to which they take recognizable legal forms or are "legalized" (part II). This discussion is used to explore the relationship between legalization of peace agreements and compliance with them.[17] The article argues (parts III–V) that peace agreements are clearly legalized documents; that they have some characteristic features that persist across examples; and that these amount to a common legal practice—*lex pacificatoria*, or law of the peacemakers (part VI).[18] Recognizing peace agreement legalization as *lex pacificatoria* is argued to be useful in further understanding the relationship of law to compliance in this context. It facilitates informed exchange between different peace processes as regards how best to promote compliance; engagement with social science debates on the factors affecting an agreement's success or failure; and understanding and challenging of the force of the *lex*.

I. PATTERNS OF PEACE AGREEMENTS

As peace processes evolve, a wide variety of documents that can be termed "peace agreement" are produced. These can usefully be classified into three main types, which tend to emerge at

Failures in Ethnic Conflict Regulation, 39 J. PEACE RES. 203 (2002); Stephen John Stedman, *Spoiler Problems in Peace Processes*, 22 INT'L SECURITY 5 (1997).

[14] Most notably, the Israeli/Palestinian Oslo Accords. GEOFFREY R. WATSON, THE OSLO ACCORDS: INTERNATIONAL LAW AND THE ISRAELI-PALESTINIAN PEACE AGREEMENTS (2000); John Quigley, *The Israel-PLO Interim Agreements: Are They Treaties?* 30 CORNELL INT'L L.J. 717 (1997); *see also* Colm Campbell, Fionnuala Ní Aoláin, & Colin Harvey, *The Frontiers of Legal Analysis: Reframing the Transition in Northern Ireland*, 66 MOD. L. REV. 317 (2003); P. H. Kooijmans, *The Security Council and Non-State Entities as Parties to Conflicts, in* INTERNATIONAL LAW: THEORY AND PRACTICE: ESSAYS IN HONOUR OF ERIC SUY 333 (Karel Wellens ed., 1998); Fionnuala Ní Aoláin, *The Fractured Soul of the Dayton Peace Agreement: A Legal Analysis*, 19 MICH. J. INT'L L. 957 (1998); Steven R. Ratner, *The Cambodia Settlement Agreements*, 87 AJIL 1 (1993); Carsten Stahn, *Constitution Without a State? Kosovo Under the United Nations Constitutional Framework for Self-Government*, 14 LEIDEN J. INT'L L. 531 (2001); Sienho Yee, *The New Constitution of Bosnia and Herzegovina*, 7 EUR. J. INT'L L. 176 (1996).

[15] *But see* STEVEN R. RATNER, THE NEW UN PEACEKEEPING: BUILDING PEACE IN LANDS OF CONFLICT AFTER THE COLD WAR 26–28 (1995) (for partial discussion of the legal obligations imposed by peace agreements in the context of their relevance to consent and UN peacekeeping), David Wippman, *Treaty-Based Intervention: Who Can Say No?* 62 U. CHI. L. REV. 607, 642–43 (1995). *Cf.* <http://www.pilg.org> (for materials approaching peace agreements as a group). Lawyers have also not looked particularly at social science insights into implementation.

[16] In Larger Freedom, *supra* note 1, ¶114; Bekoe, *supra* note 13; Roy Licklider, *The Consequences of Negotiated Settlements in Civil Wars, 1945–1993*, 89 AM. POL. SCI. REV. 681, 685 (1995).

[17] This analysis, slightly adapted, is taken from Kenneth W. Abbott, Robert O. Keohane, Andrew Moravcsik, Anne-Marie Slaughter, & Duncan Snidal, *The Concept of Legalization*, 54 INT'L ORG. 401 (2000); *see also infra* text at notes 73–77.

[18] The term *lex pacificatoria*, however, is the author's own. Cicero used the term "pacificatoria legatione," or "delegation of peacemakers" (translation by author), in CICERO PHILIPPIC, bk. XII, §1, ¶3 (n.d.), *reprinted in* CICERO PHILIPPICS 508 (Walter C. A. Kerr trans., William Heinemann Ltd. 1926).

376   THE AMERICAN JOURNAL OF INTERNATIONAL LAW   [Vol. 100:373]

different stages of a conflict: prenegotiation agreements, framework/substantive agreements, and implementation/renegotiation agreements.[19]

Prenegotiation Agreements

The prenegotiation stage of a peace process, often termed "talks about talks," typically revolves around how to get everyone to the negotiating table with an agreed-upon agenda. For parties to a long-term conflict, any move to the negotiating table is a trial-and-error process linked to whether they perceive themselves as getting more at the table than on the battlefield. For face-to-face or proximity negotiations to take place at all, parties need assurances that the talks will not be used by the other side to gain military and/or political advantages.[20] The prenegotiation stage tends to focus on who is going to negotiate and with what status, raising issues such as the return of negotiators from exile or their release from prison; safeguards as to future physical integrity and freedom from imprisonment; and limits on how the war may be waged while negotiations take place.[21] Often agreements emerging at this stage are incremental with the aim of building to a formal cease-fire that will enable multiparty talks. Typically, they do not include all the parties to the conflict but take the form of bilateral agreements between some of the parties and remain secret until a later date. Regional initiatives may also form a "pre" prenegotiation attempt to set or bolster a context for efforts at negotiations. The Harare Declaration,[22] promulgated by the Organization of African Unity in 1989, set out conditions for multiparty talks in South Africa, which began to influence the parameters for negotiations, and formed the basis of Nelson Mandela's secret talks with President F. W. de Klerk.[23] In Afghanistan in 1999, the "six plus two" group (four bordering states, the Russian Federation, and the United States) aimed at building a context for talks through their Tashkent Declaration.[24] The prenegotiation stage, if successful, will culminate in some form of cease-fire and direct talks designed to resolve the substantive issues in the conflict.

The agreements made at this stage, if published at all, have much more the feel of context-setting declarations or political pacts than binding legal agreements. They tend to be recorded as "declarations" or "records" of agreement or mutual understandings, rather than as agreements using the language of obligation.[25] These titles reflect the role of joint documents at this

---

[19] BELL, *supra* note 2, at 20–29; *cf.* Wallensteen & Sollenberg, *supra* note 1 (using different classification with some similarities).

[20] C. R. MITCHELL, THE STRUCTURE OF INTERNATIONAL CONFLICT 206–16 (1981); ZARTMAN, *supra* note 11.

[21] MITCHELL, *supra* note 20.

[22] Declaration of the OAU Ad-hoc Committee on Southern Africa on the Question of South Africa, Aug. 21, 1989, UN Doc. A/44/697, annex, *available at* <http://www.anc.org.za/ancdocs/history/oau/harare.html>.

[23] NELSON MANDELA, LONG WALK TO FREEDOM: THE AUTOBIOGRAPHY OF NELSON MANDELA 663 (Abacus ed. 1995).

[24] Tashkent Declaration on Fundamental Principles for a Peaceful Settlement of the Conflict in Afghanistan, July 19, 1999, UN Doc. A/54/174–S/1999/812, annex, *available at* <http://www.institute-for-afghan-studies.org/> [hereinafter Tashkent Declaration]; *cf.* Joint Declaration of the EC Troika and the Parties Directly Concerned with the Yugoslav Crisis, July 7, 1991, *reprinted in* YUGOSLAVIA THROUGH DOCUMENTS: FROM ITS CREATION TO ITS DISSOLUTION 311 (Snežana Trifunovska ed., 1994) (EC attempt to set a context to address escalating hostilities in former Yugoslavia).

[25] See, for example, the early agreements in South Africa between the African National Congress (ANC) and the South African National Party (SAG), and/or Inkatha (IFP), dealing incrementally with common commitments to end violence (Groote Schuur Minute, May 4, 1990, ANC-SAG); ending of armed actions and review of states of emergency (Pretoria Minute, Aug. 6, 1990, ANC-SAG); and implementing of antiviolence measures and stabilizing peace (Royal Hotel Minute, Jan. 29, 1991, ANC-IFP; DF Malan Accord, Feb. 12, 1991, ANC-SAG). These documents are available online at <http://www.anc.org.za/ancdocs/history/minutes.html>, apart from the Royal Hotel Minute, which is reprinted in SOUTH AFRICAN INSTITUTE OF RACE RELATIONS, RACE RELATIONS SURVEY 1991/92, app. E, at 519 (1992).

stage of the process: what is important to the parties is the fact of having met and having established a joint commitment to future negotiations. Prenegotiation documents are often presented as if each party were subscribing to its own understandings unilaterally, without reference to the other side's understandings and actions. The emerging documents are targeted as much at parties outside the negotiations, as at those within: they are intended to create a context in which those outside might choose to participate. A lack of legal formality enables parties to avoid the appearance of commitment to compromise, which could undermine the move toward talks and give ammunition to dissenters or outbidders (those who challenge the power base of political rivals by taking more radical stances against suggested compromises). Issues such as the scope of the talks, the range of participants, the status of the participants—all crucial issues at the prenegotiation stage—are left open by the characterization of the documents as declarations or memorandums. The documents are self-executing in the sense that they either move discussions forward toward cease-fires and negotiations, or do not. The Downing Street Declaration, for example, was issued at an early stage of the Northern Ireland peace process by the British and Irish governments in response to secret negotiations.[26] Clearly avoiding the appearance of law, the governments "recognise[d]" positions, and "confirm[ed]," "reaffirm[ed]" and "reiterate[d]" what were asserted to be past commitments.[27] Yet the declaration evidenced a new intergovernmental understanding. It sketched an embryonic framework for agreement and signaled that a cease-fire would lead to all-party talks including the previously excluded Sinn Féin. The declaratory language made this achievement possible without the appearance of direct negotiations with, or concessions to, the Provisional Irish Republican Army (IRA) or its elected political counterparts in Sinn Féin, even though both had taken place.[28]

Substantive /Framework Agreements

Substantive or framework agreements are aimed at sustaining cease-fires; they provide a framework for governance designed to address the root causes of the conflict and thus to halt the violence more permanently. The agreements reached at this stage most clearly deserve the label "peace agreement." They tend to be more inclusive of the main groups involved in waging the war by military means. They are usually public and formally recorded in written, signed form and include international participants. Those who stay outside the process are often those who choose to do so, so as to outbid the local signatories. The Burundi Peace Agreement, the Belfast Agreement, Sierra Leone's Lomé Agreement, and the South African Interim Constitution are all examples.[29]

Substantive/framework agreements establish or confirm mechanisms for demilitarization and demobilization intended to end military violence, by linking them to new constitutional structures addressing governance, elections, and legal and human rights institutions. These

---

[26] Joint Declaration on Peace: The Downing Street Declaration, Dec. 15, 1993, Ir.-U.K.; and Statement by the Taoiseach, Mr. Albert Reynolds, on the Joint Declaration on Peace (Dec. 15, 1993), *at* <http://www.cain.ulster.ac.uk/events/peace/docs/dsd151293.htm>.

[27] Joint Declaration on Peace, *supra* note 26.

[28] EAMONN MALLIE & DAVID MCKITTRICK, THE FIGHT FOR PEACE: THE SECRET STORY BEHIND THE IRISH PEACE PROCESS 105–06 (1996).

[29] Arusha Peace and Reconciliation Agreement for Burundi, Aug. 28, 2000, *available at* <http://www.usip.org/library/pa.html> [hereinafter Burundi Peace Agreement]; Agreement Reached in the Multi-Party Negotiations, Apr. 10, 1998, 37 ILM 751 (1998), *available at* <http://www.nio.gov.uk/agreement.pdf> [hereinafter Belfast Agreement]; Peace Agreement, July 7, 1999, Sierra Leone–Revolutionary United Front of Sierra Leone (RUF/SL), *available at* <http://www.usip.org/library/pa.html> [hereinafter Lomé Agreement]; INTERIM CONST. (S. Afr.) (Act No. 200, Dec. 22, 1993), *available at* <http://www.oefre.unibe.ch/law/icl/sf10000_.html>.

378   THE AMERICAN JOURNAL OF INTERNATIONAL LAW   [Vol. 100:373

agreements vary in the degree of detail they contain—either full detail or principles with accompanying processes of reform may be provided. They also vary as to whether conflicts over sovereignty, statehood, and identity are completely resolved (as they largely were in South Africa); partially resolved and partially postponed (Northern Ireland); or almost completely postponed (Kosovo and Israel/Palestine). Some processes work toward one framework agreement with lengthy and detailed provisions aimed at dealing holistically with the issues, such as the Belfast Agreement and the South African Interim Constitution.[30] Other processes, such as those of Guatemala, El Salvador, and Burundi, build up consensus issue by issue in a set of agreements that are ultimately brought together or ratified by a comprehensive final agreement.[31]

Once framework agreements are reached in formal talks, their implementation requires parties to make fundamental compromises with respect to their preferred outcome and their use of force. They will do so only if they feel that the commitments they obtained from the other side are going to be implemented. This need for reciprocity is reflected in the attention the parties pay to the detail of the wording of agreements and the frequent use of lawyers during negotiations. Peace agreements share a legal-looking structure, with preambles, sections, articles, and annexes. They also share legal-type language, speaking of parties, signatories, and binding obligations. The structure and language of peace agreements suggest that the parties mutually view them as legal documents. However, they do not easily fit within traditional legal categories such as treaty, international agreement, or constitution. The main reason is that the conflicts themselves are neither clearly interstate nor clearly internal.[32] Peace agreements deal both with the external legitimacy of the state and the transnational dimensions of the conflict, and with the state's internal constitutional order. The presence of nonstate signatories tends to take them outside international legal definitions of "treaty" or "international agreement," while the presence of multiple state parties tends to make them difficult to analyze as domestic legal documents. This feature is discussed further in part II below.

Implementation/Renegotiation Agreements

Implementation agreements begin to advance and develop aspects of the framework, fleshing out their detail. The Israeli-Palestinian Interim Agreement (Oslo II) filled out and partially implemented the framework in Oslo I; the South African final Constitution developed and implemented the Interim Constitution.[33] By their nature, implementation agreements involve new negotiations and in practice often undergo a measure of renegotiation as parties test whether they can claw back concessions made at an earlier stage. Implementation agreements typically include all the parties to the framework agreement. Sometimes implementation agreements are not documented, and sometimes they take on recognizable legal forms. Indeed, to some extent, the notion of ongoing agreements being "peace agreements" may begin to disappear at this point as the conflict resolution attempts of the peace process merge imperceptibly into the ongoing processes of public law, signifying a measure of success. Thus, treaties appear

---

[30] Belfast Agreement, *supra* note 29; INTERIM CONST., *supra* note 29.

[31] *See, e.g.,* Agreement on a Firm and Lasting Peace, Dec. 29, 1996, Guat.–Unidad revolucionaria nacional guatemalteca (URNG), UN Doc. A/51/796–S/1997/114, Annex II, 36 ILM 258 (1997) [hereinafter Guatemala Peace Agreement]; Joint Declaration, Oct. 4, 1994, El Sal.–Frente farabundo martí para la liberación nacional (FMLN), *available at* <http://www.usip.org/library/pa.html> [hereinafter El Salvador Agreement]; Burundi Peace Agreement, *supra* note 29.

[32] INTERNATIONAL LAW AND ETHNIC CONFLICT, *supra* note 4; Gleditsch & Beardsley, *supra* note 10, at 379; Regan, *supra* note 4.

[33] *See* Interim Agreement on the West Bank and the Gaza Strip, Sept. 28, 1995, Isr.-PLO, 36 ILM 551 (1997) (Oslo II); CONST. (S. Afr.) (Act No. 108, 1996, entered into force Feb. 7, 1997).

as a device to address and normalize regional relationships affected by the conflict.[34] At the domestic level, peace agreements are often taken forward in the form of constitution making or legislation, a step removed from the main peace agreement, as is dealt with further in part III below. Conversely, implementation may be uneven or nonexistent; in such cases, implementation agreements can in effect involve renegotiation and new agreements whose relationship to the former peace agreement is often unclear. The quite different examples of Sierra Leone, Liberia, and the later Israeli-Palestinian agreements all illustrate the potential ambiguity in characterizing an agreement as an implementing, renegotiated, or entirely new instrument.[35]

In summary, peace processes produce documents at the prenegotiation and implementation stage whose characterization as peace agreements could be contested. However, they indicate that many substantive/framework agreements constitute peace agreements par excellence. These agreements form the main focus of the remainder of the discussion.

II. PEACE AGREEMENT LEGALIZATION

The Difficulties of Legal Categorization

Despite appearing to be legal agreements, substantive peace agreements are difficult to place within existing international legal categories as positively understood. Such classification is hampered by the limitations of the categories, especially their unsuitability with regard to accommodating the hybrid subject matter of peace agreements and their mix of state and non-state signatories. According to Article 2 of the Vienna Convention on the Law of Treaties of 1969, much of which is accepted as restating customary international law, a treaty is "an international agreement concluded between states in written form and governed by international law, whether embodied in a single instrument or in two or more related instruments and whatever its particular designation."[36] The definition suffers from ambiguities.[37] In particular, although commentators and judicial bodies alike regard intent as crucial to treaty formation, the notion is at best implicit in the Convention.[38] Intent to be bound can be ascertained from the text of the agreement and surrounding evidence about the intentions of the parties, such as the subject matter of the obligations and the choice of language.[39] This evidence can raise difficulties for peace agreements, which deal with a state's internal institutions and structures, albeit so as to affect the nature and legitimacy (and sometimes territorial integrity) of the state on the international plane.

---

[34] *See, e.g.*, Agreement on the Normalization of Relations, Aug. 23, 1996, Croat.–Fed. Rep. Yugo. (FRY), 35 ILM 1219 (1996); Treaty of Peace, Oct. 26, 1994, Isr.-Jordan, 34 ILM 43 (1995); *see also* Agreement on the Regulation of Relations and Promotion of Cooperation, Apr. 8, 1996, FRY-Maced., 35 ILM 1246; Agreement on Special Parallel Relations, Feb. 28, 1997, FRY–Rep. Srpska, *available at* <http://www.barnsdle.demon.co.uk/bosnia/yusrp.html>.

[35] See agreements concerning Sierra Leone, 1996–99, *at* <http://www.usip.org/library/pa.html>; Accords of the Liberian Conflict, 1990–96, *at* <http://www.c-r.org/accord/lib/accord1/accords_contents.shtml>; Israel-Palestine peace agreements, 1993–present, *at* <http://www.mfa.gov.il/mfa/peace%20process/reference%20documents/>.

[36] Vienna Convention on the Law of Treaties, May 23, 1969, Art. 2, 1155 UNTS 331 [hereinafter Vienna Convention].

[37] Arguably, it places emphasis on a positivist notion of the treaty as a "formal instrument" defined by formalist criteria, rather than as a substantive "source of obligation," although these two concepts are both present to some degree. SHABTAI ROSENNE, DEVELOPMENTS IN THE LAW OF TREATIES, 1945–1986, at 14–15 (1988).

[38] *See, e.g.*, SHAW, *supra* note 6, at 812.

[39] *See* Vienna Convention, *supra* note 36, Art. 31; *cf.* MARTTI KOSKENNIEMI, FROM APOLOGY TO UTOPIA 300 (1989) (on the difficulty of constructing intention).

380   THE AMERICAN JOURNAL OF INTERNATIONAL LAW   [Vol. 100:373

Nevertheless, if the Vienna Convention's definition is used as a starting point, some peace agreements appear to be treaties. Peace agreements in "pure" interstate conflicts clearly constitute treaties, although in the last fifteen years, these have been a minority.[40] Treaties can also be used to address conflict with a mainly internal dimension. Parties to a conflict that were not states at its onset can have attained that status by the time a peace agreement is reached, as the General Framework Agreement for Peace in Bosnia and Herzegovina, or Dayton Peace Agreement (DPA), illustrates.[41] However, other agreements signed directly with nonstate parties would seem to fall outside the strict definition of a treaty under the Vienna Convention, posing the question as to what legal status, if any, such agreements have. The definition was accepted as narrow at the time the Convention was concluded, in particular because it excluded oral agreements and, critically for this discussion, agreements signed by "other subjects of international law."[42] However, these omissions were remedied by Article 3 of the Vienna Convention (and a second convention in 1986 providing for treaties between states and international organizations), which together provided for the legal status of agreements that prior to 1969 were regarded as treaties.[43] Article 3 states:

> The fact that the present Convention does not apply to international agreements concluded between states and other subjects of international law or between such other subjects of international law, or to international agreements not in written form, shall not affect:
>
> (a) the legal force of such agreements;
> (b) the application to them of any of the rules set forth in the present Convention to which they would be subject under international law independently of the Convention;
> (c) the application of the Convention to the relations of states as between themselves under international agreements to which other subjects of international law are also parties.

This provision is significant for the current discussion because it indicates that agreements between state and nonstate parties that are subjects of international law, or indeed between such nonstate parties alone, can be legally binding international agreements. Thus, customary law rules as regards formation and breach, similar to those codified in the 1969 Vienna Convention, apply.[44] However, the Vienna Convention's notion of "subjects of international law" leaves a gray area concerning who can claim such status that has assumed far greater importance than when the Convention was drafted in 1969, and is particularly relevant to practice relating to peace agreements.[45] Three main groups who sign peace agreements have some basis for

---

[40] For a review of interstate wars since 1990, see MONTY G. MARSHALL & TED ROBERT GURR, PEACE AND CONFLICT 2005: A GLOBAL SURVEY OF ARMED CONFLICTS, SELF-DETERMINATION MOVEMENTS, AND DEMOCRACY 11–12 (2005), *available at* <http://www.cidcm.umd.edu/inscr/PC05print.pdf> (references concerning five interstate conflicts, the majority of which have some relationship to intrastate conflict and follow similar peace agreement patterns, to some extent).

[41] General Framework Agreement for Peace in Bosnia and Herzegovina, Dec. 14, 1995, 35 ILM 75 (1996) [hereinafter DPA].

[42] *See, e.g.*, ROSENNE, *supra* note 37, at 11.

[43] Vienna Convention on the Law of Treaties Between States and International Organizations or Between International Organizations, Mar. 21, 1986, 25 ILM 543 (1986) (has a similarly worded Article 3); *see also* ARNOLD DUNCAN MCNAIR, THE LAW OF TREATIES (1961) (for law of treaties prior to 1969); ROSENNE, *supra* note 37, at 17–18 (noting International Law Commission drafts that included "any international agreement in written form . . . concluded between two or more States or other subjects of international law" as treaties).

[44] *See* LINDSAY MOIR, THE LAW OF INTERNAL ARMED CONFLICT 53 (2002); Antonio Cassese, *The Status of Rebels Under the 1977 Geneva Protocol on Non-international Armed Conflicts*, 30 INT'L & COMP. L.Q. 416, 423 (1981).

[45] ROSENNE, *supra* note 37, at 10–33 (noting the growth of the gray area in 1989; *id.* at 32).

claiming the status of subjects of international law. While an extended discussion of their international legal status is beyond the scope of this article, a brief summary can illustrate their claims.

Most obviously, armed opposition groups sign peace agreements as main protagonists of internal conflicts. In many peace agreements signed by armed opposition groups, grounds can be found to assert that the parties intended the agreement to be binding on the international legal plane, and that the nonstate signatories were "subjects of international law"—based on the recognition of such groups under international law, in particular through humanitarian law.[46] Many agreements potentially fulfill these criteria and could serve as examples; all use formal legal language and have international signatories. These include agreements in Angola (between the government and UNITA), Burundi (between the government, armed opposition groups, and political parties), the Democratic Republic of the Congo (between the government and armed opposition groups), Guatemala (between the government and Unidad revolucionaria nacional guatemalteca (URNG)), El Salvador (between the government and the Frente farabundo martí para la liberación nacional (FMLN)), Israel/Palestine (between the Israeli government and the Palestine Liberation Organization (PLO)), Mozambique (between the government and RENAMO), Rwanda (between the government and the Rwandese Patriotic Front), and Sierra Leone (between the government and the Revolutionary United Front of Sierra Leone (RUF)).[47]

Second, indigenous peoples also sign peace agreements and can arguably claim to be "subjects of international law."[48] They have obtained a legal status that was not envisaged in 1969 but has historical precedence in the notion of indigenous peoples as "nations" in a premodern international legal system. This status is most obviously supported by the increasing recognition in international law that indigenous peoples are "peoples" entitled to forms of self-determination short of independent statehood.[49] Throughout the last decade, various agreements have been signed with or on behalf of indigenous groups in situations involving armed violence, in what was commonly accepted as a peace process. For example, agreements were signed between the Chiapas people (through the Zapatista National Liberation Army (EZLN)) and

---

[46] *See, e.g.*, common Art. 3, Convention for the Amelioration of the Condition of the Wounded and Sick in Armed Forces in the Field, Aug. 12, 1949, 6 UST 3114, 75 UNTS 31; Convention for the Amelioration of the Condition of Wounded, Sick and Shipwrecked Members of Armed Forces at Sea, Aug. 12, 1949, 6 UST 3217, 75 UNTS 85; Convention Relative to the Treatment of Prisoners of War, Aug. 12, 1949, 6 UST 3316, 75 UNTS 135; and Convention Relative to the Protection of Civilian Persons in Time of War, Aug. 12, 1949, 6 UST 3516, 75 UNTS 287 [hereinafter Geneva Conventions]; Protocol Additional to the Geneva Conventions of 12 August 1949, and Relating to the Protection of Victims of International Armed Conflicts, *opened for signature* Dec. 12, 1977, 1125 UNTS 3 [hereinafter Protocol I]; Protocol Additional to the Geneva Conventions of 1949, and Relating to the Protection of Victims of Non-international Armed Conflicts, *opened for signature* Dec. 12, 1977, 1125 UNTS 609 [hereinafter Protocol II]; International Covenant on Civil and Political Rights, Dec. 16, 1966, Art. 1, 999 UNTS 171; International Covenant on Economic, Social and Cultural Rights, Dec. 16, 1966, Art. 1, 993 UNTS 3; Declaration on the Granting of Independence to Colonial Countries and Peoples, GA Res. 1514 (XV) ¶¶ 4, 11, 18 (Dec. 14, 1960) (referring to "national liberation movements"); MOIR, *supra* note 44; LIESBETH ZEGVELD, ACCOUNTABILITY OF ARMED OPPOSITION GROUPS IN INTERNATIONAL LAW (2002); Cassese, *supra* note 44.

[47] *See* Lusaka Protocol, Nov. 15, 1994, Angola –União nacional para a independência total de Angola (UNITA), UN Doc. S/1994/1441, *at* <http://www.usip.org/library/pa.html>; Burundi Peace Agreement, *supra* note 29; Ceasefire Agreement, July 10, 1999, Aug. 1 & 31, 1999, Dem. Rep. Congo–other Afr. states–Movement for the Liberation of the Congo–Congolese Rally for Democracy (witnessed by international organizations), *at* <http://www.usip.org/library/pa.html>; Guatemala Peace Agreement, *supra* note 31; El Salvador Agreement, *supra* note 31; Israel-Palestine peace agreements, *supra* note 35; General Peace Agreement for Mozambique, Oct. 4, 1992, Mozam.-RENAMO, *at* <http://www.usip.org/library/pa.html>; Peace Agreement, Aug. 4, 1993, Rwanda–Rwandese Patriotic Front, *at* <http://www.incore.ulst.ac.uk/services/cds/>; Lomé Agreement, *supra* note 29.

[48] S. JAMES ANAYA, INDIGENOUS PEOPLES IN INTERNATIONAL LAW 189 (2004).

[49] ILO Convention (No. 169) Concerning Indigenous and Tribal Peoples in Independent Countries, June 27, 1989, 28 ILM 1382 (1989); *see* ANAYA, *supra* note 48, at 15–31, 110; *see also* ANNA MEIJKNECHT, TOWARDS INTERNATIONAL PERSONALITY: THE POSITION OF MINORITIES AND INDIGENOUS PEOPLES IN INTERNATIONAL LAW (2001); Joshua Castellino & Jérémie Gilbert, *Self-Determination, Indigenous Peoples and Minorities*, 3 MACQUARIE L.J. 155 (2003).

382   THE AMERICAN JOURNAL OF INTERNATIONAL LAW   [Vol. 100:373

the Mexican government; between Bangladesh and the indigenous peoples of the Chittagong Hills Tract; between the Indian government and tribal groups from northeast India; between France and the Kanaks of New Caledonia; and between the Guatemalan government and Unidad revolucionaria nacional guatemalteca concerning indigenous groups (here as part of a series of agreements within a broader peace process).[50] These agreements provided for ceasefires and broad frameworks for governance designed to address key issues in the conflict. Similar agreements have been signed in situations that—while less clearly involving violent conflict—did involve ongoing land disputes connected with self-determination, and what could be called the "structural violence" of marginalization.[51] Such agreements were concluded between South Africa and the ‡Khomani San, and, in a rapidly growing number, between indigenous peoples and the Canadian government.[52] Both types of indigenous peoples' agreements evidence a legal nature, in terms of the language used, the type of commitments made by the parties, and the provision for detailed reciprocal bargains. The agreements also deal with matters integral to the notion of statehood, such as sovereignty, territory, government, and the language of "self-determination." In some cases, they provide for legislation to give commitments domestic legal status.

Finally, political and military leaders of minority groups with secessionist claims in autonomous areas often sign peace agreements with the states in which they form a minority. These agreements include those between Georgia and Abkhazia, Moldova and Transdniestria, parties on the island of Bougainville and Papua New Guinea, and Russia and Chechnya.[53] The agreements use the language of obligation and evidence intention to be bound. Treaties can, of

---

[50] Actions and Measures for Chiapas: Joint Commitments and Proposals, and related agreements (San Andrés de Larráinzar Agreements), Mex.–Chiapas–Ejército zapatista de liberación nacional (EZLN), Feb. 16, 1996, *at* <http://www.usip.org/library/pa.html>; Bangladesh: Chittagong Hill Tracts Treaty, Dec. 2, 1997, Bangl.–Parbattya Chattagram Jana Samhati Samiti–inhabitants of Chittagong Hill Tracts, *at* <http://www.satp.org>; Assam Accord, Aug. 15, 1985, India–Assam Students Union–All Assam Gana Sangram Prishad, and other agreements, *reprinted in* P. S. DATTA, ETHNIC PEACE ACCORDS IN INDIA (1995), Accord *at* <http://www.satp.org>; Accord de Nouméa, May 5, 1998, Fr.-Kanaks, *at* <http://www.gouv.nc/static/pages/outils/telechargement/telechargement.htm> (the agreement was not signed, but proposed (Art. 6(5)) that a committee of signatories be set up to take into consideration opinions of local bodies consulted on the agreement, take part in the preparation of legislation, and ensure the proper implementation of the agreement. The agreement also notes that it was approved by the partners to the earlier peace accord); Agreement on Identity and Rights of Indigenous Peoples, Mar. 31, 1995, Guat.-URNG, UN Doc. A/49/882–S/1995/256, 36 ILM 285 (1997), *available at* <http://www.usip.org/library/pa.html>.

[51] JOHAN GALTUNG, PEACE BY PEACEFUL MEANS: PEACE AND CONFLICT, DEVELOPMENT AND CIVILIZATION 197 (1996) (frames the term "structural violence" to refer to any constraint on human potential due to economic and political structures).

[52] On the Final Agreement of March 21, 1999, between South Africa and the ‡Khomani San (comprising Mier Settlement and San Settlement) (Afrikaans version on file with author), see South Africa Press Release, Deputy President Mbeki and Minister Hanekom to Officiate at Khomani/Southern Kalahari San Land Claim (Mar. 12, 1999), *at* <http://www.info.gov.za/speeches/1999/990511152p1011.htm>; Roger Chennells, *The ‡Khomani San Land Claim*, 26 CULTURAL SURVIVAL Q. 51 (2002). A summary of the Canada-Nisga'a Framework Agreement, 1991, Can.–Brit. Colum.–Nisga'a Tribal Council, and a full list of Canadian agreements are available at <http://www.atns.net.au/index.php>. The Agreement-in-Principle, Feb. 15, 1996, and the Final Agreement, Aug. 4, 1999, Can.–Brit. Colum.–Nisga'a Tribal Council, are available at <http://www.gov.bc.ca/arr//negotiation/nisgaa/default.htm> (and linked archive).

[53] For full texts of the Georgia-Abkhazia agreements, see A QUESTION OF SOVEREIGNTY: THE GEORGIA-ABKHAZIA PEACE PROCESS, ACCORD, Sept. 1999 (Jonathan Cohen ed.), *available at* <http://www.c-r.org/accord/geor-ab/accord7/index.shtml>. On Moldova-Transdniestria, see, for example, Memorandum on the Bases for Normalization of Relations, May 8, 1997, Mold.-Transdniestria, *at* <http://www.ecmi.de/cps/documents_moldova_memo.html>. On Bougainville–Papua New Guinea, see Lincoln Agreement on Peace, Security and Development on Bougainville, Jan. 23, 1998, Papua N.G.–Bougainville Transitional Gov't–Bougainville Resistance Force–Bougainville Interim Gov't–Bougainville Revolutionary Army–Bougainville leaders; Bougainville Peace Agreement, Aug. 30, 2001 (see section A regarding legal status), both available at <http://www.usip.org/library/pa.html>. On Russia-Chechnya, see Truce Agreement: Principles for Determining the Fundamentals of Relations Between the Russian Federation and the Chechen Republic [Khasavuyrt Accord], Aug. 25, 1996, Russ.-Chechnya (on file with author).

course, be signed by substate entities such as the constituent parts of a federation, depending on the powers conferred on them domestically.[54] However, in these cases the status of the substate entity and its relationship to the state are disputed and the entity is typically operating extraconstitutionally. Nonstate groups could again attempt to argue that they are "subjects of international law" because they represent minority groups. While legal documents dealing with minorities have proliferated and arguably confer on them a right as groups, their claim to international subjectivity is generally considered to be weaker than that of indigenous peoples.[55] Furthermore, there is little guiding authority on the mechanisms by which political or military leaders (mostly men) can claim to be the legitimate representatives of minority groups, although elections would provide some basis for the claim. Other claims to legal subjectivity might lie in the concept of the "state-in-the-making" whose treaty-making capacity must be recognized for statehood to be negotiated, or recognition that the minority's representatives have status as a national liberation movement or erstwhile armed group.[56] To some extent, the problem of legal status reflects international law's difficulties in dealing with transitional situations. The categorization of nonstate actors as minorities rather than armed opposition groups, national liberation movements, or even states is itself a product of transition. In the course of the peace process, both the legal regime and the humanitarian law status of nonstate groups change, as the group moves from armed opposition to inclusion in government and the level of conflict subsides.[57] A lack of governmental status (regional or otherwise) often ensues because the peace process has subsequently stalled, leaving the status of both the substate region and those who govern it in legal limbo.[58]

The difficulty is that deciding whether some or all of the above agreements constitute binding international agreements is a tautological exercise.[59] Many commentators equate the notion of international legal subjectivity with international legal personality,[60] and from this view many of the above groups appear to fall short, having some of the attributes of legal personality, but not all.[61] Other writers, most notably Anna Meijknecht, suggest that international legal subjectivity is a subcomponent of international legal personality, meaning that something less than full personality

---

[54] ANTHONY AUST, MODERN TREATY LAW AND PRACTICE 48–49 (2000).

[55] *See* MEIJKNECHT, *supra* note 49, at 225 (noting that any rational basis for this difference is difficult to find, and locating it in the acknowledgment of historical wrongs done to indigenous peoples); *see also* ANTONIO CASSESE, INTERNATIONAL LAW 63 (2d ed. 2005); HECTOR GROS ESPIELL, THE RIGHT TO SELF-DETERMINATION: IMPLEMENTATION OF UNITED NATIONS RESOLUTIONS ¶56, UN Doc. E/CN.4/Sub.2/405/Rev.1, UN Sales No. E.79.XIV.5 (1980).

[56] *Cf.* Peter Malanczuk, *Some Basic Aspects of the Agreements Between Israel and the PLO from the Perspective of International Law*, 7 EUR. J. INT'L I . 485 (1996) (effectively arguing that these concepts give the Israeli-PLO agreements international legal status).

[57] *See* Christine Bell & Johanna Keenan, *Human Rights Non-governmental Organisations and the Problems of Transition*, 26 HUM. RTS. Q. 330, 344–45 (2004).

[58] *Cf.* Wallensteen & Sollenberg, *supra* note 1, at 343 (classifying some of the peace agreements in these situations as "partial agreements").

[59] MEIJKNECHT, *supra* note 49, at 24–25.

[60] *See generally* Reparation for Injuries Suffered in the Service of the United Nations, 1949 ICJ REP. 174, 179 (Apr. 11); ANNIKA TAHVANAINEN, THE CAPACITY TO CONCLUDE TREATIES—WHICH ENTITIES CAN BECOME PARTIES TO TREATIES UNDER INTERNATIONAL LAW? (Institute for Human Rights, Åbo Akademi University, 2004) (report to the committee drafting a Nordic treaty on the Sami indigenous people's rights).

[61] *See* IAN BROWNLIE, PRINCIPLES OF PUBLIC INTERNATIONAL LAW 57 (6th ed. 2003); PETER MALANCZUK, AKEHURST'S MODERN INTRODUCTION TO INTERNATIONAL LAW 91 (1997); SHAW, *supra* note 6, at 175–246. Some of those commentators view actors with some attributes of legal personality as having "limited legal personality" or constituting "partial international legal subjects." *See* Peter Malanczuk, *Multinational Enterprises and Treaty-Making—A Contribution to the Discussion on Non-State Actors and the "Subjects" of International Law*, *in* MULTILATERAL TREATY-MAKING: THE CURRENT STATUS OF CHALLENGES TO AND REFORMS NEEDED IN THE INTERNATIONAL LEGISLATIVE PROCESS 45, 55 (Vera Gowlland-Debbas ed., 2000) [hereinafter Malanczuk, *Multinational Enterprises*].

might indicate treaty-making capacity.[62] The tautology arises because a claim to international subjectivity, on either view, involves examining what rights, powers, duties, and immunities the actors in question are accorded on the international plane, including whether they are permitted to sign treaties or international agreements.[63] Moreover, the main evidence of such permission may be the existence of an internationalized peace agreement itself.[64] Recognizing peace agreements as international agreements therefore seems to require the nonstate group and the agreement to "bootstrap" each other into the international legal realm. Rosalyn Higgins has suggested that the notion of international participants in an international legal system conceived of as a "particular decision-making process" may be more conducive to understanding the current status of nonstate actors than traditional subject-object dichotomies.[65] This approach can aid in determining whether current peace agreement practice is increasingly posing a fundamental challenge to the existing international legal order. It does not, however, assist in deciding definitively whether or not a peace agreement is a binding international agreement.

Legalization and Compliance

Does it matter whether or not peace agreements are binding legal documents? For domestic lawyers, the connection between the legal categorization of a document and its enforcement seems to be self-evident.[66] However, because the consequences of formal international legal status are less clear, international lawyers more readily question whether and how the binding legal form of an obligation affects compliance with it. Unlike political pacts or merely declaratory documents, treaties and international agreements are legally binding instruments with established enforcement mechanisms. However, their enforcement is notoriously less concrete than in domestic legal systems owing to the relative "anarchy" of the international legal order, in particular the absence of a central enforcement mechanism.[67] The Vienna Convention on the Law of Treaties provides rules for dealing with termination and suspension of the operation of treaties, which in effect encapsulate self-help in the form of either partially or completely walking away as a state's main remedy for another state party's breach of the treaty.[68] Therefore, enforcement in the domestic legal sense as backed up by courts does not exist. Implementation depends on the voluntary, ongoing assent of the parties.[69] Commentators acknowledge that formal legal status still affects compliance, as discussed in part III below.[70] However, they also

---

[62] MEIJKNECHT, *supra* note 49, at 34.

[63] *See* JAN KLABBERS, AN INTRODUCTION TO INTERNATIONAL INSTITUTIONAL LAW 43–48 (2002); *cf.* Malanczuk, *Multinational Enterprises, supra* note 61, at 55 (arguing that some subjects of international law "have legal personality only with respect to *certain* international rights and obligations").

[64] *See* ZEGVELD, *supra* note 46, at 51 (discussing the status of the El Salvador Agreement on Human Rights, July 26, 1990, El Sal.–FMLN-UN, UN Doc. A/44/971–S/21541, annex (1990)); *cf.* Antonio Cassese, *The Special Court and International Law: The Decision Concerning the Lomé Agreement,* 2 J. INT'L CRIM. JUST. 1130, 1134–35 (2004) (arguing that the Lomé Agreement was an international one, owing to the status of the nonstate actors, but also the intention of the parties in signing the Agreement). *But see* Kooijmans, *supra* note 14.

[65] ROSALYN HIGGINS, PROBLEMS AND PROCESS: INTERNATIONAL LAW AND HOW WE USE IT 50 (1994).

[66] *See, e.g.,* RICHARD A. POSNER, THE PROBLEMS OF JURISPRUDENCE (1990).

[67] *See, e.g.,* CASSESE, *supra* note 55, at 5.

[68] Vienna Convention, *supra* note 36, pt. V.

[69] Charles Lipson, *Why Are Some International Agreements Informal?* 45 INT'L ORG. 495 (1991) (describing the term "binding agreement" as "misleading hyperbole").

[70] *See generally* COMMITMENT AND COMPLIANCE: THE ROLE OF NON-BINDING NORMS IN THE INTERNATIONAL LEGAL SYSTEM (Dinah Shelton ed., 2000); 54 INT'L ORG., No. 3, *Legalization and World Politics* (2000); Anthony Aust, *The Theory and Practice of Informal International Instruments,* 35 INT'L & COMP. L.Q. 787 (1986); Richard R. Baxter, *International Law in "Her Infinite Variety,"* 29 INT'L & COMP. L.Q. 549 (1980); Lipson, *supra* note 69; Oscar Schachter, *The Twilight Existence of Nonbinding International Agreements,* 71 AJIL 296 (1977).

acknowledge that soft law or informal agreements generate some of the same pressures for compliance as the hard law or formal ones, and can be equally effective.[71] Moreover, even hard law commitments do not operate in a "monolithic or unidimensional" way.[72]

These considerations led Abbott, Keohane, Moravcsik, Slaughter, and Snidal to propose a broader concept of "legalization" as more useful to understanding an agreement's legal status than deciding whether it constitutes hard or soft law.[73] They set out a three-way matrix that maps the legalization of an agreement or norm according to (1) how "legal" the nature of the obligation is, (2) the precision with which it is drafted, and (3) the delegation to a third party of the power to interpret and enforce the agreement. Thus, an obligation expressed as a binding rule in precise language, to be enforced by an international court or organization, might stand "near the ideal type of full legalization, as in highly developed domestic legal systems."[74] A loose obligation, such as an expressly nonlegal norm, stated as a vague principle, to be enforced only by means of diplomacy, would stand at the other end of the spectrum. However, in between it is more difficult to separate and order the three dimensions:

> In some settings a strong legal obligation . . . might be more legalized than a weaker obligation . . . , even if the latter were more precise and entailed stronger delegation. Furthermore, the relative significance of delegation vis-à-vis other dimensions becomes less clear at lower levels, since truly "high" delegation, including judicial or quasi-judicial authority, almost never exists together with low levels of legal obligation.[75]

Therefore, the degree of legalization is captured by all three factors rather than just one.[76] States attempt to manage the future risks of signing an agreement by trying to manipulate all three factors so as to balance the need to lock in the other party's commitment with the importance of ensuring exit strategies for themselves.

This analysis is useful in understanding how and why the legal status of a peace agreement might matter. As Abbott and his colleagues suggest, it opens up common ground between the explorations of political scientists and lawyers as regards implementation.[77] Furthermore, although designed for the international sphere, their analysis also makes it possible to consider the relationship of a peace agreement's status as a "constitution" to what appear to be "un-constitution-like" types of obligation and third-party enforcement. In the following sections, the notion of legalization proposed by Abbott and his colleagues is adapted and applied to peace agreement practice addressing legal form (part III), the nature of the obligation (part IV), and delegation of interpretation and enforcement to third parties (part V). This examination begins to reveal the distinctive nature of peace agreement legalization, building the case for a *lex pacificatoria*.

---

[71] *See* sources cited *supra* note 70.

[72] W. Michael Reisman, *The Concept and Functions of Soft Law in International Politics, in* ESSAYS IN HONOUR OF JUDGE TASLIM OLAWALE ELIAS 135, 136 (Emmanuel G. Bello & Bola A. Ajibola eds., 1992).

[73] Abbott et al., *supra* note 17; *see also* Hartmut Hillgenberg, *A Fresh Look at Soft Law*, 10 EUR. J. INT'L L. 499 (1999) (full discussion of the mechanisms with which nontreaty commitments form "legal effect"); *cf.* JAN KLABBERS, THE CONCEPT OF TREATY IN INTERNATIONAL LAW (1996); Christine Chinkin, *Normative Development in the International Legal System, in* COMMITMENT AND COMPLIANCE, *supra* note 70, at 21, 24; Reisman, *supra* note 72.

[74] Abbott et al., *supra* note 18, at 405.

[75] *Id.* at 406.

[76] *Id.*

[77] *Id.* at 402.

386   THE AMERICAN JOURNAL OF INTERNATIONAL LAW   [Vol. 100:373

III. LEGAL FORM

An agreement's legal form remains relevant to compliance because formalized agreements raise the reputation costs of noncompliance.[78] Deciding when to use formal or informal agreements is also linked to a range of strategic choices for states concerning reputation, speed, capacity for revision, and domestic legal requirements.[79] In the context of peace agreements, however, the difficulties of legal classification mean that the choice between binding and nonbinding agreement is not straightforward. Under international law as currently constituted, state and nonstate actors that wish to sign legally binding agreements can make the terms of their agreements sound legal, can refer to international law as a basis for their commitments, and can delegate enforcement tasks to a range of international actors, as discussed in parts IV and V below. There may be good arguments that these factors take the agreements into the realm of international law, and even make them international agreements;[80] but those who wish to frame agreements clearly as treaties can best do so by framing them as between state parties only. The choice, therefore, is between a treaty whose formal parties differ from those agreeing to the obligations, and agreements whose status as binding international agreements remains in doubt. This calls for a different understanding of how legal form connects to compliance in the peace agreement context, in terms of both the reputation costs of breach and the strategic choices available with regard to how agreements are framed.

State and nonstate actors that sign agreements directly with each other can attempt to use other dimensions of legalization (such as precise language and third-party enforcement) to compensate for the lack of clear legal form, as discussed in parts IV and V below. Yet something remains lost. The lingering ambiguity over the binding status of an agreement can undo the parties' intention to be bound, by offering those who would later renege an opportunity to dismiss the agreement as not binding.[81] Looking first to the state's commitments, to the extent that the legal status of such an agreement is unclear, this deficiency undermines the notion that the state has attached its reputation to the agreement and has a self-interest in the integrity of the international legal system. Furthermore, the constraints on self-serving "auto-interpretation" brought by accepted modes of legal discourse to discussions, for example, of breach, *force majeure*, and impossibility are negated. In their place are left political and moral debates as regards breach, fault, and consequence, which have little claim to independence from the underlying disputes at the heart of the conflict, weakening their impact on conflict resolution.[82] There is also some reason to believe that parties to agreements take their obligations more seriously when they believe them to be legal.[83]

A binding legal agreement may be particularly meaningful in ensuring the commitment of nonstate actors. As the Permanent Court of International Justice noted, "[T]he right of entering into international engagements is an attribute of State sovereignty."[84] In the context of

---

[78] *See generally* sources cited *supra* note 70.

[79] *See generally* sources cited *supra* note 70.

[80] *See* Cassese, *supra* note 64; *cf.* Malanczuk, *Multinational Enterprises, supra* note 61, at 58–62 (discussing legal status of multinational companies and internationalized contracts). *But see supra* notes 59–65 and corresponding text.

[81] *See, e.g.*, Prosecutor v. Kallon, Kamara, Decision on Jurisdiction, Nos. SCSL–2004–15–AR72(E), SCSL–2004–16–AR72(E) (Mar. 13, 2004) [hereinafter *Kallon*] (discussed *infra* text at notes 88–99).

[82] *See, e.g.*, ROGER FISHER & WILLIAM URY, GETTING TO YES: NEGOTIATING AN AGREEMENT WITHOUT GIVING IN 84–98 (2d ed. 1992) (for importance of "objective criteria," as standards external to the parties in the conflict).

[83] *See* WATSON, *supra* note 14, at vii; *see also* THOMAS M. FRANCK, THE POWER OF LEGITIMACY AMONG NATIONS 35–37 (1990).

[84] S.S. "Wimbledon," 1923 PCIJ (ser. A) No. 1, at 25.

peace agreements, the imprimatur of legal form might influence nonstate actors to comply less because they have a reputation to lose if they fail to do so than because they have a new status and legitimacy to gain, which are tied up with the status of the peace agreement itself. State actors might be expected to resist conceding formal legal status to peace agreements precisely for this reason, especially given the current climate of "war against terrorism."[85] However, there are also reasons why it might be in states' interests to concede treaty status.[86] First, clarity over the binding nature of the agreement may add little to the claims of the nonstate group that has not already been conceded by the very fact of an agreement. Formal treaty status cements a cost, rather than creating it. Conversely, preserving the ambiguity over whether the agreement is binding also weakens its currency for states. The compromises of peace agreements are carefully crafted to stop terrible wars. Nonstate armed groups are less likely to abide by agreements that they know from the outset are merely "pieces of paper." Worse still for states, rejecting the legal status of both the nonstate group and the peace agreement may result in the argument that the state is bound while the nonstate actors are not.[87]

The positive legal status of peace agreements also remains important to compliance because it carries weight in legal forums: courts and tribunals use it as a starting point in determining their own jurisdiction. Here, positivist law categories hold sway, no matter how unfashionable, because they provide a rational basis for clear decision making. This can be illustrated by the *Kallon* case of the appeals chamber of the Special Court for Sierra Leone, established to prosecute persons who bear the greatest responsibility for serious violations of international humanitarian law and Sierra Leonean law during the conflict in that country.[88] In this case the defendants challenged the Special Court's jurisdiction on the basis that it contravened the amnesty provision of the Lomé Peace Agreement, and that it would constitute an abuse of process to allow the prosecution of pre-Lomé crimes.[89] The appeals chamber found itself considering the legal status of the agreement signed by the government and the RUF, so as to determine the validity of the amnesty. With respect to the status of the RUF and the Lomé Agreement, the chamber distinguished between being bound under common Article 3 of the Geneva Conventions (which it accepted as applicable), and the RUF's treaty-making ability, stating that "[i]nternational law does not seem to have vested [the RUF] with such capacity."[90] The tautologies of the decision, which relies on blank statements of law that are far from self-evident, point to the difficulties of the positivist law project in this area, but not its irrelevance.[91] Even on the decision's own terms, the question arises of whether it would have made any difference if legal provisions according a greater degree of international subjectivity to the

[85] *Cf.* Ruth Wedgwood, *Legal Personality and the Role of Non-governmental Organizations and Non-State Political Entities in the United Nations System, in* NON-STATE ACTORS AS NEW SUBJECTS OF INTERNATIONAL LAW 21, 35 (Rainer Hofmann & Nils Geissler eds., 1999) (arguing that it may prolong conflict because international status may strengthen the resistance of nonstate groups to settlement, citing the example of Georgia and Abkhazia); *cf.* AUST, *supra* note 54, at 48–54 (discussing the exercise of treaty-making capacity by parts of a state); Oliver Lissitzyn, *Territorial Entities Other Than States in the Law of Treaties,* 125 RECUEIL DES COURS 5 (1983 III) (semble).

[86] *Cf.* Wedgwood, *supra* note 85, at 34 (Wedgwood's (converse) argument relating to the difficulties of lack of legal status for nonstate actors).

[87] *See* Vienna Convention, *supra* note 36, Art. 3(c); *cf.* Cassese, *supra* note 64, at 1139–40 (noting the argument that translating Sierra Leone's Lomé Agreement into national legislation could mean that its provisions continue to bind the government, even when the underlying agreement was void, thus preventing the government from prosecuting amnestied crimes in domestic courts). There can also be arguments that notions of estoppel, precommitment, and unilateral declaration would obligate the state. *See* WATSON, *supra* note 14, at 201–64; Hillgenberg, *supra* note 73, at 505.

[88] *Kallon, supra* note 81.

[89] For the Lomé Agreement, see *supra* note 29.

[90] *Kallon, supra* note 81, ¶48.

[91] *Cf.* Cassese, *supra* note 64 (noting the tautologies of the decision and criticizing the reasoning).

388 THE AMERICAN JOURNAL OF INTERNATIONAL LAW [Vol. 100:373]

nonstate actor had been acknowledged to apply, such as Protocol II (indicating territorial control) or even Protocol I (acknowledging the group in question to be a "national liberation movement" akin to a state).[92] While Protocol I can be argued to be anachronistic, it still has some relevance, most notably in the Israeli-Palestinian conflict since the PLO signed the initial Israeli-Palestinian agreements.[93]

The need to overrule the amnesty of the Lomé Agreement might appear to demonstrate why states should not concede that peace agreements signed with nonstate actors are binding on the international level.[94] However, rejection of Lomé as a binding agreement let the RUF off the hook as regards compliance, while leaving the state subject to arguments that it was still bound to comply by virtue of its interstate commitments and its national legislation.[95] Moreover, rejection of the international legal status of Lomé was not necessary in order to invalidate its amnesty provision.[96] The *Kallon* result could have been reached by applying notions of treaty breach (the RUF having continued fighting in violation of the cease-fire commitments);[97] or by deeming the amnesty provision invalid to the extent that it covered certain crimes against humanity, serious war crimes, torture, and other gross violations of human rights;[98] or even by finding that the amnesty section applied only to future domestic law proceedings (for which a tenuous basis can be discerned in the wording).[99]

Kallon does not stand alone: a range of international tribunals may be called upon to adjudicate on the compatibility of peace agreements with international law for a variety of reasons.[100] Domestic courts, too, often end up examining the political and legal questions at the heart of the agreement, through constitutional or legislative adjudication that must determine the extent to which the peace agreement is a foundational interpretive document, or indeed a treaty, and where it is a political document to be deferred to as dealing with political questions only.[101] To be sure, in many situations the role of courts and tribunals will be marginal to an agreement's success or failure: courts and tribunals are likely to be ineffective in sustaining an

---

[92] Protocol I, *supra* note 46, Art. 2; Protocol II, *supra* note 46, Art. 1.

[93] ZEGVELD, *supra* note 46, at 16–17.

[94] *Cf.* Wedgwood, *supra* note 86, at 36 (arguing that decisions over treaty-making capacity should be made with a view to the implications of so doing).

[95] *Cf. Kallon, supra* note 81, ¶62 (where the Special Court drew a distinction between the issue of the state's obligations under the Agreement, and the validity of the treaty establishing the jurisdiction of the court).

[96] *But see* 2 WITNESS TO TRUTH: REPORT OF THE SIERRA LEONE TRUTH AND RECONCILIATION COMMISSION ¶559 (2004) (finding that the amnesty was necessary to making peace).

[97] *See* Letter Dated 9 August 2000 from the Permanent Representative of Sierra Leone to the United Nations Addressed to the President of the Security Council, UN Doc. S/2000/786, annex, *cited in Kallon, supra* note 81, ¶¶8–9; *see also* Cassese, *supra* note 64, at 1138–39 (arguing that this would have been a better legal approach).

[98] *See Kallon, supra* note 81, ¶¶66–74 (discussion of the limits of amnesty).

[99] *See* Lomé Agreement, *supra* note 29, Art. IX; *cf.* Brief of the Redress Trust (Redress), the Lawyers Committee for Human Rights, and the International Commission of Jurists, *Kallon* (n.d.), *supra* note 81, *available at* <http://www.redress.org/casework/AmicusCuriaeBrief-SCSL1.pdf>.

[100] *See, e.g.*, Legal Consequences of the Construction of a Wall in the Occupied Palestinian Territory, Advisory Opinion, 2004 ICJ REP. 131, para. 2.4(*c*) (July 9) (Elaraby, J., sep. op.) (describing the 1993 Oslo Accord as "contractual and . . . legally binding on Israel" when finding the construction of the wall contrary to international law).

[101] *See, e.g.*, Robinson v. Sec'y of State for N. Ir., [2002] UKHL 32, *available at* <http://www.bailii.org/databases.html#ew> [hereinafter *Robinson*] (the House of Lords majority judgment held that the Northern Ireland Act should be interpreted purposively, in light of the unique circumstances underlying it. The Law Lords (per Hoffmann, L.J.) described the Act as "a constitution for Northern Ireland, framed to create a continuing form of government against the background of the history of the territory and the principles agreed in Belfast"; *id.*, ¶25); Azanian People's Org. (AZAPO) v. President of S. Afr. & Others, 1996 (4) SA 671, ¶25 (CC) (challenging establishment of amnesty under Truth and Reconciliation law as a violation of international law); *cf* HCJ 4481/91, Bargil v. Israel, [1991] IsrSC 47(4) 210, *available at* <http://elyon1.court.gov.il/files_eng/91/810/044/z01/91044810.z01.pdf>, *cited in* DAVID KRETZMER, THE OCCUPATION OF JUSTICE: THE SUPREME COURT OF ISRAEL AND THE OCCUPIED TERRITORIES 23–24, 204 n.23 (2002) (where the court dismissed as nonjusticiable

agreement in the face of fundamental and violent dissent.[102] However, marginal relevance is not the same as irrelevance. Courts and tribunals have the capacity to extend and develop the agreement's meaning where they find it to be part of the legal framework.[103] More negatively, they have the capacity to terminate the operation of an agreement even in the face of political chances to sustain it.[104] The positive law status of peace agreements therefore remains important to their implementation. This importance, in turn, begins to explain innovations in legal form, which enable parties to frame obligations so that they fall within recognizable traditional legal categories.

Contrived Treaty Form

Drafters of peace agreements sometimes attempt to contrive treaty status for them. They do this by framing an agreement between state and nonstate actors as if it were simply between states (although they typically do so when the states have also been involved to some extent as participants in the conflict). Bosnia's DPA, the British/Irish treaty at the end of the Belfast Agreement, and Cambodia's Paris Accords are all framed as agreements between state parties, and yet are also attempts to bind the ethnic/national groups who were waging war within state borders.[105] This practice has precursors in the patterns of earlier peace processes, as regards Cambodia in the Indochina Conference of 1954;[106] ethnic conflict in Cyprus in the 1960s;[107] and the Camp David process in the Middle East in 1978, on which Bosnia's Dayton process was in part modeled.[108]

These treaties use state-party commitments to lock in nonstate actors in a two-way dynamic. The state parties in effect guarantee to kindred nonstate actors that the commitments to them in the agreement will be delivered; and to other parties that the commitments of nonstate actors will be honored. To achieve and reinforce this relationship between treaty and nonstate actor, some *"unique* legal features" were written into these agreements with a view to enabling the nonstate

a petition challenging the legality of the Likud government's settlement policy because the matter was a political question and the subject of intensive peace negotiations).

[102] *See infra* text at notes 131–38.

[103] *Robinson, supra* note 101 (in effect revising, to prevent the collapse of the devolved legislature, the very clear electoral procedures set out in the Northern Ireland Act, 1998).

[104] *Cf. Ex parte* Chairperson of Constitutional Assembly: *In re* Certification of Constitution of S. Afr., 1996 (4) SA 744 (CC), 1996 (10) BCLR 1253 (CC) [hereinafter *In re* Certification of Constitution] (delayed rather than prevented the certification of the final Constitution); *see also Robinson, supra* note 101, ¶¶ 42–75 (dissenting judgments of Lord Hutton and Lord Hobhouse, respectively, which would have terminated the operation of the devolved legislative Assembly that stood at the center of the Belfast Agreement).

[105] *See supra* text at note 41.

[106] Final Declaration of the Geneva Conference on the Problem of Restoring Peace in Indo-China, July 21, 1954, 31 DEP'T ST. BULL. 164 (1954), UK Cmd. 9239, at 9, 60 AJIL 643 (1966).

[107] Three agreements were signed on February 19, 1959: Basic Structure of the Republic of Cyprus; Treaty of Guarantee Between the Republic of Cyprus and Greece, the United Kingdom, and Turkey; Treaty of Alliance Between the Republic of Cyprus, Greece, and Turkey, *reprinted in* DOCUMENTS ON INTERNATIONAL AFFAIRS 1959 (Gillian King ed., 1963), *available at* <http://www.kypros.org/constitution/treaty.htm>; *see also* JEFFREY L. DUNOFF, STEVEN R. RATNER, & DAVID WIPPMAN, INTERNATIONAL LAW: NORMS, ACTORS, PROCESS: A PROBLEM-ORIENTED APPROACH 33–66 (2002); David Wippman, *International Law and Ethnic Conflict in Cyprus*, 31 TEX. INT'L L.J. 141 (1996).

[108] The Camp David Accords pointed toward a similar interstate initiation and underwriting of negotiations, although they did not reach the multilateral treaty stage. Framework for Peace in the Middle East, Isr.-Egypt, Sept. 17, 1978, 1136 UNTS 196; Framework for the Conclusion of a Peace Treaty, Isr.-Egypt, Sept. 17, 1978, 1138 UNTS 53. The accords were both signed by Israel and Egypt and witnessed by then-president of the United States Jimmy Carter. *See* GUYORA BINDER, TREATY CONFLICT AND POLITICAL CONTRADICTION: THE DIALECTIC OF DUPLICITY (1988). On the relationship of the Camp David and Dayton processes, see RICHARD HOLBROOKE, TO END A WAR 204 (1999).

390   THE AMERICAN JOURNAL OF INTERNATIONAL LAW   [Vol. 100:373

group to sign them.[109] The DPA, for example, consists of a central agreement signed by the three republics and witnessed by other states together with the European Union, and a dozen attached agreements (framed as annexes) signed by different permutations of parties and signatories, including the substate entities created by the Agreement.[110] Both state and entity treaty commitments are difficult to place within a technical legal analysis. The basis for the entity signatures is unclear: as substate regions they came into existence by virtue of the DPA, and therefore could not have had treaty-making capacity as constituent parts of the federation.[111] Neither was there any overt agreement of agency between the state and the entity.[112] As for the Belfast Agreement, it is composed of a multiparty agreement and a British-Irish treaty, which parcels out the intergovernmental commitments in treaty form. Under the terms of this treaty, however, both governments make legislative and constitutional commitments requiring the cooperation of actors beyond their control—including "the people of the island of Ireland."[113] The Agreement on a Comprehensive Political Settlement of the Cambodia Conflict of 1991 was signed "on behalf of Cambodia" by all the members of Cambodia's National Supreme Council, and Article 28 provides that "[t]he signature on behalf of Cambodia by the members of the SNC shall commit all Cambodian parties and armed forces to the provisions of this Agreement."[114] In each case, treaty status was achieved by having states alone sign the main body of the agreement directly and incorporating commitments of nonstate actors in innovative ways.

Does this strategy then remedy the deficits in legal form of peace agreements signed directly with nonstate parties? The very attempt to contrive treaty status indicates the seriousness of state commitments, raising the costs of noncompliance for the state parties. As noted, it may also be relevant to legal adjudication. Nevertheless, the lack of correlation between the parties to the conflict and the parties to the treaty negates some of the benefits of choosing a clear legal form for the obligations. Treaty status can be achieved only by forgoing the inclusion of the nonstate actor as a direct party to the treaty, even though the nonstate actor's compliance lies at the heart of the agreement's implementation. The reputation costs of formal treaty status will only attach directly to state parties, even though they may lead indirectly to political costs for nonstate actors.[115] If state guarantees *on behalf of* kindred nonstate groups are undelivered, it will be very difficult to tell whether the reason was insufficient effort or lack of capacity to influence these nonstate actors. As regards state underwriting of commitments *to* kindred nonstate groups, the state's self-interest may soon induce it to reconsider.[116] Moreover, peace-agreement treaties also suffer from two other problems, similar to those

[109] Paola Gaeta, *The Dayton Agreements and International Law*, 7 EUR. J. INT'L L. 147 (1996); *see also* AUST, *supra* note 54, at 52.

[110] The central annexes were signed by the Republic of Bosnia and Herzegovina and the entities. However, Annex 1–B (Agreement on Regional Stabilization) and Annex 10 (Agreement on Civilian Implementation) were signed by the three republics and the entities. DPA, *supra* note 41.

[111] Wedgwood, *supra* note 85, at 34.

[112] Gaeta, *supra* note 109, at 150–52.

[113] Agreement Between the Government of the United Kingdom of Great Britain and Northern Ireland and the Government of Ireland, Apr. 10, 1998, Art. 1(ii), 37 ILM 777 (1998), *available at* <http://www.nio.gov.uk/agreement.pdf>.

[114] Agreement on a Comprehensive Political Settlement of the Cambodia Conflict, Oct. 23, 1991, 31 ILM 180 (1992) [hereinafter Cambodia Political Settlement]; *see also* Ratner, *supra* note 14, at 9 (interestingly showing that this device was aimed primarily at enabling authority to be granted from a national sovereign to the UN Transitional Authority for Cambodia, without using Chapter VII of the UN Charter).

[115] *See, e.g.*, FORTNA, *supra* note 13, at 21. The Cambodian mechanism probably comes closest to including nonstate actors as parties to the treaty but is not available in contexts where the nonstate actors do not cumulatively equate to "the state."

[116] *See, e.g.*, Declaration of the Parties to the Agreement Between Ireland and the United Kingdom, Apr. 19, 2004, Ir.-UK, *available at* <http://www.taoiseach.gov.ie/index.asp?locID=199&docID=1765> (British-Irish agreement on reinterpretation of the Belfast Agreement's citizenship provisions, to accommodate Irish immigration).

Richard Baxter highlighted with respect to treaty enforcement generally.[117] They often amount to incomplete agreements, because they provide for further agreements in an attempt to stage and sequence issues and develop a peace *process*. This quality makes them susceptible to a "stop-start" dynamic in which it is difficult to assess whether failure to negotiate constitutes a treaty breach. In the context of a peace agreement, this difficulty is accentuated because parties typically test whether they can reclaim concessions, or because continuing conflict changes their self-interest and/or their capacity for compromise. Peace agreements further suffer from the problems of political treaties such as "treaties of alliance": namely, that "[a] change in a government's orientation must . . . be regarded as 'a fundamental change in circumstances,'" which changes the foundation for the treaty as well.[118] Again, such considerations have heightened relevance when it comes to peace agreements, which involve existential compromises by the state with regard to how it conceives of its own sovereignty, power, monopoly over the use of force, and capacity to resist nonstate violence. Such agreements may be uniquely vulnerable to subsequent violence and internal elections.

The limits of treaty status for peace agreements partly explain why these treaties share features with nontreaty peace agreements, such as references to the commitments of nonstate actors and the presence of a range of third-party signatories, as discussed in parts IV and V below.

Contrived Constitutional Form

An alternative way of securing a clear legal form for a peace agreement is to locate it in the domestic legal realm as a constitution. As has been pointed out, peace agreements are hybrid in a way that goes beyond the nature of their participants: they address both the external position of the state on the international plane and the internal constitutional structure of the state. Indeed, constitutional revision is often proffered by states as a means of defusing conflict,[119] resulting in the styling of some peace agreements as constitutions. The main framework peace agreement in South Africa, for example, was the Interim Constitution, which set up a transitional arrangement designed to lead to elections and a constitutional assembly that would produce a final constitution. The Interim Constitution documented the "deal" as to how the African National Congress (ANC) and the National Party/South African government would hold power, the transitional mechanisms for government, and agreed principles that were to set the parameters for the drafting of a final constitution by the newly elected representatives.[120] As other parties reached agreement with the ANC at the eleventh hour, new provisions were added to cut the Inkatha Freedom Party and right-wing Afrikaner groups into both the deal and the constitutional framework.[121] Similarly, attempts to broker cease-fires in Bosnia-Herzegovina focused on peace agreements that in effect were constitutional blueprints whose principal purpose was to accommodate the new minorities inevitably created by the disintegration

---

[117] Richard R. Baxter, *International Law in "Her Infinite Variety,"* 29 INT'L & COMP. L.Q. 549 (1980).

[118] *Id.* at 550.

[119] *See, e.g.,* Bill No. 372, The Constitution of Sri Lanka—Draft Bill to Repeal and Replace Constitution of Sri Lanka, presented to Parliament Aug. 3, 2000, *at* <http://www.priu.gov.lk/Cons/2000ConstitutionBill/Index2000ConstitutionBill.html>; Fiji Act No. 13 of 1997, Constitution Amendment Act 1997, *as amended by* Act No. 5 of 1998, *at* <http://www.oefre.unibe.ch/law/icl/>; Macedonia Framework Agreement (Ohrid Framework Agreement), Aug. 13, 2001, Annex A, Constitutional Amendments, *at* <http://www.usip.org/library/pa.html>.

[120] INTERIM CONST., *supra* note 29, ch. 5.

[121] Act No. 2 of 1994, Constitution of the Republic of South Africa Amendment Act, 1994, amend. to sched. 4 of Act 200 of 1993, §13, Art. XXXIV [hereinafter South Africa Amendment Act] (self-determination provisions addressed at the Afrikaner Brotherhood in South Africa); *see* BELL, *supra* note 2, at 49.

392   THE AMERICAN JOURNAL OF INTERNATIONAL LAW   [Vol. 100:373

of the former Yugoslavia.[122] The final deal in Bosnia reflected a correlation between peace agreement negotiations and constitution making. The Washington Agreement, designed to bring peace between Bosniacs (Bosnian Muslims) and Croats in Bosnia had two parts: a preliminary agreement of only ten lines, plus a constitution for the federation that set out a "power map" as between Croats and Bosniacs.[123] Peace agreements may include constitutions as merely one of their components: Annex 4 of the DPA is a "constitution" for the Republic of Bosnia and Herzegovina, although the peace agreement in its entirety can also be viewed as a constitution in the broadest sense.[124] The failed Rambouillet Accords in Kosovo also included both a constitution and a broad framework for governance.[125] The Bougainville Peace Agreement provided for a constitution and transitional arrangements.[126]

Here again, however, the demands of the peace process mean that the peace-agreement constitution differs from traditional constitutions in both form and substance. In stable democratic societies, constitutions are viewed as superior to domestic law and less open to revision: they are foundational documents, setting out the distribution of power and encapsulating the values, aspirations, and ethos of the state.[127] Peace-agreement constitutions, however, are also literal "social contracts" negotiated between political elites who have been at the heart of the conflict, often under pressure from the international community to conform to the notion of a constitution as establishing democratic institutions, government by law, and individual rights.[128] As a result, particularly in situations of ethnic conflict, these constitutions do not just serve as a social contract between individuals and the state (or between individuals as to the nature and limits of the state); they also constitute a horizontal contract between different groups of individuals. As a glance at these constitutions reveals, this feature often results in a degree of contractual detail that smacks of the reciprocal obligation of private law rather than the broad "founding principles" of public law. The Interim Constitution of South Africa illustrates the phenomenon: it is 227 pages long (in two languages), with copious detail.[129]

Instead of aiming at establishing permanence, peace-agreement constitutions are often explicitly transitional, providing for their imminent revision, extension, or even demise.[130] They tend to be distinctive in their heightened reference to international law, and also in their use of third-party enforcement, relying both on constitutional courts with mandates explicitly shaped by the context of conflict resolution, and on a pluralist range of enforcement mechanisms that cut across political and legal spheres, as well as domestic and international spheres (see part V, below). The lack of "fit" between peace agreements and domestic law categories represents a mirror image of the lack of fit with international law categories. It again evidences a common nature of peace agreements regardless of their legal categorization, which is located in their mix of state and nonstate signatories, the

---

[122] For more detail, see BELL, *supra* note 2, at 107.

[123] Preliminary Agreement Concerning the Establishment of a Confederation, Mar. 18, 1994, Bosn. & Herz.–Croat., 33 ILM 605 (1994); Constitution of the Federation, Mar. 18, 1994, *id.* at 740 (together, Washington Agreement), *available at* <http://www.usip.org/library/pa.html>.

[124] DPA, *supra* note 41; *see also* BELL, *supra* note 2, at 144–47.

[125] Rambouillet Accords: Interim Agreement for Peace and Self-Government in Kosovo, Feb. 23, 1999, UN Doc. S/1999/648, annex, *available at* <http://www.un.org/peace/kosovo/99648_1.pdf> [hereinafter Rambouillet Accords]. Security Council Resolution 1244 (June 10, 1999) then drew on this agreement to provide for transitional arrangements.

[126] Bougainville Peace Agreement, *supra* note 53.

[127] *See* ERIC BARENDT, AN INTRODUCTION TO CONSTITUTIONAL LAW 3–4 (1998).

[128] *Cf.* Paul R. Williams & William Spencer, *Iraq's Political Compact*, BOSTON GLOBE, Aug. 13, 2005, at A15 (arguing that Iraq's draft constitution is "first and foremost a political compact").

[129] INTERIM CONST., *supra* note 29.

[130] *See id.*, ch. 5 (The Adoption of a New Constitution); *see also* RUTI TEITEL, TRANSITIONAL JUSTICE 197–201 (2000) (documenting the use of temporary "transitional" constitutions in a range of jurisdictions).

need to address simultaneously both "internal" and "external" dimensions of intrastate conflict, and the need to address both short-term and long-term peace process goals.

As with treaty form, these distinctive attributes negate some of the "hard law" advantages of constitutional form. Even in traditional settings, constitutional interpretation is accepted as implicating politics in a deeper and more overt way than the interpretation of legislation, in opening up value debates and in requiring an ongoing working out of the relationship between the judiciary and the legislature that cuts to the heart of the relationship between law and politics itself.[131] Such controversies are dramatically accentuated in societies that are constructing both core democratic and legal institutions, using a constitution negotiated out of violent conflict and tentative beginnings in cease-fires. Indeed, it has been suggested that transitional concepts of constitutionalism require new theories of adjudication.[132] Constitutional interpretation in traditional settings draws on established notions of the rule of law and operates to buttress traditional concepts of order, community, and stability. However, in the transitional setting these concepts, and indeed the neutrality of the judiciary itself, are typically deeply contested. These circumstances point to the need for an activist, transformative approach to constitutional interpretation, and a judiciary that is willing and able to engage with the legal and political nature of transition, and the implications for its own role. Peace agreements sometimes signal this need by calling for flexible, "purposive" approaches to constitutional interpretation.[133] Yet the more judges attempt to engage in this type of interpretation, the more they risk politicizing their role, by articulating what appear to be political goals.[134] As the constitutional judicial function will be new by virtue of the context, the legitimacy of both the judiciary and the judicial function itself will be tied up with any goals that judges articulate. The stop-start nature of peace agreements also means that the judicial role is likely to be fundamentally tested by the capacity of key actors to act outside the constitution. Political violence and ongoing dissent to the legitimacy of the state "challenge[ ] the very presuppositions upon which our commitment to constitutional politics must be predicated."[135] How effective constitutional adjudication is in countering such dissent, or indeed in policing excessive responses to it, remains an open question. Such examples as exist seem to indicate that the judicial role can occasionally be effective in a bold sense,[136] but more often merely plays at the fringes of the dispute[137] or fails completely.[138]

Framing peace agreements as constitutions can also be counterproductive in terms of compliance. Constitutional status gives rise to questions about the relationship of the peace-agreement constitution to the past constitutional order. Peace-agreement constitutions tend to supplant existing constitutions outside their established processes for revision or replacement. The

---

[131] MARTIN LOUGHLIN, SWORD AND SCALES (2000) (reviewing relationship between law and politics in public law realm).

[132] TEITEL, *supra* note 130, at 5.

[133] Bougainville Peace Agreement, *supra* note 53, §A.3; INTERIM CONST., *supra* note 29, Art. 35.

[134] *Cf.* JOSEPH MARKO, FIVE YEARS OF CONSTITUTIONAL JURISPRUDENCE IN BOSNIA AND HERZE-GOVINA: A FIRST BALANCE (European Diversity & Autonomy Papers No. 7/2004), *available at* <http://www.eurac.edu/documents/edap/2004_edap07.pdf> (whose analysis illustrates the underlying politics of the reasoning of the Bosnian Constitutional Court decisions with respect to the DPA).

[135] JOHN E. FINN, CONSTITUTIONS IN CRISIS: POLITICAL VIOLENCE AND THE RULE OF LAW 6 (1991).

[136] *E.g.*, Republic of Fiji Islands v. Prasad, [2001] FJCA 2, *available at* <http://www.paclii.org/fj/cases/FJCA/2001/> (asserting the continued status of the 1997 Fijian Constitution in aftermath of coup); *see* George Williams, Republic of Fiji v. Prasad, 2 MELBOURNE J. INT'L L. 144 (2001); Venkat Iyer, *Restoration Constitutionalism in the South Pacific*, 15 PAC. RIM L. & POL'Y J. 39, 59–72 (2006).

[137] KRETZMER, *supra* note 101, at 187 (arguing that while the Israeli Supreme Court has been conservative, it has had some influence in shaping decisions in the "shadow of the law").

[138] Sallah v. Attorney-General (Const. Ct. Ghana, Apr. 20, 1970, unreported), *reprinted in* 2 SAMUEL GYAN-DOH & J. GRIFFITHS, A SOURCEBOOK OF THE CONSTITUTIONAL LAW OF GHANA 493 (1972) (concerning the validity of the dismissal of a senior civil servant belonging to the earlier regime following a coup); *see also* Tayyab Mahmud, *Jurisprudence of Successful Treason: Coup d'Etat & Common Law*, 27 CORNELL INT'L L.J. 49, 65–69 (1994).

394							THE AMERICAN JOURNAL OF INTERNATIONAL LAW							[Vol. 100:373

constitution of the DPA, for example, did not refer to or acknowledge the previous Bosnian Constitution, or attempt to work within its legal framework.[139] A peace agreement's claim to constitutional validity lies in the lack of legitimacy of the previous constitution (and by implication the state), and the need to negotiate an end to the violence that reflects the question mark over the state's legitimacy. In some cases (for example, South Africa) the lack of state legitimacy is accepted by all sides; however, in many other cases it is not. Lack of constitutional continuity, coupled with the international involvement that tends to be required to broker agreement in these circumstances, leaves the peace agreement and new regime open to charges of illegitimacy as a constitutional rupture, and an externally imposed one at that.[140] These arguments are often manipulated by opponents of the agreement on the side of the former state.[141]

Contrived "Agreement" and UN Security Council Resolutions

Another way of achieving binding legal obligations is to lock the parties to a conflict into a framework underwritten by Security Council resolutions.[142] Security Council resolutions can be used to bring the force of law to peace agreement commitments, establishing mechanisms for monitoring compliance that stand independently of the status of the agreement itself, which nevertheless forms their raison d'être.[143] Security Council resolutions can also be used to impose a framework for governance and ongoing negotiations, even in the absence of agreement.

Here the "peace process" is rooted in binding UN Security Council resolution, with international constitution brokering as a conflict resolution device. This approach has characterized processes of postconflict reconstruction consequent to the international use of force by NATO in Kosovo, the U.S.-led interventions in Afghanistan and Iraq, and the turmoil in postreferendum East Timor. The internal processes that the international community (in its different forms) has fashioned in these cases have essentially consisted of an initial framework for internationalized governance provided by a Security Council resolution, followed by constitutional processes that are used to broker agreement between the competing domestic groups. The processes in Kosovo, Afghanistan, and East Timor can be briefly sketched as having four stages: (1) adoption of a Security Council resolution providing a mandate for the international establishment of an interim administration;[144] (2) establishment of an appointed local transitional government—multiethnic where relevant—which is gradually given increasing powers (from consultation toward limited direct exercise of power),[145] in an attempt to foster cooperation

---

[139] *See* Slu beni glasnik Bosne i Hercegovine, Case U 7/97 (Const. Ct. Bosn. & Herz. Dec. 22, 1997), *available at* <http://www.ccbh.ba>; Yee, *supra* note 14, at 176–92.

[140] *See* sources cited *supra* note 139.

[141] This difficulty bolsters the argument that peace agreements face a particular set of implementation difficulties in formally democratic states. *See* Colm Campbell & Fionnuala Ní Aoláin, *The Paradox of Transition in Conflicted Democracies*, 27 HUM. RTS. Q. 172 (2005). These states are the most likely to have a functioning prior constitutional order from which to attack the constitutional manifestations of the peace agreement.

[142] *See, e.g.,* SC Res. 1023 (Nov. 22, 1995) (on which Croatian Erdut Agreement of 1995, *infra* note 190, was suspensive); SC Res. 1244 (June 10, 1999).

[143] *See, e.g.,* SC Res 788 (Nov. 19, 1992) (calling for Liberian parties to Yamoussoukro IV Accord to respect the agreement and requesting the secretary-general to dispatch a special representative to Liberia to evaluate and report on the situation, and to submit a report on the implementation of the resolution).

[144] Kosovo: SC Res. 1244, *supra* note 142; East Timor: SC Res. 1272 (Oct. 25, 1999); Afghanistan: SC Res. 1378 (Nov. 14, 2001).

[145] Kosovo: UN Doc. UNMIK/REG/2000/1 (Jan. 14, 2000) (establishing Joint Interim Administrative Structure, thereby implementing the agreement signed on December 15, 1999, by the Kosovo Albanian political party leaders present at the talks leading to the Rambouillet Accords); East Timor: UN Docs. UNTAET/REG/1999/2 (Dec. 2, 1999), 2000/23 (July 14, 2000), 2000/24 (July 14, 2000); Afghanistan: SC Res. 1383 (Dec. 6, 2001)

between competing groups and to pave the way to (3) elections;[146] and (4) drafting of a new constitution to replace the interim structures of governance with permanent structures (these last two sometimes happening in reverse order).[147] Despite not being UN-led,[148] U.S. reconstruction in Iraq appears to be following a broadly similar constitution-making pattern (albeit with further questions about its legitimacy).[149] The use of peace agreement patterns in a context where there is no initial "agreement" can be argued to be an accentuation of existing peace agreement practice as much as an aberration from it. Its extremes reflect peace process patterns that use internationalized commitments at the beginning stage, ostensibly to enable resort to local constitutionalism and politics as the permanent vehicle for ongoing conflict resolution at the end stage.

In summary, peace agreements are drafted in an attempt to use a legal form and appear to evidence an intent to be legally bound. However, these aims are somewhat frustrated at present by the limits of traditional legal categories, and in particular the difficulty of fitting direct agreements between state and nonstate parties into those categories. The compliance pull gained by achieving obligations with a clear claim to be binding as treaties or constitutions is undermined by the lack of correlation between the parties to the obligation and the formal parties to the agreement, and the peculiar nature of the peace agreement as a process document. These shortcomings point to the importance of legalized models as an alternative to formal legal status and help to explain why peace agreements are characterized by common innovations as regards form, obligations, and third-party delegation, regardless of whether or not they can be placed in a formal legal category.

IV. THE NATURE OF OBLIGATIONS

The limits and deficits of legal form may be compensated for by how an agreement's obligations are crafted, to some extent. Precise and coherent commitments, it is argued, facilitate compliance by imparting clarity regarding implementation and breach, which enhances their normative "compliance pull."[150] Conversely, imprecise language can decrease the normative compliance pull even of obligations framed in legally binding forms.[151] Peace agreement legalization, however, also points to constitutional discourse as an equally important way of framing

(endorsing Agreement on Provisional Arrangements in Afghanistan Pending the Reestablishment of Permanent Government Institutions, Dec. 5, 2001, UN Doc. S/2001/1154, §I(4) [hereinafter Bonn Agreement]).

[146] East Timor: UN Doc. UNTAET/REG/2001/2 (Mar. 16, 2001); Kosovo: UN Doc. UNMIK/REG/2001/9 (May 15, 2001) (Constitutional Framework for Provisional Self-Government); Afghanistan: Bonn Agreement, *supra* note 145, §I(4).

[147] East Timor: UN Doc. UNTAET/REG/2001/2, *supra* note 146; Kosovo: UN Doc. UNMIK/REG/2001/9, *supra* note 146; Afghanistan: Bonn Agreement, *supra* note 145, § 1(6).

[148] But note, as regards UN authorization, SC Res. 1500 (Aug. 14, 2003) (welcoming establishment of Governing Council of Iraq); SC Res. 1511 (Oct. 16, 2003) (welcoming establishment of preparatory constitutional committee); SC Res. 1546 (June 8, 2004) (endorsing proposed framework for transition).

[149] (1) Mandate: SC Res. 1483 (May 22, 2003) (recognizing the United Kingdom and the United States as occupying forces under unified command ("the Authority")). (2) Transitional government: CPA Reg. 6 (July 13, 2003), *available at* <http://www.iraqcoalition.org/regulations/index.html> (establishing the Governing Council of Iraq (GCI) as the principal body of the Iraqi interim administration with a consultative role); Law of Administration for the State of Iraq for the Transitional Period, Mar. 8, 2004, *at* <http://www.cpa-iraq.gov/government/TAL.html> (providing for vesting an Iraqi interim government consisting of a president, prime minister, and cabinet of ministers with full sovereignty [hereinafter Transitional Administrative Law]); CPA Reg. 9 (June 9, 2004), *available at* CPA Reg. 6 Web site, *supra* (dissolving the Coalition Provisional Authority (CPA)). (3) Elections: Transitional Administrative Law, *supra* (elections held on January 30, 2005). (4) New Constitution: Text of the Draft Iraqi Constitution, *available at* <http://iraqigovernment.org/constitution_en.htm> (draft approved October 15, 2005).

[150] Kenneth W. Abbott & Duncan Snidal, *Hard and Soft Law in International Governance*, 54 INT'L ORG. 421, 428–29 (2000) (citing FRANCK, *supra* note 83).

[151] *Id.*

396   THE AMERICAN JOURNAL OF INTERNATIONAL LAW   [Vol. 100:373

obligations in legal terms. In this area, the distinctiveness of peace agreements is driven by the difficulties of constructing obligations that can rely on different rationales for legalization at different stages of the peace process.

Precision for Short-Term Goals

Peace agreement commitments aimed at ending the immediate violence are clearly based on precise drafting to legalize their obligations. Establishing cease-fires, demobilization, and later demilitarization requires clear and verifiable commitments documented as precise obligations. The language of peace agreements bears this out: they are written through with agreed numbers of armed forces, specification of weaponry, timetables, and even maps.[152] Research on the success or failure of these commitments emphasizes the importance of precision to compliance.[153] Indeed, this research suggests that precision may be critical to limiting the scope for drastic "mistakes" by armies when withdrawing.[154] Precise commitments relating to demobilization and demilitarization are also especially amenable to third-party monitoring, interpretation, and enforcement. Peace agreements frequently provide full detail of mandate, role, and verification procedures, as illustrated by the extensive provisions of Angola's Lusaka Protocol of 1994, Bosnia's DPA of 1995, and Sierra Leone's Lomé Agreement of 1999.[155]

Precision and Political Institutions

Peace agreements also evidence precision and detail in the forms of internal government they aim at establishing—particularly as regards the transitional arrangements. In the same way that demobilization signifies a transfer of power, so do the new arrangements for government. The mechanics of the transfer of political power are just as important to the parties, not least because they are linked to the vulnerability created by demobilization commitments. However, precision is also needed in dealing with the technical legal issues that the transition raises as to the applicable legal regime, such as what laws are in force, the specific timing of when and how the legal regime will change, and the detail of the effect of these changes on political and legal institutions like the presidency, the police, and the courts. The transitional provisions of Burundi's Arusha Accord and South Africa's Interim Constitution are examples.[156]

In addition, a high degree of precision is often characteristic of the longer-term provisions on how power will be held and exercised. Here, the precision of peace agreement commitments is linked to the substantive content of the obligations through the notion of mutual "enlightened self-interest." The drafters of peace agreements often focus on creating incentives for cooperation and self-execution by providing for tightly reciprocal obligations at the levels both of stopping the violence and of creating democratic institutions. For political and military elites making fundamental compromises, the devil is quite literally in the details, as parties try to anticipate the consequences of any new arrangements for their own power. Thus, for an ethnic group whose separatist claims are to be accommodated with something less than its own state, the detail of which powers are to be devolved to the substate entity, the relationship of the entity

---

[152] *See, e.g.*, Angola: Lusaka Protocol, *supra* note 47; Democratic Republic of Congo: Ceasefire Agreement, *supra* note 47; El Salvador: Peace Agreement, Jan. 16, 1992, El Sal.–FMLN, UN Doc. A/46/864–S/23501, annex (1992), *available at* <http://www.usip.org/library/pa/html>.

[153] FORTNA, *supra* note 13.

[154] *Id.* at 20.

[155] Lusaka Protocol, *supra* note 47, Annex 3; DPA, *supra* note 41, Annex 1A; Lomé Agreement, *supra* note 29, Annex 1.

[156] Burundi Peace Agreement, *supra* note 29, Protocol II, ch. II; INTERIM CONST., *supra* note 29, ch. 15.

to the central state, the precise numbers of the different ethnic groups in the central and regional institutions, their weighting as regards veto powers or constitutional amendment, and the procedures for breaking deadlock will all be crucial to agreement. The peace agreements for Burundi, Northern Ireland, South Africa, Bosnia, and Bougainville illustrate the detail that results.[157] Similarly for armed groups in left-right conflicts, the move to political participation typically involves detail on the democratic principles to govern the state and its key institutions, and the precise mechanisms by which it will open up to multiparty democracy. The agreements of Mozambique, Guatemala, and El Salvador serve as examples.[158] This conflict-oriented detail also permeates the equality and human rights provisions that typically form part of the power map and are closely tied to the arrangements for government. In cases of ethnic conflict, detail is often crucial to providing for equality within centralized state structures, in particular for minorities left in the wrong territory at the subdivisional level. In the case of ideological conflicts, human rights detail plays an important role in underwriting the process of democratization, for example by providing for specific rights to political organization, or by focusing on eliminating prevalent human rights abuses. This aspect is illustrated by the emphasis on nondiscrimination in the Bosnian DPA, and the detailed provisions aimed at stopping disappearances in the El Salvadoran and Guatemalan human rights agreements, together with the detailed provision for the reform of key legal institutions found in their later agreements.[159] The level of detail and contractual "feel" of peace-agreement constitutions, as has been pointed out, is somewhat at odds with their characterization as constitutions but reflects common conflict resolution goals.

The Limits of Precision

There are limits, however, to the compliance pull of precision in the peace agreement context that point to the importance of alternative modes of legalization. Precision may be insufficient to providing incentives to cooperation where the agreement does not encapsulate any real agreement between the parties. Thus, the difficulties and failures of implementation in, for example, Rwanda, Sierra Leone, and to a lesser extent Bosnia have been put down to the absence of genuine agreement at the heart of the accords.[160] Those peace agreements became to a greater or lesser extent vehicles for pursuing largely unchanged military agendas. The Arusha Accords of Rwanda even stand charged with facilitating genocide by changing the domestic military and political power balance while failing to grapple with the parties' lack of commitment to making the accords work.[161]

Precision may also not be the key tool for managing the longer-term difficulties of implementation, which cannot be anticipated. The assumptions that underlie the fashioning of reciprocal commitments may become undone over time, particularly as the peace process

---

[157] Burundi Peace Agreement, *supra* note 29; Belfast Agreement, *supra* note 29; INTERIM CONST., *supra* note 29; DPA, *supra* note 41; Bougainville Peace Agreement, *supra* note 53.

[158] General Peace Agreement for Mozambique, *supra* note 47; Guatemala Peace Agreement, *supra* note 31; El Salvador Agreement, *supra* note 31.

[159] DPA, *supra* note 41, Annex 4, Art. 2; El Salvador Agreement on Human Rights, *supra* note 64, Art. 1; Comprehensive Agreement on Human Rights, Mar. 29, 1994, Guat.-URNG-UN, Art. 3.2, *available at* <http://www.usip.org/library/pa.html>.

[160] Yusuf Bangura, *Strategic Policy Failure and Governance in Sierra Leone,* 38 J. MOD. AFR. STUD. 551, 564 (2000); Clapham, *supra* note 5; INTERNATIONAL CRISIS GROUP, IS DAYTON FAILING? BOSNIA FOUR YEARS AFTER THE PEACE AGREEMENT (Europe Report No. 80, 1999), *available at* <http://www.icg.org>.

[161] Clapham, *supra* note 5.

enters the arena of domestic implementation.[162] Paradoxically, tightly reciprocal peace agreement commitments can often shake loose the seeds of the agreement's own demise. For example, in Northern Ireland, the operation of the devolved Assembly (a key Unionist goal) was conditioned on the operation of cross-border bodies (a key Nationalist demand), which Unionists had insisted would be subject to the Assembly.[163] However, under pressure from their antiagreement factions, the concerns of Unionists over lack of IRA decommissioning trumped their desire to self-govern. At this point, their reciprocal self-interest disappeared and the mechanism based on it in fact worked against implementation of the agreement by requiring all of the political institutions to be dismantled once one collapsed. More subtly, in South Africa the transitional consociational mechanisms and safeguards of constitutionalism that were aimed at minority protection were effectively negated by the unanticipated scale of the electoral victories of the ANC, which soon gave it the percentages required to change the Constitution unilaterally.[164] In short, while precision constitutes an important tool for short-term goals of peace agreements, it is less effective in promoting the long-term goal of constitutionalism as a mechanism of ongoing conflict transformation.[165]

Constitutional Values as Alternative Legalization

The longer-term goals of peace agreements must be achieved through the deeper constitutionalization of the commitments they embody. This requires the building of trust between the parties to the conflict, and securing their baseline commitment to the working of the new institutions, including the constitution itself. Attempts to set the foundation for a shared constitutional outlook are often contained in a peace agreement's vaguer language relating to the nature of the agreement and the nature of the state. Typically, this language is imprecise: either aspirational in outlook or deliberately employing "constructive ambiguity" to enable agreement. The agreed history of the opening chapter of the Burundi Peace Agreement, the self-determination provisions addressed to the Afrikaner Brotherhood in South Africa, the self-determination and binationalist language of the Belfast Agreement, and Guatemala's commitments on indigenous peoples, all address substantive causes of the conflict and attempt to signal the different nature of the postagreement state.[166] The lack of precision does not indicate a lack of legalization or a failure of drafting; rather, the very vagueness of what are symbolic and aspirational provisions evidences the substantive long-term goal of finding shared notions of identity and statehood.[167]

The language of constitutional values also serves other purposes, such as legitimacy and good process. Detailed precision with regard to longer-term constitutional development not merely

[162] *See* Ben D. Mor, *Peace Initiatives and Public Opinion: The Domestic Context of Conflict Resolution*, 34 J. PEACE RES. 197 (1997).

[163] *See In re* Application by de Brun and McGuinness for Judicial Review, [2001] NIQB 3.

[164] *Cf.* ADRIAN GUELKE, SOUTH AFRICA IN TRANSITION: A MISUNDERSTOOD MIRACLE (1999) (arguing that South Africa's Interim Constitution has been misunderstood as a constitutional compromise between majority and minority communities, with the strongest restraints on majority power expressly transitional). Note, however, that it can be argued that on occasion the ANC felt politically constrained to work within the existing constitution rather than to amend it unilaterally.

[165] *Cf.* Schneckener, *supra* note 13 (arguing that the key to long-term success of peace agreements lies in institutional design aimed at enabling elite leadership and cooperation).

[166] Burundi Peace Agreement, *supra* note 29, Protocol I, ch. I; South Africa Amendment Act, *supra* note 121, §13, Art. XXXIV; Belfast Agreement, *supra* note 29; Agreement on the Identity and Rights of Indigenous Peoples, pmbl., *supra* note 50.

[167] *Cf.* Abbott & Snidal, *supra* note 150.

encounters a problem of anticipation, but also is arguably undesirable.[168] A narrow range of actors tends to be involved in peace negotiations; typically, they do not have the expertise, legitimacy, or sometimes even the will necessary to design long-term constitutions and consequent institutional reform in all their value-driven complexity. Processes of ongoing institutional development and reform both serve as a risk management device with similarities to third-party delegation in other contexts and, importantly, lend legitimacy to the constitution-making project. By setting forth principles and processes rather than final provisions, peace negotiations can be concluded more quickly, while also enabling broader civic involvement in the processes of reform—involvement that is important to the local ownership and effectiveness of the new institutions. This is an alternative way of legalizing obligations.

Process Dilemmas: Legalization in Transition

Tensions, however, color the relationship between the short-term and long-term conflict resolution goals of peace agreements. While treatylike internationalized commitments are useful and even important to implementing an agreement in the short term, they may operate in subtle and not-so-subtle ways to negate and frustrate the longer-term goals of domestic constitutionalization. Thus, mediators often face a set of dilemmas as to how to achieve both short- and long-term goals, while providing for functioning institutions during the transitional period.[169] These dilemmas include whether to have elections before or after constitutional reform projects; when and how to introduce mechanisms to account for past abuses; when to use international "off-the-peg" legal tools as transitional devices; and whether these measures might undermine localized processes of constitutional development. The dilemmas, often framed as clashes of "principle" and "pragmatism," in fact reflect the tension between different short-term and long-term conflict resolution imperatives, and the fact that different international and domestic actors have different degrees of legitimacy at different stages of the implementation process.[170]

The tensions point to a central, distinctive compliance challenge for the legalization of peace agreements. The obligations must be framed so that they can depend on different rationales and mechanisms for enforcement at different stages of the peace process. In their ideal form, peace agreements attempt to incorporate internationalized treatylike commitments with a high degree of third-party enforcement, while enabling a transition to domestic constitutional commitments, implemented through normalized politics and normalized public law processes. The difficulty for drafters is to craft obligations that will pin down commitments that are clear enough to command compliance yet leave some room for the coherent holistic development also crucial to compliance.

In summary, precision is a valuable element of peace agreement legalization in the short term, particularly as regards the military commitments and transitional mechanisms of government. It suffers from limitations, however, in providing for the longer-term constitutionalization of commitments as worked out through the entrenched reform of political and legal institutions, where precise detail on wholesale constitutional reform can be counterproductive

---

[168] *See* SC Res. 1325, ¶ 15 (Oct. 31, 2000); Women, Peace and Security, *supra* note 3, ¶ 63; Principles to Combat Impunity, *supra* note 3, princ. 6 (recommending broad consultation on the composition of truth commissions), princ. 32 (reparations procedures), princ. 35 (institutional reforms aimed at preventing recurrence of violations); *see also* The Rule of Law and Transitional Justice in Conflict and Post-conflict Societies, *supra* note 3, ¶ 64(h).

[169] *See* HAMPSON, *supra* note 9; Christine Bell, *Peace Agreements and Human Rights: Implications for the UN, in* THE UN, HUMAN RIGHTS AND POST-CONFLICT SITUATIONS 241, 246–48 (Nigel D. White & Dirk Klaasen eds., 2005).

[170] *See* sources cited *supra* note 169.

400   THE AMERICAN JOURNAL OF INTERNATIONAL LAW   [Vol. 100:373

to compliance and is better served by the language of principle, values, and symbolism. The challenge is to find a way to use both forms of legalized obligation so as to bolster compliance, in a context where different forms of legalization bolster or undermine at different stages of the process.

V. DELEGATION TO THIRD PARTIES

The distinctive characteristics of peace agreements are further illustrated by the ways they delegate authority to designated third parties to interpret and implement their provisions. This element constitutes the third dimension of legalization. Abbott and colleagues plot a spectrum of legalization as regards third-party delegation, which ranges from a high end to a low end:[171] from binding decisions of international or domestic courts with general jurisdiction and direct private access; through courts with limited jurisdiction and access; to arbitration, mediation, or conciliation. At the top end of the spectrum, third-party delegation is legally binding; at the bottom end, it amounts to little more than a forum for purely political bargaining.

The range of third-party delegation in peace agreements is very broad and cannot be examined fully here. The general dynamics can be illustrated, however, by examining two persistent features, the use of third-party guarantors, and what I have termed "hybrid legal pluralism." These again, it is argued, illustrate a distinctive *lex pacificatoria*, both in types of mechanism and in related notions of how third parties can best influence the implementation of peace agreements.

Third-Party Guarantors

The majority of peace agreements employ third-party states and international organizations as signatories to agreements, either through direct signature or signature in the capacity of "witnesses," "guarantors," or "observers."[172] What this practice means, or whether the terms in which the organization signs have any technical legal implication, is unclear. (Is a "witness" different from a "guarantor," "observer," "moral guarantor," or an "outside" state as an apparently coequal signatory without specific commitments?) While these states and organizations often continue to be involved in the peace process, little discussion has been devoted to whether or how their involvement is shaped by their signature and the particular label by which they are described as a third party to the agreement.[173]

It is suggested here that their role as signatories works in various ways. Most significantly perhaps, the signature of third-party guarantors can reinforce their role as "norm promoters" by influencing the progress of the peace agreement. Mark Peceny and William Stanley have

---

[171] Abbott et al., *supra* note 17, at 404.

[172] Examples are numerous. *See, e.g.,* DPA, *supra* note 41 (United States, United Kingdom, France, Germany, Russia, and the European Union as witnesses); Lomé Agreement, *supra* note 29, Art. 34 (Togo, the United Nations, the Organization of African Unity (OAU), the Economic Community of West African States (ECOWAS), and the Commonwealth of Nations as moral guarantors); Tashkent Declaration, *supra* note 24 (the United Nations as observer).

[173] See preliminary discussion of contemporary treaty guarantees in Wippman, *supra* note 15, *passim*; BRAD R. ROTH, GOVERNMENTAL ILLEGITIMACY IN INTERNATIONAL LAW 193–94 (2000). *Cf.* Georg Ress, *Guarantee, in* 2 ENCYCLOPEDIA OF PUBLIC INTERNATIONAL LAW 626 (Rudolf Bernhardt ed., 1995); Georg Ress, *Guarantee Treaties, in id.* at 634 (discussing guarantees and treaties of guarantee and their implications for state obligations). *But see Kallon, supra* note 81, ¶41 (where Special Court interpreted third-party signatures as evidence that those parties were "moral guarantors" that "assumed no legal obligation").

argued that third-party effectiveness lies more in its norm promotion capacity than in delivering security guarantees.[174] Using Central America as an example, they argue that the peace processes followed a three-stage trajectory illustrating this role: (1) local actors in the conflicts adopted liberal practices to legitimate themselves internationally; (2) internationally mediated negotiations demonstrated to the combatants that the adversaries had changed their preferences and could be trusted to move from violence to the political rules set out in the peace agreements; and (3) international actors and the United Nations engaged in concrete and direct efforts to support liberal social reconstruction and widen participation in it.[175]

This link between third-party guarantees and norm promotion can be seen in the increasingly self-conscious approaches of the United Nations as a "normative negotiator." Involvement of the United Nations as observer, mediator, and/or signatory now appears to bring with it normative constraints as to the content of peace agreements, which helps to explain the increasing attempts to provide guidelines and standards for such agreements. In 1999 the UN secretary-general established guidelines for his representatives that, although not public, apparently dealt with the normative human rights constraints on peace agreements, in particular with reference to amnesty.[176] Shortly thereafter, in one clear example of third-party enforcement, the UN special envoy in Sierra Leone added a "disclaimer" to his signature of the Lomé Agreement with respect to the amnesty provision's inconsistency with international law.[177] This action was to play a part in the establishment of the Sierra Leone Special Court and the eventual demise of the amnesty.[178] The UN secretary-general's recent report on the rule of law affirms the constraints on UN involvement in peace agreements.[179]

The value of norm promotion also helps to explain the compliance value of having even nongovernmental actors sign peace agreements, such as the San Egidio community as mediator in Mozambique, and the Catholic Church as "moral and spiritual guide" in the Colombian peace accords.[180] Arguably, their value as signatories derives not just from their ongoing mediation function, but from the norm-promoting role they have played.[181]

Third-party signatories help to insert some of the advantages of treaty status into instruments whose status as international agreements is questionable. The presence of third-party signatories means that the treaty partners have created obligations to each other and to the third parties as well.[182] This commitment raises the compliance stakes for both state and nonstate signatories, particularly when third parties view themselves as having an active norm promotion function. As regards the state, it may counterbalance the political nature

[174] Mark Peceny & William Stanley, *Liberal Social Reconstruction and the Resolution of Civil Wars in Central America*, 55 INT'L ORG. 149, 151 (2001). *But see* Roland Paris, *The Perils of Liberal International Peacebuilding*, 22 INT'L SECURITY 54 (1997) (criticizing the same strategy for contributing to instability in war-torn societies).

[175] Peceny & Stanley, *supra* note 174; *see also* Ellen L. Lutz & Kathryn Sikkink, *International Human Rights Law and Practice in Latin America*, 54 INT'L ORG. 633 (2000).

[176] UN Press Release SG/SM/7257, *supra* note 3.

[177] *See* Seventh Report of the Secretary-General on the United Nations Observer Mission in Sierra Leone, UN Doc. S/1999/836, ¶54.

[178] *See Kallon*, *supra* note 81, ¶89.

[179] The Rule of Law and Transitional Justice in Conflict and Post-conflict Societies, *supra* note 3, ¶13.

[180] General Peace Agreement for Mozambique, *supra* note 47; Accord, Mar. 9, 1990, Colom.–political parties–M-19–Catholic Church (in the capacity of a moral and spiritual guide for the process), *available at* <http://www.c-r.org/accord/col/accord14/keytext.shtml>.

[181] *See* Dinis S. Sengulane & Jaime Pedro Goncalves, *A Calling for Peace: Christian Leaders and the Quest for Reconciliation in Mozambique, in* THE MOZAMBICAN PEACE PROCESS IN PERSPECTIVE, ACCORD, 1998 (Jeremy Armon, Dylan Hendrikson, & Alex Vines eds.), *available at* <http://www.c-r.org/accord/moz/accord3/index.shtml>.

[182] Kooijmans, *supra* note 14.

402   THE AMERICAN JOURNAL OF INTERNATIONAL LAW   [Vol. 100:373

of the commitments made to nonstate actors. As regards nonstate actors, the third party's opinions and pressures with regard to breach will not be as easy to dismiss as those of the "other side." International legitimacy may be a substantive goal of nonstate actors, and articulating a need to keep third parties on board may also increase their ability to resist their own outbidders locally.[183] As has been noted, the use of outside state signatures may also address the commitments of these states themselves to peace, less as third parties and more as regards their own involvement in the international or transnational dimensions of the "intrastate" conflict.

The inclusion of third-party guarantors as signatories of peace agreements may appear cosmetic and low on the spectrum of legalization, especially when they are not even states. However, this assessment may underestimate the ways that such guarantors can tie the status of the peace agreement to the normative direction of the commitments it contains. This norm promotion role, of course, raises important questions as to how third-party neutrality, consistency, and legal legitimacy affect third-party norm promotion capacities. It seems likely that this norm promotion function is reduced where third-party interventions are not clearly rooted in international norms, or even violate them.[184]

Hybrid Legal Pluralism

The third-party tapestry of peace agreements typically involves a wide variety of international, domestic, and hybrid mechanisms, many of which straddle the law-politics boundary and have overlapping functions and sometimes even mandates. This form of third-party delegation can be characterized as "hybrid legal pluralism" and is rooted in the hybrid nature of peace agreements, already alluded to.[185] It can be mapped loosely on the spectrum of third-party delegation running from high legalization to low legalization. While binding court decisions are often placed at the top end of the legalization spectrum, in the peace agreement context detailed peacekeeping mandates aimed at oversight and verification of security guarantees can provide equally strong mechanisms by involving third parties in the day-to-day fabric of implementation. Elaborate mandates for peacekeeping and monitoring, underwritten by Security Council resolutions, are often crucial to establishing cease-fires and consequent processes of demobilization, demilitarization, and reintegration. The relevant provisions of the DPA and the Cambodian Paris Accords all form good examples.[186]

Binding arbitration is often presented as next in the legalization spectrum. In the peace agreement context a range of different mechanisms play a similar type of role to binding arbitration. Processes of review associated with Security Council resolutions that have underwritten peace agreements fit this mold. Interestingly, Security Council resolutions can also be used to supplement matters that were not dealt with in the agreement at all, for example reform of the judiciary.[187]

---

[183] *See* Gleditsch & Beardsley, *supra* note 10 (showing how the different parties were affected by transnational input to the peace processes in Central America).

[184] *See* Outi Korhonen, *International Governance in Post-conflict Situations*, 14 LEIDEN J. INT'L L. 495 (2001); Ralph Wilde, *From Danzig to East Timor and Beyond: The Role of International Territorial Administration*, 95 AJIL 583 (2001) [hereinafter Wilde, *Danzig to East Timor*]; Ralph Wilde, *Representing International Territorial Administration: A Critique of Some Approaches*, 15 EUR. J. INT'L L. 71 (2004) [hereinafter Wilde, *Representing ITA*].

[185] *Cf.* Campbell, Harvey, & Ní Aoláin, *supra* note 14, *passim* (arguing that the Belfast Agreement should be seen as a hybrid domestic and international law instrument); Laura A. Dickinson, *The Promise of Hybrid Courts*, 97 AJIL 295 (2003) (discussion of hybrid courts and tribunals).

[186] DPA, *supra* note 41, Annex 1A (Military Aspects of the Peace Settlement); Cambodia Political Settlement, *supra* note 114, Annex 2 (Withdrawal, Ceasefire, and Related Measures).

[187] *See* William G. O'Neill, Reform of Law Enforcement Agencies and the Judiciary ¶¶ 19–24 (Int'l Council on Hum. Rts. Pol'y working paper, 2005), *at* <http://www.ichrp.org>.

International involvement in discrete peace agreement tasks or in the reform of domestic legal processes can play a similar role. International participation is often used to develop and implement specific provisions of peace agreements, with a rule-making power delegated to the international actor in question. As regards provisions on refugees and displaced persons, for example, the UN High Commissioner for Refugees is often charged with assisting in implementation, and on occasion has been vested with the power to produce its own rules or even further agreements.[188] Similarly, several agreements have given the International Committee of the Red Cross a role and rule-making power in the release of prisoners.[189] A range of international and hybrid bodies have been put in charge of supervising or monitoring elections.[190] The use of international or hybrid criminal tribunals or truth commissions with respect to dealing with the past might also fall in the category of entrusting international actors with discrete tasks. These forums involve a form of nonconsensual jurisdiction relating to one dimension of the agreement; they enjoy rule-making authority and many apply a form of international law.[191] In this context international human rights bodies can play similar specific enforcement roles through treaty monitoring functions, although these roles are ongoing. As governments ratify treaties in consequence of peace agreements, and become subject to their reporting mechanisms, they often adduce the agreement as evidence of progress on human rights issues. Human rights bodies have shown innovative responses, which operate to enforce large sections of the agreement, and sometimes the agreement in its entirety.[192] In all these areas international involvement not only reinforces compliance, but enables both detail and controversy to be

---

[188] See, e.g., DPA, supra note 41, Annex 7, Art. 1; Burundi Peace Agreement, supra note 29, Protocol IV, ch. 3, Art. 17; Quadripartite Agreement on Voluntary Return of Refugees and Displaced Persons, Georgia-Abkhazia-Russ.-UNHCR, Apr. 4, 1994, available at ACCORD, supra note 53; Comprehensive Peace Agreement, Aug. 18, 2003, Liber.–Liberians United for Reconciliation and Democracy (LURD)–Movement for Democracy in Liberia (MODEL)– political parties, Art. 12 [hereinafter Liberia Peace Agreement]; Cotonou Agreement, July 25, 1993, Liber. interim gov't–National Patriotic Front of Liber.–United Liberation Movement of Liber. for Democracy–ECOWAS–UN, pt. III, §F, Art. 18, UN Doc. S/26272 (1993); Economic Community of West African States Six-Month Peace Plan for Sierra Leone (23 October 1997–22 April 1998), Oct. 23, 1997, ECOWAS–Armed Forces Revolutionary Council regime of Sierra Leone–UN–OAU, Art. 4. The latter three agreements are available online at <http://www.usip.org/library/pa.html>.

[189] See, e.g., Lusaka Protocol, supra note 47, Annex 3.II.10; DPA, supra note 41, Annex 1, Art. 9; Final Act of the Paris Conference on Cambodia, Oct. 23, 1991, Art.13, 31 ILM 174 (1992); Cambodia Political Settlement, supra note 114, pt. XI; Democratic Republic of the Congo: Ceasefire Agreement, supra note 47, Art. 3(9); General Peace Agreement for Mozambique, supra note 47, Protocol VI(3); Agreement on Implementing the Cease-fire and on Modalities of Disarmament (Supplement to the General Agreement signed in Addis Ababa on 8 January 1993), Jan. 15, 1993, Somali movements and parties, Art. 4, available at <http://www.usip.org/library/pa.html>.

[190] See, e.g., DPA, supra note 41, Annex 3 (provides for Organization for Security and Co-operation in Europe (OSCE) to oversee elections); Basic Agreement on the Region of Eastern Slavonia, Baranja and Western Sirmium (Erdut Agreement), Nov. 12, 1995, Croat.–Local Serb Community, UN Doc. A/50/757–S/1995/951, annex, Art. 12, 35 ILM 184 (1996) (OSCE and United Nations, other international organizations, and interested states requested to oversee elections); Agreement between Guinea Bissau and the Self-Proclaimed Military Junta, Nov. 1, 1998, Art. 5, available at <http://www.usip.org/library/pa.html> (ECOWAS, Community of Portuguese-speaking countries, and the international community to observe elections); Liberia Peace Agreement, supra note 188, Art. IX (United Nations, OAU, ECOWAS, and nations elsewhere to be requested to monitor elections); General Peace Agreement for Mozambique, supra note 47, Protocol III (United Nations, OAU, and other agreed organizations to monitor elections).

[191] See, e.g., Burundi Peace Agreement, supra note 29, Protocol I, Art. 6 (delegating decision on establishing international criminal tribunal to the UN Security Council). But cf. SC Res. 1315 (Aug. 14, 2000) (establishing the Special Court for Sierra Leone, despite provision for it not being included in the terms of the Lomé Agreement); SC Res. 827 (May 25, 1993) (establishing the International Criminal Tribunal for the Former Yugoslavia, even though it was not explicitly provided for in the DPA).

[192] See International Labour Organization, Report of the Committee Set up to Examine the Representation Alleging Non-observance by Mexico of the Indigenous and Tribal Peoples Convention, 1989 (No. 169), Made Under Article 24 of the ILO Constitution by the Authentic Workers' Front (FAT) (2004), available at <http://

resolved outside the main negotiations.[193] International third-party involvement thus assists both substance and process.

Beyond this there is a broad spectrum of international participation in a variety of essentially domestic tasks, such as the organization of transitional government, constitutional and legal reform, participation in courts and tribunals, development of civil society, and general reconciliation.[194] Here, the involvement of international third parties reflects difficulties with domestic processes. Domestic legislation, for example, would seem to lie at the "high" end of the spectrum of delegation, as an internalization of international commitments that enables legal adjudication. However, in the peace agreement context, as with constitutional adjudication, it raises a particular set of compliance difficulties and can also undermine compliance.

Translating commitments into simple legislative form involves opposition groups with opposition agendas, who were not primary parties to the deal. In contrast to accepted processes of treaty ratification, the lack of formal legal status of peace agreements leaves the parameters of the incorporation debate more open. Opposition groups may force the government to backtrack on commitments so as to respond to its primary domestic constituency. Particularly in identity conflicts, a minority or indigenous group may find itself in a second, more diffuse set of negotiations where its own role is reduced to lobbying against the watering down of a finely crafted deal of which it was a coauthor. Indeed, the state's own democratic processes can be used by political outbidders on the state side to prevent implementation altogether, either in opposition, or indeed because they win the next elections on the strength of their antiagreement platform.[195] In the Middle East, the elections following the assassination of Prime Minister Yitzhak Rabin saw victory for the anti-Oslo Benjamin Netanyahu by a slim majority; as a result, the Israeli government reversed its approach to the peace process even though there had arguably been no sea change in the Israeli public's support for it.[196] In Sri Lanka in November 2003, favorable government soundings to a proposal by the Liberation Tigers of Tamil Eelam for an interim (autonomy) agreement led the antipeace-process president (from the opposition party) to fire three government ministers who had been involved in the negotiations, prorogue parliament, and declare a state of emergency.[197] Problems with passing new legislation to complete commitments in peace agreements have occurred in Macedonia and Bangladesh,[198] among other countries, where opposition political parties were able to use their positions in legislative and executive branches to undermine implementation of the agreement and the peace process itself.

---

www.ilo.org/ilolex/english/newcountryframeE.htm> (where ILO examined the complaint as regards the Convention through the framework of the San Andrés Larráinzar Agreements between the ELZN and the Mexican government, *supra* note 50, which were based on this Convention).

[193] *See* Burundi Peace Agreement, *supra* note 29, Protocol I, Art. 6.

[194] *See generally* Korhonen, *supra* note 184.

[195] *See* Mor, *supra* note 165; Stedman, *supra* note 13.

[196] *See* Ian S. Lustick, *Ending Protracted Conflicts: The Oslo Peace Process Between Political Partnership and Legality*, 30 CORNELL INT'L L.J. 741 (1997).

[197] *See* Motion for a Resolution Tabled for the Debate on Cases of Breaches of Human Rights, Democracy and the Rule of Law Pursuant to Rule 50 of the Rules of Procedure by Luigi Vinci on Sri Lanka, EUR. PARL. DOC. PE 338.629 (2003), *at* <http://www.europarl.eu.int/activities/archive/motion/search.do?language=EN>.

[198] *See* Nicholas Whyte, *Macedonia: Not out of the Woods Yet*, INTERNATIONAL CRISIS GROUP UPDATE BRIEFING (Feb. 25, 2005), *at* <http://www.crisisgroup.org>; Devasish Roy, The International Character of Treaties with Indigenous Peoples and Implementation Challenges for Intra-State Peace and Autonomy Agreements Between Indigenous Peoples and States: The Case of the Chittagong Hill Tracts, Bangladesh at 3, UN Doc. HR/Geneva/TSIP/Sem/2003/BP.8, *available at* <http://www.unhcr.ch/indigenous/treaties.htm>.

To address these difficulties, peace agreements tend to include substantive reform of legislative and constitutional processes and institutions that make international law a key reference point and give international actors a role in what are normally domestic institutions.[199] An example is the DPA's involvement of international actors in all of Bosnia's key domestic legal institutions and the role of the Office of the High Representative as "final authority in theater regarding interpretation" (a role that came to include the power to legislate in the event of political deadlock).[200] Other examples include the internationalized reform of policing and criminal justice in Northern Ireland, and the similar processes established in Central American peace agreements.[201]

Lower still on the spectrum of legalization, a range of arbitration, mediation, review, and "peace promotion" processes can be established, to operate almost completely at the political level. Examples include the British/Irish governmental review process of the Belfast Agreement,[202] the Joint Israeli-Palestinian Liaison Committee,[203] and in many agreements an assortment of peace promotion bodies[204] and provision for new agreements to be negotiated.[205]

The hybrid legal pluralism of peace agreements bears some similarity to other uses of international law alluded to by the term *lex pacificatoria*. Legal pluralism occurs in settings such as environmental law and contract compliance, where a range of quasi-legal mechanisms cut across international and domestic legal spheres in an attempt to give soft law commitments some impact on compliance.[206] As regards "hybridization," internationalized contracts have used general principles of international law either as the law governing the contract, or as a tool for *amiables compositeurs*, to prevent state parties from manipulating national law to their advantage.[207] International law can thus provide a basis for enforcement of the contract internationally and even in domestic courts, regardless of the fact that the contract itself may not constitute a binding international agreement.[208]

Nevertheless, the hybrid legal pluralism of peace agreements is arguably distinctive in several respects. While a mapping from more legalized to more political commitments (high to low) is loosely possible, it is difficult to distinguish between the implementation of the peace agreement and continuation of the peace process: postagreement does not equate to postconflict.

[199] *Cf.* Campbell, Harvey, & Ní Aoláin, *supra* note 14, at 326–28 (arguing that the Belfast Agreement must be read as a "hybrid" international/domestic agreement).

[200] DPA, *supra* note 41, Annex 10, Art. V.

[201] Belfast Agreement, *supra* note 29, Annexes A, B, respectively; El Salvador: Peace Agreement, *supra* note 152, ch. 2, Art. 3(B) (providing for international legal advisory services for police monitoring); Agreement on the Strengthening of Civilian Power and on the Role of the Armed Forces in a Democratic Society, Sept. 19, 1996, Guat.–URNG–UN, pt. IV, ¶31, 36 ILM 304 (urging international community to provide technical and financial assistance with police reform).

[202] Belfast Agreement, *supra* note 29, "Validation, Implementation and Review."

[203] Declaration of Principles on Interim Self-Government Arrangements, Sept. 13, 1993, Isr.-PLO, Art. X, 32 ILM 1525 (1993) [hereinafter Declaration of Principles].

[204] *See, e.g.,* Addis Ababa Agreement Concluded at the First Session of the Conference on National Reconciliation in Somalia, Mar. 27, 1993, Somali Movements and Parties, pt V, *available at* <http://www.usip.org/library/pa.html>.

[205] *See, e.g.,* Declaration of Principles, *supra* note 203, Art. VII.

[206] *Cf.* Harold Hongju Koh, *Why Do Nations Obey International Law?* 106 YALE L.J. 2599 (1997); Christopher McCrudden, *Human Rights Codes for Transnational Corporations: The Sullivan and MacBride Principles, in* COMMITMENT AND COMPLIANCE, *supra* note 70, at 418.

[207] Karyn S. Weinberg, *Equity in International Arbitration: How Fair is "Fair"? A Study of* Lex Mercatoria *and Amiable Composition,* 12 B.U. INT'L L.J. 227 (1994); *cf.* Derek W. Bowett, *Claims Between States and Private Entities: The Twilight Zone of International Law,* 35 CATH. U. L. REV. 929 (1986); A. A. Fatouros, *International Law and the Internationalized Contract,* 74 AJIL 134 (1980).

[208] Fatouros, *supra* note 207.

406 THE AMERICAN JOURNAL OF INTERNATIONAL LAW [Vol. 100:373

This problem, in turn, makes it difficult to distinguish between the delegation of implementation of the agreement and ongoing mediation of the agreement's development.[209] The boundary between political and legal mechanisms also tends to be particularly blurred in the transitional context. Legal institutions as both subjects and objects of reform tend to be more overtly politicized during transitions. Thus, the mixed international/domestic legal institutions of Bosnia with their multiethnic composition, and the new South African Constitutional Court's constitutional certification function (replicated in Burundi), could be viewed as examples of strong legalized delegation, or as new political negotiating forums for development and validation of constitutional law and values.[210] Conversely, political institutions established through the contractlike language of the peace agreement tend to have a legalized feel, as evidenced by some of the procedures for breaking deadlock in consociational mechanisms, which on occasion have recourse to courts.[211] Peace agreements are also difficult to plot in terms of different international and domestic forms of delegation because of the design of "hybrid" mechanisms involving both international and domestic actors in hybrid institutions. International and domestic actors work together across many aspects of the agreement to enforce and develop it: on joint military commissions,[212] joint peace-monitoring councils,[213] and consultative processes during international administrations.[214] As a result, this hybrid legal pluralism is distinctive in the depth and reach of both the "hybridization" and the pluralism of the mechanisms that simultaneously enforce and develop the agreement.

The hybrid legal pluralism of peace agreements is also distinctive with regard to its underlying rationale. Peace agreements resemble internationalized contracts in the use of international law as a basis for a legal order that is "neutral" as between the parties. However, in the peace agreement context, the use of international law is driven less by the need for an autonomous denationalized legal order, and more by the need to take processes of domestic legal reform outside their normal channels so as to address the illegitimacy of the preagreement legal and political order.[215] The use of international law reflects the fact that in internal conflicts the legitimacy and role of law itself is typically implicated, as the very notion of the rule of law has been degraded and devalued and requires rehabilitation.[216] Domestic law processes thus are both a potential enforcement tool (the subject of change) and the object of change, complicating any notion of their role in producing compliance. In rare cases, such as that of South Africa, transformation of the domestic order can be achieved through a domestically implemented fundamental reconstruction. In most cases, it cannot. At the other extreme, internationalization can bring domestic functions to the paradoxical situation where they are undertaken in their entirety by international actors. The most comprehensive internationalization

---

[209] *Cf.* RATNER, *supra* note 15, at 43–50 (noting that the most recent phase of UN peacekeeping related to negotiated agreements involves both "preserving" and "promoting" the settlement, *id.* at 44).

[210] DPA, *supra* note 41, Annex 4, Art. 6 (Constitutional Court), Annex 6, Art. 7 (Human Rights Chamber); INTERIM CONST., *supra* note 29, ch. 5, Art. 71; *see also In re* Certification of Constitution, *supra* note 104, 1996 (4) SA 774 (CC), 1996 (10) BCLR 1253 (CC); Burundi Peace Agreement, *supra* note 29, Protocol II, ch. 2, Art. 15(5) (similar provision).

[211] *See, e.g.,* DPA, *supra* note 41, Annex 4, Art. IV(3)(f).

[212] *See, e.g., id.,* Annex 1A, Art. 8; Cambodia Political Settlement, *supra* note 114, Annex 2, Art. 2 (providing for Mixed Military Working Group to be established to resolve problems arising in the observance of the cease-fire).

[213] *See, e.g.,* Burundi Peace Agreement, *supra* note 29, Protocol III, ch. 3, Art. 27; Bougainville Peace Agreement, *supra* note 53, pt. E.

[214] *See* notes 144–49 *supra* and corresponding text.

[215] But note that the distinction can also be viewed as one of degree, as peace agreements have in part developed common practices through transnational contacts, while in the commercial law setting common legal practices respond to a notion of the "illegitimacy" of national laws, albeit in a very different context.

[216] Christine Bell, Colm Campbell, & Fionnuala Ní Aoláin, *Justice Discourses in Transition,* 13 SOC. LEGAL STUD. 305, 309 (2004).

of these processes is found in the "contrived agreement" situation, and the use of an international territorial administration (ITA).[217] ITAs indicate the capacity for international "third parties" to subsume and carry out the functions of government in their totality. They are instituted in the name of conflict resolution and evidence the close connection between "implementation" and "development" of a framework for peace. As Ralph Wilde notes, international territorial administration is justified legally, morally, and politically in terms of the deficits in sovereignty and governance of the state in question, although it again gives rise to questions about the limited legitimacy of international actors in undertaking domestic governance.[218]

In summary, the examination of third-party delegation has begun to illustrate both the way that use of third-party guarantors can bring about norm promotion and the use of what has been termed "hybrid legal pluralism." The distinctiveness of hybrid legal pluralism in this context is driven by the need to respond to the politicization and degradation of domestic law in conflicts. Thus, international "third party" enforcement often necessarily includes the domestic actors whose agreement is intended to be forged in hybrid institutions. Conversely, domestic legal forms tend to be internationalized through a heightened role for international law, and by involving international actors in implementing the agreement.

VI. THE NATURE OF PEACE AGREEMENTS: A NEW *LEX PACIFICATORIA?*

Toward a Lex Pacificatoria

Peace agreements have produced practices of legalization marked by some consistency across widely varying peace processes. This legalization can be argued to constitute an emerging *lex pacificatoria* (law of the peacemakers) that draws on the idea of *lex mercatoria* (international law deriving from the practices of merchants) as a source of international commercial law.[219] This embryonic *lex pacificatoria* can now be identified as including

- a distinctive self-determination role: peace agreements address both external and internal challenges to a state's legitimacy through new permutations of government and human rights protections;

- a distinctive mix of state and nonstate signatories: peace agreements are "hybrid" agreements straddling international and domestic legal categories;

- distinctive types of obligation: peace agreements consist of both treatylike/contractual and value-driven/constitutional provisions; and

- distinctive types of third-party delegation: peace agreements rely on hybrid legal pluralism, involving multiple intertwined and overlapping legal and political mechanisms, for their implementation.

These distinctive elements reflect the conflict resolution role of peace agreements as simultaneously foundational and process-oriented documents. If we set aside legal categories and consider peace agreements on their own terms, they may be best thought of as transitional internationalized constitutions. They provide a power map and framework for governance, but

---

[217] *See generally* Wilde, *Danzig to East Timor, supra* note 184; Wilde, *Representing ITA, supra* note 184.

[218] *See* sources cited *supra* note 184.

[219] *See, e.g.,* Andreas F. Lowenfeld, Lex Mercatoria: *An Arbitrator's View, in* LEX MERCATORIA AND ARBITRATION 71, 84–85 (Thomas E. Carbonneau ed., rev. ed. 1998) (explaining that the concept of *lex mercatoria* "is not that of a self-contained system covering all aspects of international commercial law to the exclusion of national law, but rather . . . a source of law made up of custom, practice, convention, precedent—and many national laws"); *see also* A. CLAIRE CUTLER, PRIVATE POWER AND GLOBAL AUTHORITY: TRANSNATIONAL MERCHANT LAW IN THE GLOBAL POLITICAL ECONOMY 16 (2003).

408			THE AMERICAN JOURNAL OF INTERNATIONAL LAW			[Vol. 100:373

FIGURE 1. PEACE AGREEMENT GOALS OVER TIME

Internationalized implementation	Domestic implementation
Short-term/negative peace	Long-term/positive peace
Contractual/quasi-private law	Constitutional/public law
Politicized legal institutions	Normalized legal institutions
Legalized political mechanisms	Normalized political mechanisms

$\longrightarrow$

Ideal trajectory

it is often only partial and transitional, requiring further development. Contractual, treatylike commitments, backed up by delegation to mechanisms that are typically internationalized, are aimed at ensuring short-term implementation. However, domestic legal and political processes are contemplated to form the long-term vehicle for conflict transformation, and a transition to these must take place.

Figure 1, above, illustrates an idealized trajectory of peace agreement goals over time. This trajectory illustrates why peace agreements contain their distinctive mix of hybrid ingredients. It also points to peace agreement legalization as an attempt to bridge the uneasy gap between the short-term and long-term peace process goals and mechanisms. The hybrid nature of peace agreements goes beyond form, signatories, and even substance, in reaching to a need to rely on different rationales for why *pacta sunt servanda* at different stages in the process. In their initial stages peace agreements are meant to command implementation as contractual-like treaties; but it is their ability (or not) to serve as constitutions that enables them to continue as conflict resolution frameworks. Thus, Rwanda's Arusha Accords, which failed so dramatically as an internationalized agreement, were still used after the genocide to provide and legitimate the basic framework of governance: as a treaty they would have been void, but as a constitution they could live on—albeit problematically.[220]

The attempt to produce legal-type documents, and indeed the very existence of the peace agreement phenomenon, testifies to the importance of legalized commitments to peace agreement parties: they constitute a key way of doing business. Any theory of how peace agreement legalization promotes compliance would seem best located in accounts of transnational legal processes as "normative, dynamic, and constitutive."[221] Such accounts argue that the compliance pull of legalized agreements lies in their capacity to promote transactions between parties that over time interpret and internalize norms so as to "reconstitute the interests and even the identities of the participants in the process."[222] This description rings true in the peace agreement context and appears to go far in explaining how the interrelated dynamics of form, obligation, and third parties, described above, aim at inducing compliance.[223]

Yet the distinctive attributes of their legalization all reflect the fact that if peace agreements are to construct states as peaceful, democratic, and legitimate, they must reconstruct a division between political and legal order and to some extent between international, domestic, and even

[220] U.S. Dep't of State, Background Note: Rwanda (Mar. 2006), *at* <http://www.state.gov/r/pa/ei/bgn/2861.htm#gov>.

[221] Koh, *supra* note 206, at 2646.

[222] *Id.* (Koh identifies this process as having three main dynamics: interaction (between transnational actors and parties); interpretation (of the application of legal norms); and internalization (of legal norms). He argues that this theory synthesizes, rather than replaces, other theories of compliance.)

[223] *Cf. id.* at 2651–54 (using Oslo Accords as an example, Koh argues that transnational legal processes tied the antipeace-process Netanyahu into the Oslo framework to the point where he even signed and complied with a further agreement).

public and private spheres. This requirement gives rise to two difficulties for any theory of compliance. First, peace agreements focus on processes as much as outcomes, so that what constitutes compliance with them is under negotiation even as they are being implemented. This suggests a need to have some basis for distinguishing between the compliance pull of transnational legal processes on the parties and simple renegotiation.[224] Second, the notion of internalizing norms is complicated by the position of domestic law in the peace agreement setting, where it is both object and subject of negotiation. Paradoxically, these difficulties characteristically result in the internationalization of domestic legal processes. International involvement itself, however, faces increasing normative and legitimacy challenges as time passes, creating a transitional dilemma for its norm promotion capacity.

While full elaboration of how any theory of compliance can account for these complications is beyond the scope of this article, it is suggested that understanding the common dynamics of peace agreement legalization—the *lex pacificatoria*—is a key starting point. Only through identifying the essential elements of peace agreement practice and understanding the extent to which it is both a unified and a legal practice can further lines of inquiry be established.

The Case for the Lex Pacificatoria

To be characterized as *lex pacificatoria*, peace agreement legalization must make the case that it is law (*lex*), and that it is distinct to peacemakers (*pacificatoria*). As regards *lex*, this article has argued that peace agreement practice evidences a strong degree of coherence stemming from the importance of legalization to achieving agreement between parties in the first place. It is further suggested that just as the term *lex mercatoria* seeks to provide a label conducive to understanding the ways that commercial practices assert their own legalization across international and domestic spheres,[225] so the term *lex pacificatoria* usefully captures similar dynamics with regard to the legalization of peace agreement commitments. Ultimately, whether the case for the *lex* has been made depends on one's factual assessment of peace agreement practice and one's view of what constitutes law (whether—and which—essentialist functionalist definitions or nonessentialist conventionalist definitions are preferred).[226]

Whether the embryonic *lex pacificatoria* is differentiated enough to constitute a "new" form of law deserves further consideration. International law could move to accommodate peace agreements signed with nonstate actors as international agreements, just as it has accommodated agreements with international organizations.[227] Indeed, this article has demonstrated how peace agreement practice may be forcing this accommodation. However, it must also be acknowledged that to move to a clear understanding of all such peace agreements as binding international agreements would change the face of international law, even as arguments persist that it is indeed moving away from the notion of states as the primary actors.[228] Such acknowledgment would also raise the problem of what lines are to be drawn with reference to international law. While many of the agreements reviewed here have an arguable claim to be considered as international agreements because the nonstate actors enjoy some type of legal

[224] Koh's account of the role of transnational legal process in the Oslo Accords itself illustrates this difficulty, *id.* at 2653, as it can be argued that the agreements signed by Netanyahu in fact operated to dismantle key Oslo understandings rather than to implement them.

[225] CUTLER, *supra* note 219; Lowenfeld, *supra* note 219.

[226] See Brian Z. Tamanaha, *A Non-essentialist Version of Legal Pluralism*, 27 J. L. & SOC. 296 (2000) (review of nature of pluralist approaches to what constitutes "law").

[227] KLABBERS, *supra* note 63; Catherine Brölmann, *A Flat Earth? International Organisations in the System of International Law*, 70 NORDIC J. INT'L L. 319 (2001); *cf.* Malanczuk, *Multinational Enterprises, supra* note 61 (discussing whether internationalized contracts evidence a revision of international law).

[228] See Thomas M. Franck, *The Emerging Right to Democratic Governance*, 86 AJIL 46 (1992).

410   THE AMERICAN JOURNAL OF INTERNATIONAL LAW   [Vol. 100:373

subjectivity, other similar agreements are signed by actors such as domestic politicians, members of civil society, and armed groups with little claim at all to such status.[229] Moreover, domestic legal forms cannot easily accommodate peace agreements without major revision, as the discussion of peace-agreement constitutions illustrated. These categorization difficulties point to the usefulness of considering peace agreement practice on its own terms, as a distinctive use of law that cuts across international and domestic, public and private spheres. While the *lex* operates in an interstitial place similar to that of other legal documents such as internationalized contracts, it does so for quite different reasons and to quite different ends—it is the law of the peacemaker rather than the merchant.

The Lex Pacificatoria *and Compliance Inquiries*

This evaluation of the case for the *lex pacificatoria* indicates the ways that it constitutes a tool for further developing an understanding of the relationship of law to compliance in the peace agreement context. In fact, the main value of the term may be instrumental. Labeling peace agreement legalization as constituting a distinct legal practice highlights its coherence and can inform borrowings across peace processes in the search for implementation. It enables dialogue with empirical researchers, in particular with reference to their own often contradictory and unsatisfactory attempts to measure the success or failure of peace agreements.[230] While focused on "civil war" or "internal conflict," the studies use different definitions and thus compare different sets of data. Indeed, debate continues on the extent to which "civil war" can usefully be considered an undifferentiated category.[231] The authors also disagree on how to measure peace.[232] Should it be measured by the number of deaths caused by the conflict (raising the difficulty of how to define such a death)? What period of time demonstrates the existence of peace? When does the absence of deaths and lack of ostensible conflict indicate an accord's success, or repression and failure? Should indicators of democracy also be included in any quantification of success? Furthermore, the choices made by social scientists as to how to correlate peace agreement provisions with conflict outcomes often seem problematically selective, and at odds with approaches that could factor in the dynamics of processes that are much less easily tested empirically.[233] As a result, the studies find different factors to be crucial to success, with consequentially differing policy implications.

Understanding the *lex pacificatoria* embodied in peace agreement legalization makes an important contribution to these empirical debates because it reveals why some of the empirical quandaries are so intractable. If peace agreements are identified as transitional constitutions, then the difficulty of measuring success or failure lies in the difficulty of evaluating whether a constitution is successful or not. Clearly, there are empirical ways to measure success or failure, based on level of violent conflict or whether the constitution's institutions are up and running.

---

[229] *See, e.g.*, Burundi Peace Agreement, *supra* note 29 (signed by a range of political parties as well as armed opposition groups); *see also* Dili Peace Accord, Apr. 21, 1999 (signed by the National Council of Timorese Resistance and Falantil, and the Pro-integration Party); *cf.* South Africa National Peace Accord, Sept. 14, 1991, *available at* <http://www.incore.ulst.ac.uk/services/cds/agreements/pdf/sa4.pdf> (signed by ANC and National Party government, and a range of forty parties, including civic actors).

[230] *See, e.g.*, Peceny & Stanley, *supra* note 174; Nicholas Sambanis, *Using Case Studies to Expand Economic Models of Civil War*, 2 PERSP. ON POL. 259 (2004); *see also* Licklider, *supra* note 16, at 685 (discussing difficulties with definitions and research design).

[231] *See, e.g.*, Peceny & Stanley, *supra* note 174; Sambanis, *supra* note 230; *cf.* Licklider, *supra* note 16.

[232] *See, e.g.*, FORTNA, *supra* note 13; Licklider, *supra* note 16; Walter, *supra* note 10.

[233] The case study approaches do provide some process analysis. *See* Sambanis, *supra* note 230 (critiquing WORLD BANK, *supra* note 11); *cf.* Bekoe, *supra* note 13.

However, whether a constitution is actually working involves a much broader discussion of what it is that the constitution was meant to do. This includes questions such as, in what ways has the constitution provided alternatives to violent conflict? To what extent does it deliver benefits such as equality between groups and legitimacy to government? Does constitutional discourse divide or unite ethnically divided polities, and does it prevent or enable other political conversations? To have a sensible discussion about how law relates to compliance, we must have some discussion about what compliance should look like. These questions point to the benefit of examining peace agreements by means of a broad definition, and indeed of linking the discussion to ongoing debates about processes of social change and democratic renewal even outside the context of violent conflict. It suggests a need for social scientists and lawyers to talk to each other about the stuff of jurisprudence.

Recognition of a *lex pacificatoria* also indicates the need for further examination of the implications of legal pluralistic practice for compliance, particularly at the domestic level. The term *lex pacificatoria* signals the range of new inquiries. What is the relevance of the agreement's text to political discourse? How has international participation shaped this relationship? How have the various bodies charged with implementing the agreement—national monitoring commissions, peace councils, or even truth and reconciliation commissions—evolved quasi-legal regulation? Or conversely, where legal forums adjudicate on implementation, what is the role of peace agreements as regards judicial functions? At what point can legal adjudication cut free from the agreement's apparent goals, and how do we decide whether this cutting free represents a negation of the agreement or the achievement of a successful transition to "normal" political and legal structures? The compliance implications of the hybrid pluralist legal tapestry of peace agreement implementation at the domestic level have received little attention.

Finally, and perhaps most important, recognition of a *lex pacificatoria* enables engagement with the force of the *lex* and so offers the chance to question and shape its assumptions and manifestations. The phenomenal aspects of peace agreement practice point to a "univocal political meaning" on the global front, which operates to legitimate internationalized processes and blueprints.[234] This legitimating narrative presents peace agreements as always a good thing and peace processes as always moving straightforwardly from conflict to peace, and from internationalized process to domestic constitutionalization, in conformity with human rights standards. International actors appear as neutral and legitimate, and national actors as violent and equally at fault. In fact, peace processes evidence different degrees of legitimacy and neutrality of both international and domestic actors. They can move both away from and toward violence. They produce agreements that often have an ambiguous relationship to international law's normative standards, particularly those of human rights law. The fiction of a voluntary agreement crafted by equal parties, so crucial to achieving agreement, often disappears at the implementation stage, which involves supervising and enforcing what, in essence, are fundamental reallocations of power. At this point, international implementers must often abandon either their "neutrality" or their effectiveness—in practice, not all the parties can win.[235] The choice has implications for the normative basis on which international actors assert their legitimacy.[236]

---

[234] Boaventura de Sousa Santos, *Law and Democracy: (Mis)trusting the Global Reform of Courts, in* GLOBALISING INSTITUTIONS: CASE STUDIES IN REGULATION AND INNOVATION 253 (Jane Jenson & Boaventura de Sousa Santos eds., 2000).

[235] *See* Eva Bertram, *Reinventing Governments: The Promise and Perils of United Nations Peace Building*, 39 J. CONFLICT RESOL. 401 (1995).

[236] *See* sources cited *supra* note 184.

412   THE AMERICAN JOURNAL OF INTERNATIONAL LAW   [Vol. 100:373]

The above discussion has indicated that the legitimacy and the effectiveness of peace agreement legalization are related. Unless we understand the coherence of peace agreement legalization as having the force of law, we risk losing sight of a necessary discussion as to the identity of the moral and normative underpinnings of the emerging *lex*. Such a loss leaves technical devices and patterns—from constitutional blueprints to transitional justice mechanisms—to be rolled out without any coherent comparative discussion of whether they build on or undermine their possible normative justifications.[237] Without this discussion it can be somewhat puzzling why virtually identical measures seem legitimate and successful in some cases and illegitimate and unsuccessful in others.

Unveiling a *lex pacificatoria* reveals not just the normative capacity of international law, but the capacity of peace agreement practice to recast its norms.[238] This capacity reaches its height where peace agreement practice touches on normative gaps with regard to how international law deals with both mainly internal conflict and transitional situations.[239] The peace agreement phenomenon and the emerging *lex pacificatoria* therefore stand firmly at the heart of current debates over the future direction and power of international law itself and deserve further consideration.

---

[237] For evidence of the potential of "organizational" tools to promote common practice without articulating norms, see U.S. Dep't of State, Post-conflict Reconstruction Essential Tasks Matrix (Apr. 1, 2005), *at* <http://www.state.gov/s/crs/rls/52959.htm> (note, however, caveats in the preface as regards the need to be appropriate for context). *See* Post Conflict Reconstruction Unit, Post Conflict Stabilisation: Improving the United Kingdom's Contribution (Autumn 2004), *at* <http://www.postconflict.gov.uk/consultation/>.

[238] *Cf.* BELL, *supra* note 2, at 320; Nathaniel Berman, *The International Law of Nationalism: Group Identity and Legal History, in* INTERNATIONAL LAW AND ETHNIC CONFLICT, *supra* note 4, at 25.

[239] *See* sources cited *supra* note 238.

Part IV
Contemporary Challenges

[14]

From State Failure to State-Building: Problems and Prospects for a United Nations Peacebuilding Commission

SIMON CHESTERMAN*

INTRODUCTION

Tolstoy wrote that all happy families are happy alike, while every unhappy family is unhappy in its own way. It is tempting to say the same thing of states, as successful states enter an increasingly homogenous globalized economy and weaker states slip into individualized chaos. That would be only partly true. While the state-building efforts considered in this article demonstrate the importance of local context— history, culture, individual actors—they also outline some general lessons that may be of assistance in addressing problems confronting states emerging from conflict. Put another way, structural problems and root causes are part of the problem of "state failure", but an important question for policy-makers is how weak states deal with crisis. The nature of such a crisis can vary considerably. The emphasis here is on post-conflict reconstruction of states—a central concern, inasmuch as around half of all countries that emerge from war lapse back into it within five years.[1]

Post-conflict reconstruction through the 1990s saw an increasing trend towards rebuilding governance structures through assuming some or all governmental powers on a temporary basis. Such "transitional administration" operations can be divided into two broad classes: where state institutions are divided and where they have collapsed. The first class encompasses situations where governance structures were the subject of disputes, with different groups claiming power (as in Cambodia or Bosnia and Herzegovina), or ethnic tensions within the structures themselves (such as Kosovo). The second class comprises circumstances where such structures simply did not exist (as in Namibia, East Timor, and Afghanistan). A possible third class is suggested by recent experience in Iraq, where

---

*   Executive Director, Institute for International Law and Justice, New York University School of Law. The work of the Institute on governance and accountability in states at risk is generously supported by Carnegie Corporation of New York; the views expressed, however, are those of the author alone. Parts of this text draw upon passages first published in Simon Chesterman, *You, The People: The United Nations, Transitional Administration, and State-Building* (Oxford: Oxford University Press, 2004) and Simon Chesterman, Michael Ignatieff & Ramesh Thakur, eds., *Making States Work: State Failure and the Crisis of Governance* (New York: United Nations University Press, 2005). Some text also appears in Simon Chesterman, "State-Building and Human Development", *Human Development Report Office Occasional Paper* 1 (2005), 1–56. Permission to reproduce the relevant passages is gratefully acknowledged. Many thanks to Ramesh Thakur for his contributions to an earlier version of the text presented here.

1   United Nations Secretary-General, *In Larger Freedom: Towards Development, Security and Human Rights for All—Report of the Secretary-General*, UN GAOR, 59th Sess., UN Doc. A/59/2005 (2005), at para. 114 online: United Nations ‹http://daccessdds.un.org/doc/UNDOC/GEN/N05/270/78/PDF/N0527078.pdf?OpenElement›. [In Larger Freedom]

156   *Journal of International Law & International Relations*   Vol. 2(1)

regime change took place in a territory with far greater human, institutional, and economic resources than any comparable situation in which the United Nations or other actor had exercised civilian administration functions since the Second World War.[2]

The term "nation-building", sometimes used in this context, is a broad, vague, and often pejorative one. In the course of the 2000 US presidential campaign, Governor Bush used it as a dismissive reference to the application of US military resources beyond traditional mandates. The term was also used to conflate the circumstances in which US forces found themselves in conflict with the local population—most notably in Somalia—with complex and time-consuming operations such as those underway in Bosnia, Kosovo, and East Timor. Although it continues to be used in this context, "nation-building" also has a more specific meaning in the post-colonial context, in which new leaders attempted to rally a population within sometimes arbitrary territorial frontiers. The focus here is on the *state* (that is, the highest institutions of governance in a territory) rather than the *nation* (a people who share common customs, origins, history, and frequently language) as such.[3]

Within the United Nations, "peacebuilding" is generally preferred. This has been taken to mean, among other things, "reforming or strengthening governmental institutions,"[4] or "the creation of structures for the institutionalization of peace".[5] It

---

[2] See generally Simon Chesterman, *You, The People: The United Nations, Transitional Administration, and State-Building* (Oxford: Oxford University Press, 2004).

[3] Massimo D'Azeglio famously expressed the difference in the context of post-Risorgimento Italy: "We have made Italy," he declared. "Now we must make Italians." On the creation of states generally, see James Crawford, *The Creation of States in International Law* (Oxford: Clarendon Press, 1979). On nation-building, see, *e.g.*, Benedict Anderson, *Imagined Communities: Reflections on the Origin and Spread of Nationalism* (London: Verso, 1983); Ranajit Guha, ed., *A Subaltern Studies Reader, 1986-1995* (Minneapolis: University of Minnesota Press, 1997); and Jim Mac Laughlin, *Reimagining the Nation-State: The Contested Terrains of Nation-Building* (London: Pluto Press, 2001).

[4] *An Agenda for Peace: Preventive Diplomacy, Peacemaking and Peace-Keeping*, Report of the Secretary-General pursuant to the statement adopted by the Summit Meeting of the Security Council on 31 January 1992, UN Doc A/47/277-S/24111 (1992), at para 55, online: United Nations <http://www.un.org/Docs/SG/agpeace.html>.

[5] *Supplement to An Agenda for Peace: Position Paper of the Secretary-General on the Occasion of the Fiftieth Anniversary of the United Nations*, UN Doc A/50/60-S/1995/1 (1995), at para 49, online: United Nations <http://www.un.org/Docs/SG/agsupp.html>. From a UN development perspective, peacebuilding aims "to build and enable durable peace and sustainable development in post-conflict situations." See, e.g., *Role of UNDP in Crisis and Post-Conflict Situations*, Policy Paper Distributed to the Executive Board of the United Nations Development Programme and of the United Nations Population Fund, DP/2001/4 (2000), at para 51, online: United Nations <http://www.undp.org/execbrd/pdf/dp01-4.PDF>. The Development Assistance Committee (DAC) of the OECD maintains that peace-building and reconciliation focuses "on long-term support to, and

From State Failure to State-Building 157

tends, however, to embrace a far broader range of activities than those particular operations under consideration here—at times being used to describe virtually all forms of international assistance to countries that have experienced or are at risk of armed conflict.[6]

It is frequently assumed that the collapse of state structures, whether through defeat by an external power or as a result of internal chaos, leads to a vacuum of political power. This is rarely the case. The mechanisms through which political power are exercised may be less formalized or consistent, but basic questions of how best to ensure the physical and economic security of oneself and one's dependants do not simply disappear when the institutions of the state break down. Non-state actors in such situations may exercise varying degrees of political power over local populations, at times providing basic social services from education to medical care. Even where non-state actors exist as parasites on local populations, political life goes on. How to engage in such an environment is a particular problem for policy-makers in intergovernmental organizations and donor governments. But it poses far greater difficulties for the embattled state institutions and the populations of such territories.

Much discussion of "state failure" elides a series of definitional problems, most obviously about the nature of the state itself. If the state is understood as the vehicle for fulfilling a social contract, then state failure is the incapacity to deliver on basic public goods. If the state is defined by its capacity to exercise a monopoly on the legitimate use of force in its territory, state failure occurs when authority structures break down. Or if the state is constituted by its legal capacity, state failure is the incapacity to exercise such powers effectively.

Rather than choosing between these Lockean, Weberian, and juridical approaches to the state, it is argued here that such definitional questions are misleading. It is not generally the state that "fails"—it is the government or individual leaders. In extreme cases, the institutions of governance themselves may be severely undermined. But it is only through a more nuanced understanding of the state as a network of institutions that crises in governance may be properly understood and, perhaps, avoided or remedied. In many situations, the remedy will depend upon variables that are political rather than institutional, though the sustainability of any outcome depends precisely upon institutionalizing procedures to remove that dependence on politics and personality.

---

establishment of, viable political and socio-economic and cultural institutions capable of addressing the root causes of conflicts, as well as other initiatives aimed at creating the necessary conditions for sustained peace and stability": OECD, *Helping Prevent Violent Conflict, Development Assistance Committee Guidelines* (Paris: OECD, 2001), at 86, online: Organisation for Economic Co-operation and Development ‹http://www.oecd.org/dataoecd/15/54/1886146.pdf›.

[6]   Elizabeth M. Cousens, "Introduction," in Elizabeth M. Cousens & Chetan Kumar, eds., *Peacebuilding as Politics* (Boulder, CO: Lynne Rienner, 2001) 1 at 5-10.

158   *Journal of International Law & International Relations*   Vol. 2(1)

The key actors in these situations are almost always local. Nevertheless, international actors may also play a critical role, if only in creating the opportunity for local actors to establish legitimate and sustainable governance. Sometimes creating such opportunities means holding back. Humanitarian and, to some extent, development assistance flows most freely in response to crisis, but it rarely addresses the underlying causes of either poverty or conflict. If it is not well managed, such assistance may in fact undermine more sustainable recovery by establishing relationships of dependence and by distorting the economy with unsustainable allocations of resources.

This article can only explore a very small number of these issues. It focuses, therefore, on the exceptional circumstances where the United Nations assumes some or all sovereign powers.[7] Whether such operations are an appropriate activity for the United Nations remains controversial, but the expanding practice through the 1990s and early 2000s suggests that even if greater capacity is not developed the demand is unlikely to diminish. The section that follows highlights some of the difficulties inherent in such a political project of thrusting democracy and good governance on a population; section two then outlines the prospects for improvement, with particular reference to the proposed Peacebuilding Commission of the United Nations. A survey of the practice shows significant improvement in technical areas such as staging elections; the Peacebuilding Commission may remedy some of the coordination problems and funding gaps that plague post-conflict operations. It is far from clear, however, that the political contradictions inherent in such operations are being adequately understood let alone addressed.

PROBLEMS

Is it possible to establish the necessary political and economic conditions for legitimate and sustainable national governance through a period of benevolent foreign autocracy under UN auspices? This contradiction between ends and means has plagued recent efforts to govern post-conflict territories in the Balkans, East Timor, Afghanistan, and Iraq. Such state-building operations combine an unusual mix of idealism and realism: the idealist project that people can be saved from themselves through education, economic incentives, and the space to develop mature political institutions; and the realist basis for that project in what is ultimately military occupation.

Much research has focused on the doctrinal and operational difficulties experienced by such operations.[8] This is a valuable area of research, but may obscure

---

[7]   For a broader discussion of how states deal with crisis, see Simon Chesterman, Michael Ignatieff & Ramesh Thakur, eds., *Making States Work: State Failure and the Crisis of Governance* (Tokyo: United Nations University Press, 2005).

[8]   See, eg, Richard Caplan, *International Governance of War-Torn Territories: Rule and Reconstruction* (Oxford: Oxford University Press, 2005); Roland Paris, *At War's End: Building Peace after Civil Conflict* (Cambridge: Cambridge University Press, 2004).

From State Failure to State-Building 159

three sets of contradictions between means and ends that undermine such operations: the means are *inconsistent* with the ends, they are frequently *inadequate* for the ends, and in many situations the means are *inappropriate* for the ends.

Inconsistent

Benevolent autocracy is an uncertain foundation for legitimate and sustainable national governance. It is inaccurate and, often, counter-productive to assert that transitional administration depends upon the consent or "ownership" of the local population. It is inaccurate because if genuine local control were possible then a transitional administration would not be necessary. It is counter-productive because insincere claims of local ownership lead to frustration and suspicion on the part of local actors. *Clarity* is therefore required in recognizing: (a) the strategic objectives; (b) the relationship between international and local actors and how this will change over time; and (c) the commitment required of international actors in order to achieve objectives that warrant the temporary assumption of autocratic powers under a benevolent international administration.

In a case like East Timor, the strategic objective—independence—was both clear and uncontroversial. Frustration with the slow pace of reconstruction or the inefficiencies of the UN presence could generally be tempered by reference to the uncontested aim of independence and a timetable within which this was to be achieved. In Kosovo, failure to articulate a position on its final status inhibits the development of a mature political elite and deters foreign investment. The present ambiguity derives from a compromise that was brokered between the United States and Russia at the end of the NATO campaign against the Federal Republic of Yugoslavia in 1999, formalized in Security Council resolution 1244.[9] Nevertheless, it is the United Nations itself that is now blamed for frustrating the aspirations of Kosovars for self-determination. Many national and international observers have blamed lack of progress in resolving the issue of final status as a key factor in fuelling the violence that erupted in the province in March 2004.

Obfuscation of the political objective leads to ambiguity in the mandate. Niche mandate implementation by a proliferation of post-conflict actors further complicates the transition. More than five years after the Dayton Peace Agreement, a "recalibration" exercise required the various international agencies present in Bosnia and Herzegovina to perform an institutional audit to determine what, exactly, each of them did.[10] Subsidiary bodies and specialized agencies of the United Nations should in principle place their material and human resources at the direct disposal of the transitional administration: all activities should be oriented towards an agreed political goal, which should normally be legitimate and sustainable government. Ideally, the unity of civilian authority should embrace command of the military also.

---

9   UNSC Res. 1244, UN SCOR, UN Doc S/RES/1244 (1999).

10   International Crisis Group, *Bosnia: Reshaping the International Machinery* (Sarajevo/Brussels: ICG Balkans Report No 121, 29 November 2001) at 13, online: International Crisis Group ‹http://www.crisisgroup.org/home/index.cfm?id=1495&l=1›.

160 *Journal of International Law & International Relations* Vol. 2(1)

In reality, the reluctance of the United States and other industrialized countries to put their troops under UN command makes this highly improbable. Coordination thus becomes more important, to avoid some of the difficulties encountered in civil-military relations in Afghanistan.

Clarity in the relationship between international and local actors raises the question of ownership. This term is often used disingenuously—either to mask the assertion of potentially dictatorial powers by international actors or to carry a psychological rather than political meaning in the area of reconstruction. *Ownership* in this context is usually not intended to mean control and often does not even imply a direct input into political questions.[11] This is not to suggest that local control is a substitute for international administration. As the operation in Afghanistan demonstrates, a "light footprint" makes the success of an operation more than usually dependent on the political dynamic of local actors. Since the malevolence or collapse of that political dynamic is precisely the reason that power is arrogated to an international presence, the light footprint is unsustainable as a model for general application. How much power should be transferred and for how long depends upon the political transition that is required; this in turn is a function of the root causes of the conflict, the local capacity for change, and the degree of international commitment available to assist in bringing about that change.[12]

Local ownership, then, must be the end of a transitional administration, but it is not the means. Openness about the trustee-like relationship between international and local actors would help locals by ensuring transparency about the powers that they will exercise at various stages of the transition. But openness would also help the states that mandate and fund such operations by forcing acknowledgement of their true nature and the level of commitment that is required in order to effect the transition that is required.

Clarifying the commitment necessary to bring about fundamental change in a conflict-prone territory is, however, a double-edged sword. It would ensure that political will exists prior to authorizing a transitional administration, but perhaps at the expense of other operations that would not be authorized at all. The mission in Bosnia was always expected to last beyond its nominal twelve-month deadline, but might not have been established if it had been envisaged that troops would remain on the ground for a full decade or more. Donors contemplating Afghanistan in November 2001 balked at early estimates that called for a ten-year, $25 billion commitment to the country. And in the lead up to the war with Iraq, the Chief of

---

[11]   See Simon Chesterman, "The Trope of Ownership: Transfer of Authority in Post-Conflict Operations", in Agnes Hurwitz, ed., *Rule of Law Programming in Conflict Management: Security, Development and Human Rights in the 21st Century* (Boulder, CO: Lynne Rienner, 2006) [forthcoming].

[12]   Michael W. Doyle, "War-Making and Peace-Making: The United Nations' Post-Cold War Record," in Chester A. Crocker, Fen Osler Hampson & Pamela Aall, eds., *Turbulent Peace: The Challenges of Managing International Conflict* (Washington, DC: United States Institute of Peace Press, 2001) 529 at 546.

Staff of the US Army was similarly pooh-poohed by the leadership of the Defence Department when he testified to the Senate that several hundred thousand soldiers would be required for post-war duties.[13] Political considerations already limit the choice of missions, of course: not for lack of opportunity, no major transitional administration has been established in Africa, where the demands are probably greatest. The primary barrier to establishing transitional administration-type operations in areas such as Western Sahara, Somalia, and the Democratic Republic of the Congo has less to do with the difficulty of such operations than with the absence of political will to commit resources to undertake them.[14]

Resolving the inconsistency between the means and the ends of transitional administration requires a clear-eyed recognition of the role of power. The collapse of formal state structures does not necessarily create a power vacuum; as indicated earlier, political life does not simply cease. Constructive engagement with power on this local level requires both an understanding of culture and history as well as respect for the political aspirations of the population. Clarity will help here also: either the international presence exercises quasi-sovereign powers on a temporary basis or it does not. This clarity must exist at the formal level, but leaves much room for nuance in implementation.

Most obviously, assertion of executive authority should be on a diminishing basis, with power devolved as appropriate to local institutions. The transfer of power must be of more than symbolic value: once power is transferred to local hands, whether at the municipal or national level, local actors should be able to exercise that power meaningfully, constrained only by the rule of law. Unless and until genuine transfer is possible, consultation is appropriate but without the pretence that this is the same as control. Where international actors do not exercise sovereign power—because of the size of the territory, the complexity of the conflict, or a simple lack of political will—this is not the same as exercising no power at all. Certain functions may be delegated to the international presence, as they were in Cambodia and Afghanistan, and international actors will continue to exercise considerable behind-the-scenes influence either because of ongoing responsibilities in a peace process or as a gatekeeper to international development assistance. In either case, the abiding need is for clarity as to who is in charge and, equally important, who is *going* to be in charge.

Inadequate

International interest in post-conflict operations tends to be ephemeral, with availability of funds linked to the prominence of a foreign crisis on the domestic

---

[13]   Eric Schmitt, "Pentagon contradicts general on Iraq occupation force's size" *New York Times* (28 February 2003) A1.

[14]   UN envoy James Baker is said to have been asked once by Polisario representatives why the United Nations was treating Western Sahara differently from East Timor. He replied to the effect that if the Sahrawis wanted to be treated like the Timorese they had best go find themselves an Australia to lead a military action on their behalf.

162 *Journal of International Law & International Relations* Vol. 2(1)

agenda of the states that contribute funds and troops. Both have tended to be insufficient. Funds for post-conflict reconstruction are notoriously supply- rather than demand-driven. This leads to multiplication of bureaucracy in the recipient country, inconsistency in disbursement procedures, and a focus on projects that may be more popular with donors than they are necessary in the recipient country. Reluctance to commit funds is surpassed only by reluctance to commit troops: in the absence of security, however, meaningful political change is impossible. This was confirmed in the most brutal way possible with the attacks on UN personnel in Baghdad on 19 August 2003.

The ephemeral nature of international interest in post-conflict operations is, unfortunately, a cliché. When the United States overthrew the Taliban regime in Afghanistan, President Bush likened the commitment to rebuild the devastated country to the Marshall Plan. Just over twelve months later, in February 2003, the White House apparently forgot to include *any* money for reconstruction in the 2004 budget that it submitted to Congress. Legislators reallocated $300 million in aid to cover the oversight.[15] Such oversights are disturbingly common: much of the aid that is pledged either arrives late or not at all. This demands a measure of artificiality in drafting budgets for reconstruction, which in turn leads to suspicion on the part of donors—sometimes further delaying the disbursement of funds. For example, $880 million was pledged at the Conference on Rehabilitation and Reconstruction of Cambodia in June 1992. By the time the new government was formed in September 1993, only $200 million had been disbursed, rising to only $460 million by the end of 1995. The problem is not simply one of volume: Bosnia has received more per capita assistance than Europe did under the Marshall Plan, but the incoherence of funding programmes, the lack of a regional approach, and the inadequacy of state and entity institutions have contributed to it remaining in financial crisis.[16]

Many of these problems would be reduced if donors replaced the system of voluntary funding for relief and reconstruction for transitional administrations with assessed contributions, which presently fund peacekeeping operations. The distinction between funds supporting a peacekeeping operation and those providing assistance to a government makes sense when there is some form of indigenous government, but it is arbitrary in situations where the peacekeeping operation *is* the government. Given existing strains on the peacekeeping budget, however, such a change is unlikely. A more realistic proposal would be to pool voluntary contributions through a trust fund, ideally coordinated by local actors or a mixed

---

[15]   Paul Krugman, "The martial plan" *New York Times* (21 February 2003) A27; James G. Lakely, "Levin criticizes budget for Afghanistan; Says White House isn't devoting enough to rebuilding" *Washington Times* (26 February 2003) A04. Aid was later increased further: David Rohde, "US said to plan bigger Afghan effort, stepping up aid" *New York Times* (25 August 2003) A3.

[16]   See, e.g., International Crisis Group, *Bosnia's Precarious Economy: Still Not Open for Business* (Sarajevo/Brussels: ICG Balkans Report No 115, 7 August 2001), online: International Crisis Group <http://www.crisisgroup.org/home/index.cfm?id=1494&l=1>.

body of local and international personnel, perhaps also drawing upon private sector expertise. At the very least, a monitoring mechanism to track aid flows would help to ensure that money that is promised at the high point of international attention to a crisis is in fact delivered and spent. The experience of Afghanistan suggests that there is, perhaps, some learning taking place in this area, though even during one of the greatest outpouring of emergency relief fund in recent history—in response to the tsunami that struck the Indian ocean region on 26 December 2004—Secretary-General Kofi Annan felt compelled to remind donor governments that "We have often had gaps in the past [between pledges and actual donations] and I hope it is not going to happen in this case."[17] The use of PricewaterhouseCoopers to track aid flows also points to a new flexibility in using private sector expertise to avoid wastage and corruption.

Parsimony of treasure is surpassed by the reluctance to expend blood in policing post-conflict territories. In the absence of security, however, meaningful political change in a post-conflict territory is next to impossible. Unless and until the United Nations develops a rapidly deployable civilian police capacity, either military tasks in a post-conflict environment will include basic law and order functions or these functions will not be performed at all. The military—especially the US military—is understandably reluctant to embrace duties that are outside its field of expertise, but this is symptomatic of an anachronistic view of UN peace operations. The dichotomy between peacekeeping and enforcement actions was always artificial, but in the context of internal armed conflict where large numbers of civilians are at risk it becomes untenable. Moreover, as most transitional administrations have followed conflicts initiated under the auspices or in the name of the United Nations, inaction is not the same as non-interference—once military operations commence, external actors have already begun a process of political transformation on the ground. And, as the Independent Inquiry on Rwanda concluded, whether or not a peace operation has a mandate or the will to protect civilians, its very presence creates an expectation that it will do so.[18]

A key argument in the Report of the Panel on UN Peace Operations, known as the Brahimi Report, was that missions with uncertain mandates or inadequate resources should not be created at all:

> Although presenting and justifying planning estimates according to high operational standards might reduce the likelihood of an operation going forward, Member States must not be led to believe that they are doing something useful for countries in trouble when—by under-resourcing

---

[17]   Scott Shane and Raymond Bonner, "Annan nudges donors to make good on full pledges" *New York Times* (7 January 2005) A12.

[18]   *Report of the Independent Inquiry into the Actions of the United Nations During the 1994 Genocide in Rwanda*, UN Doc. S/1999/1257 (1999) at 51, Online: United Nations ‹http://www.un.org/ Docs/journal/asp/ws.asp?m=S/1999/1257›; *Report of the Panel on United Nations Peace Operations* (Brahimi Report), UN Doc. A/55/305-S/2000/809 (2000), at para 62, online: United Nations ‹http://www.un.org/peace/reports/peace_operations/›.

missions—they are more likely agreeing to a waste of human resources, time and money.[19]

This view finds some support in the report of the International Commission on Intervention and State Sovereignty, *The Responsibility to Protect*, which called for the "responsibility to rebuild" to be seen as an integral part of any intervention. When an intervention is contemplated, a post-intervention strategy is both an operational necessity and an ethical imperative.[20] There is some evidence of this principle now achieving at least rhetorical acceptance—despite his aversion to "nation-building", President Bush stressed before and during operations in Afghanistan and Iraq that the United States would help in reconstructing the territories in which it had intervened.

More than rhetoric is required. Success in state-building, in addition to clarity of purpose, requires time and money. A lengthy international presence will not ensure success, but an early departure guarantees failure. Similarly, an abundance of resources will not make up for the lack of a coherent strategy—though the fact that Kosovo has been the recipient of twenty-five times more money and fifty times more troops, on a per capita basis, compared with Afghanistan, goes some way towards explaining the modest achievements in developing democratic institutions and the economy.[21]

Inappropriate

The inappropriateness of available means to desired ends presents the opposite problem to that of the inadequacy of resources. While the question of limited resources—money, personnel, and international attention—depresses the standards against which a post-conflict operation can be judged, artificially high international expectations may nevertheless be imposed in certain areas of governance. Particularly when the United Nations itself assumes a governing role, there is a temptation to demand the highest standards of democracy, human rights, the rule of law, and the provision of services.

Balancing these against the need for locally sustainable goals presents difficult problems. A computerized electoral registration system may be manifestly ill-suited to a country with a low level of literacy and intermittent electricity, but should an international NGO refrain from opening a world-class clinic if such levels of care are unsustainable? An abrupt drop from high levels of care once the crisis and international interest passes would be disruptive, but lowering standards early implies acceptance that people who might otherwise have been treated will suffer.

---

[19]   Brahimi Report, *ibid.* at para. 59.

[20]   International Commission on Intervention and State Sovereignty, *The Responsibility to Protect* (Ottawa: International Development Research Centre, December 2001), at paras. 2.32, 5.1-5.6, online: International Commission on Intervention and State Sovereignty ‹http://www.iciss.ca/report-en.asp›.

[21]   See James Dobbins *et al.*, *America's Role in Nation-Building: From Germany to Iraq* (Santa Monica, CA: RAND, 2003) at 160-166.

From State Failure to State-Building   165

This was the dilemma faced by the International Committee of the Red Cross, which transferred control of the Dili National Hospital to national authorities in East Timor almost a year before independence.

Although most acute in areas such as health, the issue arises in many aspects of transitional administration. In the best tradition of autocracies, the international missions in Bosnia and Kosovo subscribed to the vast majority of human rights treaties and then discovered *raisons d'état* that required these to be abrogated. Efforts to promote the rule of law tend to focus more on the prosecution of the highest profile crimes of the recent past than on developing institutions to manage criminal law in the near future. Humanitarian and development assistance is notorious for being driven more by supply than demand, with the result that those projects that are funded tend to represent the interests—and, frequently, the products and personnel—of donors rather than recipients.[22] Finally, staging elections in conflict zones has become something of an art form, though more than half a dozen elections in Bosnia have yet to produce a workable government.

Different issues arise in the area of human resources. Staffing such operations always takes place in an atmosphere of crisis, but personnel tend to be selected from a limited pool of applicants (most of them internal) whose skills may be irrelevant to the tasks at hand. In East Timor, for example, it would have made sense to approach Portuguese-speaking governments to request that staff with experience in public administration be seconded to the UN mission. Instead, it was not even possible to require Portuguese (or Tetum or Bahasa Indonesia) as a language. Positions are often awarded for political reasons or simply to ensure that staff lists are full—once in place, there is no effective mechanism to assess an individual's suitability or to remove him or her quickly if this proves warranted. A separate problem is the assumption that international staffs who do possess relevant skills are also able to train others in the same field. This is an entirely different skill, however, and simply pairing international and local staff tends to provide less on-the-job training than extended opportunities to stand around and watch—a problem exacerbated by the fact that English tends to be used as the working language. One element of the "light footprint" approach adopted in Afghanistan that is certainly of general application is the need to justify every post occupied by international staff rather than a local. Cultivating relations with Diaspora communities may help address this problem, serving the dual function of recruiting culturally aware staff and encouraging the return of skilled expatriates more generally.

The "can-do" attitude of many people within the UN system is one of the most positive qualities that staffs bring to a mission. If the problem is getting a hundred tons of rice to ten thousand starving refugees, niceties of procedure are less important than getting the job done. When the problem is governing a territory,

---

22   See generally Shepard Forman & Stewart Patrick, eds., *Good Intentions: Pledges of Aid for Postconflict Recovery* (Boulder, CO: Lynne Rienner Publishers, 2000).

166   *Journal of International Law & International Relations*   Vol. 2(1)

however, procedure is more important. In such circumstances, the "can-do" attitude may become a cavalier disregard for local sensibilities. Moreover, many staffs in such situations are not used to criticism from the population that they are "helping", with some regarding it as a form of ingratitude. Where the United Nations assumes the role of government, it should expect and welcome criticism appropriate to that of the sort of political environment it hopes to foster. Security issues may require limits on this, but a central element in the development of local political capacity is encouraging discussion among local actors about these matters—apart from anything else, it enhances the legitimacy of the conclusions drawn. International staffs sometimes bemoan the prospect of endless consultation getting in the way of their work, but in many ways that conversation is precisely the point of their presence in the territory.

Just as generals are sometimes accused of planning to re-fight their last war, so the United Nations experiments in transitional administration have reflected only gradual learning. Senior UN officials now acknowledge that, to varying degrees, Kosovo got the operation that should have been planned for Bosnia four years earlier, and East Timor got that which should have been sent to Kosovo. Afghanistan's very different "light footprint" approach draws, in turn, upon the outlines of what Lakhdar Brahimi argued would have been appropriate for East Timor in 1999.

The United Nations may never again be called upon to repeat operations comparable to Kosovo and East Timor, where it exercised sovereign powers on a temporary basis. Even so, it is certain that the circumstances that demanded such interventions will recur. Lessons derived from past experiences of transitional administration will be applicable whenever the United Nations or other international actors engage in complex peace operations that include a policing function, civilian administration, development of the rule of law, establishment of a national economy, the staging of elections, or all of the above. Learning from such lessons has not, however, been one of the strengths of the United Nations.

However, even more important than learning from past mistakes, is learning about future circumstances. Modern trusteeships demand, above all, trust on the part of local actors. Earning and keeping that trust requires a level of understanding, sensitivity, and respect for local traditions and political aspirations that has often been lacking in transitional administration. How that trust is managed will, in large part, determine its legacy.

Transitional administration will remain an exceptional activity, performed on an ad hoc basis in a climate of institutional and political uncertainty. But in those rare situations in which the United Nations and other international actors are called upon to exercise state-like functions, they must not lose sight of their limited mandate to hold that sovereign power in trust for the population that will ultimately claim it.

PROSPECTS

If there is a single generalizable lesson to be learned from the recent experience of state-building, whether as transitional administration or preventing state failure, it is modesty. The challenges before the United Nations community now are not, therefore, to develop grand theories or a revivified trusteeship capacity. Rather, what are required are workable strategies and tactics with which to support institutions of the state before, during, and after conflict. As indicated earlier, doing this effectively requires clarity in three areas: (a) the strategic aims of the action; (b) the necessary institutional coordination to put all actors—especially security and development actors—on the same page; and (c) a realistic basis for evaluating the success or failure of the action.

Strategy

The accepted wisdom within the UN community, articulated most recently in the Brahimi Report, is that a successful UN peace operation should ideally consist of three sequential stages. First, the political basis for peace must be determined. Then a suitable mandate for a UN mission should be formulated. Finally, that mission should be given all the resources necessary to complete the mandate.[23] The accepted reality is that this usually happens in the reverse order: member states determine what resources they are prepared to commit to a problem and a mandate is cobbled together around those resources—often in the hope that a political solution will be forthcoming at some later date.

Strategic failure may affect all levels of an operation. The most common types of failures are at the level of overall mandate, in the interaction between different international actors with competing or inconsistent mandates, and in the relationship between international and national actors on the ground.

Kosovo's uncertain final status, for example, has severely undermined the ongoing peace operation there, contrasting starkly with the simplicity of East Timor's transition to independence. Clarity concerning the political trajectory of a territory under transitional administration is essential, but lack of strategy will also undermine efforts to prevent the collapse of state institutions. In Afghanistan, prioritising the military strategy at times undermined the professed political aims—most prominently in decisions to support warlords for tactical reasons in the hunt for al Qaeda even as they undermined Hamid Karzai's embryonic government in Kabul.

A second level at which strategic failure may take place is when different actors have competing or inconsistent mandates. Security actors are a notorious example of this—with the independence of the NATO-led KFOR in Kosovo and the ISAF in Afghanistan at times undermining the authority of the international civilian presence. Ensuring a single chain of command would be desirable, but runs against the received wisdom that the United Nations is incapable of waging war. A more achievable goal would be bringing the political process into line with development assistance. The United Nations has done this rhetorically in the term "peacebuilding",[24] but without creating any capacity to focus political attention,

---

[23] Brahimi Report, *supra* note 17 at paras. 9-83.

[24] See *supra* note 4.

design policy and strategy, and oversee operations in this area. (The proposed Peacebuilding Commission is considered in the next sub-section.)

As indicated by the discussion on political trajectory and ownership, international actors have sometimes been less than effective at managing expectations and relationships with national actors. Clarity about respective roles—and about the final authority of the population in question to determine its own future once a territory is stabilized and no longer regarded as a threat to international peace and security—would help. Where there is no existing legitimate governance structure in place, or if there are competing structures, the concept of "shadow alignment" may be helpful. This requires an assessment of available formal and informal policies and systems that can be built on, adapted, and reformed. The aim is to avoid a legacy of diverted institutions that may undermine the development of legitimate and accountable structures.[25]

Reference to strategy should not be misunderstood as suggesting that there is some template for governance that can be applied across cases. Instead, clarity about the purposes of engagement and the respective responsibilities of international and national actors provides a framework for developing a coherent strategy that takes the state itself as the starting point.

Coordination and the Peacebuilding Commission

The High-Level Panel on Threats, Challenges, and Change rightly criticized the UN experience of post-conflict operations as characterized by "countless ill-coordinated and overlapping bilateral and United Nations programmes, with inter-agency competition preventing the best use of scarce resources."[26] Its key recommendation to remedy this situation was the call for a Peacebuilding Commission to be established as a subsidiary organ of the UN Security Council under article 29 of the UN Charter.[27]

This new body was to have four functions. First, it would identify countries that are under stress and risk sliding towards state collapse. Second, it would organize, "in partnership with the national Government, proactive assistance in preventing that process from developing further". Third, it would assist in the planning for transitions between conflict and post-conflict peacebuilding. Fourth, it would marshal and sustain the efforts of the international community in post-conflict peacebuilding over whatever period may be necessary. Other guidelines mapped out institutional and procedural considerations, including the need for the

---

[25]   *Achieving the Health Millennium Development Goals in Fragile States*, Abuja: High-Level Forum on the Health MDGs (2004) at 21, online: High-Level Forum on the Health MDGs ‹http://www.hlfhealthmdgs.org/Documents/FragileStates.pdf›.

[26]   *Report of the Secretary-General's High-level Panel on Threats, Challenges and Change, A More Secure World: Our Shared Responsibility*, UN GAOR, 59th Sess., Supp. No. 565, UN Doc. A/59 (2004) at para 38, online: United Nations ‹http://www.un.org/secureworld/ report.pdf› [High-level Panel Report].

[27]   *Ibid.* at paras 261-265.

body to be small and flexible, considering both general policy issues and country-by-country strategies. It was to include representatives of the Security Council, the Economic and Social Council, the International Monetary Fund and the World Bank, donor countries, troop contributors, and regional organizations—as well as national representatives of the country under consideration.[28] A Peacebuilding Support Office would integrate system-wide policies and strategies, develop best practices, and provide support to field operations. Among other functions, the office would submit twice-yearly early warning analyses to the Peacebuilding Commission to help it in organizing its work.[29]

The Commission was generally considered to be one of the more positive ideas to come from the High-Level Panel and appeared likely to be adopted by the membership of the United Nations. When the Secretary-General drew upon this to present his own vision of the Peacebuilding Commission in his "In Larger Freedom" report of March 2005, he specifically removed any suggestion of an early warning function—presumably under pressure from governments wary that they might be the ones under scrutiny.[30] This essentially dropped the first two of the High-Level Panel's four functions, but the Secretary-General elaborated on how the other two might work in practice:

> A Peacebuilding Commission could perform the following functions: in the immediate aftermath of war, improve United Nations planning for sustained recovery, focusing on early efforts to establish the necessary institutions; help to ensure predictable financing for early recovery activities, in part by providing an overview of assessed, voluntary and standing funding mechanisms; improve the coordination of the many post-conflict activities of the United Nations funds, programmes and agencies; provide a forum in which the United Nations, major bilateral donors, troop contributors, relevant regional actors and organizations, the international financial institutions and the national or transitional Government of the country concerned can share information about their respective post-conflict recovery strategies, in the interests of greater coherence; periodically review progress towards medium-term recovery goals; and extend the period of political attention to post-conflict recovery.[31]

Two essential aspects of how the commission would function were left unresolved: what its membership would be, and to whom it would report—the Security Council or the Economic and Security Council. These ended up paralysing debate on the Commission in the lead up to the September 2005 World Summit and were deferred for later consideration. The World Summit Outcome document

---

[28]   *Ibid.* at paras. 264-265.

[29]   *Ibid.* at paras. 266-267.

[30]   In Larger Freedom, *supra* note 1 at para. 115.

[31]   *Ibid.* at para. 115.

170   *Journal of International Law & International Relations*   Vol. 2(1)

broadly endorsed the Secretary-General's view of the Peacebuilding Commission as essentially limited to mobilizing resources for post-conflict reconstruction:

> The main purpose of the Peacebuilding Commission is to bring together all relevant actors to marshal resources and to advise on and propose integrated strategies for post-conflict peacebuilding and recovery. The Commission should focus attention on the reconstruction and institution-building efforts necessary for recovery from conflict and support the development of integrated strategies in order to lay the foundation for sustainable development. In addition, it should provide recommendations and information to improve the coordination of all relevant actors within and outside the United Nations, develop best practices, help to ensure predictable financing for early recovery activities and extend the period of attention by the international community to post-conflict recovery.[32]

In one sense, the evolution of the Peacebuilding Commission is a fairly typical example of ideas and norms being diluted as they move through the policy and intergovernmental waters. Early warning died a fairly quick death even before reaching the summit. A second attempt by the High-Level Panel to strengthen early warning by creating a Deputy Secretary-General for Peace and Security was dropped entirely.[33] The outcome document of the 2005 Summit did resolve to develop early warning systems for natural disasters, in particular tsunamis, but early warning of man-made disasters was the subject for a more tepid call for the international community to support the United Nations in developing such a capability at some point in the unspecified future.[34]

On the post-conflict responsibilities of the Peacebuilding Commission, its role in planning and formulating strategy was more subtly undermined. The High-Level Panel had seen it as assisting in the "planning" for the transition from conflict to post-conflict.[35] The Secretary-General limited it to improving "United Nations planning for sustained recovery".[36] By the Summit, it was limited to "advis[ing] on and propos[ing] integrated strategies".[37] The Peacebuilding Support Office, meanwhile did not receive the requested twenty new staff or any new responsibilities beyond assisting and supporting the Commission by drawing upon existing resources within the Secretariat.[38]

---

[32]   UN General Assembly, *2005 World Summit Outcome*, GA Res 60/1, UN GAOR, 60th Sess., UN Doc. A/RES/60/1 (2005), online: United Nations <http://daccessdds.un.org/doc/UNDOC/LTD/N05/511/30/PDF/N0551130.pdf?OpenElement> [World Summit Outcome].

[33]   High-Level Panel Report, *supra* note 26 at paras. 98, 293-294.

[34]   World Summit Outcome, *supra* note 32 at paras. 56(f), 138.

[35]   High-Level Panel Report, *supra* note 26 at para. 264.

[36]   In Larger Freedom, *supra* note 1 at para. 115.

[37]   World Summit Outcome, *supra* note 31 at para. 98.

[38]   *Ibid.* at para 104.

Far from being a new Trusteeship Council, then, the Peacebuilding Commission begins to look more like a standing pledging conference, one of the most important forms of coordination for donors that currently exists.[39] If it can succeed in sustaining attention on a post-conflict situation beyond the current limits of foreign policy attention deficit disorder, the Peacebuilding Commission will have achieved a great deal. It is less clear that this additional layer of coordination will assist in how these new resources are spent.

Problems of coordination tend to arise at three levels: (a) the strategic level (for example, the final status of Kosovo); (b) the operational level (for example, competing donor agencies in Bosnia); and (c) the national level (for example, getting international actors to sign onto a national development framework in Afghanistan). The problem with the Peacebuilding Commission proposal is that its establishment under the Security Council (or the Economic and Social Council) may see it fall somewhere between (a) and (b)—lacking the authority to challenge the Security Council in New York and lacking a field presence to ensure operational cohesion on the ground. Much will, of course, depend on how the proposed commission functions. If it acts as an operational body that can bring key stakeholders— importantly including the International Financial Institutions, troop contributors, donor governments, and national representatives—onto the same page in terms of the security, humanitarian, political, and economic priorities and sequencing for a territory, it may avoid the wasted resources seen in previous operations. At the very least if it can force the United Nations to speak with one voice on post-conflict

---

[39]   Stewart Patrick, "The Donor Community and the Challenge of Postconflict Recovery" in Shepard Forman & Stewart Patrick, eds., *Good Intentions: Pledges of Aid for Postconflict Recovery* (Boulder, CO: Lynne Rienner Publishers, 2000) 35 at 40-41. In the absence of funds that can be disbursed quickly to a recovery process, significant external resources typically arrive only after such a conference, which brings donor states, UN agencies, and the International Financial Institutions together with local representatives to evaluate proposed reconstruction plans. The relative transparency of these meetings reduces the temptation of donors to 'free ride' on the efforts of others. More subtly, by involving disparate actors in providing support for post-conflict recovery as a form of public good, the pledging conference encourages the notion of a "donor community", bound by certain ethical obligations towards the recovering state. Pledging conferences also enable donors to shape and publicize recovery plans jointly, which may increase domestic support for foreign assistance as part of an international effort. For recipients, pledging conferences offer the opportunity to focus the minds of donors on a crisis and to gain public assurances that some of their needs will be met. While these aspects are positive, pledging conferences often bear the trappings of political theatre. Donors may make grand gestures that in reality double-count resources previously committed to a country, or which cannot be delivered promptly. In addition, mediating different donor interests through a conference does not remove the problems caused by the inconsistency of those interests. Donors continue to avoid controversial areas like security sector reform, preferring to fund items that will gain recognition and prestige. Finally, despite the public nature of the pledges made, there is no consistent monitoring process to ensure that pledges are realistic and transparent.

172 *Journal of International Law & International Relations* Vol. 2(1)

reconstruction—rather than being represented variously by the departments and specialized agencies—it will have achieved a significant improvement. But the key component required is some body that is able to speak truth to power: unless the commission (or the proposed Peacebuilding Support Office) is able to advise the Security Council against dysfunctional mandates or unrealistic strategies it will not fulfil its lofty aspirations.

If it is to be successful, two additional coordination dynamics need to be addressed. The first is the problem of coordination across time. This embraces both the conflicting time-tables of internationals (diminishing interest and thus reduced resources after 18 to 24 months) and locals (increasing absorptive capacity and the ability to use resources most productively only after the crisis period has passed), as well as the tension between demands for quick impact and gap-filling projects versus the development of sustainable institutions. The second coordination dynamic is the emergence of local actors as an independent political force. Consultation through an instrument such as the Peacebuilding Commission would be helpful, but not if it complicates the more important consultative mechanisms on the ground that manage day-to-day political life in the post-conflict territory. The most important aspect of this second dynamic is, once again, clarity: clarity about who is in charge at any given time, but also clarity about who will be in charge once the attention of the international community moves on.

Evaluation and Exit Strategies

In his April 2001 report on the closure or transition of complex peacekeeping operations, UN Secretary-General Kofi Annan warned that the embarrassing withdrawal of peacekeepers from Somalia should not be repeated in future operations. "No Exit Without a Strategy", the report was called.[40] For the UN Transitional Administration in East Timor (UNTAET), elections provided the basis for transfer of power to local authorities; they also set in place political processes that would last well beyond the mission and the development assistance that followed. In Kosovo, where the UN operation was determinedly called an "interim" administration, the absence of an agreed end-state has left the territory in political limbo. Reflection on the absence of an exit strategy from Kosovo, following on the apparently endless operation in Bosnia and Herzegovina, led some ambassadors to the Security Council to turn the Secretary-General's phrase on its head: "No strategy", the rallying cry went, "without an exit."

East Timor presents two contradictory stories in the history of UN peace operations. On the one hand, it is presented as an outstanding success. In two and a half years, a territory that had been reduced to ashes after the 1999 referendum on independence held peaceful elections and celebrated independence. On the other hand, however, East Timor can be seen as a series of missed opportunities and

---

[40] *No Exit Without Strategy: Security Council Decision-Making and the Closure or Transition of United Nations Peacekeeping Operations*, Report of the Secretary-General, UN Doc. S/2001/394 (2001), online: United Nations ‹http://daccess-ods.un.org/TMP/3169153.html›.

wastage. Of the UN Transitional Administration's annual budget of over $500 million, around one-tenth actually reached the East Timorese. At one point, $27 million was spent annually on bottled water for the international staff— approximately half the budget of the embryonic Timorese government, and money that might have paid for water purification plants to serve both international staff and locals well beyond the life of the mission. More could have been done, or done earlier to reconstruct public facilities. This did not happen in part because of budgetary restrictions on UN peacekeeping operations that, to the Timorese, were not simply absurd but insulting. Such problems were compounded by coordination failures, the displacement of local initiatives by bilateral donor activities, and the lack of any significant private sector investment. When East Timor (now Timor-Leste) became independent, it did so with the dubious honour of becoming the poorest country in Asia.[41]

Evaluations of the UN operation in Cambodia (1992 to 1993) varied considerably in the course of the mission and have continued to do so with the benefit of hindsight. Prior to the 1993 election, prophecies of doom were widespread, with questions raised about the capacity of the United Nations to complete a large military and administrative operation.[42] Immediately after the election was held with minimal violence, Cambodia was embraced as a success and a model for future such tasks.[43] Subsequent events suggested that these initially positive evaluations were premature. Many commentators outside the United Nations now regard the UN Transitional Authority in Cambodia (UNTAC) as a partial failure, pointing to the departure from democratic norms in the 1997 coup. Within the United Nations, UNTAC continues to be regarded as a partial success. The important variable is how one views the political context within which UNTAC operated. If the purpose of the mission was to transform Cambodia into a multiparty liberal democracy in 18 months, it clearly did not succeed. If, however, one takes the view that Hun Sen— who had led Cambodia from 1979 and later seized power from his coalition partners in a coup four years after the 1993 elections—was always going to be the dominant political force in Cambodia, and that the purpose of the mission was to mollify the exercise of that power through introducing the language of human rights to Cambodian civil society, fostering the establishment of a relatively free press, and taking steps in the direction of a democratic basis for legitimate government, the mission was indeed a partial success.

Two lessons were (or should have been) learned in Cambodia. The first was to underscore the fragility of complex peace operations. Even though UNTAC was, at the time, the largest and most expensive operation in UN history, it still faced enormous difficulties in bringing about a fundamental change in the psyche of the country. Without peace and security, and without the rule of law, democratic

---

41 "Getting Ready for Statehood" *The Economist* (13 April 2002) 64.

42 See, e.g., William Branigin, "U.N. performance at issue as Cambodian vote nears" *Washington Post* (20 May 1993) A25.

43 "A UN success in Cambodia" *Washington Post*, (18 June 1993) A24.

processes may in themselves be unsustainable. Providing these foundations, if it was possible at all, would have required a more sustained commitment to remaining in Cambodia after the elections. The counterfactual is hypothetical as there was no willingness before or after the vote for UNTAC to remain beyond the completion of its mandate.

Secondly, the aftermath of the UN engagement in Cambodia—the 1997 coup, the flawed elections in 1998—began to raise questions about the relative importance of democracy. Though it may not be directly traceable to Cambodia, a shift began to occur in the rhetoric that saw "good governance" sometimes replace democracy in the peacebuilding and development jargon.[44]

Clarity about the objectives of an operation, then, may be helpful—even if it requires a retreat from the rhetoric that justifies the expenditure of resources for a peace effort. Often it will not be possible—even if it were desirable—to transform a country over the course of eighteen months into, say, Canada. Instead, perhaps the most that can be hoped for is to create the conditions in which a vulnerable population can start a conversation about what kind of country they want theirs to be.

CONCLUSION

In his book *In My Father's House*, Kwame Anthony Appiah notes that the apparent ease of colonial administration generated in some of the inheritors of postcolonial nations an illusion that control of the state would allow them to pursue as easily their much more ambitious objectives. Once the state was turned to the tasks of massive developments in infrastructure, however, it was shown wanting: "When the postcolonial rulers inherited the apparatus of the colonial state, they inherited the reins of power; few noticed, at first, that they were not attached to a bit."[45]

Given the fraught history of so many of the world's states, it is not remarkable that some states suffer basic crises in their capacity to protect and provide services for a population—on the contrary, it is remarkable that more do not. As indicated in the introduction, discussion of such institutional crises frequently suggests that, when a state "fails", power is no longer exercised within

---

[44] "Good governance" was an intentionally vague term that spoke less to the formal structures of government than how a state is governed. The term "governance" itself emerged within the development discourse in the 1990s as a means of expanding the prescriptions of donors to embrace not merely projects and structural adjustment but government policies. Though intergovernmental organizations like the World Bank and the International Monetary Fund are technically constrained from referring to political processes as such, "governance" provides a convenient euphemism for precisely that. See, e.g., Goran Hyden, "Governance and the Reconstitution of Political Order" in Richard Joseph. ed., *State, Conflict and Democracy in Africa* (Boulder, CO: Lynne Rienner, 1999) 179.

[45] Kwame Anthony Appiah, *In My Father's House: Africa in the Philosophy of Culture* (New York: Oxford University Press, 1992) at 266.

From State Failure to State-Building   175

the territory. In fact, the control of power becomes more important than ever—even though it may be exercised in an incoherent fashion.

Engagement with such states requires, first and foremost, understanding the local dynamics of power. The much-cited Weberian definition of the state as claimant to a monopoly of the legitimate use of force is less a definition of what the state *is* than what it *does*. The legitimacy and sustainability of local power structures depends, ultimately, upon local actors. Certain policies can help—channelling political power through institutions rather than individuals, and through civilians rather than the military; imposing term limits on heads of state and government; encouraging and regulating political parties—but their implementation depends on the capacity of local leaders to submit themselves to the rule of law, and local populations to hold their leaders to that standard.

For international actors, a troubling analogy is to compare engagement with weak states to previous models of trusteeship and empire. Current efforts at state-building attempt—at least in part—to reproduce the better effects of empire (inward investment, pacification, and impartial administration) without reproducing its worst features (repression, corruption, and confiscation of local capacity). This is not to suggest nostalgia for empire or that such policies should be resurrected. Only two generations ago, one-third of the world's population lived in territory considered non-self-governing; the end of colonialism was one of the most significant transformations in the international order since the emergence of sovereign states. But the analogy may be helpful if it suggests that a realistic assessment of power is necessary to formulate effective policies rather than effective rhetoric.

States cannot be made to work from the outside. International assistance may be necessary but it is never sufficient to establish institutions that are legitimate and sustainable. This is not an excuse for inaction. Action is necessary, if only to minimize the humanitarian consequences of a state's incapacity to care for its vulnerable population. Beyond that, however, international action should be seen first and foremost as facilitating local processes, providing resources and creating the space for local actors to start a conversation that will define and consolidate their polity by mediating their vision of a good life into responsive, robust, and resilient institutions.

[15]

'Security starts with the law': The role of international law in the protection of women's security post-conflict

AMY MAGUIRE

Introduction

The concept of security is often simplified and misunderstood in post-conflict societies – those in which 'predominately male combatants have ceased to engage in "official" war'.[1] During post-war transition, women's victimhood has been emphasised at the expense of careful inquiry into women's unique experiences of conflict or their security needs during the peace-building process.[2] Women's interactions with the notion of security are varied and complex, and extend far beyond a desire for an end to the 'official' war.[3] This chapter explores two questions: what are the views of women regarding the role of law in protecting their security, and to what extent is law – both international and domestic – capable of transforming approaches to women's security? These questions respond to the demand, commonly expressed by women living through post-conflict transition, for a transformation rather than a mere reinterpretation of existing socio-political structures.[4]

Meintjes, Pillay and Turshen describe transformation as distinct from reconstruction of the past. They interpret women's demands for

---

[1] Lori Handrahan, 'Conflict, gender, ethnicity and post-conflict reconstruction' (2004) 35 *Security Dialogue*, 429–45, 429

[2] Codou Bop, 'Women in conflicts, their gains and their losses' in Sheila Meintjes, Anu Pillay and Meredeth Turshen (eds.), *The Aftermath: Women in post-conflict transformation* (London: Zed Books, 2001), 19–34, 19.

[3] Brandon Hamber, Paddy Hillyard, Amy Maguire, Monica McWilliams, Gillian Robinson, David Russell and Margaret Ward, 'Discourses in transition: Re-imagining women's security' (2006) 20 *International Relations*, 487–502, 491–4.

[4] Sheila Meintjes, Anu Pillay and Meredeth Turshen, 'Introduction' in Sheila Meintjes, Anu Pillay and Meredeth Turshen (eds.), *The Aftermath: Women in post-conflict transformation* (London: Zed Books, 2001), 3–18, 4.

transformation to mean the 'substantive advancement' of women, the permanent removal of 'traditional gender restrictions' and a recasting of social and political structures to enable gender equality in post-conflict societies.[5] In the context of security, such a transformation requires the increased representation of women in peace-building roles. However, transformation also demands a new framework for security dialogue – the ongoing conversation between international, state and non-state actors engaged in the policy and practice of security in post-conflict societies. This new framework ought to ensure that women's voices are not marginalised in security dialogue,[6] explore how gender influences peoples' capacity 'to both articulate their security needs and mobilize resources to meet those security needs',[7] and compel states and other powerful actors to take seriously the positions and security needs of women in post-conflict societies.[8]

This chapter is a step in an ongoing inquiry into the role of international law in the protection of women's security post-conflict.[9] Part I explores the direct testimony of women respondents in post-conflict societies about their hopes for law and its capacity to protect women's security during transition from conflict. In Part II, I discuss two competing theoretical perspectives that may shed some light on law's capacity to protect women's security, namely the discourses of 'transitional justice' and 'law's violence'. Part III describes women-specific international laws relating to security, before considering the degree to which international

---

[5] *Ibid.*, 4–5.

[6] Gunhild Hoogensen and Svein Vigeland Rottem, 'Gender identity and the subject of security' (2004) 35 *Security Dialogue*, 155–71, 166.

[7] Beth Woroniuk, *Women's Empowerment in the Context of Human Security: A discussion paper* (Bangkok: United Nations Economic and Social Commission for Asia and the Pacific (ESCAP), 1999), 5.

[8] Anu Pillay, 'Violence against women in the aftermath' in Sheila Meintjes, Anu Pillay and Meredeth Turshen (eds.), *The Aftermath: Women in post-conflict transformation* (London: Zed Books, 2001), 35–45, 36.

[9] For contributions to this field of commentary, see Mary-Jane Fox, 'Girl soldiers: Human security and gendered insecurity' (2004) 35 *Security Dialogue*, 465–79; Heidi Hudson, '"Doing" security as though humans matter: A feminist perspective on gender and the politics of human security' (2005) 36 *Security Dialogue*, 155–74; Paul Higate and Marsha Henry, 'Engendering (in)security in peace support operations' (2004) 35 *Security Dialogue*, 481–98; and Meenakshi Gopinath and Sumona DasGupta, 'Structural challenges, enabling spaces: Gender and non-traditional formulations of security in South Asia' in Ralf Emmers, Mely Caballero-Anthony and Amitav Acharya (eds.), *Studying Non-Traditional Security in Asia: Trends and issues* (Singapore: Marshall Cavendish Academy, 2006), 192–209.

standards are reflected in the peace agreements and/or constitutions of post-conflict societies. I argue that legal efforts achieve the best outcomes for women when they are driven by women's direct participation in peace-building and their demands for social transformation.

The data used in this chapter was gathered between 2004 and 2006 through a study on 'Re-imagining women's security and participation in post-conflict societies'.[10] Research was conducted in three societies at various stages of post-conflict transition: Lebanon (before the 2006 conflict with Israel), Northern Ireland and South Africa. A concern of the study was to give women and men experiencing transition an opportunity to describe the meaning of security with reference to their own experiences. The major data-collection strategy was to convene thirty focus groups, each of which brought together women or men from a particular interest group from a wide range of social spheres.[11] In addition to the focus groups, twenty interviews were conducted with a range of prominent persons in each research site. A 'gender audit'[12] was also conducted in each site, which brought together a range of quantitative data regarding the security and participation of women.

The data considered in this chapter is drawn from focus groups conducted with women in each of the research sites. It was selected by searching across each of the focus groups for transcripts that discuss in detail law's role in the promotion of women's security. The data represents a cross-section of perspectives on the role of law in protecting security. The wide range of the women's responses indicates both the breadth of women's security concerns and the challenge of defining law's role in addressing them.

Two frameworks dominate the global discussion of security: 'state security' discourse and 'human security' discourse.[13] The former is an institutionalised approach that focuses on the protection of state borders[14]

---

[10] Funded by UK Economic and Social Research Council Award RES 223-25-0066.

[11] These groups included people in economic reconstruction, NGOs, political parties, ex-combatants, victims and campaigners.

[12] Audits are methods of quantitative data analysis in which statistics are compiled to support the qualitative and quantitative data gathered through empirical research. This method was used in this research and termed a 'gender audit' as it canvassed the representation and roles of women and men in a range of areas relevant to security, including governance, cultural, political, economic and constitutional issues.

[13] For further discussion, see Hamber et al., 'Discourses in transition', 489–91.

[14] Sverre Lodgaard, *Human Security: Concept and operationalization* (Oslo: Norwegian Institute of International Affairs, 2000), 2.

and defines security as the absence of violent conflict.[15] State-security discourse tends to be hierarchical and patriarchal, and particularly ill-suited to addressing the security needs of women in post-conflict environments.[16] As Eric Blanchard notes:

> Statesmen, diplomats, and the military conduct the business of states, and too often war, imbuing the relations and processes of the society of nation-states with an atmosphere seemingly devoid of women and an interest in issues of concern to women.[17]

In contrast, the idea of human security identifies the person, rather than the state, as the primary referent of security policy.[18] This approach recognises that security is a holistic concept encompassing seven inter-related areas – economic, food, health, environmental, personal, community and political – and aims to ensure both 'freedom from want' and 'freedom from fear'.[19] Human security has become a powerful notion within the peace-building work of the United Nations, and the United Nations Development Programme has published annual Human Development Reports since 1990, each of which reflects on the notion of human security. Alongside the freedoms from fear and want, more recent human-security discourse also emphasises the importance of giving people the 'freedom to live in dignity'.[20] As promoted in the international arena by the UN,

---

[15] According to Hans Morgenthau, the state's role in protecting its security is to struggle for power: 'The statesman must think in terms of the national interest, conceived as power among other powers': Hans Morgenthau and Kenneth W. Thompson, *Politics Among Nations: The struggle for power and peace*, 6th edn (New York: McGraw Hill, 1985), 165.

[16] Hoogensen and Rottem, 'Gender identity and the subject of security', 158; Edward Newman, 'Human security and constructivism' (2001) 2 *International Studies Perspectives*, 239–51, 240.

[17] Eric M. Blanchard, 'Gender, international relations, and the development of feminist security theory' (2003) 28 *Signs: Journal of Women in Culture and Society*, 1289–312, 1289.

[18] Newman, 'Human security and constructivism', 239. For other commentary on human security discourse, see, e.g., Sabina Alkire, *A Conceptual Framework for Human Security* (Oxford: Centre for Research on Inequality, Human Security and Ethnicity, Working Paper 2, 2003); Rob McRae and Don Hubert (eds.), *Human Security and the New Diplomacy: Protecting people, promoting peace* (Montreal: McGill-Queen's University Press, 2001); Ramesh Thakur, 'The UN and human security' (1999) 7 *Canadian Foreign Policy*, 51–9.

[19] United Nations Development Programme, *Human Development Report 1994* (New York: United Nations, 1994), 24.

[20] UN Doc. A/59/2005 (21 March 2005) In larger freedom: Towards development, security and human rights for all: Report of the secretary-general, 34.

222 ROLE OF INTERNATIONAL LAW IN REBUILDING SOCIETIES

human-security discourse aims to empower people through security policies to which they freely contribute.[21]

Women respondents to the study described security in a way that is consistent with the human-security literature. They did not project a utopian image of what security could be in the post-conflict environment, but rather recognised a wide range of practical measures that could be taken to reinforce women's security at all levels of social life.[22] The following exchange between three South African women illustrates this understanding of security as a holistic concept:

R1:   ... when I think of security the first thing that comes to mind is safety. I think of safety and especially as far as women are concerned ... you look at the figures in our country of the high rate of rape ...

R2:   ... in addition I think it's the issue of education and jobs. That women need to have skills, need to be educated in order to secure jobs, in order to have safe living areas and all those types of things ...

R3:   I think as well, I suppose in a South African context especially, when you refer to economic security it is commonly referred to as independence, especially in relation to women. Being financially independent, that comes with a lot of security, and just the freedom and will to do as you wish and when you want to, because you have that economic security.

(South Africa, women in economic reconstruction)

Since the 1990s, the human-security approach has gained prominence in security dialogue and is increasingly informing international legal approaches to problems of security policy.[23] This is a positive development as women's layered and complex conceptions of security are better incorporated by the human-security approach than by the traditional state-security discourse. The strong support for the growth of human-security discourse internationally, especially within the UN and civil society, encourages states to acknowledge those who have been made insecure by statist notions of security and move to address these human insecurities.[24]

---

[21] Commission on Human Security, *Human Security Now* (New York: Commission on Human Security, 2003), 6.

[22] For further discussion of this process of reimagining, see Hamber et al., 'Discourses in transition', 487–502.

[23] See for example SC Res. 1325 (31 October 2000); UN Doc. S/2002/1154 (16 October 2002) Report of the secretary-general on women, peace and security.

[24] Katrina Lee Koo, 'Confronting a disciplinary blindness: Women, war and rape in the international politics of security' (2002) 37 *Australian Journal of Political Science*, 525–36, 535.

A particularly important contemporary development is the 'gendered' security approach to human-security discourse. This approach recognises that human security carries significant potential as a counter-balance to the dominance of state concerns in security dialogue, but argues that the notion of human security is insufficiently conscious of the gendered aspects of security policy and provision. Indeed, human-security discourse has marginalised both women's inequalities as subjects of security[25] and women's capacities to make distinctive contributions to peace-building.[26] Gopinath and DasGupta describe the 'engenderment' of security thus:

> 'Engendering' security goes significantly beyond mainstreaming. It attempts to construct an alternative discourse, resocializing men and women into a qualitatively nuanced understanding of security ... shifting priorities from threat perceptions and deterrence vocabularies to a language that cognizes 'structural challenges' and 'enabling spaces'.[27]

A gendered security approach argues that women's security must be made a central concern of contemporary security discourse. Gopinath and DasGupta point out, however, that this does not mean the 'main-streaming' of gender into an existing and male-dominated security dialogue. Nor can it be achieved simply through increasing the representation of women in a patriarchal arena. Instead, the gendered security approach aims to empower women to participate in, and indeed drive, a process of transforming their post-conflict societies. For this to occur, structural challenges – inbuilt societal inequalities between men and women – must be recognised and addressed. One means by which this may be achieved is through opening 'enabling spaces' and empowering women in post-conflict societies to express both their unique experiences of conflict and their particular security needs during transition and beyond. This chapter is one small 'enabling space' in which women's views of security during transition are explored.

I. Women's voices in post-conflict societies

In this part, I consider a range of women's perspectives on law's role in promoting their security during post-conflict transition. The testimonies are a selection from the focus groups conducted with women in Lebanon,

---

[25] Woroniuk, *Women's Empowerment in the Context of Human Security*, 4.
[26] Betty A. Reardon, *Women and Peace: Feminist visions of global security* (Albany: State University of New York Press, 1993), 141.
[27] Gopinath and DasGupta, 'Structural challenges, enabling spaces', 206.

224 ROLE OF INTERNATIONAL LAW IN REBUILDING SOCIETIES

Northern Ireland and South Africa. Five themes emerged through the analysis of women's responses in relation to law's role in protecting women's security, and each of these themes is sketched here.

A. The role of law in the protection of security

Several respondents, particularly in Lebanon, attributed a powerful role to law in the post-conflict period:

> Specifically, the primary role of laws is to ensure security for human beings.
>
> > (Lebanon, women in NGOs).

> For me [security] would be that a woman lives in a society that assumes she should be protected in some way.
>
> > (Northern Ireland, women in NGOs).

> *Security starts with the law* ... I think that when there is a law that protects me ... when you know there is a law that punishes the offender, violence stops in the home ... So, in my opinion, the law is a necessary condition for one to feel secure.
>
> > (Lebanon, women ex-combatants (emphasis added)).

Through such comments, women respondents identified law as a powerful, possibly the most powerful, force in transitional societies. In such a conception, law sets the example for society and reflects the values which that society seeks to entrench in all fields of life. As discussed below in Part III, the wide range of women-specific rights-protections in international law support the demands of some women that law take on a transformative role in promoting their security during post-conflict transition. It is also interesting that women in Lebanon – which, of the three research sites, provides the least legal protection for women's rights and security – were most likely to attribute to law a capacity to bring about radical change in security policy and practice.

B. The constitutive force of law in post-conflict society

For some women respondents, again particularly in Lebanon, the logical consequence of the positive roles they ascribed to law in the context of security was their recognition of law's constitutive potential. Comments in this context asserted that law has the power to establish new frameworks to replace established orders, thus providing powerful advocacy tools and helping to promote social transformation:

> As an activist, as a lawyer, I cannot change anything unless I have the law on my side. In order to be able to change the mentality, I have to change the law in order to have a framework to guide this change.
>
> (Lebanon, women in NGOs)

> Unless the laws are amended to protect women, how do you expect the women to start claiming their rights? On what basis do you expect them to take action unless they have the means to protect themselves? The laws are the tools which women need to start the change and put an end to abuse.
>
> (Lebanon, women in political parties)

It appears that the heightened degree of state-sanctioned sex discrimination and ongoing social conflict experienced by Lebanese women made them more likely than other participants in this research to attribute constitutive potential to law. For women with direct experience of discriminatory laws, the contrasts between those laws and laws that aim to protect women's security are compelling.

C. Failures of implementation and the limits of law's power

One area in which there was significant commonality across the research sites was in relation to the gap between legal measures and their implementation. Women in each of the three research sites reflected upon the prevailing patriarchy and discriminatory attitudes as key limitations on law's power to protect their security. In this context, however, women tended to advocate for law reform accompanied by attitudinal change, rather than an abandonment of legal advocacy:

> We have to ... change the whole of our society and actually organise it so that it suits us just as well as men ... Having legislation, rules and laws, they do help ... but if it is begrudgingly and there is a ... resentment that you should be protected by law, it's going to be given as a shake of the hand you know, and women know that very quickly.
>
> (Northern Ireland, pilot group)

> ... I think no matter how much laws change, unless the outlook changes, there will always be shrewd lawyers who would manipulate the laws and the woman will keep losing. I say this because we have seen several instances where the law has been amended, however the implementation of these laws ... let us take for example the testimony of women in real estates, [by law women's testimony in real estate is valid] yet you still find many people who insist to fetch two men instead of one woman to testify.
>
> (Lebanon, women in NGOs)

Women respondents commented upon the failure of law to make a real difference to their security during transition if there is an absence of political will:

> I think it's a lack of implementation, because if the laws are there, I mean what else is left except to put them into practice. It's good and fine to have all these laws. I mean you can take them to Lebanon and say 'here, we have our nice laws', but in actual fact what is happening back there?
>
> (South Africa, women in economic reconstruction)

The recurrence in this research of the three themes identified above reflects the strong sense among women that law can be used to achieve dramatic change in their security situations if it is well intentioned, well designed and thoroughly implemented. However, the remaining two themes to emerge from women's views on the role of law in protecting security demonstrate respondents' awareness of the negative potential of law.

D. Legal silences

Beyond the limitations of law imposed by failings of implementation lie actual legal silences or spaces in which many women respondents argued law ought to intervene to protect their security. For example:

> At work, young women feel insecure, especially those who are not highly qualified … They are the ones who are the most subjected to sexual harassment and there are no laws to protect them. Whenever we, the League of Working Women, approach officials regarding passing a law to protect women against sexual harassment we are laughed at and all we get are sarcastic answers.
>
> (Lebanon, women in NGOs)

Such legal silences occur not only in areas where the law has failed to intervene, but also through laws which fail to properly consider the impact of law on social relations:

> I think, in as much as the law of the country allows women to be empowered, that is going to have a spin-off effect on men's behaviour and men's attitudes towards women. In particular, those so-called empowered women. They'll always be subject of abuse … everywhere you go … I am not only referring to perhaps males who they have relationships with, their husbands and partners; even complete strangers … if you are perceived to be an empowered woman you are subject to a lot of abuse from society in general.
>
> (South Africa, women in economic reconstruction)

Some women respondents asserted that legal silences are created or entrenched by the marginalisation of women from lawmaking and security policy development:

> Most of the ... laws, which were put in place – women were not involved in those laws. We were not there; we were forgotten altogether.
>
> (South Africa, women victims)

Legal silences can actually increase the degree of fear faced by women in post-conflict societies, as is revealed by the following comment:

> During the war, there was shelling and bombs were falling on our heads. We did not think about the rule of law and things like this. When Ta'if came, it failed to bring about the rule of law, so now I feel more afraid than before.
>
> (Lebanon, women victims)

This reflection on the relationship between law and security highlights the conflict between law's potential to promote justice and security during transition, and the potential violence of law, to be discussed in Part II. It is clear that women identify a parallel between their own absence from security policymaking and practice, and the legal silences that inhibit their security. However it is not only women themselves who are marginalised from security dialogue – legal silences are also created when women's contextualised conceptions of their security needs are not given space to inform policy or practice.

E. Violent laws

A final theme to emerge across all the research sites was the inhibiting effect that overtly violent laws have on women's security. These laws, as described by women respondents, do violence in a range of ways, for example by entrenching harsh discriminatory practices against women, by failing to protect women from physical violence or by making women subject to structural inequalities. Women shared a concern that laws that discriminate against women mirror the broader patriarchy against which women battle for equality:

> In my opinion the patriarchal system prevails in all aspects of life. It regulates the lives of all social classes and religious groups. This reality is revealed and reinforced in the laws. All laws clearly instruct women to be submissive and passive.
>
> (Lebanon, women in NGOs)

228 ROLE OF INTERNATIONAL LAW IN REBUILDING SOCIETIES

> I still think [violence against women] is not addressed and you still hear
> of people charged with rape getting six months' suspended sentences ...
> We get messages all the time that crimes against the female body aren't
> really that important.
>
> (Northern Ireland, pilot group)

Even where positive laws are developed to enhance women's security, the
problem of patriarchy can limit their potential, as one woman made clear:

> But there are still men ... [inaudible] ... they don't fear the law.
>
> (South Africa, women political campaigners)

Lebanese respondents repeatedly referred to law's violence with regard
to 'personal status' laws. Although the 1989 Ta'if amendments to the
constitution refer to the eventual aim of abolishing political confession-
alism, all Lebanese remain subject to personal-status laws that regulate
their personal lives differently according to their religious denomination/
ethnicity.[28] For example, separate codes and court systems regulate the
age of consent, marriage, custody and citizenship disputes according to
a Lebanese person's ethnic or religious identity.[29] Lebanese women's
testimonies in relation to these laws identify the need not only to develop
positive law but to do away with violent law:

> You cannot imagine the extent of violence imposed on women as a result
> of implementing these laws which discriminate against them to a great
> extent. I am currently working on improving the laws that regulate the
> issue of custody. I keep meeting women, receiving complaints from
> women; you cannot imagine the extent of violence they are being subject
> to. Can you imagine the suffering of a woman when they take away her
> son who is barely one year and a half old? Another woman – the father
> who does not know his son, he had not seen him for six years, and yet he
> comes forward insisting to take him from her.
>
> (Lebanon, women in NGOs)

> ... our laws are still far from establishing equality between men and
> women when it comes to nationality, crime, punishment.
>
> (Lebanon, women in public life)

[28] Constitution of the Republic of Lebanon 1926, preamble (h); 'Ta'if Accord' (22 October
1989) (also known as the 'National Reconciliation Accord' or 'Document of National
Accord'); Mona Chemali Khalaf, 'Re-imagining women's security: A comparative study
of Lebanon, Northern Ireland and South Africa – Draft Lebanon Gender Audit', 2005.

[29] See the following Lebanese legislation: Ottoman Law of Family Rights 1917; Codified
(Druze) Personal Status Law 1948; Law on the Rights of the Family 1962; Law on
Organisation of the Sharia Courts 1962.

One Lebanese woman argued that law's capacity to achieve social trans-formation was fundamentally weakened by government acceptance of religious laws that regulate women's lives and status. Nevertheless, for this woman, despite the violence done by personal status codes, law is not stripped of its constitutive potential:

> It is the duty of the government to pass these laws. Christianity or Islam should not be blamed. We should blame the government in the case of gender-based violence. There is no solution but to resort to the power of the law.
>
> (Lebanon, women in political parties)

One unifying thread across the five themes discussed above is that women in general regarded law as having a significant potential role in the protection of their security. Respondents demanded that law do more to protect women's security and the security of their families, commu-nities and societies as a whole. By revealing their negative experiences of law's power, however, women also demonstrated their awareness and concern that laws that do not centralise women's security concerns are capable of doing women further violence beyond the conflict experi-ence. In the following section I discuss two perspectives that theorise law's capacity to bring about social change in very different ways. Elements of each theory could assist in developing legal approaches to security that are better adapted to meeting women's security needs.

II. Theoretical perspectives

A. The role of law in transitional-justice theory

'Transitions', Teitel states, 'imply paradigm shifts in the conception of justice.'[30] The study of 'transitional justice', then, constitutes a useful means of understanding how societies emerge from violent conflict towards long-term peace. Theories of transitional justice recognise that the legitimacy of law is generally weakened during conflict, suggesting that in the transitional period law must become both the subject and object of change,[31] renewing itself and playing a role in societal renewal.[32] Such

---

[30] Ruti G. Teitel, *Transitional Justice* (Oxford: Oxford University Press, 2000), 6.
[31] Christine Bell, Colm Campbell and Fionnuala Ní Aoláin, 'Justice discourses in transi-tion' (2004) 13 *Social and Legal Studies*, 305–28, 309.
[32] Colm Campbell, Fionnuala Ní Aoláin and Colin Harvey, 'The frontiers of legal analysis: Reframing the transition in Northern Ireland' (2003) 66 *Modern Law Review*, 317–45, 334.

theories favour a strong focus on the capacity of law to contribute to societal transformations. It is argued:

> law in transitional societies has to engage with the imperatives of moving between radically different political contexts. The need to compensate for domestic rule of law 'gaps', coupled with internationally imposed impera-tives, means that international law typically forms a heightened and important legal reference point during transition by virtue of its extern-ality to the parties to the conflict.[33]

By focusing on the role of law, transitional-justice theories offer a means of analysing the efficacy of peace agreements, constitutions and other transitional legal mechanisms. Such analyses recognise that these legal mechanisms are structured by the paradoxical role law plays during transition, simultaneously guiding processes of legitimation of state institutions and of gradual change across the transitional society.[34] An example of such a legal intervention is the 1998 Good Friday Agreement which is constitutive of the ongoing peace process in Northern Ireland.[35]

Transitional-justice theories identify law's transitional role as one of *transformation* rather than *reformation*.[36] This requires that legal and political institutions in transitional societies be evaluated to account for their role in creating the justice gaps that led to or perpetuated conflict. For justice to develop, social institutions must be transformed in aware-ness of the expressed needs of all people, rather than reformed to reflect old patterns and structural inequalities. This claim parallels women's demands for social transformation in the post-conflict environment.

Transitional-justice theories, however, contain some gaps of their own. First, these theories have not yet paid sufficient attention to women's experiences of conflict and transition. For example, it is clear that processes of negotiation and decision-making during transition remain dominated by men, marginalising women's experiences of the 'continuum' of violence.[37] A lack of direct engagement with the gendered aspects of transition weakens the transformative potential of legal analyses driven by transitional-justice theory. Second, the theories also face the challenge

---

[33] Bell, Campbell and Ní Aoláin, 'Justice discourses in transition', 308.

[34] Teitel, *Transitional Justice*, 223.

[35] 'Good Friday Agreement' (10 April 1998) (also known as the 'Belfast Agreement').

[36] Campbell, Ní Aoláin, and Harvey, 'The frontiers of legal analysis', 336.

[37] Bell, Campbell and Ní Aoláin, 'Justice discourses in transition', 321. See also Christine Bell, 'Women address the problems of peace agreements' in Radhika Coomaraswamy and Dilrukshi Fonseka (eds.), *Peace Work: Women, armed conflict and negotiation* (New Delhi: Women Unlimited, 2004), 96–126.

of maintaining analytical and problem-solving roles in the altered global political context post-September 11, 2001. Current United States uni-lateralism in security policy, as typified by the 'war on terror', threatens the capacity of international law to bind states. In turn, changes in global political attitudes to security policy threaten the human-rights body of law within the international law framework, weakening the influence of transitional justice arguments.[38]

Teitel notes that, in the contemporary global political climate, transitional justice has come to focus more heavily on peace and stability than on the larger goals of democracy and the rule of law.[39] This is a troubling development in the context of women's security, considering that women's demands for transformation during transition require an approach that recognises that security operates on several levels, not simply the cessation of conflict. If transitional-justice approaches are to properly address women's unique security needs, they must address not only formal peace-building processes, but also incorporate the holistic and multi-layered conceptions of security that women express during transition.

B. Theory of 'law's violence'

One means by which transitional justice theories may better address women's security needs is through acknowledging the capacity of law to do violence as well as justice. Since Robert Cover's work in the 1980s,[40] a critique of law has developed that asserts that law functions in relationship to violence. Austin Sarat describes a 'violence of law' perspective in the following terms:

> Law depends on violence and uses it as a counterpunch to the allegedly more lethal and destructive violence situated just beyond law's boundaries.

---

[38] Several prominent theorists of transitional justice have noted the potential stifling impact of US 'exceptionalism' on transitional justice approaches: Martti Koskenniemi, 'Between impunity and show trials' (2002) 6 *Max Planck Yearbook of United Nations Law*, 1–32; Ruti G. Teitel, 'Transitional justice genealogy' (2003) 16 *Harvard Human Rights Journal*, 69–94; Christine Bell and Catherine O'Rourke, 'Does feminism need a theory of transitional justice? An introductory essay' (2007) 1 *International Journal of Transitional Justice*, 23–44, 24.

[39] Ruti G. Teitel, 'Transitional justice in a new era' (2003) 26 *Fordham International Law Journal*, 893–906, 898.

[40] Robert M. Cover, 'The Supreme Court 1982 Term – Foreword: NOMOS and narrative' (1983) 97 *Harvard Law Review*, 4–68; Robert M. Cover, 'Violence and the word' (1986) 95 *Yale Law Journal*, 1601–29.

> But the violence on which law depends always threatens the values for
> which law stands … Moreover the pain that these acts produce is every-
> where, in the drama of law's sporadic vengeance as well as in the ordinary
> lives of those subject to legal regulation.[41]

As women made clear in response to the study on which this chapter
is based, a wide range of forms of violence threaten their security in the
post-conflict period.[42] There was agreement across each of the research
sites, and particularly among Lebanese women respondents, that laws
continue to inflict violence upon women.

The relationship between law and violence raises an important question: if there is a link between law and justice (this being a fundamental
proposition of transitional-justice theory), must there also be a link
between law's violence and its capacity to attain justice?[43] The women's
responses set out above indicate a complex interrelationship between
law, justice and violence in the post-conflict period. For example, many
of the Lebanese respondents who condemned laws that do violence
through discrimination or social repression also demanded that the
state employ law to achieve justice and security during transition. This
relationship between law, justice and violence is a significant one in the
context of legal efforts to protect women's security during transition,
although it has not yet been investigated. The complexity of the relationship may be one reason why most approaches to the provision of security
during transition have failed to interrogate law's dual power to bring
about justice and to inflict violence. I argue, however, that legal
approaches to the protection of women's security would be enhanced
by a consideration of the theories of transitional justice and law's violence in a complementary fashion. In practice, this requires security
approaches that confirm law's transformative potential, whilst tempering
the ambition of transitional-justice theory with the recognition that laws
can inflict violence upon women. A crucial step towards developing this
approach is to listen to women's views on how to reform laws in order to
protect security. Also important is the recognition that no one theory –
whether transitional justice, human security or otherwise – ought to

---

[41] Austin Sarat, 'Situating law between the realities of violence and the claims of justice: An
introduction' in Austin Sarat (ed.), *Law, Violence, and the Possibility of Justice*
(Princeton: Princeton University Press, 2001), 3–16, 3.

[42] See Hamber et al., 'Discourses in transition', 487–502.

[43] Sarat, 'Situating law', 3; Alisa Rosenthal, 'Law, violence, and the possibility of justice –
Book review' (2002) 12 *Law and Politics Book Review*, 339–42, 339.

usurp what Bell and O'Rourke describe as the 'larger political project of securing substantial material gains for women in transition'.[44]

III. Women-specific laws

In this part, I introduce women-specific laws that relate to security at both the international and domestic levels. Some of these legal measures, particularly at the international level, reflect transitional-justice approaches and emphasise the transformative power of law. However, other international and domestic legal instruments reflect the complexity of the relationship between law, justice and violence.

A. International law, women's rights, and women's security

The early period of international lawmaking in the human-rights field was characterised by a strong focus on what are frequently termed 'first generation' rights: civil and political rights. Measures in this area are important in the establishment of a baseline of political participation. In 1952 the UN General Assembly adopted the first international-law mechanism directed specifically towards protecting the rights of women, the Convention on the Political Rights of Women.[45] Through this Convention, women's equal rights to vote, stand for election, and hold public office are confirmed. The preamble to the UN General Assembly Resolution adopting the Convention expresses a transitional-justice-style faith in the transformative potential of law:

> *Believing* that an international convention on the political rights of women will constitute *an important step towards* the universal attainment of equal rights of men and women.[46]

By 1974, when the Declaration on the Protection of Women and Children in Emergency and Armed Conflict was adopted,[47] the international law of human rights had developed to emphasise economic, social, cultural and collective rights.[48] This was a major development in relation to women's security, as it broadened the focus of rights discourse

---

[44] Bell and O'Rourke, 'Does feminism need a theory of transitional justice?', 44.

[45] Opened for signature 20 December 1952, 193 UNTS 135 (entered into force 7 July 1954).

[46] GA Res. 7/640 (20 December 1952), preamble (emphasis added).

[47] GA Res. 29/3318 (14 December 1974).

[48] See, e.g., International Covenant on Economic, Social and Cultural Rights, opened for signature 16 December 1966, 993 UNTS 3 (entered into force 3 January 1967).

234 ROLE OF INTERNATIONAL LAW IN REBUILDING SOCIETIES

to include the wide range of areas which women identify as essential to security.[49] The 1974 Declaration reveals an important shift in focus towards the range of insecurities faced by women, and the myriad forms of intervention open to international law in relation to women's security. It reflects the concerns of international humanitarian law, with specific focus on women and children, for example by emphasising the prohibition on attacking civilian targets, employing chemical warfare and denying aid and shelter to non-combatants. The Declaration is more closely aligned with the human-security approach than earlier legal interventions, in the sense that it recognises that security is a layered concept which does not involve simply freedom from conflict.

Some aspects of the Declaration, however, indicate that international law-making of the time was still not adequately informed by women's advocacy and experiences. First, the language contains patronising elements, particularly its references to '*defenceless* women and children'.[50] In this sense, not only are women denied a degree of agency, but they are categorised alongside children, which arguably further emphasises their disempowerment. Second, there are no explicit references to sexual violence against women during conflict, despite the overwhelming weight of evidence pointing to sexual violence being one of the most confronting, common and damaging conflict experiences for women.[51] The Declaration reflects the complex interaction between law, justice and violence which was highlighted by the women's voices recorded earlier in this chapter.

In contrast, by the time the Convention on the Elimination of All Forms of Discrimination against Women (CEDAW) was adopted in 1979,[52] women's advocacy and voices had become more powerful within international lawmaking processes.[53] CEDAW was developed in response to the recognition that, despite the existence and broad acceptance of international human-rights mechanisms promoting the equality of men and women, extensive discrimination against women continued to exist.[54] A Bill of Rights for Women was required to stand alongside the

---

[49] Hamber et al., 'Discourses in transition', 491–4.
[50] GA Res. 29/3318 (14 December 1974) Declaration on the Protection of Women and Children in Emergency and Armed Conflict, Art. 2 (emphasis added).
[51] Lee Koo, 'Confronting a disciplinary blindness', 528, 531.
[52] Opened for signature 18 December 1979, 1249 UNTS 13 (entered into force 3 September 1981).
[53] Elizabeth Evatt, 'Finding a voice for women's rights: The early days of CEDAW' (2002) 34 *George Washington International Law Review*, 515–53, 515–17.
[54] Arvonne S. Fraser, 'Becoming human: The origins and development of women's human rights' (1999) 21 *Human Rights Quarterly*, 853–906, 890.

International Bill of Rights, to define and develop the notions of equality and non-discrimination. Significantly in the context of this study of women's security and participation in post-conflict societies, Art. 2 of the Convention enshrines the agreement of state parties to embody gender equality in their constitutions or other legislation, to use law to prohibit discrimination against women, to take all steps to eliminate discrimination against women, and to reform domestic law to ensure that no provisions discriminate against women.

Through Art. 2 of the Convention, the international community endorsed the idea that law can bring about significant change in relation to women's rights and security, so long as legal standards are effectively implemented at the domestic level. Many women, particularly those familiar with the experience of conflict and its accompanying insecurities, have used this provision as a benchmark to measure against domestic laws and institutions. Legal silences that fail to protect women's security are revealed by the examples of national constitutions that do not measure up to international standards, some of which will be considered below.

One area particularly relevant to security with which international law has engaged is the elimination of violence against women. In December 1993, the General Assembly adopted the Declaration on the Elimination of Violence against Women, which recognises violence as one of the central obstacles in the path of ensuring women's equality, security and participation.[55] This instrument condemns all forms of gender-based violence, and requires states to protect women from such violence, no matter the motivation or perpetrator (Art. 4). This is an important adoption of the human-security approach, in that it recognises that women's experiences of violence are not confined to conflict experiences, and that women's intimate partners are often responsible for inflicting violence upon them. The Declaration is also significant in terms of the role it envisages for international agencies in the elimination of violence and discrimination against women. However, the Declaration is a document of 'soft' law and it has been criticised for being too modest in its language and goals, for example by failing to acknowledge violence against women as a human-rights violation, thus situating this harm on a lesser plane than other rights violations.[56]

---

[55] GA Res. 48/104 (20 December 1993).
[56] Hilary Charlesworth, 'Human rights as men's rights' in Julie Peters and Andrea Wolper (eds.), *Women's Rights, Human Rights: International feminist perspectives* (New York: Routledge, 1995), 103–13, 108.

236 ROLE OF INTERNATIONAL LAW IN REBUILDING SOCIETIES

The 1993 Declaration was a precursor to what is now frequently described as one of the central legal mechanisms in the promotion of women's rights and security,[57] UN Security Council Resolution 1325 (2000) on women and peace-building.[58] Resolution 1325 reflects the persuasive power of women's advocacy in the international arena. Indeed, it was largely through the efforts of women in the international forum, notably through the Women's International League for Peace and Freedom and International Alert, that this resolution was passed.[59] Through its emphasis on the need for women to be equally involved in peacemaking and peace-building, the resolution recognises that women-focused mechanisms are made meaningful and useful only through women's involvement and engagement at all levels of policymaking and lawmaking. In his first report on progress following Resolution 1325, then UN Secretary-General Kofi Annan asserted that women's full engagement in peace processes was essential to 'build the founda-tions for enduring peace development, good governance, human rights and justice'.[60]

Resolution 1325 has been welcomed due to the importance it places on the participation of women in security dialogue, yet it paints an inadequate picture of women's security needs. The language of the resolution implies that women's participation in security policymaking and lawmaking will result in vastly improved outcomes, without acknowledging that increasing women's representation is only part of the problem. As is clear from the women's voices explored earlier in this chapter, security dialogue must also consider how to acknowledge and address women's particularised security needs. Charlesworth argues that Resolution 1325 would have achieved greater clarity on the sig-nificance of 'gender' during post-conflict transition if it had considered

---

[57] Carol Cohn, Helen Kinsella and Sheri Gibbings, 'Women, peace and security: Resolution 1325' (2004) 6 *International Feminist Journal of Politics*, 130–40, 130; Victoria Brittain, 'The impact of war on women' (2003) 44(4) *Race and Class*, 41–51, 41–2.

[58] SC Res. 1325 (31 October 2000).

[59] Felicity Hill, Mikele Aboitiz and Sara Poehlman-Doumbouya, 'Nongovernmental organ-izations' role in the buildup and implementation of security council resolution 1325' (2003) 28 *Signs: Journal of Women in Culture and Society*, 1255–69.

[60] Kofi Annan, *Women, Peace and Security: Study submitted by the secretary-general pursuant to Security Council Resolution 1325 (2000)* (New York: United Nations, 2002), ix. See also UN Doc. S/2002/1154 (16 October 2002) Report of the secretary-general on women, peace and security; UN Doc. S/2004/814 (13 October 2004) Women and peace and security: Report of the secretary-general.

the relationship between women's security needs and men's identities during and after conflict.[61] Instead, the resolution reflects the notion of 'mainstreaming' rather than the notion of 'engenderment'. Whereas mainstreaming advocates the consideration of 'women's issues' in the mainstream security discourse, the engenderment of that discourse goes beyond this to construct spaces in which women's and men's unique experiences and perspectives are explored and allowed to generate 'bottom-up' solutions to security problems. To return to Gopinath and DasGupta's argument, this process requires participants in security dialogue to confront structural challenges and open up enabling spaces.[62]

This survey of the women-specific international laws that relate to security demonstrates the complexity of the relationship between law, justice and violence, in the sense that even the more progressive legal instruments suffer from legal silences that prevent them from adequately addressing women's experiences of conflict and transition. It is clear from the responses to this study that women demand equal participation in lawmaking and security policy. International law is increasingly responding to that demand, by seeking to encourage women's participation and by exploring a wider range of women's insecurities. However, women's calls for social transformation in the post-conflict period warrant a more integrated approach to women's security than has been evident to date in international law. Such an approach would require recognition that women's and men's roles and experiences during conflict have significance for their experience during transition.[63] It also demands legal instruments that address women's security as a concept comprising more than the absence of violent conflict, and including, for example, the significance of financial security, women's experiences of violence during transition and the need to empower women's participation in the institutions of transition.[64] An integrated approach might also explore ways of encouraging transitional states to include international law and other standards in domestic peace agreements and constitutions.

---

[61] Hilary Charlesworth, 'Not waving but drowning: Gender mainstreaming and human rights in the United Nations' (2005) 18 *Harvard Human Rights Journal*, 1–18, 15.

[62] Gopinath and DasGupta, 'Structural challenges, enabling spaces', 207.

[63] Brandon Hamber, 'Masculinity and transitional justice: An exploratory essay' (2007) 1 *International Journal of Transitional Justice*, 375–90, 384.

[64] Hamber et al., 'Discourses in transition', 498–500.

238 ROLE OF INTERNATIONAL LAW IN REBUILDING SOCIETIES

B. Domestic peace agreements/constitutions and the protection of women's security

The peace agreements and/or constitutions of Lebanon, Northern Ireland and South Africa indicate that the implementation of international standards remains inadequate and haphazard in the domestic laws of post-conflict societies. The peace agreements/constitutions of these three transitional societies display varying degrees of commitment to the standards of equality, participation and security for women that are set out in international law, and reflect an ambivalence towards international law.[65]

i. Lebanon

The Lebanese constitution, as amended by the 1989 Ta'if Accord,[66] contains two brief equality provisions:

> Preamble
> c. Lebanon is a parliamentary democratic republic based on respect for public liberties, especially the freedom of opinion and belief, and respect for social justice and equality of rights and duties among all citizens without discrimination.

> Article 7 (Equality)
> All Lebanese are equal before the law. They equally enjoy civil and political rights and equally are bound by public obligations and duties without any distinction.

The constitution does not make any mention of gender equality or discrimination against women. Focus groups conducted with women in Lebanon revealed a low degree of faith in the capacity of the Ta'if Peace Agreement to promote women's equality, security and participation. Many Lebanese women argued that gains made by women in the post-conflict period were due to women's direct advocacy, and that the absence of women in the text of the Peace Agreement reflected their lack of status more broadly:

> Now it is mere coincidence that women's achievements, as far as their status and rights are concerned, happened following Ta'if, but they are not in any way an outcome of the Accord.
>
> (Lebanon, women ex-combatants)

---

[65] Bell, Campbell and Ní Aoláin, 'Justice discourses in transition', 308.
[66] Constitution of the Republic of Lebanon 1926; 'Ta'if Accord' (22 October 1989).

Lebanon's constitution does not implement the range of international standards that would provide women with a broad complement of advocacy tools at the domestic level. Indeed, Lebanon's initial and second reports to the Committee on the Elimination of Discrimination against Women, presented in 2004–5, note the reservations Lebanon placed on its ratification of CEDAW,[67] and recognise that women are actively discriminated against through Lebanese law in terms of honour crimes, adultery, abortion, assault on honour and prostitution.[68] In other words, the Lebanese state admits its failure to abolish discriminatory laws, and implicitly recognises that its own laws do violence to women.

ii. Northern Ireland

The 1998 Good Friday Agreement, a hybrid peace agreement and constitution, is more explicit in terms of women's equality than parallel Lebanese measures, an outcome that is largely attributable to the interventions of the Northern Ireland Women's Coalition in pre-agreement negotiations. The Agreement confirms 'the right of women to full and equal political participation'.[69] The Agreement also affirms equal opportunity of men and women in relation to all social and economic activity, and establishes a foundation for legislation requiring all public bodies to ensure equal opportunity on gender terms. The Agreement was the first step in the creation of the Equality Commission, an equal opportunity monitoring body.

Nevertheless, the Agreement does not directly address women's security needs. For example, the provisions relating to 'victims' do not consider women's unique experiences of the conflict, but rather focus on the experiences of the ethno-religious communities involved.[70] Furthermore, the provisions that reconfigure the police service set a quota for Catholic membership, but do not propose equivalent measures to address the under-representation of women.[71] Women's responses to the Agreement and its capacity to advance their situations are mixed:

[67] The Lebanese Government has entered reservations regarding Arts. 9(2), 16(1)(c), (d), (f), (g), 29(1).

[68] UN Doc. CEDAW/C/LBN/1 (2 September 2004) Consideration of reports submitted by states parties under Article 18 of the Convention on the Elimination of All Forms of Discrimination against Women: Initial report of states parties: Lebanon.

[69] 'Good Friday Agreement' (10 April 1998), Part 6, Art. 1.

[70] *Ibid.*, Part 6, Arts. 11–13.

[71] Independent Commission on Policing for Northern Ireland, *A New Beginning: Policing in Northern Ireland* (Belfast: Independent Commission on Policing for Northern Ireland, 1999), para. 15.11.

> When I think back to before the Agreement, there wouldn't have been an Equality Commission, there wouldn't have been section 75 [the provision of the Northern Ireland Act which imposes equal opportunity requirements on all public bodies].
>
> (Northern Ireland, women in public life)

> ... the engagement of the Women's Coalition meant that you didn't feel [during] the last period of the Agreement that you were passed over because they were engaging in issues of a solid contribution that women could make, and that was very much what gave more commitment to it and seeing it as something active rather than ... all this goes on outside of you or round you or over your head. ... in that sense I suppose I feel a lot of the [subsequent activity] at the Assembly has been very demotivating.
>
> (Northern Ireland, women in economic reconstruction)

This latter response reflects the gap in representation that many women in Northern Ireland identify now that the Women's Coalition no longer holds seats in the Northern Ireland Assembly, and the majority of sitting political parties remain heavily dominated by men.[72] The domestic law in Northern Ireland has failed to implement fully international legal demands for women's equal participation in public life and an end to all forms of discrimination against women. Although the law in Northern Ireland does not do active violence to women in the same sense as the law in Lebanon, the gaps in the legal protection afforded to women's security by the Good Friday Agreement and parallel measures demonstrate that the same body of law can simultaneously promote justice in some senses while doing violence in others.

iii. South Africa

The National Peace Accord of South Africa of 1991 contained few references to women, but does indirectly reflect on the relationship between women and the security forces. The South African constitution of 1996, however, is progressive in containing a comparable number of women-directed rights protections to the Northern Ireland Good Friday Agreement. Article 1 states that the Republic is founded on the values of achieving equality and fundamental human rights. The constitution

---

[72] Margaret Ward, *The Northern Ireland Assembly and Women: Assessing the gender deficit* (Belfast: Democratic Dialogue, 2000), 1–30. Current data on the representation of men and women in the Northern Ireland Assembly is available at www.niassembly.gov.uk/mem.htm.

is distinctive in its attention to women's representation, for example Art. 46's reference to women and men as members of the National Assembly.

As part of its broader statement of the rights of all people to equality, Art. 9 of the constitution prohibits the state from discriminating, directly or indirectly, against any citizen on the basis of gender. Article 174 seeks to promote the development of a judiciary 'broadly representative' of the gender balance in South African society. A Commission for Gender Equality is established by Arts. 181(1)(d) and 187.

One woman respondent to this study regarded the constitution as the key legal framework for women's advancement in South Africa:

> I think that the constitution we have is one of the most democratic constitutions in the world. And if you look at the constitution of our country it gives everybody, whether male or female, the same rights. So I don't think that we could have legislated something better. I think ... it's just the implementation. It's the implementation and, you know it's easy to say the law, but you need to change attitudes.

> (South Africa, women in economic reconstruction)

Indeed, many South African women responding to this study reported positive views on the capacity of constitutional and legislative reform to improve the position of women in South African society.[73] However, legal measures directed primarily towards increasing the representation of women in fields of public life do not, on their own, adequately address the myriad forms of insecurity faced by women in post-conflict societies. This is apparent from the very high rates of sexual violence and violence in the home experienced by women in South Africa, and by statistics which suggest that such violence has increased in the post-conflict period.[74]

Each of the three domestic legal mechanisms described here contains some degree of protection for women's right to equality, but even the most progressive does not directly address the role that law ought to play in protecting the security of women in the post-conflict environment. In each society the domestic law, either through legal silences or through

---

[73] See Hamber et al., 'Discourses in transition', 495.

[74] For example, in 2004–5, 55,114 rapes were reported to the South African police, which represents 118.3 rapes per 100,000 persons, and a 1.5 per cent increase on the previous year: Crime Information Analysis Centre, *Rape in the RSA for the Period of April to March 2001/2002 to 2004/2005* (Pretoria: South African Police Service, 2005). See also Hamber et al., 'Discourses in transition', 497.

242 ROLE OF INTERNATIONAL LAW IN REBUILDING SOCIETIES

overt discrimination, inflicts violence upon women in some sense. The transitional-justice discourse might regard some gaps in the transitional legal framework as unfortunate but unavoidable,[75] arguing that, during transition, law must simultaneously legitimate existing social structures and bring about change.[76] However, the problem for women who are experiencing post-conflict transition is that international legal standards would be more influential in women's lives if they were fully incorporated in domestic constitutions and laws.

Conclusion

An analysis of women's perspectives, theories of law's capacity to bring about positive social change, and international and domestic laws that regulate security, suggests a paradox: law, especially during post-conflict transition, is bound up with the competing forces of justice and violence because the process of transition both brings into question the role of law in prior conflict and the capacity of law to reform social institutions. Despite being aware of this complex relationship, women continue to demand that law take on a constitutive role in the protection of their security. This is striking considering that the women respondents to this study who most strongly advocated for law's role in the protection of their security also spoke of traumatic encounters with law. This confirms that the confidence of transitional-justice theories in law's capacity to bring about positive social transformation does have a place in contemporary security dialogue. Although there are inconsistencies in the international legal standards, the growing concern for women's rights, equality and security evident in international law further confirms the significance of transitional-justice theories in security discourse.

Women's testimonies regarding legal silences and the violence inflicted upon them by law, and the gaps in international and domestic legal protections for women's security, also suggest that transitional-justice approaches should be tempered by an awareness of law's capacity to do violence as well as justice. The full and equal participation of women at all levels of lawmaking in relation to security is crucial to the achievement of women's security in post-conflict societies. Women's security will however only be adequately protected when the laws

---

[75] Christine Bell, 'Dealing with the past in Northern Ireland' (2003) 26 *Fordham International Law Journal*, 1095–147, 1099, 1128.

[76] Teitel, *Transitional Justice*, 223.

regulating security are engendered; that is, security dialogue must provide enabling spaces within which women may express their security needs and contribute to the development of laws aimed at protecting their security. Women require legal intervention that is explicitly concerned with the capacity of law to deliver justice, rather than laws that are silent about women's experiences of violence or insecurity, or laws that can actually do violence to women. If security is to start with the law, then the law must start by listening to the voices of those seeking the full protection of their security, in the broadest sense, during post-conflict transition.

[16]

Framing the Issue: UN Responses to Corruption and Criminal Networks in Post-Conflict Settings

VICTORIA K. HOLT and ALIX J. BOUCHER

This article examines the links between peace operations and combating transnational organized crime. It argues that while UN Security Council mandates direct UN missions to support establishing the rule of law in states that host peace operations, their role in addressing organized crime is more implicit than explicit. This article notes, however, that UN panels of experts, small fact-finding teams appointed to monitor targeted sanctions, may offer insight into, and options for addressing, such criminal networks. Panel findings and recommendations, however, are not integrated with related UN efforts to build the rule of law. This lack of integration reflects a need, on the part of the UN and its member states, to address better the ability of peace operations, UN panels of experts, and other tools for peacebuilding to contribute more effectively to fighting spoiler networks and organized crime.

> *The Panel has received numerous reports and allegations which indicate that the Government of the Sudan and rebel groups continue to violate the arms embargo …. Since the Security Council imposed an arms embargo on all non-governmental groups on 30 July 2004, by resolution 1556 (2004), SLA/M and JEM have continued to receive arms, ammunition and/or equipment from Chad, Eritrea, the Libyan Arab Jamahiriya, non-governmental groups and other unknown sources.*[1]

UN peace operations focus on offering security and support for political processes to take hold. Even as UN missions play broader roles in transitions from war to peace – with ever-growing mandates to support state capacity and governance – their role in halting corruption and transnational crime is neither well defined nor central to their work. States that host peace operations often face corruption, transnational organized crime, illegal resource exploitation and weapons trafficking. In contrast, the UN sends panels (and groups) of experts, primarily to Africa, to monitor and identify transnational crime and corruption, part of their role in assessing implementation of UN-targeted sanctions. While they vary in quality, panel reports not only analyse such problems, but also increasingly go further to consider remedies for corruption and transnational crime. Where both UN missions and UN expert groups operate – such as today in Côte d'Ivoire, the Democratic Republic of Congo (DRC), Sudan and Liberia – the UN has the potential to harmonize these separate functions towards a more common effort. Some integration could help develop more approaches to transnational crime and corruption; strengthen the effectiveness of peace operations and targeted sanctions regimes; and, ultimately, build security, improve peace-building and establish the rule of law.[2]

This article argues that there is an implicit link between the objectives of peace operations and combating transnational crime, based on UN peacekeeping mandates to support the rule of law. Indeed, if these missions aim to build peace, security and the rule of law, then, logically, they need to be part of a strategy that addresses threats to these objectives, including transnational crime. Similarly, we argue that UN panels of experts play a vital role in identifying aspects of transnational criminal networks and in offering ways for the 'international community' to address them. We consider the role of UN panels of experts in monitoring transnational crime and illicit networks, and of UN peace operations in fostering state legitimacy, rule of law and sustainable peace. We identify early links between these UN tools and argue that their better integration could enhance peacebuilding and rule of law efforts. Finally, we offer recommendations for these efforts in post-conflict states.

Grappling with Frameworks and Conceptual Questions

A few challenges facing the UN should be considered before examining the role of peace operations and panels in addressing corruption and transnational crime. First, the UN is often asked to play multiple, potentially conflicting, roles in a post-conflict country. The organization's roles include those of a neutral purveyor of support or mediation (for ceasefire observation, humanitarian aid), a political office bolstering a government (peacebuilding assistance, development aid), an impartial enforcer (a Chapter VII peace operation), and a judge naming and penalizing 'spoilers' (UN-targeted sanctions, the International Criminal Court).[3] It is easy for the UN to send mixed messages about its priorities. Indeed, in some cases, Chapter VII peace operations (such as in Kosovo) may play a role in enforcing the rule of law but fail to take active steps to arrest, detain and try people accused of war crimes.[4] Likewise, in Sudan, the UN often plays conflicting roles in mediating and maintaining access for humanitarian assistance providers, in leading a peacekeeping force and joining the African Union for another in Darfur (both under Chapter VII), and in implementing targeted sanctions and supporting the International Criminal Court's activities.

Second, in 2008, the UN was increasingly overstretched by its current commitments and Security Council ambitions. Over the last decade, peace operations have grown dramatically, not just in numbers, but also in scope and objectives. Today, the UN Department of Peacekeeping Operations (DPKO) leads peace operations in 16 countries from Liberia to Timor-Leste and from Sudan to Haiti. Over 80,000 troops are deployed, with another 11,000 police and 17,000 civilian staff. The mandates for these operations range from traditional monitoring of peace agreements (such as in Cyprus) to assisting with the organization of elections and the rebuilding of national institutions (as in the DRC and Liberia), to administering the areas in which they are deployed (such as in Kosovo). UN operations can struggle to implement these wide mandates, as well as to integrate their activities with other UN programmes and agencies, and international and local actors. Within the UN Secretariat, reforms have led to the creation of offices dedicated to bolstering the rule of law, and the enhancement of DPKO's capacity.[5] Beyond New York (and DPKO), UN efforts concerning transnational crime and corruption are spread across the globe, ranging from the UN Office on Drugs and Crime (UNODC) to the UN Development Programme (UNDP), with limited coordination with Interpol and other international bodies, such as the Organization for Security and Cooperation in Europe (OSCE).

Even as it faces the twin challenges of setting priorities and meeting current ambitions for peace operations, the UN needs, in our view, to look at how transnational crime, corruption and efforts to build the rule of law affect the success of its missions.

Defining the Problem: Transnational Crime, Corruption and the Rule of Law

Until the 1990s, transnational crime was equated with multinational organized crime, such as the activities of national and multinational mafias. Experts, however, now seek a more comprehensive view of how such crime functions. The UN's definition of transnational crime, based on the 2000 UN Convention on Transnational Crime, is wide-ranging: it considers an organized criminal group as a 'structured group of three or more persons, existing for a period of time and acting in concert with the aim of committing one or more serious crimes or offenses established in accordance with this Convention'.[6] Based on this definition, scholars now use the phrases 'illicit networks', 'transnational crime' or the even wider-ranging 'illicit enterprise and illegal economies',[7] to capture the nature of modern networks in the global economy, how these networks affect societies, and, in many cases, the ability of those societies to maintain and build peace.[8]

Corruption, similarly, is seen as the abuse of entrusted office for illegitimate private gain, as well as both a cause of conflict and an impediment to peacebuilding.[9] Combined with involvement in illicit networks, it can lead to renewed grievances and conflict.[10] Together, illicit networks and corruption undermine the rule of law, which UN Secretary-General Kofi Annan described in 2004 as

> a principle of governance in which all persons, institutions and entities, public and private, including the State itself, are accountable to the laws that are publicly promulgated, equally enforced and independently adjudicated, and which are consistent with international human rights norms and standards. It requires, as well, measures to ensure adherence to the principles of supremacy of law, equality before the law, accountability to the law, fairness in the application of the law, separation of powers, participation in decision-making, legal certainty, avoidance of arbitrariness and procedural and legal transparency.[11]

In post-conflict settings, the distribution of political and/or military power can institutionalize corruption and create incentives for opposing democratic governance and the rule of law. Both government and rebel groups can be key players in trafficking weapons and commodities such as diamonds and timber.[12]

In Liberia and the DRC, the transitional governments included important roles for former rebel leaders, many of whom continued to participate in illegal activities, such as smuggling commodities to finance arms purchases and ultimately to support continuing violence.[13] During the transitional period in Liberia, for example, the government collected less than 20 per cent of taxes and fees due first on timber exports and second on petroleum imports.[14] Former rebels, meanwhile, refused to vacate a national park for two years after the war: while they exploited only small amounts of timber, they did not want to lose that revenue and continued to threaten peace and security.[15] Following revelations of corruption during the transitional period, members of the National Transitional Government, including its chair, Gyude Bryant, were investigated and in 2008 were being tried for misappropriating funds.[16]

The Role of Peace Operations in Responding to Corruption and Criminal Networks

Certainly UN missions would benefit from a better understanding of criminal and illicit trade networks, as well as of the sources of corruption, that impede their efforts to help establish security and the rule of law. Moreover, most peace operations, even if they are mandated to support the rule of law, are not well designed to address corruption and transnational crime. Indeed, the UN must decide what tasks are associated with these mandates and whether peace operations should try to hinder criminal networks and corruption explicitly; whether they should build host-state capacity to immediately address these challenges; or whether the longer-term outcome of their wider efforts will increase a state's ability to prevent such activities. The Security Council mandates for current UN peace operations generally offer little direct guidance to address illicit and criminal networks. Nonetheless, many peace operations have some implicit direction to counter these activities through mandates to help build security and the rule of law in the host state. Thus, where the UN decides to support a weak government or to limit so-called spoilers, it needs to develop systematic responses to corruption and transnational crime. Finally, in all of its activities, the UN must also avoid peacekeepers themselves becoming involved in crime and develop a system of accountability to ensure that its own field personnel are systematically held to account for criminal behaviour.[17]

UN-led operations in Liberia, Côte d'Ivoire, the DRC, Sudan, Haiti, Timor-Leste, Kosovo and Chad/Central African Republic, for example, have mandates to assist in building the judicial institutions of host states. These mandates suggest that peace operations should therefore pay attention to transnational crime.[18] This section examines missions that have such mandates, discusses steps they may take to impede illicit trade, and offers suggestions to improve their effectiveness.

One indicator of how peace operations may address criminal networks is the role given to UN police forces in supporting the rule of law. Police roles can be variously distinguished as traditional, transformational or executive in format.[19] With a traditional mandate, UN police monitor the host state's police

24   INTERNATIONAL PEACEKEEPING

activities and report on potential human rights violations and other problems, as seen in peacekeeping missions in the early 1990s. Transformational mandates engage more in supporting the development of the rule of law capacity by helping to vet, train and rebuild local police forces. Most UN missions since 2000 have had such mandates, including operations in Liberia (UNMIL), Côte d'Ivoire (UNOCI), DRC (MONUC), Sudan (UNAMID), the Central African Republic and Chad (MINURCAT), Haiti (MINUSTAH) and Burundi (ONUB).[20] Intrusive, executive mandates, such as those for the missions in Kosovo and Timor-Leste, remain rare but involve missions carrying out rule-of-law actions themselves and assuming law enforcement authority while the host state forces are (re)built. Indeed, UNMIK appears to be one of the only operations directly assigned to prevent and disrupt organized crime.[21] UNMIK police officers therefore take part in such tasks as border and customs control, anti-trafficking operations and assisting in the removal of illegal checkpoints. Still, UN police lack training and specialized skills for fighting organized crime, and these are significant impediments in their ability to address the challenges.

Associated with rule of law promotion, other missions do have more crime-fighting tasks, though they are less explicitly mandated to combat criminality by the Security Council. The UN operation in Haiti (MINUSTAH), while not an executive mission, conducts anti-drug-trafficking operations. Tasks assigned to UN police in several other missions – UNOCI, UNMIK and UNMIT (Timor-Leste) – include enforcing the law and arresting suspects.[22] Further, MONUC may also detain crime suspects.[23] Moreover, UNOCI, UNMIK, MONUC, UNMIT and UNMIL are involved in border and customs control.[24] Several missions are tasked with investigating police and government abuses or corruption, including UNMIL, the various Timor missions, MINUSTAH, MONUC and UNMIK.

What missions actually do to track and deter transnational crime is a different matter. According to the Secretary-General's reports (in particular, reports on UNMIL, MONUC and UNMIT), their activities consist mostly, as prescribed by their mandates, of efforts to build capacity in the country's rule-of-law sectors, particularly police, corrections and the judiciary. As such, peace operations support the training of rule-of-law professionals, the building of courthouses and police stations, and the assessing of progress in recruiting and training sufficient personnel for these tasks.[25] The role of UNMIK is an interesting case study because of the wide authority it derives from its mandate. UNMIK tracked human traffickers with the help of NATO troops, for example. In its early years, NATO forces would gather information on these networks, and with the help of NATO police forces (mostly Italian *carabinieri*) raid the relevant establishment. NATO turned over suspects to UNMIK for detention and trial. The mission was subsequently reduced to supporting the nascent Kosovan forces to tackle the remaining networks.[26]

Another problem with fighting illicit networks, however, is that peace operations may actually lead to increased activity within these networks and undermine rule of law. The UN High Commissioner for Human Rights estimated that '30 percent of those visiting Bosnia's brothels were UN personnel, NATO peacekeepers, or aid workers'.[27] Human Rights Watch found that during the late 1990s, many women were lured to jobs in Bosnia, mostly in bars and restaurants, only to be forced into prostitution.[28] In November 2007, over 100 Sri Lankan peacekeepers were sent home from the UN mission in Haiti for suspected involvement in sexual exploitation of local women. Similarly, a Pakistani unit deployed with the UN mission in the DRC was investigated for trafficking gold and weapons with militia groups in that country.[29] UN peace operations, therefore, while they already attempt to take some steps to deter criminal networks and illicit trade, do not do so in a systematic fashion. Moreover, they need to ensure they do not increase criminality in the host state. The following section examines the role of another UN instrument – panels of experts – that monitor these networks and illicit trade. The Security Council has used targeted sanctions to direct that certain commodities and individuals no longer be permitted to fund war and to threaten peace, and has then charged a panel of experts to monitor their implementation and report on the success of the sanctions.

The Role of UN Panels of Experts in Monitoring Transnational Crime and Illicit Trade Networks

While not formally acknowledged as a UN tool to track transnational criminal networks, *per se*, the UN uses panels of experts to this effect. The Security Council appoints these small fact-finding teams to monitor UN targeted sanctions – embargoes on arms, diamonds and timber; asset freezes and travel bans – and to investigate how they are violated. Initially created to monitor the arms embargo on Rwanda and then sanctions on Angola, panels of experts have since looked into how sanctions are violated in Sierra Leone, Liberia, the DRC, Côte d'Ivoire, Sudan, and Somalia, and by Al Qaida and the Taliban. The panels were among the first to link criminal networks to continuing conflict, detailing how spoilers secure arms and undermine peace, and in some cases how governments use these networks to continue war.[30]

Through their investigations, the panels have gained a detailed understanding, particularly in Central and West Africa, of how weapons, diamonds, timber and commodities such as coltan (essential material used in mobile phones and computers) have been used to fund war in these countries. In 2000, the panel of experts on Sierra Leone documented former Liberian President Charles Taylor's role in arming the Revolutionary United Front (RUF) in Sierra Leone. Taylor also admitted to violating the UN-imposed arms embargo by ordering weapons from Serbia in March 2003. The panel found that Taylor's list of weapons almost entirely matched the list of weapons delivered with a fake Nigerian end-user certificate. The consequences were serious: the panel later reported seeing both government and Liberian rebel soldiers using the weapons that had been delivered.[31]

Panel reporting also highlights the deep problems and the mix of challenges that greatly affect the UN's ability to conduct peacekeeping missions. A key aspect of panel reporting is highlighting the practices of weapons traffickers. Panels have repeatedly found that weapons are purchased from remaining stocks in post-Communist countries and flown to the relevant nation by falsified flight plans. To better conceal their activities (and benefit from the impression or even 'evidence' that the UN is involved in these activities), several panels (including the DRC and Sudan groups) have found that businessmen suspected of trafficking weapons paint their aircraft white, the colour of UN aircraft, to hide their activities.[32] The weapons are then traded for valuable commodities, such as gold, loaded onto the aircraft, and traded on the leading world markets.

This trafficking has other, longer-term implications. The DRC group of experts has reported that incomplete and falsified cargo manifests prevent the authorities from collecting customs duties, which are essential to funding national reconstruction and development efforts.[33] Moreover, corrupt border officials allow armed groups to traffic weapons and other commodities with impunity and extort customs fees at border crossings for personal gain. In the Ituri and Kivus, for example, corrupt officials fail to send the fees they collect to the DRC central bank. In 2005, the shortfall to government coffers was an estimated US$4m, representing an unknown amount of weaponry, natural resources and other commodities.[34] This trafficking is so valuable to the officials involved that it leads to suspected criminal behaviour: the DRC group found that officers who had reported the illegal import of uniforms to an army unit were killed, reportedly for having raised the possibility that the shipment violated the sanctions.[35]

In addition to documenting detailed violations of the UN arms embargo, the panel on Sudan reported that while the Security Council had referred specifically to the Janjaweed militia in its resolution imposing an arms embargo on belligerents in Sudan, the Janjaweed's ability to continue obtaining weapons was due to their close links, if not full integration, with Sudanese security forces.[36] Later in 2006, the panel again detailed the arms violations, demonstrating the kinds of information it had gained from its field research in mid-2006:

> The Panel witnessed approximately seven Toyota pickup trucks mounted with light machine guns and a large number of troops of the Sudanese armed forces being unloaded from an Ilyushin 76 at the El-Fasher airport. ...
> Reliable sources stated that this was only one of approximately 10 such flights that had landed during the past week. Such daylight transfers of military personnel and equipment using commercial air cargo companies are blatant violations for the arms embargo and are indicative of a significant attitude shift on the part of the Government of the Sudan regarding its adherence to the sanctions imposed by the United Nations.[37]

Not all panel reports offer such detail about these types of activities and behaviour. In some cases, panel reports have also been watered down to limit political fallout over findings that are controversial or difficult to verify *in situ*. Similarly, the role of UN peace operations in practically addressing these challenges remains limited by their mandates and capacity. The following section argues that increased cooperation between peace operations, panels of experts, and other actors concerned with stemming these activities could improve their overall effectiveness and build a more enduring rule of law in the countries concerned.

Panels of Experts and UN Peace Operations: Current Cooperation

Most current panels – on Liberia, the DRC, Côte d'Ivoire, Sudan, and Somalia, and on Al Qaida and the Taliban – work in countries that host UN peace operations. Only the panels for Côte d'Ivoire, the DRC and Sudan have specific mandates to work with the corresponding peace operations. Likewise, only the UN peace operations in Côte d'Ivoire, the DRC and Liberia have mandates referencing work with the corresponding panels. For these 'co-deployments', both UN tools have developed mechanisms for increasing their cooperation, information-sharing and integration. Cooperation between panels and peacekeeping missions has potential benefits. The panels report that peacekeeping missions in Côte d'Ivoire, the DRC, Liberia and Sudan provide them invaluable support, mostly by sharing information and offering logistical assistance while they are in the field. In turn, panels share findings and information with peace operations.

In the DRC, the group of experts reported that MONUC provided liaison points within its headquarters that greatly increased cooperation. The panel worked particularly closely with the mission's Joint Mission Analysis Cell (JMAC). Moreover, the panel worked with MONUC's Disarmament, Demobilization and Reintegration (DDR) unit to obtain detailed information on weapons flows within the country.[38] This cooperation, whether initiated by the panel or MONUC, remains *ad hoc*, however, and depends on the personalities involved, the consent of the Secretary-General's Special Representative, and the ability of both parties to use the information effectively.

In Côte d'Ivoire, the UN mission, UNOCI, is mandated to monitor the sanctions, providing another avenue for cooperation with the panel. UNOCI is the only mission with an embargo cell to monitor the UN arms embargo. The cell conducts random inspections of cargo at border crossings and reports suspicious incidents to the panel for investigation. The five-person cell serves as 'the eyes of the panel' when the panel itself is not in the country and often conducts joint investigations when it is there.[39] In turn, the panel assists UNOCI with its mandate by helping to train border and customs police officers. Ideally, peace operations with this type of mandate would create such a cell, use opportunities for experts to provide training, and develop formal mechanisms for cooperation between the panel and the peace operation.

Next Steps

It is widely recognized that ignoring criminal networks and pervasive corruption can be fatal to international efforts to restore peace and security. No single UN tool, however, is designed to address this suite of vexing problems. Nonetheless, cooperation between panels and peace operations could be more extensive and arrangements more systematic. In the field, UN peace operations and panels of experts both play a role in documenting some criminal networks, and combined, these UN efforts could bear fruit, as seen in Liberia. Following panel findings, the Security Council conditioned the lifting of its targeted sanctions on the Liberian government's creation of adequate financial controls to prevent the continued operations of illicit networks. The Security Council then charged the panel with assessing the progress of Liberian authorities in meeting these objectives. The Security Council also asked UNMIL to assist Liberia to meet those conditions – by helping Liberian authorities to patrol timber areas, for example.[40] In a sense, UNMIL and the panels helped to stem illicit criminal networks and support the establishment of the rule of law. Such peacebuilding efforts are a useful approach and offer an avenue for improving UN assistance with developing the rule of law, undermining corruption and fighting international criminal networks to create sustainable security. Further study is needed to assess the potential to strengthen such approaches and whether the strategy in Liberia was unique or could be reproduced elsewhere.

Such cooperative efforts by panels and UN peace operations remain limited and anecdotal. There are four areas, however, in which nations could help UN missions to be more effective in contributing to stemming transnational crime and criminal networks. First, transnational crime should be recognized and evaluated as a potential – and central – threat to peace and stability, as well as to the success of peace operations. In establishing UN missions, the Security Council would benefit from clearer assessments of such threats in the host nation and their potential to undermine missions. If UN-targeted sanctions are failing in a country with a peace operation, the Security Council needs to know why. The panel on Sudan, for example, has provided highly detailed, and devastating, descriptions not just of arms embargo violations, but also of the human rights atrocities committed by the parties to the conflict. Panel information and analysis, in concert with related JMAC efforts, can support longer-term UN analytical efforts to clarify the characteristics, motivations and strength of 'spoilers'. Such analysis can help the mission leadership set priorities, identify requirements to support its rule-of-law mandates and refine its broader peacebuilding strategy. In addition, resources to institutionalize cooperation with Interpol and the UN Peacebuilding Commission, for example, should be increased.

Second, when they operate in the same countries, the efforts of panels of experts and peace operations to assist the rule of law should be better coordinated. Specifically, the Security Council should consider directing them to work with each other in common mission areas. Member states should back this approach, both by providing data to the panels and by supporting UN peacekeeping missions. In addition to information sharing and logistical support, the UN could gain from more systematic cooperation over specific joint tasks, such as where peace operations (such as MONUC or UNOCI) have a mandate to monitor borders. Expanding on the early success of mission-specific initiatives, such as UNOCI's embargo cell, could lead the way to additional avenues for coordination.

Third, stronger institutional and financial support at UN headquarters is badly needed, especially for panels, their investigations, and the professional staff in the Department of Political Affairs (DPA) who back them up and work with the Security Council's sanctions committees. The DPA unit that supports panels is small: its political affairs officers support at least two panels and corresponding sanctions committees each, making it impossible for them to provide as much support as is needed.

The challenges for the DPA are many: they must continue to work on developing an improved roster of experts to expedite and facilitate panel member recruitment (one of the most time-consuming aspects of their work). There is no central repository for panel research and findings. There is discussion about creating a database to host panel findings, but another, related, database for tracking the implementation of their recommendations is also necessary. Indeed, neither the Security Council nor the UN Secretariat has a regular mechanism to know what steps – if any – countries take to disrupt the networks that violate these targeted sanctions.[41] The Security Council should first require UN member states to report regularly on their activities to support and implement targeted sanctions. Second, to ease tracking of sanctions implementation, the UN needs a mechanism to report and track efforts to uphold targeted sanctions regimes. This tracking will require increasing staff resources in this area at UN headquarters. Additional options include expanding the structures created for the UN counter-terrorism efforts and the creation of a sanctions coordinator.[42]

Finally, on a broader scale, the UN needs to develop a deeper political strategy to address these networks and to fill the gaps in programmes currently aimed at tackling the problems.[43] Indeed, panels offer only periodic analysis and they cannot (and should not) be expected to enforce sanctions or fight spoiler networks themselves. On the other hand, further expanding the mandates and responsibilities of heavily overstretched UN peace operations is also risky. Indeed, unless matched with capacity, the Security Council is setting up peace operations for failure if they are not sufficiently staffed and resourced for their tasks.[44]

To maximize its resources and effectiveness, the UN and its member states need to assess how best to marry its ambitions for peace and security with various tools. Indeed, expanding the number of actors involved in monitoring and addressing these phenomena could lead to confusion on the ground, with each actor unsure of who bears responsibility for implementing ever-expanding mandates. Especially in the area of peace operations, expanding mandates need support, clarity and feasibility, and adequate means for their effective implementation. The creation of the Peacebuilding Commission is such an example, as it remains unclear when it is optimal for that institution to begin its activities in a post-conflict setting.

Stemming corruption and transnational crime are urgent issues for those concerned with state fragility and peace operations. Nevertheless, the link between transnational crime, corruption, and conflict requires that nations take a harder look at these relationships and devise better tools and systems for addressing them. New efforts to better address criminality and corruption must be developed with a sound understanding of the challenges and contradictions facing different UN teams in meeting their goals, without being at odds with one another.

UN peace operations and panels of experts have both developed a variety of tools to address these issues, and should be better linked to get the best results. Their effectiveness, however, depends on greater cooperation, the backing of the Security Council and member states, and improved resources. The challenge

30   INTERNATIONAL PEACEKEEPING

is to focus on what each has accomplished and to build on their successes to enhance international willingness and the ability to support the rule of law and sustainable peace in post-conflict societies.

NOTES

1. UN, 'Report of the United Nations Panel of Experts on Sudan', UN Doc., S/2006/65, 30 Jan. 2006, paras.79, 80.
2. This article is partly based on Alix J. Boucher and Victoria K. Holt, *Targeting Spoilers: The Role of United Nations Panels of Experts*, Washington, DC: Henry L. Stimson Center, 2008. This article focuses on targeted sanctions and the fact that panels of experts can help identify the criminalization associated with their imposition. Peter Andreas explains why, in the case of comprehensive sanctions, the failure to recognize this link had lasting effects on efforts to build peace in the Balkans. Andreas acknowledges that targeted sanctions may have less of a criminalizing effect, but without further research their impact cannot be adequately assessed. 'Criminalizing Consequences of Sanctions: Embargo Busting and Its Legacy', *International Studies Quarterly*, Vol.49, 2005, pp.335–60.
3. The UN provides interim administration to Kosovo and Timor-Leste, accessed at www.unmikonline.org; www.unmit.org. Another international effort to root out corruption is the Governance and Economic Management Assistance Program (GEMAP), run by the World Bank, which consists of technical assistance to key Liberian natural resource administrations. The head of the timber and diamond administrations, for example, shares his job with an international civil servant, accessed at www.gemapliberia.org.
4. For an example of such 'mixed messages', see Majbritt Lyck, 'International Peace Enforcers and Indicted War Criminals: The Case of Ramush Haradinaj', *International Peacekeeping*, Vol.14, No.3, 2007, pp.418–32.
5. For example, the UN created an Office of Rule of Law and Security Institutions (OROLSI) in DPKO, which 'brings together a wide range of entities including the police division, judicial, legal and corrections unit, mine action, DDR, as well as security reform functions'. The office's priority is to translate policy into implementable programmes under an Assistant Secretary-General. See UN News Service, 'UN Rule of Law, Security Officials Outline Key Priorities for 2008', 21 Jan. 2008. A second initiative is the creation of a Rule of Law Coordination and Resource Group chaired by Deputy Secretary-General Asha-Rose Migiro, which gathers the heads of eight UN departments, including DPKO, UNDP, UNODC, to discuss better integration of rule-of-law efforts. UN News Service, 'Migiro: rule of law drives work and mission of UN', 1 Nov. 2007.
6. United Nations Convention Against Transnational Organized Crime (2000), articles 2–3. According to the convention, a serious crime is punishable by at least four years in prison. A crime is transnational when it is planned, committed, and has effects in more than one state.
7. For an extensive discussion of how the scholarly community has moved from studying organized crime to transnational crime, and 'illicit enterprise and illegal economies', see Andre Standing, 'Rival Views of Organized Crime', Monograph 77, Institute for Security Studies, Pretoria, Feb. 2003.
8. James Cockayne, *Transnational Organized Crime: Multilateral Response to a Rising Threat*, New York: International Peace Academy, Apr. 2007.
9. US Agency for International Development (USAID), *Anticorruption Strategy*, Washington, DC, Jan. 2005, pp.5–8.
10. Alix J. Boucher, William J. Durch, Margaret Midyette, Sarah Rose and Jason Terry, *Mapping and Fighting Corruption in War-Torn States*, Washington, DC: Henry L. Stimson Center, Mar. 2007.
11. UN Secretary-General, 'The Rule of Law and Transitional Justice in Conflict and Post-Conflict Societies', Report of the Secretary-General, UN Doc., S/2004/616, 23 Aug. 2004, para.2.
12. See the reports of the panels of experts on Liberia (for instance, from Apr. 2003), Sierra Leone (Dec. 2000), the DRC (for example, Apr. 2001 and July 2006), and Sudan (for example, Oct. 2007).
13. International Crisis Group, 'The Congo's Transition Is Failing: Crisis in the Kivus', Africa Report No. 91, Mar. 2005, p.30; UN, 'Report of the Secretary-General to the Security Council on Liberia', UN Doc., S/2003/875, 11 Sept. 2003, para.15.
14. UN, 'Report of the Panel of Experts on Liberia', UN Doc., S/2006/379, paras. 24–25,102.

15. The approximately 200 fighters were eventually persuaded to leave the national park. UN, 'Report of the Panel of Experts on Liberia', UN Doc. S/2005/745, 7 Dec. 2005, para.65.
16. UN, 'Report of the Panel of Experts on Liberia', UN Doc., S/2007/340, paras.106–7.
17. For a detailed discussion of gaps in accountability, see Katherine N. Andrews, William J. Durch, Madeline L. England and Matthew C. Weed, *Improving Criminal Accountability for Police and Civilian Personnel in UN Peace Operations*, Washington, DC: Henry L. Stimson Center, 2008.
18. Even with such mandates, surprisingly few current peace operations actually had explicit mandates to monitor borders and impede illicit trade. See Kathleen A. Walsh, Katherine N. Andrews, Brandon L. Hunt and William J. Durch, *Post-Conflict Borders and UN Peace Operations*, Washington, DC: Henry L. Stimson Center, Aug. 2007.
19. For more on these distinctions, see Joshua G. Smith, Victoria K. Holt and William J. Durch, *Enhancing United Nations Capacity to Support Post-Conflict Policing and Rule of Law*, Washington, DC: Henry L. Stimson Center, Dec. 2007.
20. Ibid., Table 2, p.18.
21. UNMIK derives its executive mandate from UN Security Council Resolution 1244 (1999), specifically para.10 i). See 'Report of the Secretary-General', UN Doc., S/1999/779, 12 July 1999, paras.60–64.
22. For UNTAET's mandate, see UN Doc. S/RES 1272 (1999), paras.2–3; UN, 'Report of the Secretary General', UN Doc., S/1999/1024, para.59, which explains that the civilian police unit will have 'executive enforcement functions'.
23. See UN Doc., S/RES/1355 (2004) and UN Doc., S/RES/1565 (2004).
24. UN Doc., S/RES/1528 (2004), para.6. The mandate for the mission to Haiti (MINUSTAH) is virtually identical; see UN Doc. S/RES/1542 (2004), para.1. See Smith et al. (n.19 above). See Walsh et al., *Post-Conflict Borders and UN Peace Operations* (n.18 above).
25. For examples of these activities, see 'Report of the Secretary-General on the United Nations Integrated Mission to Timor-Leste', UN Doc. S/2008/26, 17 Jan. 2008; 'Report of the Secretary-General on the United Nations Mission to the Democratic Republic of Congo', S/2007/671, 17 Nov. 2007.
26. Author interview with former NATO officer, Washington, DC, 14 Nov. 2007. See 'Report of the Secretary General on UNMIK,' UN Doc. S/2003/996, 15 Oct. 2003, para.19.
27. Cited in Refugees International, 'Conflict, Sexual Trafficking and Peacekeeping', accessed at www.refugeesinternational.org/content/article/detail/4146, 8 Oct. 2004. See also Sarah E. Mendelson, *Barracks and Brothels: Peacekeepers and Human Trafficking in the Balkans*, Washington, DC: Center for Strategic and International Studies, 2005.
28. Martina E. Vandenberg, Juris Doctor, 'Testimony on Trafficking of Women and Girls to Bosnia and Herzegovina', House Committee on International Relations Subcommittee on International Operations and Human Rights, 24 Apr. 2002, accessed at http://hrw.org/backgrounder/wrd/trafficking-testim-april.pdf.
29. UN, IRIN, 'DRC: Probe into MONUC Gold, Arms Trafficking Allegations "Well Advanced"', 25 May 2007, accessed at www.irinnews.org/Report.aspx?ReportId=72373; Martin Plaut, 'Eastern DRC, UN Troops "Traded Gold for Guns"', *BBC News*, 23 May 2007; Martin Plaut, 'Trading Guns for Gold: Pakistani Peacekeepers in the Congo', *Review of African Political Economy*, Vol.34, No.113, 2007, pp.580–8. Plaut reports that the investigation was unfinished, in part because of political reluctance to implicate this major troop contributor. He points to the detrimental impact of failing to investigate fully such allegations on MONUC's (and the UN's) credibility, legitimacy and ability to fulfil its mandate.
30. NGOs, including Global Witness and Human Rights Watch, have also done pioneering reporting on the link between sanctions violations, international networks and conflict.
31. 'Report of the Group of Experts on Liberia', UN Doc, S/2003/937, 28 Oct. 2003, para.87.
32. 'Report of the Group of Experts on the DRC', UN Doc. S/2005/30, 25 Jan. 2005, paras.66–70; 'Report of the Panel of Experts on the Sudan', UN Doc., S/2007/584, 3 Oct. 2007, paras.200–11.
33. 'Report of the Group of Experts on the DRC', UN Doc. S/2005/30, 25 Jan. 2005, paras.45–50.
34. 'Report of the Group of Experts on the DRC', UN Doc. S/2006/53, 26 Jan. 2006, paras.49–52.
35. Ibid.
36. 'Report of the Group of Experts on the Sudan', 30 Jan. 2006, UN Doc. S/2006/65, 20 Jan. 2006, para.81.
37. 'Report of the Group of Experts on the Sudan', UN Doc., S/2006/795, 3 Oct. 2006, para.84.
38. 'Report of the Group of Experts on the DRC', UN Doc., S/2006/525, 18 July 2006, paras.44, 45, 217.

39. Author telephone interview with UN official, 31 Aug. 2007. 'Report of the Panel of Experts on Côte d'Ivoire', UN Doc., S/2007/611, 18 Oct. 2007. Efforts to curb trade in conflict zone diamonds, such as the Kimberley process (which offers to certify that the gems do not come from war zones), cannot deter all trading from conflict areas, mainly because of the volume of diamond trading and the difficulty in determining the exact origin of the stones.

40. 'Report of the Panel of Experts on Liberia', UN Doc., S/2006/976, 15 Dec. 2006, para.64.

41. Alix J. Boucher and Victoria K. Holt, 'Tracking Bad Guys, Small Arms, and Illicit Trade: The Role of the United Nations Panels of Experts', Issue Brief, Washington, DC: Henry L. Stimson Center, July 2007.

42. David Cortright and George Lopez, 'A Sanctions Coordinator', in Peter Wallensteen and Carina Staibano, *International Sanctions: Between Words and Wars in the Global System*, London: Frank Cass, 2005, pp.65–74.

43. The UN could improve its cooperation across many agencies, such as the UN Office on Drugs and Crime (UNODC), which has 20 field offices (beyond its Vienna headquarters), but only one office in Africa (in Egypt). The UNODC has an office in Afghanistan, the only office located in a country that also has a UN field mission.

44. Where targeted sanctions regimes have not been imposed, the UN could seek to support strengthening border capacity. See Walsh et al. (n.18 above).

[17]

Corrupting Peace? Peacebuilding and Post-conflict Corruption

PHILIPPE LE BILLON

Many conflict-affected countries are among the most corrupt in the world, and corruption is frequently reported as a major concern of local populations and foreign aid agencies during transition to peace. Tackling corruption is part of 'liberal peacebuilding', which seeks to consolidate peace through democracy and free markets economy. Yet liberalization policies may also foster corruption. Using a preliminary analysis of selected corruption perception indicators, this article finds tenuous and divergent support for post-conflict patterns of corruption. Three main arguments linking liberal peacebuilding with higher levels of corruption are then presented for further elaboration, and a research agenda is outlined.

Corruption has recently become a major item on the international security agenda.[1] Many conflict-affected countries are among those perceived to be the most corrupt in the world, and corruption is reported among the key concerns of local populations during the so-called post-conflict reconstruction period.[2] Concerns among rich countries about corruption and security have largely focused on terrorism, narcotics, organized crime and 'state failure'.[3] Corruption is further perceived as an impediment to peacebuilding.[4] By weakening the effectiveness and legitimacy of public institutions, undermining economic recovery and jeopardizing international aid and foreign direct investment (FDI), corruption increases the risk of renewed violence and undermines the wellbeing and political empowerment of local populations.[5] The pervasiveness of corruption in Bosnia and Herzegovina (BiH), for example, is widely portrayed as a major cause of the country's political and economic setbacks since the 1995 Dayton Accord.[6] The most prominent United Nations (UN) report on peace operations argues that 'support for the fight against corruption' is the first priority among the 'essential complements to effective peacebuilding'.[7]

Concerns about the effects of corruption on the transition to peace add to a growing literature on corruption and armed conflict.[8] Research on the political economy of corruption and collective violence has yielded important insights on the relationships between corruption, regime types and processes of transition (such as rural protests and agricultural modernization in India).[9] Yet until recently, few analytic works have been conducted on post-conflict corruption, and much of the research derives from the work of aid agencies themselves or policy-oriented research institutes.[10] Relevant literature mostly comes from the sub-fields of the political economy of war, corruption in transitional processes, and econometric studies of conflicts.[11] Critiques of the 'good governance' agenda have also pointed at the pathologization of 'domestic' corruption in relation to state failure arguments and liberalization policies, for example in the context of post-conflict and post-natural disaster countries such as Nicaragua.[12] It has also been suggested that different forms of corruption have different effects on conflict likelihood and peacebuilding.[13]

In this essay, standard explanations are presented for the reported prevalence of corruption in 'post-conflict' countries, which largely focus on the 'domestic' roots of corruption. In short, corruption resulting from the legacies of war economies and a culture of impunity undermines liberal reforms, resulting in suboptimal outcomes. Using a preliminary analysis of selected corruption perception indicators, post-conflict corruption patterns are then investigated, where tenuous and divergent evidence is found. I then discuss arguments linking corruption and 'liberal peacebuilding', which is a widespread form of international intervention that seeks to consolidate peace through political and economic liberalization. Three major arguments are presented for further consideration:

- First, liberal peacebuilding can exacerbate and transform corruption, to the point of undermining its objectives of democratization and economic liberalization. The risk is that more competitive forms of corruption within a weak institutional setting result in greater instability and chronic conflict, with donors and populations then acquiescing in the institutionalization of more monopolistic forms of corruption for the sake of economic and political stability.
- Second, corruption is institutionalized within peacebuilding and reconstruction initiatives. Although it may not be corruption *stricto sensu*, nepotism, fraud, over-invoicing, lack of transparency and accountability, and tax avoidance have characterized various forms of foreign engagement during the transition process. The risk is that these types of 'corruption' undermine the integrity, efficiency, legitimacy and role-modelling of peacebuilding and reconstruction initiatives.
- Third, there is a frequent dilemma faced by donors and recipients with the 'corruption problem', most notably with bureaucratic corruption. Donors do not directly support recipient governments because of their presumed corruption; in turn, recipient governments rely even more heavily on corruption to supplement government incomes.

Each of these arguments requires detailed research and a more balanced treatment of the issues that they engage. I thus conclude with some thoughts on a future research agenda.

Corruption, Peacebuilding and Reconstruction

Between 1989 and 2002, international donors have spent in excess of US$60 billion to 'reconstruct' 32 conflict-affected countries.[14] Unprecedented since the reconstruction efforts following the second world war, this amount seems large, but in fact averaged out to only US$14 per conflict-affected person per year, with major differences between recipient countries. This figure leaves little room for wastage and embezzlement.[15] This entire amount has since been surpassed by three years of 'peacebuilding and reconstruction' in the context of the US-led 'war on terror'. Iraq's reconstruction budget alone was about US$60 billion between 2003 and 2006. The wastage, fraud and lack of transparency in this context have been denounced as staggering.[16] Official overseas development assistance by OECD members to Afghanistan climbed from US$87 million in 2000 to US$2.2 billion in 2005. In Lebanon, international donors pledged US$7.6 billion after the destruction wrought by the Israeli military in 2006. Overall, peacebuilding and reconstruction monies have been 'disbursed' in countries with some of the poorest corruption indicators, often falling well below the average 'corruption level' for their income group.[17] Afghanistan, like Iraq, Haiti, Somalia and Sudan, ranks supposedly among the 10 per cent most corrupt in the world according to the 2007 Transparency International (TI) compilation of surveys. Anecdotal evidence also suggests that corruption sharply increases during post-conflict transition.[18]

A prevalent explanation for high levels of corruption in post-conflict contexts lies in their historical 'domestic' context. Corruption often pre-dates the conflict, sometimes having contributed to it. Wartime generally sees an entrenchment and diffusion of corrupt practices as governmental structures break down and the 'politics of survival' take over any semblance of 'public ethics'. Armed factions often justify corruption through reference to the war while using corrupt practices – equivalent to 'protection rackets' by state security agencies and government militias – to strengthen their hold on power.[19] For lack of an alternative, ordinary people also resort to corruption and illegal economic activities to cope with the hardships of war or economic sanctions.[20] Corruption by local and regional authorities along with participation in the informal economy by ordinary people can also sustain chronic conflicts.[21]

The 'weakness' of institutions is another recurring theme in the post-conflict literature. Economic and political transition often takes place in a weak or highly politicized institutional framework. Recurrent problems affecting the level of corruption include poor fiscal leverage, judicial backlogs and bias, corruption related to low wages, and shadow economic control. Anti-corruption institutions frequently remain weak or instrumentalized, and critics are often silenced or co-opted. In a context of scarcity and high demand, the position of suppliers is privileged, resulting in rapid inflation, predatory pricing and corrupt practices. Yet reconstruction is also generally a moment of great opportunity, with improved economic flexibility and rapid improvements to freedom of movement, and increases in transportation capacity and imported goods. Immediate private gain is undeniably attractive when facing the uncertainties and opportunities of transition. The threat of dismissal, electoral loss and short-term postings in transition governments all increase the incentives of corruption. Personal financial wealth also becomes a greater symbol of social status in a peaceful era. For war veterans and exiles freshly brought to power, reconstruction can become a payback scheme, with wartime 'sacrifices' justifying the misuse of newly controlled public offices and positions. Years of discrimination, repression and fraud, however, can mobilize the political will of progressive politicians and citizens to 'fight' corruption.

If much of the blame is frequently ascribed to 'local' factors, corruption should be recognized as a highly politicized issue, to be fought not only at the domestic state level, but also at multiple sites, interconnections and processes. This essay addresses only some of these concerns, by raising issues with the 'empirics' of corruption measurement instruments, the roles of liberal peacebuilding in post-conflict corruption, and their consequences.

Measuring Corruption Perception Trends

There is no systematic and comprehensive study of corruption trends in relation to post-conflict transition and liberal peacebuilding.[22] I attempt to draw some preliminary findings from two publicly available sources: TI and Political Risk Service/International Country Risk Guide (PRS). Table 1 provides a first attempt, using publicly available Corruption Perception Index (CPI) data from TI.[23] The table includes 22 major 'peacebuilding and reconstruction' operations

TABLE 1:
CORRUPTION PERCEPTION INDEX TRENDS IN 'POST-CONFLICT' COUNTRIES
(1990–2006)*

Location	Duration	Return to war	Annual corruption trend	Corruption index (2006)	Corruption index (year)
Namibia	1989–90	No	−0.15	4.1	5.3 (1998)
Nicaragua	1989–92	No	−0.05	2.6	3 (1998)
Cambodia	1991–93	Yes	−0.2	2.1	2.3 (2005)
Angola	1991–97	Yes	0.4	2.2	1.7 (2002)
El Salvador	1991–95	No	0.4	4	3.6 (1998)
Mozambique	1992–95	No	−0.7	2.8	3.5 (1999)
Somalia	1992–95	Yes	n.a.	n.a.	2.1 (2005)
Rwanda	1993–96	Yes	−0.6	2.5	3.1 (2005)
Croatia	1995–98	No	0.7	3.4	2.7 (1999)
Bosnia	1995–present	No	−0.4	2.9	3.3 (2003)
Palestine†	1995–present	Yes	−0.2	2.4	3 (2004)
Guatemala	1997	No	−0.5	2.6	3.1 (1998)
East Timor	1999–2005	No	n.a.	n.a.	n.a.
Sierra Leone	1999–2005	Yes	0	2.2	2.2 (2003)
Kosovo	1999–present	No	n.a.	n.a.	n.a.
Congo, D.R.	2001–present	Yes	0	2	2 (2004)
Afghanistan	2002–present	Yes	n.a.	n.a.	2.5 (2005)
Liberia	2003–present	No	n.a.	n.a.	2.2 (2005)
Iraq	2003–present	Yes	−0.3	1.9	2.2 (2003)
Côte d'Ivoire	2003–present	Yes	0	2.1	2.1 (2003)
Haiti	2004–present	No	0.3	1.8	1.5 (2004)
Sudan	2004–present	Yes	−0.1	2	2.2 (2004)

*Duration refers to the military presence of the peace operation; the corruption index ranks countries from one to ten, with one being the highest level of perceived corruption; worsening perceptions of corruption are in italics; n.a., not available; standard deviation can range from 0.3 to 1.9.
†Peacebuilding in Palestine had no international military component, and the CPI for 2006 is based on two surveys, rather than the minimum of three required for inclusion into Transparency International's corruption survey.
Source: Corruption Perception Indexes from Transparency International (www.transparency.org/policy_research/surveys_indices/; www.icgg.org/downloads/overview05.csv).

since 1989, with data available for only 17 cases. In ten out of these 17 cases, corruption was generally perceived to be worsening in the period following these operations (according to data available, which are sometimes available after the operation has concluded and for only a few years). Perceptions of corruption reported an improvement in only four cases (Angola, El Salvador, Croatia and Haiti). These data may suggest that peacebuilding operations in these countries generally did not reduce perceptions of corruption. Yet the data are clearly insufficient to support the argument that peace operations increased corruption, notably owing to methodological limitations in comparing the CPI over time and other alternative explanations. Nor is it possible to draw conclusions about the possible impact of corruption perception trends on conflict recurrence, as the data are historically incomplete. Of the ten countries in which perceptions of corruption worsened, six of them did not experience renewed conflict, while hostilities recommenced in the other four countries. Again, the criteria for statistical significance limit the validity of these observations.

The utility of the analysis presented in Table 1 is notably limited by the lack of historical data, which prevents the analysis of trends in perceptions of corruption according to the timeframe of the peacebuilding and reconstruction operations. Such data are available for only four cases – Guatemala, Iraq, Haiti and Côte d'Ivoire – and no obvious trend can be observed.

The second attempt at examining quantitative data builds upon survey data collected by PRS, which offers the advantage of a longer time series, and greater time consistency allowing for comparative assessment. However, data are not available for all countries that have experienced post-conflict peacebuilding, and the data set is limited to 14 countries and suffers from time series gaps.[24] Figure 1 presents an average of the variation in the perception of corruption across countries with available data for these years, both before and after the cessation of hostilities (time = 0). The findings suggest that corruption perception is relatively stable throughout the end and immediate aftermath of hostilities (with the noticeable exception of Sierra Leone, where corruption was perceived as having increased immediately after the end of hostilities in early 2002). After six years there is a sharp increase in the perception of corruption.

Several methodological biases could explain this pattern. First, the PRS corruption assessment focuses on investor confidence. This may explain the inverse trend with the CPI data set and much of the literature: corruption may not be perceived as threatening for investors during the initial post-conflict period owing to the presence of peacekeeping forces and the backing of foreign donors. After the departure of troops and decreasing donor interest and leverage, this confidence may disintegrate. The apparent perception that corruption increases six years after the end of hostilities could also reflect a selection bias resulting from data availability, as well as a 'built-in' PRS survey bias that the longer a regime is in place the more corrupt it is supposed to be.[25]

In order to compare the two data sets, the case of Côte d'Ivoire is examined. Both the CPI and the PRS have corruption data available for this country prior to the conflict (see Figure 2).[26] For both CPI and PRS data sets, corruption is perceived to have increased since the 1999 *coup d'état* and to have momentarily

FIGURE 1
CORRUPTION PERCEPTION TRENDS, PRS DATA SET

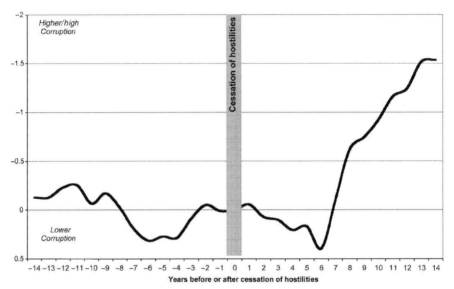

decreased around 2002, prior to the signing of the Linas–Marcoussis Accords in
January 2003, although the PRS data suggest a larger and longer reduction than
the CPI. The conflict has remained in a stalemate with a de facto partition of the
country. The northern part is controlled by an army rebel faction and experiences

FIGURE 2
CORRUPTION PERCEPTION INDEX TREND IN CÔTE D'IVOIRE (1998–2006)

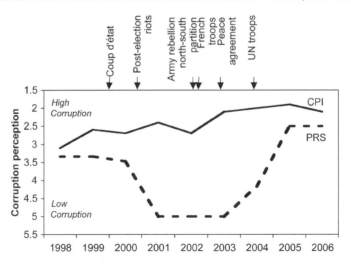

recurrent violence. In 2004, the initial UN observation mission was replaced by the United Nations Operation in Côte d'Ivoire, mandated with peacekeeping and the demobilization of combatants, as well as providing electoral, human rights, and law and order support. Between 2005 and 2006, corruption was perceived to have stabilized (PRS) or even decreased (CPI). This single case suggests the importance of considering multiple surveys and country-specific longitudinal studies that can differentiate between different types of corruption.

Corruption and Liberal Peacebuilding

The number of armed conflicts has declined since the early 1990s, at the same time as there has been an increase in liberal peacebuilding interventions. Yet Roland Paris argues that the political and economic liberalization characterizing these interventions has had destabilizing effects through increased societal competition and weakened domestic institutions.[27] Indeed, more wars (re)started and (re)ended in the 1990s than in any previous decade since 1946, suggesting that violent political instability had increased, although in most cases large-scale organized violence in the form of war was not sustained.[28] For Oliver Richmond and Jason Franks, liberal peacebuilding has, in practice, 'created very weak states and institutions that are dependent upon foreign support and subject to tests over power-sharing and corruption'.[29] Beyond simply being 'tested' by corruption, liberal peacebuilding has had contradictory relationships with corruption. On the one hand, peacebuilding interventions may provide the resources and institutions to curtail corruption. On the other, these may motivate and create opportunities for new forms of corruption. I briefly discuss below three main arguments linking liberal peacebuilding with higher levels of corruption.

Corruption and Democratization

The transition from war to peace, at least since the end of the cold war, has generally been shaped around negotiated settlements and democratization. This 'negotiated democracy' has potential impacts on corruption. First, 'national reconciliation' in the context of a peace process often results in a politically driven distribution of state assets and positions, with a tacit agreement on corruption included within the peace accords.[30] The resulting mix of electoral politics and power-sharing arrangements can undermine institution building and reduce accountability as each faction asserts 'sovereignty' over its territorial or institutional turf. The biased control of public assets by political factions has been characteristic of many transitions to peace. Eager not to 'jeopardize the peace', international donors often turn a blind eye to such practices or even portray them as a 'normal route to capitalist development'.[31] There is therefore a high risk that a transition to democracy increases political corruption, notably in the absence of formal instruments for party financing.

More generally, political liberalization represents a critical moment in terms of political party financing and the mode of governance in 'authoritarian' regimes. A shift from overtly coercive modes of political control to more democratically savvy forms of clientelism and vote buying may aggravate the intensity of corruption and cause it to change forms. Deleterious forms of political corruption include illegal (or dubious) political donations and economic activities, misappropriation of public funds, or the abuse of state resources.[32]

Corruption and Economic Liberalization

The process of economic liberalization offers major corruption opportunities that post-conflict institutions may be unwilling or unable to address. This process often results in the 'spontaneous' or unregulated privatization of state assets, and the liberalization of markets and landholding. Corrupt practices spread in some former socialist countries, such as Algeria and Mozambique, at least partly as a result of economic liberalization.[33]

As in other transition countries, prioritization of private over public ownership by international agencies may unintentionally play into the hands of local corrupt elites. The post-conflict context is often dominated by informal and sometimes criminal activities. Greater 'market' access to land and other assets along with a booming private sector favours local actors with access to seed capital, often generated by the proceeds of wartime criminal activities and corruption.[34] In some cases, international Western donors and financial institutions are aware and even accepting of this evolution, characterizing this process as a 'normal'.

More controversially, the 'endgame' of liberal peacebuilding may not be peace but market access, and corruption is tolerated or even promoted (by donors and investors) if it fosters the 'right kind' of stability (for geopolitical and economic objectives). This type of donor behaviour was particularly noticeable towards governments – such as Mozambique and Uganda – that were 'successfully' carrying out (neo-liberal) donor-sponsored reforms.[35] Liberalization policies are opportunistically imposed and manipulated, imposing heavy and unequally spread social and environmental burdens on populations still recovering from war.[36] In this regard, there is a vast literature on the economics of 'civilizing missions'. There is also some good evidence that FDI 'follows the flag', at least in the case of US corporations investing following US troop deployments.[37] The evidence is more ambivalent in the case of peacebuilding, where FDI does not immediately increase with UN peacebuilding missions, but rather follows the departure of UN troops.[38] This three- to five-year window provides a period of market and investment project 'maturation' and signals improving political stability.

Donors, Exceptions and a Corruption Dilemma

Donors and governments frequently face a mutually constructed corruption dilemma as assistance results in 'rent-seeking' through two main possible channels. Using a broader definition of corruption, the first channel links revenue windfalls with not only domestic authorities, but also the peacebuilding apparatus itself. The 'urgency' of political and economic transformations can take priority over democratic modes of governance, prudent management and due process, thereby creating a 'state of exception' for the organizations involved.[39] Much has been written on the abuses of the so-called 'disaster industry', ranging from cronyism in subcontracting and direct collusion in corrupt practices by local authorities, to issues such as poor transparency and lack of accountability.[40]

As demonstrated by the 'state of exception' in Iraq during the rule of the Coalition Provisional Authority (CPA), spending rules are far from systematic and reflect in part the sources of available funding and the mix of political and corporate interests at play. Iraqi government funds were sent in cash by the plane-load and disbursed without much regard to accountability. By contrast, funds allocated by the US Congress 'trickled' because of red tape constraining recon-struction activities by USAID and State Department agencies (reflecting in part an internal power struggle). From March 2003 to the end of June 2004, the US-run CPA was directed by US presidential executive order and a resolution of the UN Security Council to control Iraqi government funds representing US$20.6 billion.[41] Over that period, the CPA disbursed or committed 85 per cent of the funds, including US$11.8 billion in freshly minted US bills shipped to Iraq. This was hailed by the US Under Secretary of Treasury for International Affairs as 'one of the most successful and carefully planned operations of the war', before adding that the lack of accountability did not matter so much because it was 'Iraqi' money.[42] The management of this massive cash transfer was repeat-edly criticized by auditors, who suggested that there was a systematic haste to spend Iraqi funds before the Iraqi interim government 'took over' from the CPA.[43] By contrast, only 20 per cent of US taxpayers' reconstruction money was actually spent over the same period, in part because of much stricter disbur-sement rules. Beyond the lack of accountability over Iraqi funds, the relative imbalance between the disbursement of Iraqi and US funds also conveniently allowed for future US aid leverage over Iraqi authorities (and the subsequent redirection of funds to the 'security' budget), without having to ask for more money from Congress.[44]

The corruption dilemma also comes about because donors often distrust the government and prefer not to support it directly while still imposing significant demands upon the state. Simultaneously faced by a limited supply and increased demand for funds, governments turn to corruption. Part of this 'anti-state' liberal inclination relates to donor assessments of government corruption. This 'corrup-tion dilemma' leaves most resources in the hands of private subcontractors and non-governmental organizations (NGOs). Unfortunately, this strategy does not put assistance monies out of the reach of 'grabbing hands' so much as divert it away from public sector actors and towards private sector actors. If a broad defi-nition of corruption is adopted, the 'brain drain' from government departments to the private sector actually undermines the public interest and corrupts the 'state-building' agenda. Even the inflationary effects of aid flows and personnel can prove propitious for corruption.

The arguments presented above can help to explain high levels of corruption in many post-conflict countries. However, only a detailed analysis of socio-economic contexts and power relations can provide a nuanced understanding of the specific context, motivations and mechanisms behind multiple forms of corruption during transition.

Assessing the Consequences of Corruption

The first major consequence of corruption is a higher risk of renewed conflict. To the extent that economic variables such as the level, structure and growth of income influence the risk of armed conflict, corruption can undermine peacebuilding.[45] Corruption often plays a major role in informal economic activities, having negative effects on public revenue, economic formalization, and the protection of workers and the environment. Yet any attempts at tackling corruption by formalizing the economy should consider the social consequences and the possible impact on conflict, since informal economic activities support local livelihoods and act as a valuable 'social pressure valve'. In many countries, the formalization and legalization of the economy would do more harm than good.

Another political consequence of corruption may be the entrenchment of an imbalance of power or the political status quo inherited from the conflict. As groups empowered by the outcome of the war continue to sustain dominant political and economic positions through corruption, they may prevent the redistribution of power by stifling institutional checks and balances. At the extreme, donors may end up dealing with war criminals as official interlocutors – a situation that has been avoided in some cases by granting executive powers to international agencies through trusteeship and transitional authority mandates, as in the case of the Office of the High Representative in Bosnia.[46]

Post-conflict mismanagement and embezzlement of reconstruction assistance can also delegitimize the local government and lead to social unrest. To cover this up, local political leaders may, once again, resort to a divisive politics of hatred and fear, pushing corruption issues into the background. Following Hurricane Mitch in 1998, the US administration, for example, was eager to prevent a repetition of the political fallout resulting from the 1972 earthquake assistance offered to Nicaragua. In this case, the Somoza regime embezzled international emergency assistance monies, thus contributing to its forceful demise and the rise of the Sandinistas. The US Congress and USAID took strong measures to prevent the diversion of this assistance, with some degree of success in terms of the probity of the operation.[47] Critics have pointed out, however, that whereas these measures may have limited cases of narrowly defined corruption ('abuse of public office for private gain'), US assistance failed to challenge this narrow definition, thus perpetuating high levels of inequality and undermining the public interest.[48]

Corruption also facilitates criminality and violence in post-conflict societies by compromising the conduct and independence of the police and judiciary and by recycling former combatants into the private militias of corrupt politicians or organized crime. In extreme cases, corruption can help turn post-conflict countries into criminal hubs, as in Cambodia, Liberia or some of the Caucasus states in the 1990s. Corruption in the police and judiciary – along with weapons availability, endemic poverty and score settling – may also help to explain the higher homicide rate in post-conflict situations.[49]

According to the 'good governance' agenda and 'aid selectivity' principles of key Western development agencies, the most immediate consequence of corruption should be a negative effect on the volume, quality and targeting of reconstruction assistance provided by international donors and local authorities. However, an empirical test of the effect of corruption on aid provision between 1975 and 1995 indicates that this relationship is valid only for Scandinavian and Australian bilateral donors, but that the United States actually provided more aid to more corrupt countries.[50]

When local politicians make decisions about aid delivery based on politically or economically corrupt premises, rather than on competence and/or need, this results in inadequate infrastructure and services, higher costs and sometimes delays, and the entrenchment of inequalities.[51] A lack of commitment towards reconstruction goals and corruption in local public finances often deters donors, particularly when local authorities appear to have the resources to finance some of the reconstruction. For example, despite massive needs for reconstruction in Angola, Western donors have expressed reluctance to assist a government that has been accused of large-scale corruption in the oil and mineral industries – a position that facilitated 'constructive' engagement by China.[52] In Liberia, the cynicism and greed of fighters and politicians who were willing to jeopardize peace to secure a hoped-for lucrative position in the new government undermined donors' confidence in and support for the reconstruction process, eventually leading to quasi-trusteeship measures.[53]

Aid projects set up under circumstances of corruption will have a long-term impact. Beneficiary targeting for political purposes, incompetent or wasteful contractors, rigged bidding processes favouring political interest – these will impair security and negatively affect overall economic growth. For example, the privatization of the reconstruction of Beirut's Central District through Solidere, a company in which late Prime Minister Rafik Hariri and his associates were shareholders, led to widespread suspicion of conflicts of interests and corruption. The priority of the first Hariri government was not to provide public services for the poor, but to promote highly visible, prestige construction projects, which fanned the resentment of the have-nots and left the country with a staggering debt of US$33 billion.[54]

Finally, as argued earlier, corruption should be thought of more broadly, reaching beyond the 'domestic'. In this regard, a critical feature of peacebuilding concerns the fiscal aspects of market liberalization. Post-conflict transitions offer renewed economic opportunities that require careful fiscal management in order to consolidate the state and improve the wellbeing of the population.[55] Liberalization policies can be interpreted as a form of broadly defined 'corruption' of such fiscal priorities. The taxation of FDI projects is key here, precisely because these projects often benefit from a 'liberal' transition to peace. Following recurring calls by civil society and opposition politicians for contractual reviews, a government commission in the Democratic Republic of Congo (DRC) concluded that out of 61 mining contracts, many of them signed during the 'transition' period, 38 contracts had to be renegotiated and 23 cancelled because of irregularities.[56] Another example was provided through the renegotiation of a US$900 million international iron-mining contract signed by the transitional government in Liberia. Whereas the country's new elected government has since been under tight anti-corruption supervision through the Liberia Governance and Economic Management Assistance Programme (GEMAP), it was an NGO that highlighted contractual problems that would harm the Liberian public interest.[57] In both the DRC and Liberia, the transition period thus proved to be an opportune moment to capture lucrative contracts while potentially undermining the public interest.

Although the main consequences of corruption are overwhelmingly negative, functionalist arguments about corruption suggest that some forms of corruption may occasionally have positive effects. Corruption may help in securing some degree of political, economic and social stability. Although corruption needs to be 'rooted out' as early as possible, it is often very difficult rapidly and effectively to address local sources of grievances and conflict. In this respect, some of the political and social effects of corruption may provide a short-term solution – such as buying out 'peace spoilers' or authorizing illegal but licit (i.e. accepted by custom or morality) economic activities that sustain local livelihoods.[58] Donors should thus ensure that reconstruction programmes and interventions are sensitive to local contexts. Many examples, however, suggest that such 'quick fixes', tempting though they may be, may have long-lasting negative effects. Buying out spoilers is a risky venture, as impunity and economic rewards can sustain rebel movements, as demonstrated in Angola with UNITA or Sierra Leone with the RUF. Informal economic activities strengthen the grip of quasi-criminal groups in the economic and government sphere, as well as negatively affect future economic development. In this light, every effort should be made to move beyond 'buying peace' to ensure short-term stability, to achieve the goals of social justice and sustainable peace. The difficulty, of course, is in achieving these goals.[59]

Discussion

The challenges faced by conflict-affected countries are formidable. Less corruption in 'post-conflict' peacebuilding and reconstruction not only means better-targeted, higher quality and more efficient development assistance, but also a greater contribution to the positive transformation of the local political economy as well as the consolidation of state institutions and legitimate political parties. In short, less corruption should help build a stronger peace. Corruption, however, should not only be 'fought' in domestic governance at the state level, but must also be addressed in a broader sense at multiple sites and interconnections.

A very broad definition of corruption encompasses 'abuses of the public interest by narrow sectional interests', rather than simply 'the abuse of public office for private gain', as often stated.[60] From this perspective, a definition of corruption should encompass profiteering from peacebuilding and reconstruction, as well as the drastic economic policies that frequently end up serving narrow interest groups.[61] Rethinking the concept of corruption would thus promote the public interest of post-conflict countries by addressing the lucrative subcontracting networks, the tax-free salaries of overpaid consultants, donor agencies' aggressive promotion of FDI ventures over domestic entrepreneurship, the fire-sale privatization of public assets, and the liberalization of trade and tax policies.[62]

Defining corruption more broadly means engaging with the involvement of a large number of non-domestic actors, ranging from aid agencies to foreign investors and international banks. In fact, the policies of some international agencies and financial institutions have compounded and transformed corruption, notably through economic sanctions, structural adjustments and the privatization of state assets.[63] In Iraq, the oil-for-food programme exacerbated corruption while demonstrating a politically motivated lack of oversight by both the UN Secretariat and the Security Council.[64] In the private sector, many companies investing in post-conflict countries also seek to minimize the amount of tax they pay. For reasons of incapacity or vested interests, transitional governments often do not maximize the public interest, signing highly lucrative contracts that favour the private sector. More generally, the geography of post-conflict corruption should encompass the vast financial apparatus deployed in the creation and redistribution of wealth during transition, ranging from large commercial banks and well-established tax havens to fly-by-night financial intermediaries.[65]

To conclude, this essay has presented some of the arguments linking liberal peacebuilding with higher levels of corruption. Alternative arguments, however, have not been discussed and the preliminary evidence collected begs further enquiry. The most basic ambivalence suggested relates to the effect of anti-corruption efforts on short-term political stability. The first priority in this regard is to maintain security for the population. An assessment of the capacity of corrupt peace-spoilers is thus required before moving against them. The international community may wisely let corruption buy a temporary peace when the risk of renewed conflict is too high. However, the legacy of such an approach is risky. Rather than risk complacency or complicity, a better tactic is to drive a wedge between peace-spoilers and their source of power: their economic interests. Amnesty and enticing demobilization, disarmament and reintegration (DDR) packages can ensure the co-operation of middle- and low-ranking combatants, whereas war-crime indictments can isolate leaders. International supervision can help to protect public finances and key economic sectors from embezzlement and secure a smoother transition towards accountable and transparent economic management.

The other ambivalences suggested concern the 'democratic institutions' and 'markets' that are likely to foster competitive corruption, resulting in deteriorating legitimacy with the population. A second priority in this regard is to restore the confidence of the population, most notably in the government and the political process. A corrupt government rarely has the support of its population, but in many cases patronage and clientelism are the legitimating link between individual rulers and the ruled. In order to move beyond corruptly financed modes of redistribution, both institutional arrangements and political culture have to change.

Accusations of corruption are also a prominent political dimension in the reconstruction period: better detection and accountability mechanisms should prevent manipulation. Foreign interveners also need to have greater confidence in the local population and political parties to ensure an optimal partnership. Institutional reforms are key to building transparency and accountability, but implementation can be slow and difficult. Thus, a short-term priority needs to be placed on informing the public: about what is being done, by whom and how, and how it affects the average citizen. Too often a climate of fear, (feigned) ignorance and opportunism pervades so-called post-conflict situations. Widely broadcast and high-quality information is crucial to ensure that the goals of transparency and accountability are more rapidly achieved.

From a research agenda perspective, further empirical studies should track trends in corruption perceptions according to the timeframe of peacebuilding and reconstruction operations. For quantitative approaches to succeed, a broader data set (covering the entire period and all countries) and multivariate analysis would be required; but the reliability of these data should be closely examined, in so far as reported corruption data rely heavily on perceptions, and thus to some extent on expectations and informational context as well as the survey targets. For example, those surveyed may expect less corruption after the transition to peace (and thus rank corruption levels higher) and they may be exposed to more media information about corruption (thanks, for example, to the work of anti-corruption 'watchdogs' and a more open public media). Perceptions are nevertheless important in understanding possible links between corruption and renewed conflict. Survey data should thus be disaggregated according to the characteristics of informants. Alternative methods of data collection have included tracking media reporting of corruption-related conflicts. Sub-national surveys and media reporting can also be particularly useful, especially in the case of separatist conflicts such as Aceh.[66]

Future enquiries into corruption and liberal peacebuilding projects should pay particular attention to the differentiating effects of corruption and anti-corruption programmes. The reworking of sovereignty, place-based politics and 'fast-track' integration into global markets provide grounds for detailed field-based and archival research. Ethnographic and social survey studies of post-conflict violence could also yield more insights into the political geography of the 'state of exception' at work during recent liberal peacebuilding operations. Not only could this research be of interest in assessing the risk of renewed armed conflict, but it could also provide a better understanding of the broader relations between violence, conflict and corruption.

NOTES

1. UN, 'Corruption: Threats and Trends in the Twenty-first Century', UN doc., A/CONF.203/6, 2005.
2. See, for example, opinion polls: 'South East Europe Public Agenda Survey' by the South East Europe Democracy Support, 2002; Nicaragua, 'National Integrity Survey', CIET International, 1998; 'Governance and Anti-corruption Report for Sierra Leone', World Bank, 2003; 'Cambodia Governance and Corruption Diagnostic', World Bank, May 2000.
3. In the UK, a new anti-corruption and anti-bribery measure was enacted as part of the Anti-terrorism, Crime and Security Act 2001. In the United States, see the 1998, 2002 and 2006 'National Security Strategy of the United States'; see also 'Terrorism, Corruption and War', posted by the US State Department (at: usinfo.state.gov/products/pubs/iraq/war.htm); D. Kaufmann, 'Corruption, Governance and Security: Challenges for the Rich Countries and the World', *Global Competitiveness Report 2004/2005*, Washington, DC: World Bank, 2004; William Reno, 'The Politics of Insurgency in Collapsing States', *Development and Change*,

Vol.33, No.5, 2002, pp.837–58; K. Thachuk, 'Corruption and International Security', *SAIS Review*, Vol.25, No.1, 2005, pp.143–52.

4. I refer to peacebuilding as complementary to peacemaking (bringing an end to hostilities) and peacekeeping (maintaining peace through military force to separate conflicting parties). As such, peacebuilding aims to create a 'self-sustaining' peace, one that does not require external peacekeeping.

5. Emil Bolongaita, 'Controlling Corruption in Post-conflict countries', Kroc Institute Occasional Paper No. 26, January 2005; Philippe Le Billon, 'Corruption, Reconstruction and Oil Governance in Iraq', *Third World Quarterly*, Vol.26, No.4, 2005, pp.679–98; Le Billon, 'Overcoming Corruption in the Wake of Conflict', *Global Corruption Report*, Berlin: Transparency International, 2005, pp.73–82; A. Alix Boucher, William J. Durch, Margarete Midyette, Sarah Rose and Jason Terry, 'Mapping and Fighting Corruption in War-torn States', Washington, DC: Henry L. Stimson Centre, 2006; Madelene O'Donnell, 'Post-conflict Corruption: A Rule of Law Agenda?', in Agnes Hurwitz and Reyko Huang (eds) *Civil War and the Rule of Law*, Boulder, CO: Lynne Rienner, 2008.

6. General Accounting Office (GAO), 'Bosnia Peace Operation: Crime and Corruption Threaten Successful Implementation of the Dayton Peace Agreement', *GAO/ NSIAD-00-156*, Washington, DC, 2000; International Crisis Group (ICG), 'Courting Disaster: The Misrule of Law in Bosnia and Herzegovina, Balkans', Report No. 127, Brussels, 2002; Vera Devine, 'Corruption in Post-war Reconstruction: The Experience of Bosnia and Herzegovina', in David Large (ed.), *Corruption in Post War Reconstruction. Confronting the Vicious Circle*, Beirut: Lebanese Transparency Association, TIRI and UNDP, 2005.

7. Yet the report does not locate the 'fight against corruption' *within* effective peacebuilding, and only refers twice more to corruption as an 'economic' cause of conflict, and in discussing the employment of UN volunteers as cheap labour potentially 'corrupting' the programme as these volunteers 'work alongside colleagues who are making three or four times their salary for similar functions'. UN 'Report of the Panel on United Nations Peace Operations', UN doc., A/55/305; S/2000/809, 2000, p.24.

8. Bolongaita (see n.5 above).

9. Akhil Gupta, *Postcolonial Development. Agriculture in the Making of Modern India*, Durham, NC: Duke University Press, 1998.

10. Large (see n.6 above); Jens C. Andvig, 'Corruption and Armed Conflict. Some Stirring Around in the Governance Soup', Working Paper 720, Norwegian Institute of International Affairs (NUPI), 2007.

11. Paul Collier, Lance Elliot, Håvard Hegre, Anke Hoeffler, Marta Reynal-Querol and Nicholas Sambanis, 'Breaking the Conflict Trap: Civil War and Development Policy', Washington, DC: World Bank, 2003; David Keen, *The Economic Functions of Civil Wars*, Adelphi Paper No. 320, Oxford: IISS/Oxford University Press, 1998; William Reno, *Warlord Politics and African States*, Boulder, CO: Lynne Rienner, 1998; Joel S. Hellman, Geraint Jones and Daniel Kaufmann, 'Seize the State, Seize the Day: State Capture and Influence in Transition Economies', *Journal of Comparative Economics*, Vol.31, No.4, 2003, pp.751–73; Jens C. Andvig, 'Corruption and Fast Change', *World Development*, Vol.34, No.2, 2006, pp.328–40.

12. Ed Brown and Jonathan Cloke, 'Neoliberal Reform, Governance and Corruption in the South: Assessing the International Anti-corruption Crusade', *Antipode*, Vol.36, No.2, 2004, pp.272–94; Brown and Cloke, 'Neoliberal Reform, Governance and Corruption in Central America: Exploring the Nicaraguan Case', *Political Geography*, Vol.24, No.5, 2005, pp.601–30.

13. Le Billon (see n.5 above), pp.679–98; Le Billon, 'Buying Peace or Fuelling War: The Role of Corruption in Armed Conflicts', *Journal of International Development*, Vol.15, 2003, pp.413–26.

14. OECD Creditor Reporting System for the period 1989–2002, this figure includes reconstruction and development assistance and excludes food aid, emergency relief, debt relief, and military intervention or peacekeeping costs.

15. While conflict situations grab the attention of the media, aid has been lower than usual in non-conflict situations over the past decade; Collier et al. (see n.11 above).

16. The 'reconstruction' budget for the period 2003–06 amounted to more than US$62 billion (Development Fund for Iraq: US$28.2 billion; US government Iraq Relief and Reconstruction Fund: US$20.9 billion; Official Development Assistance from other donors: US$13 billon (for 2003–05 only), including World Bank Iraqi Trust Fund: US$0.4 billion. Sources: www.state.gov/p/nea/rls/rpt/60857.htm; World Bank Operations in Iraq, 28 Feb. 2007; See Looney, this issue.

17. Daniel Kaufmann and Massimo Mastruzzi, *Governance Matters V: Governance Indicators for 1996–2005*, Washington, DC: World Bank, 2006.

18. Large (see n.6 above).

19. Charles Tilly, 'War Making as State Making', in Peter Evans, Dietrich Rueschemeyer and Theda Skocpol (eds), *Bringing the State Back*, Cambridge: Cambridge University Press, 1985; William D. Stanley, *The Protection Racket State: Elite Politics, Military Extortion, and Civil War in El Salvador*, Philadelphia, PA: Temple University Press, 1996. Ideals and strict discipline in armed movements have also limited corruption, as with the Eritrean People's Liberation Front. In Afghanistan, the Taliban regime was initially well received by the population for putting an end to the corruption of mujahedin warlords; Christopher Cramer and Jonathan Goodhand, 'Try Again, Fail Again, Fail Better? War, the State, and the "Post-conflict" Challenge in Afghanistan', *Development and Change*, Vol.33, No.5, 2002, pp.885–909.

20. David Keen, *The Economic Functions of Civil Wars*, Adelphi Paper No. 320, Oxford: IISS/ Oxford University Press, 1998.

21. Ibid. Widespread participation in the 'illegal' logging in Cambodia helped sustain the conflict for several years, see Le Billon, 'The Political Ecology of Transition in Cambodia 1989–1999: War, Peace and Forest Exploitation', *Development and Change*, Vol.31, No.4, 2000, pp.785–805.

22. Several donor agencies have streamlined assessments of corruption in many 'post-conflict' governance analyses, most notably the World Bank and USAID through its 'Office of Democracy and Governance'.

23. TI's Corruption Perception Index is a composite index, PRS's corruption index essentially measures the risk posed by corruption to the private sector (and especially foreign investors).

24. Including: Angola, Côte d'Ivoire, Croatia, Democratic Republic of Congo, El Salvador, Ethiopia, Guatemala, Haiti, Liberia, Mozambique, Namibia, Sierra Leone, Somalia and Sudan.

25. Theresa Thompson and Anwar Shah, 'Transparency International's Corruption Perceptions Index: Whose Perceptions Are They Anyway?' Discussion Paper, World Bank, 2005 (at: siteresources.worldbank.org/INTWBIGOVANTCOR/Resources/ TransparencyInternationalCorruptionIndex.pdf).

26. The CPI data are available from 1998 to 2006. Note that PRS data were included in the CPI until 2000, and that PRS data are converted to match CPI index range (zero to ten).

27. Roland Paris, *At War's End: Building Peace after Conflict*, Cambridge: Cambridge University Press, 2004; see also M. Duffield, *Global Governance and the New Wars. The Merging of Development and Security*, London: Zed, 2001; Oliver P. Richmond, *The Transformation of Peace*, Basingstoke: Palgrave, 2005.

28. *Human Security Brief 2006*, Vancouver: Human Security Report Project, Simon Fraser University (at: www.humansecuritybrief.info).

29. Oliver P. Richmond and Jason Franks, 'Liberal Hubris? Virtual Peace in Cambodia', *Security Dialogue*, Vol.38, No.1, 2007, p.30.

30. Le Billon (see n.13 above), pp.413–26.

31. Joe Hanlon, 'Do Donors Promote Corruption? The Case of Mozambique', *Third World Quarterly*, Vol.25, No.4, 2004, pp.747–63.

32. Jon Moran, 'Democratic Transitions and Forms of Corruption', *Crime, Law and Social Change*, Vol.36, No.4, 2001, pp.379–93; Marcin Walecki, 'Political Money and Corruption', in *Global Corruption Report 2004: Political Corruption*, London: Transparency International and Pluto Press, 2004; Alan Doig and Heather Marquette, 'Corruption and Democratization – The Litmus Test of International Donor Agency Intentions?', *Futures*, Vol.37, 2005, pp.199–213.

33. Fatiha Talahite, 'Économie Administrée, Corruption et Engrenage de la Violence en Algérie: Corruption, Libéralisation, Démocratisation', *Tiers Monde*, Vol.161, 2000, pp.49–74; Graham Harrison, 'Corruption as "Boundary Politics": The State, Democratisation, and Mozambique's Unstable Liberalisation', *Third World Quarterly*, Vol.20, No.3, 1999, pp.537–50.

34. R.T. Naylor, *Wages of Crime: Black Markets, Illegal Finance, and the Underworld Economy*, Ithaca, NY: Cornell University Press, 2004.

35. Hanlon (see n.31 above), pp.747–63; Roger Tangri and Andrew M. Mwenda, 'Politics, Donors and the Ineffectiveness of Anti-corruption Institutions in Uganda', *Journal of Modern African Studies*, Vol.44, No.1, 2006, pp.101–24.

36. Naomi Klein, *The Shock Doctrine: The Rise of Disaster Capitalism*, Toronto: Knopf, 2007.

37. Glen Biglaiser and Karl DeRouen, 'Following the Flag: Troop Deployment and U.S. Foreign Direct Investment', *International Studies Quarterly*, Vol.51, 2007, pp.835–54.

38. Stephanie R. Ahern, 'Foreign Direct Investment and the Economic Wilderness States: The Effects of War and Foreign Military Intervention', paper at the Annual Meeting of the International Studies Association, Honolulu, 2005.

39. Frederik Galtung, 'Introduction: The Corruption Dimension of Post-war Reconstruction', in Large (see n.6 above); Giorgio Agamben, *State of Exception*, Chicago: University of Chicago Press, 2004.

40. With respect to humanitarian relief, see Barnaby Willitts-King and Paul Harvey, *Managing the Risks of Corruption in Humanitarian Relief Operations*, London: Overseas Development Institute, 2005.

41. Cash inflow represented close to US$20.6 billion, half from oil sales, the rest from transfers of the oil-for-food programme and repatriated funds from the Saddam Hussein regime (at: govinfo.library.unt.edu/cpa-iraq/budget/DFI_26jun2004.xls).

42. John B. Taylor, 'Billions over Baghdad', *New York Times*, 27 Feb. 2007.

43. Jeremy Kahn, 'Where did all the Cash go in Iraq? Treasury's Reconstruction Efforts are just as Flawed as the Rest', *The New Republic*, 6 Mar. 2007; Henry A. Waxman, 'Cash transfers to the Coalition Provisional Authority', Committee on Oversight and Government Reform, Congress of the United States, 6 Feb. 2007 (at: oversight.house.gov/Documents/20070206130101-80952.pdf).

44. For example, Deputy Defense Secretary Paul Wolfowitz stressed to Congress that: 'There's a lot of money to pay for this [reconstruction] that doesn't have to be U.S. taxpayer money, and *it starts with the assets of the Iraqi people*', House Committee on Appropriations Hearing on a Supplemental War Regulation, 27 Mar. 2003 [emphasis added]; Le Billon (see n.5 above), pp. 679–98.

45. Collier et al. (see n.11 above).

46. If transitional international administration helped keep peace-spoilers and war criminals out, it also struck bargains with corrupt politicians deemed non-threatening to the political status quo; Richard Caplan, *A New Trusteeship: The International Administration of War torn Territories*, Adelphi Paper 341, Oxford: IISS/Oxford University Press, 2002.

47. Mitchell A. Seligson, *Good Governance and Transparency in Honduras After Hurricane Mitch: A Study of Citizen Views*, Alexandria, VA: Casals and Associates, 2001; T.E. Cox, 'An Ounce of Prevention. Oversight of Disaster Reconstruction Activities in Central America and the Caribbean', *Journal of Public Inquiry*, Fall/Winter, 2001, pp.33–6.

48. Ed Brown, 'Still their Backyard? The US and Post-Mitch Development Strategies in Nicaragua', *Political Geography*, Vol.19, 2000, pp.543–72; Brown and Cloke 'Neoliberal Reform, Governance and Corruption in Central America: Exploring the Nicaraguan Case' (see n.12 above); B. Wisner, 'Risk and the Neoliberal State: Why Post-Mitch Lessons didn't Reduce El Salvaldor's Earthquake Losses', *Disasters*, Vol.25, No.3, 2001, pp.251–68.

49. Paul Collier and Anke Hoeffler, 'Murder by Numbers: Socio-economic Determinants of Homicide and Civil War', WPS/2004-10, Oxford: Centre for the Study of African Economies Series, 2004.

50. Alberto Alesina and Beatrice Weder, 'Do Corrupt Governments Receive Less Foreign Aid?', *American Economic Review*, Vol.92, No.4, 2002, pp.1126–37.

51. Pete Ewins, Paul Harvey, Kevin Savage and Alex Jacobs, *Mapping the Risks of Corruption in Humanitarian Action*, London: Overseas Development Institute and Management Accounting for NGOs, 2006.

52. Norwegian Refugee Council, *Angola: Lack of Assistance Undermines Sustainable Return of IDPs*, Oslo, 2004; Human Rights Watch (HRW), *Some Transparency, No Accountability: The Use of Oil Revenue in Angola and its Impact on Human Rights*, New York, 2004.

53. ICG, 'Rebuilding Liberia: Prospects and Perils', ICG Africa Report No. 75, Brussels, 2003. See also Reno, this issue.

54. The plan was replete with 'irregularities such as under-pricing and buying real estate under the guise of rebuilding the city', i.e., predatory expropriation. The Hariri government was suspected of having initiated an anti-corruption administrative reform only to pressure coalition politicians and MPs to approve the plan. The plan was approved and no high-ranking official or politicians faced sanctions. See, Richard W. Carlson, 'Mr. Hariri Goes to Washington', *The Weekly Standard*, Vol.8, No.34, 12 May 2003; Lara Marlowe, 'Up From Despair', *Time*, Vol.147, No.3, 15 Jan. 1996; Abeer El-Gazzawi, 'Lebanon's Financial Crisis: A Recipe for Disaster?', *World Press Review*, 24 June 2002.

55. See James Boyce and Madelene O'Donnell, *Peace and the Public Purse: Economic Policies for Postwar Statebuilding*, Boulder, CO: Lynne Rienner, 2007; Tony Addison and Alan Roe, *Fiscal Policy for Development: Poverty, Reconstruction and Growth*, Basingstoke: Palgrave, 2004.

56. Jonathan Clayton, 'Mining Groups Face Congo Shake-up after Review', *The Times*, 8 Nov. 2007.

57. The initial contract gave Mittal Steel 'complete freedom to set the price of the iron ore', which affected the amount to be paid in taxes to the Liberian government. See Global Witness, *Heavy Mittal? A State within a State: The Inequitable Mineral Development Agreement between the Government of Liberia and Mittal Steel Holdings NV*, London: Global Witness, 2006, p.7. Mittal's parent was domiciled in Netherlands Antilles, and later in the 'tax-friendly' Swiss canton of Zug; its Liberian subsidiary was domiciled in Cyprus; on GEMAP, see Reno, this issue.

58. Le Billon (see n.13 above), pp. 413–26; Willem Van Schendel and Itty Abraham, *Illicit Flows and Criminal Things: States, Borders, and the Other Side of Globalization*, Bloomington, IN: Indiana University Press, 2005.
59. A detailed discussion of anti-corruption initiatives in 'post-conflict' countries falls beyond the scope of this article (see n.5 above).
60. Tax Justice Network, 'Corruption and the Offshore Interface', 2006 (at: www.taxjustice.net/cms/front_content.php?idcat=100).
61. Klein (see n.36 above).
62. M. Carnahan, *Options for Revenue Generation in Post-conflict Environments*, New York and Amherst, MA: Centre on International Co-operation and Political Economy Research Institute, 2007; Morris Szeftel, 'Clientelism, Corruption and Catastrophe' *Review of African Political Economy*, Vol.27, No.85, 2000, pp.427–41.
63. R. Cooksey, 'Aid and Corruption: A Worm's-eye View of Donor Policies and Practices', paper at the 11th International Anti-corruption Conference, Seoul, South Korea, 26–29 May 2003.
64. Le Billon (see n.5 above), pp.678–98.
65. Naylor (see n.34 above); Raymond Baker, *Capitalism's Achilles Heel. Dirty Money and How to Renew the Free-market System*, Hoboken, NJ: John Wiley, 2005; Tax Justice Network, *Tax Us if You Can. The True Story of a Global Failure*, London, 2005.
66. See Aceh Conflict Monitoring Update (at: www.conflictanddevelopment.org).

[18]

Closing the Gap Between Peace Operations and Post-Conflict Insecurity: Towards a Violence Reduction Agenda

ROBERT MUGGAH and KEITH KRAUSE

This article highlights how the instruments for addressing the presumed source(s) of armed violence need to be sharpened and extended to address the heterogeneous character of armed violence present in many post-conflict situations. These extensions require the development of practical armed violence prevention and reduction programmes that draw upon scholarship and practice from the criminal justice and public health sectors. The article argues that reducing organized violence and insecurity in post-conflict contexts requires responding to the wider dynamics of armed violence rather than focusing exclusively on insecurity directly connected to what are traditionally defined as armed conflict and post-conflict dynamics; and this requires attention not just to the instruments of violence, but also to the political and economic motives of agents and institutions implicated in violent exchanges at all levels of social interaction.

Despite the oft-repeated mantra that sustainable development requires security, and sustainable security requires development, international agencies and actors have struggled to reconcile peace and security with development concerns. Yet, in practice, a number of links and synergies have emerged, in most cases more by default than design. For example, from a narrow peacekeeping focus on separating well-defined parties under a negotiated ceasefire, multilateral peace and security operations have expanded to deal with irregular forms of war, up to and including peace enforcement operations, and to engage in the longer-term process of post-conflict peacebuilding, statebuilding and democracy promotion.[1] The development community has also come to treat underdevelopment as 'dangerous' and to invest in interventions to bolster governance and security in so-called fragile or weak states.[2] This 'mission creep' was driven to some extent by institutional learning: a growing awareness of the ways in which warring parties (and the international actors) were caught in cycles of violent conflict and insecurity.[3] In some cases, both development and security actors concluded that a failure to address effectively and comprehensively the immediate and underlying causes of armed violence meant that the embers smouldered, waiting for the next spark to reignite into violence.[4]

Yet the effectiveness of this broad-spectrum treatment for contemporary armed conflicts remains unproven, from Afghanistan to Iraq to sub-Saharan Africa. This article focuses on one particular gap in the international arsenal of responses: the weak responses to the large-scale armed violence, both criminal and political, that often characterizes unstable post-conflict environments, in places such as Timor-Leste, Guatemala or Burundi. To date, the main policy instruments for dealing with the presumed sources of post-conflict violence and insecurity have included disarmament, demobilization, and reintegration (DDR) of ex-combatants, and small arms control programmes. Comprising a cluster of activities designed to secure the peace, these interventions are regularly advanced at the national level and targeted at potential spoilers (individual combatants and groups of civilians).[5] While exhibiting certain differences in approach, both DDR and small arms control reflect the strategic and bureaucratic priorities of the security and development sectors and perpetuate the discourse and policy priorities of international donors and power-holding local elites. Each cluster of activities also lacks clear metrics of success or evidence of whether they are effective in achieving even their stated objectives. The little evidence that has been assembled indicates that DDR and small arms control are often unable, when pursued in isolation, to contend with the criminal and quasi-political violence that often supersedes purely political violence in the post-conflict period.[6]

This article highlights how the instruments for addressing the presumed source(s) of armed violence need to be sharpened and extended to address the heterogeneous character of armed violence present in many (if not most) post-conflict situations. These extensions will require the development of practical armed violence prevention and reduction programmes that draw upon scholarship and practice from the criminal justice and public health sectors. Analysts in these areas are increasingly cognisant of the ways in which violence is spatially, temporally and demographically concentrated among particular 'at-risk' groups, as both potential perpetrators and victims. A range of examples of armed violence prevention and reduction are emerging that build on bottom-up analyses, prioritize evidence-based programming, and target risk factors alongside spoilers and the tools of violence. These activities offer a new paradigm for addressing post-conflict armed violence and a compelling alternative to more narrowly focused DDR and small arms control activities.

This article first reviews conventional DDR and small arms control activities – their priorities, characteristics and uneven outcomes. Second, it analyses the complex landscape of armed violence – particularly conflict, criminal and urban dynamics – offering some tentative explanations for the modest returns associated with narrowly conceived approaches to post-conflict insecurity. The final section examines the evolution of armed violence reduction activities and interventions that have been particularly effective in developed and middle-income countries throughout Latin America and the Caribbean. Overall, the article finds that dealing with the most widespread forms of organized violence and insecurity in post-conflict contexts will require responding to the wider dynamics of armed violence rather than focusing exclusively on insecurity directly connected to what are traditionally defined as armed conflict and post-conflict dynamics. Adequately addressing post-conflict organized violence – whether criminal or political (or both) – will require attention not just to the instruments of violence, but also to the political and economic motives of agents and institutions implicated in violent exchanges at all levels of social interaction. While more systemic evaluations are required to determine the extent to which experiences from one part of the world can be adapted to another, the article concludes that second-generation activities – including municipal-level armed violence interventions – can potentially complement more conventional approaches.

Conventional DDR and Small Arms Control

Post-conflict demobilization and the disarming of former combatants have long been understood in multilateral peace operations as a key component of re-establishing peace and stability.[7] At a general level, these interventions are expected to prevent or minimize war recurrence and, as the World Bank described it, 'a successful demobilization and reintegration program (DRP) for ex-combatants is the key to an effective transition from war to peace'.[8] Peace support operations and post-conflict recovery packages regularly adopted DDR and small arms control measures according to the mandates of UN Security Council resolutions or mediated peace agreements, particularly since the 1970s (Table 1). The programmes focused on specific categories of individuals who potentially could challenge the newly established (or re-established) Weberian monopoly on the legitimate use of force by state institutions.

Most DDR and weapons management activities introduced in the wake of war have had a supply-side focus. They emphasized a reduction in the number of arms in circulation and offered straightforward (often monetized) demobilization packages (including integration into newly created national armed forces) to former combatants. The disarmament phase recognized that ex-combatants from irregular armed forces often kept their weapons, or surrendered old or non-functional ones, with the result that large numbers of military-style weapons entered into society, with potentially negative consequences for human security. But because the issues of the instruments (small arms) and agents (spoilers) are considered by warring parties to be especially politically sensitive, provisions for DDR and small arms control tended to be watered down or relegated to the end of peace negotiations (if at all), with conflicting parties either maximizing their future freedom of action or their short-term economic gains.

TABLE 1:
GEOGRAPHIC DISTRIBUTION OF DDR: 1974–PRESENT

Region	Number of operations	Percentage of total
Africa	34	65
Central America	3	6
Caribbean	2	4
South America	1	2
Asia*	8	15
Pacific	2	4
Balkans	2	4

*Asia includes Afghanistan and Iraq.
Source: Robert Muggah (ed.), *Security and Post-Conflict Reconstruction Dealing with Fighters in the Aftermath of War*, New York: Routledge, 2008.

Originally conceived as a security or military activity that focused on disarmament and demobilization, in the 1990s, DDR programmes expanded to include the creation of formal programmes for the reinsertion and reintegration of ex-combatants into civilian life. Programmes such as those undertaken in Uganda and Ethiopia also focused on correcting distortions in national budgeting and a shift from military to social welfare spending.[9] One of the most prominent examples is the World Bank's Multi-Donor Demobilization and Reintegration Programme (MDRP) undertaken in nine countries of the Great Lakes Region (GLR) of Africa.[10] In parallel, security sector reform (SSR) initiatives and, in rare cases, enhanced firearm legislation and weapons management activities targeting civilians (as opposed to combatants) were occasionally included in UN Security Council-mandated operations.[11] Thus, DDR and post-conflict small arms control efforts were increasingly implemented in the context of broader socio-economic development and human security goals, an extension of the initial logic that had been much more politically focused on (re)establishing the security of state institutions. More specifically, DDR and small arms control were expected to alter the incentives for ex-combatants in civilian life to resort to predatory and criminal activities (usually involving the use of arms), and promote a process of integration into ostensibly 'normal' civilian socio-economic structures.[12] Again, this was based on the assumption that the instrument and agent – small arms and the demobilized ex-combatants, respectively – posed the greatest potential threat not only to state but also to human security.

But while the discourse and practice of DDR and small arms control may reflect the merging of the security and development agendas,[13] the extent to which such interventions practically enhance safety remains largely unknown. There has been comparatively little serious discussion of how to measure whether DDR and small arms regulation is effective. In fact, there were two competing implicit benchmarks of success: the first focused on eliminating short-term threats to the stability of the peace agreement and the security of the state and regime; the second has been associated with broader peacebuilding and state-building goals, including socio-economic and development considerations. Most recent evidence suggests that DDR rarely yields durable reintegration at the political, economic, or social level.[14] DDR and arms reduction programmes associated with peace support operations may also be less effective at minimizing violence than expected.[15] The extent to which such failures are attributed to the way in which DDR is (under)conceptualized or implemented remains a poorly researched area.

Although DDR focused on weapons held by ex-combatants, this was usually only one aspect of the policy arsenal deployed to deal with the potential impact of arms availability and misuse on post-conflict peace and security. Parallel to the relatively large investments in DDR, Western donors and the development community more generally have been preoccupied with the role of arms in fuelling armed conflict and other forms of collective violence.[16] Formal measures adopted under the ambit of peace support operations to contain and deter arms availability usually included such activities as arms embargoes and sanctions, no-fly zones to reduce arms trafficking, increased border controls and enforced cordon and search operations. Within these operations, arms availability has been conceived largely in supply-side terms. This entails a relatively simplistic causal assumption that constraining illegal trade and promoting reductions in a given stock of arms in a conflict-affected society will generate positive returns for domestic security. Beyond the immediate measures focused on peace support operations, prominent international initiatives have focused on enhancing export controls, strengthening border policing, establishing an international instrument for tracing illicit weapons, restricting illicit arms brokering activities, improving the security of state-held stocks and tightening controls over the availability of ammunition.[17]

These essentially supply-side initiatives are important, because in 'bad neighbourhoods' marked by porous borders, state collapse and unsecured arsenals, the easy availability of arms – particularly those in local circulation – can contribute to and exacerbate the severity of armed conflict.[18] While arms do not cause conflicts in a simplistic sense, they can extend their effects and lead to protracted armed violence and so-called 'excess deaths' long after wars are brought to a formal end.[19] For example, the sheer abundance of left-over weapons and munitions in the wake of Somalia's collapse in 1991 lowered the costs of acquiring arms and increased the attractiveness of violent solutions to long-standing conflicts. It has subsequently been impossible to break the hold of violent actors over Somali politics (except in quasi-independent Northern Somaliland and Puntland). Similar trends are evident in Central America[20] and the GLR.[21]

But focusing on the supply of weapons alone is likely to be insufficient to address the dynamics of weapons proliferation and misuse in post-conflict contexts. Notwithstanding reductions in overall levels of armed conflict between (and perhaps within) states, the demand for arms varies considerably between and within countries and communities. Structural factors such as underdevelopment, poverty, and unemployment do not by themselves adequately explain the resort to violence by politically – or criminally – motivated actors (and the line between the two is often blurry). The use of arms that occurs in contexts of warfare, crime, and collective violence is often highly concentrated among specific demographic groups and in specific places: the direct perpetrators and victims of armed violence are generally young males.[22] Perpetrators often include combatants, ex-combatants, and their dependants, but in the aftermath of an armed conflict, they also include mercenaries, paramilitary or militia groups, criminal and predatory gangs, and others who may not have been directly involved in the earlier 'conflict-associated violence'. For example, during violent conflicts, arms are often integrated into localized 'self-defence' strategies – whether through the vigilante groups that operate in parts of Nigeria, Uganda and Cameroon,[23] or in accelerated forms of pastoralist violence such as that affecting much of the Horn of Africa and across the Sahel.[24]

In 'fragile states', particularly those exhibiting weak and poorly maintained public services, the easy availability of arms that develops in a conflict situation can be especially pernicious, spreading well beyond groups that were directly implicated in the conflict. Pre-existing vulnerabilities can expose already marginalized populations to even greater suffering from what is often misleadingly labelled 'criminal violence' in post-conflict settings, but which in reality is often a form of highly organized predatory behaviour that is facilitated by elite patrons and the weak institutional apparatus of a fragile state. Prominent examples include Guatemala and El Salvador in Central America, Venezuela and Brazil in South America, Timor-Leste and Papua New Guinea in the Asia-Pacific region, and numerous examples in sub-Saharan Africa, including such major states as Sudan, Nigeria and the Democratic Republic of Congo.[25] Characterizing the large-scale violence that afflicts these – often post-conflict – contexts as 'criminal' in the liberal Western sense does not facilitate the incorporation of violence prevention and reduction programmes into peace support operations, concerned as they traditionally have been with stabilizing the post-conflict state.

The Many Faces of Armed Violence

A major challenge confronting peace support operations and conventional DDR and small arms control thus relates to their almost exclusive focus on armed conflict contexts. Such interventions typically adopt a narrow conception of arms availability and violent actors in which the weapons of concern are considered to be those in the hands of individuals directly implicated in conflict violence. As a result, they fail to apprehend the many categories of armed violence before, during, and after wars come to a close. Armed violence does not necessarily follow a diachronic continuum – peaking during an armed conflict and subsiding in its aftermath. Rather, armed violence is often perpetrated by a wide spectrum of state and non-state actors and armed groups with competing motives and interests, and it ebbs and flows according to opportunities, risks and alternatives. Armed violence also takes place across a wide array of spatial contexts – from war zones, and border and grazing areas to urban slums. As a result, many conventional DDR and small arms control operations are ill-equipped to deal with the many facets of armed violence in post-conflict, crime-affected and urban environments.

One way of graphically illustrating this is to contrast the relative burden of violent deaths[26] in armed conflict and non-armed conflict contexts. Globally, armed conflict and its associated violence exact a major toll on developing countries. More than 50,000 and perhaps as many as double or triple that number were fatally wounded each year in war-affected societies at the turn of the millennium, and 2–10 times more (depending on the nature of the armed conflict and the associated humanitarian crisis) died from preventable, non-violent causes ('indirect' or 'excess' deaths) due to the effects of war on the health of populations.[27] Although the incidence of armed conflicts worldwide appears to be declining overall,[28] the burden of conflict-related armed violence on developing countries remains significant, with severe impacts on priorities such as poverty reduction, good governance, gender equality, health, education, public service delivery and the environment, all of which are undermined by a climate of fear and insecurity. Internal and cross-border displacement generated by armed violence undermines agricultural productivity, commercial and market-based activity, and the functioning of local institutions.[29] In Africa alone, the opportunity cost of the continent's wars was estimated at more than US$280bn from

1990 to 2005, and amounted to 15 per cent of continental GDP.[30] Other studies estimate the annual burden at 2–20 per cent of national GDP in affected countries.[31]

Meanwhile, 'criminal' or non-conflict armed violence results in at least 490,000 homicides every year – with several times more non-fatally wounded.[32] Despite the fact that non-conflict violence is associated with many more direct fatalities than is war, the security and development establishments are only slowly acknowledging its relevance as a development disabler.[33] The impacts are important because large-scale predatory criminal violence – ranging from systematic armed robbery, to extortion, carjacking, kidnapping and other violent crimes – can undermine productivity, distort livelihoods and sustain cycles of poverty, especially in contexts where risk aversion is high and 'insurance' is unavailable. Paradoxically, security-related interventions designed to contain criminal violence – including slum clearances, cordon and search operations, and weapons collection programmes – while immensely popular among the elite, tend to focus disproportionately on the poor.[34]

Another way to illustrate the importance of non-conflict as opposed to conflict-related violence is through case studies. Guatemala experiences one of the highest rates of homicide in Central America, if not the world. The country's homicide rate in 2007 was 47 per 100,000, compared to the global average of 7.3 per 100,000 and the Western European rate of 0.5–2.0 per 100,000. Although homicides declined following the 1996 peace agreement, reaching some 2,655 in total by 1999, they more than doubled by 2007, exceeding 5,780.[35] The absolute number of deaths is greater than during many of the peak years of the long civil war in Guatemala, which claimed between 119,300 and 145,000 lives between 1960 and 1996.[36] The aetiological and demographic patterns of violence have also changed, with civil war-related violence concentrated among the indigenous populations and in the less-populated highlands, while contemporary armed violence is associated with drugs, gangs, border areas and cities. The homicide rate in Guatemala City is 110 per 100,000 – at least twice the national average. In Colombia, a similar pattern emerges, where less than 10 per cent of the more than 20,000 annual deaths from armed violence per year are conflict-related (the rest comprising homicide).[37]

Criminal armed violence has important implications for development and aid effectiveness. On the one hand, it leads to diverted national spending. Expenditures on law enforcement consume up to 5 per cent of the GDP in countries such as Colombia and El Salvador, although with only limited effectiveness in reducing rates of armed violence.[38] Large-scale criminal armed violence also has a negative impact on urban investment, access to goods and services and mobility, as residents in high-crime areas (usually the poor) lose access to shops and services that can no longer do business profitably or safely. Perhaps more worryingly in the long run, when public confidence in security and legal institutions declines – as it has in many countries in Africa, Latin America and the Caribbean and Asia – households and communities may take security provision into their own hands.[39]

Beyond the numbers alone, violent conflicts and criminal or non-conflict violence have overlapping, but somewhat different risk factor profiles. The structural risk factors associated with the onset and duration of violent armed conflict include such things as sharp economic shocks, rising levels of income inequality, the expansion of unemployed youth populations,[40] demographic youth 'bulges',[41] horizontal inequalities between groups,[42] and unresolved grievances. The risk factors that contribute to criminal armed violence include (in addition to some of those listed above), such things as exposure of children – particularly young males – to domestic, interpersonal and collective violence, as well as social and economic exclusion, unregulated urbanization, unequal access to basic public services, underemployment, and living in poorer and socially marginalized areas.[43] Reactive and severe policing – coupled with corruption in the security sector, criminal impunity and extra-judicial killings – can widen the gap between people and their security providers, triggering a crisis of confidence, as was the case in the wake of contested elections in Kenya in 2007.[44]

One additional feature that complicates the picture is rapid urbanization, which now means that a considerable proportion of contemporary armed conflict and criminal violence is concentrated in urban spaces. Indeed, the majority of the world's population today resides in cities and peri-urban areas.[45] Rapid urban growth is associated with persistent armed violence – presenting a growing challenge to both the development and security communities.[46] The city constitutes a magnet for the young, particularly as the relative returns from agriculture and subsistence living decline. As rural–urban migration continues, cities assume a central role in formal and informal commerce, trade and investment. In the context of war or crime, youth – particularly the urban youth – are the most likely to perpetrate, and be victimized by, armed violence.[47]

The destruction of traditional (often family-centred) social networks and creation of newer networks associated with informal groups or gangs often plays a central role in identity and community formation, without necessarily being crime-related in all cases.[48] Rapidly expanding city spaces further contribute to the exposure of youth populations to informal labour opportunities, sometimes in organized and petty crime. With municipal institutions unable to provide adequate social infrastructure – whether schools, recreational spaces or alternative livelihoods – there are few 'pull factors' to deter young males from resorting to armed violence. The involvement of youth in organized drug and arms trafficking networks, protection rackets and gangs is evidence of this. In some of the most dramatic cases, as in Medellin, Rio de Janeiro, Dili, Port-au-Prince, Nairobi and Lagos, youth are recruited (voluntarily and forcibly) from urban slums into more structured political institutions such as militia or even rebel groups.

What are the implications of this picture for post-conflict peacebuilding, including DDR and small arms control strategies, and for the role of the development community in security building? First, traditional armed conflict-prevention and peacebuilding interventions have proved only partly successful in redressing conflict-related violence,[49] and it is little surprise, therefore, that DDR and small arms control interventions that focus narrowly on the armed conflict itself without taking into account these larger issues associated with large-scale armed violence have so far yielded similarly modest returns. Second, development donors and public authorities have been relatively blind to the security needs of their target populations and to the need to incorporate violence prevention and reduction strategies into their programmes. The result is an important policy gap, where neither the post-conflict nor the development communities pursue opportunities to prevent and reduce armed violence through development initiatives or more effective peacebuilding strategies.

Reducing and Preventing Organized Armed Violence

Conventional DDR and arms reduction activities tend to focus on mitigating the onset of armed conflict through national-level institutions and processes. External support is thus focused on creating or strengthening national commissions and focal points and nurturing 'local ownership'. But armed violence knows no borders, is heterogeneous, and is spatially, temporally and demographically differentiated. Development and security practitioners are beginning to acknowledge that traditional classifications of countries according to categories such as 'armed conflict', 'crime', 'crisis' and 'at peace' only imperfectly capture the real and perceived transnational, municipal, and household dynamics and impacts of armed violence. They are also starting to explore alternative approaches to addressing these dynamics through lending support to local institutions.

Although armed violence is increasingly acknowledged by states and civil society as a major constraint in achieving the Millennium Development Goals (MDGs) and to aid effectiveness,[50] donors and development agencies still lack the language, tools, and experience to deal with the changing landscapes of armed violence. Consequently, they often overlook or underfund opportunities to prevent and reduce armed violence. In some cases, governments and donors support top-down enforcement operations to crack down on would-be perpetrators. But there exists comparatively little evidence that such actions are effective in the medium to long term, certainly not unless they are combined with other bottom-up interventions that address risk factors and structural determinants.[51] Although some governments and international agencies are demonstrating an increasing willingness to support voluntary and participatory approaches to preventing and reducing armed violence, there are few demonstrated cases of what works and what does not.[52]

An array of tested approaches to containing and in some cases reducing armed violence is starting to emerge, however, particularly in Latin America and the Caribbean. In contrast to some of the more narrowly focused DDR and small arms control efforts, these second-generation approaches tend to endorse evidence-led policies focusing on identifying risk factors, enhancing resilience at the municipal level, and constructing realistic interventions based exclusively on identified needs. Armed violence prevention and reduction programmes launched in municipal centres in Colombia, Mexico, Brazil and Haiti during the 1990s and early 2000s adopted a host of programmes ranging from voluntary weapons collection, temporary weapons carrying restrictions, targeted environmental design in areas affected by acute violence, and focused interventions in at-risk groups and paramilitaries, leading to a significant decline in homicidal violence.[53] These and other interventions explicitly targeted the diverse dimensions of arms availability, including the preferences of actors using them, and real and perceived factors contributing to armed violence.

Such second-generation activities tend to adopt a more holistic, organic approach than has been advanced within the rubric of DDR and micro-disarmament programmes in the past.[54] Second-generation initiatives also tend to favour a bottom-up approach by focusing on community security promotion rather than more narrowly on the formation of national institutions expected to coordinate activities from above. In parts of Africa, the introduction of 'weapons for development' programmes in the Republic of Congo, Mali and Liberia; 'weapons lotteries' in Mozambique; and 'gun-free zones' in South Africa all reflect the emergence of a more 'people-centred' approach to reducing arms availability and armed violence.[55] In Latin America, building on the experience of some municipalities in El Salvador, Nicaragua, Colombia and elsewhere, interventions focus on locally defined and sustained action plans and indicators, intersector violence prevention and reduction activities, and efforts gradually to scale up successful activities (in order to capture potentially important demonstration or multiplier effects). Such activities complement the emerging preoccupation of security and development actors with, *inter alia*, strengthening the national regulatory framework associated with arms transfers and trafficking, enhancing the security of the weapons holdings of public security providers, and reinforcing civilian oversight over the security sector.

Finally, because violence reduction programmes tend to be formulated by municipal authorities in concert with public and private security actors, academic institutions, and civil society, they often (unconsciously) adopt an 'all-of-government' or integrated approach. They explicitly acknowledge the long-term nature of activities aimed at reducing arms availability and armed violence – with priorities extending long after donors have come and gone. Rather than being entrenched in formal national institutions, programmes are embedded in both formal and informal municipal authority structures, including elected officials, university faculties, faith-based centres, councils of elders and customary authorities, so as to promote a degree of local legitimacy. These interventions also purposefully seek to build up confidence and legitimacy through the deliberate engagement of local actors.

Despite some positive developments, second-generation armed violence prevention and reduction initiatives still require further development and deepening in two ways. First, in spite of growing recognition among some parts of the security and development communities with regard to the importance of enhancing controls on arms availability, the most important work has so far been led by criminologists and the public health community. Second, violence reduction initiatives ultimately have to rely on the (re)construction of robust national and local public authorities (especially in the security sector). These are the very institutions that may be critically weakened or delegitimized by prolonged periods of violent conflict, and hence such activities are not always possible in situations of acute state fragility. While many second-generation interventions are only nascent, and evidence of their effectiveness is only gradually being produced, they still offer a promising approach to dealing with the aftermath of armed conflict and persistent non-conflict violence, especially as we move beyond addressing short-term post-conflict reconstruction needs to dealing with the wider problems of human insecurity in post-conflict societies.

Conclusions

The easy availability of arms, particularly given locally driven demand, circulation, and misuse, can contribute to and enhance the severity of armed violence in a variety of contexts. While arms do not by themselves cause violent conflicts or crime, they can exacerbate the effects of war and lead to protracted armed violence long after formal hostilities have been brought to a close. In fragile states, particularly those exhibiting weak and poorly performing security sectors, the impacts of arms availability can be far-reaching, especially where pre-existing patterns of vulnerability expose already marginalized populations to even greater suffering. Although a range of interventions have been introduced over the past two decades in various post-conflict countries to stem arms availability and neutralize violent actors, activities such as DDR and small arms control have generated only modest returns – in part because they do not adequately address the many different faces of armed violence. This final section offers several ways in which to promote more comprehensive approaches to armed violence reduction in post-conflict or high violence environments:

1. *Develop policies that transcend the conventional categories of armed conflict, post-conflict and criminal violence.* While neatly separated for bureaucratic clarity, the categories of conflict and crime are unable to explain adequately the diverse patterns of armed violence affecting many societies. The international development and peace and security architecture is structured according to specific sectors that deal with such things as the rule of law, health, education, governance, gender and the environment, treating issues of insecurity and armed violence in an isolated and not a holistic fashion.
2. *Recognize the heterogeneous characteristics of violent actors in different contexts.* There is a need for both donors and national agencies to rethink the incentives and behaviour of armed groups and 'violence entrepreneurs'. While the availability of resources is a significant determinant in shaping rent-seeking behaviour, armed groups are highly heterogeneous in character and origin, with many displaying a combination of political and economic or criminal objectives. They are frequently a direct product of weakened or fragile state institutions and deeply interconnected to political economies of war and peace. It is critical that their motivations and means are better recognized,[56] and that innovative interventions focus as much on redressing systemic governance failures as on controlling or eliminating armed groups themselves.
3. *Adopt a broad understanding of the forces determining weapons flows and arms availability.* It is important to move beyond a narrow approach to small arms control that focuses mainly on supply-side issues such as export and import controls, regulation of brokering and countering the illegal

trade. While these are all legitimate priorities, arms availability is also demand-driven and development agencies must acknowledge the multiple ways arms are supplied, acquired, recirculated and used. Recognizing the ways in which many states produce and leak weapons from their security sectors (unintentionally or otherwise), how informal armed groups are deployed as proxies for state elites, the mechanisms by which civilian motiv-ations (profit, predation, self-defence) fuel the domestic trade, and the factors leading to their misuse are critical to securing safety and security in post-conflict and high-violence environments.

4. *Strengthen the evidence base behind DDR, SSR and small arms control pro-grammes.* Despite the primacy that donors, UN agencies, and governments have accorded to DDR and small arms control in the aftermath of war, it is important to recognize the limitations of such interventions. Policy-relevant and experimental research needs to be encouraged in order to identify key risk factors facilitating armed violence, resilience factors that mitigate it, and the effectiveness of external interventions to contain and regulate it in the medium term. While the political economy of security promotion cannot be ignored, the focus on short-term wins over long-term investment in programmes needs to be reconsidered. Investment in evidence-generation (e.g., national surveillance and monitoring systems), decentralized long-term planning strategies at the local level (e.g., commissions, task forces, and com-mittees), and capacities to implement targeted interventions is a priority.

5. *Acknowledge the potentially important role that could be played by armed violence prevention and reduction programmes adopting a public health or criminal justice approach, especially at the local or municipal level.* There is growing awareness that activities focusing on alternative livelihood/employ-ment schemes for at-risk urban youth and former gang members, and reinfor-cing customary management of common property resources in areas of pastoral conflict or strengthening the role and influence of 'peace promoters' in affected communities can generate significant reductions in violence. Along with this, strengthening the capacity of local or municipal governments to identify, respond to, and monitor armed violence can increase their ability to manage, finance and evaluate armed violence prevention and reduction activities. Especially in Africa, local governments are weak in relation to the state-building interests of the central government, unlike the case of Latin America and the Caribbean, where municipalities have comparatively more robust governance and tax generation capacities, and are hence better able to develop effective armed violence-reduction programmes. A priority for donors and African governments, then, is to enhance the capacity of munici-palities to develop integrated interventions, to 'bargain' with central auth-orities and to pursue sustainable interventions.

This article finds that DDR and small arms control programmes are often ill-equipped to contend with the emergent and dynamic forms of armed violence in countries affected by systemic politically and economically motivated violence or emerging from armed conflict. A growing cadre of scholars and practitioners acquainted with public health, criminology, and sociology are increasingly cognisant of the ways in which armed violence itself is spatially, temporally and demographically distributed, particularly at the subnational level. A host of pioneering examples of armed violence prevention and reduction activities are emerging that construct interventions on the basis of solid longitudinal and epidemiological evidence, prioritize bottom-up engagement, and target recurrent risk factors. While such activities would require considerable tailoring to each post-conflict context, by privileging an evidence-based approach, they can potentially complement – and enhance the effectiveness of – conventional DDR and small arms control activities.

NOTES

1. Roland Paris and Timothy D. Sisk, 'Managing Contradictions: The Inherent Dilemmas of Postwar Statebuilding', International Peace Academy, New York, Nov. 2007; Roland Paris, *At War's End*, Cambridge: Cambridge University Press, 2004; Alex Bellamy, *Understanding Peacekeeping*, London: Polity, 2004, Alex Bellamy and Phil Williams (eds), *Peace Operations and Global Order*, London: Routledge, 2007.
2. Mark Duffield, *Development, Security, and Unending War*, London: Polity, 2007; Jennifer Welsh and Ngaire Woods, *Exporting Good Governance*, London: Wilfred Laurier, 2007.
3. Paul Collier, Vani Elliott, Harvard Hegre, Anke Hoeffler, Marta Reynal-Querol and Nicholas Sambanis (eds), *Breaking the Conflict Trap: Civil War and Development Policy*, Oxford: Oxford University Press and World Bank, 2003.
4. Ibid.; Otta Harbom and Peter Wallensteen, 'Armed Conflict, 1989–2006', *Journal of Peace Research*, Vol.44, No.5, 2006, pp. 623–34. But see especially Astri Suhkre and Ingrid Samset for a critical analysis of these claims that argues that the risk of conflict recurrence is considerably lower than the oft-cited 50 per cent: 'What's in a Figure? Estimating Recurrence of Civil War', *International Peacekeeping*, Vol.14, No.2, 2007, pp.195–203.
5. Stephan Stedman, 'Spoiler Problems in Peace Processes', *International Security*, Vol.22, No.2, 2007, pp.5–53.
6. Torunn Chaudhary and Astri Suhrke developed a typology of different categories of post-war violence, ranging from political and routine state violence to economic and crime-related violence, community and informal justice, and post-war displacement and land/property disputes: 'Postwar Violence', background paper for the Small Arms Survey, Geneva, 2008.
7. Robert Muggah (ed.), *Security and Post-Conflict Reconstruction: Dealing with Fighters in the Aftermath of War*, New York: Routledge, 2008 (forthcoming); Mats Berdal, 'Disarmament and Demobilisation After Civil Wars', *Adelphi Paper* No.303, Oxford: International Institute for Strategic Studies.
8. Nat Colletta, Markus Kostner and Ingo Wiederhofer, 'Case Studies in War-to-Peace Transition', *World Bank Discussion Paper* No.331, Washington, DC: World Bank, 1996.
9. Ibid.
10. World Bank, 'Greater Great Lakes Regional Strategy for Demobilization and Reintegration', *Report No.23869-AFR*, Washington, DC, World Bank: 2002. Details of MDRP activities accessed at www.mdrp.org.
11. For a review of the evolution of UN Security Council resolutions in Haiti from 1990 to 2006, see Robert Muggah and Keith Krause, 'The True Measure of Success? Considering the Emergence of Human Security in Haiti', in Sandra McLean, David Black and Tim Shaw (eds), *A Decade of Human Security: Global Governance and New Multilateralisms*, London: Ashgate 2006, pp.113–126.
12. For a critique of the rationalist approaches to DDR favoured by the World Bank and UN agencies that privilege a narrow *homo economicus* interpretation of combatant and civilian incentives, see Muggah, *Security and Post-Conflict Reconstruction* (see n.7 above).
13. Mark Duffield describes how development – far from benevolent – constitutes a 'technology of security that is central to liberal forms of power and government'. In its effort to control and ameliorate the unintended consequences of 'progress', development makes and remakes societies and continues the 'civilizing' process of state consolidation (see n.2 above); see also his *Global*

Governance and the New Wars: The Merging of Development and Security, London: Zed Books, 2001.

14. Macartan Humphreys and Jeremy Weinstein, 'Assessing Progress Toward Demobilization and Reintegration in Sierra Leone'; James Pugel, 'DDR in Liberia: Questioning Scope and Informing Evaluation', in Muggah, *Securing Protection* (see n.7 above) pp.47–69.
15. Jorge Restrepo and Robert Muggah, 'Disarming and Demobilising Colombia's Paramilitaries', in Muggah, *Securing Protection* (see n.7 above) pp.30–46.
16. See UN, 'UN Programme of Action on Combating the Illicit Trade and Trafficking of Small Arms in All Its Aspects', accessed at www.iansa.org/un/programme-of-action.htm; the 'Arms Trade Treaty', accessed at www.armstradetreaty.com; and OECD–DAC (Organisation for Economic Cooperation and Development – Development Assistance Committee), *Guidance on Armed Violence Reduction and Development*. Paris: OECD–DAC (forthcoming).
17. *Small Arms Survey 2007*, Cambridge: Cambridge University Press, 2007; Keith Krause, 'Small Arms and Light Weapons: Towards Global Public Policy', New York: International Peace Academy, 2007.
18. *Small Arms Survey 2005*, Oxford: Oxford University Press, 2005.
19. Ibid.; Hazem Ghoborah, Paul Huth and Bruce Russett, 'Civil Wars Kill and Maim People – Long After the Shooting Stops', *American Political Science Review*, Vol.97, No.2, 2003, pp.189–202.
20. Robert Muggah and Chris Stevenson, 'On the Edge: Causes and Consequences of Armed Violence in Central America', *Central America Development Report*, Washington, DC: World Bank (forthcoming); Bill Godnick, Camilla Waszink and Robert Muggah, 'Stray Bullets: Arms Availability and Misuse in Central America', Occasional Paper No.8, Small Arms Survey, Geneva, 2004.
21. Ryan Nichols and Robert Muggah, 'Quoi de neuf sur le front congolais? Évaluation de base sur la circulation des armes légères et de petit calibre en République du Congo' ['What's New on the Congo Front? Base Evaluation of the Circulation of Light and Small Calibre Weapons in the Democratic Republic of Congo'], Geneva: UNDP/Small Arms Survey, 2007.
22. World Health Organization (WHO), *WHO Report on Violence on Africa*, Oxford: Oxford University Press, 2008; *Small Arms Survey 2006*, Oxford: Oxford University Press, 2006.
23. See *Small Arms Survey 2006* (see n.22 above) for a review of vigilante groups in Africa.
24. For a review of pastoral violence in the Horn of Africa, see Human Security Baseline Assessment, 'Responses to Pastoral Wars: A Review of Violence Reduction Efforts in Sudan, Uganda and Kenya', Issue Brief 8, Geneva: Small Arms Survey, 2007.
25. WHO 2006 (see n.22 above).
26. Violent deaths are of course only one indicator among many to illustrate the intensity and burden of armed violence. They are nevertheless a good proxy of the manifold impacts of violence, including nonfatal intentional injury, assault and harassment, sexual and gender-based violence and displacement.
27. Geneva Declaration Secretariat, *The Global Burden of Armed Violence*, Geneva: Geneva Declaration Secretariat, 2008; *Small Arms Survey 2005*, Oxford: Oxford University Press, 2005.
28. There were 32 armed conflicts in 23 locations in 2006, according to Harbom and Wallensteen, 'Armed Conflict, 1989–2006' (see n.4 above), far fewer than the peak of 52 in 1991 and 1992. See Andy Mack, *Human Security Brief 2006*, Vancouver: Simon Fraser University, 2007, accessed at www.hsrgroup.org/images/stories/HSBrief2006/contents/finalversion.pdf.
29. See OECD–DAC (see n.16 above).
30. Oxfam-GB, *Africa's Missing Billions*, Oxford: Oxfam, 2007.
31. Frances Stewart and Valpy Fitzgerald, *War and Underdevelopment*, Vol.1, Oxford: Oxford University Press, 2001.
32. Geneva Declaration Secretariat, 2008 (see n.27 above); *Small Arms Survey 2004*, Oxford: Oxford University Press, 2004.
33. The OECD–DAC is supporting the production of guidance on armed violence reduction in order to enhance donor capacities to diagnose and respond to various forms of violence, including crime and victimization.
34. Oliver Jütersonke, Keith Krause and Robert Muggah, 'Guns and the City: Analysing Urbanisation and Armed Violence', *Small Arms Survey 2007*, Cambridge: Cambridge University Press, 2007.
35. Crucially, more than 80 per cent (83 per cent) of all reported homicides in 2007 were the result of firearms. See Muggah and Stevenson, 'On the Edge' (see n.20 above).
36. Patrick Ball, Paul Kobrak and Herbert Spirer, *State Violence in Guatemala, 1960–1996: A Quantitative Reflection*, Washington, DC: American Association for the Advancement of Science and International Center for Human Rights Research, 1999.

37. *Small Arms Survey 2006*, Oxford: Oxford University Press, 2006, p.215.
38. See Inter-American Development Bank (IADB), 'How Is Violence Measured?', *Technical Note 2*, Washington, DC: IADB [n.d.].
39. Actions encouraging social investment in youth to reduce criminal delinquency or interventions to reduce victimization have a return of more than US$7 on every dollar spent. Geneva Declaration Secretariat (see n.27 above).
40. Collier et al. (see n.3 above).
41. Richard Cincotta, Environmental Change and Security Program, *Report No.10*, Washington, DC: Woodrow Wilson Center, 2004.
42. Stewart and Fitzgerald (see n.31 above).
43. *Small Arms Survey 2007*, Oxford: Oxford University Press, 2007.
44. See Robert Muggah and Oliver Jütersonke, 'Considering the Contribution of Public and Private Security Providers to Endemic Urban Violence', Ottawa: Ministry of Foreign Affairs and International Trade, 2008, accessed at www.humansecurity-cities.org/page119.htm.
45. The UN estimates that by 2015 there will be more than 550 cities with populations exceeding 1 million, up from 86 in 1950. Several urban areas are expected to grow beyond 20 million residents, often including vast slums, with a global slum population expected to reach more than 1.4 billion by 2020. See Jütersonke et al. (see n.34 above).
46. Muggah and Jütersonke (see n.44 above).
47. Dennis Rodgers, 'The State as a Gang: Conceptualizing the Governmentality of Violence in Contemporary Nicaragua', *Critique of Anthropology*, Vol.26, No.3, 2006, pp.315–30.
48. See Kees Koonings and Dirk Kruijt (eds), *Societies of Fear: The Legacy of Civil War, Violence and Terror in Latin America*, London: Zed Books, 1999. See also Kees Koonings and Dirk Kruijt (eds), *Armed Actors: Organised Violence and State Failure in Latin America*, London: Zed, 2004.
49. See, for example, OECD–DAC (see n.16 above) and the review of efforts to monitor and evaluate conflict-prevention and peace-building activities.
50. See, for example, the Geneva Declaration (www.genevadeclaration.org) for a review of the specific impacts of armed violence on MDG priorities.
51. OECD–DAC (see n.16 above); *Small Arms Survey 2007* (see n.17 above).
52. By August 2008, 94 countries had signed the Geneva Declaration on Armed Violence and Development, with clear commitments to achieving measurable reductions in armed violence by 2015, accessed at www.genevadeclaration.org; WHO (see n.22 above).
53. OECD–DAC (see n.16 above).
54. The UN has sought to develop its approach to DDR and arms reduction through the design of integrated missions. While experiencing growing pains in countries such as Haiti and Sudan, integrated missions involving UNDP and the Department of Peacekeeping Operations are expected to enhance coherence and coordination in relation to DDR, address civilian possession, and reduce transaction costs and collective action dilemmas between agencies.
55. Adelé Kirsten, *A Nation Without Guns?* Scottsville: South Africa: University of KwaZulu-Natal Press, 2007; Centre for Humanitarian Dialogue, 'Preventing Misuse: National Regulation of Small Arms', in *Missing Pieces: Directions for Reducing Gun Violence through the UN Process on Small Arms Control*, Geneva, 2005, pp.15–35.
56. See Robert Muggah and Jurgen Brauer, 'Completing the Circle: Building a Theory of Small Arms Demand', *Contemporary Security Policy*, Vol.27, No.1, 2006, pp.138–154.

Name Index